D1539767

MSU/Detroit College of Law

AMERICANS WITH DISABILITIES ACT HANDBOOK

Fourth Edition

Volume 2

Henry H. Perritt, Jr.

PUBLISHERS

1185 Avenue of the Americas, New York, NY 10036

www.aspenpublishers.com

This publication is designed to provide accurate and authoritative information in regard to the subject matter covered. It is sold with the understanding that the publisher is not engaged in rendering legal, accounting, or other professional services. If legal advice or other professional assistance is required, the services of a competent professional person should be sought.

—From a *Declaration of Principles* jointly adopted by
a Committee of the American Bar Association and a
Committee of Publishers and Associations

SUMMARY OF CONTENTS

CONTENTS

Volume 2

A complete table of contents for each chapter is included in the beginning of the chapter.

Chapter 17
REMEDIES

Chapter 18
PREVENTIVE MATERIALS

APPENDIX A
AMERICANS WITH DISABILITIES ACT

APPENDIX B
EEOC REGULATIONS FOR ADA TITLE I—CODE OF FEDERAL REGULATIONS, TITLE 29 PART 1630

APPENDIX C
APPENDIX TO PART 1630—INTERPRETIVE GUIDANCE ON TITLE I OF THE AMERICANS WITH DISABILITIES ACT

APPENDIX D
DEPARTMENT OF TRANSPORTATION REGULATIONS

CONTENTS

CHAPTER 13

DISCOVERY

§ 13.01 INTRODUCTION AND OVERVIEW

This chapter presents forms and other materials related to discovery for Americans with Disabilities Act (ADA)[1] cases. It provides a significant amount of strategic and tactical analysis for discovery techniques utilizing time extensions,[2] as well as the full text of Rule 26 of the Federal Rules of Civil Procedure, which changes federal discovery by imposing uniform obligations of disclosure and limiting the use of depositions and interrogatories.

It is important to understand that modern discovery significantly shapes the subsequent handling of a lawsuit by forming the record on which summary judgment can be based and by identifying the specific evidence and issues for trial.

§ 13.02 DISCOVERY APPROACHES

[A] Discovery Strategy

Counsel for any party in an ADA case should formulate a clear strategy for discovery. The strategy should distinguish the roles of interrogatories[3] and depositions[4] and assign an appropriate place to requests for production of documents and things[5] and requests for physical and mental examinations.[6] Counsel also should recognize that modern discovery serves two different purposes: (1) the discovery of specific facts and evidence; and (2) the preservation and packaging of evidence for use in summary judgment proceedings and at trial.

The second purpose is particularly important in ADA litigation. The best way for a plaintiff to show the qualifications of the plaintiff may be to demonstrate in a videotape deposition the plaintiff actually performing the essential functions in controversy. This possibility makes videotape depositions particularly important and increases the likelihood that plaintiff's counsel may wish to arrange for the deposition of the plaintiff.

Videotape depositions can also be of particular value to defendants in ADA litigation. If the plaintiff has unusual difficulty performing certain functions, an effective way to prove this may be to ask the plaintiff to perform those functions during a videotape deposition. Or if the plaintiff

---

[1] Pub. L. No. 101-336, 104 Stat. 327 (1990) (codified at 42 U.S.C. §§ 12,101–12,213 (1994); 47 U.S.C. §§ 225, 711 (1994)) [hereinafter ADA].

[2] *See* Forms 13–1 through 13–5.

[3] *See* Forms 13–15 to 13–24.

[4] *See* Forms 13–6 to 13–14.

[5] *See* Forms 13–25 to 13–29.

[6] *See* Forms 13–30 and 13–31.

has a mental disability that causes outbursts or other behavioral problems, it is effective to capture these during a videotape deposition. The videotape deposition then could be used at trial either for direct evidence or for impeachment purposes.

Obviously, the possibility and importance of these trial-oriented discovery techniques make it essential to anticipate their use by opponents. Demonstrative depositions are persuasive only if the assumptions underlying the demonstration match the position of the opponent. For example, the ADA defers — at least to some extent — to the employer's definition of the essential functions of positions. The probative value and probable admissibility of a deposition demonstrating the plaintiff's performance of job functions is greater if the job functions demonstrated are the ones defined unilaterally by the employer. If the plaintiff and the defendant disagree about the essentiality of certain job functions, it is possible that a deposition structured around the plaintiff's definition of essential job functions would be admissible, but there would be additional challenges to its materiality and relevancy.

From the opposing perspective, the defendant obviously is in a better position to protect its interests at a demonstrative deposition if the defendant knows what functions will be demonstrated, based on the plaintiff's position. Accordingly, an important part of the discovery strategy, the discovery conference, and the joint discovery planning process must be to determine whether the opponent intends to use videotape depositions and demonstrations in depositions. In this way, the parties can use the appropriate discovery tools to determine the scope of any demonstrations.

[B] Rule 26: General Provisions Governing Discovery; Duty of Disclosure

This section provides the full text of subsection (a) and of paragraphs (b)(1) and (2) of Rule 26 of the Federal Rules of Civil Procedure, adopted by the Supreme Court in April 1993. This Rule went into effect on December 1, 1993, and was amended thereafter.

(a) Required Disclosures; Methods to Discover Additional Matter.
(1) Initial Disclosures. Except in categories of proceedings specified in Rule 26(a)(1)(E), or to the extent otherwise stipulated or directed by order, a party must, without awaiting a discovery request, provide to other parties:

(A) the name and, if known, the address and telephone number of each individual likely to have discoverable information that the disclosing party may use to support its claims or defenses, unless solely for impeachment, identifying the subjects of the information;

(B) a copy of, or a description by category and location of, all documents, data compilations, and tangible things that are in the possession, custody, or control of the party and that the disclosing party may use to support its claims or defenses, unless solely for impeachment;

(C) a computation of any category of damages claimed by the disclosing party, making available for inspection and copying as under Rule 34 the documents or other evidentiary material, not privileged or protected from disclosure, on which such computation is based, including materials bearing on the nature and extent of injuries suffered; and

(D) for inspection and copying as under Rule 34 any insurance agreement under which any person carrying on an insurance business may be liable to satisfy part or all of a judgment which may be entered in the action or to indemnify or reimburse for payments made to satisfy the judgment.

(E) The following categories of proceedings are exempt from initial disclosure under Rule 26(a)(1):

(i) an action for review on an administrative record;

(ii) a petition for habeas corpus or other proceeding to challenge a criminal conviction or sentence;

(iii) an action brought without counsel by a person in custody of the United States, a state, or a state subdivision;

(iv) an action to enforce or quash an administrative summons or subpoena;

(v) an action by the United States to recover benefit payments;

(vi) an action by the United States to collect on a student loan guaranteed by the United States;

(vii) a proceeding ancillary to proceedings in other courts; and

(viii) an action to enforce an arbitration award.

These disclosures must be made at or within 14 days after the Rule 26(f) conference unless a different time is set by stipulation or court order, or unless a party objects during the conference that initial disclosures are not appropriate in the circumstances of the action and states the objection in the Rule 26(f) discovery plan. In ruling on the objection, the court must determine what disclosures — if any — are to be made, and set the time for disclosure. Any party first served or otherwise joined after the Rule 26(f) conference must make these disclosures within 30 days after being served or joined unless a different time is set by stipulation or court order. A party must make its initial disclosures based on the information then reasonably available to it and is not excused from making its disclosures because it has not fully completed its investigation of the case or because it challenges the sufficiency of another party's disclosures or because another party has not made its disclosures.

(2) Disclosure of Expert Testimony.

(A) In addition to the disclosures required by paragraph (1), a party shall disclose to other parties the identity of any person who may be used at trial to present evidence under Rules 702, 703, or 705 of the Federal Rules of Evidence.

(B) Except as otherwise stipulated or directed by the court, this disclosure shall, with respect to a witness who is retained or specially employed to provide expert testimony in the case or whose duties as an employee of the party regularly involve giving expert testimony, be accompanied by a written report prepared and signed by the witness. The report shall contain a complete statement of all opinions to be expressed and the basis and reasons therefor; the data or other information considered by the witness in forming the opinions; any exhibits to be used as a summary of or support for the opinions; the qualifications of the witness, including a list of all publications authored by the witness within the preceding ten years; the compensation to be paid for the study and testimony; and a listing of any other cases in which the witness has testified as an expert at trial or by deposition within the preceding four years.

(C) These disclosures shall be made at the times and in the sequence directed by the court. In the absence of other directions from the court or stipulation by the parties, the disclosures shall be made at least 90 days before the trial date or the date the case is to be ready for trial or, if the evidence is intended solely to contradict or rebut evidence on the same subject matter identified by another party under paragraph (2)(B), within 30 days after the disclosure made by the other party. The parties shall supplement these disclosures when required under subdivision (e)(1).

(3) Pretrial Disclosures. In addition to the disclosures required by Rule 26(a)(1) and (2), a party must provide to other parties and promptly file with the court the following information regarding the evidence that it may present at trial other than solely for impeachment:

(A) the name and, if not previously provided, the address and telephone number of each witness, separately identifying those whom the party expects to present and those whom the party may call if the need arises;

(B) the designation of those witnesses whose testimony is expected to be presented by means of a deposition and, if not taken stenographically, a transcript of the pertinent portions of the deposition testimony; and

(C) an appropriate identification of each document or other exhibit, including summaries of other evidence, separately identifying those which the party expects to offer and those which the party may offer if the need arises.

Unless otherwise directed by the court, these disclosures must be made at least 30 days before trial. Within 14 days thereafter, unless a different time is specified by the court, a party may serve and promptly file a list disclosing (i) any objections to the use under Rule 32(a) of a deposition designated by another party under Rule 26(a)(3)(B), and (ii) any objection, together with the grounds therefor, that may be made to the admissibility of materials identified under Rule 26(a)(3)(C). Objections not so disclosed, other than objections under Rules 402 and 403 of the Federal Rules of Evidence, are waived unless excused by the court for good cause.

(4) Form of Disclosures. Unless the court orders otherwise, all disclosures under Rules 26(a)(1) through (3) must be made in writing, signed, and served.

(5) Methods to Discover Additional Matter. Parties may obtain discovery by one or more of the following methods: depositions upon oral examination or written questions; written interrogatories; production of documents or things or permission to enter upon land or other property under Rule 34 or 45(a)(1)(C), for inspection and other purposes; physical and mental examinations; and requests for admission.

(b) Discovery Scope and Limits. Unless otherwise limited by order of the court in accordance with these rules, the scope of discovery is as follows:

(1) In General. Parties may obtain discovery regarding any matter, not privileged, that is relevant to the claim or defense of any party, including the existence, description, nature, custody, condition, and location of any books, documents, or other tangible things and the identity and location of persons having knowledge of any discoverable matter. For good cause, the court may order discovery of any matter relevant to the subject matter involved in the action. Relevant information need not be admissible at the trial if the discovery appears reasonably calculated to lead to the discovery of admissible evidence. All discovery is subject to the limitations imposed by Rule 26(b)(2)(i), (ii), and (iii).

(2) Limitations. By order, the court may alter the limits in these rules on the number of depositions and interrogatories or the length of dep-

ositions under Rule 30. By order or local rule, the court may also limit the number of requests under Rule 36. The frequency or extent of use of the discovery methods otherwise permitted under these rules and by any local rule shall be limited by the court if it determines that: (i) the discovery sought is unreasonably cumulative or duplicative, or is obtainable from some other source that is more convenient, less burdensome, or less expensive; (ii) the party seeking discovery has had ample opportunity by discovery in the action to obtain the information sought; or (iii) the burden or expense of the proposed discovery outweighs its likely benefit, taking into account the needs of the case, the amount in controversy, the parties' resources, the importance of the issues at stake in the litigation, and the importance of the proposed discovery in resolving the issues. The court may act upon its own initiative after reasonable notice or pursuant to a motion under Rule 26(c).

The remainder of Rule 26 has been omitted.

[C]   Discovery Checklist

_____ 1. Obligations under Federal Rules of Civil Procedure 26(b)(1), 26(g), and local rules
          _____ Sanctions under Federal Rules of Civil Procedure 16, 26, and 37

_____ 2. Filing and Service Requirements
          _____ Nonfiling of discovery materials under Federal Rules of Civil Procedure 5(d)
          _____ All discovery requests/responses
          _____ Confidential materials
          _____ Defer transcribing/filing depositions
          _____ Filing when needed in connection with motions
          _____ Reports regarding discovery
          _____ Periodic reports
          _____ Filing abbreviated notices of discovery requests/responses
          _____ Reducing service requirements under Federal Rule of Civil Procedure 5(c)
          _____ Use of liaison counsel/coordinating secretaries
          _____ Special service on need-to-know basis
          _____ Use of electronic bulletin boards, databases accessible through the Internet, and/or joint databases to track requests and status

_____ 3. Preclusion (failure to disclose proposed facts/proof/evidence may result in preclusion from use at trial)

____ 4. Identification of Issues for Discovery Purposes
    ____ Issues for early discovery
    ____ Sources of information (documents/witnesses/other litigation)
    ____ Existence of compiled/computerized data
    ____ Issues for early discovery
    ____ Class action discovery
    ____ Special issues for early resolution
    ____ Limiting scope of discovery
    ____ Time periods
    ____ Priority to particular claims/defenses
    ____ Damages issues — whether to defer
    ____ Interrelationship between discovery and issues
    ____ Revision of discovery plan in light of intervening discovery and refinement/modification of issues
    ____ Attempt to structure discovery so that any additional discovery will be supplementary, not duplicative

____ 5. Control of Discovery
    ____ Limitations
    ____ Time limits
    ____ Completion of all discovery (or set trial date)
    ____ Schedule for completing particular phases/forms
    ____ Limits based on issues
    ____ Priority of specified issues
    ____ Deferring discovery on specified issues
    ____ Limits on quantity
    ____ Number/length of depositions
    ____ Number of interrogatories
    ____ Requiring joint interrogatories/document requests
    ____ Precluding discovery already obtained by coparties
    ____ Special situations
    ____ Class members/representatives
    ____ Limitations on scope of discovery from class representatives and counsel
    ____ Approval from court before discovery from class members
    ____ Limits on quantity/scope/form of discovery from class members
    ____ Discovery outside country
        ____ Advance approval from court required
        ____ Need shown
        ____ Specific information/documents sought
    ____ Sequencing of discovery
    ____ Identify sources of information

_____ Location/form of documents
_____ Identification/location of witnesses
_____ Computerized data; summaries
_____ Governmental studies/reports
_____ Other litigation
_____ Priority of discovery on specific issues, time periods, geographic areas; common discovery before individual discovery
_____ Sequencing common discovery, with concurrent individual discovery; priority/preference according to party
_____ From one side before other side
_____ By one side before other side
_____ Alternatively by weeks/months
_____ According to form of discovery
_____ Document production
_____ Depositions
_____ Interrogatories
_____ Requests for admission
_____ Reducing cost/time of discovery
_____ Cooperation among counsel
_____ Stipulations
_____ Informal discovery
_____ Document inspection
_____ Interviews of possible witnesses
_____ Consultation before formal discovery requests prepared
_____ Nontechnical reading of discovery requests
_____ Disclosing/providing similar information already available
_____ Combining forms of discovery (requests for admission, document requests, interrogatories, identification of potential deponents)
_____ Conference-type depositions
_____ Limiting number of counsel
_____ Resolving discovery disputes
_____ Good-faith effort by counsel to resolve voluntarily
_____ Procedures for obtaining court ruling
_____ Form of motion/request — written or oral
_____ When briefs required/permitted
_____ Telephonic conferences
_____ Reference to magistrates
_____ Appointment of special master
_____ Use of other judges on special matters (for example, privileges)
_____ Depositions in other districts
_____ Monitoring progress of discovery

_____ Periodic written reports
_____ Reports at conferences
_____ Sanctions for failure to meet schedules

_____ 6. Privileges and Confidential Information
    _____ Identification of potential problem areas
    _____ Discovery from parties
    _____ Discovery from third parties
    _____ Access sought by others
    _____ Related litigation
    _____ News media; public interest groups
    _____ Governmental investigations
    _____ Confidential orders
    _____ To whom disclosure authorized without prior court approval
    _____ Extent of disclosure to clients
    _____ Disclosure to experts
    _____ Disclosure for trial support services
    _____ Execution of agreements precluding further disclosure
    _____ Counsel in related litigation
    _____ Procedures for additional disclosures
    _____ Advance notification of proposed disclosure
    _____ Disputes whether documents should be considered confidential; declassification
    _____ Power of court to modify terms of order
    _____ Special terms regarding depositions
    _____ Availability of protection to third parties
    _____ Subpoenas from other courts/agencies
    _____ Copying
    _____ Claims of privilege, including work product protection
    _____ Possible avoidance of or delaying certain discovery
    _____ Need to identify items for which privilege claimed
    _____ Use of another judge/magistrate for in camera inspections
    _____ Need for appointment of special master
    _____ Consideration of nonwaiver agreements

_____ 7. Documents
    _____ Identification system
    _____ Same number throughout litigation
    _____ When copies separately identified
    _____ Log of documents produced; relationship to computer databases or electronic bulletin boards and access through Internet
    _____ Preservation orders

_____ Modification of interim order against destruction

_____ Exemption to avoid unnecessary hardship

_____ Limiting scope as issues narrowed

_____ Procedure for giving advance notice of proposed destruction

_____ Expiration

_____ Return of documents after litigation concluded

_____ Retention for specified period of time

_____ Special problems with computerized data

    _____ Format compatibility

    _____ Identification of existing data/printouts

    _____ Description of files/fields/records; other documentation

    _____ Direct communications between parties' experts

    _____ Identification of data prepared/compiled for trial

    _____ Time for disclosure

    _____ Format

    _____ Preservation of source documents

    _____ Verification

    _____ Production of source documents

    _____ Inquiry regarding input, storage, retrieval

    _____ Opportunity for testing

    _____ Feasibility of requiring admission regarding accuracy production

    _____ In machine-readable form

    _____ Formats

    _____ Protection of confidential information, including programming

    _____ Requests for special programming/formats

    _____ Cost

    _____ Feasibility of jointly developed trial support systems

    _____ Accessibility through Internet

_____ Coordinating requests for documents

_____ Joint request for production

_____ Limiting request to documents not previously produced

_____ Standard/deemed requests in multiple litigation

    _____ Discovery from third parties

    _____ Sufficient advance notice

    _____ Applicability of confidentiality orders

    _____ Cost-sharing

    _____ Outside district

    _____ Exercise of powers outside district

    _____ Use of special master to supervise

_____ 8. Depositions
  _____ Limitations
  _____ Number/length of depositions
  _____ Requiring court approval
  _____ Depositions of class members
  _____ Depositions outside country
  _____ Cost-saving measures
  _____ Informal interviews
  _____ Tape-recorded interviews
  _____ Tape-recorded depositions
  _____ Encouragement by court
  _____ Stipulations as to submission/filing
  _____ Provision for transcriptions
  _____ Tape recording as supplement to regular reporting
  _____ Telephonic depositions
  _____ Videotape depositions
  _____ Stipulations as to oath
  _____ Restrictions on attendance/coaching
  _____ Providing documents to deponent
  _____ Written questions under Federal Rule of Civil Procedure 31
  _____ Conference-type depositions
  _____ Affidavit from proposed deponent claiming no knowledge
  _____ Limited attendance by counsel
  _____ Authorizing supplemental examination after review of transcript
  _____ Participation by telephone
  _____ Providing written questions under Federal Rules of Civil Procedure 30(c) and 31
  _____ Deferring transcription/filing until need arises
  _____ Adoption of previously given depositions/report/affidavit
  _____ Videotape depositions; teleconferencing
  _____ Scheduling
  _____ Time periods
  _____ Exclusive periods for particular parties
  _____ Preferential rights during specified periods
  _____ According to subject matter
  _____ Special time periods for deposing experts
  _____ Arranging depositions in logical or geographic sequence
  _____ Conducting depositions in central locations
  _____ Multiple, concurrent depositions
  _____ Ordinarily no postponement for attorney scheduling conflicts
  _____ Other litigation

_____ Cross-noticing
_____ Adoption of previously given testimony
_____ Coordination of scheduling
_____ Order to show cause why not usable in other cases
_____ Disputes
_____ Telephonic presentations
_____ Acting as deposition judge outside district
_____ Use of master/magistrate/judge to supervise deposition
_____ Guidelines
_____ Improper objections; suggesting answers
_____ Instructions not to answer
_____ Privileges
_____ Bad faith/oppressive examination
_____ Who may be present
_____ Advance approval for telephonic and nonstenographic depositions
_____ Confidential information-examination/production
_____ Providing copies of documents to deponent/other counsel
_____ Procedures for supplemental examination
_____ Procedures for obtaining court ruling

_____ 9. Interrogatories
       _____ Uses
       _____ Identifcation of witnesses/documents
       _____ Identification/description of computerized data
       _____ Specific information known in part by different persons
       _____ Initial discovery of expert opinions
       _____ Explanation of denials of requests for admission
       _____ Contention interrogatories
       _____ Timing
       _____ Scope
       _____ Limitations
       _____ Number
       _____ Restricting over inclusive definitions
       _____ Scope/purpose; timing
       _____ No repetition of interrogatories previously answered
       _____ Exchange in machine-readable form, including electronic mail (e-mail) or the World Wide Web
       _____ Improving utility
       _____ Consolidated interrogatories in multiple-party litigation
       _____ Standard/master interrogatories in multiple-party litigation
       _____ Use of answers from other litigation
       _____ Nontechnical reading
       _____ Respond with available information similar to that requested

_____ Successive responses as information obtained
_____ Resolving disputes promptly — voluntarily if possible
_____ Continuing obligation to supplement

_____ 10. Stipulations; Admissions; Uncontested/Contested Facts
_____ Timing; adequate opportunity for discovery
_____ Acknowledging facts that will not be disputed or contested
_____ Federal Rule of Civil Procedure 36 procedures
_____ Timing
_____ Duty to make reasonable inquiry
_____ Obligation to clarify denial, admit other parts
_____ Interrogatories to clarify further
_____ Negotiated stipulations
_____ Timing
_____ Use of special master to facilitate
_____ Development of uncontested/contested facts; statements of contentions and proof
_____ Sequential preparation
_____ Timetable
_____ Scope
  _____ All facts
  _____ Principal facts
  _____ Facts that may be admitted and, if admitted, will reduce scope of trial
  _____ Fact of particular issues (for example, summary judgment)
_____ Use of special hearings (for example, class certification, preliminary injunctions)
_____ Interlineation/deletion to clarify position
_____ Annotations by reference to witnesses/documents
_____ Permissive
_____ Mandatory, with preclusive effect
_____ Objections
  _____ Not basis for refusing to admit
  _____ Requiring certain objections (for example, authentication)
  _____ Requiring all objections
  _____ Effect
_____ Admitted for purpose of trial; when independent evidence permitted
_____ Precluding proof of unlisted facts
_____ Sanctions under Federal Rule of Civil Procedure 36 for unwarranted denial
_____ Withdrawal from admission under Federal Rule of Civil Procedure 36 standards

17

_____ 11.   Special Problems
        _____ Expert opinions
        _____ At initial conference
        _____ Identify subjects on which expert opinions may be offered
        _____ Set timetables for
                _____ Identifying experts to be called
                _____ Disclosure of reports/information under Federal Rule
                      of Civil Procedure 26
                _____ Deposing experts
        _____ Any revision to opinions/reasons
        _____ Materials on which opinions based
        _____ General requirement for preservation/production
        _____ Consider whether aborted/discarded preliminary studies
              should be preserved/produced
        _____ Potential problem when using information protected by at-
              torney-client privilege or work product doctrine
        _____ Disclosure of publications/treatises
        _____ Critiques of opinions by other experts — time for disclo-
              sure
        _____ Costs of depositions
        _____ Paid by deposing party under Federal Rule of Civil Pro-
              cedure 26
        _____ Each party by agreement pays costs to own expert
        _____ Limiting length of deposition
        _____ Pretrial consideration of objections to expert's qualifica-
              tions or opinions
        _____ Discovery from court-appointed expert(s)
        _____ Governmental investigations/reports
        _____ Early identification of relevant investigations/reports
                _____ Production
                _____ From parties
                _____ From public records
                _____ Subpoena
                _____ Requests under Freedom of Information Act[7]
        _____ Grand jury materials
        _____ Admissibility
        _____ Discovery regarding trustworthiness
        _____ Pretrial consideration of objections
        _____ Summaries; compilations
        _____ Timetable for disclosure
        _____ Production of underlying data

---

[7] 5 U.S.C. § 552 (1994).

_____ Verification procedures
_____ Detect/correct errors if feasible
_____ Stipulation as to estimated range of errors
_____ Polls; surveys; other sampling techniques
_____ Timetable for disclosure of potential use
_____ Consultation between experts prior to conducting survey
_____ Disclosure of results/underlying data
_____ Admissibility
_____ Discovery
_____ Pretrial consideration of objections
_____ Settlements
_____ Continuing duty to disclose settlements/special agreements
_____ Discovery regarding fairness/adequacy of proposed class settlements
_____ Discovery not postponed for settlement discussions
_____ Potential problems with settlements limiting discovery
_____ Attorneys' fees
_____ Scope of discovery
_____ Inquiry into hourly rates of opposing counsel[8]

§ 13.03   Time Extensions

[A]   Generally

Civil discovery reforms have shifted management of discovery timing from the parties to the court. When deviation from stipulated or court-ordered schedule for discovery is contemplated, formal requests are necessary.

[B]   Sample Forms

[1]   Motion to Extend Discovery Time

FORM 13–1   Sample Motion to Extend Discovery Time

DEFENDANTS' MOTION FOR ENLARGEMENT OF TIME IN WHICH TO CONDUCT DISCOVERY

Defendants, [A.I.C. SECURITY INVESTIGATIONS, LTD.]; [A.I.C. INTERNATIONAL, LTD.]; and [unnamed defendant C], by and through their attorneys, [WESSELS AND PAUTSCH, P.C.], by [Charles A. Pautsch], [attorney A], and [attorney B], pursuant to Rule 6(b), Fed. R. Civ. P., hereby request this Court to

---

[8] Adapted from Manual for Complex Litigation (Second) § 40.2 (1985).

enlarge the time in which parties to this action may conduct discovery and state in support hereof as follows:

1. This action was filed by Plaintiff on [November 5, 1992].

2. On or about [November 12, 1992], this Court, upon motion of Plaintiff, set forth an order closing discovery in this matter as of [January 1, 1993].

3. Thus far, Plaintiff has taken the depositions of six (6) individuals, five (5) of whom are current employees of Defendants, has scheduled depositions for two (2) more employees of the Defendant companies, and has sought to depose the individually named Defendant [C].

4. Defendants have served upon Plaintiff answers to interrogatories, documents in response to Rule 34, Fed. R. Civ. P., document requests, and objections to certain written discovery inquiries.

5. Thus far, Defendants have taken the depositions of two (2) treating physicians and two (2) individuals. Defendants intend to depose two (2) additional individuals prior to [December 31, 1992].

6. Plaintiff has served upon Defendants answers to interrogatories.

7. On [November 17, 1992], Defendants served upon Plaintiff Defendants' First Requests for Production of Documents. According to this Court's [November 12, 1992], Order, Plaintiff's responses to Defendants' First Request for Production of Documents were due on [November 27, 1992].

8. As of the date below, Defendants have not received from Plaintiff responses to Defendants' First Requests for Production of Documents.

9. On [December 1, 1992], Defendants sent to Plaintiff a Notice of Deposition for [Charles H. Wessel ("Wessel")].

10. Plaintiff refused to produce [Wessel] for his deposition scheduled for [December 10, 1992].

11. Plaintiff has failed to set forth an adequate reason for the failure of [Wessel] to appear for his deposition, did not seek a protective order, and has produced no verification that [Wessel] is unfit to be deposed.

12. Defendants promptly filed a Motion to Compel the attendance of [Charles H. Wessel] for deposition.

13. On or about [December 15, 1992], this Court referred Defendants' Motion to Compel the Attendance of [Charles H. Wessel] for Deposition to Magistrate Judge [Guzman] for determination. Thus far there has been no ruling on Defendants' Motion nor has a hearing date for said motion been set.

14. If Defendants are not allowed to depose [Wessel] prior to trial, they will be unfairly prejudiced.

15. On [November 13, 1992], Defendants made a motion to this Court for an Order allowing the physical and mental examination of [Wessel].

16. On or about [November 24, 1992], this Court referred Defendants' Motion to Magistrate Judge [Guzman] for determination. Thus far there has been no ruling on Defendants' Motion nor has a hearing date been set for said motion.

17. Defendants have retained a physician who can make a physical and mental examination of [Wessel] within a reasonable time after this Court so orders.

18. If Defendants are not allowed a physical and mental examination prior to trial, they will be unfairly prejudiced.

19. Due to upcoming holidays, it will be nearly impossible to complete discovery before [January 1, 1993].

WHEREFORE, in light of the foregoing, Defendants, through counsel, respectfully request that

(1) the discovery deadline in this action be moved to [Friday], [January 22, 1993]; and

(2) the pretrial conference, presently scheduled for [January 15, 1993], be moved ahead accordingly.

Dated this [22nd] day of [December] [1992].

[2] Motion to Extend Time for Written Discovery/Supporting Affidavit

FORM 13–2   **Sample Motion to Extend Time for Written Discovery**

IN THE UNITED STATES DISTRICT COURT
FOR THE [NORTHERN] DISTRICT OF [ILLINOIS]
[EASTERN] DIVISION

U.S. EQUAL EMPLOYMENT OPPORTUNITY COMMISSION,

Civil Action No. [92 C 7330]

Plaintiff,

v.

[A.I.C. SECURITY INVESTIGATIONS, LTD.];
[A.I.C. INTERNATIONAL, LTD.];
and [unnamed defendant C]

Honorable [Marvin E. Aspen]

Defendants.

DEFENDANTS' MOTION FOR ENLARGEMENT OF TIME IN WHICH TO RESPOND TO PLAINTIFF'S WRITTEN DISCOVERY

Defendants, [A.I.C. SECURITY INVESTIGATIONS, LTD.], [A.I.C. INTERNATIONAL, LTD.], and [C], by and through their attorneys, [WESSELS & PAUTSCH, P.C.], by [Charles W. Pautsch], [attorney A], and [attorney B], pursuant to Rule 6(b), Fed. R. Civ. P., hereby request that this Honorable Court grant Defendants an extension of time in which to respond to Plaintiff's written discovery and state in support hereof as follows:

1. On or about [November 9, 1992], Plaintiff Equal Employment Opportunity Commission (EEOC) served upon Defendants its First Set of Interrogatories, First Request for Production of Documents, and First Request for Admissions.

2. Along with the discovery requests served upon Defendants, as referenced in paragraph 1 above, Plaintiff also filed a motion with this Court to expedite discovery asking that the Court order (1) that all written discovery be answered by

any party within seven days of receipt, and (2) that all discovery be completed by [December 31, 1992].

3. Upon information and belief, on or about [November 12, 1992], this Court, without the parties coming forward for argument, granted Plaintiff's motion. Defendants' attorneys were never served with the Court's order and have knowledge of it only through subsequent conversations with the Court's Minute Clerk.

4. The undersigned counsel for Defendants subsequently discussed the Court's order over the telephone with Attorney [name] of the EEOC and each party agreed that the Court's Order meant Defendants' answers to Plaintiff's First Set of Written Discovery would be due on or before [November 24, 1992].

5. Upon the date Defendants' attorneys were served with Plaintiff's First Request for Production of Documents, First Set of Interrogatories, and First Request for Admissions, the same were immediately forwarded to the Defendants' place of business in order to facilitate the gathering of the requested information.

6. Plaintiff's First Set of Interrogatories to Defendants number in excess of 50, including subparts, and Plaintiff's First Request for Production of Documents requests voluminous materials.

7. Defendants in good faith have attempted to respond to Plaintiff's First Set of Interrogatories and First Request for Production of Documents by [November 24, 1992] but, however, were unable to comply with such an expedited deadline.

8. On or about [November 18, 1992], Defendants served upon the EEOC Defendants' Responses to Plaintiff's First Request for Admissions.

9. Defendants' delay in serving their responses to Plaintiff's First Set of Interrogatories and First Request for Production of Documents was the result of excusable neglect.

10. Defendants will need until [December 15, 1992], to set forth adequately responses to the EEOC's First Set of Interrogatories and First Request for Production of Documents.

WHEREFORE, Defendants request an order allowing them until [December 15, 1992], in which to set forth responses to Plaintiff's First Set of Interrogatories and First Request for Production of Documents.

FORM 13–3   Sample Affidavit in Support of Motion to Extend Time

IN THE UNITED STATES DISTRICT COURT
FOR THE [NORTHERN] DISTRICT OF [ILLINOIS]
[EASTERN] DIVISION

U.S. EQUAL EMPLOYMENT OPPORTUNITY COMMISSION,
Plaintiff,
v.   Civil Action No. [92 C 7330]
[A.I.C. SECURITY INVESTIGATIONS, LTD.];
[A.I.C. INTERNATIONAL, LTD.];
and [unnamed defendant C],

Honorable [Marvin E. Aspen]

Defendants.

AFFIDAVIT OF [attorney B]
STATE OF [WISCONSIN]
COUNTY OF [MILWAUKEE]

The affiant [attorney B], being first duly sworn upon oath, hereby deposes and states as follows:

1. Affiant is an attorney duly admitted to practice before this Honorable Court and has filed an appearance on behalf of the Defendants in the above-captioned cause.

2. Neither Affiant nor any other attorney of the law firm of [Wessels & Pautsch, P.C.] was served with the Court's Order dated [November 12, 1992], expediting discovery in the above-captioned cause, and affiant only has knowledge of the Court's [November 12, 1992], Order through conversation with the Court's Minute Clerk.

3. After receiving knowledge of the Court's [November 12, 1992], Order expediting discovery, Affiant talked with [Attorney A], attorney for Plaintiff, regarding an interpretation of the Order and agreed that the Order instructed Defendants to set forth responses to Plaintiff's First Set of Written Discovery on or before [November 24, 1992].

4. On or about [November 9, 1992], Affiant, on behalf of Defendants, was served with Plaintiff's First Set of Interrogatories and First Request for Production of Documents. On that same day, Affiant immediately forwarded via facsimile Plaintiff's First Request for Production of Documents and First Set of Interrogatories to Defendants' place of business in order to facilitate the gathering of the requested information.

5. Affiant has read these five (5) paragraphs and two (2) pages, and certifies by his signature below that they are true and correct to Affiant's best information and belief.

[3]   Response to Motion to Extend Time for Discovery (EEOC)

FORM 13–4   Sample Response to Motion to Extend Time for Discovery

EEOC'S RESPONSE TO DEFENDANTS' MOTION FOR ENLARGEMENT OF
TIME IN WHICH TO CONDUCT DISCOVERY

Plaintiff, the Equal Employment Opportunity Commission (the "EEOC"), respectfully submits this Memorandum in response to Defendants' Motion for Enlargement of Time in Which to Conduct Discovery.

This is an action under the Americans with Disabilities Act (ADA), 42 U.S.C. §§ 12,101 *et seq.,* in which the EEOC alleges that [Charles H. Wessel ("Wessel")] was discharged from his employment because of his disability, terminal brain cancer. [Wessel] suffers from malignant brain tumors, and his condition has been diagnosed as terminal. See depositions of Drs. [A] and [B].

Because of [Wessel]'s condition, the EEOC requested, and the Court ordered, a discovery cutoff date of [December 31, 1992], and a date for final pretrial order of [January 15, 1993]. Defendants now seek a three-week extension of those dates. The EEOC respectfully requests that the Motion be denied, because any delay in setting the case for trial may result in [Wessel's] being unable to testify and because Defendants' Motion demonstrates on its face that no extension is necessary.

Defendants' Motion relies on two bases for an extension: that the EEOC has not yet responded to an outstanding document request; and that the Court has not yet ruled upon Defendants' Motion for a Mental and Physical Examination of [Charles H. Wessel]. None of these bases justifies an extension of discovery cutoff.

The EEOC produced its investigative file to Defendants on [November 24, 1992]. The documents sought in Defendants' First Request for Production of Documents were documents belonging to [Wessel], and those obtained by the EEOC were produced on [December 28, 1992].

Defendants' Motions to Compel a Second Deposition by [Wessel] and to compel a Mental and Physical Examination have been fully briefed. In the event that the Court were to order that either take place, they would, of course, need to be scheduled outside the discovery period. This would not, however, require any extension of discovery for any other purpose.[9]

As set forth in Defendants' Motion for Enlargement of Time, both parties have noticed and taken numerous depositions during the discovery period. In addition, Defendants have subpoenaed voluminous documents from health care providers and others. Defendants have not noticed any depositions, other than that of [Wessel], which they have been unable to schedule. Defendants do not claim a need for any discovery in addition to that which is the subject of the two pending motions; therefore, no extension of time is necessary.

This is an unusual case in that Plaintiff's most important evidence, [Wessel]'s testimony, may be unavailable if the matter is not brought quickly to trial.[10] Defendants have identified no discovery that they need that either has not been obtained or is the subject of pending motions. No extension of discovery is necessary, and the EEOC therefore requests that the dates for discovery cutoff and for final pretrial order stand, and that the matter be set for trial at the earliest convenient date.

---

[9] There is also a pending Motion to Compel answers to interrogatories and answers to document requests filed by EEOC and fully briefed by the parties. Ruling on that motion will not require any delay in the discovery cutoff date. Similarly, ruling on a pending motion by defendants to disqualify counsel for A.I.C. should not be permitted to delay discovery.

[10] Wessel's videotape deposition was taken on November 5, 1992, in response to a Petition to Perpetuate Testimony made by Wessel and by the defendants. That deposition will not be as probative of the issues in the case as live testimony by Wessel would be.

[4]   Transcript of Hearing on Defendants' Request for Extension of Time for Discovery

FORM 13–5   Sample Hearing Transcript on Request for Extension of Time

IN THE UNITED STATES DISTRICT COURT
FOR THE [NORTHERN] DISTRICT OF [ILLINOIS]
[EASTERN] DIVISION

U.S. EQUAL EMPLOYMENT OPPORTUNITY DIVISION
Plaintiff,   Docket No. [92 C 7330]
v.
[A.I.C. SECURITY INVESTIGATIONS, LTD.];
[A.I.C. INTERNATIONAL, LTD.];
and [unnamed defendant C],
Defendants.
[Chicago, Illinois]
[December 29, 1992]

TRANSCRIPTS OF PROCEEDINGS BEFORE THE HON. [MARVIN E. ASPEN]
APPEARANCES:
For the Plaintiff:
[plaintiff attorney A] and
[plaintiff attorney B]
(United States Equal Employment Opportunity Commission)
[536 South Clark St.]
[Chicago], [Illinois] [60605]
For Defendant [A.I.C.]:
[WESSELS & PAUTSCH], by
[defense attorney B]
[330 East Kilbourn Avenue]
[Milwaukee], [Wisconsin] [53202]
For Defendant [Wessel]:
[injured party's attorney]
[address]
Court reporter:
[court reporter]
[address]
[telephone number]
THE CLERK: [92 C 7330], EEOC versus [A.I.C. Security Investigations]
[DEFENSE ATTORNEY B]: Good morning, your Honor,

THE COURT: Good morning.
[DEFENSE ATTORNEY B]: [Defense attorney B name] appearing on behalf of the defendants.

25

[PLAINTIFF ATTORNEY A]: [Plaintiff attorney A] and [Plaintiff attorney B] representing the EEOC.

[INJURED PARTY'S ATTORNEY]: Your Honor, I, [injured party's attorney name], am appearing on behalf of — for [attorney D], who represents Charles Wessel. She was unable to be here today, and she requested that I appear here for her.

THE COURT: Okay, I don't have the motion here. I think I might have left it on my desk, Gladys, with — I know what it's about.

Do you have an objection to the extension of time for —

[PLAINTIFF ATTORNEY A]: Yes, your Honor, the EEOC, we do have an objection to the extension of time.

Your Honor, this is a case under the Americans with Disabilities Act. Charles Wessel has terminal cancer. His prognosis is not good. He is at the moment well; he will be able to testify.

The discovery cutoff at this point is December 31st, and both sides have virtually completed all discovery. There are a couple of pending motions, and if those were granted, some additional discovery would be necessary, but I don't think that would require an extension on other matters.

Our primary concern is to get the case to trial, and what we would ask for is an early trial date. Then beyond that we would have no particular concern about discovery until then.

THE COURT. Yes.

[DEFENSE ATTORNEY]: If I may reply.

We feel that discovery is not almost over. This case has been on the expedited docket, and our client is working with a small administrative staff that has been overburdened, especially in the past month, attempting to comply with numerous discovery requests, written discovery, and the many depositions. We have had 12 depositions scheduled together in December. It's been a short month, only 19 working days. We haven't had time to conduct discovery — complete discovery.

We have asked for the deposition of Mr. Wessel, who is the subject of the case, and without moving for a protective order —

THE COURT: What you have asked for, really, is an extension of about a month, right, to complete discovery?

[DEFENSE ATTORNEY]: 21 days, I believe. Until January 22nd, I believe.

THE COURT: It's not realistic if the case is going to be tried in that time period anyway. So I am going to allow the motion, but I am not going to give you any further extensions, so you're going to have to do what you have to do during that time period. If you don't complete discovery in that period, it won't be done.

I will also set the date for filing the written pretrial order in open court. Let's set that down for February the 9th at 10:00 o'clock.

How long is it going to take to try this case?

[PLAINTIFF ATTORNEY A]: Four or five days I would think, your Honor.

[DEFENSE ATTORNEY]: We believe longer than that, your Honor.

THE COURT: Okay. I am going to — who's the Magistrate Judge in this case?

[DEFENSE ATTORNEY]: Guzman.

[PLAINTIFF ATTORNEY A]: Guzman.

THE COURT: All right. Do you have any objections to Magistrate Judge Guzman trying the case?

[PLAINTIFF ATTORNEY A]: No, your Honor. We want the earliest possible trial date.

THE COURT: Okay.

[DEFENSE ATTORNEY]: Your Honor, at this time I would like to be able to discuss with other counsel an objection to that. At this point we are going to maintain an objection to that.

THE COURT: I'm sorry?

[DEFENSE ATTORNEY B]: At this point we are going to maintain an objection going to the Magistrate.

THE COURT. It would be helpful, because otherwise I am going to have to interrupt another trial to try this case, and I will; it's going to be tried quickly.

Why don't you —

[DEFENSE ATTORNEY B]: Can we have time to consider that?

THE COURT. Sure. Come back Friday at —

THE CLERK: Friday is a holiday, Judge.

THE COURT: Okay. Why don't you come back on January the 12th at 9:30, if you want, and let me know at that time whether your clients will accept it, all right?

§ 13.04   Depositions

[A]   Generally

As previously noted, one of the purposes of discovery is the preservation and packaging of evidence for use in summary judgment proceedings and at trial. This is particularly important in ADA litigation. The best way for a plaintiff to show the qualifications of the plaintiff may be to demonstrate in a videotape deposition the plaintiff actually performing the essential functions in controversy. This possibility makes videotape depositions particularly important and increases the likelihood that plaintiff's counsel may wish to arrange for the deposition of the plaintiff.

As noted in § 13.02[A], videotape depositions can also be of particular value to defendants in ADA litigation. If the plaintiff has unusual difficulty performing certain functions, an effective way to prove this may be to ask the plaintiff to perform those functions during a videotape deposition. Or if the plaintiff has a mental disability that causes outbursts or other behavioral problems, it is effective to capture these during a videotape deposition. The videotape deposition then could be used at trial either for direct evidence or for impeachment purposes.

Rule 31 of the Federal Rules of Civil Procedure permits depositions to be taken where the presiding officer reads written questions submitted in advance by the party convening the deposition. This technique may be appropriate if the deponent is some distance away, making it expensive for the person taking the deposition to travel to the place at which it is taken. On the other hand, telephone depositions also are authorized by Federal Rule of Civil Procedure 30, and they preserve much of the spontaneity and ability to follow up questions and answers that are lost in depositions on written interrogatories. Accordingly, when distance is a problem, telephonic depositions are preferable to depositions on written questions.

The discovery plan now required by Federal Rules of Civil Procedure 16 and 26 can ensure that telephonic depositions as well as videotapes and other modern technologies play their appropriate role in the overall discovery plan.

[B]   Sample Forms

[1]   Order for Deposition Guidelines

FORM 13–6   Sample Order for Deposition Guidelines

It is ORDERED that depositions be conducted in accordance with the following rules:

1. Cooperation. Counsel are expected to cooperate with, and be courteous to, each other and deponents.

2. Stipulations. Unless contrary to an order of the court, the parties (and, when appropriate, a nonparty witness) may stipulate in any suitable writing to alter, amend, or modify any practice relating to noticing, conducting, or filing a deposition. Stipulations for the extension of discovery cutoffs set by the court are not, however, valid until approved by the court.

3. Scheduling. Absent extraordinary circumstances, counsel shall consult in advance with opposing counsel and proposed deponents in an effort to schedule depositions at mutually convenient times and places.

4. Attendance.

(a) Who may be present. Unless otherwise ordered under Fed. R. Civ. P. 26(c), depositions may be attended by counsel of record, members and employees of their firms, attorneys specially engaged by a party for purpose of the deposition, and potential witnesses. While the deponent is being examined about any stamped confidential document or the confidential information contained therein, persons to whom disclosure is not authorized under the Confidentiality Order shall be excluded.

(b) Unnecessary attendance. Unnecessary attendance by counsel is discouraged and may not be compensated in any fee application to the court. Counsel who have only marginal interest in a proposed deposition or who expect their interests to be adequately represented by other counsel may elect not to attend and to conduct pursuant to paragraph 13(b) of this order supplemental interrogation of the deponent should a review of deposition reveal the need for such examination.

5. Conduct.

(a) Examination. Each side should ordinarily designate an attorney to conduct the principal examination of the deponent, and examination by other attorneys should be limited to matters not previously covered.

(b) Objections. The only objections that should be raised at the deposition are those involving a privilege against disclosure or some matter that may be remedied if presented at the time, such as to the form of the question or the responsiveness of the answer. Objections on other grounds are unnecessary and should generally be avoided. All objections should be concise and must not suggest answers to (or otherwise coach) the deponent. Argumentative interruptions will not be permitted.

(c) Directions not to answer. Directions to the deponent not to answer are improper except on the ground of privilege or to enable a party or deponent to present a motion to the court for termination of the deposition on the ground that it is being conducted in bad faith or in such a manner as unreasonably to annoy, embarrass, or oppress the party or the deponent. When a privilege is claimed, the witness should nevertheless answer questions relevant to the existence, extent, or waiver of the privilege, such as the date of a communication, who made the statement, to whom the contents of the statement have been disclosed, and the general subject matter of the statement.

(d) Private consultation. Private conference between deponents and their attorney during the actual taking of the deposition are improper except for the purpose of determining whether a privilege should be asserted. Unless prohibited by the court for good cause shown, such conferences may, however, be held during normal recesses and adjournments.

6. Documents.

(a) Production of documents. Witnesses subpoenaed to produce numerous documents should ordinarily be served at least 30 days before the scheduled deposition. Depending upon the quantity of documents to be produced, some time may be needed for inspection of the documents before the interrogation commences.

(b) Confidentiality order. A copy of the Confidentiality Order shall be provided to the deponent before the deposition commences if the deponent is to produce or may be asked about documents that may contain confidential information.

(c) Copies. Extra copies of documents about which counsel expect to examine the deponent should ordinarily be provided to opposing counsel and the deponent. Deponents should be shown a document before being examined about it except when counsel seek to impeach or test the deponent's recollection.

7. Depositions of witnesses who have no knowledge of the facts. An officer, director, or managing agent of a corporation or a governmental official served with a notice of a deposition or subpoena regarding a matter about which such person has no knowledge may submit to the noticing party a reasonable time before the date noticed an affidavit so stating and identifying a person within the corporation or government entity believed to have such knowledge. Notwithstanding such affidavit, the noticing party may proceed with the deposition, subject to the right of the witness to seek a protective order.

8. Expert witnesses. Leave is granted to depose expert witnesses in addition to or in lieu of discovery through interrogatories. Objection to such depositions may be made by motion.

9. Tape-recorded depositions. By indicating in its notice of a deposition that it wishes to record the deposition by tape recording in lieu of stenographic recording (and identifying the person before whom the deposition will be taken), a party shall be deemed to have moved for such an order under Fed. R. Civ. P. 30(b)(4). Unless an objection is filed and served within [number of] days after such notice is received, the court shall be deemed to have granted the motion pursuant to the following terms and conditions.[11]

(a) Transcript; filing. Subject to the provision of paragraph 12, the party noticing the deposition shall be responsible for preparing a transcript of the tape recording and for filing within applicable time limits this transcript together with the original tape.

(b) Right of other parties. Other parties may at their own expense arrange for stenographic recording of the deposition, may obtain a copy of the tape and transcript upon payment of a prorata share of the noticing party's actual cost, and may prepare and file their own version of the transcript of the tape recording.

10. Videotape depositions. By indicating in its notice of a deposition that it wishes to record the deposition by videotape (and identifying the proposed videotape operator), a party shall be deemed to have moved for such an order under Fed. R. Civ. P. 30(b)(4). Unless an objection is filed and served within [number of] days after such notice is received, the court shall be deemed to have granted the motion pursuant to the following terms and conditions.[12]

(a) Stenographic recording. The videotape deposition shall be simultaneously recorded stenographically by a qualified court reporter. The court reporter shall on camera administer the oath or affirmation to the official record of the deposition for purposes of Fed. R. Civ. P. 30(e) (submission to witness) and 30(f) (filing exhibits).

(b) Cost. The noticing party shall bear the expense of both the videotaping and the stenographic recording. Any party may at its own expense obtain a copy of the videotape and the stenographic transcript.
Requests for taxation of these costs and expenses may be made at the conclusion of the litigation in accordance with applicable law.

(c) Video operator. The operator(s) of the videotape recording equipment shall be subject to the provisions of Fed. R. Civ. P. 28(c). At the commencement of the deposition the operator(s) shall swear or affirm to record the proceedings fairly and accurately.

(d) Attendance. Each witness, attorney, and other person attending the deposition shall be identified on camera at the commencement of the deposition. Thereafter, only the deponent (and demonstrative materials used during the deposition) will be videotaped.

(e) Standards. The deposition will be conducted in a manner to replicate to the extent feasible the presentation of evidence at a trial. Unless physically incapacitated, the deponent shall be seated at a table or in a witness box except when reviewing or presenting demonstrative materials for which a change in position is

---

[11] This provision is unnecessary under the 1993 amendments to Fed. R. Civ. P. 30(b).
[12] *Id.*

needed. To the extent practicable, the deposition will be conducted in a neutral setting, against a solid background, with only such lighting as is required for accurate video recording. Lighting, camera angle, lens setting, and field of view will be changed only as necessary to record accurately the natural body movements of the deponent or only as necessary to record satisfactorily the voices of counsel and the deponent. Eating and smoking by deponents or counsel during the deposition will not be permitted.

(f) Interruptions. The videotape shall run continuously throughout the active conducting of the deposition. Videotape recording will be suspended during all "off the record" discussions.[13]

(g) Examination; exhibits; rereading. The provisions of paragraph 5 and 6 of this order apply to videotape depositions. Rereading of questions or answers, when needed, will be done on camera by the stenographic court reporter.

(h) Index. The videotape operator shall use a counter on the recording equipment and after completion of the deposition shall prepare a log, cross-referenced to counter numbers, that identified the positions on the tape at which examination by different counsel begins and ends, at which objections are made and examination resumes, at which exhibits are identified, and at which any interruption of continuous tape recording occurs, whether for recesses, "off the record" discussions, mechanical failure, or otherwise.

(i) Filing. The operator shall preserve custody of the original videotape in its original condition until further order of the court. Subject to the provisions of paragraph 12 of this order, the original of the tape recording, together with the operator's log index and a certificate of the operator attesting to the accuracy of the tape, shall be filed with the Clerk. No part of a videotape deposition shall be released or made available to any member of the public unless authorized by the court.

(j) Objections. Requests for pretrial rulings on the admissibility of evidence obtained during a videotape deposition shall be accompanied by appropriate pages of written transcript. If the objection involves a matter peculiar to the videotaping, a copy of the videotape and equipment for viewing the tape shall also be provided to the court.

(k) Use at trial, purged tapes. A party desiring to offer a videotape deposition at trial shall be responsible for having available appropriate playback equipment and a trained operator. After the designation by all parties of the portions of a videotape to be used at trial, an edited copy of the tape, purged of unnecessary portions (and any portions to which objections have been sustained), [may/shall] be prepared by the offering party to facilitate continuous playback, but a copy of the edited tape shall be made available to other parties at least [number of] days before it is used, and the unedited original of the tape shall also be available at the trial.

11. Telephonic depositions. By indicating in its notice of a deposition that it wishes to conduct the deposition by telephone, a party shall be deemed to have

---

[13] If, as in this sample order, a simultaneous stenographic transcript is being made, many courts prefer that the off-the-record discussions be eliminated from the videotape.

moved for such an order under Fed. R. Civ. P. 30(b)(7). Unless an objection is filed and served within [number of] days after such notice is received, it is deemed that the court shall have granted the motion. Other parties may examine the deponent telephonically or in person. However, all persons present with the deponent shall be identified in the deposition and shall not by word, sign, or otherwise coach or suggest answers to the deponent.

12. Waiver of transcription and filing. The parties and deponents are authorized and encouraged to waive transcription and filing of depositions that prove to be of little or no usefulness in the litigation or to agree to defer transcription and filing until the need for using the depositions arises.

13. Use; supplemental depositions.

(a) Use. Depositions may, under the conditions prescribed in Fed. R. Civ. P. 32(a)(1)–(4), or as otherwise permitted by the Federal Rules of Evidence, be used against any party (including parties later added and parties in cases subsequently filed in, removed to, or transferred to this court as part of this litigation)

(1) who was present or represented at the deposition,

(2) who had reasonable notice thereof, or

(3) who, within 30 days after the filing of the deposition (or, if later, within 60 days after becoming a party in this court in any action that is part of this litigation), fails to show just cause why such deposition should not be usable against such party.

(b) Supplemental depositions. Each party not present or represented at a deposition (including parties later added and parties in cases subsequently filed in, removed to, or transferred to this court) may, within 30 days after the filing of the deposition (or, if later, within 60 days after becoming a party in this court in any action that is a part of this litigation), request permission to conduct a supplemental deposition of the deponent, including the right to take such deposition telephonically and by nonstenographic means. If permitted, the deposition shall be treated as the resumption of the deposition originally noticed; and each deponent shall, at the conclusion of the initial deposition, be advised of the opportunity of nonattending parties to request a resumption of such deposition, subject to the right of the deponent to seek a protective order. Such examination shall not be repetitive of the prior interrogation.

14. Rulings.

(a) Immediate presentation. Disputes arising during depositions that cannot be resolved by agreement and that, if not immediately resolved, will significantly disrupt the discovery schedule or require a rescheduling of the deposition, may be presented by telephone to the court. If the judge will not be available during the period while the deposition is being conducted, the dispute may be addressed to Magistrate [name]. The presentation of the issue and the court's ruling will be recorded as part of the deposition.

(b) Extraterritorial jurisdiction. The undersigned will exercise by telephone the authority granted under 28 U.S.C. § 1407(b) to act as district judge in the district in which the deposition is taken.[14]

---

[14] This specifies the power to exercise authority over nonparty deponents outside the district circuit or intercircuit assignment.

Date: [date]
United States District Judge[15]

[2] Notice of Videotape Deposition

FORM 13–7   **Sample Notice of Videotape Deposition**

To: [names of each party and his or her attorney]

You are hereby notified that the deposition of [name of plaintiff] will be taken by oral examination pursuant to Rule [number] of the Federal Rules of Civil Procedure by videotape before [name of court reporter or other person authorized to administer oath] at [location] in [city, state] on [date] at [time].

The deponent is obligated by Rule 30 to appear and may bring counsel. Others named in this notice may appear and examine the deponents.

Federal Rule 30 permits you to make your own arrangements for the preparation of a traditional transcript of this deposition. The videotape will remain in the custody of the person before whom it is taken, and copies will be made available to you at your cost.

Commentary. In *State ex rel. Anderson v. Miller,*[16] the Oregon Supreme Court granted mandamus against a trial court judge who prohibited a videotape deposition. The pertinent Oregon rule of civil procedure not only allowed depositions to be videotaped if so specified in the notice of deposition but also provided for protective orders to eliminate harassment or unduly burdensome discovery. In prohibiting the use of videotape, the trial judge simply expressed his view that videotaping was unnecessary and might impose a certain amount of inconvenience. The Oregon Supreme Court said that the trial judge was substituting his policy judgment for that of the rule drafters and concluded that mandamus was the appropriate remedy for this abuse of discretion. However, in *Cherry Creek School District No. 5 v. Voelker,*[17] the Colorado Supreme Court reversed the intermediate court. The court found plaintiff not entitled to videotape plaintiff's deposition after the end of discovery and on the eve of trial because she was unable to attend trial. Plaintiff's inability to attend had long been known, and the videotape deposition, even though a superior means of presenting testimony compared with a reading discovery deposition, would have worked an inconvenience on the defendant.

---

[15] These deposition guidelines have been adapted from *Sample Deposition Guidelines, in* Manual for Complex Litigation (Second) § 41.38 (1985).

[16] 882 P.2d 1109 (Or. 1994).

[17] 859 P.2d 805, 810 (Colo. 1993).

[3]   Notice of Deposition of Unknown Corporate Deponent

FORM 13–8   **Sample Notice of Deposition of Unknown Corporate Deponent**

To: [names of each party and his or her attorney]

You are hereby notified that the deposition of [name of corporation] will be taken by oral examination pursuant to the Federal Rules of Civil Procedure before [name of court reporter or other person authorized to administer oath] by videotape at [location] in [city, state] on [date] at [time].

[Name of corporation] is directed, pursuant to Fed. R. Civ. P. 30(b)(6), to designate one or more of its officers, directors, managing agents, or other persons to appear on its behalf and testify on each of the subject matters set forth below:

1. The employment history of the plaintiff in this action;

2. The knowledge possessed by any employee of the corporation as to physical or mental disabilities, real or perceived, of the plaintiff;

3. Any request for accommodation to disability made by the plaintiff;

4. Any discussions, analysis, reports, or correspondence from, by, or to employees of the corporation with respect to the disabilities of the plaintiff or possible accommodation to disabilities by the corporation.

The deposition will continue from day to day until completed. Parties and their attorneys other than the corporation and the designated deponent may appear and examine the witness. The corporation is obligated to appear through its designated officer, director, managing agent, or other person.

Any party may cause a traditional transcript to be made of the deposition at its own expense. The videotape will be retained in the custody of the officer taking the deposition, and copies will be made available to any party at that party's request and expense.

[4]   Notice of Deposition/Response Letter

FORM 13–9   **Sample Notice of Deposition**

IN THE UNITED STATES DISTRICT COURT
FOR THE [NORTHERN] DISTRICT OF [ILLINOIS]
[EASTERN] DIVISION

U.S EQUAL EMPLOYMENT OPPORTUNITY COMMISSION,
Plaintiff,
and

Civil Action No. [92 C 7330]

[A.I.C. SECURITY INVESTIGATIONS, LTD.];
[A.I.C. INTERNATIONAL, LTD.];
and [unnamed defendant C],

Honorable [Marvin E. Aspen]
Defendants.

NOTICE OF DEPOSITION

To: [plaintiff attorney A]
Equal Employment Opportunity Commission
[536 South Clark Street] [Room 982]
[Chicago], [IL] [60605]
[defense attorney D]

PLEASE TAKE NOTICE that, pursuant to Rule 30 of the Federal Rules of Civil Procedure, the Defendants, [A.I.C. SECURITY INVESTIGATIONS, LTD.], [A.I.C. INTERNATIONAL, LTD.], and [unnamed defendant C], by and through their attorneys, [WESSELS & PAUTSCH, P.C.], by [Charles W. Pautsch], [attorney A], and [attorney B] will take the deposition upon oral examination of the following:

DEPONENT: [Charles H. Wessel]
DATE: [Thursday], [December 10, 1992]
TIME: [10:00 A.M.]
PLACE: [Wessels & Pautsch, P.C.],
[Dunham Center]
[2035 Foxfield Drive]
[St. Charles], [IL] [60174]

FORM 13–10   Sample Response Letter to Deposition Notice

[December 4, 1992]

[defense attorney B]
[Wessels & Pautsch, P.C.]
[330 East Kilbourn Avenue]
[Suite 1475]
[Milwaukee], [WI] [53202]
Re: EEOC v. A.I.C., *et al.*
[92 C. 7330] [(N.D. Ill.)]

Dear [attorney B]:
I am writing to you concerning the Notice of Deposition for [Charles H. Wessel], which we received today. As I advised [defense attorney A] this afternoon, we consider another deposition of [Mr. Wessel] to be unduly burdensome in light of the lengthy deposition he has already given.

If you believe that there are areas that need to be covered that were not inquired about during the previous deposition, please let me know. If not, we will move for a protective order.

I will give you a call on [Monday], [December 7], so that we can have a conference as required by Rule [12(k)] of the Local Rules of the [Northern District] of [Illinois].

I look forward to hearing from you.

[plaintiff attorney A]

[5]   Motion to Compel Deposition of Victim

FORM 13–11   Sample Motion to Compel Deposition of Victim

IN THE UNITED STATES DISTRICT COURT
FOR THE [NORTHERN] DISTRICT OF [ILLINOIS]
[EASTERN] DIVISION

U.S. EQUAL EMPLOYMENT OPPORTUNITY COMMISSION,
Plaintiff,
and   Civil Action No. [92 C 7330]
[A.I.C. SECURITY INVESTIGATIONS, LTD.];
[A.I.C. INTERNATIONAL, LTD.];
and [unnamed defendant C],
                                                          Honorable [Marvin E. Aspen]
Defendants.

DEFENDANTS' MOTION TO COMPEL ATTENDANCE
OF CHARLES H. WESSEL FOR DEPOSITION

Defendants [A.I.C. SECURITY INVESTIGATIONS, LTD.], [A.I.C. INTERNATIONAL, LTD.], and [C], by and through their attorneys, [WESSELS & PAUTSCH, P.C.], by [Charles W. Pautsch], [attorney A], and [attorney B], pursuant to Rule 37, Fed. R. Civ. P., hereby move this Honorable Court for an Order compelling the attendance of [Charles H. Wessel] for Deposition and state in support hereof as follows:

1. On [November 5, 1992], prior to the instigation of this present action, [Charles H. Wessel ("Wessel")] was deposed by his attorney, [attorney C], pursuant to a Court Order made by Judge [Kocoras] upon [Wessel]'s Petition to Perpetuate Testimony under Rule 27, Fed. R. Civ. P.

2. On [November 5, 1992], counsel for Defendants had a limited opportunity to cross-examine [Wessel]. (See Memorandum in support hereof, served herewith and incorporated herein.)

3. Prior to [November 5, 1992], counsel for Defendants had no opportunity whatsoever to conduct any background discovery, including the collection and review of documents and medical records.

4. On [November 5, 1992], Plaintiff Equal Employment Opportunity Commission ("EEOC") filed this present action on behalf of [Wessel] and served the Complaint upon Defendants on or about [November 10, 1992].

5. On [November 12, 1992], this Court ordered discovery to be conducted on an expedited basis with discovery closing [December 31, 1992].

6. On [December 1, 1992], Defendants' counsel sent to Plaintiff EEOC via facsimile and U.S. Mail a Notice of Deposition instructing Plaintiff EEOC to have [Wessel] appear for his deposition on [Thursday], [December 10, 1992], at [10:00 A.M.] (See copy of Notice of Deposition and Proof of Service attached hereto as Exhibit No. 1 and incorporated herein.)

7. On [Friday], [December 4, 1992], [attorney A], attorney for Plaintiff EEOC, sent a letter to Defendants' counsel expressing a desire to conduct a [12(k)] (Local Court General Rule [12(k)]) conference on [December 7, 1992]. (See letter attached hereto as Exhibit No. 2 and incorporated herein.)

8. On [Monday], December 7, 1992], [attorney B], another attorney for Plaintiff EEOC, telephoned Defendants' counsel; however, Defendants' counsel was in meeting and unable to take Attorney [B]'s telephone call. (See copy of message note attached hereto as Exhibit No. 3 and incorporated herein.)

9. Twice on [Monday], [December 7, 1992], at approximately [1:00 P.M.] and [3:00 P.M.], Defendants' counsel [B] returned the telephone call of EEOC Attorney [B]; however, EEOC Attorney [B] did not accept the calls and did not return the message left by Defense Attorney [B]. (See Affidavit of [defense attorney B] attached hereto and incorporated herein.)

10. On [Tuesday], [December 8], [1992], one of Defendants' counsel, [attorney A], telephoned Plaintiff's EEOC Attorney [A], and was informed by her that Plaintiff refused to produce [Wessel] for deposition.

11. Prior to the date of filing of this present motion, Defendants' attorneys' attempts to engage in personal consultation have been unsuccessful due to no fault of Defendants' attorneys. [Local Court Gen. Rule 12(k)].

12. Prior to the date of filing of this present motion, Plaintiff EEOC has not moved for a protective order pursuant to Rule 26(c), Fed. R. Civ. P., nor has Plaintiff put forward a legitimate reason for not producing [Wessel] for deposition.

WHEREFORE, Defendants respectfully request the Court to set forth an Order

(1) commanding [Charles H. Wessel] to appear for deposition; and

(2) awarding Defendants just and equitable relief pursuant to Rule 37(d), Fed. R. Civ. P., including but not limited to reasonable attorneys' fees and costs for having to file this present motion.

FORM 13–12   Sample Affidavit for Motion to Compel

IN THE UNITED STATES DISTRICT COURT
FOR THE [NORTHERN] DISTRICT OF [ILLINOIS]
[EASTERN] DIVISION

U.S. EQUAL EMPLOYMENT OPPORTUNITY COMMISSION,
Plaintiff,
and   Civil Action No. [92 C 7330]
[A.I.C. SECURITY INVESTIGATIONS, LTD.];

[A.I.C. INTERNATIONAL, LTD.];
and [unnamed defendant C],

Honorable [Marvin E. Aspen]

Defendants.
AFFIDAVIT OF [attorney B]
STATE OF [WISCONSIN]
COUNTY OF [MILWAUKEE]

I, [attorney B], being first duly sworn under oath, depose and state:

1. Affiant is an attorney duly admitted to practice before this Court and has filed an Appearance on behalf of the Defendants in the above-captioned action.

2. On [Monday], [December 7, 1992], Affiant received a written telephone message from his secretary, [name], that Attorney [B] from the Equal Employment Opportunity Commission ("EEOC") had telephoned.

3. At approximately [1:00 P.M.] on [December 7, 1992], Affiant telephoned the EEOC in [Chicago] and asked for Attorney [B]. The person answering the phones at the EEOC indicated that [attorney B] was unavailable to come to the phone. The affiant then asked the receptionist at the EEOC to take down his name and number and have [attorney B] return the call.

4. At approximately [3:00 P.M.] on [Monday], [December 7, 1992], Affiant made a second telephone call to the EEOC and asked for Attorney [B]. The person answering the phones for the EEOC indicated that [attorney B] was still not available to talk. Affiant requested that a telephone message be given to [attorney B] so she could promptly return Affiant's phone call.

5. On [Monday], [December 7, 1992], Affiant was at his office until approximately [6:30 P.M.] and did not at any time receive a telephone call from either Attorney [B] or Attorney [A].

6. I have read these six (6) paragraphs and two (2) pages, and certify by my signature below that they are true and correct to my best information and belief.

[6]   Defendant's Motion to Compel Deposition of Victim's Wife

FORM 13–13   **Sample Motion to Compel Deposition of Victim's Wife**

DEFENDANTS' MOTION TO COMPEL DEPOSITION OF DEPONENT
[ALICE E. WESSEL]

Defendants, [A.I.C. SECURITY INVESTIGATIONS, LTD.], [A.I.C. INTERNATIONAL, LTD.], and [unnamed defendant C], by and through their attorneys [WESSEL AND PAUTSCH, P.C.], by [Charles A. Pautsch], [attorney A], and [attorney B], pursuant to Rule 37(a)(2), Fed. R. Civ. P., hereby move this Honorable Court to set forth an Order compelling Deponent [Alice H. Wessel] to answer certain questions posed to her at deposition and state in support hereof as follows:

1. On [January 27, 1993], [Alice H. Wessel] was deposed at the offices of the Equal Employment Opportunity Commission ("EEOC") pursuant to a sub-

poena issued to her under Rule 45, Fed. R. Civ. P., by Defendants' attorneys, [Wessel & Pautsch, P.C.]

2. Deponent [Alice H. Wessel] was represented at the deposition by Attorney [C].

3. During the course of the deposition of [Alice H. Wessel], Attorney [C] instructed his client not to answer a number of questions posed to her based upon an assertion of spousal privilege.

4. During the course of this deposition, the parties presented an argument to this Court via a telephone conference call on the deponent's refusal to testify regarding assets owned by her and her husband, the Plaintiff in intervention, [Charles Wessel] (which issue was ruled upon during said conference with the Court), and also regarding the deponent's refusal to answer any questions concerning communications between the deponent and [Charles Wessel].

5. The Court proposed that the parties stipulate to the deponent's answering the objectionable questions and that the transcript be sealed and forwarded to the Court for its ruling on the asserted application of spousal privilege; when the deponent's counsel refused to so stipulate, the Defendants were instructed to certify to the Court any objected to questions pursuant to the Federal Rules of Civil Procedure.

6. Accordingly, the Defendants hereby move to compel the deponent [Alice Wessel]'s testimony on questions posed on the following pages and lines (hereinafter referenced as TR [Page #], [Line #s]) of the attached transcript: [enumerated page citations omitted].

(See transcript of deposition of [Alice H. Wessel] filed herewith and incorporated herein.)

7. Defendants are entitled to the questions set forth in paragraph six (6) above. (See Memorandum in support of this motion filed herewith and incorporated herein.)

WHEREFORE, Defendants respectfully request this Court to set forth an Order compelling Deponent [Alice H. Wessel] to answer the foregoing questions noted from the transcript of her [January 27, 1993] deposition. Defendants further request attorneys' fees and costs in having to prepare and file this present motion and attorneys' fees and costs in reconvening the deposition of [Alice H. Wessel].

Dated this [8th] day of [February] [1993].

[7] Order to Compel Attendance at Deposition

FORM 13–14   **Sample Order to Compel Attendance at Deposition**

IN THE UNITED STATES DISTRICT COURT
FOR THE [NORTHERN] DISTRICT OF [ILLINOIS]
[EASTERN] DIVISION

U.S. EQUAL EMPLOYMENT OPPORTUNITY COMMISSION,
Plaintiff,

and　　　　　　　　　　　　　　　　Civil Action No. [92 C 7330]
[A.I.C. SECURITY INVESTIGATIONS, LTD.];
[A.I.C. INTERNATIONAL, LTD.];
and [unnamed defendant C],

　　　　　　　　　　　　　　　　Honorable [Marvin E. Aspen]
　　Defendants.

ORDER

Pending is Defendants' [A.I.C. SECURITY INVESTIGATIONS, LTD.], [A.I.C. INTERNATIONAL, LTD.], and [defendant C] ("Defendants") motion to compel attendance of plaintiff [Charles H. Wessel ("Wessel")] for deposition. For the reasons listed below, [Mr. Wessel] is hereby ordered to appear.

BACKGROUND FACTS

This is an action under the Americans with Disabilities Act, 42 U.S.C. §§ 12,101 *et seq.,* ("the Act") alleging that [Charles Wessel ("Wessel")] was terminated from his employment because of his disability, terminal cancer. On [November 5, 1992], prior to the commencement of this action, [Wessel] was deposed by defense Attorneys [C] and [B], pursuant to a Court Order entered by the Honorable [Charles Kocoras] upon [Wessel]'s Petition to Perpetuate Testimony under Fed. R. Civ. P. 37. At this time, counsel for Defendants had no opportunity to conduct any background discovery, including the collection and review of documents and medical records. At the time of the deposition, it appears that Defendants had been forwarded a list of all the medical practitioners who had provided treatment or examined [Mr. Wessel]'s medical condition or status. This list included the hospitals where [Mr. Wessel] had been treated. [Mr. Wessel] did not have any medical records in his possession with one exception: he had the last two MRIs that were performed on him at the [Center for Magnetic Imaging]. He did not, however, have the radiologist's report that interpreted those MRIs. At this time, [Mr. Wessel]'s attorney also produced payment records provided by [Mr. Wessel]'s insurance company.

On [November 6, 1992], the Equal Employment Opportunity Commission ("EEOC") filed the instant complaint on behalf of [Wessel] and served the Complaint upon Defendants on or about [November 10, 1992]. On [December 1, 1992], Defendants' counsel sent to the EEOC a Notice of Deposition instructing the EEOC to have [Wessel] appear for his deposition on [Thursday], [December 10, 1992], at [10:00 A.M.]. On [Tuesday], [December 8, 1992], one of Defendants' counsel, [attorney A], telephoned [Wessel]'s attorney at the EEOC, [attorney A], and was informed by her that [Wessel] would not be produced for his deposition. Prior to the filing of this motion, negotiations pursuant to [Local Court Gen. Rule 12(k)] proved unsuccessful.

The EEOC objects to producing [Wessel] because such a deposition would be unduly burdensome, and because of alleged misstatements made in Defendants' Motion to Compel Attendance. In particular, the EEOC points out that the initial Petition to Perpetuate Testimony of [Wessel] as well as to Produce Documents and for a Physical and Mental Examination were initiated by Defendants. Similarly, the EEOC argues that Defendants' counsel had ample opportunity to examine [Wessel] during the [November 5, 1992] deposition. The EEOC also points out that attorneys for Defendants requested and received information and documents from [Wessel]'s attorneys in accordance with an order issued by Judge [Kocoras] at a hearing on [October 15, 1992].

The EEOC further argues that it would be unduly burdensome to produce [Wessel] a second time especially in light of the fact that he was questioned extensively concerning his medical condition and its effect upon his ability to perform his job duties. The EEOC contends that Defendants have made no showing that there were material issues that were not covered during the deposition.

DISCUSSION

While I agree with the EEOC that Defendants have failed to make a showing of the material issues not covered during [Mr. Wessel]'s deposition of [November 5, 1992], it is also clear that Defendants were required to take [Mr. Wessel]'s deposition with little or no medical evidence as to [Mr. Wessel]'s terminal cancer condition. The list of health care providers forwarded to Defendants' counsel on [October 21, 1992], would not have adequately prepared Defendant for this deposition nor would the two MRIs.

As provided in the Act, the Act currently provides for a three-pronged definition of disability, which provides as follows:

A person with disability is

(a) a person with a physical or mental impairment that substantially limits that person in some major life activity;

(b) a person with a record of such a physical or mental impairment; or

(c) a person who is regarded as having such an impairment.

ADA § 3, 42 U.S.C. § 12,102(2).

The EEOC regulations to the ADA, which implement the employment title of the law (Title I), repeat this three-prong definition of disability. [See 29 C.F.R. § 1630.2(g)]. As indicated by the definition, this impairment must be one that substantially limits the person in a major life activity. [Id.] In determining whether a person is substantially limited in a life activity, the potential limitation must be analyzed without regard to the existence of mitigating devices or medicines. See [29 C.F.R. § 1630.2(h), (j) (EEOC GUIDANCE at 35,741)]. While most serious medical conditions do have a substantial impact on basic life activities, this impact on [Mr. Wessel] must be established by [Mr. Wessel] to enjoy the protection of the Act.

Further, [Mr. Wessel] must show that he is a qualified individual with a disability. Under the ADA, a *qualified individual with a disability* is a person who, with or without reasonable accommodation can perform the "essentials functions" of the job that the person holds or desires. ADA § 101(8), 42 U.S.C. § 12,111(8). [Mr. Wessel]'s qualifications or lack thereof could be used by Defendants as a defense.

In light of the fact that [Mr. Wessel]'s condition is a cerebral progressive condition and the effects of this condition vary from case to case, it is only appropriate that [Mr. Wessel] appear for a second deposition where the limitations of his medical condition as well as the essential functions of the job are explored. Defendants could not have adequately prepared for this line of questioning without having reviewed [Mr. Wessel]'s medical records.

I am limiting, however, the scope of this second deposition in accordance with Fed. R. Civ. P. 26(c) from questioning [Mr. Wessel] on issues not covered in the [November 5, 1992] deposition. Fed. R. Civ. P. 26(c) provides that a court may limit the discovery of a party "to protect a party . . . from annoyance, embarrassment, oppression, or undue burden or expense" on a showing of good cause.

Defendants are not to take this opportunity to harass [Mr. Wessel]. If such becomes the case, [Mr. Wessel] may petition the court for a protective order.

§ 13.05   Interrogatories

[A]   Drafting Interrogatories

The author of interrogatories must never forget that interrogatories are answered in an adversarial context. If the form of an interrogatory affords room for an opponent to object or to give a vague or unhelpful answer, the opponent is motivated to do so. Accordingly, interrogatories should be narrowly framed, precise, and unambiguous. When preparing interrogatories, it is even more useful than in complaint drafting to change roles or have someone play devil's advocate to see what kinds of objections or useless responses can be made to a preliminary draft of interrogatories. Properly drafted interrogatories support motions for sanctions if an opponent is unresponsive.

One useful technique for minimizing unhelpful responses is to provide branching questions, for example, "State what accommodations you provided plaintiff; if you provided no accommodation, state why not." This reduces the probability of the respondent getting off the hook with a simple "no," or "none were provided."

When a court order or local rule limits the number of interrogatories that may be propounded without special permission,[18] attention must be given to efficiency in drafting interrogatories. For example, by asking, "Who was involved in the decision not to provide accommodation to plaintiff's disability?," only one interrogatory is used. By asking, "Was A involved in deciding not to accommodate plaintiff's disability? Was B involved in failing to accommodate plaintiff's disability? Was C involved in failing to accommodate plaintiff's disability?," three interrogatories are used.

---

[18] Even if Congress postpones or rejects these amendments, a growing number of judges and local rules already limit the number of interrogatories.

It is more convenient for everyone if interrogatories are propounded and answered in computer-readable form.

[B] Objections to Interrogatories

Federal Rule of Civil Procedure 33(a) authorizes objections to interrogatories rather than answers, as long as the objections are asserted with particularity and are served more or less contemporaneously with the answers. Counsel objecting to interrogatories should consider at least the following objections, which are usually valid if supported by the form of the question in the underlying factual circumstances:

1. Outside the scope of discovery, for example, privileged or not likely to lead to admissible evidence;
2. Vague or ambiguous;
3. Overbroad (for example, all documents pertaining to the employer's personnel policies or actions taken pursuant thereto);
4. Unduly burdensome, in light of the cost to respond and the probable utility to the propounding party;
5. Request for purely legal conclusions.

The following objections are not likely to be sustained:

1. Inadmissible information;
2. Information available to the requesting party through other sources;
3. Requests for an admission;
4. Opinions or contentions.

Objections can be asserted in the response to the interrogatories or, if they relate to an entire set of interrogatories, they may be asserted in a request for a protective order.

[C] Interrogatory Preparation

The following is a list of the types of information to be requested in interrogatories in an ADA case:

1. Names of persons providing statements to the responding person or entity;
2. Persons who have been interviewed in connection with the litigation;
3. Other persons with knowledge of the transactions material to the litigation;
4. Existence, nature, description, location, and custodian of documents, including witness statements;
5. Summaries of technical data and statistics, reports, studies, personnel policies, and position evaluations and descriptions ma-

terial to the litigation and reflecting an employer's overall approach to accommodation under the ADA;

6. Business and corporate information, including the state of incorporation, the relationship between the employing entity and its corporate affiliates, and the assets and income of both the employing entity and its corporate affiliates for relevant time periods;
7. Names of expert witnesses who will testify at trial, or who have been retained or consulted whether or not they will testify;[19]
8. Opinions and bases for opinions of experts expected to testify at trial;
9. Existence and extent of insurance coverage;
10. Information that may be pertinent to an ultimate writ of execution, with appropriate attention to possible garnishment;
11. Facts pertinent to establishing personal jurisdiction;
12. Basis for contentions expressed or implied by the pleadings or anticipated in amendments to the pleadings.[20]

Interrogatories typically are divided into sections, which include:

1. Prefaces explaining the request and the authority for making the request, including time limits for answering;
2. Instructions, including a reminder to conduct a reasonable investigation and an obligation to include information, even if it is hearsay;
3. Definitions, including definitions of commonly used words like *describe, document,* and *identify.*

[D]   Sample Forms

[1]   Interrogatories with Detailed Definitions

FORM 13–15   Sample Interrogatories with Detailed Definitions

[JKL]'S FIRST SET OF INTERROGATORIES TO THE DEFENDANTS
    The Plaintiff, [JKL Corporation], hereby requests that the defendants each answer the following interrogatories in accordance with Rule 33 of the Federal Rules of Civil Procedure.

---

[19] By limiting discovery of facts and opinions held by experts who are not expected to be called, Fed. R. Civ. P. 26(b)(4)(B) implies that the names of such experts are discoverable. Moreover, the phrase "who has been retained or specially employed" implies that the facts known to and opinions held by experts who are regular employees are discoverable like any other information.
[20] Fed. R. Civ. P. 33(b) expressly permits "contention interrogatories."

Definitions and Instructions

1. As used herein, the designation [JKL] refers to the named plaintiff [JKL Corporation] and any and all predecessor or successor companies, corporations, partnerships, or other business entities; any company, corporation, partnership, or other business entity affiliated with [JKL] or owned by it in whole or in part; and the partners, directors, agents, employees, and attorneys of any of them, including all persons acting or purporting to act on behalf of, or who are subject to the direction or control of, any of the foregoing.

2. The term *document* or *documents* as used herein shall mean any recordation of any intelligence or information, and includes, wherever applicable and without limitation, letters, correspondence, memoranda, notes, reports, compilations, data, notebooks, work papers, graphs, charts, blueprints, books, ledgers, drawings, sketches, schematic diagrams, layouts, logic diagrams, flow charts, part lists, photographs, movies, slides, video recordings, diaries, sales literature, brochures, employee handbooks, employee benefit plans, summary plan descriptions, agreements, minutes of meetings, punch cards, magnetic disks, diskettes, tape or wire, optical disks, printout sheets, and any and all other writings, typings, printings, drafts, copies, and/or mechanical, electronic, or photographic reproduction or recordations thereof in the possession, custody, or control of the defendants or any of its representatives, or known to any of the foregoing, whether or not prepared by the defendants. *Document* or *documents* also includes all copies that are not identical with the original.

3. *Water Recreation Equipment* means boats, skis, motorized ski equipment, as well as related and unrelated equipment used for recreational boating.

4. *Individual Defendant(s)* means [defendant A], [defendant B], [defendant C], or [defendant D] individually and in any permutation.

5. Whenever an interrogatory or response refers to a document, the answer shall state the following information with respect to each such document:

(a) the date appearing on such document, and if no date appears thereon, the answer shall so state and shall give the date or approximate date such document was prepared;

(b) the identifying or descriptive code number (including production number if already produced), file number, title, or label of such document;

(c) the general nature or description of such document (i.e., whether it is a letter, memorandum, drawing, etc.) and the number of pages of which it consists;

(d) the name of the person who signed such document, and if it was not signed, the answer shall so state and shall give the name of the person or persons who prepared it;

(e) the name of the person to whom such document was addressed and the name of each person other than such addressee to whom such document or copies thereof were given or sent;

(f) the name of the person(s) having possession, custody, or control of such document and any copy thereof;

(g) whether or not any draft, copy, or reproduction of such document contains or has been subject to any postscript, notation, change, amendment, or addendum not appearing on said document itself, and if so, the answer shall identify as herein required each such draft, copy, or reproduction.

(h) the source or origin of said document, and if the document was not generated by defendants, the answer shall specify from whom the document was obtained and identify said person and the relationship of that person to defendants;

(i) if any such document was but is no longer in the possession or subject to the control of defendant, the disposition made of it and when;

(j) if any such document is claimed to be privileged, in addition to the foregoing information,

      (i) the basis on which the claim of privilege is asserted, and

      (ii) a general description of the content thereof;

6. The term *communication* refers to any exchange or transfer of information whether documentary, oral, or otherwise.

7. The term *things* refers to any physical object other than documents, including without limitation models, structures, components, circuit boards, prototypes, or other devices, and any parts, portions, or assemblies thereof.

8. Whenever an interrogatory or response refers to a person, state to the extent known, his or her

(a) full name;

(b) present or last known home address;

(c) present or last known business address;

(d) present or last known title or occupation;

(e) present or last known employer; and

(f) if associated with defendants, the period of times so associated, the nature of the association, and the area of responsibility during such times.

9. Whenever an interrogatory or response refers to a company, corporation, partnership, joint venture, foundation, educational institution, or other entity, state to the extent known

(a) its full name;

(b) its address;

(c) its state of incorporation;

(d) its location of its headquarters;

(e) its location of the division(s), branch(es), or office(s) that is (are) connected with or handled the matter(s) referred to in the interrogatory; and

(f) the identity of the person or persons acting or purporting to act on behalf of the entity in connection with the matter(s) referred to in the interrogatory.

10. Whenever an interrogatory or response refers to "information" or "beliefs," to the extent known

(a) identify the person, document, communication, or other source of said information or belief;

(b) identify the person or other recipient of said information or belief;

(c) state the date said information or belief was communicated;

(d) state what information or belief was communicated;

(e) identify all acts, transactions, occurrences, or other activities undertaken to verify or otherwise investigate the veracity of said information or belief;

(f) state what information was relied upon to form any belief; and,

(g) identify all documents and communications referring or relating to said information or belief or the information referred to in subsections (a)–(f) hereof.

11. Whenever an interrogatory or response refers to or seeks a description of an act, transaction, occurrence, dealing, omission, or instance, state to the extent known

(a) the date, including year, month, and date, when it occurred;

(b) the place where it occurred;

(c) the identity of each person participating therein;

(d) on whose behalf each said person participated or purported to participate.

(e) the nature, subject matter, and circumstances surrounding it;

(f) the nature and substance of all communications occurring during, or in connection with it; and

(g) all documents referring or relating thereto or the information referred to in subsections (a)–(f) hereof.

12. Whenever an interrogatory seeks the basis for an allegation, include all facts, beliefs, acts, transactions, occurrences, dealings, omissions, instances, and communications, and identify all documents and persons that refer or relate to said allegation.

13. These interrogatories shall be deemed continuing so that with respect to any interrogatory herein, or part thereof, as to which defendants, after answering, acquire additional knowledge or information, [JKL] requests that a supplemental response be made within thirty (30) days after acquiring such additional knowledge or information.

INTERROGATORY NO. 1

Identify all related and predecessor corporations and business entities (including subsidiaries, divisions, affiliated, or parent corporations) of the defendants [A, B, C, and D] and identify each officer, director, employee, and shareholder for such corporation or business entity.

INTERROGATORY NO. 2

Identify the persons, with tenure dates, who have had for the past 10 years responsibility for the following functions of defendants [A, B, C, and D], their predecessors, and related corporations identified in the Answer to Interrogatory No. 1:

(a) chief executive officer;

(b) chief operating officer or general manager;

(c) manufacturing;

(d) sales;

(e) engineering;

(f) research and development;

(g) patent activities;

(h) contract and license;

(i) the manufacture, marketing, sale, or distribution of water treatment equipment;

(j) personnel or human resources;

(k) labor relations;

(l) employee benefits;

(m) risk management;

(n) training;

(o) legal;
(p) Board of Directors;
(q) Treasurer; and
(r) Secretary.

INTERROGATORY NO. 3

Describe any and all business relationships that presently exist or have in the past existed between or among each of the defendants (in any combination or permutation) and locate and identify all documents and things that refer to, relate to, or comment upon any such relationship.

INTERROGATORY NO. 4

Identify all documents and things in the possession, custody, or control of [A, B, C, or D] and/or the Individual Defendants that
(a) any Individual Defendant obtained during or by reason of his employment at [JKL] or during any period of consultancy for [JKL];
(b) embody or in any way refer to information obtained during and by reason of any individual Defendant's employment at [JKL]; and/or
(c) embody or in any way refer to information secured, directly or indirectly, from [JKL].

INTERROGATORY NO. 5

As to each individual Defendant for the whole of the time period subsequent to his employment at [JKL] and for [RDP] from [1988] to the present, identify all documents and things that were at one time in his or its possession, custody, or control that are no longer in his or its possession, custody, or control and that
(a) constitute documents or things of [JKL]; and/or
(b) embody or in any way refer to information secured, directly or indirectly, from [JKL].

INTERROGATORY NO. 6

State whether any representative of [A, B, C, or D] (including the Individual Defendants for the time periods subsequent to the respective dates of termination of their employment at [JKL]) has ever seen any documents, or excerpts thereof, or orally received any information that refers to, relates to, or comments upon
(a) plaintiff's mental or physical condition;
(b) plaintiff's ability to perform job functions;
(c) any request for modification in job functions for plaintiff;
(d) any evaluation of plaintiff's performance and conduct as an employee; and
(e) plaintiff's prospects for future employment with any defendant.

INTERROGATORY NO. 7

If the response to any part of Interrogatory No. 6 is affirmative, state for each occurrence

(a) when and where each such document was seen or such oral information was received;

(b) by whom and to whom each document was shown or such oral information was disclosed;

(c) how each such document or oral information was obtained;

(d) whether [ABC] and/or any individual Defendant now has each such document,

and, if not, when and how it lost possession thereof and the present location of each such document; and

(e) the identity of all such documents presently in the possession, custody, or control of any defendant.

INTERROGATORY NO. 8

Identify all documents that refer or relate in any way to a need or desire on the part of defendants [A, B, C, or D] to respond to or meet their obligations under any law covering mental or physical disabilities of

(a) employees;

(b) suppliers; and

(c) customers.

[2] Sample Employee Interrogatories for ADA Claim

FORM 13–16   Sample Employee Interrogatories for ADA Claim

§ 1 Reasons for Employee Termination and Employer Justification

1. Why was the plaintiff/employee terminated?

2. Are there any documents reflecting this reason for termination? Please describe briefly each such document, and provide copies of them.

3. What, if anything, was the plaintiff told was the reason for termination? By whom? When? Please give dates and names of persons participating, and describe what was said to the plaintiff and by the plaintiff on each occasion.

4. At what time did you begin contemplating the discharge of the plaintiff? Please state the exact date.

5. Did the plaintiff ever make any complaints about your policies or practices? If the answer is "yes," provide dates, times, and a summary of the complaints, and identify by name, address, and telephone number the person to whom the complaints were made.

6. Please describe the incident or series of incidents that prompted you first to consider terminating the plaintiff. In your answer, please describe exactly what the plaintiff did or did not do.

7. What was your response to this conduct of the plaintiff? Include the date, the name of any person designated to act in your behalf, and the action you took.

8. If you told the plaintiff about plaintiff's conduct, please state as precisely as you can what you said, and state the time, date, and place of this communication. If you communicated to the plaintiff in writing, please describe the content of the communication, and state the date the communication was sent or given to the plaintiff.

9. Why do you feel that the plaintiff's conduct could not be tolerated, consistent with the business needs of your firm?

§ 2 Contract Formation and Terms of the Employment Relation

10. Was the employee/plaintiff ever told anything orally, or in writing, regarding how long employment would last, or the conditions under which the employment would end?

11. Did you ever tell the plaintiff that it would take a certain discrete period of time to complete fully the task or tasks for which she was hired? If so, state the date and circumstances under which the statement was made, and the time period mentioned.

12. Did you ever represent to the plaintiff that the job would last for a specific length of time? If so, how long?

13. Did you ever represent to the plaintiff that plaintiff's job was dependent on the performance of tasks or on the fulfillment of certain conditions? If so, please specify the date on which the representations were made, by whom, in what form, and the precise details of the tasks and conditions.

14. Did you ever represent to the plaintiff that plaintiff would never have to worry about being discharged? If so, state the time, place, and form of the representation, and the name of the person(s) who made such a representation.

15. Did you ever represent to the plaintiff that all employees of the company would be treated fairly? If so, state the time, date, place, and form of such representations, and the name of the person(s) who made the representations.

16. Did you ever represent to the plaintiff that plaintiff would be dismissed if plaintiff engaged in certain conduct or failed to meet certain performance requirements? If so, please state the time, date, and place such representations were made, the name of the person(s) who made the representations, and the form of the representations.

17. Do you believe that you treat your employees fairly? If so, please state your reasons why. How do you ensure that first-level supervisors treat your employees fairly?

18. Do you have a written personnel policy handbook or an employee manual? If so, please state when it was created, describe any revisions made since it was created, and describe its contents. Please provide a copy.

19. What is the purpose of the employee handbook or manual?

20. Do you give the employee manual or policy handbook to the employees? If so, please state when the manual or policy handbook is given to employees.

21. Was the plaintiff given a copy of the employee handbook or manual? If so, please state the time, date, and place of the distribution.

22. Did a person authorized to make representations on your behalf explain the meaning of the handbook or policy manual to the plaintiff? If so, please state the name of the person who made such representation, as well as his/her address and position/job title. In addition, please describe the explanation that this representative made at the time of distribution of the manual or handbook.

23. Do other documents exist that were written in connection with the creation of the employee handbook or manual? If so, please describe their content.

24. Who wrote the employee handbook or manual? Please state their names, addresses, and positions.

25. Do you believe the employee handbook or manual to be a part of the plaintiff's employment contract with you? If not, please state your reasons for this belief.

26. Is there any reason why the plaintiff would believe that you do not follow the policies articulated or procedures outlined in the handbook or manual? If so, please give your reasons.

27. When you gave the plaintiff the handbook or manual, did you intend to be bound by it? If not, please explain why.

28. Do you expect employees to comply with provisions of the handbook or manual? Which provisions?

29. Do you have a standard application for employment form? If the answer is "yes," please provide a copy.

30. Did the plaintiff fill out an application for employment form? If the answer is "yes," please provide a copy.

31. Why do you think that the plaintiff came to work for you?

32. After you hired the plaintiff, were you aware of any offers made to plaintiff for new employment? If so, please state the date and substance of the offers, to the best of your knowledge.

33. Did the plaintiff discuss these offers with anyone in your enterprise? If the answer is "yes," summarize the nature of such discussions and state what was said to the plaintiff.

34. After you hired the plaintiff, did plaintiff arrive for work at the stated time? Please state the date upon which plaintiff's work began.

§ 3 Procedures Utilized in Connection with the Termination

35. When the plaintiff was terminated, what procedure was followed? Please list each step, the result, the date upon which the step was taken, and the person in charge of administering the particular steps.

36. Please describe any additional actions that you took, or actions taken by any person designated by you to act, in response to any conduct by the plaintiff.

37. If you told the plaintiff anything regarding plaintiff's conduct, please state as well as you can what you said, and the date, time, and place of such statements.

38. If you had any written communication with the plaintiff regarding plaintiff's conduct, please describe the content of the communication, and the date on which it was sent or given to the plaintiff.

39. Did you at any time cause anyone to investigate any fact of the plaintiff's life, including conduct on or off the job? If so, please state the investigator's name, address, and time period during which the investigations were conducted.

40. If an investigation was made of the plaintiff, were reports made to you? If the answer is "yes," please state the date on which the reports were made, the nature of the reports, and their content.

41. What means were used to investigate the plaintiff? Please describe the means in detail.

42. If an investigation of the plaintiff was made, were any reports made? If so, please state the dates of the reports, and their nature and content.

43. Did you ever tell the plaintiff that plaintiff would be terminated on a date other than the date the plaintiff was actually terminated? If so, please state the date and place such statements were made, and the name, address, and position of the person who made the statements.

44. If you did not tell the plaintiff prior to the date that plaintiff was terminated that plaintiff would be terminated, please explain why you did not.

45. Was the decision to terminate the plaintiff subject to review by someone else before the termination was effected? If so, by whom?

46. Before you terminated the plaintiff's employment, did you consider how the plaintiff would feel when plaintiff was terminated? If you did, please describe your thoughts at the time.

47. Do you believe that the plaintiff expected to be terminated? If so, please state your reasons for this belief.

48. Was the plaintiff afforded any kind of internal hearing or review before plaintiff was terminated? If so, please describe, giving the dates and the names of the persons participating in each step. Are there any written records or documents summarizing, or otherwise memorializing, what transpired while these procedures were being followed? Please describe each of these documents.

49. If you personally terminated the plaintiff, please describe plaintiff's reaction to the termination. If another employee terminated the plaintiff, please state the person's name, address, and position.

50. When you were contemplating terminating the employment of the plaintiff, did you talk with anyone about this pending decision? If so, please state the person's name, address, and position (if employed by you), and describe the nature and content of the communication.

51. During the termination, was any other person present? If so, please state the person's name, address, and position, if employed by you.

52. Did the plaintiff undertake to arbitrate or mediate the termination? If so, please describe the steps taken, the results, the dates upon which the steps were taken, and the names and addresses of all persons involved.

53. After the plaintiff's termination, did you communicate with any other person about the decision, excluding attorneys? If so, state the other person's name, address, and position (if your employee), and describe the nature and content of the discussion.

§ 4 Employer's Assessment of the Plaintiff's Job Performance

54. Are there any written evaluations of the plaintiff's performance during plaintiff's tenure with the company? Do you have any other documents reflecting the plaintiff's performance during the time that plaintiff was employed by you? If so, please describe, and please provide copies of such documents.

55. Do you have documents describing your initial evaluation of the plaintiff prior to the time plaintiff started working for you? If do, please describe them, and provide copies.

56. Do you have any documents describing any disciplinary action taken against the plaintiff? If so, please describe, and provide copies.

57. Was the plaintiff ever counseled in any way regarding plaintiff's conduct or performance? If so, please give the dates, and names of persons participating in such counseling. What was said on each occasion to the plaintiff and by the plaintiff?

58. How would you characterize the plaintiff's overall work performance?

59. Did the plaintiff receive any awards or commendations? If so, please give the dates on which the awards or commendations were given, and describe the awards or commendations, the reasons for them, and the occasions on which they were given.

60. Why did the plaintiff's employment continue for as long as it did?

§ 5 Discovering Similarly Situated Personnel

61. Have any other employees ever been terminated for the same reason as the plaintiff? Please give the names of these employees and the dates of termination.

62. What other employees performed at the same level as the plaintiff and engaged in conduct similar to the plaintiff's? Please give the names and a brief summary of their performance, conduct, and any personnel actions taken.

63. Who, if anyone, is now filling the plaintiff's job?

64. Is anyone now performing the plaintiff's job duties? Who?

§ 6 Background Information about the Employer

65. Describe the nature of your business. Include the number of employees, the type(s) of work they do, and the institutions or persons they serve, if applicable.

66. How many distinct plants or facilities are part of the employing enterprise? Please provide a list of all such plants and facilities.

67. What is the legal form of the employing enterprise (e.g., partnership, corporation, proprietorship)?

68. In what state is the employing enterprise registered or incorporated?

69. If the employing enterprise is a corporation, is the stock publicly traded? If so, what is its symbol, and on which exchange is it traded?

70. If the employing enterprise is a corporation, please provide a list of the 10 most significant owners of stock in the company.

71. Are you required to be licensed by state, local, or federal governments to perform your business functions? If so, please describe the licenses held, and provide the name and address of the issuing agency.

72. Are you subject to any state or federal civil service laws or regulations? If so, please briefly describe their nature, or state in what publication they may be found.

73. When did the plaintiff first begin working for you? Please state the exact date.

74. Who was the plaintiff's supervisor?

75. Who made the decision to terminate the plaintiff's employment?

76. Has this person ever terminated any other employees? If so, please give the employees' names and the dates of termination.

§ 7 Witness Identification

77. What are the names, telephone numbers, and addresses of employees who can testify to (i) employer policies or statements, or (ii) conduct showing employer policy, practice, and performance, or (iii) conduct of the plaintiff?

§ 8 Other Formal Proceedings Related to the Termination

78. Was any hearing held on an unemployment claim by the plaintiff? Were any other documents or records made memorializing the hearing?

79. Did the company contest any claim for unemployment benefits made by the plaintiff? If not, why not? Do you have any internal procedures for grievance processing? If so, please state (i) when such procedures came into effect, (ii) the name, address, and position of the person or persons responsible for administering them, and (iii) the nature of the procedures.

80. Did you have in effect any arbitration or mediation procedure, either formal or informal, at the time of the plaintiff's termination? If so, please describe the steps taken under this procedure, and describe the procedure as a whole.

81. Do you know of any company or official investigation or inquiry into the circumstances surrounding the plaintiff's termination?

§ 9 Reasonable Accommodation by Employer/Undue Hardship

82. Did your company perform a preemployment medical examination on the plaintiff? If so, were any major medical problems discovered? Please attach a copy of the doctor's written report pertaining to plaintiff's examination. Does your company as a practice subject all employees to a medical examination prior to the commencement of their employment?

83. When the plaintiff began working for you, did you believe her to be a *qualified individual with a disability,* as defined by the Americans with Disabilities Act ("ADA"), 42 U.S.C. §§ 12,101 *et seq.*?

84. If the answer to the preceding question is "yes," what mental or physical impairment did you or do you believe the plaintiff to have? Please explain.

85. Do you contend that you attempted to make a *reasonable accommodation,* as defined by the ADA, to cope with the plaintiff's disability? What steps, if any, did you take to accommodate the plaintiff's disability?

86. Do you contend that to make an accommodation for the plaintiff's disability would constitute an *undue hardship,* as defined by the ADA? If the answer is "yes," please state in some detail why such an accommodation would constitute an undue hardship.

87. Why is the plaintiff, in your opinion, no longer qualified to perform plaintiff's job? What essential job functions is the plaintiff unable to perform?

88. Are there any other jobs with your company similar to the plaintiff's former job that plaintiff would be capable of performing? Did you attempt to have the plaintiff try another job after you concluded that plaintiff was no longer capable of performing plaintiff's previous job?

89. Do you contend that even if you make reasonable accommodations, the plaintiff still will be unable to perform essential job functions? If so, please specifically describe what functions plaintiff cannot perform.

90. Do you contend that the demand for accommodation for the plaintiff requires elimination of an essential function of the job? If you do, identify the function or functions.

91. What do you believe would be the economic cost to you in order to accommodate the disability of the plaintiff?

92. Would it be possible for you to reassign the plaintiff to a lower-graded position because you cannot make the accommodations to allow plaintiff to remain in plaintiff's former position?

93. Could you conceivably restructure the plaintiff's job requirements in order to allow plaintiff to continue working in the position occupied prior to the termination of employment?

94. Do you have any employees who suffer from the same disability suffered by the plaintiff? If so, please state their names, positions, and addresses.

95. Do you contend that the plaintiff's disability poses a health or safety threat to other employees of your company? Do you contend that the plaintiff's disability poses a direct threat to plaintiff? Specifically identify the threat or threats.

96. Do you contend that the plaintiff has a substance abuse problem? If so, what leads you to this conclusion? Please provide copies of any drug test results or relevant other materials. Do you believe that the plaintiff has ever completed a supervised drug rehabilitation program?

97. Do you have notices posted in accessible format to applicants, employees, and members describing the applicable portions of the ADA? If so, where are such notices posted? Please provide a specific geographical description.

98. What major life activities of the plaintiff do you believe are substantially limited by plaintiff's disability?

99. Are there certain preemployment tests associated with the plaintiff's former job that you believe plaintiff is presently unable to pass? If so, please describe the tests as best you can, and provide a copy of them, if possible. Are all entering employees subject to this examination regardless of disability?

100. Do you contend that business necessity forces you to deny continuing employment to the plaintiff, given plaintiff's disability? Please describe in detail what business necessity, if any, makes you unable to make a reasonable accommodation for the plaintiff's disability.[21]

---

[21] These interrogatories were compiled by Mark R. Lisker, assistant to Henry H. Perritt, Jr., in June 1993.

[3]   First Interrogatories (EEOC)

FORM 13–17   Sample First Interrogatories (EEOC)

IN THE UNITED STATES DISTRICT COURT
FOR THE [NORTHERN] DISTRICT OF [ILLINOIS]
[EASTERN] DIVISION

U.S. EQUAL EMPLOYMENT OPPORTUNITY COMMISSION,
Plaintiffs,

Civil Action No. [92 C 7330]

v.

[A.I.C. SECURITY INVESTIGATIONS, LTD.];
[A.I.C. INTERNATIONAL, LTD.];
and [unnamed defendant C],
Defendants.

Judge [Marvin E. Aspen]

EQUAL EMPLOYMENT OPPORTUNITY COMMISSION'S
FIRST SET OF INTERROGATORIES TO DEFENDANTS

Pursuant to Rule 33 of the Federal Rules of Civil Procedure, Plaintiff Equal Employment Opportunity Commission (the "EEOC") hereby propounds the following Interrogatories to Defendants [A.I.C. Security Investigations, Ltd. ("A.I.C.")], [A.I.C. International, Ltd. ("A.I.C. International")], and [defendant C], to be answered fully in writing and under oath within forty-five (45) days from the date of receipt of this request, or such shorter period as may be ordered by the Court.

DEFINITIONS AND INSTRUCTIONS

For each of these Interrogatories, and unless a different meaning is clearly required by the context, the following definitions shall apply:

1. *Defendants* as used herein includes Defendants and their attorneys and agents, including but not limited to any agent or consultant employed by said attorneys in connection with this litigation.

2. *Person* as used herein refers to a natural person, or, if applicable, any form of legal entity such as a partnership, association, or corporation.

3. *Document* as used herein refers to and includes but is not limited to all writings of any kind, including the original and all non-identical copies (whether different from the original by reason of notations made on such copies, or otherwise) of all letters, telegrams, memoranda, reports, forms, invoices, advertisements, statements, studies, contracts, calendar or diary entries, pamphlets, notes, charts, diagrams, plans, outlines, tabulations, proposals, minutes and records of meetings, conferences, and telephone or other communications, and every form of mechanical, electronic, or electrical recording or date compilation, including all forms of machine or computer storage or retrieval.

4. *Identify,* when used herein with respect to a document, means to state the title of the document, the date of the document, the author(s) of the document, the addressees of the document, a detailed description of the contents of the document, and the present location and possessor(s) of the original and each copy of the document.

5. *Identify,* when used in reference to a person, means to state the name, Social Security number, last known business address, last known home address, and last known position held by the person being identified.

6. If asked to state the facts upon which Defendants base an allegation or contention, state all of the facts known or available to Defendants, whether in possession of Defendants' attorneys, or other agents, and state the identity of the person who has knowledge of said facts, together with the identity of any documents relating to each of said facts.

7. If Defendants identify any documents that have been lost, discarded, or destroyed, such documents shall be identified in a written response as completely as possible, including the following information: author, addressee, date, subject matter, date of disposal, person authorizing the disposal, and person disposing of the document.

INTERROGATORIES

1. With respect to Defendant [A.I.C.], state

a. Its correct legal name;

b. Any other name(s) by which [A.I.C.] has been known, and dates when such name(s) was (were) used;

c. The state and date of incorporation;

d. The identification of all its officers from [January 1, 1986], to the present;

e. The identification of all its owners from [January 1, 1986], to the present;

f. Its relationship to [A.I.C. International] and to [defendant C].

g. The number of its employees on [July 29, 1992], and the identification of all documents reflecting the number of employees on that date;

h. The number of its employees on [November 5, 1992], and the identification of all documents reflecting the number of employees on that date.

2. With respect to [A.I.C. International], state

a. Its correct legal name;

b. Any other name(s) by which [A.I.C. International] has been known, and dates when such name(s) was (were) used;

c. The state and date of its incorporation;

d. The identification of all its officers from [January 1, 1986], to the present;

e. The identification of all its owners from [January 1, 1986], to the present;

f. The nature of its business;

g. The number of its employees on [July 29, 1992], and the identification of all documents reflecting the number of employees on that date;

h. The number of its employees on [November 5, 1992], and the identification of all documents reflecting the number of employees on that date; and

i. The names and the nature of all businesses held by [A.I.C. International], and the number of employees of each such business on [July 29, 1992], and on [November 5, 1992].

3. State every reason for the termination of [Charles H. Wessel ("Wessel")], and identify all documents that relate to or support such reasons, and all persons having knowledge of any such reason.

4. With respect to the decision to terminate [Wessel],

a. Identify all persons who participated in the decision, and describe the nature of their participation;

b. State the date, location, and identity of all participants with respect to all conversations of any of the persons identified in subpart *a* with each other and/or with [Wessel] concerning the termination and the reasons for the termination;

c. State the substance of each conversation identified in subpart b.

d. Identify all documents reflecting any such conversations.

5. Identify all customers of [A.I.C.] whose contracts were overseen by an [A.I.C.] employee other than [Wessel] from [January 1, 1992], through [July 31, 1992].

6. Identify all customers of [A.I.C.] whose contracts were overseen by an [A.I.C.] employee other than [Wessel] from [January 1, 1992], through [July 31, 1992]. For each such customer state

a. The name of the [A.I.C.] employee who had responsibility for the account;

b. The date on which the [A.I.C.] employee assumed responsibility for the account;

c. The identity of the individual who represented the customer with respect to the account.

7. Identify all conversations between [defendant C], or any employee of Defendants, whether in person or by telephone, with any physician or employee of a physician, concerning [Wessel]'s health and/or his ability to work. For each such conversation state

a. The date of the conversation;

b. The identity of the participants;

c. The substance of the conversation;

d. The identity of any documents that reflect the conversation.

8. With respect to [Wessel], state

a. His date of hire;

b. His salary at hire;

c. The dates and amounts of all salary increases throughout his employment, and the identity of the person(s) determining each such salary increase;

d. The dates and amounts of all bonuses paid to [Wessel] throughout his employment, and the identity of the person(s) determining each such bonus;

9. Describe every accommodation offered to [Wessel] because of his disability, and with respect to each such accommodation state

a. Whether [Wessel] requested the accommodation, and, if so, on what date;

b. The identity of the person(s) who decided to make the accommodation;

c. Whether the accommodation was necessary in order to allow [Wessel] to perform the essential functions of the job;

d. The date on which the accommodation was made, and whether the accommodation was a continuing one;

e. The identity of all documents reflecting or pertaining to such accommodation.

10. Describe any accommodation [Wessel] requested that was not made by Defendants. For each such requested accommodation, state

a. The date the accommodation was requested;

b. The identity of the person(s) denying the accommodation;

c. Every reason that the accommodation was denied;

d. If defendants claim that the accommodation would have created an undue hardship, describe the nature of the undue hardship;

e. The identity of all documents that reflect or pertain to the requested accommodation and its denial.

11. Identify and describe each essential function and each marginal function of the position of Executive Director of [A.I.C.].

12. Describe each essential function of the position of Executive Director that was reassigned to another employee between [January 1, 1987], and [August 1, 1992]. For each such reassignment state

a. The date of the reassignment;

b. The identity of the person making the reassignment;

c. The identity of the person(s) to whom the essential function was reassigned;

d. The duration of the reassignment;

e. The identity of the person(s) who have performed the function since [August 1, 1992];

f. The identity of all documents that reflect or pertain to the transfer of the essential function.

13. State the annual earnings of [A.I.C.] for each year from [1987–1992].

14. State every reason for the termination of [David P.], identify all documents that relate to or refer to the reasons for his termination, and identify all persons with knowledge of any reason for the termination of [David P.].

15. For each refusal to admit a Request to Admit propounded by the EEOC, describe all facts that support the refusal to admit, and identify all persons with knowledge of said facts, and all documents that reflect or pertain to such facts.

[4] Objections to Interrogatories and First Request for Production (EEOC)

FORM 13–18   **Sample Objections to Interrogatories and First Request for Production (EEOC)**

IN THE UNITED STATES DISTRICT COURT
FOR THE [NORTHERN] DISTRICT OF [ILLINOIS]
[EASTERN] DIVISION

U.S. EQUAL EMPLOYMENT OPPORTUNITY COMMISSION,
Plaintiffs,

Civil Action No. [92 C 7330]

v.

[A.I.C. SECURITY INVESTIGATIONS, LTD.];
[A.I.C. INTERNATIONAL, LTD.];

and [unnamed defendant C],
Defendants.   Judge [Marvin E. Aspen]

DEFENDANTS' OBJECTIONS TO PLAINTIFF'S FIRST SET OF
INTERROGATORIES AND
FIRST REQUEST FOR PRODUCTION OF DOCUMENTS

Defendants, [A.I.C. SECURITY INVESTIGATIONS, LTD.], [A.I.C. INTER-
NATIONAL, LTD.], and [defendant C], by and through their attorneys, [WESSELS
& PAUTSCH, P.C.], by [Charles W. Pautsch], [attorney A], and [attorney B], hereby
set forth the following objections to Plaintiff Equal Employment Opportunity Commission's First Set of Interrogatories and First Request for Production of Documents:

Interrogatory No. 13: State the annual earnings of [A.I.C.] for each year from
[1987–1992].

OBJECTION: Defendants object. The information sought by Interrogatory
No. 13 is not reasonably calculated to lead to the discovery of admissible evidence
and would be unduly burdensome to produce. In addition, Defendants object because the term "annual earnings" is vague.

Interrogatory No. 14: State every reason for the termination of [David P.],
identify all documents that relate to or refer to the reasons for his termination, and
identify all persons with knowledge of any reason for the termination of [David
P.].

OBJECTION: Defendants object. The information sought by Interrogatory
No. 14 is not reasonably calculated to lead to the discovery of admissible evidence.

Interrogatory No. 15: For each refusal to admit a Request to Admit propounded by the EEOC, describe all facts that support the refusal to admit, and
identify all persons with knowledge of said facts, and all documents that reflect or
pertain to such facts.

OBJECTION: Defendants object. The information sought in part by Interrogatory No. 15 was either properly objected to in Defendants' responses to Plaintiff's
Request to Admit or seeks legal conclusions that do not constitute proper inquiries
under Rule 33, Fed. R. Civ. P. In addition, Defendants object because the information sought in part by Interrogatory No. 15 seeks extended narrative that Plaintiff
will have a proper opportunity to gather through depositions. Furthermore, Defendants object to Interrogatory No. 15 because it is vague.

Request No. 2: Personnel files of [Charles H. Wessel ("Wessel")], [Victor
V.], [David P.], [Lawrence R.], [Edward B.], [Jan D.], and [Beverly K.].

OBJECTION: Defendants object. The documents that Request No. 2 seeks
are not reasonably calculated to lead to the discovery of admissible evidence and
would impose an unreasonable burden and expense upon Defendants in having to
produce such documents. Without waiving said objection, Defendants state that
they will produce the personnel files of [Charles H. Wessel].

Request No. 3: All contracts between [A.I.C.] and its customers that were
overseen by [Wessel] from [February 1, 1986], through [July 31, 1992].

OBJECTION: Defendants object. The documents that Request No. 3 seeks
are not reasonably calculated to lead to the discovery of admissible evidence and

would impose an unreasonable burden and expense upon Defendants in having to produce such documents. In addition, Defendants object because the contracts that Request No. 3 seeks are confidential, containing proprietary information, and therefore are not properly discoverable.

Request No. 3: All documents that show profits and liabilities for [A.I.C.] for the years [1987–1992], including but limited to year-end balance sheets or financial statements.

OBJECTION: Defendants object. The documents that Request No. 3 seeks are not reasonably calculated to lead to the discovery of admissible evidence and would impose an unreasonable burden and expense upon Defendants in having to produce such documents. In addition, such documents are confidential, containing proprietary information, and therefore are not properly discoverable.

Dated this [27th] day of [November 1992].

[5] Plaintiff's Motion to Compel

FORM 13–19   Sample Plaintiff's Motion to Compel

IN THE UNITED STATES DISTRICT COURT
FOR THE [NORTHERN] DISTRICT OF [ILLINOIS]
[EASTERN] DIVISION

U.S. EQUAL EMPLOYMENT OPPORTUNITY COMMISSION,
Plaintiffs,
v.

Civil Action No. [92 C 7330]

[A.I.C. SECURITY INVESTIGATIONS, LTD.];
[A.I.C. INTERNATIONAL, LTD.];
and [unnamed defendant C],
Defendants.   Judge [Marvin E. Aspen]

PLAINTIFF'S MOTION TO COMPEL

Plaintiff, the Equal Employment Opportunity Commission (the "EEOC"), respectfully moves the Court, pursuant to Rule 37 of the Federal Rules of Civil Procedure, for an Order compelling Defendants [A.I.C. Security Investigations, Ltd.], [A.I.C. International, Ltd.], and [defendant C] [(collectively, "A.I.C.")] to respond to EEOC's First Set of Interrogatories and EEOC's First Request for Production of Documents. In support of its Motion, EEOC states as follows:

1. This is an action brought pursuant to the Americans with Disabilities Act of 1990 (ADA), 42 U.S.C. §§ 12,101 *et seq.*, alleging that [A.I.C.] discharged [Charles H. Wessel], a qualified individual with a disability, because of his disability, terminal cancer. The action was filed on [November 5, 1992], and, because of the nature of the disability, EEOC moved for expedited discovery.

2. On [November 6, 1992], EEOC served [A.I.C.], by facsimile and by U.S. mail to their attorney, with EEOC's First Set of Interrogatories (attached as Exhibit 1) and First Request for Production of Documents (attached as Exhibit 2).

3. On [November 12, 1992], the Court granted EEOC's Motion for Expedited Discovery and ordered that all written discovery is to be answered by any party within seven days of receipt. The Order also provided a discovery cutoff date of [December 31, 1992]. Pursuant to the Order, responses to EEOC's written discovery were due no later than [November 17, 1992].

4. On [November 30, 1992], EEOC received Defendants' Objections to Plaintiff's First Set of Interrogatories and First Request for Production of Documents (attached as Exhibit 3). No responses were received to the Interrogatories and Document Requests to which there were no objections.

5. On [December 1, 1992], a telephone conference was conducted pursuant to [Rule 12(k)] of the Local Rules of the [Northern District] of [Illinois]. Participants were [A], attorney for the EEOC, [B], attorney for the EEOC, and [defense attorney B], attorney for [A.I.C.]. During the conference it was agreed that [A.I.C.] would withdraw its objections to certain Interrogatories and Document Requests if EEOC would agree to a protective order concerning proprietary information. [A.I.C.] maintains its objections to Interrogatory No. 14 and Document Request No. 3.

6. During the [12(k)] conference, [defense attorney B] stated that he would attempt to provide interrogatory answers by [December 4, 1992]. He did not know when the requested documents would be available.

7. As of the date of this Motion, no responses have been received.

For the foregoing reasons, EEOC respectfully requests that the Court issue an Order compelling [A.I.C.] to provide forthwith full responses to EEOC's First Set of Interrogatories and First Request for Production of Documents, including those objected to by [A.I.C.]. In further support of its Motion, EEOC submits a Memorandum and requests that the case be set for a pretrial conference pursuant to Rule 16(a) of the Federal Rules of Civil Procedure.

[6]   Memorandum Supporting Motion to Compel Answers to Interrogatories

FORM 13–20   **Sample Memorandum Supporting Motion to Compel Answers to Interrogatories**

IN THE UNITED STATES DISTRICT COURT
FOR THE [NORTHERN] DISTRICT OF [ILLINOIS]
[EASTERN] DIVISION

U.S. EQUAL EMPLOYMENT OPPORTUNITY COMMISSION,
Plaintiff,
v.

Civil Action No. [92 C 7330]
[A.I.C. SECURITY INVESTIGATIONS, LTD.];
[A.I.C. INTERNATIONAL, LTD.];
and [unnamed defendant C],
Defendants.

Judge [Marvin E. Aspen]

EEOC REPLY MEMORANDUM IN SUPPORT OF MOTION TO COMPEL

Plaintiff, Equal Employment Opportunity Commission (the "EEOC"), respectfully submits this Reply Memorandum in support of its Motion to Compel Answers to its First Set of Interrogatories and First Request for Production of Documents.

Since the filing of EEOC's Motion, the Court on [December 8, 1992], granted Defendants' [("A.I.C.'s")] Motion for an extension of time to answer written discovery to [December 15, 1992]. On [December 7, 1992], EEOC received responses to EEOC's First Set of Interrogatories, in which [A.I.C.] maintained its objections discussed in the previous Memoranda. [A.I.C.] further objected to two additional Interrogatories, which EEOC counsel had believed to be resolved. See Letter from [EEOC attorney A] to [A.I.C. attorney B], dated [December 2, 1992], attached as Exhibit 1; Letter from [A.I.C. attorney B] to [EEOC attorney A] dated [December 3, 1992], attached as Exhibit 2. The Answers to Interrogatories were not made under oath as required by Rule 33 of the Federal Rules of Civil Procedure. This Memorandum will address Defendants' continued objections: (1) to production of information concerning the termination of [David P.]; (2) to information concerning [A.I.C.]'s annual earnings; (3) to identification of documents and persons with knowledge concerning [A.I.C.]'s failure to admit certain requests for admissions; and (4) to information concerning contracts overseen by [Charles Wessel].

1. In their Memorandum in Response to the Motion to Compel, [A.I.C.] asserts that it should not be compelled to provide information concerning the reasons for the termination of [David P.], former President of [A.I.C.], and [Wessel]'s immediate supervisor, because "the reasons for his [David P.'s] termination from [A.I.C. International, Ltd.] do not relate in any way to the issues to be tried." Defendants' Memorandum, p. 2. The argument is refuted by Defendants' subpoena of [David P.] for deposition on [December 16, 1992], requiring him to produce any and all documents that relate in any way to "(1) [David P.]'s termination of employment with [A.I.C. International, Ltd.]" (Attached as Exhibit 3.)

2. Interrogatory No. 13 requests information concerning the annual earnings of [A.I.C.]. Defendants objected on grounds of relevance, burdensomeness, and vagueness. EEOC counsel believed that these objections had been withdrawn, based on EEOC's willingness to agree to a protective order covering any proprietary information. See Exhibits 1 and 2. However, the earnings of the Division of which [Wessel] was Executive Director are obviously relevant to his capabilities as the Manager of the Division. There is minimal burden in producing audited financial statements, as testified to by [Philip W.], Comptroller of [A.I.C.], at his deposition on [December 8, 1992].

3. Interrogatory No. 15 requests facts concerning [A.I.C.]'s refusals to admit, identification of documents that support such refusals, and identification of persons with knowledge of the alleged facts. During the [12(k)] conference, EEOC agreed to limit the request to identification of documents and witnesses. *See* Exhibit 1. The disputed requests to admit concern [Wessel]'s ability to perform the essential functions of his job (Request Nos. 9 and 10), [Wessel]'s qualifications (Request No. 13), and his disability (Request Nos. 11 and 12). EEOC is clearly entitled to all documents pertaining to, and witnesses with knowledge of, these issues.

4. Finally, Defendants' objection to producing customer contracts overseen by [Wessel] during his tenure as Executive Director is without merit. In its Answers to Interrogatories, [A.I.C.] admits that one of the essential functions of the Executive Director position is to "direct and represent the company regarding customer relations." Answer to Interrogatory No. 11. Defendants' "most important" objection to production of the documents — that they contain valuable proprietary information — fails to acknowledge that EEOC has offered to agree to a protective order that would require confidentiality of any proprietary information.

For the foregoing reasons, and for the reasons set forth in EEOC's previous memorandum, EEOC respectfully requests that Defendants be ordered to submit Answers to Interrogatories under oath, that they be compelled to Answer Interrogatory No. 14 concerning the reasons for the termination of [David P.], and that they be ordered to produce contracts overseen by [Wessel] during his tenure as Executive Director.

[7]   Defendants' Motion to Compel Answers to Interrogatories and Responses to Requests for Admission

FORM 13–21   **Sample Motion to Compel Answers to Interrogatories and Responses to Requests for Admission**

IN THE UNITED STATES DISTRICT COURT
FOR THE [NORTHERN] DISTRICT OF [ILLINOIS]
[EASTERN] DIVISION

U.S. EQUAL EMPLOYMENT OPPORTUNITY COMMISSION,
Plaintiff,
v.

Civil Action No. [92 C 7330]

[A.I.C. SECURITY INVESTIGATIONS, LTD.];
[A.I.C. INTERNATIONAL, LTD.];
and [unnamed defendant C],
Defendants.

Honorable [Marvin E. Aspen]
Magistrate Judge [Ronald A. Guzman]

DEFENDANTS' EMERGENCY MOTION TO COMPEL ANSWERS TO DEFENDANTS' SECOND SET OF INTERROGATORIES AND FIRST SET OF REQUESTS FOR ADMISSIONS TO PLAINTIFF [WESSEL]

Defendants, [A.I.C. SECURITY INVESTIGATIONS, LTD.], [A.I.C. INTERNATIONAL, LTD.], and [unnamed defendant C], by and through their attorneys, [WESSELS & PAUTSCH, P.C.], by [Charles W. Pautsch], [attorney A], and [attorney B], pursuant to Rule 37, Fed. R. Civ. P., and [Local Court General Rule 12], hereby set forth their Emergency Motion to Compel Answers to Defendants' Second Set of Interrogatories and First Set of Requests for Admissions to Plaintiff [Wessel] as follows:

1. On [January 19, 1993], Defendants served upon Plaintiff [Wessel] Defendants' Second Set of Interrogatories to be answered pursuant to Court Order, within seven (7) days of receipt.

2. Defendants' Second Set of Interrogatories to Plaintiff [Wessel] seek information reasonably calculated to lead to the discovery of admissible evidence. Specifically, Defendants' Second Set of Interrogatories inquires into the financial status of Plaintiff [Wessel]. Such information is relevant to this action since Plaintiff's claim of compensatory and punitive damages is premised, in part, upon allegations that the Defendants' actions caused [Wessel] extreme financial hardship after his termination.

3. Defendants' Second Set of Interrogatories to Plaintiff [Wessel] violate no rules of procedure and were served in a timely fashion.

4. On [January 22, 1993], Defendants served upon Plaintiff [Wessel] Defendants' First Set of Requests for Admissions.

5. Thereafter, attorneys for Plaintiff [Wessel] have taken the position that Defendants' First Set of Requests for Admissions are untimely and have refused to answer same.

6. Defendants' First Set of Requests for Admissions to Plaintiff [Wessel] violate no rules of procedure and were served in a timely fashion.

7. Attempts to resolve the foregoing discovery conflicts would be futile in light of Plaintiff's position that Defendants' discovery is untimely, irrespective of the Court's Order that discovery could proceed until [January 22, 1993].

WHEREFORE, Defendants respectfully request this Court to set forth an Order compelling Plaintiff [Wessel] to set forth responses to Defendants' Second Set of Interrogatories and Defendants' First Set of Requests for Admissions and to grant Defendants' costs and attorneys' fees incurred in bringing this present motion.

Dated this [25th] day of [January 1993].

[A.I.C. SECURITY INVESTIGATIONS, LTD.];
[A.I.C. INTERNATIONAL, LTD.];
and [unnamed defendant C].
By: [defense attorney A]

[8]   **Responses to Interrogatories**

FORM 13–22   Sample Response to Interrogatories

DEFENDANTS' [__], [__], and [__] ANSWERS TO
PLAINTIFF'S INTERROGATORIES

1. [R __] Company]: [January 1, 1978]–[June 30, 1980], sole proprietorship.
[R.B.C., Inc., d/b/a RBC Company]: [July 1, 1980] to present.
Officers: [__ Sr.], President;
Board of Directors: [__ Sr.], [__], [__, Jr.], [__], [__].
Shareholders: [__, Jr.], [__] and [__].
2. a. [Robert W. M__, Jr.], [1978]–present.
   b. [Robert W. M__, Sr.], [1978]–present.
   c. [Paul G. M[__], [September 1978]–present.
   d. [Richard W. M__], [1978]–present.
   e. [Paul G. M__] and [Richard W. M__], [September 1978]–present.
   f. [Robert W. M__, Sr.], [T.H. Wentz], [Dorothy S. M__], [Robert W. M__, Jr.], [Richard W. M__], and [Paul G. M__].
   g. [Dorothy S. M__], [1978]–present.
3. All of the Defendants, with the exception of Defendants [K] and [G,] are employees of [RBC]. [K] has been employed as a consultant on an independent contractor basis. [G] is not currently employed but in the past has been employed on an independent contractor basis. All documents relating to the business relationships between the Defendants are contained in their individual personnel files, which, insofar as they are relevant, are available for inspection and copying in the office of [RBC].
4. a. All documents are being copied and will be supplied to Plaintiff. In addition to the documents that are in the process of being copied, Defendant [W], upon leaving, retained three manuals identified as follows: [Personnel Policy Manual for Supervisors]; [Handling Employee Problems]; [Writing Employee Evaluations]. Copies of these documents will be made available if requested.

Except with regard to [K], all documents that were in the possession of the individual defendants when they left [JKL]'s employ have been produced. No documents have been destroyed or otherwise discarded or removed from the control of any of the answering Defendants. With respect to [K], shortly after his consulting relationship with [JKL] terminated, [JKL] sent a representative to [K]'s offices who removed a large number of documents. [K] does not recall the identity of each of these documents.

5. Defendants object to Interrogatory No. 5 insofar as it assumes that Defendants are aware of the identity of each customer or supplier of [JKL]. Insofar as this interrogatory requests information relating to contacts between [RBC Company] and [JKL], correspondence relating to such contacts is attached. Furthermore, each of the individual defendants had contact with [Robert W. M__, Sr.], and other representatives of [RBC] before they were offered and accepted employment. Such information is available in the individual defendants' personnel files. [Robert W. M__, Sr.], met with [H.D.] in [March 1985] in [RBC]'s [Delaware] office about

employment. [M_] contacted [J.S.] in the [Spring] of [1985]. He has also had contact with [J.W.], [A.I.], and [G.E.]. [Robert M_] had contact with several others who remain in [JKL]'s employ. Defendants object to Interrogatory No. 5 insofar as it requests information relating to contacts between [RBC Company] and others who may currently be employed by [JKL] on the grounds that such contacts were confidential and are privileged. Defendants are unwilling to supply this information to Plaintiff until the terms of a confidentiality agreement and protective order have been negotiated by the parties.

    6. a. No.

      b. No.

      c. Defendants were aware that [JKL]'s Material Handling Division was having financial trouble. Defendants also were told that [JKL] had instituted an employee performance monitoring program.p

      d. Yes, [RBC] was told about [ABC]'s disability by [J.B.] in [June 1993].

      e. Defendants do not understand what information Plaintiff seeks in response to this interrogatory, and if it is clarified, Defendants will respond accordingly.

    7. See reply to No. 6. No documents exist.

    8. None, except insofar as other documents produced or made available reflect such a desire.

    9. Yes

      a. [Robert W. M__], President, overall involvement in design, development, manufacture, marketing, etc., of water recreation equipment.

      [J.G.], designer, provided design services to [RBC] on a contract basis.

      [__], draftsman/designer.

      [__], draftsman.

      [__], draftsman.

      [__, Jr.], draftsman.

      [__], engineering consultant.

      b. The time sheets of the individual defendants, as well as lists of [RBC]'s product codes, are available at Defendants' offices and will be made available to Plaintiff upon execution of an acceptable confidentiality agreement and protective order.

      c. Previously supplied.

      d. [__]: Contract employee [April 29, 1985]–[April 30, 1985]. Full-time employee [May 1, 1985] to present.

      [__]: Contract employee [April 11, 1985]–[April 29, 1985]. Full-time employee [May 1, 1985] to present.

      [__]: Full-time employee [April 15, 1985] to present.

      [__: Jr.]: Contract employee [August 12, 1985]–[August 31, 1985]. Full-time employee [September 1, 1985] to present.

      [K]: Engineering consultant [1982] to present.

      [G]: [June 5, 1985], contract employee.

      e. Objected to as being a request for privileged material. Moreover, the request is overbroad and unrelated to any specific product that is at issue in this proceeding. This interrogatory seeks, essentially, every document in Defendants' offices, and the request is burdensome. Without waiver of this objection, Defendants are willing to advise that no written contracts exists between [RBC] and any of the individual defendants.

10. No.

11. a. [Robert W. M__, Sr.], [Richard W. M__], [Robert W. __, Jr.], and [Paul G. M__].

b. [Robert W. M__, Sr.], [Richard W. M__], [Robert W. M__, Jr.], and [Paul G. M__].

c. [Robert W. M__, Sr.], [Richard W. M__], [Robert W. M__, Jr.], and [Paul G, M__].

d. [Robert W. M[__, Sr.], [Richard W. M__], [Robert W. M__, Jr.], and [Paul G. M__].

e. Personnel files will be available as previously noted. These files contain resumes of the Defendants.

12. See answer to 11e.

13. The specific duties and assignments are listed on the individual Defendants' time sheets, which will be made available once the conditions noted previously are satisfied. Defendants object to providing listings of every trip undertaken by any of them on the grounds that the information will lead to the disclosure of the identities of [RBC]'s suppliers. This information is considered confidential by Defendants and is privileged.

14. a. Yes. [RBC] was contacted by [H] regarding employment when the company was located in [Newark], [Alabama]. During the meeting with [Mr. H], he was instructed by [RBC]'s representatives to disclose any impediments to his ability to perform job functions. During their interviews with [RBC], [A] and [M] were instructed to make the same disclosures.

b. No documents exist.

c. No documents exist.

15. Insofar as this interrogatory seeks information relating to [RBC]'s development and manufacture of water recreation equipment, it is objected to as being overbroad and burdensome. This interrogatory seeks virtually every document relating to [RBC]'s business. The interrogatory makes no effort to limit its request or to have it relate to matters that are in dispute in this litigation. With respect to [JKL]'s products, Defendants have no documents other than those previously supplied.

16. All [JKL] documents that Defendants retained are being supplied.

17. See answer to 16.

18. See answer to 16.

19. Yes.

20. With respect to all of the individual defendants, such information will be made available to Plaintiff upon execution of an appropriate confidentiality agreement and protective order. Upon execution of an appropriate confidentiality agreement and protective order, such information will be made available. Former [JKL] employees contacted, in addition to the individual defendants, are [H.C.], [G.G.], [J.W.], and [A.S.].

VERIFICATION

I, [Robert W. M___], verify that I am the President of [RBC Company]; as such I am authorized to make this verification on its behalf; and that the foregoing Answers to Interrogatories are true and correct to the best of my knowledge, information, and belief. I understand that false statements herein are made subject to the penalties of [18 Pa. Cons. Stat. Ann. § 4904] relating to unsworn falsification to authorities.

[9] Supplemental Responses to Interrogatories (EEOC)

FORM 13–23   **Sample Supplemental Responses to Interrogatories (EEOC)**

IN THE UNITED STATES DISTRICT COURT
FOR THE [NORTHERN DISTRICT] OF [ILLINOIS]
[EASTERN] DIVISION

U.S. EQUAL OPPORTUNITY COMMISSION
Plaintiff,

v.

Civil Action No. [92-C-7330]

[A.I.C. SECURITY INVESTIGATIONS, LTD.];
[A.I.C. INTERNATIONAL, LTD.];
and [unnamed defendant C],
Defendants.

Judge [Marvin E. Aspen]
Magistrate Judge [Guzman]

EQUAL EMPLOYMENT OPPORTUNITY COMMISSION'S SUPPLEMENTAL
RESPONSES TO DEFENDANTS' FIRST SET OF INTERROGATORIES TO
PLAINTIFF

Interrogatory No. 36: List all experts retained by Plaintiff or [Wessel] in anticipation of litigation and state
(a) the name of the expert;
(b) the specialty of the expert;
(c) the address and telephone number of the expert.

Supplemental Response:
[A], M.D., Radiation Oncology, [address], [telephone number].
[C], M.D., Neurology, [address], [telephone number].

Respectfully submitted,

[attorney A]
Supervisory Trial Attorney

Equal Employment Opportunity Commission
[536 South Clark], [Room 982]
[Chicago], [Illinois] [60605]
[(312) 353-7546]

[10] Order to Compel Answers

FORM 13–24   Sample Order to Compel Answers

IN THE UNITED STATES DISTRICT COURT
FOR THE [NORTHERN] DISTRICT OF [ILLINOIS]
[EASTERN] DIVISION

U.S. EQUAL OPPORTUNITY COMMISSION
Plaintiff,
v.   No. [92-C-7330]
[A.I.C. SECURITY INVESTIGATIONS, LTD.];
[A.I.C. INTERNATIONAL, LTD.];
and [unnamed defendant C],
Defendants,

ORDER

Pending is Plaintiff's motion to compel pursuant to Rule 37 of the Federal
Rules of Civil Procedure, for an order compelling Defendants, [A.I.C. Security
Investigations, Ltd.], [A.I.C. International, Ltd.], and [unnamed defendant C] [(col-
lectively "A.I.C.")], to respond to the EEOC's First Set of Interrogatories and the
EEOC's First Request for Production of Documents. For the reasons listed below,
plaintiff's motion is hereby granted in part and denied in part.

BACKGROUND FACTS

This is an action brought pursuant to the Americans with Disabilities Act of
1990 (ADA), 42 U.S.C. §§ 12,101 *et seq.,* alleging that [A.I.C.] discharged [Charles
Wessel] because of his disability, terminal cancer. On [November 6, 1992], the
EEOC served [A.I.C.] with the EEOC's First Set of Interrogatories and First Request for Production of Documents.

DISCUSSION

Defendants have objected to Plaintiff's Interrogatory No. 14, which inquires
into the reasons for the termination of [David P.], the former president of [A.I.C.
International, Ltd.]. This interrogatory also seeks documents pertaining to his termination and a list of all persons with knowledge of [David P.]'s termination.
Defendants claim that the information sought is not reasonably calculated to lead
to the discovery of admissible evidence. Plaintiff responds that the reason for seek-

ing information regarding [David P.]'s termination is that Defendants may use this evidence at trial.

I agree with Defendants that Plaintiff has failed to establish that Interrogatory No. 14 seeks information that is reasonably calculated to lead to the discovery of admissible evidence. Further, I assume that [Mr. P.]'s entire personnel file is being produced pursuant to Document Request No. 2, which Defendants have failed to raise any objections to. In light of this, Plaintiffs' Motion to Compel Answers to Interrogatory No. 14 is hereby denied.

Plaintiffs also seek, through its request for Document No. 3, all contracts between [A.I.C. Security Investigations, Ltd.] (a subsidiary of [A.I.C. International, Ltd.]) and its customers that were overseen by [Mr. Wessel] from [February 1, 1986] through [July 31, 1992]. Defendants object to this request for three reasons. First, Defendants objected because such documents are not easily calculated to lead to the discovery of admissible evidence. Defendants contend that these contracts have no bearing on the issue whether [Wessel] was able to perform the essential functions of his job position. Second, the production of these contracts over more than a [six]-year period is unduly burdensome. Third, Defendants object because the contracts in question are confidential and contain valuable proprietary information.

I agree with Defendants that the production of this information would divulge information that could create irreparable harm. The terms of a contract between a business and its customers are often confidential, and Plaintiff has failed to establish that the specific terms of the contracts are relevant. I have concluded, however, that the number of contracts [Mr. Wessel] negotiated and monitored during his employment with Defendant is entirely relevant for purposes of determining what the job requires and whether [Wessel] is a qualified person. In light of such, Defendants are hereby ordered to compile a list summarizing the contracts [Wessel] was responsible for securing and/or monitoring. This list is to indicate the name of the client, the date the contract was negotiated, and any other information Defendants deem appropriate to include.

Defendants are further ordered to produce information concerning [A.I.C.]'s annual earnings pursuant to Interrogatory No. 13. I agree with Plaintiff that the annual earnings of [A.I.C.] are obviously relevant to [Wessel]'s capabilities as Manager of the Division. As Plaintiff points out, there is minimal burden in producing audited financial statements.

Likewise, Defendants are hereby ordered to answer Interrogatory No. 15 The disputed Requests to Admit concern [Wessel]'s ability to perform essential functions of his job, [Wessel]'s qualifications, and his disabilities. The EEOC is clearly entitled to all documents pertaining to witnesses with knowledge of these issues.

CONCLUSION

Plaintiff's motion to compel is hereby GRANTED IN PART and DENIED IN PART.

The parties are to contact my clerk to schedule a Pretrial Conference.

SO ORDERED

Enter: [January 29, 1993]
[Ronald A. Guzman]
United States Magistrate Judge

§ 13.06   REQUEST FOR PRODUCTION OF DOCUMENTS

[A]   Generally

Requests for production of documents or things are mainstays of building the documentary case for both sides. In framing such requests, it is essential not to omit electronic formats such as archived e-mail messages and word processing files.

[B]   Sample Forms

[1]   Request for Production of Documents

FORM 13–25   Sample Request for Production of Documents

PLAINTIFF'S FIRST REQUEST FOR PRODUCTION OF
DOCUMENTS AND THINGS

Plaintiff, [ABC Corporation ("ABC")], hereby requests, pursuant to Rule 34, Fed. R. Civ. P., that defendants permit plaintiff to inspect and copy the following documents and things on or before the date specified in Rule 34.

For purposes of this request, the term *employment policies* means letters, e-mail messages, Web pages, computer files, memoranda, and notes of meetings as well as formal personnel procedure manuals or employee handbooks. The abbreviations ["ABC"] and ["JKL"] include any parent, subsidiary, affiliates, or related corporations or business entities. The term *Individual Defendants* means [defendant A], [defendant B], [defendant C], [defendant D], and [defendant E], both individually and in all permutations.

1. All documents and things requested to be identified in [X]'s First Set of Interrogatories to Defendants.

2. All agreements (including employment agreements) of any kind, type, or description between any of the Individual Defendants and (a) [X] or (b) [JKL].

3. All documents and things obtained directly or indirectly by any of the individual Defendants from [JKL].

4. Any and all employment advertisements of [JKL], including particularly all advertisements referring in any way to equal opportunity.

5. All employment agreements between [X] and [JKL].

6. All personnel policies.

7. All documents referring to [X]'s disability or [ABC]'s ability to perform job functions, essential or otherwise.

[2] Response to Request for Production

FORM 13–26   Sample Response to Request for Production

REPLY OF DEFENDANTS TO PLAINTIFF'S REQUEST FOR
PRODUCTION OF DOCUMENTS

1. Supplied, except those to which we have previously objected. Defendants incorporate their objections contained in their Answers to Interrogatories as appropriate.

2. a. None in possession of Defendants.

   b. None exist.

3. Supplied.

4. Attached.

5. See reply to 2a above.

[3] First Request for Production (EEOC)

FORM 13–27   Sample First Request for Production

IN THE UNITED STATES DISTRICT COURT
FOR THE [NORTHERN] DISTRICT OF [ILLINOIS]
[EASTERN] DIVISION

U.S. EQUAL EMPLOYMENT OPPORTUNITY COMMISSION,
Plaintiff,

v.

Civil Action No. [92-C-7330]

[A.I.C. SECURITY INVESTIGATIONS, LTD.];
[A.I.C. INTERNATIONAL, LTD.];
and [unnamed defendant C],
Defendants.

Judge [Marvin E. Aspen]

EQUAL EMPLOYMENT OPPORTUNITY COMMISSION'S FIRST REQUEST
FOR PRODUCTION OF DOCUMENTS TO DEFENDANTS

Plaintiff Equal Employment Opportunity Commission (the "EEOC"), pursuant to Rule 34 of the Federal Rules of Civil Procedure, hereby requests that Defendants, [A.I.C. Security Investigations, Ltd. ("A.I.C.")], [A.I.C. International, Ltd. ("A.I.C. International")], and [unnamed defendant C], produce the documents listed in this Request that are within their possession, custody, or control, for inspection and copying at the office of the EEOC, [536 South Clark Street], [Room 982], [Chicago], [Illinois], within 45 days from the date of receipt of this Request, or within such shorter period as may be ordered by the Court.

DEFINITIONS AND INSTRUCTION

1. This request incorporates by reference the definitions and instructions contained in EEOC's First Set of Interrogatories to Defendants.

2. With respect to any document that Defendants deem privileged and withhold from production, Defendants shall provide a written response on the date of the production pursuant to this Request, setting forth as to each document:

a. The date appearing on the document or if no date appears, the date on which the document was prepared;

b. The identity of the person(s) to whom the document was addressed;

c. The identity of the person(s) to whom the document or a copy thereof was sent or with whom the document was discussed;

d. The identity of the person(s) who prepared it;

e. The general nature or description of the subject matter and contents of the document and the number of pages of which it consists;

f. The identity of the person(s) who has custody of the document; and

g. The specific ground(s) on which the claim of privilege rests.

DOCUMENTS TO BE PRODUCED

1. All documents identified in Defendants' Answers to EEOC's First Set of Interrogatories.

2. Personnel files of [Charles H. Wessel ("Wessel")], [Victor V.], [David P.], [Lawrence R.], [Edward B.], [Jan D.], and [Beverly K.].

3. All contracts between [A.I.C.] and its customers that were overseen by [Wessel] from [February 1, 1986], through [July 31, 1992].

4. All EEO-1 reports filed with the joint Reporting Committee for the years [1986]–[1992] for [A.I.C.], [A.I.C. International], and for each other entity held by [A.I.C. International].

5. All documents that describe or relate to the essential functions of the position of Executive Director of [A.I.C.] for each year from [1986] through [1992], including but not limited to written job description, written performance evaluations, and written performance goals.

6. All documents that describe or relate to the essential functions of the positions held by [David P.], [Lawrence R.], [Edward B.], [Jan D.], and [Beverly K.] for each year from [1986] through [1992].

7. All documents that relate or refer to [Wessel]'s medical condition, including but not limited to notes of conversations with his doctors and letters from doctors concerning his condition, internal memoranda between Defendants' employees, documents prepared by [Wessel] concerning his medical condition, and letters or notes of conversations between Defendants and outside experts.

8. All documents pertaining to policies of [A.I.C.] concerning sick leave and/or attendance.

9. All documents that reflect or relate to attendance and/or time off from work by [Wessel] from [1987]–[1992].

10. All documents that support the contention that [Wessel] was unable to perform any essential function of his job from [1987]–[1992].

11. All documents that support the contention that [Wessel] was unable to perform any marginal function of his job from [1987]–[1992].

12. All documents that support the contention that any essential function of the position of Executive Director was transferred from [Wessel] to another employee or agent of [A.I.C.] from [January 1, 1992], to [July 31, 1992].

13. All documents that show profits and liabilities for [A.I.C.] for the years [1987]–[1992], including but not limited to year-end balance sheets or financial statements.

14. All documents that describe or relate to Defendants' policies with respect to termination or management of employees, including but not limited to policies with respect to discharge, layoff, retirement, and permanent disability retirement.

15. All documents that reflect or relate to any accommodations provided to [Wessel] or considered for [Wessel].

[4] Request for Production Under Rule 34 (Refusal to Hire)

FORM 13–28   **Sample Request for Production of Documents (Refusal to Hire)**

Plaintiff [A.B.] requests defendant [C.D.] to respond within [number] days to the following request:

That defendant produce and permit plaintiff to inspect and copy each of the following documents:

(1) Any written statement of the job description and/or essential job functions of the position that the plaintiff applied for;

(2) All documents reflecting the reason why the plaintiff was not hired;

(3) Any written personnel policy or handbook or employee manual;

(4) Any documents written in connection with the creation of the employee handbook or manual;

(5) The standard application for employment form, as well as the completed application form filled out by the plaintiff;

(6) Any written communication between your company and the plaintiff regarding potential employment;

(7) Any investigative reports of the plaintiff made by you or for you;

(8) Any documents describing your initial evaluation of the plaintiff prior to your decision not to hire plaintiff;

(9) Any publication that describes the nature of your business, including the number of employees, the type of work they do, and the institutions or persons they serve;

(10) Any documents stating the number of offices or distinct plants or manufacturing facilities that are part of the employing enterprise as well as listing the location of all such facilities;

(11) A copy of the registration or incorporation certificate of the employing enterprise;

(12) A list of the 10 most significant owners of stock in the company, if the employing enterprise is a corporation;

(13) A copy of the doctor's written report if a preemployment physical examination was conducted;

(14) Any documents reflecting accommodations that you offered to make to deal with the plaintiff's disability;

(15) A copy of all notices posted in accessible format to applicants, employees, and members describing the applicable portions of the ADA.

Signed: [attorney for plaintiff]
[address]

[5]   Request for Production of Documents (Employee Termination)

FORM 13–29   Sample Request for Production of Documents (Employee Termination)

Plaintiff [A.B.] requests defendant [C.D.] to respond within [number] days to the following request:

That defendant produce and permit plaintiff to inspect and copy each of the following documents:

(1) Any written statement of the plaintiff's job description and/or listing of the essential job functions associated with plaintiff's position;

(2) All documents reflecting the reason why the plaintiff was terminated;

(3) Any written personnel policy, handbook, or employee manual;

(4) Any documents written in connection with the creation of the employee handbook or manual;

(5) The standard application for employment form, as well as the completed application form filled out by the plaintiff;

(6) Any written communication between your company and the plaintiff regarding plaintiff's conduct;

(7) Any investigative reports of the plaintiff made by you or for you;

(8) Any written records of any internal hearing or review afforded to the plaintiff prior to plaintiff's termination;

(9) All written evaluations of the plaintiff's performance during plaintiff's tenure with the company, as well as any other documents reflecting the plaintiff's performance during the time that plaintiff was employed by you;

(10) Any documents describing any initial evaluation of the plaintiff prior to the time plaintiff started working for you;

(11) Any documents describing any disciplinary action taken against the plaintiff;

(12) Any documents that describe the nature of your business, including the number of employees, the type of work they do, and the institutions or persons they serve;

(13) Any documents stating the number of offices or distinct plants or manufacturing facilities that are part of the employing enterprise as well as listing the location of all such facilities;

(14) A copy of the registration or incorporation certificate of the employing enterprise;

(15) A list of the 10 most significant owners of stock in the company, if the employing enterprise is a corporation;

(16) Any documents or records regarding any unemployment claim made by the plaintiff;

(17) A copy of the doctor's written report if a preemployment physical examination was conducted;

(18) Any documents reflecting accommodations made by you to deal with the plaintiff's disability;

(19) A copy of all notices posted in accessible format to applicants, employees, and members describing the applicable portions of the ADA;

(20) A copy of any preemployment tests that the plaintiff took as well as an evaluation of the results.

Signed: [attorney for plaintiff]
[address][22]

[6] Request for Production of Computer-Readable Materials

Most enterprises, even relatively small ones, maintain some or all of their records in computer-readable form. Discovery requests should encompass such format. For example, in *Zapata v. IBP, Inc.,*[23] national origin discrimination plaintiffs included the following requests in their First Request for Production of Documents:

7. A complete copy of all computer data, including but not limited to computer tapes, disks, and hard copies of the computer data, including personnel and /or employment files for all employees of the [Garden City], [Kansas], and [Emporia], [Kansas], plants employed during any period of time between [January 1, 1988], to the present.

8. A list of all computer codes and decoders related to the computer data requested in Request No. 7.

9. A complete copy of all dispensary records or documents, including computer records, for all employees of the [Garden City], [Kansas], and [Emporia], [Kansas], plants employed during any period of time between [January 1, 1988], to the present.

The defendants objected to these requests on the grounds that the personnel files and records of nonparty employees were irrelevant and immaterial, that the breadth and scope of the request would impose an undue burden and expense, and that some of the documents were privileged attorney-client communications or work product. The district court overruled these objections. It concluded that in-

---

[22] This document was compiled by Mark R. Lisker, assistant to Henry H. Perritt, Jr., in June 1993.

[23] Civ. A. No. 93-2366-EED, 1994 WL 649322 (D. Kan. Nov. 10, 1994).

formation on salaried employees was relevant because that would permit statistical analysis of promotion paths available. It overruled the objection on burdensomeness because the defendant failed to produce specific facts showing how responding to the request for production would be burdensome.

This request can easily be tailored to an ADA action in which statistical evidence about other employees is likely to be or to lead to admissible evidence. The language of paragraph 8 can be improved upon, however. It would be better to refer to "copies of all computer programs or routines in such form as will permit the data to be read and analyzed." It also might be appropriate to delete the request for hard copies and to add a request for magnetic cassettes and optical media of any kind and magnetic cassettes.

In *Alexander v. FBI,*[24] the following requests sought discovery of electronic data:

> EOP shall designate "one or more" representatives to testify on: (1) the system of files maintained to store, protect, and preserve documents including audio and videotape recordings, computer files, and electronic mail sent, received, forwarded, transmitted, etc. in or from the EOP, offices of White House Counsel, or the office of the First Lady; (2) the systems used since January 1, 1992 to create, store, retrieve, and delete electronic mail; (3) the system of recording devices used to record sounds or pictures in any of the office, common, residential, and/or other areas of the White House and the Entirety of the Executive Office of the President; (4) the White House Office Database ("WHODB"); . . . (7) systems for recording the acquisition, location, and/or disposition of personal electronic computers used by any official, employee, detailee, resident, volunteer, intern, visitor, or overnight guest in the EOP; (8) any recording, transcription, communication, printing, filming, and any and all recordation devices used by Hillary Rodham Clinton and others in the White House in the governmental, official, or private capacities; and (9) any other matters relevant to this case, or which may lead to the discovery of relevant evidence.

When hearing-impaired persons are involved in ADA litigation, discovery may be sought of transcripts of telecommunications device for the deaf (TDD) communications. In *People v. Mid-Hudson Medical Group, PC,*[25] the district court applied conventional attorney work product analysis to TDD transcripts to justify denying a motion for an order to compel disclosure. The court held, "Hearing-impaired lawyers deserve the same expectation of confidentiality as hearing lawyers. To hold otherwise would sanction opposing counsel's eavesdropping on TTY conversations between lawyers and their witnesses in anticipation [of] litigation."

§ 13.07 Physical and Mental Examination

[A] Generally

ADA cases often put the physical or mental condition of the plaintiff or others in question. Accordingly, requests for physical or mental exami-

---

[24] 188 F.R.D. 111 (D.D.C. 1998).
[25] 877 F. Supp. 143 (S.D.N.Y. 1995).

nation may be appropriate to develop evidence as to impairments and their effects.

[B]   Sample Forms

[1]   Motion for Physical and Mental Examination

FORM 13–30   Sample Motion for Physical and Mental Examination

IN THE UNITED STATES DISTRICT COURT
FOR THE [NORTHERN] DISTRICT OF [ILLINOIS]
[EASTERN] DIVISION

U.S. EQUAL EMPLOYMENT OPPORTUNITY COMMISSION,
Plaintiff,
and

Civil Action No. [92 C 7330]

[A.I.C. SECURITY INVESTIGATIONS, LTD.];
[A.I.C. INTERNATIONAL, LTD.];
and [unnamed defendant C],
Defendants.

Honorable Judge [Marvin E. Aspen]

DEFENDANTS' MOTION FOR A PHYSICAL AND MENTAL EXAMINATION
OF [CHARLES H. WESSEL]

Defendants, by and through their attorneys, [WESSELS & PAUTSCH, P.C.], by [Charles W. Pautsch], [attorney A], and [attorney B], and pursuant to Rule 35, Fed. R. Civ. P., hereby move this Court for an Order compelling [Charles H. Wessel] to submit to a physical and mental examination and state in support hereof as follows:

1. On or about [November 5, 1992], the Equal Employment Opportunity Commission ("EEOC") filed this present action on behalf of [Charles H. Wessel ("Wessel")] alleging certain violations of the Americans with Disabilities Act ("ADA"), 42 U.S.C. §§ 12,101 *et seq.,* on the part of Defendants.

2. Within the EEOC's Complaint filed herein at paragraph ten (10), it states that [Wessel] was a qualified individual with a disability who was able to perform the essential functions of his job with or without reasonable accommodation.

3. Defendants contend, *inter alia,* that [Wessel], due to his condition, could not perform the essential functions of his job with or without reasonable accommodation.

4. Medical evidence and expert medical testimony will play a key role in determining issues at trial.

5. The mental and physical condition of [Wessel] is in controversy.

6. Defendants will be unduly prejudiced if unable to have [Wessel] examined by a physician.

7. If allowed by this Court, [Wessel]'s examination will be performed by Dr. [Susan S.] (neurologist), located at [clinic name], [address], and [telephone number], on [Tuesday], [December 29, 1992], at [2:00 P.M.].

8. If ordered by this Court, [Dr. S.] shall examine [Wessel]'s mental and physical capacity to function in his previous position with [A.I.C.] and produce a report enabling other experts in the fields of oncology and radiology to testify regarding [Wessel]'s ability to perform the essential functions of his prior position.

WHEREFORE, Defendants, by and through counsel, hereby respectfully request this Court to order a physical and mental examination of [Charles H. Wessel].

[2]   Order to Compel Physical and Mental Examination

FORM 13–31   Sample Order to Compel Physical and Mental Examination

IN THE UNITED STATES DISTRICT COURT
FOR THE [NORTHERN] DISTRICT OF [ILLINOIS]
[EASTERN] DIVISION

U.S. EQUAL OPPORTUNITY COMMISSION
Plaintiff,
v.   No. [92-C-7330]
[A.I.C. SECURITY INVESTIGATIONS, LTD.];
[A.I.C. INTERNATIONAL, LTD.];
and [unnamed defendant C],
Defendants.

ORDER

Pending is Defendants' [A.I.C. Security Investigation, Ltd.], [A.I.C. International, Ltd.], and [defendant C]'s [(collectively, "A.I.C.")] motion to compel [Charles H. Wessel] to submit to a physical and mental examination. For the reasons listed below, [A.I.C.]'s motion is hereby granted.

BACKGROUND FACTS

On or about [November 5, 1992], the Equal Opportunity Commission ("EEOC") filed this present action on behalf of [Charles H. Wessel ("Wessel")] alleging certain violations of the Americans with Disabilities Act (ADA), 42 U.S.C. §§ 12,101 *et seq.* The EEOC in its complaint alleges that [Wessel] is an individual who was able to perform the essential functions of his job with or without reasonable accommodation. Defendants contend, however, that [Wessel] is not able to perform the essential functions of his job with or without reasonable accommodation. In light of this defense, [A.I.C.] argues that the mental and physical condition of [Wessel] is in controversy and that [A.I.C.] will be unduly prejudiced if they are unable to have [Wessel] examined by a physician.

DISCUSSION

The Act currently provides for a three-pronged definition of *disability*, which states as follows:
A person with a disability is
(a) a person with a physical or mental impairment that substantially limits that person in some major life activity,
(b) a person with a record of such a physical or mental impairment; or
(c) a person who is regarded as having such an impairment.
ADA § 3, 42 U.S.C. § 12,102(2).

The EEOC regulations to the ADA, which implement the employment title of the law (Title 1), repeat this three-pronged definition of *disability. See* [29 C.F.R. § 1620.2(g)]. As indicated by the definition, this impairment must be one that substantially limits the person in a major life activity; the potential limitation must be analyzed without regard to the existence of mitigating devices or medicines. *See* [29 C.F.R. § 1630.2(h), (j) (EEOC GUIDANCE at 35,741)]. Although most serious medical conditions do have a substantial impact on basic life activities, this impact on [Wessel] must be established by [Wessel] to enjoy the protection of the Act.
Furthermore, [Wessel] must show that he is a qualified individual with a disability. Under the ADA, a *qualified individual with a disability* is a person who, with or without reasonable accommodation, can perform the "essential functions" of the job that the person holds or desires. ADA § 101(8), 42 U.S.C. § 12,111(8). [Wessel]'s qualifications or lack thereof could be used by Defendants as a defense.
In light of the fact that [Wessel]'s condition is a cerebral progressive condition and the effects of this condition vary from case to case, it is only appropriate that [A.I.C.] be given the opportunity to have its medical experts examine [Wessel] from both a mental and physical perspective.

CONCLUSION

[Wessel] is hereby ordered to appear before [Doctor L.] for a mental and physical examination.

ORDERED

Entered: [February 2, 1993]
[Ronald A. Guzman]
United States Magistrate Judge

§ 13.08   Requests for Admissions

[A]   Generally

The reason for requests for admissions[26] overlaps with the purpose of interrogatories and the preparation of pretrial orders and stipulated facts for partial summary judgment purposes. Now that the number of interrogatories is limited (under amendments to the Federal Rules of Civil Procedure transmitted to Congress in April 1993), it may be appropriate to shift some requests for admissions from interrogatories to requests for admissions explicitly denominated as such. On the other hand, the need for separately denominated requests for admissions is diminished by the increasing formality and standardization of pretrial orders that declare uncontested facts. The form of requests should be such that each can be answered with a simple "admitted" or "denied." Obviously, they should be framed with such particularity that a "denied" response exposes the responder to sanctions if the request subsequently is proved. Form 25 appended to the Federal Rules of Civil Procedure illustrates the form:

Plaintiff [A.B.] requests defendant [C.D.] within [number] days after service of this request to make the following admissions for the purpose of this action only and subject to all pertinent objections to admissibility which may be interposed at the trial:

(1) That each of the following documents, exhibited with this request, is genuine. [List the documents and describe each document.]
(2) That each of the following statements is true. [List the statements.]

As with interrogatories, a preface and definition may be appropriate.

A request for admissions should be more like questions asked on cross-examination than questions asked on direct examination. In other words, requests for admissions, unlike interrogatories, should be closed-ended, and suitable for yes or no answers. It is important to ask, "Do you admit that plaintiff has been diagnosed with dyslexia?" instead of "From what mental disabilities does the plaintiff suffer?"

It is important to remember that limiting phrases or words, such as adjectives, gives the responding party wiggle room. Asking for an admission to the statement, "the plaintiff suffers from severe depression," permits a "denied" response based on the word "severe" when the responding party would admit that "the plaintiff suffers from depression."

---

[26] *See* Forms 13–32 through 13–34.

With requests for admissions, it is also wise to avoid compound assertions, because the responding party may deny all of the assertions based on a denial of one part.

[B] Sample Forms

[1] Motion to Compel Responses to Requests for Admissions

FORM 13–32   Sample Motion to Compel Responses to Requests for Admissions

IN THE UNITED STATES DISTRICT COURT
FOR THE [NORTHERN] DISTRICT OF [ILLINOIS]
[EASTERN] DIVISION

U.S. EQUAL EMPLOYMENT OPPORTUNITY COMMISSION,
Plaintiff,
v.

Civil Action No. [92 C 7330]

[A.I.C. SECURITY INVESTIGATIONS, LTD.];
[A.I.C. INTERNATIONAL, LTD.];
and [unnamed defendant C],
Defendants.

Honorable [Marvin E. Aspen]
Magistrate Judge [Ronald A. Guzman]

DEFENDANTS' EMERGENCY MOTION TO COMPEL ANSWERS TO
DEFENDANTS' FIRST SET OF REQUESTS FOR ADMISSIONS TO
PLAINTIFF EQUAL EMPLOYMENT OPPORTUNITY COMMISSION

Defendants, [A.I.C. SECURITY INVESTIGATIONS, LTD.], [A.I.C. INTERNATIONAL, LTD.], and [C], by and through their attorneys, [WESSELS & PAUTSCH, P.C.], by [Charles W. Pautsch], [attorney A], and [attorney B], pursuant to Rule 37, Fed. R. Civ. P., and [Local Court General Rule 12], hereby set forth their Emergency Motion to Compel Answers to Defendants' First Set of Requests for Admissions to Plaintiff Equal Employment Opportunity Commission (EEOC) as follows:

1. On [January 22, 1993], Defendants served upon Plaintiff Equal Employment Opportunity Commission Defendants' First Set of Requests for Admissions.

2. The Plaintiff, Equal Employment Opportunity Commission, has taken the position that Defendants' previously served Second Set of Interrogatories are untimely, and therefore, any attempts to resolve the foregoing discovery conflicts would be futile in light of Plaintiff's position that Defendants' discovery is untimely, irrespective of the Court's order that discovery could proceed until [January 22, 1993].

WHEREFORE, Defendants respectfully request this Court to set forth an Order compelling Plaintiff Equal Employment Opportunity Commission to set forth responses to Defendants' First Set of Requests for Admissions within seven (7) days of service to grant Defendants costs and attorneys' fees incurred in bringing this motion.

Dated this [25th] day of [January 1993].
[A.I.C. SECURITY INVESTIGATIONS, LTD.];
[A.I.C. INTERNATIONAL, LTD.];
and [defendant C].
By: [attorney A]

[2]   Memorandum Supporting Plaintiff's Motion to Compel

FORM 13–33   Sample Memorandum Supporting Plaintiff's Motion to Compel

IN THE UNITED STATES DISTRICT COURT
FOR THE [NORTHERN] DISTRICT OF [ILLINOIS]
[EASTERN] DIVISION

U.S. EQUAL EMPLOYMENT OPPORTUNITY COMMISSION,
Plaintiff,
v.   Civil Action No. [92 C 7330]
[A.I.C. SECURITY INVESTIGATIONS, LTD.];
[A.I.C. INTERNATIONAL, LTD.];
and [unnamed defendant C],
Defendants.

Judge [Marvin E. Aspen]

MEMORANDUM IN SUPPORT OF PLAINTIFF'S MOTION TO COMPEL

Plaintiff, the Equal Employment Opportunity Commission (the "EEOC"), respectfully submits this Memorandum in support of its Motion to Compel.

This is an action brought pursuant to the Americans with Disabilities Act of 1990 (ADA), 42 U.S.C. §§ 12,101 *et seq.*, alleging that [Charles H. Wessel ("Wessel")] was discharged from his employment by Defendants, [A.I.C. Security Investigations, Ltd.], [A.I.C. International, Ltd.], and [defendant C] [(collectively, "A.I.C.")].

The facts pertaining to the Motion are not disputed. [Wessel] suffers from cancer, and his condition has been diagnosed as terminal. [Wessel] was hired by [A.I.C.] as Executive Director of [A.I.C.]'s security guard division in [February 1986]. He held that position until his discharge on [July 29, 1992]. In that position he reported directly to the President of [A.I.C. International, Ltd.], [David P.], until [David P.]'s termination on [July 2, 1992], less than a month prior to [Wessel]'s discharge. [Wessel]'s duties include the oversight of contracts to provide security guards to managers of commercial property who were customers of [A.I.C.].

EEOC alleges that [Wessel] was, at the time of his discharge and continuing to the present, able to perform the essential functions of his position as Executive Director, with or without reasonable accommodations, an allegation denied by [A.I.C.]. EEOC's most important witness at trial will be [Wessel], if he remains able to testify. Because of his condition, his deposition was taken by videotape transcription on [November 5, 1992]. Also because of his condition, EEOC requested expedited discovery, and the Court ordered expedited discovery on [November 12, 1992]. EEOC also expects to call [David P.] to demonstrate, *inter alia*, that [Wessel] continued to perform his duties of oversight of contracts. [A.I.C.] intends to argue that [David P.] is a biased witness because of his own termination.

The Court's Order of [November 12, 1992], requires that all written discovery be answered within seven days of receipt, that discovery be concluded by [December 31, 1992], and that a Final Pretrial Order be filed with the court on [January 15, 1993].

The disputed discovery consists of Answers to Interrogatories and Requests for Production of Documents that were due on [November 17, 1992].[27] To date, no answers have been received, although Defendants' Objections were mailed on [November 27, 1992].[28]

EEOC respectfully submits that the Court should order that the answers be provided immediately. Rule 37(a) of the Federal Rules of Civil Procedure provides that a party may move the Court to compel answers to interrogatories and document requests if the opposing party fails to answer, as is the case here. EEOC has scheduled nine depositions between [December 4, 1992], and [December 28, 1992]. The written discovery responses will assist EEOC in preparing for those depositions.

EEOC also requests that the Court order [A.I.C.] to respond to Interrogatory No. 14 and Document Request No. 3, the discovery requests to which [A.I.C.] maintained its objections following the conference held pursuant to [Rule 12(k)] of the Local Rules for the [Northern] District of [Illinois]. Interrogatory No. 14 requests [A.I.C.] to "[s]tate every reason for the termination of [David P.] and identify all documents that relate to or refer to the reasons for [David P.]'s termination, and identify all persons with knowledge of the reasons for the termination of [David P.]." Document Request No. 3 requests [A.I.C.] to produce "[a]ll contracts between [A.I.C.] and its customers that were overseen by [Wessel] from [February 1, 1986], through [July 31, 1992]."[29]

---

[27] Counsel for the EEOC agreed on November 13, 1992, to an informal extension of time to provide answers by November 24, 1992.

[28] A.I.C.'s Answers to EEOC's First Request for Admissions, also due on November 17, 1992, were mailed to the EEOC on November 18, 1992. A.I.C.'s Answers to EEOC's Second Set of Interrogatories (dealing with proposed expert witnesses), which were due on November 30, 1992, were received on December 3, 1992. These responses are not the subject of the Motion.

[29] EEOC had agreed to a protective order that would have protected any proprietary information contained in those contracts.

The general rule is that failure to make timely objection to a discovery request results in waiver of the objection, even if the objection is based on privilege. *See* [Davis v. Fendler, 650 F.2d 1154, 1160 (9th Cir. 1981)]; [United States v. 58.16 Acres of Land, 66 F.R.D. 570 (E.D. Ill. 1975)]. In this case, the only objections are that "the . . . information sought is not reasonably calculated to lead to the discovery of admissible evidence," and, with respect to production of the contracts, undue burden. Here, where expedited discovery is so crucial, [A.I.C.] should be deemed to have waived any objection to the discovery sought.

In any event, the objections are without merit. Interrogatory No. 13 seeks information concerning [David P.], the former President of [A.I.C.]. He is expected to testify for the EEOC, and his credibility may well be a major issue to be determined by the jury.[30] Reasons for his discharge are obviously relevant to a determination of that credibility.

Similarly, contracts overseen by [Wessel] requested by Document Request No. 3 are clearly relevant to the issue whether [Wessel] was performing that particular essential function of his position. [A.I.C.] has made no attempt to demonstrate any undue burden that would be created by copying the contracts.

EEOC will be ready for trial on [January 15, 1993], when the Final Pretrial Order is filed. Because of the nature of the case, EEOC will ask for the earliest possible trial date. [A.I.C.]'s refusal to comply with the expedited discovery schedule should not be permitted to delay trial and thus increase the possibility that [Wessel] may be unable to testify or to obtain the relief of reinstatement that he seeks.

For the foregoing reasons, EEOC respectfully requests that its Motion to Compel be granted. EEOC also requests that the case be set for a Pretrial Conference pursuant to Rule 16 of the Federal Rules of Civil Procedure, to resolve all discovery disputes and to set a trial date.

[3]   Response to Motion to Compel (EEOC)

FORM 13–34   **Sample Response to Motion to Compel**

IN THE UNITED STATES DISTRICT COURT
FOR THE [NORTHERN] DISTRICT OF [ILLINOIS]
[EASTERN] DIVISION
U.S. EQUAL EMPLOYMENT OPPORTUNITY DIVISION

Plaintiff,

v.

Civil Action No. [92 C 7330]

[A.I.C. SECURITY INVESTIGATIONS, LTD.];
[A.I.C. INTERNATIONAL, LTD.];
and [unnamed defendant C],

---

[30] A.I.C. had subpoenaed David P. for deposition on December 16, 1992.

Defendants.

Honorable [Marvin E. Aspen]
Magistrate Judge [Guzman]

PLAINTIFF EQUAL EMPLOYMENT OPPORTUNITY COMMISSION'S RESPONSE TO DEFENDANT'S EMERGENCY MOTION TO COMPEL ANSWERS TO FIRST SET OF REQUESTS FOR ADMISSIONS

The Defendants have filed an Emergency Motion to Compel the Equal Employment Opportunity Commission ("EEOC") to respond to Defendant's First Set of Requests for Admissions and Second Set of Interrogatories. Defendant's Motion misstates both the facts and the rules applicable to this matter. First, the Defendants' contention that the EEOC has refused to answer a Second Set of Interrogatories is simply wrong. The fact is that the Defendants never served the EEOC with a Second Set of Interrogatories. Therefore, the EEOC cannot be compelled to answer discovery with which it was never served.

Next, Defendants' contention that their First Set of Requests for Admissions were timely served under the rules and must be answered by EEOC is likewise unfounded. On [December 29, 1992], Defendants requested and were granted by Judge [Aspen] an extension of the discovery cutoff date from [December 31, 1992], to [January 22, 1993]. Judge [Aspen] also stated to both parties at that time that there would be no more extensions of discovery beyond the [January 22, 1993], date. Specifically, Judge [Aspen] stated, "I am going to allow the motion, but I am not going to give you any further extensions, so you're going to have to do what you have to do during that time period. If you don't complete discovery in that period it won't be done." Transcript of the [December 29, 1992], hearing before the Honorable [Marvin Aspen] at pages 3, 4. Attached hereto as Exhibit 1.

On [January 19, 1993], the EEOC received a copy of Defendants' First Requests for Admissions. On [January 22, 1993], the EEOC informed Defendants' counsel by letter (Exhibit 2) that the 34 Requests for Admissions were not timely under the Local Rules and that, as a result, the EEOC would not be submitting responses to the Requests. The EEOC also noted in its [January 22nd] letter that because 24 of the requests dealt with the authenticity of documents, the EEOC would be happy to discuss stipulations as to authenticity as a part of the pretrial order process. On that same date, Defendants' counsel requested assistance in locating the Local Rule that supports the EEOC's position that Defendants' Requests for Admissions were not timely served. The EEOC informed Defendants' counsel by telephone which Local Rule applied — specifically, paragraph three of the Standing Order Establishing Pretrial Procedure (Exhibit 3) — which states:

> Except to the extent specified by the Court on motion of either party, discovery must be completed before the discovery closing date. Discovery requested before the discovery closing date, but not scheduled for completion before the discovery closing date, does not comply with this order.

On [January 25, 1993], counsel for Defendants informed the EEOC by letter that the Local Rule the EEOC had been relying on had been repealed in [1982] (Exhibit 4). On [January 26, 1993], the EEOC sent counsel for Defendants a copy of the rule in question showing that the Rule is still in effect, and asked for Defendants' counsel to produce evidence to the contrary if any existed (Exhibit 5). Defendants have produced no such evidence.

The facts here are simple. Judge [Aspen] set a discovery cutoff date in this case of [January 22, 1993], and stated that all discovery in the case was to be completed by that date and that there would be no further extensions. In an effort to circumvent Judge [Aspen]'s order, Defendants chose not to serve further written discovery until three days prior to the close of discovery in direct contravention of the Local Rules for this District and in complete defiance of Judge [Aspen]'s order. In sum, the Defendants are trying to do indirectly what Judge [Aspen] stated they would not be allowed to do directly — extend the discovery cutoff date in this case. The Defendants should not be allowed to circumvent either the discovery cutoff date or the requirements of the Local Rules by delaying service of written discovery until three days before the discovery cutoff and then seeking an order compelling the EEOC to answer them outside the discovery period. To allow the Defendants' motion would reward Defendants for their decision to ignore the Local Rules of this District and would in effect nullify Judge [Aspen]'s clear order regarding the discovery cutoff in this case.

For the reasons stated herein, Defendants' motion should be denied in its entirety.

Respectfully submitted,
[EEOC attorney B]
Trial Attorney

§ 13.09   Orders

[A]   Points for Memorandum on Protective Order

Federal Rule of Civil Procedure 26(c) authorizes protective orders[31] to prevent "annoyance, embarrassment, oppression, or undue burden or expense." One of the clearest reasons for the entry of a protective order is to protect well-recognized privileges. The doctor-patient privilege is one such recognized privilege, and it clearly extends to any form of psychological counseling as long as the counselor is a professional.[32]

A person seeking a protective order must do so in advance, rather than by simply refusing to answer questions and then raising that privilege or other matter justifying a protective order after the fact.[33]

The language of the interrogatories, attached as an exhibit to the motion for a protective order, demonstrated on the face of the interrogatories a

---

[31] *See* Form 13–35.

[32] Cunningham v. Southlake Ctr. for Mental Health, 125 F.R.D. 474, 477 (N.D. Ind. 1989) (denying privilege to supervisor).

[33] *See* Hudson Tire Mart, Inc. v. Aetna Cas. & Sur. Co., 518 F.2d 671 (2d Cir. 1975).

request for disclosure of information within the psychiatrist-patient privilege.[34]

The likelihood of privilege claims in ADA litigation suggests that the convenience of court and counsel might be served by appointing a master to decide such claims.[35]

[B] Sample Forms

[1] Motion for Protective Order

FORM 13–35   Sample Motion for Protective Order

Plaintiff moves this court for an order pursuant to Fed. R. Civ. P. 26(c) prohibiting defendant from asking plaintiff questions in discovery that invade the psychiatrist-patient privilege.

The basis for this motion is certain interrogatories propounded by the defendant, shown in Exhibit A to this motion, presenting the likelihood that plaintiff will be subject to sanctions for refusing to answer these questions unless a protective order is issued, and also making it probable that defendant will ask similar questions in depositions already scheduled or to be scheduled in the future.

This motion is based on the attachments, including the plaintiff's affidavit (Exhibit B) and the attached Memorandum of Law.

[2] Sample Order Referring Privilege Claims to Master

FORM 13–36   Sample Order Referring Privilege Claims to Master

Referral of Privilege Claims to Master

It appears that submission of claims of privilege to a special master appointed under Fed. R. Civ. P. 53 is warranted by the expected volume of such claims and by the likelihood that in camera inspection may be needed to rule on these claims and should be accomplished, to the extent possible, by someone other than the judge to whom this litigation has been assigned, the court hereby, with the consent of the parties, ORDERS:

1. Appointment. [Name] is appointed under Rule 53 as special master for the purpose of considering all claims of privilege (including assertion of protection against disclosure based on the "work product" doctrine) that may be asserted

---

[34] Calloway v. Marvel Entertainment Group, 110 F.R.D. 45, 50 (S.D.N.Y. 1986) (question not implicating psychiatrist-patient privilege because dealing with communications outside scope of treatment).

[35] See Form 13–36.

during the course of discovery in this litigation and for such other matters as may be referred to such master by the court, such as resolution of disputes under the Confidentiality Order.

2. Procedures. The master shall have the rights, powers, and duties as provided in Rule 53 and may adopt such procedures as are not inconsistent with that Rule or with this or other orders of the court. Until directed otherwise by the master or the court, any person asserting a privilege shall specifically identify the document or other communication sought to be protected from disclosure, including the date, the person making the statement, the persons to whom or in whose presence the statement was made, other persons to whom the contents were or have been revealed, the general subject matter of the communication (unless itself claimed to be privileged), the particular privileges (or doctrines) upon which protection against disclosure is based, and any other circumstances affecting the existence, extent, or waiver of the privilege. When appropriate, the master may require that this documentation of claims of privilege be verified.

3. Reports. The master shall make findings of fact and conclusions of law with respect to the matters presented by the parties and report expeditiously to the court pursuant to Rule 53(e) as applicable in nonjury actions. Unless directed by the court or believed advisable by the master, the report shall not be accompanied by a transcript of the proceedings, the evidence, or the exhibits. Such parts of the report, if any, as may be confidential shall be filed under seal pending further order of the court.

4. Fees and Expenses. Compensation at rates mutually agreeable to the master and the parties shall be paid to the master on a periodic basis by the parties. The master may employ other persons to provide clerical and secretarial assistance; such persons shall be under the supervision and control of the master, who shall take appropriate action to ensure that such persons preserve the confidentiality of matters submitted to the master for review. Final allocation of these amounts shall be subject to taxation as costs at the conclusion of the case at the discretion of the court.

5. Distribution. A copy of this order shall be mailed by the Clerk to the Special Master and to Liaison Counsel for the parties.

Dated: [date]
United States District Judge

CHAPTER 14

EARLY PRETRIAL PLANNING, MOTIONS FOR SUMMARY JUDGMENT, AND SUPPORTING MEMORANDA

§ 14.01   INTRODUCTION

This chapter presents materials for Americans with Disabilities Act (ADA)[1] cases for initial pretrial conferences,[2] scheduling,[3] and summary judgment,[4] as well as a reply memorandum on summary judgment.[5] A significant trend in modern civil procedure is to increase judicial management of cases by mandating more explicit scheduling and planning for the handling of discovery and the framing of issues for trial. Implicitly, this involves removing certain issues from the trial agenda by deciding them as a matter of law through summary judgment.

§ 14.02   RULE 16: PRETRIAL CONFERENCES, SCHEDULING, AND MANAGEMENT

[A]   Generally

One of the 1993 amendments to the Federal Rules of Civil Procedure expands Rule 16 to make it more specific about judicial control of litigation. The full text of the amended rule follows.

[B]   Sample Forms

[1]   Pretrial Conference

FORM 14–1   Pretrial Conference

(b) Scheduling and Planning. Except in categories of actions exempted by district court rule as inappropriate, the district judge, or a magistrate judge when authorized by district court rule, shall, after receiving the report from the parties under Rule 26(f) or after consulting with the attorneys for the parties and any unrepresented parties by a scheduling conference, telephone, mail, or other suitable means, enter a scheduling order that limits the time

(1) to join other parties and to amend the pleadings;
(2) to file motions; and
(3) to complete discovery.

The scheduling order may also include

---

[1] Pub. L. No. 101-336, 104 Stat. 327 (1990) (codified at 42 U.S.C. §§ 12,101–12,213 (1994); 47 U.S.C. §§ 225, 711 (1994)) [hereinafter ADA].

[2] *See* Form 14-1.

[3] *See* Form 14-2.

[4] *See* Forms 14-3 through Form 14-5.

[5] *See* Form 14-6.

(4) modifications of the times for disclosures under Rules 26(a) and 26(e)(1) and of the extent of discovery to be permitted;

(5) the date or dates for conferences before trial, a final pretrial conference, and trial; and

(6) any other matters appropriate in the circumstances of the case.

The order shall issue as soon as practicable but in any event within 90 days after the appearance of a defendant and within 120 days after the complaint has been served on a defendant. A schedule shall not be modified except upon a showing of good cause and by leave of the district judge or, when authorized by local rule, by a magistrate judge.

(c) Subjects for Consideration at Pre-trial Conferences. At any conference under this rule consideration may be given, and the court may take appropriate action, with respect to

(1) the formulation and simplification of the issues, including the elimination of frivolous claims or defenses;

(2) the necessity or desirability of amendments to the pleadings;

(3) the possibility of obtaining admissions of fact and of documents which will avoid unnecessary proof, stipulations regarding the authenticity of documents, and advance ruling from the court on the admissibility of evidence;

(4) the avoidance of unnecessary proof and of cumulative evidence, and limitations or restrictions on the use of testimony under Rule 702 of the Federal Rules of Evidence;

(5) the appropriateness and timing of summary adjudication under Rule 56;

(6) the control and scheduling of discovery, including orders affecting disclosures and discovery pursuant to Rule 26 and Rules 29 through 37;

(7) the identification of witnesses and documents, the need and schedule for filing and exchanging pretrial briefs, and the date or dates for further conferences and for trial;

(8) the advisability of referring matters to a magistrate judge or master;

(9) settlement and the use of special procedures to assist in resolving the dispute when authorized by statute or local rule;

(10) the form and substance of the pre-trial order:

(11) the disposition of pending motions;

(12) the need for adopting special procedures for managing potentially difficult or protracted actions that may involve complex issues, multiple parties, difficult legal questions, or unusual proof problems;

(13) an order for a separate trial pursuant to Rule 42(b) with respect to a claim, counterclaim, cross-claim, or third-party claim, or with respect to any particular issue in the case;

(14) an order directing a party or parties to present evidence early in the trial with respect to a manageable issue that could, on the evidence, be the basis for a judgment as a matter of law under Rule 50(a) or a judgment on partial findings under Rule 52(c);

(15) an order establishing a reasonable limit on the time allowed for presenting evidence; and

(16) such other matters as may facilitate the just, speedy and inexpensive disposition of the action.

At least one of the attorneys for each party participating in any conference before trial shall have authority to enter into stipulations and to make admissions regarding all matters that the participants may reasonably anticipate may be discussed. If appropriate, the court may require that a party or its representative be present or reasonably available by telephone in order to consider possible settlement of the dispute.

[2]   Checklist for Initial Conference[6]

1.   Court
　　_____ Early assumption of active supervision over litigation
　　_____ Assignment to single judge
　　_____ Review potential conflicts; recusal/disqualification
　　_____ Related litigation
　　_____ Cases pending in same court
　　_____ Reassignment of cases
　　_____ Consolidation for pretrial
　　_____ Coordination of cases not consolidated
　　_____ Cases pending in other courts
　　_____ Civil cases pending in other federal courts
　　_____ Potential multidistrict transfers under 28 U.S.C. § 1407
　　_____ Potential transfers under 28 U.S.C. § 1404 or 1406
　　_____ Potential removal of state cases
　　_____ Coordination with cases not removed
　　_____ Related criminal cases
　　_____ Coordination order
　　_____ Joint hearings
　　_____ Joint special master
　　_____ Joint appointment of lead counsel
　　_____ Designation of lead case
　　_____ Deference to prior rulings
　　_____ Suspension of local rules
　　_____ Procedures for attending to emergency matters; telephonic conferences
　　_____ Referrals to magistrate judges, special masters, and other judges
　　_____ Schedule and set format for initial pretrial conference (see paragraph 3 below)

2.   Counsel
　　_____ Admission *pro hac vice*
　　_____ Present/potential problems of disqualification/withdrawal
　　_____ Responsibilities

---

[6] Adapted from checklist, Manual for Complex Litigation (Second) § 40.1 (1985).

_____ Coordination of counsel/designated counsel
_____ Organizational structure
_____ Liaison counsel
_____ Lead counsel
_____ Committees
_____ Trial counsel
_____ Designated counsel
_____ Powers and responsibilities
_____ Compensation
_____ Maintenance and submission of time and expense records
_____ Establishing policies and guidelines
_____ Avoidance of unnecessary attendance or other expenditure of time
_____ Obligations under Federal Rules of Civil Procedure and local rules
_____ Cooperation and courtesy; resolving disputes without resort to court
_____ Use of _Manual for Complex Litigation_ (_Third_)
_____ Responsibility for preparation/maintenance of service list

3. **Initial pretrial conference**
_____ Appearances
_____ Counsel
_____ Parties
_____ Counsel from other cases
_____ Others
_____ Agenda
_____ Identification and narrowing of issues (see paragraph 5 below)
_____ Deadlines and limits on joinder and pleadings
_____ Coordination with related federal or state litigation
_____ Jurisdiction of subject matter and parties
_____ Consolidation and severance
_____ Referral to magistrate judge or special master (see paragraph 10 below)
_____ Organization of counsel and maintenance of time and expense records (see paragraph 2 above)
_____ Reducing filing and service (see paragraph 4 below)
_____ Suspension/revision of local rules/orders
_____ Reference to ADR procedures
_____ Class-action issues (see paragraph 7 below)
_____ Disclosure and discovery (see paragraphs 8 and 9 below)
_____ Preservation orders
_____ Experts
_____ Judge's expectations and practices
_____ Case management plan
_____ Scheduling orders
_____ Scheduling next conference
_____ Sanctions
_____ When court will impose
_____ Requirement of good-faith effort to resolve disputes

_____ Procedure
_____ Settlement

4. **Filing and service**
   _____ Reducing filing
   _____ Creation of master file
   _____ Filing in master file
   _____ When to file in individual cases also
   _____ Nonfiling of discovery except on court order
   _____ Reducing service under Fed. R. Civ. P. 5
   _____ Use of liaison counsel to receive/distribute orders
   _____ Use of liaison counsel to receive/distribute documents from parties
   _____ Parties to be served separately
   _____ Maintenance of service list

5. **Issues**
   _____ Preparation for initial conference
   _____ Identifying, narrowing, and resolving issues
   _____ Duplicative, irrelevant, or frivolous issues
   _____ Uncontested issues
   _____ Use of stipulation
   _____ Target discovery on issues for early resolution
   _____ Class certification (see paragraph 7 below)
   _____ Dispositive motions
   _____ Motions affecting scope of discovery

6. **Pleadings and motions**
   _____ Suspension of time for filing certain pleadings and motions
   _____ Deadlines
   _____ Adding/changing claims or defenses
   _____ Joining additional parties
   _____ Counterclaims, cross-claims, third-party complaints
   _____ Relief from deadlines if justified by discovery
   _____ Refiling of amended/consolidated complaint after discovery
   _____ Procedure for motions
   _____ Requirement of good-faith attempt to resolve
   _____ Determine if discovery needed; set scope
   _____ Schedule for submission, argument, and decision
   _____ Standard and "deemed" pleadings, motions, and orders
   _____ Provision for later filed cases
   _____ Supplementing/revising standard pleadings
   _____ Summary judgment
   _____ Partial
   _____ Discovery allowed
   _____ Time for filing, argument, and decision
   _____ Alternative early trial of severed issues under Fed. R. Civ. P. (b)
   _____ Interlocutory appeal

7. **Class certification**
   _____ Time/procedures for presenting certification question
   _____ Relation to other proceedings in the litigation
   _____ Whether formal motion required and, if so, when
   _____ Discovery
   _____ Schedule; completion date
   _____ From class representatives
   _____ From class members
   _____ Briefing; statement of uncontested/contested facts
   _____ Schedule
   _____ Identify factual disputes on which evidentiary hearing needed
   _____ Proposed method and form of certification notice
   _____ Hearings
   _____ Dates
   _____ Evidence presented by affidavit, witnesses, or other
   _____ Need to define class in objective terms and identify particular claims of class
   _____ Possible class conflicts
   _____ Within class
   _____ With other classes sought/certified
   _____ With nonclass actions
   _____ Conflicts involving counsel
   _____ Communications with class

8. **Prediscovery disclosure**
   _____ Meeting of counsel
   _____ Modification of requirements of Fed. R. Civ. P. 26(a)(1).
   _____ Defining/scheduling prediscovery exchange of information
   _____ Schedule for supplementation under Fed. R. Civ. P. 26(e)

9. **Preliminary plan for discovery**
   _____ Obligations under Fed. R. Civ. P. 26(g)
   _____ Discovery plan
   _____ Advance meeting of counsel under Fed. R. Civ. P. 26(f)
   _____ Court adopts discovery plan after conference
   _____ Periodic progress reports by counsel
   _____ Limitations
   _____ Time limits and schedules
   _____ Cutoff date for discovery
   _____ Limits on quantity
   _____ General limitations under Fed. R. Civ. P. 26(g)
   _____ Sequencing of discovery

Checklists
   _____ Procedures for resolving disputes
   _____ Attempts by counsel to resolve voluntarily
   _____ Procedures for obtaining court ruling
   _____ Form of motion—written/oral

_____ When briefs required/permitted
_____ Telephonic rulings
_____ Use of magistrate judges
_____ Appointment of special master
_____ Special provisions
_____ Confidential information; protective orders
_____ Provisions for allocation of costs
_____ Documents
_____ Adoption of identification system
_____ Preservation
_____ Depositories
_____ Evidentiary foundation
_____ Depositions
_____ Cross-noticing
_____ Coordination with related litigation
_____ Guidelines/time limits
_____ Timing; scope
_____ Limits on number
_____ Deferred supplemental depositions
_____ Requests for admission
_____ Expert discovery
_____ Discovery of class members/representatives
_____ Discovery in other countries
_____ Governmental investigations/grand jury materials
_____ Computerized data
_____ Summaries
_____ Surveys; other sampling techniques
_____ Schedule for amendments under Fed. R. Civ. P. 26(e)
_____ Duty to disclose agreements affecting discovery

10. **Special appointments and referrals**
_____ Court-appointed experts under Fed. R. Evid. 706
_____ Magistrate judges
_____ Special masters under Fed. R. Civ. P. 53
_____ Scope of referral
_____ Timing
_____ Procedure for selection
_____ Nominations by parties
_____ Suggestions by other groups; peremptory challenges
_____ Use of magistrate judge as special master
_____ Compensation
_____ Discovery from court-appointed experts
_____ Communication with parties/experts/court
_____ Agreements as to effect of findings
_____ Report
_____ Referrals to alternative dispute resolution mechanisms

11. Settlement

_____ Raising settlement with the parties
_____ Techniques to encourage settlement
_____ Firm trial date
_____ Settlement conferences with parties
_____ Confidential discussions with judge
_____ Contribution bar orders
_____ Offer of judgment
_____ Trial of representative cases
_____ Severance
_____ Referral to other judges/magistrate judges/special masters
_____ Settlement counsel
_____ Use of alternate processes
_____ Mediation
_____ Summary jury trial
_____ Summary bench trial
_____ Minitrial
_____ Special problems
_____ Class actions
_____ Partial settlements
_____ Settlement classes
_____ Side agreements
_____ "Mary Carter" agreements
_____ Most-favored-nation clauses
_____ Agreements affecting discovery
_____ Tolling agreements
_____ Ethical considerations

12. Subsequent conferences

_____ Scheduling the next conference
_____ Interim status reports
_____ Additional conferences
_____ Prescheduled
_____ On request
_____ For emergency matters

[3] Report of Parties' Planning Meeting (Form 35)[7]

FORM 14–2   Sample Report of Parties' Planning Meeting

1. Pursuant to Fed. R. Civ. P. 26(f), a meeting was held on [date] at [place] and was attended by

---

[7] Form 35 (see Form 14-2), provided in the Federal Rules of Civil Procedure, covers essentially the same issues as the checklist in § 14.02[2]. That checklist could be used as the starting point for a more detailed report of a planning meeting, in lieu of the simpler form presented here.

name for plaintiff(s) [name]

name for defendant(s) [name]

name for defendant(s) [name]

2. Pre-Discovery Disclosures. The parties [have exchanged/will exchange] by [date] the information required by [Fed. R. Civ. P. 26(a)(1)/Local Rules —].

3. Discovery Plan. The parties jointly propose to the court the following discovery plan: (Use separate paragraphs or subparagraphs as necessary if parties disagree.)

Discovery will be needed on the following subjects: (brief description of subjects on which discovery will be needed).

All discovery commenced in time to be completed by [date]. (Discovery on [issue for early discovery] to be completed by [date])

Maximum of [___] interrogatories by each party to any other party. (Responses due [___] days after service.)

Maximum of [___] requests for admission by each party to any other party. (Responses due [___] days after service.)

Maximum of [___] depositions by plaintiff(s) and [___] by defendants.

Each deposition (other than of [___]) limited to maximum of [___] hours unless extended by agreement of parties.

Reports from retained experts under Rule 26(a)(2) due

from plaintiff(s) by [date]

from defendant(s) by [date]

Supplementations under Rule 26(e) due [time/interval].

4. Other Items. (Use separate paragraphs or subparagraphs as necessary if parties disagree.)

The parties [request/do not request] a conference with the court before entry of the scheduling order.

The parties request a pretrial conference in [month, year].

Plaintiff(s) should be allowed until [date] to join additional parties and until [date] to amend the pleadings.

Defendant(s) should be allowed until [date] to join additional parties and until [date] to amend the pleadings.

All potentially dispositive motions should be filed by [date].

Settlement [is likely/is unlikely/cannot be evaluated prior to [date]]. [Settlement may be enhanced by use of the following alternative dispute resolution procedure:]

Final lists of witnesses and exhibits under Rule 26(a)(3) should be due

from plaintiff(s) by [date]

from defendant(s) by [date]

Parties should have [___] days after service of final lists of witnesses and exhibits to list objections under Rule 26(a)(3).

The case should be ready for trial by [date] (and at this time is expected to take approximately [length of time]).

[Other matters.]

Date: [date]

[4]   Sample Schedule Order

FORM 14–3   Sample Schedule Order

Schedule Order

It is ORDERED:

1. Discovery shall be conducted according to the following schedule:

   Discovery Time

   Interrogatories by all parties to ascertain identity and location of witnesses and documents, including computerized records

   Document production by all parties

   Lay witness depositions

   ___ noticed by plaintiffs

   ___ noticed by defendants

   Expert(s):

   Plaintiff

   ___ identification; reports

   ___ depositions

   Defendant

   ___ identification; reports

   ___ depositions

   Production of proposed computerized summaries and samples:

   ___ by plaintiffs

   ___ by defendants

   Requests for admission and interrogatories by all parties

2. Except for good cause shown,

(a) relief from the above schedule shall not be granted and all discovery shall be completed by [date];

(b) discovery shall be limited to matters occurring after [date], and before [date];

(c) no more than [___] interrogatories (including subparts) may be propounded to any party (exclusive of interrogatories seeking the identity and location of witnesses and documents);

(d) no more than [___] depositions may be taken by either plaintiffs or defendants, nor may they take more than [___] days;

(e) no amendment of pleadings may be made after [date], and no additional parties may be joined as plaintiff, defendant, or third-party defendant after [date].

3. The parties are expected to be prepared for trial on all issues (except [___]) by [date].

Dated:

United States District Judge

§ 14.03 SUMMARY JUDGMENT ISSUES

[A] Generally

Summary judgment is the mechanism for cutting litigation short when pleading and discovery do not reveal triable issues of fact. The party resisting summary judgment must point to specific discovery materials or burdens of production that entitle that party to trial of one or more issues material to the case.

[B] Sample Forms

[1] Statement of Material Facts

FORM 14–4   Sample Statement of Material Facts

IN THE UNITED STATES DISTRICT COURT
FOR THE [NORTHERN] DISTRICT OF [ILLINOIS]
[EASTERN] DIVISION

U.S. EQUAL EMPLOYMENT OPPORTUNITY COMMISSION,

Plaintiff,   Civil Action No. [92 C 7330]

v.

[A.I.C. SECURITY INVESTIGATIONS, LTD.];

[A.I.C. INTERNATIONAL, LTD.];

and [unnamed defendant C],   Honorable [Marvin E. Aspen]

Defendants.   Magistrate Judge [Guzman]

DEFENDANTS' STATEMENT OF MATERIAL FACTS

Defendants, [A.I.C. SECURITY INVESTIGATIONS, LTD. ("A.I.C.")], [A.I.C. INTERNATIONAL, LTD. ("A.I.C. INTERNATIONAL")], and [unnamed defendant C], by and through their attorneys [WESSEL & PAUTSCH, P.C.], by [Charles W. Pautsch], [attorney A], and [attorney B], pursuant to Rule 56 of the Federal Rules of Civil Procedure, and [Rule 12(*l*)] of the General Rules of the United States District Court for the [Northern] District of [Illinois], hereby proffer the following material facts to which there exists no material issue to be tried:

A. ESSENTIAL FUNCTIONS OF [CHARLES WESSEL]'S POSITION

1. [Charles Wessel (hereinafter "Wessel")] was hired in [February 1986], as the Executive Director of [A.I.C. Security Investigations, Ltd. (hereinafter, "A.I.C.")], a wholly owned subsidiary of A.I.C. International, Ltd. (hereinafter, "A.I.C. International"); [A.I.C.] was and is the largest division of [A.I.C. International] [citation to record].

2. The Executive Director position that [Wessel] held was at all times during his employment the highest management position in [A.I.C.], and, accordingly, [Wessel] was responsible for the overall management and profitability of [A.I.C.] [citations to record].

3. The business of [A.I.C.] at all pertinent times has been to provide security guards and related services for commercial and residential properties in and around [Chicago], [Illinois] [citations to record].

4. The security guard business, as compared to other service industries, is highly competitive; it is a dynamic, unpredictable business that requires continual and prompt adaptations to the clients' needs as they arise [citation to record].

5. The position of Executive Director for [A.I.C.] required, as an essential function, regular and predictable attendance of as many hours as necessary to meet the needs of the clients; it was not a "9 to 5" job [citation to record].

6. The position of Executive Director for [A.I.C.] required, as an essential function, overall management and direction of the 300-plus employees of the company, from all management-level personnel to watch commanders, and ultimately the hundreds of security guards employed by [A.I.C.] [citation to record].

7. The position of Executive Director for [A.I.C.] required, as an essential function, dealing with labor unions . . . . supervising investigations . . . , and tracking litigation [A.I.C.] was involved in [citations to record].

8. The position of Executive Director for [A.I.C.] required, as essential functions, developing policy, conducting site walk-throughs, handling labor matters, establishing price rates, and monitoring and disciplining subordinates [citation to record].

B. [CHARLES WESSEL]'S CLAIMED DISABILITY

9. When [Wessel] started with [A.I.C.], he had emphysema caused by smoking 2–4 packs of cigarettes/day for approximately 25 years and 8–10 cigars a day for 15 years, and he had a back injury rendering him 20-percent disabled under his V.A. disability.

10. [Wessel] had cancer for five of the approximately six years he worked for [A.I.C.], with the first diagnosis of lung cancer in his left lung in [1987]; a recurrence of cancer in his right lung in [1991]; and, a diagnosis of inoperable brain tumors in early [April of 1992].

11. The cancerous brain tumors are believed by [Wessel]'s doctors to have "metastasized" (i.e., moved to the brain from their primary site of development, Wessel's lungs) approximately three to six months before they were diagnosed, sometime in late [1991] [citation to record].

12. [Wessel]'s condition is believed by his doctors to be terminal, and he was told sometime in [April 1992] that he had 6 to 12 months to live; his treatments since [April] of [1992] have been "palliative," that is, not for the purpose of a cure but rather to prolong and ensure some quality of [Wessel]'s life.

13. [Wessel] was initially diagnosed in [April 1992] with two tumors, and subsequently in [June 1992], two additional tumors were diagnosed, for a total of four.

C. [CHARLES WESSEL]'S INABILITY TO CONTINUE TO PERFORM THE ESSENTIAL FUNCTIONS OF THE POSITION HE HELD AS EXECUTIVE DIRECTOR FOR [A.I.C.]

14. As of [July 29, 1992], [Charles Wessel] was absent from work approximately 25 percent of the previous year:

(a) He missed 16 days between [July 29] and [August 13, 1991], when he experienced a pneumothorax (collapsed lung) during what was supposed to have been a routine one-day biopsy [citation to record];

(b) He missed 2 half-days and one full day following the above, in [August] of [1991];

(c) He missed approximately 33 days between [October 3] and [November 4], [1991], for surgery to remove a portion of his right lung due to recurring cancer [citation to record];

(d) He missed approximately 3 hours per day as a result of each day he received radiation treatments, which would have included:

(i) several days in [December 1991], following his lung operation;
(ii) 15 workdays in [April] and [May], [1992] (Ex. 2, 63);
(iii) several workdays in [June] [1992];
(iv) 2 days in [July] [1992].

D. [CHARLES WESSEL]'S RISK OF INJURY TO HIMSELF AND OTHERS

15. An additional brain tumor in the occipital area of [Charles Wessel]'s brain was identified on or about [June 22, 1991] [citation to record].

16. Dr. [A], [Wessel]'s primary treating physician, restricted [Wessel]'s driving because of lesions in the occipital lobe of the brain [citation to record].

17. In [June] of [1992], [Wessel] developed new brain tumors in the parietal area of the brain [citation to record].

18. [Wessel] experienced seizures in [December] of [1992] [citation to record].

19. Dr. [B], a radiation oncologist treating [Wessel], informed [defendant C] in a telephone conversation that [Wessel] had been advised not to drive [citation to record].

20. [Larry R.], the Executive Vice President of [A.I.C. International]'s Systems Division, offered [Wessel] a driver as an accommodation, which [Wessel] refused [citation to record].

Dated this [24th] day of [February] [1993].

[counsel for defendants]

[2]   Response to Statement of Material Facts

FORM 14–5   **Sample Response to Statement of Material Facts**

IN THE UNITED STATES DISTRICT COURT
FOR THE [NORTHERN] DISTRICT OF [ILLINOIS]
[EASTERN] DIVISION

U.S. EQUAL EMPLOYMENT OPPORTUNITY COMMISSION
AND [CHARLES H. WESSEL]
Plaintiffs,   Civil Action No. [92 C 7330]
v.
[A.I.C. SECURITY INVESTIGATIONS, LTD.];
[A.I.C. INTERNATIONAL, LTD.];
and [unnamed defendant C],
Defendants.   Magistrate Judge [Guzman]

PLAINTIFFS' RESPONSE TO DEFENDANTS' STATEMENT OF MATERIAL FACTS

Pursuant to Rule 56 of the Federal Rules of Civil Procedure and [Rule 12(n)] of the General Rules of the United States District Court for the [Northern] District of [Illinois], Plaintiffs hereby file their response to Defendants' Statement of Material Facts.

Paragraph 1: The Plaintiffs admit this statement.
Paragraph 2: The Plaintiffs admit this statement.
Paragraph 3: The Plaintiffs admit this statement.
Paragraph 4: The security industry is a changing business requiring adaptation to resolve issues as they arise [citation to record].

Paragraph 5: The security industry is not always a nine-to-five business [citation to record].

Paragraphs 6, 7, and 8: The essential functions of the position of Executive Director at [A.I.C. Security Investigations, Ltd.] were the supervision over and responsibility for the guard division to ensure both profitability and legal compliance [citation to record].

Paragraphs 9 and 10: Defendants have not cited any support in the record for the information contained in these paragraphs. As the moving parties, Defendants have the burden of proving that there is no genuine issue of fact as to these assertions. Because Defendants failed to provide any support for these assertions, the statements should not be considered for purposes of the pending Motion for Summary Judgment.

Paragraph 11: [Charles Wessel] was diagnosed with brain lesions in [April 1992]. There is no way of determining within a reasonable degree of medical certainty how long the brain tumors were present before they were diagnosed [citation to record].

Paragraphs 12 and 13: Defendants have not cited any support in the record of the information contained in these paragraphs. As the moving parties, Defendants have the burden of proving that there is no genuine issue of fact as to these assertions. Because Defendants failed to provide any support for these assertions, the statements should not be considered for the pending Motion for Summary Judgment.

Paragraph 14:[8] Initially, Plaintiffs note that Defendants have not cited any support in the record for the assertions in subparagraphs (b), (d)(i), (d)(iii), and (d)(iv). As the moving parties, Defendants have the burden of proving that there is no genuine issue of fact as to these assertions. Because Defendants failed to provide any support for these assertions, the statements should not be considered for purposes of the pending Motion for Summary Judgment.

Plaintiffs admit subparagraphs 14(a) and (c); however, the statement that the 49 days that [Wessel] missed work represents 25 percent of the workdays between [July 1991] and [July 1992] is simply incorrect.

Paragraphs 15 and 17: In [June 1992], [Charles Wessel] was found to have a new small lesion, less than one centimeter, in the parietal area of the brain [citation to record].

Paragraph 16: The Defendants cite to pages 189–91 of Dr. [A]'s deposition in support of the statement; however, no such pages exist in the deposition transcript. Dr. [A], [Wessel]'s primary treating physician, never instructed [Charles Wessel] not to drive. As of [September 3, 1992], Dr. [A] would place some driving restrictions on [Wessel] [citations to record].

Paragraph 18: In [December 1992], [Wessel] experienced a seizure [citation to record].

Paragraph 19: Plaintiffs admit this paragraph.

---

[8] Defendants originally had two Paragraph Nos. 13 in their Statement of Material Facts, but they did not have a Paragraph No. 14 in their statement. Therefore, Plaintiffs labeled the second Paragraph No. 13 as Paragraph No. 14 for purposes of this response.

Paragraph 20: [Charles Wessel] did not require a driver to and from his employment in 1991 and does not recall being offered a driver by [Larry R.] at that time. Deposition of [Charles Wessel] [(February 10, 1993)], p. 44, lines 20–24; and p. 45, lines 1–4.

Respectfully submitted,

[attorney B]

Trial Attorney

Equal Employment Opportunity Commission
[536 South Clark], [Room 982]
[Chicago], [Illinois] [60605]
[(312) 886-9120]

[attorney D]

Attorney for [Charles Wessel]

[3]   Reply Memorandum on Summary Judgment

FORM 14–6   Sample Reply Memorandum on Summary Judgment

DEFENDANTS' REPLY MEMORANDUM ON SUMMARY JUDGMENT

I. THE PLAINTIFFS HAVE NOT REBUTTED THE CONCLUSIVE EXPERT MEDICAL EVIDENCE THAT [CHARLES WESSEL] WAS UNABLE TO PERFORM THE ESSENTIAL FUNCTIONS OF HIS JOB

Defendants' motion for summary judgment was supported by uncontroverted medical opinions from both of [Wessel]'s treating physicians. (Defendants' initial memorandum, pages 16–17.) Defendants also supplied for the record medical opinions of the two physicians Defendants intend to call at trial, if necessary [citation to record]. As the record makes clear, all four physicians who would give expert medical testimony at trial have declared [Charles Wessel] unable to perform his former position of Executive Director for [A.I.C.]. This conclusive medical testimony is not disputed anywhere in the Plaintiffs' response.

Specifically, [Wessel]'s primary treating physician, Doctor [A], completed a medical report for the Bureau of Disability Determination Service, stating that [Wessel] was "frequently fatigued," was "unable to perform routine tasks," and was "unable to perform any work-related activities at this time" [citation to record].[9]

---

[9] This opinion was rendered on or about August 24, 1992, one week after Doctor [A] examined Wessel. The most recent examination of Wessel prior to this August examination

Defendants have also made pertinent portions of the deposition transcript of Doctor [B] a part of the record. Doctor [B] similarly indicated that [Wessel] was unable to perform his position.[10] Doctor [C] also testified that [Wessel] was not able to perform the essential function of his job as Executive Director at [A.I.C.] [citation to record].

Finally, Doctor [D], the only neurologist among the parties' expert witnesses for trial, testified:

Q. Okay. Dr. [D], do you have any opinions, within a reasonable degree of medical certainty, as to whether or not, in [July 1992], [Charles Wessel] was able to perform the essential functions of his job?

A. I do.

Q. And what is that opinion?

A. Well, because of the neurological condition that [Wessel] had, it was my opinion that he was very likely to have cognitive impairments; neurological problems in terms of various functions involving reasoning, judgment, other personality-related functions that go along with having had metastatic brain tumors, as well as a course of radiation therapy, as well as medications that he was receiving.

[citation to record].

II. THE PLAINTIFFS HAVE NO SUPPORTIVE MEDICAL EVIDENCE FOR A TRIAL

It comes as no surprise that Plaintiffs have completely ignored the medical opinions of even their own expert witnesses in their response. Their medical expert, Doctor [A], has admitted to supplying false medical reports to the bureau of Disability Determination Services on the very issue about which he is to testify at trial (i.e., [Wessel]'s ability to work).

On or about [August 24, 1992], Doctor [A] completed a medical report for the Bureau of Disability Determination Services in connection with [Wessel]'s application for Social Security disability benefits. . . . This medical report stated that [Wessel] was "frequently fatigued," was "unable to perform routine tasks," and was "unable to perform any work-related activities at this time" [citations to record].

By contrast, a little more than one week after filling out this disability medical report, Doctor [A] signed an affidavit prepared for him by the EEOC . . . . This

---

was performed on July 13, 1992. Because Wessel's last day of work for defendants was July 29, 1992, the August examination is the most relevant to Wessel's condition on his last day at work. This conclusion is particularly compelling in light of Doctor [B]'s testimony that, if anything, Wessel's condition had improved in August [citations to record].

[10] Defendants' citation in its original memorandum, page 17, incorrectly cited to page 67 rather than page 127. This was a typographical error. Page 163 may have been omitted from Defendants' Exhibit 4 of Doctor [B]'s deposition transcript, and it is attached hereto as Exhibit A, as a Supplement to Exhibit 4.

document provided: "I have assessed that [Wessel] can work full-time in the position he held as Executive Director with A.I.C. Security" [citations to record].

On [December 18, 1992], Dr. [A] was confronted with these two contradictory medical reports at his deposition. Having testified in support of his EEOC affidavit that [Wessel] could work, Dr. [A] was asked to explain his conflicting medical report that Wessel could not work:

Q. What does it state under No. 11 [of the report]?

A. It states, "Patient is unable to perform any work-related activities at this time."

Q. Do you want to distinguish between that and your previous testimony?

A. The reason for this now is that he had been fired from his job, and we felt that he should be able to get some compensation because no one is going to hire him anymore. He is not going to be able to get any income at all, and so this is for the Social Security to say that, yes, he is not able to work.

Q. And you know that by writing what you were writing under No. 11 that would help him qualify for benefits?

A. That's correct.

Q. Is it your testimony today that despite what you put in response to Question No. 11, that's not what you believe?

A. Absolutely not.

Q. You emphatically disagree with what you wrote on that?

A. Yes.

Clearly, Doctor [A] was without any legitimate explanation for his two completely contradictory medical opinions. Instead, the doctor testified that one of the opinions — the one given to the Bureau of Disability Determination Services — was entirely fabricated because "we felt he [Wessel] should be able to get some compensation. . . ."

At the same time, Doctor [A] testified that he knew almost nothing about [Wessel]'s job at [A.I.C.] (including its title) even though he had signed the EEOC's affidavit that stated: "I am aware of the essential functions that comprise the job of Executive Director" [citation to record].[11]

Doctor [A] admittedly committed a felony by lying on the very issue that Plaintiffs are attempting to prove through his expert medical opinion. The Social Security Act contains severe criminal penalties for the filing of false medical reports, and upon conviction of such a felony, the law provides for a fine of not more than $5,000.00 or imprisonment for not more than five years, or both. 42 U.S.C. § 408(c); *cf.* [*United States v. Toler*, 440 F.2d 1242 (5th Cir. 1971)].

---

[11] In fact, Doctor [A] testified that he was not under oath when he signed the EEOC affidavit. Furthermore, he admitted, "I sign a lot of things without reading them," so he was not sure if he had ever read the EEOC's affidavit [citations of record]. Defendants submit that, given the fact that Doctor [A] had just prepared a medical report on August 24 that stated that Wessel was unable to work, a proper investigation into the facts of this matter required more than just obtaining a busy doctor's signature on a form affidavit that he may not even have read.

This Court is justified in excluding Doctor [A]'s opinions from its consideration of the merits of this case. The [Seventh] Circuit Court of Appeals has held that a Rule 702 (Fed. R. Evid.) Expert Witness's "declaration, full of assertion but empty of the facts and reasons, won't get a case past summary judgment, for the judge must look behind [the expert's] ultimate conclusion. . . ." (citations omitted; emphasis added). [*Mid-State Fertilizer Co. v. Exchange National Bank*, 877 F.2d 1333, 1339 (7th Cir. 1989)].

In this case, Doctor [A]'s testimony that he flat out lied about [Wessel]'s medical condition should be so offensive to the Court that anything he may say now is without one scintilla of value to the findings of fact in this action. As Judge [James M.] of this Court noted in [*Soderlund v. Ben Franklin Stores, Inc.*, 41 Fair Empl. Prac. Cas. (BNA) 1709, 1711 (N.D. Ill. 1986)], some testimony is so unworthy of consideration in court that it may be termed "incredible as a matter of law" (citing [*Draeger v. Jockey International, Inc.*, 583 F. Supp. 570 (S.D.N.Y.), *aff'd mem.*, 751 F.2d 368 (2d Cir. 1984)]).

Under circumstances such as these, the United States Court of Appeals for the [Seventh] Circuit has declared that district courts have a "duty to ignore sham issues in determining the appropriateness of summary judgment." [*Babrocky v. Jewel Food Co.*, 773 F.2d 857, 861 (7th Cir. 1985)].

In [*Babrocky*], the court of appeals stated that parties (or, Defendants submit, their expert witnesses) should not be allowed to create credibility issues contradicting their own earlier testimony: "Otherwise, the very purpose of the summary judgment motion — to weed out unfounded claims, specious denials, and sham defenses [—] would be severely undercut." [*Id.* at 861]. Here, Doctor [A] must not be allowed to pick between his medical opinions, especially to state that his opinion of [August 24] was a felonious lie, but that his opinion of [September 2] is now credible for this Court.

Significantly, Doctor [B] has never rendered any medical opinion about [Wessel]'s ability to work other than her assessment to the Bureau of Disability Determination Services that [Wessel] could not do so [citation to record]. Doctor [B] apparently will not contradict her earlier opinion that [Wessel] could not work, and in any event, Plaintiffs have not any favorable opinion from [Dr. B] for purposes of the instant motion.

Doctor [B] testified generally about the effects of tumors in various portions of the brain . . . but when asked specifics about memory processes, she replied: "That's really beyond area [*sic*] of, you know, my personal expertise since I'm not a neurologist or neurosurgeon" [citation to record].

At her deposition, Doctor [B] would only testify that the physiological aspects of the human brain fall outside her expertise and within the expertise of neurosurgeons and neurologists:

Q. Is it safe to say generally that those portions of the brain we're talking about where [Mr. Wessel]'s tumors were in [April] are more related to motor functions?

A. No, they are not so much related to motor functions. Really, the area which is referred to motor function is parietal [*sic*] area of the brain.

Again, I think you are trying to simplify the question, you know. The brain cannot be just separated, you know, 9 or 10 pieces. It is all connected together.

Q. Again, the experts that talk about this type of subject would be a neuro-surgeon or neurologist?

A. That's correct.

[citation to record].

Given the uncontroverted fact that [Wessel] suffers from a dynamic neuro-logical condition, and given the uncontroverted fact that [Wessel]'s position in-volved reasoning, judgment, and, generally, running an entire company in the de-manding security guard industry, no fair-minded jury could find that [Wessel] was qualified without the benefit of expert medical testimony.

All of the expert medical opinions in this record state that [Wessel] could not do the job anymore.

III. GIVEN THE NATURE OF [WESSEL]'S ILLNESS AND HIS JOB, PLAINTIFFS CANNOT MEET THEIR PRIMA FACIE BURDEN TO SHOW THAT [WESSEL] WAS QUALIFIED WITHOUT COMPETENT EXPERT MED-ICAL EVIDENCE

The instant action involved [Charles Wessel]'s condition of "metastatic can-cer," that is, cancer initially of the lungs that subsequently moved to his brain in the form of multiple, growing tumors [citation to record].

[Wessel]'s position of Executive Director of [A.I.C.], as the top management position, meant that he ran the company [citation to record]. The essential functions of the position are, admittedly, largely intellectual.[12]

Given these facts, competent medical evidence is required in order to address the issue of [Wessel]'s ability to continue to perform, with or without reasonable accommodation, the essential functions of his job while suffering from a degen-erative brain disease.

In [*School Board of Nassau County v. Arline*, 480 U.S. 273, 287 (1987)], the Supreme Court observed that "in most cases, the district court will need to conduct an individualized inquiry and make appropriate findings of fact" in order to deter-mine if an individual is "qualified" for a particular job.

The [*Arline*] court held that its inquiry "should include '[findings of]' facts based upon reasonable medical judgments given the state of medical knowledge" about [Arline]'s communicable disease. [(*Id.* at 288.)]

The instant action requires that the Court's inquiry include findings of fact based upon the reasonable medical judgments in the record concerning [Wessel]'s degenerative brain cancer. The [District of Columbia] Court of Appeals addressed a similar situation involving the complexities of diseases of the brain:

> Unlike some other handicaps, the causes and effects of manic-depressive syn-drome and the extent to which the symptoms of the illness can be controlled by medication and therapy [i.e. "accommodated"] are beyond the ken of the av-erage lay person. Where proof of an issue is related to a science or profession

---

[12] However, the defendants do dispute the plaintiff's characterization of his job as purely mental.

beyond the ken of an average lay person, expert testimony is required. (Citations omitted.)

[*American University v. DCCHR,* 57 Fair Empl. Prac. Cas. (BNA) 245, 250, 598 A.2d 416 (D.C. Ct. App. 1991)].

Indeed, expert medical testimony is a commonplace necessity in handicap/disability litigation. *See, e.g.,* [*Chiari v. City of League City,* 920 F.2d 311, 316 (5th Cir. 1991) (on review of district court's decision of summary judgment, court of appeals rejected Plaintiff's argument that "despite the testimony of three physicians, a jury still could find that he is capable of performing his job . . .")]; [*Sanders v. United Parcel Service,* 491 N.E.2d 1314, 1318, 142 Ill. App. 3d 362, 96 Ill. Dec. 854 (1986) (dismissal of complaint upheld where Plaintiff failed to provide medical documentation and therefore failed to meet initial burden on handicap claim)]; [*Connecticut General Life Insurance Co. v. DILHR,* 86 Wis. 2d 393, 407–08, 273 N.W.2d 206 (1979) (court's determination regarding alcoholism as a handicap "is a matter of expert medical opinion proved by a physician and not a layman")].

The circumstances of the present case call for expert medical opinions just as the Supreme Court required in [*Arline*], and just as numerous forums have required in similar case law. The neurological consequences of brain tumors in various portions of the brain simply are not within the knowledge of the lay person juror.

IV. THE PLAINTIFFS' RESPONSE TO DEFENDANTS' MOTION FOR SUMMARY JUDGMENT FAILS TO CREATE THE GENUINE ISSUES OF MATERIAL FACT NECESSARY TO TAKE THIS CASE TO TRIAL, AND SUMMARY JUDGMENT IN DEFENDANTS' FAVOR IS THEREFORE APPROPRIATE

Plaintiffs concede that it is their burden to prove that [Wessel] was qualified for the position of Executive Director at the time of his discharge [citation to record]. Having admitted this burden, however, Plaintiffs have failed to designate specific facts showing a genuine issue for trial on the matter of whether [Wessel] was qualified to remain in his position beyond [July 29, 1992].

Instead of putting forth specific facts that would create a genuine issue regarding the material fact of [Wessel]'s ability to continue working, Plaintiffs' memorandum treats the issue as though this were Defendants' burden, which they need only disprove.[13]

The only evidence Plaintiffs put forth in support of their prima facie burden to show that [Wessel] was qualified is that [Wessel] had "experience and expertise in the security industry." . . .[14] This misses the mark. [Wessel] would not have been

---

[13] For instance, Plaintiffs concede Wessel's short-term memory loss but argue that this fact does not evidence any impact upon Wessel's performance [citation to record].

[14] Plaintiffs' memorandum argues several points that are not supported in the record. First, the entire "Factual Summary" is without one single citation to record evidence; second, Plaintiffs' assertion regarding the financial performance of A.I.C. is likewise unsupported by Fed. R. Civ. P. 56 evidence (defendants could show that A.I.C.'s profitability was actually

hired as A.I.C.'s Executive Director in [1986] had he not had experience in the security industry. The relevant issue is whether [Wessel] was able to perform the essential functions of the job beyond [July 1992] given his degenerative condition. In these regards, it must be noted that Plaintiffs' heavy reliance on [David P.] is meaningless considering Plaintiffs' admission that [David P.] was fired on [July 6, 1992] [citations to record].

The severe lack of probative evidence offered by Plaintiffs is simply insufficient to overcome Defendants' Motion for Summary Judgment, and Rule 56(c) of the Federal Rules of Civil Procedure provides that Summary Judgment "shall be rendered forthwith" where the moving party is entitled to judgment as a matter of law based upon the record before the court.

In [*EEOC v. Clay Printing Co.,* 955 F.2d 936, 942–43 (4th Cir. 1992)], the Court noted that "[i]n overcoming a motion for summary judgment," the EEOC has to "produce direct evidence" supporting its prima facie case. Holding that the EEOC failed to "marshall enough evidence," the Court upheld summary judgment, stating as follows:

> A fair-minded jury simply could not return a verdict for the EEOC on the evidence presented. [*Anderson v. Liberty Lobby, Inc.,* 477 U.S. 242, 252 (1986)]. "The mere existence of a scintilla of evidence in support of the plaintiff's position will be insufficient; there must be evidence on which the jury could reasonably find for the plaintiff." [*Id.*]

Here, Plaintiffs do not even attempt to rebut [Wessel]'s own admissions that he turned over his essential functions to his assistants. (*See* Defendants' initial memorandum, pp. 15–16 and citations to evidence.) Furthermore, such transfers of essential functions do not even fall into the analysis of whether reasonable accommodations can be made.

In another handicap case involving the security guard industry (albeit a managerial position was not involved), the Court of Appeals for the [Tenth] Circuit held that the company did not have to provide an assistant to a legally blind security guard. [*Coleman v. Darden,* 595 F.2d 533 (10th Cir. 1979)]. The court in [*Coleman*] reasoned that the "assistant" would be performing the job for the individual rather than assisting the individual to perform his job. [*Id.* at 536.]

Similarly, when [Wessel], as Executive Director, required that his "assistants" perform what had always been the essential functions of his job, in essence he ceased doing the job and was no longer "qualified." Again, these compelling facts are uncontroverted.

---

drastically down in 1992 from 1991, had Plaintiffs properly put the matter at issue in this motion); and finally, Plaintiffs' so-called "powerful" evidence that a subordinate on-site employee (that is, an employee who did not work at A.I.C.'s premises with Wessel) held Wessel in high esteem is less than the scintilla of evidence rejected on summary judgment in *Brownell* [citations to record]. *See* Brownell v. Figel, 950 F.2d 1285, 1289 (7th Cir. 1991).

V. PLAINTIFFS HAVE FAILED TO RAISE ANY ISSUE OF MATERIAL FACT THAT DEFENDANTS ARE NOT ENTITLED TO SUMMARY JUDGMENT BECAUSE [WESSEL] POSED A DIRECT THREAT AS DEFINED IN THE ADA

Plaintiffs' memorandum [citation to record] does not raise any issues of fact on the matter of [Wessel]'s medically verified risk of injury to himself and others. Therefore, the following facts are now undisputed:

(1) [Wessel] was at risk of unpredictable seizures and was advised as early as [April] [1992] to avoid the use of an automobile [citation to record];

(2) Based upon the discovery of new tumors in the parietal area of his brain in [June] [1992], [Wessel] was considered by his physicians to be at an acute and heightened risk of seizures [citation to record];

(3) [Wessel] drove to, from, and during work and included his subordinate employees as passengers in his automobile [citation to record];

(4) Defendants offered [Wessel] a personal driver to pick him up at his house and take him to and from his work [citation to record];

(5) [Wessel] refused Defendants' offer of a driver [citation to record]; and

(6) [Wessel] continued driving despite his doctors' advising him not to drive [citation to record].

Instead of challenging these facts, Plaintiffs argue that the direct-threat defense of the ADA does not apply as a matter of law. Obviously, this is a matter to be decided by the Court and not a jury.

Plaintiffs' argument is based upon two erroneous legal arguments. First, they argue that Defendants' direct-threat defense must fail because Defendants cannot establish that driving was an essential function of the position of Executive Director. Second, Plaintiffs apparently argue that Defendants may not assert the direct-threat defense without proving that their motive was particular concern over the health or safety of [Wessel] and/or his subordinates. Both of these legal arguments must fail.

A. Under the ADA, a direct threat need only be "job-related" and in any event, getting to and from work was an essential function inherent in [Wessel]'s position.

It is expressly stated in the pertinent provisions of the ADA that the direct threat need only be "job-related." 42 U.S.C. §§ 12,113(a), (b).

To apply the direct-threat standard only to essential functions of the job would mean that employers would have to tolerate serious safety risks in all instances where a "direct threat" employee is performing only marginal functions or is simply on the employer's premises. Although the ADA mandates reasonable accommodations to avoid the risks involved with a direct-threat employee, there clearly can be risks associated with nonessential functions that simply cannot be reasonably accommodated.[15]

For example, an engineer with Parkinson's disease poses no direct threat to safety while performing the essential functions of his engineering job. However, if in performing those essential functions, he needs to get to, from, and about in the buildings he is inspecting, he may pose a serious risk to health and safety. These were the actual facts in the case of [*Chiari v. City of League City*, 920 F.2d 311 (5th Cir. 1991)].

The Court in [*Chiari*] held that the Plaintiff was not "otherwise qualified" under the Rehabilitation Act when three neurologists/neurosurgeons testified that his Parkinson's disease posed a significant risk to health and safety. [*Id.* at 316.]

In the instant action, Plaintiffs did not challenge their own expert witness's, Dr. [B]'s, determination that [Wessel] posed a significant risk while driving due to the high probability of seizures. When [Wessel] in fact experienced seizures, Dr. [B] was not in the least surprised [citation to record].

As with [*Chiari*], driving did not constitute the majority of [Wessel]'s job, yet he clearly needed to get to and from work. Furthermore, [Wessel] himself testified that approximately 5 percent of his job involved making on-site visits, although he became more selective in [1992] [citation to record].

Thus, driving was inherently an essential function of [Wessel]'s job, even though this is not required under the law.

Plaintiffs' hypothetical argument that [Wessel] could easily have used other modes of transportation is unavailing under the uncontroverted circumstances of this case. [Wessel] insisted on driving. [Wessel] drove despite his doctors' orders. [Wessel] refused Defendants' offer to provide a personal driver for him. These facts are not contested.

Under these circumstances, Defendants attempted to provide [Wessel] more than "reasonable accommodations," all to no avail.

Similar to [Wessel], the Plaintiff in [*Chiari*] argued to the Court that he should be able to make his own choices regarding his personal safety. [*Id.* at 316.] However, the [*Chiari*] Court upheld summary judgment against Plaintiff based upon objective and credible medical evidence that [Chiari] posed a risk to health and safety, with no consideration given to the subjective arguments of [Chiari]. [*Id.* at 317.]

B. Plaintiffs' argument that defendants must show a genuine concern for [Wessel]'s health and safety sets a standard for the direct-threat defense that does not exist in the law.

Plaintiffs' argument that Defendants may not assert the direct-threat defense because their motives were in the wrong place is simply unavailing. Plaintiffs would

---

[15] Even the EEOC interpretative rules (29 C.F.R. § 1630.2(r)) do not go so far as to say that a threat must be directly connected to an essential function of the employer's job. To an extent, the rules could be read in the fashion argued in Plaintiffs' response. The defendants submit that the rules are inconsistent with the congressional directive that the threat be "job-related." 42 U.S.C. §§ 12,113(a), (b).

have Defendants bear a burden of demonstrating genuine concern over the health and welfare of [Charles Wessel] in order to assert the defense. This is not the law.

The ADA requires only that "an individual shall not pose a direct threat to health or safety . . . ." 42 U.S.C. § 12,113(b). This language does not support Plaintiffs' conclusion that an employer's motive be humane versus financial versus any other motive. All that the law requires is that, as here, medical experts have determined that [Wessel] posed a significant risk to health and safety to either himself or other employees in the workplace, and that these circumstances caused his exclusion from work with Defendants.

VI. CONCLUSION

In a very recent civil rights action before this Court, District Judge [Charles N.] summarized [Seventh] Circuit and Supreme Court precedent on the circumstances that favor the granting of a motion for summary judgment:

> Rule 56(c) of the Federal Rules of Civil Procedure provides that for a party to prevail on a summary judgment motion "the pleadings, depositions, answers to interrogatories, and admissions on file, together with the affidavits, if any, [must] show that there is no genuine issue as to any material fact and the moving party is entitled to a judgment as a matter of law." Fed R. Civ. P. 56(c). Even though all reasonable inferences are drawn in favor of the party opposing the motion, [*Beraha v. Baxter Health Care Corp.*, 956 F.2d 1436, 1440 (7th Cir. 1992)], a scintilla of evidence in support of the non-movant's position will not suffice to oppose a motion for summary judgment. [*Brownell v. Figel*, 950 F.2d 1285, 1289 (7th Cir. 1991)]. Instead, the non-moving party must elucidate specific facts demonstrating that there is a genuine issue for trial. [*Matsushita Elec. Indus. Co. v. Zenith Radio Corp.*, 475 U.S. 574, 586 (1986)]. Moreover, to preclude summary judgment the disputed facts must be those that might affect the outcome of the suit, [*First Indiana Bank v. Baker*, 957 F.2d 506, 508 (7th Cir. 1992)], and a dispute about a material fact is "genuine" only if the evidence is such that a reasonable jury could return a verdict for the non-moving party. [*Anderson v. Liberty Lobby, Inc.*, 477 U.S. 242, 248 (1986)]. "One of the principal purposes of the summary judgment rule is to isolate and dispose of factually unsupported claims and defenses . . . ." [*Celotex Corp. v. Catrett*, 477 U.S. 317, 323–24 (1986)]. Accordingly, the non-moving party is required to go beyond the pleadings, affidavits, depositions, answers to interrogatories and admissions on file to designate specific facts showing a genuine issue for trial. [*Bank Leurni Le-Isreal, B.M. v. Lee*, 928 F.2d 232, 236 (7th Cir. 1991)].

[*Seward v. General Motors Corp.*, 805 F. Supp. 623, 627 (N.D. Ill. 1992)].

Plaintiffs' response to Defendants' Motion for Summary Judgment leaves untouched the unanimous medical opinions that [Wessel] could not perform. There are no genuine issues of material fact on the expert medical opinions in this action.

As the nonmoving party, Plaintiffs were required to come forward with specific facts creating genuine issues for trial. This is particularly necessary as to issues which Plaintiffs concede are their burden to prove in order to maintain any action under the ADA, and they have failed to provide evidence under Rule 56(c) that would permit a rational jury to determine that [Wessel] was qualified to remain the Executive Director for [A.I.C.].

On the matter of [Wessel] having also been excluded as posing a direct threat to health and safety, Plaintiffs have likewise wholly ignored the uncontroverted medical consensus that [Wessel] indeed posed such a probable risk. The legal arguments Plaintiffs raise are for the Court's determination (not a jury's) and the arguments are insufficient to avoid summary judgment,

Because no rational jury could return a verdict for Plaintiffs based upon the record now before the Court, Defendants are entitled to have their motion for summary judgment granted.

See [*Anderson v. University of Wisconsin,* 841 F.2d 737 (7th Cir. 1988)].

Respectfully submitted this [1st] day of [March] [1993].

[name and address of counsel]

[4] Record for Summary Judgment[16]

FORM 14–7   **Sample Record for Summary Judgment**

The Court simply is not persuaded for purposes of summary judgment that Plaintiffs's medical restrictions do not create "a significant barrier to employment in positions that are comparable in stature to her former position at [Kitterman]" — especially given her limited educational, training, and employment background. As to the different jobs Plaintiff has held since Defendant told her she could not return to [Kitterman], there is evidence before the Court that either (1) those jobs required her to perform restricted tasks prohibited by Plaintiff's doctor in her medical release report and/or tasks that caused her pain in connection with her carpal tunnel syndrome; (2) the jobs involuntarily [. . .] ended due to layoff; or (3) the jobs were not permanent or not available full-time. Not only does this evidence to which Defendant cites fail to support Defendant's proposition that Plaintiff's "physical impairment has not created a significant barrier to employment positions that are comparable in stature to her former positions at [Kitterman]," but it actually flies in the face of such a conclusion given Plaintiff's sworn testimony regarding the duties of the full-time and permanent jobs she actually secured. Notably, beyond Defendant's conclusory allegations to the contrary, there is no evidence before the Court to dispute Plaintiff's claim that she is significantly restricted in the ability to perform a class of jobs or a broad range of jobs in various classes, when compared with the ability of a person with comparable training, qualifications, skills, and

---

[16] This section contains an actual court record (Form 14-7) from Smith v. Kitterman, 897 F. Supp. 423, 427–28 (W.D. Mo. 1995), and the portions of the deposition exchanges (Form 14-8) upon which the court based its record. In this case, the referenced deposition exchanges saved the plaintiff from summary judgment on the employer's argument that her carpal tunnel syndrome did not constitute a disability because it disqualified her from only one job. In the court record, the cross-references to the deposition exchanges are omitted.

abilities to perform those same jobs. *See* EEOC Interpretive Guide, § 1630.2(j) [footnotes omitted].

FORM 14–8   Sample Deposition Exchange

Q. In your position at [Bio Mat], is there anything that you do that causes you problems with your hands?

A. There is some things, yes.

Q. What would those things be?

A. For instance, like turning things, like the ratchet type thing. It causes pain, but I still do it, if I have to turn it really super hard. [Karen Smith] Dep. at 8–9.

Q. While you were working at [Henry Wurst], did you experience any problems with either your right hand or your left hand?

A. Yes, I did at different times, yes.

Q. What type of problems did you have?

A. Well, just normal problems like I always have, pain. [Karen Smith] Dep. at 12–13.

Q. What did you do for [Haldex]?

A. Put brakes together.

Q. Can you describe for me or tell me how you did that job, what was involved?

A. Yes. You had to — I guess I can tell you exactly how it was done. You had to put a lot of greasy parts together, and you had to screw them down, and you had to use an air driver to put them in.
You had a lot of twisting and turning to do.

* * *

Q. Did you have any troubles with either your right hand or your left hand using the air driver?

A. Yes, I did.

Q. What about the twisting and the turning?

A. I had trouble with that.

Q. Which hand bothered you?

A. The right hand. [Karen Smith] Dep. at 21–22.

Q. [I]n October of '93, [Dr. Vilmer] gave you certain restrictions as far as the type of work you could perform. I was wondering if you're under any of the same restrictions today or different restrictions?

A. Well, I haven't been back to him. I do just what I have to do. I do it and if it hurts, I still do it anyway. [Karen Smith] Dep. at 14.

Q. What type of work did you do for [Westport Research]?

A. Electronics.

Q. What type of work was that?

A. We had to put boards together, electronic boards.

Q. Okay. To do this job, did you need to use small hand tools?

A. I had to use like little pliers. [Karen Smith] Dep. at 32–33.

* * *

Q. How long did you work for [Stuart Hall]?

A. I think I worked for them three months.

Q. What caused you to leave [Stuart Hall]?

A. Layoff.

Q. [T]he work you did at [Stuart Hall], was [*sic*] there any tasks that you performed that would cause you problems with either your right or your left hand?

A. I really didn't have anything that I had to twist or pull or —

Q. So would that mean no?

A. That would mean no. [Karen Smith] Dep. at 27.

Q. Before [Stuart Hall], where did you work?

A. Oh. Yeah, I was in [Interstate Inn], and I did that basically part-time.

Q. Did any of your job duties at [Interstate Inn] require twisting and turning with your hands?

A. No.

Q. Did you have to use small hand tools?

A. No.

Q. Why did you leave [Interstate Inn]?

A. Because I needed to make more money. [Karen Smith] Dep. at 27–29.

Q. Do you have any recollection as to how long you were with [Westport Research]?

A. I think I was with them for like a couple of months. However long the job lasted.

Q. And it was a temporary position?

A. Yes. [Karen Smith] Dep. at 33.

CHAPTER 15

PRETRIAL PROCESS

§ 15.01 INTRODUCTION AND OVERVIEW

[A] Generally

This chapter provides materials for Americans with Disabilities Act (ADA)[1] cases related to the pretrial process.[2]

[B] Sample Forms

[1] Order of Reference

FORM 15–1 **Sample Order of Reference**

UNITED STATES DISTRICT COURT

DISTRICT OF [name]

Plaintiff, [name]

v.   Docket No. [case number]

Defendant, [name].

ORDER OF REFERENCE

IT IS HEREBY ORDERED that the above-captioned matter be referred to United States Magistrate Judge [name] for all further proceedings and entry of judgment in accordance with Title 28 U.S.C. § 636(c) and the consent of the parties.

U.S. District Judge

[2] Motion to Extend Time for Pretrial Order

FORM 15 2 **Sample Motion to Extend Time for Pretrial Order**

DEFENDANTS' EMERGENCY MOTION FOR AN ENLARGEMENT OF TIME FOR FILING THEIR FINAL PRETRIAL ORDER

The Defendants, [A.I.C. SECURITY INVESTIGATIONS, LTD.], [A.I.C. IN-TERNATIONAL, LTD.], and [unnamed defendant C], by and through their attor-

---

[1] Pub. L. No. 101-336, 104 Stat. 327 (1990) (codified at 42 U.S.C. §§ 12,101–12,213 (1994); 47 U.S.C. §§ 225, 711 (1994)) [hereinafter ADA].

[2] *See* Forms 15–1 to 15–5.

neys, [WESSELS & PAUTSCH, P.C.], by [Charles W. Pautsch], [attorney A], [attorney B], and [William H., Esq.], pursuant to Rule 6(b) of the Federal Rules of Civil Procedure, hereby move for an enlargement of time in which to file the parties' Final Pretrial Order in the above-captioned action based upon the following.

1. By Order dated [December 29, 1992], the Court established [February 9, 1993], as the due date for the parties' Final Pretrial Order in the above-captioned action.

2. On [December 8, 1992], Defendants filed their motion to compel the deposition of the Plaintiff in intervention, [Charles Wessel], after he had refused to appear for his deposition, noticed pursuant to the Federal Rules of Civil Procedure for [December 10, 1992].

3. To date, there has been no ruling on Defendants' Motion to Compel, and it is the Defendants' position that their ability to defend against this action is being severely prejudiced without this essential discovery.

4. On or about [November 13, 1992], Defendants filed their Motion to Compel the Physical and Mental Examination of [Charles Wessel].

5. To date, there has been no ruling on Defendants' Motion to Compel the foregoing examination of [Charles Wessel], and it is the Defendants' position that their ability to defend against this action is being severely prejudiced without this essential discovery.

6. On [December 24, 1992], Defendants filed their motion to disqualify [attorney D] and the law firm of [firm name] from appearing on behalf of and representing [Charles Wessel] in this litigation due to an obvious conflict of interest in that [attorney D] is a witness in this action and she and her firm have rendered legal services to Defendant [A.I.C. Security Investigations, Ltd.] on matters of employment law related to this action.

7. To date, there has been no ruling on Defendants' motion to disqualify counsel for Plaintiff [Charles Wessel], and it is Defendants' position that their ability to defend against this action is being severely prejudiced by the involvement of challenged counsel.

8. This action was filed on or about [November 5, 1992], and, as a result of an expedited discovery schedule procured by motion of the Equal Employment Opportunity Commission, the cutoff for discovery was [December 31, 1992], a mere [35] working days ([56] actual days) from the initiation of this action by the Plaintiff and approximately one month after the Defendants' answer was due.

9. By Order dated [December 29, 1992], the Court extended discovery until [January 22, 1993], with no further extensions permitted, and established [February 9, 1993], as the due date for final pretrial orders; no other extensions have been granted.

10. Pursuant to the above-referenced discovery timetable, Defendants scheduled three depositions for [Thursday], [January 21, 1993]; however, one of the depositions — that of [Alice Wessel] — was unexpectedly canceled without notice based upon her attorney's ([attorney C] of the law firm [firm name]) representation that his flight to [Chicago] from [city] was canceled on that date due to the weather. By stipulation, the parties have agreed to reschedule [Alice Wessel]'s deposition on [Wednesday], [January 27, 1993], on account of the foregoing unavoidable "act of God."

11. Defendants are unable to obtain transcripts of depositions already taken until approximately early [February], and the deposition transcript of [Alice Wessel] may not be available until perhaps a week later — the current week of the due date for final pretrial orders.

12. Many responses to discovery are either still pending, incomplete, or challenged, and Defendants are currently attempting to resolve same or, if necessary, will move to compel responses.

13. Because of all the foregoing, the Defendants are being unduly prejudiced in their defense of the charges brought in this litigation, and there will be no adequate opportunity for motions in limine, statements of stipulated/uncontested facts, schedules of exhibits, and all other materials necessary for full compliance with the Court's final pretrial order.

WHEREFORE, the Defendants respectfully request that the final pretrial order in this action, currently due on or before [February 9, 1993], be enlarged by a reasonable time period to allow for rulings on all pertinent outstanding motions and to allow for all discovery issues to be resolved; Defendants propose that a status conference be set in this matter in early [February] to determine the status of the foregoing matters and to set a subsequent date for the pretrial order that will permit the parties an adequate opportunity to provide all required materials and documents.

Dated this [22nd] of [January] [1993].

[3] Statement of Cause of Action

FORM 15–3 Sample Statement of Cause of Action

IN THE UNITED STATES DISTRICT COURT FOR THE [NORTHERN] DISTRICT OF [ILLINOIS] [EASTERN] DIVISION

U.S. EQUAL EMPLOYMENT OPPORTUNITY COMMISSION,

Plaintiff

v.   Civil Action No. [92 C 7330]

[A.I.C. SECURITY INVESTIGATIONS, LTD.];

[A.I.C. INTERNATIONAL, LTD.];

and [unnamed defendant C],

Judge [Marvin E. Aspen]

Defendants.

Magistrate Judge [Guzman]

DEFENDANTS' STATEMENT OF CAUSE OF ACTION

Defendants, [A.I.C. SECURITY INVESTIGATIONS, LTD.], [A.I.C. INTER-NATIONAL, LTD.], and [defendant C], by and through their attorneys, [WESSELS & PAUTSCH, P.C.], by [Charles W. Pautsch], [attorney A], and [attorney B], hereby submit to this Honorable Court Defendants' Statement of Cause of Action:

1. At the Pretrial Conference held [Thursday], [March 4, 1993], in the above-referenced case, the Court requested that Defendants submit a "Statement of Cause of Action" to be read to the jury.

2. Defendants submit as the "Statement of Cause of Action" as follows:

This is an action filed under the Americans with Disabilities Act of 1990 (the "ADA"), in which Plaintiffs allege that Defendants discriminated against [Charles H. Wessel] by discharging him from his employment because of a disability, cancer, in violation of the ADA. Defendants deny any violation of the ADA occurred and instead contend, among other things, that [Charles Wessel] was justifiably excluded from the position of Executive Director because he could no longer perform the essential functions of that position.

Dated this [5th] day of [February] [1993].

[4]   Checklist for Final Preparation for Trial

_____ 1. Review of Proceedings
 _____ Schedule
 _____ Reports on completion of discovery
 _____ Items remaining to be completed
 _____ Requests for relief from deadlines/preclusion orders
 _____ Review statements of uncontested/contested facts, statements of contention and proof, witness/documents lists
 _____ Outstanding motions
 _____ Rule on all outstanding motions
 _____ Challenges to jurisdiction or venue
 _____ Transfer under 28 U.S.C. § 1404 or 1406
 _____ Summary judgment, including motions under Federal Rule of Civil Procedure 56(d)
 _____ Motions seeking to limit period/scope of proof
 _____ Issues regarding right to jury trial
 _____ Possible rulings on objections to evidence
 _____ Immediate rulings
 _____ Schedule hearing under Federal Rule of Evidence 104
 _____ Consider whether to recommend remand under 28 U.S.C. § 1407

_____ 2. Trial
     _____ Set/modify/confirm date and place of trial
     _____ Continuance only in extreme circumstances
     _____ Deadline for partial settlements in class actions
     _____ Trial schedule:
         _____ Normal hours
         _____ Days when no trial or trial day reduced
         _____ Holidays; recesses
     _____ Consolidation under Federal Rule of Civil Procedure 42(a):
         _____ Class actions and individual actions
         _____ Jury and nonjury cases
         _____ Transfer as appropriate under 28 U.S.C. § 1404 or 1406
     _____ Severance under Federal Rule of Civil Procedure 42(b):
         _____ Define/confirm issues for trial and those severed for later trial
     _____ If both jury and nonjury issues to be tried:
         _____ Receive additional nonjury evidence at completion of trial
         _____ Receive additional nonjury evidence at close of each day
     _____ Schedule for subsequent trials of severed issues:
         _____ Immediately after initial trial
         _____ Later, perhaps after additional discovery
     _____ Order of proof/issue/evidence:
         _____ Standard order of presentation
         _____ Issues presented in specified sequence
         _____ Plaintiffs' evidence presented in specified sequence, followed by defendants' evidence in same sequence
         _____ Parties present all evidence on first issue before proceeding with evidence on next issue(s)
         _____ Arguments presented as evidence on issue completed
         _____ Verdict/findings on first issue before proceeding with evidence on next issue
     _____ Jury selection:
         _____ Principal jurors
         _____ Number of peremptory challenges
         _____ Selection of alternate jurors
         _____ Number
         _____ When disclosure made as to identity of alternates
     _____ Stipulations:
         _____ Agreement to receive verdict from remaining jurors, avoiding need to select alternatives
         _____ Agreement to accept less than unanimous verdict

_____ Agreement on excusing juror after deliberations begin

_____ Agreement to accept nonjury decision if jury not unanimous

_____ Number of jurors to be called/impaneled

_____ Submission of suggested voir dire questions:

_____ Written questionnaires

_____ Before jury reports

_____ After jurors given initial instructions

_____ Special procedures to handle problems of publicity

_____ Review of practices used in court for exercising challenges

_____ 3. Witness and Exhibit Lists

_____ Deadline for submitting:

_____ Sequentially

_____ Concurrently by all parties

_____ Contents

_____ All potential witnesses and exhibits

_____ Exception for impeachment evidence

_____ Indicate whether probable or improbable

_____ Key witnesses and exhibits

_____ Expected length of direct examination of witnesses

_____ Nature of expected testimony

_____ Depositions:

_____ Indicate which witnesses to be presented by deposition

_____ Designation of portions to be offered

_____ Preparation of agreed summaries of depositions

_____ Identify evidence to be offered against fewer than all parties

_____ Provide copies of exhibits not previously produced

_____ Responses

_____ Cross-examination

_____ Expected length

_____ Additional substantive topics

_____ Designation of additional portions of depositions

_____ Objections to evidence:

_____ Certain objections waived if not raised (for example, authenticity, best evidence, requirement for foundation)

_____ All objections waived if not raised

_____ Effect

_____ Precluding evidence not listed:

_____ Except solely for impeachment purposes

_____ Authenticating/laying foundation for exhibits

_____ Precluding all or certain objections not raised

____ 4. Limits on Evidence; Facilitating Presentation of Evidence
    ____ Precluding proof of facts not disclosed on statement of contentions or statement of contested facts
    ____ Precluding witnesses/exhibits not listed
    ____ Precluding expert testimony unless report filed
    ____ Limits on quantity of evidence
    ____ Preliminary steps:
        ____ Review lists of witnesses/exhibits in light of disputed facts
        ____ Consider views of counsel
        ____ Limit number of expert witnesses
        ____ Limit number of lay witnesses/exhibits on particular subjects
        ____ Limit time for presentation by parties
        ____ Limit time for direct examination of own witnesses and for cross-examination of other witnesses
        ____ Limit gross time for each party's case-in-chief
        ____ Depositions
        ____ Summaries
        ____ Selected extracts, purged of unnecessary materials
        ____ Adoption of prepared reports as direct testimony, subject to cross-examination
        ____ Permitting all/specified witnesses to remain in courtroom by not invoking Federal Rule of Evidence 615
        ____ Limiting cross-examination on additional subjects under Federal Rule of Evidence 611(b)
        ____ Pretrial ruling on objections
        ____ Use of summaries or samples in lieu of voluminous source documents

____ 5. Briefs
    ____ Timetable:
        ____ Sequential
        ____ Concurrent
    ____ Supplemental briefs as trial progresses
    ____ Contents:
        ____ Specific issues or all probable issues
        ____ Jury voir dire
        ____ Suggested questions for oral examinations
        ____ Suggested written questionnaire
        ____ Suggested instructions
        ____ Initial instructions
        ____ Limiting instructions on particular evidence
        ____ Final instructions

_____ Glossary/index of key terms, events, persons
_____ Suggested special verdict/interrogatories
_____ Proposed findings/conclusions in nonjury cases

_____ 6. Administrative Details
_____ Arrangements for facilities/equipment
_____ Representatives from parties
_____ Courtroom arrangement, tables, name plates
_____ Witness/exhibit/conference rooms
_____ Copying/computer equipment
_____ Exhibits:
_____ Premarked and listed on clerk's exhibit sheets
_____ Absent objection, deemed as offered and received when identified
_____ Notify counsel before using (to avoid interruptions while they review/locate copies)
_____ Glossaries, indexes, demonstrative aids
_____ Provide copies for court/jurors
_____ Exhibit books
_____ Enlargement/slides
_____ Representatives assist clerk in maintaining/indexing list of exhibits received
_____ Schedule of evidence:
_____ Advance notification of expected order of presenting witnesses and documents
_____ Notification of changes in schedule as soon as known
_____ Notification of changes in deposition designations
_____ Notification if portion of document to be offered
_____ Guidelines/discussion of courtroom protocol/decorum:
_____ Examination of witnesses
_____ Manner of making objections
_____ Submission of exhibits to witnesses
_____ Publication of exhibits to jurors
_____ Side-bar/chambers conferences
_____ How/when offer of proof made
_____ Witness demonstrations
_____ Approaching witnesses
_____ Use of podium
_____ Transcript of proceedings:
_____ Expedited/daily/hourly transcript
_____ Representatives review daily
_____ Suggested corrections submitted promptly to court
_____ Whether to permit independent tape recording of proceedings

_____ Interpreters, translation of documents
_____ Special arrangements if jury to be sequestered:
    _____ Hotel/meals
    _____ Transportation
    _____ Family visitation
    _____ Recreation
    _____ Security
_____ Schedule for interim conferences during trial:
    _____ Jurors
    _____ Note-taking
    _____ Exhibit books
    _____ Questions by jurors[3]

[5]   Motion to Amend Witness List

FORM 15–4   Sample Motion to Amend Witness List

DEFENDANTS' MOTION TO AMEND WITNESS LIST

Defendants, [A.I.C. SECURITY INVESTIGATIONS, LTD.], [A.I.C. INTER-NATIONAL, LTD.], and [unnamed defendant C], by and through their attorneys, [WESSELS & PAUTSCH, P.C.], by [Charles W. Pautsch], [attorney A], and [attorney B], hereby set forth their Motion to Amend Witness List as follows:

1. On [Monday], [February 22, 1993], Defendants and Plaintiffs in the above-referenced case filed a joint Pretrial Order.
2. Within the Pretrial Order referenced above was included Defendants' List of Witnesses.
3. Due to an oversight by Defendants' counsel, [A], M.D. was left off the Defendants' Witness List.
4. Defendants now wish to add [Dr. A] to Defendants' Witness List.
5. Plaintiffs will not be prejudiced in any manner by the adding of [Dr. A] to Defendants' Witness List since [Dr. A] was a treating physician of Plaintiff [Wessel] and was previously deposed in this matter.

WHEREFORE, Defendants respectfully request this Court to grant Defendants' Motion to Amend Witness List to add the name of [A], M.D.

Dated this [26th] day of [February] [1993].

---

[3] This checklist was adapted from Manual for Complex Litigation (Second) § 40.3 (1985).

[6]   Support for Calling Witness Named in Pretrial Order

FORM 15–5   Sample Support for Calling Witness Named in Pretrial Order

IN THE UNITED STATES DISTRICT COURT FOR THE [NORTHERN] DISTRICT OF [ILLINOIS] [EASTERN] DIVISION

U.S. EQUAL EMPLOYMENT OPPORTUNITY COMMISSION,

Plaintiff

v.   Civil Action No. [92 C 7330]

[A.I.C. SECURITY INVESTIGATIONS, LTD.];
[A.I.C. INTERNATIONAL, LTD.];
and [unnamed defendant C],

Honorable [Marvin E. Aspen]

Defendants.

Magistrate Judge [Ronald A. Guzman]

DEFENDANTS' RESPONSE TO PLAINTIFFS' OBJECTION TO

DEFENDANTS' CALLING [JODIE C.] AS A WITNESS AT TRIAL

Defendants, [A.I.C. SECURITY INVESTIGATIONS, LTD.], [A.I.C. INTERNATIONAL, LTD.], and [unnamed defendant C], by and through their attorneys, [WESSELS & PAUTSCH, P.C.], by [Charles W. Pautsch], [attorney A], and [attorney B], hereby submit to this Honorable Court Defendants' Response to Plaintiffs' Objection to Defendants' calling [Jodie C.] as a Witness at Trial and state in support hereof as follows:

1. On [February 22, 1993], the parties submitted to the Court a Final Pretrial Order signed by all parties.
2. Schedule D-2 to the Final Pretrial Order is Defendants' List of Witnesses with Plaintiffs' objections noted.
3. Within Schedule D-2, Defendants list as a witness [Jodie C.], and Plaintiffs object because she was not identified in answer to Plaintiff EEOC's First Set of Interrogatories No. 3.
4. Plaintiff EEOC's First Set of Interrogatories No. 3 states:
State every reason for the termination of [Charles H. Wessel ("Wessel")], and identify all documents that relate to or support reasons, and all persons having knowledge of any such reason.
5. Defendants answered Plaintiff EEOC's Interrogatory No. 3 as follows:

ANSWER: [Charles H. Wessel] was terminated because he could not perform, with or without reasonable accommodation, the essential functions of his job position. See also defenses enumerated in Defendants' Answers and Defenses previously filed with the Court. Persons having knowledge of the reasons for [Wessel]'s termination are [defendant C], [Beverly K.], [Lawrence R.], [Ken D.], [Ed B.], and [Jan D.]. Defendants have not identified any documents that relate to or support such reasons. Investigation continues.

6. Defendants in good faith answered Interrogatory No. 3, listing each and every individual who may have had involvement in the decision-making process and who may have had possible knowledge for the reasons for the decision that was made.

7. The language of Plaintiff EEOC's Interrogatory No. 3 seeks, in part, those individuals with knowledge of the actual reasons for [Wessel]'s "termination." This interrogatory does not ask for individuals with knowledge of any fact that supports a claim or defense to this action.

8. [Jodie C.] is an individual who worked in a separate division from [Wessel]. Her work station happened to be near the back entrance to the building. Thus, [witness] was able to observe Wessel entering and leaving the building on a daily basis. Also [witness] would see Wessel in the building at various times during the business day. [Witness] will testify to these facts.

9. [Jodie C.] in no way was part of any decision-making process regarding [Wessel] nor was she privy to any information whatsoever regarding the decision-making process and the reasons for [Wessel]'s separation from employment, Thus, [witness] had no knowledge whatsoever of the information sought by Plaintiff EEOC's Interrogatory No. 3. Her ignorance on the issues as to the reasons for [Wessel]'s "termination" was verified by the undersigned counsel for Defendants by a direct interview with her wherein she stated in essence that she did not have knowledge of the reasons why [Wessel] was not working at [A.I.C.] any longer. Defendants' counsel would be willing to set forth an affidavit to this effect if so requested by the Court.

10. Plaintiffs cannot claim that they are surprised or suffer unfair prejudice due to Defendants' calling [Jodie C.] at trial. At [Charles Wessel]'s first deposition on [November 5, 1992], the same day this action was filed, [Wessel] testified in substance that he would pass [Jodie C.] when entering and leaving the building at [A.I.C.]. (*See* Transcript of [Wessel] Deposition of [November 5, 1992], at 125, line 9.) Defendants will call [Jodie C.] at trial to testify to those very same observations. Thus, for Plaintiffs to claim unfair surprise or prejudice to a witness they knew about before the filing of this suit is baseless and should be overruled by this Court.

11. Defendants would be willing to submit [Jodie C.] to deposition before trial.

Wherefore, Defendants respectfully request the Court to overrule Plaintiffs' objection to [Jodie C.]'s being called as a witness at trial.

Dated this [5th] day of [February] [1993].

§ 15.02   MOTIONS IN LIMINE

[A]   Generally

Technically, motions in limine[4] must include not only a request that the court make a determination as to the admissibility or nonadmissibility of certain evidence but also a request that the court make a determination as to the permissibility of asking for it at trial.[5] Unless the second finding is necessary to avoid prejudice from the mere asking of a question, there is no principled reason for deciding the evidentiary question in advance, as opposed to deciding it at trial, when the question is asked. Nevertheless, the increasing emphasis on efficient litigation management and the growing importance of the pretrial process may make it appropriate to have motions in limine as a part of the pretrial order drafting step even when the asking of questions or the offering of nontestimonial evidence would not be particularly prejudicial. The authority for motions in limine is generally thought to reside in the inherent power of a trial judge to supervise the trial,[6] in Federal Rule of Civil Procedure 16(c)(3), allowing advance rulings on admissibility, or in Federal Rule of Evidence 103(d), which requires that proceedings be conducted so as to prevent inadmissible evidence from being suggested to the jury by any means.[7]

[B]   Sample Forms

[1]   Motion in Limine to Exclude Videotape

FORM 15–6   Sample Motion in Limine to Exclude Videotape

MOTION TO EXCLUDE VIDEOTAPE

Plaintiffs filed a motion on [October 24, 1985], to admit a job qualification videotape into evidence. The videotape is intended to show how Plaintiff [name] can perform the essential duties of various office jobs despite significant physical disabilities. Defendant objects to Plaintiff's motion on the grounds that the videotape is hearsay and will provide only cumulative evidence.

---

[4] *See* Forms 15–6 to 15–12.

[5] The term *motion in limine* conventionally refers to a motion to exclude evidence. However, for ease of exposition, Chapter 15 uses the term expansively to refer also to pretrial motions seeking determinations that evidence is admissible.

[6] *See* Sperburg v. Goodyear Tire & Rubber Co., 519 F.2d 708 (6th Cir. 1975) (evaluating pretrial order in context of overall management of trial).

[7] Oswald v. Laroche Chems., Inc., 894 F. Supp. 998 (E.D. La. 1995) (granting motion in limine in ADA case to exclude evidence of pre-effective-date conduct).

Defendant has several specific objections to the contents of the tape regarding its representational character and potential for undue prejudice. Several aspects of the film indicate that the activities depicted are not typical of those found in Defendant's workplace and are unduly prejudicial toward the Defendant. The filming of Plaintiff unduly emphasizes telephone conversations with customers and fellow employees, even though these constitute a relatively small part of all the clerical jobs in Defendant's workplace. Conversation in the unedited version of the film suggests that the photocopying may be done in a way that is totally unlike the requirements of the physical layout of Defendant's offices. The edited version of the film minimizes the difficulties Plaintiff would encounter in delivering mail and does not fairly convey the totality of Plaintiff's actual experience. The manner in which Plaintiff is depicted using a personal computer is simply not believable.

The question of permitting the showing of a motion picture film or videotape at trial is one for the sound discretion of the Court. [*Szeliga v. General Motors Corp.,* 728 F.2d 566, 567 (1st Cir. 1984)]. The propriety of allowing videotapes of this type into evidence is questionable for several reasons. Almost always, an edited tape necessarily raises issues as to every sequence portrayed of whether the event shown is fairly representational of fact after the editing process, and whether it is unduly prejudicial because of the manner of presentation. Further, the fact that a plaintiff is aware of being videotaped for such a purpose is likely to cause self-serving behavior, consciously or otherwise. *See* [*Haley v. Byers Transportation Co.,* 414 S.W.2d 777, 780 (Mo. 1967)]. Next, use of a videotape for such purposes is troublesome because it dominates evidence more conventionally adduced simply because of the nature of its presentation. "[T]he very obvious impact of these films would have been to create a sympathy for the plaintiff out of proportion to the real relevancy of the evidence." [*Id.*] Finally, such a videotape may serve to distract the jury from other cogent issues that properly must be considered to produce a fair verdict conscientiously derived from an impartial consideration of the evidence with strict attention to applicable principles of law.

Fed. R. Evid. 1001(2) defines *photographs* as inclusive of videotapes and motion pictures, and therefore properly authenticated tapes do not appear to be inadmissible on grounds of hearsay. *See also* [*Grimes v. Employers Mutual Liability Insurance Co.,* 73 F.R.D. 607, 610–11 (D. Alaska 1977)]. However, policy issues akin to hearsay are also raised even if the tapes are not hearsay. Even in instances where the videotaping is attended by opposing counsel, the conduct filmed is not subject to cross-examination at the time it is made and, therefore, lacks some of the safeguards of the adversary system.

For all of the above reasons, videotapes should be admitted as demonstrative evidence only when the tapes convey the observations of a witness to the jury more fully or accurately than, for some specific, articulable reason, the witness can convey them through the medium of conventional, in-court examination. These requirements are not met here. [*Szeliga v. General Motors Corp.,* 728 F.2d 566, at 567]. [Plaintiff] can testify on her own behalf. [Plaintiff] can demonstrate to the jury in open court activities similar to those depicted in the videotape. Further, relatives and physicians of Plaintiff may offer similar testimony. Vocational rehabilitation specialists can testify as to the capabilities of Plaintiff and the correspondence between those capabilities and the job functions actually required in Defendant's workplace. Thus, the videotape will be merely cumulative of testimonial evidence that is available to Plaintiff. *See* [*Helm v. Wismar,* 820 S.W.2d 495, 496 (Mo. 1991) (affirming exclusion of "day in the life" videotape because plaintiff was in court for jury's observation; emphasizing trial judge's discretion)]; [*Bolstridge v. Central Main Power Co.,* 621 F. Supp. 1202, 1203 (D. Me. 1985) (order denying use at trial of "day in the life" videotape because no showing that traditional testimony by plaintiff could not adduce same facts and risk of prejudice because of claims that portrayal was not accurate portrayal of regular activities)]; [*Johnson v. William C. Ellis & Sons Iron Works,* 604 F.2d 950 (5th Cir.), *modified on other grounds,* 609 F.2d 820 (5th Cir. 1979)]; [*Finn v. Wood,* 178 F.2d 583 (2d Cir. 1950)]; [*DeCamp v. United States,* 10 F.2d 984 (D.C. Cir. 1926)]. Also, admission of the tape into evidence will create the risk of distracting the jury and unfairly prejudicing Defendant, principally, though not exclusively, because the benefit of effective cross-examination is lost. *See* [*Haley v. Byers Transportation Co.,* 414 S.W.2d 777 (Mo. 1967)]. Therefore, it should be excluded under Fed. R. Evid. 403. [*Johnson,* 604 F.2d at 958]. *See also* [*Foster v. Crawford Shipping Co.,* 496 F.2d 788 (3d Cir. 1974)]; [*Finn,* 178 F.2d at 584]; [*DeCamp,* 10 F.2d at 985]; [5 J. Weinstein, M. Berger, Weinstein's Evidence 1001–36 (1983) ("where the motion picture is not necessary to prove or disprove a material proposition, it should not be allowed into evidence")].

This policy is consistent with that set in Fed. R. Civ. P. 32(a)(3), which provides for the admission of videotape depositions only in instances where the witness is unavailable or "such exceptional circumstances exist as to make it desirable, in the interest of justice and with due regard to the importance of presenting the testimony of witnesses orally in open court."[8]

[2] Objection to Use of Videotape Deposition

[a] Generally

Recent case law provides a wide spectrum of opinions in regard to videotape depositions. For example, in *General Motors Corp. v. Mosely,*[9] the court found it was error to admit a videotape deposition from another case and that, with the videotape deposition, there was no incentive to cross-examine the witness on the point for which the videotape deposition was admitted. However, that opinion can be compared with *Verdict v. State.*[10] In *Verdict,* the videotape deposition of the medical expert was validly admitted at a murder trial because the expert was unavailable. The court affirmed conviction. In *Miller v. Solaglas California, Inc.,*[11] the defendants unsuc-

---

[8] The language of this motion is adapted from the opinion in Bolstridge v. Central Maine Power Co., 621 F. Supp. 1202 (D. Me. 1985) (excluding day-in-the-life videotape in personal injury case).

[9] 447 S.E.2d 302, 308 (Ga. Ct. App. 1994).

[10] 868 S.W.2d 443 (Ark. 1993).

[11] 870 P.2d 559 (Colo. Ct. App. 1993).

cessfully argued on appeal that the trial court had erred in refusing to grant a new trial based upon the admission of a videotape deposition in lieu of live testimony, the rejection of certain objections to the showing of the videotape, and the trial judge's leaving the bench in the courthouse during the jury's viewing of the videotape deposition. The use of the deposition was authorized by the Colorado rules, and, more important, the plaintiff had listed his intention to use the videotape deposition in lieu of live testimony in his "trial data certificate," and the defendant had failed to timely object.[12] On the other point, the defendants had stipulated that the trial judge's presence during the playing of the videotape was unnecessary.[13]

In *Web v. Thomas,*[14] the court found that no prejudice was shown from a refusal to admit the transcript of the videotape deposition in addition to the videotape deposition itself. In *State v. Vaughn,*[15] the court affirmed conviction. The videotape testimony of a witness who was on vacation at the time of trial was validly admitted because the witness was under oath and was cross-examined during videotaping. However, in *Carter v. Sowders,*[16] the court overturned a conviction. The only evidence was a video deposition that was improperly admitted because of the refusal of defendant's counsel to participate in the videotaping, and because the use of the videotape deposition violated the confrontation clause. The court, in *Miller v. National Railroad Passenger Corp.,*[17] denied the costs of the videotape deposition because it saved no time and was otherwise unnecessary, and because the medical expert witness was available to testify in person. The *Miller* court disagreed with the court's opinion in *Commercial Credit Equipment Corp. v. Stamps.*[18] The court in *Kirby v. Ahmad*[19] found that the expert witness fee of $750 per hour for a videotape deposition was unreasonable, and the fee request was reduced to $250 per hour for all depositions.

---

[12] *Id.* at 569–70.

[13] *Id.* at 570.

[14] 873 S.W.2d 875, 878 (Ark. 1992).

[15] 768 P.2d 1051, 1056 (Ariz. Ct. App. 1989).

[16] 5 F.3d 975, 979 (6th Cir. 1993).

[17] 157 F.R.D. 145, 146 (D. Mass. 1994).

[18] 920 F.2d 1361, 1368 (7th Cir. 1990).

[19] 635 N.E.2d 98 (Ohio C.P. 1994).

[b]   Sample Form

FORM 15–7   Sample Objection to Use of Videotape Deposition

IN THE UNITED STATES DISTRICT COURT FOR THE [NORTHERN] DISTRICT OF [ILLINOIS]

[EASTERN] DIVISION

U.S. EQUAL EMPLOYMENT OPPORTUNITY COMMISSION,

Plaintiff

v.   Civil Action No. [92 C 7330]

[A.I.C. SECURITY INVESTIGATIONS, LTD.];
[A.I.C. INTERNATIONAL, LTD.];
and [unnamed defendant C],

                                              Honorable [Marvin E. Aspen]

Defendants.

                                    Magistrate Judge [Ronald A. Guzman]

DEFENDANTS' OBJECTIONS TO PLAINTIFFS' DEPOSITION

DESIGNATION OF [CHARLES H. WESSEL]

The Defendants, [A.I.C. SECURITY INVESTIGATIONS, LTD.], [A.I.C. INTERNATIONAL, LTD.], and [defendant C], by and through their attorneys, [WESSELS & PAUTSCH, P.C.], by [Charles W. Pautsch], [attorney A], and [attorney B], hereby object to Plaintiffs' deposition designation of [Charles H. Wessel] based upon the following:

1. Defendants maintain their objection to showing the videotape deposition of [Charles Wessel ("Wessel")] at trial. No portion of this videotape should be used at trial if [Wessel] is available to testify. The use of this videotape at trial will cause undue delay, will cause waste of time, and will present unnecessary cumulative evidence. Fed. R. Evid. 403.

2. In the event the Court does allow the videotape deposition of [Wessel] to be played at trial, the following portions should be omitted from evidence as inadmissible hearsay:

(a) page 17, lines 2–13;
(b) page 62, line 12–23; and
(c) page 127, lines 8–18.

3. In the event the Court does allow the videotape deposition of [Wessel] to be played at trial, the following portions should be added to Plaintiffs' deposition designation in the interest of fairness:

(a) page 30, line 13, to page 31, line 17;
(b) page 74, lines 21–22;
(c) page 73, line 8, to page 74, line 20; and
(d) page 114, lines 30–20.

Respectfully submitted,

[A.I.C. SECURITY INVESTIGATIONS, LTD.];
[A.I.C. INTERNATIONAL, LTD.];
and [unnamed defendant C]

[3] Motion in Limine to Exclude Evidence

FORM 15–8   Sample Motion in Limine to Exclude Evidence

IN THE UNITED STATES DISTRICT COURT FOR THE [NORTHERN]
DISTRICT OF [ILLINOIS]
[EASTERN] DIVISION

U.S. EQUAL EMPLOYMENT OPPORTUNITY COMMISSION,

Plaintiff
v.   Civil Action No. [92 C 7330]
[A.I.C. SECURITY INVESTIGATIONS, LTD.];
[A.I.C. INTERNATIONAL, LTD.];
and [unnamed defendant C],

Honorable [Marvin E. Aspen]

Defendants.

Magistrate Judge [Ronald A. Guzman]

DEFENDANTS' EMERGENCY MOTION IN LIMINE

TO EXCLUDE FROM EVIDENCE PLAINTIFFS' EXHIBIT NO. 26 —
"DISABILITY EVALUATION UNDER SOCIAL SECURITY"

The Defendants, [A.I.C. SECURITY INVESTIGATIONS, LTD.], [A.I.C. IN-
TERNATIONAL, LTD.], and [defendant C], by and through their attorneys, [WES-
SELS & PAUTSCH, P.C.], by [Charles W. Pautsch], [attorney A], and [attorney
B], hereby move to exclude from evidence Plaintiffs' Exhibit No. 26 — "Disability
Evaluation under Social Security" — based upon the following:

1. On [February 22, 1993], the parties in the above-captioned action submitted
a Final Pretrial Order to the Court.

2. Attached as Schedule C-1 to the Final Pretrial Order is Plaintiffs' List of Exhibits.

3. Exhibit No. 26 of Plaintiffs' List of Exhibits is "Disability Evaluation under Social Security — May, 1992."

4. Defendants were served with Plaintiffs' Exhibit No. 26 on or about [March 1, 1993].

5. After having a chance to review Plaintiffs' Exhibit No. 26, Defendants have taken the position that said exhibit should be excluded from evidence at trial for the reasons listed below.

6. Plaintiffs' Exhibit No. 26 is an incomplete document. Specifically, Plaintiffs have intentionally excluded pages 12, 14, 16–74, and 82–118 from the document labeled "Disability Evaluation under Social Security" (Plaintiffs' Exhibit No. 26).

7. Plaintiffs' Exhibit No. 26 cannot be relied upon in evidence as a trustworthy document since major omissions have been made to the document by Plaintiff EEOC's Counsel.

8. Plaintiffs' Exhibit No. 26 is an out-of-court statement that Defendants believe Plaintiffs will introduce for the truth of the matters asserted in the document; and, therefore, said exhibit is inadmissible hearsay.

WHEREFORE, Defendants respectfully request this Court to exclude from evidence Plaintiffs' Exhibit No. 26 — "Disability Evaluation Under Social Security."

Dated this [4th] day of [March] [1993].

[A.I.C. SECURITY INVESTIGATIONS, LTD.];
[A.I.C. INTERNATIONAL, LTD.];
and [defendant C]

By: [attorney A]

[4] Response to Motion in Limine

FORM 15–9   Sample Response to Motion in Limine

IN THE UNITED STATES DISTRICT COURT FOR THE [NORTHERN]
DISTRICT OF [ILLINOIS]
[EASTERN] DIVISION

U.S. EQUAL EMPLOYMENT OPPORTUNITY COMMISSION,

Plaintiff
v.   Civil Action No. [92 C 7330]
[A.I.C. SECURITY INVESTIGATIONS, LTD.];
[A.I.C. INTERNATIONAL, LTD.];
and [unnamed defendant C],

Honorable [Marvin E. Aspen]

Defendants.

Magistrate Judge [Ronald A. Guzman]

DEFENDANTS' RESPONSE TO PLAINTIFFS' MOTION IN LIMINE

TO EXCLUDE EVIDENCE OF UNEMPLOYMENT COMPENSATION
AND DISABILITY BENEFITS

INTRODUCTION

[A.I.C. Security Investigations, et al. ("A.I.C.")] hereby opposes the Plaintiff's Motion for the Exclusion of Evidence relating to unemployment compensation, Social Security disability payments, and private disability payments paid to [Mr. Wessel]. Unemployment compensation is a not a collateral benefit and is subject to deduction from any damages award. Furthermore, disability payments, including private disability funded by the employer, do not derive from an independent collateral source and should also be deducted from any damages award.

Evidence of unemployment compensation and disability payments will not be presented by the Defendant solely on the issue of damages. Evidence with regard to these payments is relevant to both the damages award and other matters in the trial. Furthermore, certain discussions relating to the potential for disability payments are relevant as to the motivation of both the Employer and the Plaintiff at the cessation of [Wessel]'s employment.

Under the Americans with Disabilities Act, a Plaintiff may be entitled to receive compensatory damages, including damages for "future pecuniary losses, emotional pain, suffering, inconvenience, mental anguish, loss of enjoyment of life and other nonpecuniary losses." 42 U.S.C. § 1981a(b)(3). The Plaintiff in this case has argued that he should receive compensatory damages, and has further indicated that he will argue that his emotional distress was compounded by financial problems. Undoubtedly, his receipt of other income is relevant to these claims.

1. UNEMPLOYMENT COMPENSATION SHOULD BE DEDUCTED FROM ANY DAMAGES AWARD

Backpay awards are within the court's discretion. [*Olshock v. Village of Skokie*, 541 F.2d 1254 (7th Cir. 1976)]. Unemployment compensation should be deducted from any backpay damages due from the employer, as the amount of the benefits paid should be credited to the party who financed them. [*Nottelson v. Smith Steelworkers D.A.L.U.*, 643 F.2d 445 (7th Cir. 1981)]. In the [*Nottelson*] case, the [Seventh] Circuit held, in a Title VII case, that the Plaintiff's backpay award should reflect a credit for the employer for any unemployment benefits paid to the Plaintiff. [*Id.* at 456.] For purposes of a backpay order under Title VII, the sum of the backpay shall be reduced by the amount of any welfare or unemployment compensation received. [*Association Against Discrimination in Employment, Inc. v. Weeks*, 454 F. Supp. 758 (D. Conn. 1978)].

In [*Diaz v. Pan American World Airways*, 346 F. Supp. 1301 (S.D. Fla. 1972)], the court held that the backpay awarded in a Title VII case should be reduced by the amount of unemployment insurance received by the Plaintiff during the relevant backpay period. [*Id.* at 1309].

Defendant also intends to introduce into evidence information on unemployment compensation as relevant to other issues in addition to the award of backpay. Therefore, based on case precedent that backpay should be reduced by unemployment benefits, and that the Defendant intends to utilize this evidence as to other issues, such evidence is relevant and should not be excluded from presentation at trial.

II. DISABILITY PAYMENTS DO NOT CONSTITUTE A COLLATERAL SOURCE

Under the collateral source rule, courts are prohibited from considering payments received from third parties in determining the extent of Plaintiff's damages; however, when those payments are received from Defendant, the collateral source rule does not apply. [*Barkanic v. General Administration of Civil Aviation*, 923 F.2d 957, 964 n.8 (2d Cir. 1991)]. The Plaintiff's reliance on [*Whatley v. Skaggs Co.*, 707 F.2d 1129 (10th Cir. 1983)], is misplaced.

In [*Whatley*], the court refused to deduct payments that Plaintiff received for an on-the-job injury from the total backpay award. This case fails to state what the source of these payments were. However, due to the language in the case, and the fact that it was an on-the-job injury that resulted in the disability payments, one can assume that the payments were made from workers' compensation insurance. However, deductions made under workers' compensation are excluded based on the collateral source rule because they are obligatory benefits paid by the employer. [*Stifle v. Marathon Petroleum Co.*, 876 F.2d 552 (7th Cir. 1989)]. This situation is different as there is no claim for workers' compensation and the disability compensation was not obligatory on the part of the employer.

Plaintiff's reliance on [*Spulak v. K-Mart Corp.*, 894 F.2d 1150 (10th Cir. 1990)], is also misplaced. In [*Spulak*] the court simply held that an award of Social Security disability benefits to the employee did not extinguish his right to receive damages for wrongful discharge. It is important to note that the Social Security disability benefits were based on emphysema and back problems, both conditions not related to the termination of his employment. Thus, the [*Spulak*] case does not stand for the proposition alleged by Plaintiff and is cited in error.

It is also important to point out that in Plaintiff's cited case of [*Johnson v. Harris County Flood Control District*, 869 F.2d 1565 (5th Cir. 1989)], the court states that it is within the trial court's discretion to decide what deductions are to be made from the backpay award. Thus, due to the fact that any deductions from a backpay award are within the trial court's discretion, it is appropriate to state as a matter of law that these types of deductions are improper and should be excluded as irrelevant evidence.

Plaintiff also argues in error that "[t]he Plaintiff should not be penalized for having had the foresight to obtain insurance." This argument is misplaced as Plaintiff did not pay the premium for the disability insurance — the Employer did. As a result, the funds do not derive from a collateral source and should be deducted from any backpay award.

Where benefits are paid to Plaintiff from Defendant, the collateral source rule does not apply. [*Barkanic v. General Administration of Civil Aviation,* 923 F.2d 957 (2d Cir. 1991)]. "The collateral source rule prohibits courts from considering benefits received from third parties in determining the extent of Plaintiff's recovery." [*Id.* at 964 n.8]. Therefore, due to the fact that the disability insurance was provided by Defendant, the collateral source rule does not apply. Thus, Defendant is entitled to an offset in an amount of disability payments made to Plaintiff.

CONCLUSION

Evidence relating to unemployment or disability payments should not be excluded from consideration for two reasons. First, such payments are not from a collateral source and thus should be deducted from a collateral source and any backpay award. Second, such evidence is relevant to other issues to be presented at trial, specifically, Plaintiff's claim for compensatory damages and the motivation of Defendant and Plaintiff in the events leading up to the cessation of [Wessel]'s employment. Thus, the jury should not be prohibited from being advised of the fact that unemployment and disability payments were made to Plaintiff. The refusal to exclude such evidence would not be prejudicial to Plaintiff. Accordingly, Defendants respectfully request that the motion to exclude evidence of unemployment compensation, Social Security, or private disability payments made to Plaintiff, be denied.

[WESSELS & PAUTSCH, P.C.]
By: [attorney A]

[attorney B]
Attorneys for Defendant

[5]   Defendant's Response to Plaintiff's Motion in Limine

FORM 15–10   Sample Defendant's Response to Plaintiff's Motion in Limine

IN THE UNITED STATES DISTRICT COURT FOR THE [NORTHERN] DISTRICT OF [ILLINOIS] [EASTERN] DIVISION

U.S. EQUAL EMPLOYMENT OPPORTUNITY COMMISSION,

Plaintiff,
v.   Civil Action No. [92 C 7330]
[A.I.C. SECURITY INVESTIGATIONS, LTD.];
[A.I.C. INTERNATIONAL, LTD.];
and [unnamed defendant C],

Judge [Marvin E. Aspen]

Defendants.

Magistrate Judge [Guzman]

DEFENDANTS' RESPONSE TO PLAINTIFFS' MOTION IN LIMINE

Defendants, [A.I.C. SECURITY INVESTIGATIONS, LTD.], [A.I.C. INTER-NATIONAL, LTD.], and [defendant C], by and through their attorneys, [WESSELS & PAUTSCH, P.C.], by [Charles W. Pautsch], [attorney A], and [attorney B], hereby submit to this Honorable Court Defendants' Response to Plaintiffs' Motion in Limine and state in support hereof as follows:

1. On [February 22, 1993], the parties to this action filed a Pretrial Order within the Court.
2. Attached as Schedule N to the Pretrial Order is Plaintiffs' Motion in Limine, which seeks to exclude from evidence the reasons for [David P.]'s termination.
3. [David P.] will be called as a witness in Plaintiffs' case-in-chief. (Plaintiff EEOC's First Set of Interrogatories No. 14.)
4. In an early set of interrogatories sent from the EEOC to Defendants (Plaintiff EEOC's First Set of Interrogatories No. 14), the reasons for [David P.]'s termination were requested. These interrogatories were served and answered prior to [David P.]'s and [defendant C]'s depositions.
5. Defendants objected to Plaintiff EEOC's Interrogatory No. 14 because it did not at that time appear to be relevant to this action.
6. The reasons for [David P.]'s termination may be used on cross-examination by Defendants' counsel to impeach [David P.]'s credibility.
7. Plaintiffs can claim no surprise or unfair prejudice regarding the information about [David P.]'s termination.
8. Specifically, [David P.] has been a cooperative witness for the EEOC and filled out and executed an affidavit to support the charges of [Charles Wessel]. Thus, the EEOC could ask [David P.] himself the reasons for his termination.
9. In addition, counsel for Plaintiff EEOC extensively and exhaustively questioned [defendant C], the person who solely decided to terminate [David P.], regarding the reasons for his termination. (*See* Transcript of [defendant C] Deposition at 46–55 attached hereto and incorporated herein).

Wherefore, Defendants respectfully request the Court to deny Plaintiff's Motion In Limine to exclude evidence regarding [David P.]'s termination and rule that such evidence may be used at trial.

Dated this [5th] day of [February] [1993].

[6] Motion in Limine to Exclude Plaintiff's Expert Witness

FORM 15–11 **Sample Motion in Limine to Exclude Plaintiff's Expert Witness**

DEFENDANTS' EMERGENCY MOTION IN LIMINE TO EXCLUDE [Dr. B] FROM TESTIFYING AT TRIAL

The Defendants, [A.I.C. SECURITY INVESTIGATIONS, LTD.], [A.I.C. IN-TERNATIONAL, LTD.], and [unnamed defendant C], by and through their attorneys, [WESSELS & PAUTSCH, P.C.], by [Charles W. Pautsch], [attorney A], and [attorney B], hereby move to exclude [Dr. B] from testifying at trial based upon the following:

1. On [February 22, 1993], the parties in the above-captioned action submitted a Final Pretrial Order to the Court.
2. Attached as Schedule D-1 to the Final Pretrial Order is Plaintiffs' List of Witnesses.
3. [Dr. B.], M.D., is listed as a "will call" witness in Plaintiffs' List of Witnesses.
4. [Dr. B.] was Plaintiff [Wessel]'s primary testing physician.
5. Plaintiffs will attempt at trial to qualify [Dr. B.] as an expert witness and to elicit opinions from [Dr. B.] to further their claims against Defendants.
6. For the reasons stated in Defendants' Memorandum and Reply Memorandum in Support of Their Motion for Summary Judgment, the Court should hold, as a matter of law, that [Dr. B.] is a completely incredible witness and should not be allowed to testify at trial as an expert witness or in any other capacity. (*See* Defendants' Memorandum in Support of Their Motion for Summary Judgment at 16–17 and Defendants' Reply Memorandum on Summary Judgment at 3–8.)

WHEREFORE, Defendants respectfully request this Court to preclude from trial the testimony of [Dr. B.], M.D.

Dated this [4th] day of [March] [1993].

[7] Motion in Limine to Preclude Testimony on Rebuttal

FORM 15–12 **Sample Motion in Limine to Preclude Testimony on Rebuttal**

DEFENDANTS' EMERGENCY MOTION IN LIMINE TO EXCLUDE

[Dr. C], M.D., FROM TESTIFYING AT TRIAL IN REBUTTAL OR OTHERWISE

The Defendants, [A.I.C. SECURITY INVESTIGATIONS, LTD.], [A.I.C. IN-TERNATIONAL, LTD.], and [unnamed defendant C], by and through their attorneys, [WESSELS & PAUTSCH, P.C.], by [Charles W. Pautsch], [attorney A], and [attorney B], hereby move to exclude from testifying at trial [Dr. C.], M.D., in rebuttal or otherwise, based upon the following:

1. On [February 22, 1993], the parties to the above-captioned action submitted a Final Pretrial Order to the Court.

2. Attached as Schedule D-1 to the Final Pretrial Order is Plaintiffs' List of Witnesses.

3. Included in Plaintiffs' List of Witnesses is [Dr. C.] as a rebuttal witness.

4. On or about [February 19, 1993], Defendants filed a Motion to Exclude [Dr. C.] as an expert witness at trial.

5. Thereafter in open court Plaintiff EEOC's counsel conveyed that [Dr. C.] will not be called in Plaintiffs' case-in-chief. The Court then ruled that [Dr. C.] would be excluded from testifying in Plaintiffs' case-in-chief, but the Court reserved ruling on the issue of whether [Dr. C.] could testify for Plaintiff in rebuttal.

6. For the reasons stated in Defendants' previous Motion to Exclude [Dr. C.] as an expert witness in Plaintiffs' case-in-chief, Defendants now object to his testimony at trial in rebuttal or otherwise.

WHEREFORE, Defendants respectfully request this Court to preclude from trial the testimony of [Dr. C.] in rebuttal or otherwise.

Dated this [4th] day of [March] [1993].

§ 15.03   PRETRIAL ORDERS

[A]   Generally

The materials in this chapter and in Chapter 16 are closely related because the pretrial order[20] resulting from a final pretrial conference governs the course of the trial. In addition, as the *A.I.C.* pretrial order[21] shows, a comprehensive pretrial order actually contains material, such as rulings on facts,[22] evidentiary issues, and jury instructions that will take effect as the trial proceeds.

---

[20] *See* Forms 15–15 to 15–17.
[21] *See* Form 15–18.
[22] *See* Forms 15–13 to 15–14.

[B] Sample Forms

[1] Order to Establish Uncontested and Contested Facts[23]

FORM 15–13   Sample Order to Establish Uncontested and Contested Facts

STATEMENT OF UNCONTESTED AND CONTESTED FACTS

It is ORDERED:

1. Development of Joint Statement of Uncontested and Contested Facts.

(a) Plaintiffs' Proposed Facts. By [_____] 19[__], Plaintiffs shall serve on opposing parties a narrative statement listing all facts proposed to be proved by them at trial in support of their claim(s) as to liability and damages (except on the issue(s) of [_____]).

(b) Defendants' Response and Proposed Facts. By [_____], 19[_____], Defendants shall serve on opposing parties a statement

(1) indicating the extent to which they contest and do not contest the Plaintiffs' proposed facts;

(2) listing all additional facts proposed to be proved by them at trial in opposition to, or in special defense of, the Plaintiffs' claim(s) as to liability and damages; and

(3) listing all facts proposed to be proved by them at trial in support of their counterclaim(s), cross-claims(s), and third-party claim(s).

(c) Replies.

(1) By [_____], 19[__], Plaintiffs shall serve on opposing parties a statement indicating the extent to which they contest and do not contest the Defendants' proposed facts (including defendants' modifications to the facts initially proposed by plaintiffs) and listing all additional facts proposed to be proved by them at trial in opposition to, or in special defense of, the defendants' counterclaims; and

(2) By [_____], 19[__], Defendants to cross-claims and third-party claims shall serve on opposing parties a statement indicating the extent to which they contest and do not contest the proposed facts of the cross-claimant or third-party claimant and listing all additional facts proposed to be proved by them at trial in opposition to, or in special defense of, such cross-claims or third-party claims.

(d) Final Response. By [_____], 19[__], defendants making counterclaims, cross-claims, or third-party claims shall serve on opposing parties a statement indicating the extent to which they contest and do not contest their adversary's proposed facts (including modifications to the facts initially proposed by them).

---

[23] These statements are sometimes also known as statements of contentions (and proof) or final pretrial statements (FPSs). Form 15–13 was adapted from a Sample Order to Establish Uncontested and Contested Facts, Manual for Complex Litigation (Second) § 41.6 (1985).

(e) Joint Statement of Uncontested and Contested Facts. By [_____], 19__],
the parties shall file with the court a joint statement listing the facts that are not
contested and those that are contested, indicating as to the latter the precise nature
of their disagreement. These facts, both uncontested and contested, will to the
extent practicable be organized and collected under headings descriptive of the
claim or defense to which they may be relevant (and, where appropriate, subdivide
into factual categories descriptive of particular parties and time periods).

2. Directions.

(a) Narration of Proposed Facts. In stating facts proposed to be proved, counsel shall do so in simple, declarative, self-contained, consecutively numbered sen-
tences, avoiding all "color words," labels, argumentative language, and legal conclusions. If a fact is to be offered against fewer than all parties, counsel shall
indicate the parties against which the fact will (or will not) be offered. (The facts
to be set forth include not only ultimate facts but also all subsidiary and supporting
facts except those offered solely for impeachment purposes.)

(b) Agreement and Disagreement. Counsel shall indicate that they do not
contest a proposed fact if at trial they will not controvert or dispute the fact. In
indicating disagreement with a proposed fact, counsel shall do so by deletion or
interlineation of particular words or phrases so that the nature of their disagreement
(and the extent of any agreement) will be clear.

(c) Objections. Objections to the admissibility of a proposed fact (either as
irrelevant or on other grounds) may not be used to avoid indicating whether or not
the party contests the truth of that fact. (Counsel shall, however, indicate any objections, both to the facts they contest and those they do not contest.)

3. Annotations. Facts, not evidence, are to be listed by the parties. However,
a party may identify in parentheses at the end of a proposed fact the witness(es),
deponent(s), document(s), or other evidence supporting the truth of the fact. No
party, however, will be required to admit or deny the accuracy of such references.

4. Effect.

(a) Elimination of Proof. The uncontested facts shall be taken at the trial as
established under Fed. R. Civ. P. 36 without the need for independent proof. To
the extent relevant to a resolution of the contested facts and otherwise admissible,
these facts may be read to the jury. Independent proof of the uncontested facts will
be allowed only if incidental to the presentation of evidence on the contested facts
or if such proof will better enable the jury to resolve the contested facts.

(b) Preclusion of Other Facts. Except for good cause shown, the parties shall
be precluded at trial from offering proof of any fact not disclosed in their listing
of proposed facts (except purely for impeachment purposes).

5. Sanctions. Unjustified refusal to admit a proposed fact or to limit the extent
of disagreement with a proposed fact shall be subject to sanctions under Fed. R.
Civ. P. 37(c). Excessive listing of proposed facts (or of the evidence to be submitted
in support of or denial of such facts) that imposes an onerous burden on opposing
parties shall be subject to sanctions under Rule 16(f).

Dated: [_____], 19[__]

United States District Judge

[2] Motion to Amend Statement of Facts

FORM 15–14   Sample Motion to Amend Statement of Facts

DEFENDANTS' EMERGENCY MOTION FOR LEAVE TO SUPPLEMENT THEIR STATEMENT OF UNCONTESTED MATERIAL FACTS

Defendants, [A.I.C. SECURITY INVESTIGATIONS, LTD.], [A.I.C. INTER-NATIONAL, LTD.], and [unnamed defendant C], by and through their attorneys, [WESSELS & PAUTSCH, P.C.], by [Charles W. Pautsch], [attorney A], and [attorney B], and pursuant to [Rule 12] of the Court's Local Rules, hereby move for leave to supplement their statement of uncontested facts as follows:

1. On or about [August 5, 1992], just one week after his last day of work at [A.I.C.], [Charles Wessel] applied for disability benefits through Social Security. (Attached hereto and incorporated herein as Exhibit B, following Defendants' previously submitted Exhibits 1–12.)
2. [Wessel]'s application was signed under penalty of perjury and criminal punishment. (*Id.*)
3. [Wessel]'s application was not received by Defendants until very recently after his deposition, despite Defendants' efforts to subpoena said documents in [December 1992], because the Social Security Administration refused to release them without [Wessel]'s authorization.
4. As the disability report states, paragraph 20, daily radiation that [Wessel] underwent between [April 7, 1992], and [July 14, 1993] "caused a reduction in work activity and slowed production time."

WHEREFORE, because the foregoing represents a sworn statement, because Defendants did not have access to the documents until recently in this expedited trial, and finally, because the foregoing evidence is extremely probative as to one of the key issues on summary judgment, Defendants seek leave to submit the attached Exhibit No. 13 as an uncontested fact.

Dated this [1st] day of [March] [1993].

[3] Pretrial Order Draft

FORM 15–15   Sample Pretrial Order Draft

FINAL PRETRIAL ORDER

This case came before the court at a pretrial conference held on [date], pursuant to Fed. R. Civ. P. 16, at which [name] appeared as counsel for the plaintiff and [name] appeared as counsel for the defendant. Accordingly, the following Order is hereby entered:

I. Pleadings and Discovery Material

Only the following pleadings, answers to interrogatories, and depositions listed below will be admitted into evidence. Any objections to such admission are hereby waived unless set forth below:

A. Pleadings

The complaint, except for Count 6.

B. All answers to interrogatories, except the answer to Interrogatory No. [____].

The videotape deposition of the Plaintiff demonstrating her capacity to engage in word processing and answer the phone.

II. Witnesses

A. Plaintiff's Witnesses

1. Plaintiff will call the following witnesses with respect to liability:
2. Plaintiff will call the following witnesses with respect to damages:

B. Defendant's Witnesses

1. Defendant will call the following witnesses with respect to liability:
2. Defendant will call the following witnesses with respect to damages:

C. Expert Witnesses

No expert may testify unless identified in this section. No experts may testify unless their qualifications are summarized in an attachment to this order. No objections to qualifications may be made unless they are summarized in this section. No expert witness may testify unless all opposing counsel had been informed in advance of testimony of the substance of the expert's anticipated testimony.

1. Plaintiff's expert witnesses and reference to summaries of substance of testimony:
2. Defendant's objections to the qualifications of any of plaintiff's experts:
3. Defendant's expert witnesses and reference to written summaries of the substance of their testimony:
4. Plaintiff's objections to defendant's experts:

III. Exhibits

Only the exhibits listed in this section may be introduced at trial. Any objection to these exhibits is waived unless summarized in this section. It shall not be necessary to produce the custodian of an exhibit unless that requirement is set forth below:

A. Plaintiff's Exhibits

1. Description and number of each exhibit:
2. Defendant's objections, by number and basis for objection:

B. Defendant's Exhibits:

1. Number and description of each exhibit defendant intends to introduce:
2. Plaintiff's objections, by number and basis for objection:

IV. Facts

A. Uncontested Facts [list each uncontested fact, along with a determination of whether it shall or shall not be read to jury at beginning of trial]

B. Plaintiff's Presentation on Contested Facts

1. Plaintiff will prove these contested facts with respect to liability:
2. Plaintiff will prove these contested facts with respect to damages:

C. Defendant's Proof of Contested Facts

1. Defendant will prove the following contested facts with respect to liability:
2. Defendant will prove these contested facts with respect to damages:

V. Legal Propositions

A. Uncontested Legal Propositions
B. Plaintiff's Position on Contested Legal Issues
C. Defendant's Position on Contested Legal Issues

VI. Other Trial Management Issues

A. Length of Trial (including allowance for various stages, such as plaintiff's case-in-chief and defendant's case-in-chief, opening and closing arguments, and jury instructions)
B. Draft Jury Instructions
C. Sequestration of Witnesses and of Jury

[4]   Final Pretrial Order

FORM 15–16   **Sample Final Pretrial Order**

FINAL PRETRIAL ORDER

It is ORDERED:

1. Rulings on outstanding motions. [Resolve all outstanding motions seeking summary judgment, challenging jurisdiction or venue, requesting transfer, seeking to limit the period of proof, regarding jury demands, and similar matters.]

2. Trial. Trial is [tentatively] scheduled to commence at [_____] A.M. 19[__], at the Federal Courthouse, [_____].

(a) Consolidation. Under Fed. R. Civ. P. 42(a), the following cases are consolidated for purposes of this trial:

(Define by inclusion or exclusion the cases consolidated for trial. To the extent appropriate, order transfer of cases under 28 U.S.C. § 1404 or 1406.)

(b) Severance. Under Fed. R. Civ. P. 42(b), the following issues are scheduled for trial at this time:

(Define the issues to be tried, indicating whether jury or nonjury.)

After this trial has been concluded, the court will establish a schedule for trial of the remaining issue(s) as may be necessary.

(c) Order of proof. (Identify special provisions as to the order in which the issues, evidence, or arguments will be presented.)

(Indicate any anticipated changes, such as federal holidays, days on which trial will not be held or on which the trial hours will be reduced, any religious holidays to be observed, and any planned recesses.)

(d) Jury. A jury of [__] persons and [__] alternates shall be selected. The parties shall by [_____], 19[__], file any special voir dire question they request the panel be asked; additional questions may be suggested after the initial examination of the panel. Each side shall be permitted [__] peremptory challenges to the principal jurors and [__] peremptory challenges to the alternate jurors. (By stipulation of the parties under Fed. R. Civ. P. 48, a verdict may be accepted if returned by a unanimous jury of at least [__] jurors.)

(e) Continuances; deadline for partial settlements. Postponement of trial will be granted only for compelling reasons. Illness or unavailability of counsel will not justify a continuance if other members of counsel's firms or attorneys representing parties with similar interests are available to proceed with the trial.

3. Witness lists. Plaintiffs shall file and serve by [_____], 19[__], and defendants shall file and serve by [_____], 19[__], a list identifying all persons (including expert and rebuttal witnesses) whose testimony they may offer at trial in person or by deposition. Counsel will separately list their "major" witnesses (whose testimony they expect to offer) and their "minor" witnesses (whose testimony will probably not be needed but who have been listed merely to preserve the right to offer such testimony should it be needed in the light of developments during trial).

(a) Witnesses to testify in person. For witnesses to be examined in person, the list will contain an estimate of the time expected to be needed for direct examination and include a brief summary of the witnesses' expected direct testimony/ indicate the subjects on which they are expected to testify. For any witness who is to express any opinion under Fed. R. Evid. 702, the list shall include, if not previously provided, the information prescribed under Fed. R. Civ. P. 26(b)(4)(A)(i).

(b) Depositions. Each party will attach to the list the pages of any deposition to be used at trial, with the portions to be offered by the proponent indicated by the blue marking in the margin.

(c) Response. Within [___] days after receiving these lists, each party shall, with respect to witnesses not previously listed by it but listed by another party, file and serve a notice

(1) indicating for each witness who is to testify in person the estimated time expected to be needed for cross-examination and [a brief summary of the expected cross-examination/any additional subjects on which the witness will likely be examined on cross-examination] (other than for impeachment); and

(2) attaching for each witness whose testimony will be presented by deposition the portions of the deposition, marked in yellow, that are objected to (specifying the grounds for the objections) and, marked in red, that in fairness should be considered with the portions already designated or that will be offered as cross-examination. Unless indicated to the contrary in the notice, the party shall be deemed to have agreed that the conditions of Fed. R. Civ. P. 32(a) are satisfied with respect to each person identified in another party's witness list as someone whose testimony will be presented by deposition.

(d) Effect. Except for good cause shown, the parties will be precluded from offering substantive evidence through any person not so listed. The listing of a witness does not commit the listing party to have such person available at trial or to offer the testimony of such person. Any party may offer the testimony of a witness listed by another party.

4. Exhibit lists. Plaintiffs shall file and serve by [_____], 19[__], and defendants shall file and serve by [_____], 19[__], a list identifying all writings, recordings, documents, bills, graphs, charts, models, summaries, compilations, reports, records, photographs, and other exhibits (collectively called "exhibits") they expect to offer at trial, to use as demonstrative exhibits, or to be used or referred to by any of their witnesses, including expert witnesses.

(a) Identification. The list shall describe each exhibit and give its identification number, if any. Although some exhibits may be adequately identified through a group description (for example, "invoices from C.D. Inc., to A.B., dated from [_____], 19[__], to [_____], 19[__], bearing identification #[_____] through #[_____]") general references (for example, "documents identified in the deposition of _____)" are insufficient.

(b) Exhibits. Unless beyond the party's control (for example, exhibits from an independent third party being obtained through subpoena), the party shall at the time of serving the list make all exhibits not previously produced available to other parties for their inspection and copying at [_____] (city in which trial will be held, or some other convenient location).

(c) Objections. Except to the extent a party in its listing of exhibits or within [___] days after receiving another party's exhibit list gives notice to the contrary, it shall be deemed to have agreed (for purposes of this trial only) that

(1) the originals of the listed exhibits are authentic within Fed. R. Evid. 901 or 902;

(2) duplicates, as defined in Fed. R. Evid. 1001, of the listed exhibits are admissible to the same extent as the originals;

(3) any listed exhibits purporting to be correspondence were sent by the purported sender (and received by the purported recipients) on approximately the dates shown or in accordance with customary delivery schedules;

(4) any disputes regarding the accuracy of any of the listed exhibits that purport to be summaries under Fed. R. Evid. 1006 affect only the weight, not the admissibility, of such exhibits;

(5) any listed exhibits purporting to be records described in Fed. R. Evid. 803(6) meet the requirements of that Rule without extrinsic evidence; and

(6) any listed exhibits purporting to be public records or reports described in Fed. R. Evid. 803(8) meet the requirements of that Rule.

(d) Effect. Except for good cause shown, the parties may not offer in evidence, use as demonstrative evidence, or examine any of their witnesses concerning any exhibit not so identified (except solely for impeachment purposes). The listing of any exhibit does not commit the listing party to use it. Subject to any objections that have not been waived under subparagraph (c), any party may use any exhibit that has been listed by another party.

(e) Rulings. Requests for a ruling under Fed. R. Evid. 104 in advance of trial with respect to any objections made under subparagraph (c) or with respect to any other expected objection to admissibility of evidence must be made by motion filed not later than [_____], 19[__].

5. Limits on evidence. (Except for good cause shown, counsel may not offer proof of facts not disclosed in the joint statement of uncontested and contested facts previously submitted, nor may they offer independent evidence of the agreed facts except to the extent incidental to the presentation of evidence on the disputed facts.) Counsel are expected to be selective in deciding on (and listing) the witnesses and documents to be presented at trial and in deciding as trial progresses which of the listed witnesses and documents will be offered. If warranted after review of the lists of witnesses or documents, the court will consider (after hearing from the parties) whether to impose any limits on the length of trial, number of witnesses, or number of exhibits.

6. Briefs. By [_____], 19[__], plaintiffs (and any defendants asserting counterclaims, cross-claims, or third-party claims) shall file and serve comprehensive trial briefs covering all significant legal issues expected to arise at trial with respect to their claims and the defenses made to such claims. By [_____], 19[__], defendant (and any plaintiffs against whom counterclaims are asserted) shall file and serve comprehensive trial briefs responding to the legal contentions of their adversaries and covering any additional significant legal issues expected to arise at trial with respect to the claims against them and their defenses. Any reply briefs shall be filed by [_____], 19__.

(a) Suggested preliminary and interim instructions. In a separate section of their briefs, the parties shall include their suggestions as to the contents of preliminary instructions to be given the jury at the beginning of the trial and of any interim instructions regarding evidence that will likely be received only for a limited purpose. (The time for filing requests for final jury instructions will be set by the court during trial).

(b) Proposals for special verdicts or interrogatories. In a separate section of their briefs, the parties shall outline the special verdicts or interrogatories that, depending upon the evidence, may be appropriate for submission to the jury. (The time for filing revisions to these proposed special verdicts or interrogatories will be set by the court during trial.)

7. Administrative Details.

(a) Facilities. Each side shall by [_____], 19[__], designate a representative to confer with the Clerk of the court and the [GSA Building Manager] and make any special arrangements with respect to the courtroom, witness and conference rooms, facilities for storage of documents, installation of copying machines or computer equipment, and similar matters.

(b) Schedule of witnesses and documents. Counsel shall, absent unusual circumstances, give notice to opposing parties at least [__] hours before calling a witness or offering (or otherwise using) any exhibit during direct examination. This shall be accomplished during trial by daily providing a schedule, updated as trial progresses, reflecting the order in which witnesses are expected to be presented during the next [__] trial days and the exhibits that are expected to be offered or used during the examination of such witnesses.

(1) If less than a complete exhibit (or less than all of the portions of a deposition previously designated by the parties) is to be introduced, the schedule shall so indicate.

(2) Revisions to this projected sequence of witnesses and documents (or to the portions of the deposition to be read) shall be disclosed as soon as known.

(c) Interim conferences. A short conference will usually be held at the end of each trial day and [__] minutes before the start of each trial day to consider problems that may be expected to arise, including last-minute revisions in the sequence or scope of evidence to be presented and objections that have not previously been ruled on or that should be reconsidered.

(d) Presentation of exhibits. Exhibits shall be premarked by the proponent. Unless impractical, the proponent shall provide extra copies for the court and for each juror at the time of offering or first referring to an exhibit. Use of an exhibit shall, unless specifically disclaimed or limited, be deemed an offer of the exhibit in evidence; and, unless excluded on objection promptly made, the exhibit shall be deemed received in evidence. If notice of the proposed use has been given under subparagraph (b) or (c), the presentation of evidence shall not be interrupted for opposing counsel to examine the exhibit. Each side shall designate a representative to aid the courtroom deputy in maintaining current lists and indexes of the exhibits that have been received.

8. Additional conferences. The court will be available to confer with the parties as trial approaches to consider any details of trial not resolved in this order or any part of this order that should be changed.

Dated: [   ]

United States District Judge[24]

[5]   Pretrial Order (Mock Trial)

FORM 15–17   Sample Pretrial Order

UNITED STATES DISTRICT COURT FOR THE [EASTERN]
DISTRICT OF [PENNSYLVANIA]

[Steve Lyons],
Plaintiff

v.   Civil Action No. [820130]

[Eastern Pharmaceuticals, Incorporated],
Defendant

PRETRIAL ORDER

It is ORDERED:

1. Trial is scheduled to commence at [9:00] A.M., [June 29, 1993], at the Federal Courthouse for the [Eastern] District of [Pennsylvania], [Independence Mall West], [Philadelphia], [Pennsylvania].

2. Subject to further order, the court sessions will be held from 9:00 A.M. until 5:00 P.M. each weekday, except for [Monday] [July 5], on which there will be no session, in honor of the celebration of Independence Day.

3. A jury of twelve (12) persons and three (3) alternates shall be selected. The parties shall by [June 15, 1993], file any special voir dire questions they request to be presented to the panel. Any additional questions may be suggested after the initial examination of the panel. Pursuant to Fed. R. Civ. P. 47(b) and 28 U.S.C. § 1870, each side shall be permitted three (3) peremptory challenges to the jurors.

4. In general, Plaintiff claims that he suffers from multiple sclerosis ("MS"), which substantially limits the major life activities of reading, speaking, and walking. He further claims that Defendant employer terminated him due to his disability, without making reasonable accommodations that would allow him to continue to perform his essential job functions, in violation of the Americans with Disabilities Act ("ADA").

5. In general, Defendant claims that they did not terminate Plaintiff due to his alleged ailment. Defendant does not admit that Plaintiff suffers from MS and denies that the ADA applies to this action. Further, Defendant alleges that even if

---

[24] Form 15–16 was adapted from the "Final Pre-Trial Order Form" in Manual for Complex Litigation (Second) § 41.7 (1985).

Plaintiff is given the additional accommodations that he requested, he will still be unable to perform his essential job functions.

6. The following facts are established by admissions in the pleadings or by stipulations of counsel:

(a) Plaintiff is a citizen of the United States and resides in [Norristown], [Pennsylvania].

(b) Defendant, [Eastern Pharmaceuticals, Incorporated ("Eastern")], is a [Delaware] corporation with its manufacturing plant and principal place of business in [Fort Washington], [Pennsylvania].

(c) [Eastern] is a "person," is engaged in "industry affecting commerce," is an "employer," and is a "covered entity," all as defined by the ADA. In addition, [Eastern] employed more than 25 employees for each working day in more than 20 weeks during the preceding year.

(d) Plaintiff was hired by [Eastern] on [July 7, 1972], as an accounting clerk. After several promotions, Plaintiff was employed as a staff accountant in [Eastern]'s finance department. Plaintiff was promoted to this position on [July 11, 1989], and held the job until he was terminated on [August 5, 1992].

(e) [Lisa Brown], [Eastern]'s accounting manager, was Plaintiff's direct supervisor at all relevant times. She terminated Plaintiff on [August 5, 1992].

(f) Plaintiff's essential job functions as a staff accountant were producing financial reports through spreadsheet applications, operating an adding machine to perform various mathematical functions, maintaining the general ledger, and communicating with outside vendors and [Eastern]'s purchasing agents regarding fixed-asset acquisitions.

(g) [Eastern] provided Plaintiff with a device that magnifies the computer screen and also rerouted Plaintiff's incoming calls so that another employee answered the phone for Plaintiff. After these accommodations were provided, Plaintiff was able to perform the essential functions of his job as a staff accountant.

7. The following constitutes the witness lists as they presently stand:

(a) Plaintiff's witnesses:

(i) [Steve Lyons], Plaintiff, will be the first witness called. He will be called on the morning of [June 29, 1993].

(ii) [Dr. Willard Allen], Plaintiff's expert medical witness, will be the second witness called. He will be called in the afternoon of [June 29, 1993].

(b) Defendant's witnesses:

(i) [Henry Bell], the controller at Defendant [Eastern], will be the first witness called by the defense. He will likely be called on the morning of [June 30, 1993].

(ii) [Arthur Smith], Defendant's expert, will be the second witness called by Defendant. He will likely be called in the afternoon of [June 30, 1993].

(c) In the event that there are any other witnesses to be called at trial, their names and addresses will be reported to opposing counsel at least 10 days prior to trial. This restriction shall not apply to rebuttal witnesses, for the need for such testimony cannot reasonably be anticipated prior to the time of trial.

8. As this is a jury trial, requests for jury instructions must be submitted to the Court at the commencement of the case, subject to the right of counsel to supplement such requests during the course of trial as to matters that cannot reasonably be anticipated.

9. This pretrial order has been formulated after a final pretrial conference, at which counsel for the respective parties appeared. Reasonable opportunity has been given to counsel to submit corrections or additions prior to the signing of the Order by the Court. From this point forward, this Order will control the course of the trial and may not be amended, except by consent of the parties and the Court or by Order of the Court to prevent manifest injustice, pursuant to Fed. R. Civ. P. 16(e). The pleadings will be deemed merged herein. If any provision of this Order proves to be ambiguous, reference may be made to the record of this conference to the extent reported by stenographic notes, and reference may also be made to the pleadings.

10. The probable length of this trial is ten (10) days. The case is scheduled to commence with a jury on [June 29, 1993], at [10:00] A.M.

11. The court will be available to confer with the parties as trial approaches to consider any details of the trial not adequately resolved in this order.

Dated this [_____] day of [_____], 19[__].

United States District Judge

[6]   Final Pretrial Order (EEOC)

FORM 15–18   Sample Final Pretrial Order

IN THE UNITED STATES DISTRICT COURT FOR THE [NORTHERN] DISTRICT OF [ILLINOIS] [EASTERN] DIVISION

U.S. EQUAL EMPLOYMENT OPPORTUNITY COMMISSION and

[CHARLES H. WESSEL],
Plaintiff,
v.   Civil Action No. [92 C 7330]
[A.I.C. SECURITY INVESTIGATIONS, LTD.];
[A.I.C. INTERNATIONAL, LTD.];
and [unnamed defendant C],   Judge [Aspen]

Defendants.

Magistrate Judge [Guzman]

FINAL PRETRIAL ORDER

This matter is scheduled to be heard before the Court at a pretrial conference pursuant to Fed. R. Civ. P. ("Rule") 16 on [February 19, 1993], at [2:00 P.M.]. The following attorneys will appear at trial on behalf of Plaintiff, Equal Employment Opportunity Commission (the "EEOC"):

[attorney A]

[attorney B]

Equal Employment Opportunity Commission
[536 South Clark Street], [Room 982]
[Chicago], [IL] [60605]
[(312) 353-7582]

The following attorneys will appear at trial on behalf of Intervening Plaintiff [Charles H. Wessel ("Wessel")]:

[attorney C]

[attorney E]

The following attorneys will appear on behalf of Defendants [A.I.C. Security Investigations, Ltd. ("A.I.C.")], [A.I.C. International, Ltd. ("A.I.C. International")], and [defendant C]:

[Charles W. Pautsch]
[attorney A]

[attorney B]

[Wessels & Pautsch]
[Two Plaza East]
[330 E. Kilbourne Avenue]
[Suite 1475]
[Milwaukee], [WI] [53202]
[(414) 291-0600]

This is an action filed under the Americans with Disabilities Act of 1990 (the "ADA"), 42 U.S.C. §§ 12,101 *et seq.,* in which Plaintiffs allege that Defendants discriminated against [Wessel] by terminating his employment because of his disability, terminal cancer, in violation of the ADA. The jurisdiction of this Court is invoked pursuant to 28 U.S.C. §§ 451, 1331, 1337, 1343, and 1345. Jurisdiction and venue are not disputed.

The following stipulations and statements are attached and are made part of this Order:

SCHEDULE A STATEMENT OF UNCONTESTED FACTS

SCHEDULE B AGREED STATEMENT OF CONTESTED ISSUES OF FACT AND LAW

Schedule B-1 Plaintiffs' Proposed Contested Facts
Schedule B-2 Defendants' Proposed Contested Issues of Fact or Law
Schedule B-3 Agreed Statement of Contested Issues of Law

SCHEDULE C EXHIBITS

Schedule C-1 Plaintiffs' List of Exhibits
Schedule C-2 Plaintiffs' Exhibits to Which Defendants Do Not Object
Schedule C-3 Plaintiffs' Exhibits to Which Defendants Object, with Defendants' Objections Noted
Schedule C-4 Defendants' List of Exhibits
Schedule C-5 Defendants' Exhibits to Which Plaintiffs Do Not Object
Schedule C-6 Defendants' Exhibits to Which Plaintiffs Object, with Plaintiffs' Objections Noted

SCHEDULE D WITNESSES

Schedule D-1 Plaintiffs' List of Names and Addresses of Potential Witnesses to Be Called (specifying those who will be called and those who may be called), with Defendants' Objections to the Calling or to the Qualifications of Plaintiffs' Witnesses
Schedule D-2 Defendants' List of Names and Addresses of Potential Witnesses to Be Called (specifying those who will be called and those who may be called), with Plaintiffs' Objections to the Calling or Qualifications of Defendants' Witnesses

SCHEDULE E STIPULATION OF QUALIFICATIONS OF EXPERT WITNESSES

Schedule E-1 Plaintiffs' Proposed Stipulated Qualifications of Experts
Schedule E-2 Statement of Qualifications of Defendants' Expert Witnesses

SCHEDULE F DEPOSITION DESIGNATIONS

Schedule F-1 Statement of Plaintiffs' Deposition Designations and Defendants' Objections
Schedule F-2 Statement of Defendants' Deposition Designations and Defendants' Objections

SCHEDULE G ITEMIZED STATEMENT OF SPECIAL DAMAGES

Schedule G-1 Defendants' Objections to Statement of Special Damages

SCHEDULE H PLAINTIFFS' TRIAL BRIEF

SCHEDULE I DEFENDANTS' TRIAL BRIEF

SCHEDULE J JURY INSTRUCTIONS

Schedule J-1 Plaintiffs' Proposed Jury Instructions and Verdict Forms
Schedule J-2 Defendants' Proposed Jury Instructions and Verdict Forms

SCHEDULE K LIST OF PROPOSED VOIR DIRE QUESTIONS

SCHEDULE L DEFENDANTS' LIST OF PROPOSED VOIR DIRE QUESTIONS

SCHEDULE M HISTORY OF SETTLEMENT NEGOTIATIONS

SCHEDULE N MOTIONS IN LIMINE (TO BE ADDED TO IF NECESSARY)

Each party has completed discovery. Except for good cause shown, no further discovery shall be permitted. Trial of this case is expected to take between 8 and 10 business days. The Court has set trial of this case for [March 8, 1993].

The case will be tried by a six-person jury. Plaintiffs prefer that alternates deliberate. Defendants prefer that alternates not deliberate.

It is the preference of the parties that the issues of liability and damages should not be bifurcated for trial.

The parties have agreed that this case may be tried before a Magistrate Judge.

This Order will control the course of the trial and may not be amended except by consent of the parties and the Court, or by order of the Court to prevent manifest injustice.

Possibility of settlement of this case was considered by the parties.

SCHEDULE A

STATEMENT OF UNCONTESTED FACTS

1. Plaintiff Equal Employment Opportunity Commission (the "EEOC") is the agency of the United States charged with the administration and enforcement of Title I of the Americans with Disabilities Act of 1990, 42 U.S.C. §§ 12101 *et seq.* ("ADA").

2. Intervening Plaintiff, [Charles H. Wessel ("Wessel")] is a former employee of [A.I.C. Security Investigations, Ltd.].[25]

3. At all times relevant to the issues in this lawsuit, Defendant [A.I.C. Security Investigations, Ltd. ("A.I.C.")] has been an [Illinois] corporation doing business in the State of [Illinois] and the City of [Chicago]. At all relevant times [A.I.C.] has had more than 200, but less than 500, employees.

4. At all times relevant to the issues in this lawsuit, Defendant [A.I.C. International, Ltd. ("A.I.C. International")] has been an [Illinois] corporation doing business in the State of [Illinois] and the City of [Chicago]. At all relevant times [A.I.C. International] has been a holding company holding all shares of [A.I.C.].

5. Since [June 6, 1992], and to the present, Defendant [C] has owned all shares of stock of [A.I.C. International].

---

[25] This stipulation will be read to the jury, unless the court determines that Wessel has not properly intervened in the case.

6. [Wessel] was employed by [A.I.C.] from [February 2, 1986], through [July 31, 1992], as Executive Director.

7. [Wessel] was diagnosed with lung cancer in [June 1987], at which time he had surgery; he was hospitalized from [June 6, 1987], until [June 19, 1987]. He returned to work at [A.I.C]. on [July 6, 1987].

8. In [July] of [1991], [Wessel] suffered pneumothorax during a routine biopsy and was hospitalized from [July 29, 1991], until [August 12, 1991]. He returned to work on [August 13, 1991].

9. In [October 1991], [Wessel] had surgery for lung cancer of the right lung; he was hospitalized from [October 3, 1991], until [October 18, 1991]. He returned to work at [A.I.C.] on approximately [November 4, 1991].

10. [Wessel] was diagnosed with inoperable metastatic brain cancer in [April 1992]. The condition was and is considered by his doctors to be terminal.

11. [A.I.C. Security Investigations, Ltd.], is the largest of the entities held by [A.I.C. International]. [A.I.C.] provides licensed private security guards for residential and commercial property in the [Chicago] area.

12. [Wessel] was hired by [Victor V.], owner of [A.I.C. International] in [February 1986] as Executive Director of [A.I.C.].

13. During all relevant times, the Executive Director position at [A.I.C.] was the top management position of [A.I.C].

14. [Victor V.], owner of [A.I.C. International], died on [June 5, 1992]. [David P.], President of [A.I.C. International], was involuntarily terminated from his employment on [July 6, 1992].

15. As of [July 31, 1992], [Wessel] was earning [$46,725] per year plus [$350] per month designated as car allowance and reported to the IRS on a Form 1099.

16. If [Wessel] had continued to be employed by [A.I.C.], he would have earned a salary of [$3893.75] per month, excluding any miscellaneous income designated as car allowance and any bonuses and raises, for each month during which he remained employed by [A.I.C.], after [July 1992].

17. Following [July 31, 1992], [Wessel] has received unemployment compensation.

18. Beginning in [January 1993], and retroactive to [October 29, 1992], [Wessel] has received payments at the rate of 60 percent of his former salary pursuant to a disability policy maintained by [A.I.C.] for its management employees.

19. In [August 1992], [Wessel] applied for Social Security disability benefits. He has been found eligible for such benefits beginning in [January 1993].

20. If [Wessel] had continued to be employed by [A.I.C.], the company would have maintained his health insurance by paying premiums of [$598.84] per month for insurance for himself and his wife, for each month that he continued to be employed by [A.I.C.] after [July 1992].

21. If [Wessel] had continued to be employed by [A.I.C.], the company would have maintained his life insurance, paying [$237.72] per quarter in premiums for each quarter that he continued to be employed by [A.I.C.] after [July 1992].

22. Since [July 1987], Dr. [B] has been [Charles Wessel]'s primary treating physician. Dr. [B] is an oncologist and a hematologist.

SCHEDULE B

AGREED STATEMENT OF CONTESTED ISSUES OF FACT AND LAW

1. Whether [Wessel] was involuntarily terminated from his employment as Executive Director of [A.I.C.].

2. Whether, in [July 1992], [Wessel] was able to perform the essential functions of his position as Executive Director, with or without reasonable accommodation.

3. Whether, since [July 29, 1992], [Wessel] has continued to be able to perform the essential functions of his position as Executive Director, with or without reasonable accommodation.

4. Whether, and in what amount, [Wessel] suffered emotional pain, suffering, inconvenience, mental anguish, loss of enjoyment of life, or other nonpecuniary losses as a result of his discharge from [A.I.C.].

5. Whether [Wessel] is an individual with a disability within the meaning of the Americans with Disabilities Act.

6. Whether throughout his employment with [A.I.C.], [Wessel] met all of the skill and experience requirements for the position of Executive Director of [A.I.C.].

7. What were the essential functions of [Wessel]'s job as Executive Director of [A.I.C.].

8. Whether, during the following fiscal years (each ending [July 3]), [A,I.C.] (the security guard division) had net earnings of:

1986 [$1,446,659]
1987 [$1,681,644]
1988 [$2,188,535]
1989 [$2,315,051]
1990 [$2,367,729]
1991 [$2,267,277]
1992 [$2,454,627]

9. Whether [Wessel] received a salary increase and a bonus in each year that he was employed by [A.I.C.], except [1991], when no bonuses were given. Whether [Wessel] did not receive a raise or bonus in [1992] because no appraisals were performed, or raises or bonuses awarded, by [A.I.C.] prior to [July 31, 1992].

10. Whether [Wessel] was terminated because he suffers from cancer.

11. Whether [Wessel] was paid through [July 31, 1992]. Whether he received accrued vacation pay.

12. Whether [Wessel] had diligently sought employment since his discharge by [A.I.C.].

13. Whether, at the time of his discharge, [Wessel] did not meet the job-related qualification standards consistent with [A.I.C.]'s business necessity because he posed a direct threat to the health and safety of others in the workplace.

14. Whether [Wessel] was terminated from [A.I.C.] for legitimate business reasons.

15. Whether [Wessel] was discharged on [July 30, 1992], effective [July 31, 1992].

16. Whether during his employment with [A.I.C.], [Wessel] did or did not ever request an accommodation in order to perform the essential functions of his position as Executive Director.

SCHEDULE B-1

PLAINTIFFS' PROPOSED CONTESTED FACTS

1. Whether [defendant C], [A.I.C.], and/or [A.I.C. International] acted with malice or reckless indifference to [Wessel]'s federally protected rights in discharging him.

2. Whether [Wessel] is a widely recognized leader in the security guard industry. Whether he has worked in the industry for approximately 30 years.

3. Whether [Wessel] is licensed as a private detective and as a private security contractor by the State of [Illinois]. Whether he holds similar licenses from the State of [Florida].

4. Whether [Wessel] is a member of, and has served on the Boards of, numerous professional associations, including the [Associated Detectives of Illinois], the [Associated Guard and Patrol Agencies, Inc.], and the [Special Agents Association].

5. Whether [Wessel] was the principal drafter of the [Illinois] licensing act for private investigators. Whether he served as chair of the [Legislative Rewrite Committee], which drafted the [Illinois Private Detective, Private Security Contractor, and Private Alarm Act of 1983], the statute which licenses private investigators and security guards in [Illinois].

6. What were the marginal functions of [Wessel]'s position as Executive Director of [A.I.C.].

7. Whether the decision to terminate [Wessel]'s employment was made by [defendant C].

8. Whether, prior to making the decision to terminate [Wessel], [defendant C] did not consult with any employees of [A.I.C.], other than [Beverly K.], who was hired on approximately [June 10, 1992].

9. Whether, at the direction of [defendant C], [Beverly K.], on [July 29, 1992], advised [Wessel] that [defendant C] had determined that he should retire.

10. Whether, on [July 30, 1992], [Beverly K.] advised [Wessel] by telephone that he was terminated, effective [July 31, 1992].

11. Whether [Wessel] was never subjected to any employment performance warnings or disciplinary action prior to his discharge.

12. Whether [defendant C], [A.I.C.], and [A.I.C. International] were aware of the requirements of the ADA in [July] [1992], at the time [defendant C] made the decision to discharge [Wessel].

SCHEDULE B-2

DEFENDANTS' PROPOSED CONTESTED ISSUES OF FACT OR LAW

1. Whether [Wessel] was advised by any of his treating physicians in [April 1992], and/or at other subsequent times, that he was not to drive an automobile due to the significant risk posed by his brain cancer and treatment for same.

2. Whether [Wessel] was offered a driver by [A.I.C.] to get him to and from work in [1991] and [1992].

3. Whether [Wessel] refused [A.I.C.]'s offer to provide him with a driver to get him to and from work in [1991] and [1992].

4. Whether [Wessel]'s brain tumors and treatments, including medications and radiation, affected his mental capacities prior to [July 29, 1992], and if so, whether the symptoms relate to [Wessel]'s performance of any of the essential functions of his job of Executive Director of [A.I.C.].

5. Whether [Wessel] was given a parking place next to the entrance at [A.I.C.]'s building as an accommodation to his condition.

6. Whether [Wessel] was given an office next to the elevator at [A.I.C.]'s building as an accommodation to his condition.

7. Whether [Wessel] was physically assisted with his walking in and around [A.I.C.]'s premises by [A.I.C.]'s personnel as an accommodation to his condition.

8. Whether [Wessel] was assisted by [A.I.C.] personnel in obtaining insurance coverage for an air purifier that he kept in his office at [A.I.C.] as an accommodation to his condition.

9. Whether [Wessel], on account of his terminal illness, personally conducted interviews in or around [May] of [1992] for the purpose of hiring his replacement as Executive Director.

10. Whether [Wessel] personally, during the course of [1992], turned over to other [A.I.C.] personnel many of the duties that had always been essential functions of the position of Executive Director.

11. Whether [Wessel]'s position of Executive Director for [A.I.C.] required, as essential functions of the job, regular and predictable full-time attendance.

12. Whether [Wessel] voluntarily proposed retirement terms of his own choosing on [July 29, 1992], to [Beverly K.], an employee of [A.I.C.].

13. Whether [A.I.C.] agreed to give [Wessel] the retirement terms he had proposed on [July 29, 1992], and communicated this agreement to [Wessel].

14. The amount of time [Wessel] missed work during the last year he was employed with [A.I.C.].

15. Whether [Wessel] determined to file his Charge, and, in fact, did file his Charge with the EEOC before he attempted to provide [A.I.C.] with any information from his treating physicians.

16. Whether [Wessel] has diligently sought to mitigate any damages claimed in the instant litigation.

17. Whether [Wessel], during his employment with [A.I.C.] in the year [1992], told any [A.I.C.] personnel that his doctor had told him not to drive, but he ([Wessel]) was not going to listen and, in fact, [Wessel] did not follow his doctor's instruction.

SCHEDULE B-3

AGREED STATEMENT OF CONTESTED ISSUES OF LAW

1. Whether [Wessel] was, on [July 29, 1992], a qualified individual with a disability covered by the protections of the Americans with Disabilities Act.

a. Whether [Wessel]'s condition of terminal cancer constitutes a physical impairment that substantially limits him in one or more major life activities.

b. Whether, on [July 29, 1992], [Wessel] met the skill and education requirements for his position as Executive Director of [A.I.C.].

2. Whether [Wessel] was, from [July 29, 1992], to the present, a qualified individual with a disability covered by the protections of the Americans with Disabilities Act.

a. Whether [Wessel]'s condition of terminal cancer constitutes a physical impairment which substantially limits him in one or more major life activities.

b. Whether, from [July 29, 1992], to the present, [Wessel] met the skill and education requirements for his position as Executive Director of [A.I.C.].

3. Whether [Wessel] is "otherwise qualified" in that he satisfies the prerequisites for the position of Executive Director of [A.I.C.], possessing the appropriate educational background, employment experience, skills, licenses, etc.

SCHEDULE C EXHIBITS

SCHEDULE C-1

PLAINTIFFS' LIST OF EXHIBITS

Exhibit #1: Affidavit of [Charles H. Wessel] to EEOC dated [August 11, 1992].

Exhibit #2: Notes of [Charles Wessel] dated [July 29 and 31, 1992].

Exhibit #3: [August 20, 1992], letter from [Phil W.] to [Charles H. Wessel] advising [Wessel] of the cost of continuing his health benefits for him and his wife.

Exhibit #4: [September 14, 1992], letter from [Charles H. Wessel] to [Phil W.] enclosing payment for continuation of health insurance.

Exhibit #5: Memorandum from [Larry R.] to all [A.I.C.] Building Staff regarding [Charles Wessel].

Exhibit #6: [November 25, 1992], letter from [Unum] Insurance Company to [Charles H. Wessel] informing him that [Unum] had not yet received the employer section of his application for his disability insurance.

Exhibit #7: Letter from [A.I.C. attorney B] to [EEOC attorney A] dated [January 25, 1993], regarding discovery.

Exhibit #8: Videotape deposition of [Charles H. Wessel] #1.

Exhibit #9: Videotape deposition of [Charles H. Wessel] #2.

Exhibit #10: Resume of [Charles H. Wessel].

Exhibit #11: List of potential employers from whom [Charles H. Wessel] sought employment subsequent to his discharge from [A.I.C.].

Exhibit #12: [February 10, 1993], letter from [Dr. Peter A. L.], M.D. to [A.I.C. attorney B].

Exhibit #13: Letter to Whom It May Concern from Dr. [B].

Exhibit #14: [A.I.C. International, Ltd.] and Subsidiaries Consolidated Financial Statements, Year Ended [July 31, 1986].

Exhibit #15: [A.I.C. International, Ltd.] and Subsidiaries Consolidated Financial Statements, Year Ended [July 31, 1987].

Exhibit #16: [A.I.C. International, Ltd.] and Subsidiaries Consolidated Financial Statements as of [July 31, 1989] and [1988], together with Auditor's Report.

Exhibit #17: [A.I.C. International, Ltd.] and Subsidiaries Consolidated Financial Statements as of [July 31, 1991] and [1990], together with Auditor's Report.

Exhibit #18: [A.I.C. International, Ltd.] and Subsidiaries Consolidated Financial Statements as of [July 31, 1992], together with Auditor's Report.

Exhibit #19: Curriculum Vitae of Dr. [B].

Exhibit #20: Curriculum Vitae of Dr. [A].

Exhibit #21: Amended Charge of Discrimination.

Exhibit #22: [Wessel] computer printout — New Local 73 Format–[July 7, 1992].

Exhibit #23: EEOC First Request for Production of Documents, Requests 10 and 11.

Exhibit #24: Defendants' Response to EEOC's First Request for Production of Documents, Requests 10 and 11.

Exhibit #25: Curriculum Vitae of Dr. [C] (for rebuttal only).

Exhibit #26: "Disability Evaluation under Social Security" — [May 1992].

Exhibit #27: Chart showing annual net revenue from [A.I.C. Security Investigations, Ltd.] and [A.I.C. International, Ltd.].

Exhibit #28: Plaintiff's First Set of Interrogatories, Interrogatory #8; Defendants' Answer to Plaintiff's First Set of Interrogatories, Interrogatory #8.

Plaintiffs reserve the right to offer additional exhibits as impeachment or rebuttal.

SCHEDULE C-2

PLAINTIFFS' EXHIBITS TO WHICH DEFENDANTS DO NOT OBJECT

EXHIBIT NO./DESCRIPTION

1: Affidavit of [Charles H. Wessel] to EEOC, dated [8/11/92].

2: Notes of [Charles Wessel], dated [7/29] and [7/31/92].

3: [8/20/92] Letter from [P.W.] to [C. Wessel] advising [Wessel] of the cost of continuing his health benefits for him and his wife.

4: [9/14/92] Letter from [C. Wessel] to [P. W.] enclosing payment for continuation of health insurance.

6: [11/25/92] Letter from [Unum] to [C. Wessel].

7: [1/25/93] Letter from [A.I.C. attorney B] to [attorney A] regarding discovery. [8–9: In original.]

10: Resume of [C. Wessel].

11: [C. Wessel] — List of Potential Employers.

12: [2/10/93] Letter from [Dr. L.] to [A.I.C. attorney B].

13: Letter from Dr. [B] to Whom It May Concern.

14–18: [A.I.C. International, Ltd.] and Subsidiaries Consolidated Financial Statements Years Ended [7/31/86], [7/31/87], [7/31/89] and [1988], [7/31/91] and [1990], [7/31/92].

19: Curriculum Vitae of Dr. [B].
20: Curriculum Vitae of Dr. [A].
21: Amended Charge of Discrimination.
22: Computer printout of New Local 73 Format [7/7/91].

SCHEDULE C-3

PLAINTIFF'S EXHIBITS TO WHICH DEFENDANTS OBJECT, WITH DE-
FENDANTS' OBJECTIONS NOTED

EXHIBIT NO./DESCRIPTION AND OBJECTION

5: Memo from [Larry R.].

Defendants object because this document was prepared in the course of litigation per specific instructions of counsel and, therefore, is attorney-client privilege
and attorney work product that was not produced to Plaintiff by any proper means.

8: Videotape Deposition of [C. Wessel].

Defendants object. This videotape deposition should not be used at trial if
[C. Wessel] is available to testify. If [C. Wessel] is available to testify, the use of
his videotape deposition at trial will cause undue delay, will waste time, and will
needlessly present cumulative evidence. Rule 403, Fed. R. Evid.

9: Videotape of the Roast of [C. Wessel].

Defendants object. *See* Schedule N, Defendants' Motion in Limine.

23: EEOC First Document Requests Nos. 10 and 11.

Defendants object based upon the expedited discovery schedule.

24: Defendants' Responses to EEOC's First Request for Production of Documents, Requests Nos. 10 and 11.

Defendants object based upon the expedited discovery schedule.

25: Curriculum Vitae of Dr. [C.].

Defendants object to Plaintiff's calling Dr. [C.] at trial for the reasons stated
in Defendants' Motion to Exclude Expert Witness. To the extent Dr. [C.] is excluded, his Curriculum Vitae is irrelevant.

26: Defendants reserve the right to object to Plaintiffs' Exhibit No. 26.
27: Chart showing annual net revenue from [A.I.C. Security Investigations,
Ltd.] and [A.I.C. International, Ltd.].

Defendants object based upon lack of foundation and authenticity.

28: Plaintiff's First Set of Interrogatories, Interrogatory #8; Defendants' Answer to Plaintiff's First Set of Interrogatories, Interrogatory #8.

Defendants object based upon the expedited discovery schedule.

SCHEDULE C-4

DEFENDANTS' LIST OF EXHIBITS

EXHIBIT NO./DESCRIPTION

1: Social Security Administration Form 2417, Determination of Benefit Rights, undated (2 pages).

2: Social Security Administration Form 831-U3, Disability Determination and Transmittal, dated [8/31/92] (1 page).

3: Letter from [Charles Wessel] to Social Security Administration allowing release of records, dated [1/20/93] (1 page).

4: Social Security Administration computer printout of disability payments made to [Charles Wessel], undated (1 page).

5: Disability Development Worksheet, dated [8/6/92] to [8/27/92] (2 pages).

6: Neoplasm Report, Bureau of Disability Determination Services, dated [8/19/92] (2 pages).

7: [Illinois] Disability Determination Services Medical Release Form, dated [8/5/92] (1 page).

8: Data Form for Cancer Staging, undated (1 page).

9: [South Suburban Hospital] Tissue Report, dated [6/10/87] (1 page).

10: [South Suburban Hospital] Data Form for Cancer Staging — Pathology, undated (1 page).

11: [South Suburban Hospital], Report of Frozen Section, dated [6/10/87] (1 page).

12: [South Suburban Hospital], Tissue Report, dated [6/12/87] (2 pages).

13: [South Suburban Hospital], Cytology (Form 11), dated [6/10/87] (1 page).

14: [South Suburban Hospital], Data Form for Cancer Staging, Pathology, undated (1 page).

15: [South Suburban Hospital], Data Form for Cancer Staging, Pathology, undated (1 page).

16: [South Suburban Hospital], Tissue Report, dated [6/11/87] (1 page).

17: [Loyola University Hospital] Admission/Discharge Record, dated [10/18/91] (1 page).

18: [Loyola University Hospital] Admission Discharge Summary, dated [11/23/91] (1 page).

19: [Loyola University Hospital], Report of Operation, dated [10/16/91] (1 page).

20: [Loyola University Hospital], Clinical Laboratory Summary Report dated [10/19/91] (4 pages).

21: [Loyola University Hospital], Final Report, dated [10/10/91] (4 pages).

22: [Loyola University Hospital], Progress Notes, dated [10/3/91] to [10/11/91] (34 pages).

23: [Illinois] Bureau of Disability Determination Services, Records Request to [South Suburban Hospital], dated [8/11/92] (1 page).

24: [Illinois] Bureau of Disability Determination Services, Records Request to [Palos Community Hospital], dated [8/11/92] (1 page).

25: [Illinois] Bureau of Disability Determination Services, Records Request to [Loyola University Hospital], dated [8/11/92] (1 page).

26: [Illinois] Bureau of Disability Determination Services, Records Request to [Ingalls Memorial Hospital], dated [8/11/92] (1 page).

27: [Illinois] Bureau of Disability Determination Services, Records Request to [SWC Cancer Center], dated [8/11/92] (1 page).

28: [Illinois] Bureau of Disability Determination Services, Records Request to [Craig A.], M.D., dated [8/11/92] (1 page).

29: [Illinois] Bureau of Disability Determination Services, Records Request to [B], M.D., dated [8/11/92] (1 page).

30: [Palos Community Hospital], Surgical Pathology Report, dated [7/30/91] (1 page).

31: Social Security Administration Form 3368-13K, Disability Report, dated [8/5/92] (8 pages).

32: Preliminary Information Sheet — Disability Claim, dated [8/5/92] (1 page).

33: Application for Disability Insurance Benefits, dated [8/5/92] (4 pages).

34: Progress Notes of [Susan L., M.D.], dated [6/2/92], [11/5/92], [5/5/92] (2 pages).

35: Report of Consultation and Operation from [Susan L.], M.D., dated [8/2/91] (2 pages).

36: [Dependicare Home Health, Inc.], Initial Contact Sheet, dated [1/24/92] (1 page).

37: [Dependicare] Patient Evaluation, dated [10/25/91] (1 page).

38: [Dependicare] Initial Sheet, dated [1/18/91] (1 page).

39: [Dependicare] Service Pickup Form, dated [10/17/91] (1 page).

40: [Dependicare] Service Order Form, dated [10/19/91] (1 page).

41: Letter to Dr. [C] from [Dependicare], dated [10/28/91] (1 page).

42: [Dependicare] Certificate of Medical Necessity, dated [9/7/92] (1 page).

43: [Dependicare] Certificate of Medical Necessity, undated (1 page).

44: [Dependicare] Certificate of Medical Necessity, undated (1 page).

45: [Guardian] Health Insurance Claim Form, dated [10/27/92] (1 page).

46: [Guardian] Health Insurance Claim Form, dated [9/29/92] (1 page).

47: [Guardian] Health Insurance Claim Form, dated [8/28/92] (1 page).

48: [Guardian] Health Insurance Claim Form, dated [7/28/92] (1 page).

49: [Guardian] Health Insurance Claim Form, dated [6/29/92] (1 page).

50: [Guardian] Health Insurance Claim Form, dated [5/27/92] (1 page).

51: [Guardian] Health Insurance Claim Form, dated [7/21/92] (1 page).

52: [Guardian] Health Insurance Claim Form, dated [4/28/92] (1 page).

53: [Guardian] Health Insurance Claim Form, dated [6/18/92] (1 page).

54: [Guardian] Health Insurance Claim Form, dated [3/27/92] (1 page).

55: [Guardian] Health Insurance Claim Form, dated [2/27/92] (1 page).

56: [Guardian] Health Insurance Claim Form, dated [1/28/92] (1 page).

57: [Guardian] Health Insurance Claim Form, dated [12/27/91] (1 page).

58: [Guardian] Health Insurance Claim Form, dated [11/26/91] (1 page).

59: [Guardian] Health Insurance Claim Form, dated [11/15/91] (1 page).

60: [Guardian] Health Insurance Claim Form, dated [10/24/91] (1 page).

61: [Guardian] Health Insurance Claim Form, dated [10/31/91] (1 page).

62: [Radiation Therapy Consultants, Ltd. (SWC Cancer Center)], description of treatments and billings, dated [11/11/92] (3 pages).

63: [SWC Cancer Center] Progress Notes, dated [6/26/87] to [6/29/92] (6 pages).

64: Letter of Consultation from [S.R.], M.D., dated [6/9/87] (1 page).

65: Letter to Dr. [B] from Dr. [A], dated [7/17/92] (1 page).

66: Letter to Dr. [B] from Dr. [A], dated [6/23/92] (1 page).

67: Letter to Dr. [B] from Dr. [A], dated [5/19/92] (1 page).

68: Letter to Dr. [B] from Dr. [G.], dated [8/25/87] (1 page).

69: Letter to Dr. [B] from Dr. [G.], dated [7/8/87] (1 page).

70: Letter to Dr. [B] from Dr. [A], dated [4/15/92] (1 page).

71: [Center for Magnetic Imaging] Report of Examination, dated [6/3/92] (1 page).

72: [Palos Community Hospital] Report of Examination, dated [4/7/92] (1 page).

73: [Palos Community Hospital] Report of Examination, dated [4/30/92] (1 page).

74: [Center for Magnetic Imagining] Report of Examination, dated [4/14/92] (1 page).

75: Pulmonary Function Laboratory, [South Suburban Hospital] Test Result, dated [6/9/87] (1 page).

76: [SWC Cancer Center] Authorization of Administration of Radiation, dated [4/13/92] (1 page).

77: [Illinois] Bureau of Disability Determination Services Neoplasm Report, dated [8/19/92] (1 page).

78: [SWC Cancer Center], Plan of Radiation Therapy, dated [6/18/92] (1 page).

79: [SWC Cancer Center], Record of Radiation Therapy, dated [6/16/92] to [7/2/92] (2 pages).

80: [SWC Cancer Center] Plan of Therapy, dated [4/13/92] (1 page).

81: [SWC Cancer Center] Record of Radiation Treatments, dated [4/14/92] to [5/11/92] (2 pages).

82: [SWC Cancer Center] Plan of Therapy, dated [6/26/87] (1 page).

83: [SWC Cancer Center] Record of Radiation Treatments, dated [7/10/87] to [8/19/87] (2 pages).

84: [SWC Cancer Center] Computer Diagram of Brain, dated [4/28/92] (1 page).

85: Progress Note from [C.A.], M.D., dated [6/29/92] (1 page).

86: Report from [C.A.], M.D., dated [7/31/91] (3 pages).

87: Report from Pulmonary Function Lab of [Palos Community Hospital], dated [9/11/91] (2 pages).

88: Report of Operation by [C.A.], dated [9/6/91] (2 pages).

89: Excerpt from [Unum Insurance] Policy (4 pages).

90: [Unum] form record of payment, undated (1 page).

91: Letter from [Unum] to [Wessel], dated [12/18/92] (1 page).

92: [Unum] Benefit Memo, dated [12/18/92] (1 page).

93: Letter to [Unum] from [Charles M.], dated [11/2/92] (1 page).

94: Letter to [Unum] from [Wessel], dated [10/26/92] (1 page).

95: [Unum] Application for Disability Benefits, dated [10/26/92] (1 page).

96: [Unum] Application for Disability Benefits, dated [9/27/92] (1 page).

97: [Unum] Notes of Telephone Call to [A.I.C.], dated [12/18/92] (1 page).

98: [Unum] Benefit Memo, dated [12/15/92] (1 page).

99: [Center for Magnetic Imaging] Report of Examination, dated [8/12/92] (1 page).

100: [July 1992] Letter to Dr. [B] from Dr. [A] (1 page).

101: Report from Dr. [B], dated [10/7/92] (1 page).

102: [Unum] — Employer's Statement, dated [11/27/92] (4 pages).

103: [SWC Cancer Center] Letter to Dr. [B] from Dr. [G], dated [8/25/87] (1 page).

104: [SWC Cancer Center] Letter to Dr. [B] from Dr. [G], dated [7/8/87] (1 page).

105: [South Suburban Hospital] Consultation Report, dated [6/9/87] (1 page).

106: [South Suburban Hospital] Radiology Report, dated [6/9/87] (1 page).

107: [South Suburban Hospital] Admission Summary, dated [6/19/87] (1 page).

108: [South Suburban Hospital] Consultation Report, dated [6/7/87] (1 page).

109: [South Suburban Hospital] Pulmonary Function Report, dated [6/9/87] (2 pages).

110: [Palos Community Hospital] Outpatient Record, dated [9/6/91] (1 page).

111: [Palos Community Hospital] Consent for Procedure Form, dated [9/6/91] (1 page).

112: [Palos Community Hospital] Outpatient Registration, dated [8/13/92] (1 page).

113: [Palos Community Hospital] Report of Examination, dated [8/13/92] (1 page).

114: [Palos Community Hospital] Report of Examination, dated [9/24/92] (1 page).

115: [Palos Community Hospital] Report of Examination, dated [9/28/92] (1 page).

116: [Palos Community Hospital] Report of Examination, dated [7/22/91] (1 page).

117: [Palos Community Hospital] Report of Examination, dated [4/30/92] (1 page).

118: [Palos Community Hospital] Report of Examination, dated [4/7/92] (1 page).

119: [Palos Community Hospital] Report of Examination, dated [12/31/90] (1 page).

120: [Palos Community Hospital] Report of Examination, dated [9/27/88] (1 page).

121: [Palos Community Hospital] Record of Admission, dated [7/29/91] (1 page).

122: [Palos Community Hospital] Discharge Summary, dated [8/12/91] (1 page).

123: [Palos Community Hospital] Emergency Department Assessment, dated [7/29/91] (1 page).

124: [Palos Community Hospital] Admission History, dated [7/29/91] (1 page).

125: [Palos Community Hospital] Physical Examination Report, dated [7/29/91] (1 page).

126: [Palos Community Hospital] Consultant's Report, dated [7/29/91] (2 pages).

127: [Palos Community Hospital] Consultant's Report, dated [7/31/91] (3 pages).

128: [Palos Community Hospital] Consultant's Report, dated [8/2/91] (1 page).

129: [Palos Community Hospital] Report of Examination, dated [7/29/91] (1 page).

130: [Palos Community Hospital] Report of Examination, dated [7/30/91] (1 page).

131: [Palos Community Hospital] Report of Examination, dated [7/31/91] (1 page).

132: [Palos Community Hospital] Report of Examination, dated [8/1/91] (1 page).

133: [Palos Community Hospital] Report of Examination, dated [8/2/91] (1 page).

134: [Palos Community Hospital] Report of Examination, dated [7/31/91] (1 page).

135: [Palos Community Hospital] Report of Examination, dated [8/3/91] (1 page).

136: [Palos Community Hospital] Report of Examination, dated [8/4/91] (1 page).

137: [Palos Community Hospital] Report of Examination, dated [8/6/91] (1 page).

138: [Palos Community Hospital] Report of Examination, dated [8/7/91] (1 page).

139: [Palos Community Hospital] Report of Examination, dated [8/8/91] (1 page).

140: [Palos Community Hospital] Report of Examination, dated [8/9/91] (1 page).

141: [Intermed Oncology Associates] List of appointments and billings, dated [8/26/87] to [11/5/91] (27 pages).

142: [Intermed Oncology Associates] List of appointments and billings, dated [12/30/91] to [2/25/92] (5 pages).

143: [South Suburban Hospital] Discharge Summary, dated [12/27/87] (1 page).

144: [South Suburban Hospital] History and Physical, dated [12/31/87] (1 page).

145: [Dr. G.]'s Radiology Report, dated [8/3/88] (1 page).

146: [Dr. G.]'s Radiology Report, dated [3/6/89] (1 page).

147: [South Suburban Hospital] Consultation Report, dated [10/18/87] (2 pages).

148: Letter to Dr. [B] from [Wessel] dated [10/22/91] (1 page).

149: [Illinois] Bureau of Disability Determination Services Letter to Dr. [B], dated [8/11/92] (3 pages).

150: [Illinois] Bureau of Disability Determination Services, Neoplasm Report, dated [8/24/92] (1 page).

151: Letter to Dr. [B] from [Wessel], dated [9/27/92] (1 page).

152: Memorandum to Dr. [B] from [Wessel], dated [9/27/92] (3 pages).

153: Letter from Dr. [B] to Whom It May Concern, dated [9/2/92] (1 page).

154: [Palos Community Hospital] Report of Examination, dated [6/29/92] (1 page).

155: [Palos Community Hospital] Admission History, dated [9/27/88] (1 page).

156: [Palos Community Hospital] Admission History, dated [7/29/91] (1 page).

157: [Wessel] Medical Notes, dated [2/19/89] (1 page).

158: [Loyola University Hospital] Outpatient Registration, dated [8/24/91] (1 page).

159: [Loyola University Hospital] Provisional Discharge Summary, dated [10/18/91] (1 page).

160: [Loyola University Hospital] Examination Report, dated [11/26/91] (1 page).

161: [Loyola University Hospital] Examination Report, dated [9/23/91] (1 page).

162: Letter from Dr. [G] to Dr. [A], dated [8/29/91] (1 page).

163: [Loyola University Hospital] [Wessel] Patient Record, dated [10/3/91] (2 pages).

164: [Loyola University Hospital] Admission — Discharge Record, dated [10/3/91] (1 page).

165: [Loyola University Hospital] Discharge Summary, dated [10/18/91] (1 page).

166: [Loyola University Hospital] Pulmonary Function Report, dated [9/5/91] (1 page).

167: [Loyola University Hospital] Final Report, dated [10/3/91] (1 page).

168: [Loyola University Hospital] Final Report, dated [10/4/91] (1 page).

169: [Loyola University Hospital] Final Report, dated [10/5/91] (1 page).

170: [Loyola University Hospital] Final Report, dated [10/6/91] (1 page).

171: [Loyola University Hospital] Final Report, dated [10/7/91] (1 page).

172: [Loyola University Hospital] Final Report, dated [10/8/91] (2 pages).

173: [Loyola University Hospital] Final Report, dated [10/9/91] (1 page).

174: [Loyola University Hospital] Final Report, dated [10/10/91] (1 page).

175: [Loyola University Hospital] Final Report, dated [10/11/91] (1 page).

176: [Loyola University Hospital] Patient Database, dated [10/3/91] (4 pages).

177: [Loyola University Hospital] Discharge Medication Schedule, dated [10/3/91] (1 page).

178: Letter to [Charles Wessel] from [Vince G.], dated [1/29/92] (1 page).

179: Letter to [Vince G.] from [Charles Wessel], dated [1/27/92] (1 page).

180: Letter to [Charles Wessel] from [Phyllis M.], dated [11/23/92] (1 page).

181: Determination of Unemployment Insurance Benefits to [Wessel], dated [1/16/93] (1 page).

182: Letter from [Unum] to [Wessel], dated [1/5/93] (1 page).

183: Letter to [A.I.C. attorney B] from Dr. [M], dated [1/18/93] (2 pages).

184: Letter to [A.I.C. attorney B] from Dr. [M], dated [2/8/93] (1 page).

185: Letter to [A.I.C. attorney B] from Dr. [L], dated [2/10/93] (2 pages).

186: Notes of Dr. [M], undated (1 page).

187: Updated Curriculum Vitae of Dr. [M], undated (4 pages).

188: Curriculum Vitae of Dr. [M], undated (4 pages).

189: Curriculum Vitae of Dr. [L], undated (12 pages).

190: Letter to [defendant C] from [Richard F.], dated [8/4/92] (1 page).

191: [Advocare] Bill to [Guardian] Insurance Company, dated [9/1/92] (1 page).

192: [Advocare] Memorandum to Attorneys for [Wessel], dated [11/16/92] (1 page).

193: [Advocare] Initial Report, dated [12/13/91] (5 pages).

194: [Advocare] Letter to [Alice Wessel], dated [12/11/91] (1 page).

195: [Advocare] Provider Agreement, dated [1/3/92] (1 page).

196: [Advocare] Bill to [Guardian] Insurance Company, dated [10/30/91] to [12/16/91] (1 page).

197: [Advocare] Interim Report, dated [9/1/92] (2 pages).

198: [Shay Health] Care Services Letter to [Wessel], dated [12/12/91] (1 page).

199: [Shay Health] Carrier Inquiry Sheet, dated [12/12/91] (1 page).

200: [Shay Health] Home Health Certification and Plan of Treatment, dated [10/18/91] (1 page).

201: [Shay Health] Progress Notes, dated [11/1/92] to [12/12/92] (6 pages).

202: [Loyola University Hospital] Community Nursing Referral Form, undated (2 pages).

203: [Shay Health] Nurses' Notes, dated [10/18/91] to [10/22/91] (4 pages).

204: [Shay Health] Admit Note, dated [10/18/91] (1 page).

205: [Shay Health] Patient Assessment Form, dated [10/18/91] (8 pages).

206: Medicine List and Times, dated [4/27/92] (1 page).

207: Medicine List and Times, dated [8/4/92] (1 page).

208: Medical Information List for [Wessel], dated [10/26/92] (4 pages).

209: Telephone Notes of [Janice D.], undated, and Fax Cover Sheet, dated [1/22/93] (2 pages).

210: Letter to [Judy A.] from [Wessel], dated [9/7/92] (1 page).

211: Fax Transmittal Sheet from [Wessel] to [A.I.C. attorney D], dated [9/13/90] (1 page).

212: EEOC Initial Determination, dated [9/10/92] (2 pages).

213: EEOC Charge of Discrimination, dated [8/3/92] (1 page).

214: Letter to [Wessel] from [Judy A.], dated [9/3/92] (1 page).

215: [Wessel] EEOC Affidavit, dated [8/11/92] (4 pages).

216: List of General Accommodations Given to [Wessel], undated (2 pages).

217: Statement of [defendant C], dated [9/8/92] (5 pages).

218: Letter to [John R.] from [Lawrence R.], dated [8/20/92] (1 page).

219: Signed EEOC Affidavit of [Ken B.] (1 page).

220: Unsigned EEOC Affidavit of [Ken B.] (1 page).

221: Unsigned EEOC Affidavit of Dr. [B] (1 page).

222: Signed EEOC Affidavit of Dr. [B] (1 page).

223: Memo to [Larry R.] from [Charles B.], dated [9/1/92] (1 page).

224: Medicine List and Times, dated [7/20/92] (1 page).

225: Memo to [Larry R.] from [Ed B.], dated [9/2/92] (1 page).

226: Memo to [Larry R.] from [Jan D.], dated [9/2/92] (2 pages).

227: Letter to [Daniel M.] from [Lawrence R.].

228: Handwritten Letter to [David P.] from [Judy A.], dated [9/10/92] (3 pages).

229: Handwritten Statements of [Wessel], undated (5 pages).

230: EEOC Interview Notes of [Wessel], dated [8/1/92] (9 pages).

231: EEOC Interview Notes of [Wessel], undated (13 pages).

232: Draft Affidavit of Dr. [B], undated (1 page).

233: Draft EEOC Charge of Discrimination of [Wessel], undated (1 page).

234: Handwritten EEOC Affidavit of [Wessel] with Attachments, undated (6 pages).

235: Draft Affidavit of [Ken B.] and Facsimile Cover Sheets of EEOC and [Premisys Real Estate Services, Inc.], dated [9/10/92] (4 pages).

236: Facsimile Cover Sheet and Letter to Dr. [B] from [Judy A.], dated [9/2/92] (2 pages).

237: [A.I.C. International, Ltd.] Drug and Alcohol Abuse Policy, undated (3 pages).

238: [A.I.C. International, Ltd.] Drug Free Awareness Program, undated (1 page).

239: [A.I.C. International, Ltd.] AIDS Policy, undated (2 pages).

240: [A.I.C. International, Ltd.] Drug and Alcohol Abuse Policy and Procedures for Applicants (2 pages).

241: [A.I.C. International, Ltd.] Drug and Alcohol Abuse Policy and Procedures for Employees, undated (5 pages).

242: Memo to [A.I.C. International, Ltd.] from [law firm] re: Drug Free Workplace Act Obligations.

243: Life Threatening Illness Policy, dated [1/1/90] (1 page).

244: Facsimile Cover Sheet and Attachments from [Wessel] to [A.I.C. attorney D], dated [9/10/90] (7 pages).

245: Letter from Social Security Administration to [Wessel], dated [9/8/92] (3 pages).

246: [Wessel]'s W-2 Wage and Tax Statements for [1992] from [Unum] Insurance Company (1 page).

247: [IDES] Benefit Payment Stub and Explanation, dated [12/12/92] to [1 /2/93] (2 pages).

248: [Wessel]'s Personal Automobile Policy Premium Statements, dated [3/ 12/92], [6/17/92], [9/12/92] (3 pages).

249: EEOC Case Log, Charge No. [210922899], dated [8/3/92] to [9/10/ 92] (2 pages).

250: Memorandum to [Beverly K.] from [Wessel], dated [7/21/92] (1 page).

251: Memorandum to [David P.] from [Wessel], dated [2/6/91] (1 page).

252: Memorandum to [David P.] from [Wessel] re: Drug-Free Workplace Policy, dated [9/18/90] (1 page).

253: Memo to [David P.] from [Wessel] re: Vacation, dated [5/8/90] (1 page).

254: Vacation/Day Off Requisition of [Wessel], dated [5/7/90] (1 page).

255: Memo to [David P.] from [Wessel] re: Medical Checkup, dated [1/27/ 88] (1 page).

256: Memo to [David P.] from [Wessel], dated [7/18/86] (1 page).

257: Letter to [A.I.C. attorney B] from [A.I.C. attorney D] re: [Wessel]'s Answers to Defendants' First Set of Interrogatories to Plaintiff [Wessel], dated [2 /15/93] (14 pages).

258: Plaintiff [Wessel]'s Responses to Defendants' First Set of Interrogatories (24 pages).

259: List of [Wessel]'s Assets (3 pages).

260: [Randall Wessel]'s Notes re: _____ [8/3/92] (4 pages).

261: Resume Questionnaire of [Wessel], dated [8/16/92] (6 pages).

262: [Wessel] Resume List, dated [8/6/92] to [10/22/92] (3 pages).

263: Resume of [Wessel], undated (2 pages).

264: EEOC's Answers to Defendants' First Set of Interrogatories to Plaintiff EEOC, dated [12/4/92] (18 pages).

265: Letter to [Wessel] from [Phil W.], dated [8/12/92] (1 page).

266: Letter to [Wessel] from [Phil W.], dated [8/20/92] (1 page).

267: [Wessel]'s [1991] Income Tax Return with Attachments (14 pages).

268: [Wessel]'s [1990] Income Tax Return with Attachments (9 pages).

269: [Wessel]'s [1989] Income Tax Return with Attachments (6 pages).

270: [Wessel]'s [1988] Income Tax Return with Attachments (7 pages).

271: [Wessel]'s [1987] Income Tax Return with Attachments (14 pages).

272: Medicine List as of [11/21/92] (1 page).

273: Description Notes of Dental Work Performed on [Wessel] (7 pages).

274: [Wessel] Resume ([1984]) (2 pages).

275: [Wessel] Application for Employment, dated [2/19/86] (5 pages).

276: [Shay Health] Care Services Notes re: Habits and Behavior, undated (1 page).

277: [Wessel] Resume Draft ([1992]) (3 pages).

278: Letter to [David P.] from [Jack H.], dated [3/3/92] (1 page).

279: [A.I.C. International, Ltd.] and Subsidiaries Consolidated Financial Statements, Year Ended [7/31/86] (13 pages).

280: [A.I.C. International, Ltd.] and Subsidiaries Consolidated Financial Statements, Year Ended [7/31/87] (14 pages).

281: [A.I.C. International, Ltd.] and Subsidiaries Consolidated Financial Statements, Year Ended [7/31/89] (12 pages).

282: [A.I.C. International, Ltd.] and Subsidiaries Consolidated Financial Statements, Year Ended [7/31/91] (9 pages).

283: [A.I.C. International, Ltd.] and Subsidiaries Consolidated Financial Statements, Year Ended [7/31/92] (11 pages).

284: Statement of [Lawrence R.], dated [9/4/92] (5 pages).

285: Memo to [Phil W.] from [Wessel], dated [7/24/92] (1 page).

286: Memo to [Phil W.] from [Wessel], dated [7/27/92] (1 page).

287: EEOC Telephone Interview Notes of Conversation with Dr. [A], dated [8/25/92] (1 page).

288: EEOC Telephone Notes of Conversation with Dr. [B], dated [8/25/92] (1 page).

289: [Local 73] Wage/Revenue Spreadsheet, dated [7/7/92] (2 pages).

290: [A.I.C. Security Investigations, Ltd.] List of Duties of Executive Director [1986]–[1992] (2 pages).

291: [A.I.C. Security Investigations, Ltd.] List of Reassignment of Duties [1987]–[1992] (7 pages).

292: Memo to [Larry R.] from [R.E.B.] and [Jan D.], dated [8/28/92] (2 pages).

293: [Illinois] Bureau of Disability Determination Services, Signed Records Request to [SWC Cancer Center], dated [8/11/92] (1 page).

294: [Shay Health] Care Services Nurses' Notes, dated [10/18/91] to [10/22/91] (4 pages).

295: List of [Wessel]'s Health Care Providers, dated [10/20/92] (4 pages).

296: EEOC Intake Questionnaire, dated [8/3/92] (1 page).

297: List of Medicine and Doctors, undated (1 page).

298: Handwritten Note to [EEOC attorney A] from [Judy A.], re: [Ken B.], dated [9/9/92] (3 pages).

299: Notes of [Judy A.], dated [8/13/92] (3 pages).

300: [Unum] Disability Insurance Policy (23 pages).

301: [Guardian] Group Health Insurance Policy (83 pages).

302: Memo from [David P.] to All Employees, dated [1/1/89] (3 pages).

303: Moving Violation Driving Citation [Wessel] Received in [1992] (referred to in [Wessel]'s second deposition).

Defendants reserve the right to introduce as exhibits additional medical records regarding [Charles Wessel] obtained after the time period encompassed in his health care providers' responses to previous discovery subpoenas served in late [1992]. Defendants also reserve the right to introduce exhibits in rebuttal.

SCHEDULE C-5

DEFENDANTS' EXHIBITS TO WHICH PLAINTIFFS DO NOT OBJECT

Exhibit 152: Memorandum to Dr. [B] from [Wessel], dated [4/27/92].

Exhibit 153: Letter from Dr. [B] to Whom It May Concern, dated [9/2/92].

Exhibit 181: Determination of Unemployment Insurance Benefits to [Wessel], dated [1/16/93].

Exhibit 185: Letter to [A.I.C. attorney B] from Dr. [L], dated [2/10/93].
Exhibit 188: Curriculum Vitae of Dr. [M].
Exhibit 189: Curriculum Vitae of Dr. [L].
Exhibit 206: Medicine List and Times, dated [4/27/92].
Exhibit 207: Medicine List and Times, dated [8/4/92].

Plaintiffs do not object to admission of evidence concerning [Wessel]'s health after [July 31, 1993], for the limited purpose of determining whether he remained able to work and is, therefore, entitled to backpay for the period.

Exhibit 208: Medical Information List for [Wessel], dated [10/6/92].
See qualification to admission of Exhibit 207.

Exhibit 210: Letter to [Judy A.] from [Wessel], dated [9/7/92].
Exhibit 212: EEOC Letter of Determination, dated [9/10/92].
Exhibit 213: EEOC Charge of Discrimination, dated [8/3/92].
Exhibit 215: [Wessel] EEOC Affidavit, dated [8/11/92].
Exhibit 224: Medicine List and Times, dated [7/20/92].
Exhibit 229: Handwritten Statement of [Wessel].
Exhibit 230: EEOC Interview Notes of [Wessel], dated [8/11/92].
Exhibit 231: EEOC Interview Notes of [Wessel].
Exhibit 233: Draft EEOC Charge of Discrimination of [Wessel].
Exhibit 234: Handwritten EEOC Affidavit of [Wessel] with Attachments. (Plaintiffs anticipate no objection but are unable to identify the attachments.)
Exhibit 246: [Wessel]'s W-2 Statements for [1992].
Exhibit 250: Memorandum to [Beverly K.] from [Chuck Wessel], dated [7/21/92].
Exhibit 251: Memorandum to [David P.] from [Chuck Wessel], dated [2/6/91].
Exhibit 253: Memo from [Wessel] to [David P.] re: Vacation, dated [5/8/90].
Exhibit 254: Vacation/Day Off Requisition of [Wessel], dated [7/18/86].
Exhibit 255: Memo to [David P.] from [Wessel] re: medical checkup, dated [1/27/88].
Exhibit 256: Memo to [David P.] from [Wessel], dated [7/18/86].
Exhibit 260: [Randall Wessel]'s Notes, dated [8/30/92].
Exhibit 261: Resume Questionnaire of [Wessel], dated [8/16/92].
Exhibit 262: [Wessel] Resume List, dated [8/6/92].
Exhibit 263: Resume of [Wessel].
Exhibit 265: Letter to [Wessel] from [Phil W.], dated [8/12/92].
Exhibit 266: Letter to [Wessel] from [Phil W.], dated [8/20/92].
Exhibit 272: Medicine List as of [11/21/92].
See qualification to admission of Exhibit 207.

Exhibit 274: [Wessel] Resume ([1984]).
Exhibit 275: [Wessel] Application for Employment, dated [2/6/86].
Exhibit 277: [Wessel] Resume Draft ([1992]).
Exhibit 279: [A.I.C. International, Ltd.] and Subsidiaries Consolidated Financial Statements, Year Ended [7/31/86].

Exhibit 280: [A.I.C. International, Ltd.] and Subsidiaries Consolidated Financial Statements, Year Ended [7/31/87].

Exhibit 281: [A.I.C. International, Ltd.] and Subsidiaries Consolidated Financial Statements, Year Ended [7/31/89].

Exhibit 282: [A.I.C. International, Ltd.] and Subsidiaries Consolidated Financial Statements, Year Ended [7/31/91].

Exhibit 283: [A.I.C. International, Ltd.] and Subsidiaries Consolidated Financial Statements, Year Ended [7/31/92].

Exhibit 285: Memo to [Phil W.] from [Wessel], dated [7/24/92].

Exhibit 286: Memo to [Phil W.] from [Wessel], dated [7/27/92].

Exhibit 289: [Local 73] Wage/Revenue Spreadsheet, dated [7/7/92].

Exhibit 295: List of [Wessel]'s Health Care Providers, dated [10/20/92]. See qualification to admission of Exhibit 207.

Exhibit 296: EEOC Intake Questionnaire.

Exhibit 297: List of Medicine and Doctors. See Qualification to Admission of Exhibit 207.

Exhibit 300: [Unum] Disability Insurance Policy.

Exhibit 301: [Guardian] Group Health Insurance Policy.

Exhibit 302: Memo from [David P.] to All Employees, dated [1/1/90].

SCHEDULE C-6

DEFENDANTS' EXHIBITS TO WHICH PLAINTIFFS OBJECT, WITH PLAINTIFFS' OBJECTIONS NOTED

Exhibits 1–8: Documents from Social Security Administration File

Plaintiffs object to the Exhibit(s) because the documents submitted to the agency and the proceedings and actions of the agency are pursuant to statutes, rules, and/or regulations different from those applicable to the Plaintiffs' claims herein. If the Court allows Defendants to offer the agency documents into evidence, the entire file contents should be admitted with the limiting instruction requested by Plaintiffs.

Exhibit 9–16: Documents from [South Suburban Hospital]

Plaintiffs object because documents are incomplete. If Defendants offer the entire [South Suburban] file, Plaintiffs will withdraw their objection.

Exhibit 17–22: Documents from [Loyola Hospital]

Plaintiffs object because documents are incomplete. If Defendants offer the entire [Loyola Hospital] file, Plaintiffs will withdraw their objection.

Exhibits 23–33: Documents from [Illinois] Bureau of Disability Determination

Plaintiffs object to the Exhibit(s) because the documents submitted to the agency and the proceedings and actions of the agency are pursuant to statutes, rules, and/or regulations different from those applicable to the Plaintiffs' claims herein. If the Court allows Defendants to offer the agency documents into evidence, the entire file contents should be admitted with the limiting instruction requested by Plaintiffs.

Exhibits 34–35: Documents from [Susan L.], M.D., [Southwest Head and Neck Surgical Association]

Plaintiffs object because documents arc incomplete. If Defendants offer the entire file from [Susan L.], M.D., [Southwest Head and Neck Surgical Association], Plaintiffs will withdraw their objection.

Exhibits 36–61: Documents from [Dependicare]

Plaintiffs object because the documents are incomplete. If Defendants offer the entire file from [Dependicare], Plaintiffs will withdraw their objection.

Exhibits 62–84: Documents from Dr. [A], [Southwest Cancer Center]

Plaintiffs object because the documents are incomplete. If Defendants offer the entire file from Dr. [A], [Southwest Cancer Center], Plaintiffs will withdraw their objection.

Exhibits 85–88: Documents from [Craig A.], M.D.

Plaintiffs object because the documents are incomplete. If Defendants offer the entire file from [Dr. Craig A.], Plaintiffs will withdraw their objection.

Exhibits 89–102: Documents from [Unum]

Plaintiffs object because the documents are incomplete. If Defendants offer the entire file from [Unum], Plaintiffs will withdraw their objection.

Exhibits 103–109: Documents from [South Suburban Hospital]

Plaintiffs object because the documents are incomplete. If Defendants offer the entire file from [South Suburban Hospital], Plaintiffs will withdraw their objection.

Exhibits 110–140: Documents from [Palos Hospital]

Plaintiffs object because the documents are incomplete. If Defendants offer the entire file from [Palos Hospital], Plaintiffs will withdraw their objection.

Exhibits 141–151 and 154–157: Documents from Dr. [B], M.D., [Intermed Oncology Associates, P.C.]

Plaintiffs object because the documents are incomplete. If Defendants offer the entire file from Dr. [B], [Intermed Oncology Associates, P.C.], Plaintiffs will withdraw their objection.

Exhibits 158–177: Documents from [Loyola University Hospital]

Plaintiffs object because the documents are incomplete. If Defendants offer the entire file from [Loyola University Hospital], Plaintiffs will withdraw the objection.

Exhibit 178: Letter to [Charles Wessel] from [Vince G.], dated [1/29/92]

Plaintiffs object to the extent that the document is intended to support the contention that [Wessel] was unable to perform the essential or the marginal functions of his position. The document was not disclosed in response to EEOC's First Request for Production of Documents, Request Nos. 10 and 11, which asked for all documents supporting such contentions. Defendants answered that no such documents existed. Plaintiffs also object to lack of foundation.

Exhibit 179: Letter to [Vince G.] from [Charles Wessel], dated [1/7/92]

Plaintiffs object for the reasons set forth in Objection to Exhibit 178. Plaintiffs also object to lack of foundation.

Exhibit 180: Letter to [Charles Wessel] from [Phyllis M.], dated [11/23/92]

Plaintiffs object for the reasons set forth in Objection to Exhibit 178. Plaintiffs also object to lack of foundation.

Exhibit 182: Letter from [Unum] to [Wessel], dated [1/5/93]

Objection — *See* Objection to Exhibits 89–102.

Exhibit 183: Letter to [attorney B] from Dr. [M], dated [1/18/93]

Objection — Hearsay.

Exhibit 184: Letter to [attorney B] from Dr. [M], dated [2/8/93]

Objection — Hearsay.

Exhibit 186: Notes of Dr. [M], undated

Objection — Hearsay.

Exhibit 187: Undated Curriculum Vitae of Dr. [M].

Objection — Duplicative of Exhibit 190.

Exhibit 190: Letter to [defendant C] from [Richard F.], dated [8/4/92]

Plaintiffs object for the reasons set forth in Objection to Exhibit 178. Plaintiffs also object to lack of foundation.

Exhibits 191–197: Documents from [Advocare] file

Plaintiffs object because the documents are incomplete. If Defendants offer the entire file from [Advocare], Plaintiffs will withdraw their objection.

Exhibits 198–205: Documents from [Shay Health] Care Services

Plaintiffs object because the documents are incomplete. If Defendants offer the entire file from [Shay Health] Care Services, Plaintiffs will withdraw their objection.

Exhibit 209: Telephone Note of [Janice D.], undated, and Fax Cover Sheet, dated [1/22/93]

Objection — Hearsay.

Exhibit 211: Fax Transmittal Sheet from [Wessel] to [A.I.C. attorney D], dated [9/13/90]

Objection — Relevance. *See also* Objection to Exhibit 178.

Exhibit 214: Letter to [Wessel] from [Judy A.], dated [9/3/92]

Objections — Hearsay, Relevance.

Exhibit 216: List of General Accommodations Given to [Wessel]

Objection — Hearsay.

Exhibit 217: Statement of [defendant C], dated [9/8/92]

Objection — Hearsay.

Exhibit 218: Letter to [John R.] from [Lawrence R.]

Objection — Hearsay.

Exhibit 219: Signed EEOC Affidavit of [Ken B.]

Objection — Hearsay.

Exhibit 220: Unsigned EEOC Affidavit of [Ken B.]

Objection — Hearsay.

Exhibit 221: Unsigned EEOC Affidavit of Dr. [B]

Objections — Hearsay, Relevance.

Exhibit 222: Signed EEOC Affidavit of Dr. [B]

Objection — Hearsay.

Exhibit 223: Memo from [Larry R.] to [Charles B.], dated [9/1/92]

Objection — Hearsay.

Exhibit 225: Memo to [Larry R.] from [Ed B.], dated [9/2/92]

Objection — Hearsay.

Exhibit 226: Memo to [Larry R.] from [Jan D.], dated [9/2/92]

Objection — Hearsay.

Exhibit 227: Letter to [Daniel M.] from [Lawrence R.]

Objection — Hearsay.

Exhibit 228: Letter to [David P]. from [Judy A.], dated [9/10/92]

Objections — Hearsay, Relevance.

Exhibit 232: Draft Affidavit of Dr. [B]

Objections — Hearsay, Relevance.

Exhibit 235: Draft Affidavit of [Ken B.] and Facsimile Cover Sheets, dated [9/10/92]

Objections — Hearsay, Relevance.

Exhibit 236: Facsimile Cover Sheet and Letter to Dr. [B] from [Judy A.], dated [9/2/92]

Objections — Hearsay, Relevance.

Exhibit 237: [A.I.C. International, Ltd.] Drug and Alcohol Abuse Policy

Objection for the reasons set forth in Objection to Exhibit 178; objection to relevance.

Exhibit 238: [A.I.C. International, Ltd.] Drug Free Awareness Program

Objection for the reasons set forth in Objection to Exhibit 178; objection to relevance.

Exhibit 239: [A.I.C. International, Ltd.] AIDS Policy

Objection for the reasons set forth in Objection to Exhibit 178; objection to relevance.

Exhibit 240: [A.I.C. International, Ltd.] Drug and Alcohol Abuse Policy and Procedures for Applicants

Objection for the reasons set forth in Objection to Exhibit 178; objection to relevance.

Exhibit 241: [A.I.C. International, Ltd.] Drug and Alcohol Abuse Policy and Procedures for Employees

Objection for the reasons set forth in Objection to Exhibit 178; objection to relevance.

Exhibit 242: Memo to [A.I.C. International, Ltd.] from [Lindquist & Vennum] re: Drug Free Workplace Act Obligations

Objection for the reasons set forth in Objection to Exhibit 178; objection to relevance.

Exhibit 243: Life-Threatening Illness Policy, dated [1/1/90]

Objection for the reasons set forth in Objection to Exhibit 178; objection to relevance.

Exhibit 244: Facsimile Cover Sheet and Attachments from [Wessel] to [A.I.C. attorney D], dated [9/10/90]

Objection for the reasons set forth in Objection to Exhibit 178; objection to relevance.

Exhibit 245: Letter from Social Security Administration to [Wessel], dated [9/8/92]

Plaintiffs object to the Exhibit because the document submitted to the agency and the proceedings and actions of the agency are pursuant to statutes, rules, and /or regulations different from those applicable to the Plaintiffs' claims herein. If the Court allows Defendants to offer the agency document into evidence, the entire file contents should be admitted with the limiting instruction requested by Plaintiffs.

Exhibit 247: [IDES] Benefit Payment Stub and Explanation

Objection — Relevance.

Exhibit 248: [Wessel]'s Personal Automobile Policy Premium Statements

Objection — Relevance.

Exhibit 249: EEOC's Case Log, Charge No. [210922899]

Objections — Hearsay, Relevance.

Exhibit 252: Memorandum to [David P.] from [Wessel] re: Drug-Free Workplace Policy

Objection for the reasons set forth in Objection to Exhibit 178; objection to relevance.

Exhibit 257: Letter to [A.I.C. attorney B] from [A.I.C. attorney D] re: [Wessel]'s Answer to Defendants' First Set of Interrogatories to Plaintiff [Wessel], dated [2/15/93]

Objection — Relevance.

Exhibit 258: Plaintiff [Wessel]'s Responses to Defendants' First Set of Interrogatories

Objection — Relevance.

Exhibit 259: List of [Wessel]'s Assets

Objection — Relevance.

Exhibit 264: EEOC's Answers to Defendants' First Set of Interrogatories, dated [12/4/92]

Objection — Relevance.

Exhibit 267: [Wessel]'s [1991] Income Tax Return with Attachments

Objection — Relevance.

Exhibit 268: [Wessel]'s [1990] Income Tax Return with Attachments

Objection — Relevance.

Exhibit 269: [Wessel]'s [1989] Income Tax Return with Attachments

Objection — Relevance.

Exhibit 270: [Wessel]'s [1988] Income Tax Return with Attachments

Objection — Relevance.

Exhibit 271: [Wessel]'s [1987] Income Tax Return with Attachments

Objection — Relevance.

Exhibit 273: Description Notes of Dental Work Performed on [Wessel]

Objection — Relevance.

Exhibit 276: [Shay Health] Care Services Notes re: Habits and Behavior

Plaintiffs object because the documents are incomplete. If Defendants offer the entire file from [Shay Health] Care Services, Plaintiffs will withdraw their objection.

Exhibit 278: Letter to [David P.] from [Jack H., dated [3/3/92]

Objection — Hearsay, lack of foundation. *See also* Exhibit 178.

Exhibit 284: Statement of [Lawrence R.], dated [9/4/92]

Objection — Hearsay.

Exhibit 287: EEOC Telephone Interview Notes of Conversation with Dr. [A]

Objection — Hearsay.

Exhibit 288: EEOC Telephone Notes of Conversation with Dr. [B], dated [8/25/92]

Objection — Hearsay.

Exhibit 290: [A.I.C. Security Investigations, Ltd.] List of Duties of Executive Director, [1986]–[1992]

Objection — Hearsay.

Exhibit 291: [A.I.C. Security Investigations, Ltd.] List of Reassignment of Duties, [1987]–[1992]

Objection — Hearsay.

Exhibit 292: Memo to [Larry R.] from [R.E.B.] and [Jan D.], dated [8/28/92]

Objection — Hearsay.

Exhibit 293: [Illinois] Bureau of Disability Determination Services, Signed Records Request to [SWC Cancer Center], dated [8/11/92]

Plaintiffs object to the Exhibit(s) because the documents submitted to the agency and the proceedings and actions of the agency are pursuant to statutes, rules, and/or regulations different from those applicable to the Plaintiffs' claims herein. If the Court allows Defendants to offer the agency documents into evidence, the entire file contents should be admitted with the limiting instruction requested by Plaintiffs.

Exhibit 294: [Shay Health] Care Services Nurses' Notes, dated [10/18/91]–[10/22/91]

Plaintiffs object because the documents are incomplete. If Defendants offer the entire file from the [Shay Health] Care Services, Plaintiffs will withdraw their objection.

Exhibit 298: Handwritten Note to [EEOC attorney A] from [Judy A.] re: [Ken B.], dated [9/9/92]

Objections — Hearsay, Relevance.

Exhibit 299: Notes of [Judy A.], dated [8/13/92]

Objections — Hearsay, Relevance.

Exhibit 303: Moving Violation Driving Citation [Wessel] Received in [1992]

Plaintiff objects to admission of any documents not identified by number in this order that have not been produced to Plaintiffs.

SCHEDULE D WITNESSES

SCHEDULE D-1

PART I

PLAINTIFFS' LIST OF NAMES AND ADDRESSES OF POTENTIAL WITNESSES TO BE CALLED

Plaintiffs will call as witnesses the following persons:

[names and addresses of witnesses]

Plaintiffs may call as witnesses:

[names and addresses of witnesses]

Plaintiff [Wessel] may call as witnesses:

[names and addresses of witnesses]

Plaintiffs expect to call as a rebuttal witness:

[name and address of witness]

Plaintiffs reserve the right to call any witness named by Defendants and additional witnesses for purposes of impeachment and/or rebuttal.

SCHEDULE D-1

PART 2

DEFENDANTS' OBJECTIONS TO THE CALLING OR TO THE QUALIFICATIONS OF PLAINTIFFS' WITNESSES

1. It appears from Plaintiffs' List of Witnesses that Plaintiffs are waiving their right to call at trial Dr. [C]. To the extent Plaintiffs attempt to call Dr. [C] at trial (for rebuttal or otherwise), Defendants object for reasons stated in Defendants' Motion to Exclude Expert Witness.

SCHEDULE D-2

PART I

DEFENDANTS' LIST OF NAMES AND ADDRESSES OF POTENTIAL WITNESSES TO BE CALLED

Witnesses Defendants will call at trial:

[names and addresses of witnesses]

Witnesses Defendants may call at trial:

[names and addresses of witnesses]

Defendants reserve the right to call additional witnesses in rebuttal and/or to verify the authenticity of documents listed in Schedule C-6.

SCHEDULE D-2

PART 2

PLAINTIFFS' OBJECTIONS TO THE CALLING OR TO THE QUALIFICA-
TIONS OF DEFENDANTS' WITNESSES

Plaintiffs object to the calling of [Scott M.] because he was not identified by
Defendants as a person with knowledge of the reasons for [Charles Wessel]'s termination in Defendants' answer to EEOC's First Set of Interrogatories, No. 3.

Plaintiffs object to calling any witness to authenticate documents where Plaintiffs have not challenged authenticity.

[names and addresses of witnesses]

SCHEDULE E STIPULATION OF QUALIFICATIONS OF EXPERT WIT-
NESSES

SCHEDULE E-1

PLAINTIFFS' PROPOSED STIPULATED QUALIFICATIONS OF EXPERTS

[Dr. B] is a doctor of medicine specializing in treatment of cancer patients.
He received his M.D. at [name] Medical College in [location] in the year [1963].
He served an internship at [name] Hospital during the years [1965]–[1966]. He
performed a residency in the field of internal medicine at [name] Hospital between
[1966] and [1968]. He performed a residency in the field of hematology at the
[name] Clinic in [city, state] from [1969]–[1971]. In [1971] he was an assistant
professor of medicine at the [name] Medical School of the University of [city].

Dr. [B] has been certified as a specialist in internal medicine by the American
Board of Internal Medicine since [1972], as a specialist in hematology by the
American Board of Hematology since [1972], and in oncology, that is, the field of
cancer treatment, by the American Board of Oncology since [1975].

Dr. [B] has engaged in the private practice of medicine since [1971]. He has
specialized in treatment of cancer patients since [1975]. He is affiliated with [name]
Hospital in [city, state]; with [name] Hospital in [city, state]; with [name] Hospital
in [city, state]; and with [name] Hospital in [city, state].

Dr. [B] has been [Mr. Wessel]'s primary treating physician since [July 1987].
The substance of Dr. [B]'s testimony is that [Mr. Wessel]'s disability did not significantly interfere with his mental abilities, and that he was able to perform the
essential functions of his position as Executive Director.

Dr. [A] is a doctor of medicine specializing in radiation treatment of cancer
patients. She obtained her medical degree from the University of [city], in [coun-
try], in the year [1972]. She served as a resident at the [name] Hospital from [1974]
though [1977] and at the University of [city] Medical Center from [1977] through
[1978].

Dr. [A] has been certified as a specialist in the fields of radiology and radiation
oncology by the American Board of Radiology and Radiation Oncology since

[1978]. *Radiation oncology* is the branch of oncology that treats cancer patients with radiation treatments, as opposed to medical oncology, which treats cancer patients with chemotherapy.

Between [1978] and [1990] Dr. [A] practiced at the [name] Medical Center and acted as a consultant at several hospitals in that area. Since [1990] Dr. [A] has participated in a group practice at [firm name], providing radiation treatments for patients at [name] Hospital and [name] Hospital.

Dr. [A] has provided radiation treatments to [Mr. Wessel] since [April 1992]. The substance of Dr. [A]'s testimony is that [Mr. Wessel]'s disability and treatment did not significantly interfere with his mental abilities and that he was able to perform the essential functions of his position as Executive Director.

SCHEDULE E-2

STATEMENT OF QUALIFICATIONS OF DEFENDANTS' EXPERT WITNESSES

Defendants will call as an expert witness [Larry S. M.], M.D., a doctor who specializes in the treatment of cancer patients. [Dr. M.] is a board-certified oncologist, hematologist, and doctor of internal medicine. [Dr. M.] received his undergraduate and medical school training from the University of [state] and in [1966] graduated from [name] Medical School with high honors. From [1966] to [1968] [Dr. M.] worked as an intern and resident at the University of [state] Hospital in [city]. [Dr. M.] then went on to conduct research at [name] Institute in [city, state] from [1968] to [1970]. From [1970] to [1971] [Dr. M.] worked at [name] Hospital in the hematology department. Thereafter from [1971] to [1972], [Dr. M.] worked for the department of Hematology and Oncology at the University of [state] Hospital.

[Dr. M.]'s professional experience includes but is not limited to the following:

(1) Attending physician at [name] and [name] Hospitals;
(2) Private Practice in Hematology and Oncology;
(3) Member Board of Directors of American Cancer Society, [name] and [name] units;
(4) Chairman of the tumor boards at [name] and [name] Hospitals;
(5) President of the American Cancer Society, [name] unit;
(6) Deputy Chief Police Surgeon, [city] Police Department;
(7) Attending Physician at [name] Hospital.

[Dr. M.] is also a member of the American College of Physicians, American Medical Association, American Society of Hematology, and American Society of Clinical Oncology.

Among [Dr. M.]'s many publications are the following:

[list published articles]

[Dr. M.] will testify at trial. The substance of [Dr. M.]'s testimony is that due to brain tumors, respiratory insufficiencies, radiation treatments, and medication,

[Charles H. Wessel] was unable to perform the essential functions of his job position in [July] of [1992].

Defendants will also call as an expert witness [Peter H. L.], M.D., a doctor who specializes in the treatment of people with mental diseases and impairments. [Dr. L.] is a board-certified Psychiatrist and Neurologist. [Dr. L.] received his undergraduate and medical school training from [name] University in [state]. From [1975] to [1976] [Dr. L.] worked as a resident in medicine at [name] Hospital, from [1977]–[1980] was a resident in Neurology at [name] Medical Center, and from [1979]–[1980] was the chief resident at that facility. From [1980]–[1983] [Dr. L.] worked as a clinical associate at [name] Institute in [city, state]. From [1984] to present [Dr. L.] has been an Associate Professor of Neurology and Psychiatry at [name] School of Medicine in [city, state]. From [1988] to the present, [Dr. L.] has worked at the clinical Neuroscience Program at [name] Hospital.

[Dr. L.] is an elected member of the Academy of Neurology and American Neurological Association, Chairman of the Scientific Program Committee of the [state] Neurological Association, Chairman of the Medical Advisory Board of the [state] Parkinson's Foundation, a member of the Medical Advisory Board of the United Parkinson's Foundation, and a member of the Scientific Advisory Board of the [state] Chapter of the Alzheimer's Disease Association.

Among many professional activities throughout his career, [Dr. L.] was the Director of a Postgraduate Neurology Course for the Foundation of [name] in [city, state] from [1981]–[1982] and was on the faculty of [name] Medical School in [city, state] in [1983].

[Dr. L.] has had more than 100 of his works published, including several publications in the *New England Journal of Medicine*.

[Dr. L.] will testify at trial. The substance of [Dr. L.]'s testimony is that due to brain tumors, medication, and high doses of radiation, [Charles H. Wessel] suffered cognitive impairments to his higher mental functions in [July] of [1992]. [Dr. L.] will further testify that such cognitive impairments can affect reasoning, judgment, personality, and memory.

SCHEDULE F DEPOSITION DESIGNATIONS

SCHEDULE F-1

PART ONE

STATEMENT OF PLAINTIFFS' DEPOSITION DESIGNATIONS AND DEFENDANTS' OBJECTIONS

p. 5, line 8 — p. 16, line 19

p. 17, line 2 — p. 30, line 12

p. 31, line 18 — p. 74, line 20

p. 75, line 16 — p. 78, line 6

p. 78, line 18 — p. 98, line 17

p. 99, line 2 — p. 107, line 5

p. 107, line 15 — p. 114, line 17

p. 114, line 20 — p. 130, line 16

p. 130, line 21 — p. 151, line 23

p. 152, line 15 — p. 188, line 22

p. 189, line 7 — p. 193, line 7

Deposition of [defendant C] — p. 124, lines 14–18

Deposition of [Kenneth D.] — p. 15, lines 7–15

Deposition of [Larry R.] — p. 35, lines 5–22, p. 171, lines 7–14

SCHEDULE F-1

PART TWO

DEFENDANTS' OBJECTIONS TO PLAINTIFFS' DEPOSITION DESIGNATIONS

1. Videotape deposition of [Charles Wessel]. Defendants object. No portion of this videotape should be used at trial if [Charles Wessel] is available to testify. If [Wessel] is available to testify, the use of this videotape will cause undue delay, will waste time, and will needlessly present cumulative evidence. Rule 403, Fed. R. Evid.

2. Deposition of [defendant C]. Defendants object. No portion of this transcript should be read into evidence at trial if defendant is available to testify. If [defendant C] is available to testify, the reading of this transcript will cause undue delay, will waste time, and will needlessly present cumulative evidence. Rule 403, Fed. R. Evid.

3. Deposition of [Ken D.]. Defendants object for the same reasons stated in paragraph two (2) above.

4. Deposition of [Larry R.]. Defendants object for the same reasons stated in paragraph two (2) above.

SCHEDULE G ITEMIZED STATEMENT OF SPECIAL DAMAGES

1. Lost wages from [August 1, 1992], through [August 1, 1993] — [$36,013]. [$4,244] per month for eight months; plus 5% raise effective [November 1, 1992]; plus [$1,000] bonus

193

2. Health insurance premiums through [March 1993] — [$4,790.72]
3. Life insurance premiums for two quarters — [$475.44]
4. Job search expenses — [$100]
5. Prejudgment interest
6. Emotional distress
7. Punitive damages

SCHEDULE G-1

DEFENDANTS' OBJECTIONS TO STATEMENT OF SPECIAL DAMAGES

Defendants do not stipulate to the Statement of Special Damages drafted by Plaintiff's attorneys and object to same.

Specifically, Defendants object to Paragraph 1 in Schedule G because it does not apportion [Wessel]'s car allowance and assumes, without foundation, that [Wessel] would have received a raise and bonus in [1992].

Defendants also object to paragraphs 4–7 of Schedule G. Prejudgment interest, emotional distress, and punitive damages are not special damages. Also, Plaintiffs have listed a round figure of [$100] for job search expenses without providing any foundation for the calculation of this figure.

Defendants list the following as special damages:

1. Lost wages of [$3,893.75] per month from [August 1, 1992], to a date to be determined at trial, when [Wessel] was no longer able to perform the essential functions of the job position with or without reasonable accommodation.

2. A car allowance of [$350] per month from [August 1, 1992], to a date to be determined at trial, when [Wessel] was no longer able to perform the essential functions of the job position with or without reasonable accommodation.

3. Health insurance premiums of [$598.84] per month from [August 1, 1992], to a date to be determined at trial, when [Wessel] was no longer able to perform the essential functions of the job position with or without reasonable accommodation.

4. Life insurance premiums of [$237.72] per quarter from [August 1, 1992], to a date to be determined at trial, when [Wessel] was no longer able to perform the essential functions of the job position with or without reasonable accommodation.

5. Job search expenses of an amount to be proved by Plaintiffs at trial.

SCHEDULE H PLAINTIFFS' TRIAL BRIEF[26]

SCHEDULE I DEFENDANTS' TRIAL BRIEF[27]

SCHEDULE J JURY INSTRUCTIONS[28]

---

[26] Plaintiffs' trial brief appears in Chapter 17.

[27] Defendants' trial brief appears in Chapter 16.

[28] Agreed jury instructions appear in Chapter 16.

SCHEDULE J-1

PLAINTIFFS' PROPOSED JURY INSTRUCTIONS AND VERDICT FORMS[29]

SCHEDULE J-2

DEFENDANTS' PROPOSED JURY INSTRUCTIONS AND VERDICT FORMS[30]

SCHEDULE K LIST OF PROPOSED VOIR DIRE QUESTIONS[31]

SCHEDULE L DEFENDANTS' LIST OF PROPOSED VOIR DIRE QUESTIONS[32]

SCHEDULE M HISTORY OF SETTLEMENT NEGOTIATIONS

On [November 16, 1992], counsel for the EEOC wrote a letter to counsel for Defendants setting forth full relief for the violations alleged in the Complaint. On [November 20, 1993], counsel for Defendants wrote a letter to counsel for the EEOC rejecting full relief.

Defendants made a counteroffer to Plaintiff [Wessel] on [January 18, 1993]. That offer was rejected.

Counsel for the parties have discussed the possibility of settlement on [February 17], [February 19], and [February 20, 1993], and agree that further discussions will be pursued.

SCHEDULE N MOTIONS IN LIMINE

IN THE UNITED STATES DISTRICT COURT FOR THE [NORTHERN] DISTRICT OF [ILLINOIS] [EASTERN] DIVISION

U.S. EQUAL EMPLOYMENT OPPORTUNITY COMMISSION and

[CHARLES H. WESSEL],
Plaintiffs
v.   Civil Action No. [92 C 7330]
[A.I.C. SECURITY INVESTIGATIONS, LTD];
[A.I.C. INTERNATIONAL, LTD.];
and [unnamed defendant C],

Defendants.

---

[29] Plaintiffs' proposed jury instructions appear in Chapter 16.
[30] Defendants' proposed jury instructions appear in Chapter 16.
[31] Plaintiffs' proposed voir dire questions appear in Chapter 16.
[32] Defendants' list of proposed voir dire questions appears in Chapter 16.

Judge [Aspen]

Magistrate Judge [Guzman]

PLAINTIFFS' MOTION IN LIMINE

Plaintiffs hereby move for the exclusion of evidence, relating to the reason(s) for [David P.]'s termination as President of [A.I.C. International]. The use of evidence of the reasons for [David P.]'s termination is precluded based upon the Court's previous denial of the EEOC's Motion to Compel. Defendants argued in opposition to the Motion to Compel that such evidence was nondiscoverable and not reasonably calculated to lead to the discovery of admissible evidence. Therefore, Defendants cannot now be heard to say that such evidence can be used at trial. A denial of the Motion in Limine would essentially permit Defendants to withhold evidence from the Plaintiffs, arguing that it is not admissible, and thereafter introduce the very same evidence at trial. Surely such an anomalous result cannot be permitted.

The Court's acceptance of the Defendants' argument in denying the Motion to Compel also precludes the use of evidence of the reasons for [David P.]'s termination, because the Court expressly stated that the EEOC had "failed to establish that Interrogatory No. 14 seeks information that is reasonably calculated to lead to the discovery of admissible evidence." Defendants should not be permitted to use evidence at trial that was previously determined not to be admissible.

Finally, the Court's order on the Motion to Compel was partially premised on its understanding that [David P.]'s personnel file would be provided to the EEOC pursuant to Document Request No. 2, to which Defendants did not raise an objection. In his deposition of [December 8, 1992], [Philip A. W.] testified as follows:

Q. What about personnel files of other management employees; do you have custody of those?
A. Yes.
Q. If you wanted to give them to me, how long would it take you to do that?
A. If I wanted to give them to you?
Q. Right.
A. First I have to see who's there. With the people that have come and gone lately —
Q. What if I wanted, for example, [David P.]'s personnel file?
A. [David P.]'s could be in the other building. That may take a while to find.

Deposition of [Philip A. W.], page 34, lines 12–24. To date, Defendants have not provided the Plaintiffs with a copy of [David P.]'s personnel file, stating that it cannot be located. The Defendants' failure to provide [David P.]'s personnel file, despite the Court's understanding that it had done so, is yet another basis for excluding the admission of any evidence as to the reasons for [David P.]'s termination by the Defendants at trial.

WHEREFORE, Plaintiffs respectfully request that evidence relating to the reasons for [David P.]'s termination be excluded from the evidence presented by Defendants at trial.

[Elaine M. C.]
Trial Attorney
Equal Employment Opportunity Commission
[536 South Clark], [Room 982]
[Chicago], [Illinois] [60605]

DEFENDANTS' MOTION IN LIMINE

MOTION NO. 1: Defendants hereby move to exclude the purported May Roast Videotape of [Charles Wessel] proffered as Exhibit No. 9 by Plaintiff EEOC based upon the following:

1. The video is of a "roast" held for the benefit of [Charles Wessel] by the security guard association to which he belonged; it has absolutely no relevance to any of the issues involved in this case, including the issue whether [Wessel] could perform the essential functions of his position of Executive Director. (*See* Rules 401 and 402, Fed. R. Evid.)
2. The contents of the video are inadmissible hearsay, especially in view of the fact that many of the individuals speaking at the event — [Wessel] himself, [David P]., [Richard F.] — are named witnesses of the parties, and the other participants in the event are available as witnesses to testify in Court.
3. The videotaped roast is akin to a eulogy, wherein the various speakers pay tribute to a colleague they know to be terminally ill, and thus, their statements are, as [Wessel] himself indicated at the event, far too generous.
4. The tenuous value of the videotape at trial is substantially outweighed by the danger of unfair prejudice, confusion of the issues, and misleading the jury. (*See* Rule 403, Fed. R. Evid.)
5. The video cannot be adequately authenticated, and the copy that Defendants obtained during discovery appears to have been only a portion of what actually may have been recorded at this event. (*See* Rules 901(a) and 401(b), Fed. R. Evid.)

WHEREFORE, Defendants respectfully request that this video be excluded from evidence at trial.

By:

[attorney A]

CHAPTER 16

TRIAL MATTERS

§ 16.01 INTRODUCTION AND OVERVIEW

[A] Generally

This chapter contains Americans with Disabilities Act (ADA)[1] trial materials, from motions to exclude[2] to jury verdict forms.[3] Because there have been relatively few complete ADA jury trials, this chapter relies to a significant extent on materials developed in simulated ADA trials.[4]

Transcripts of simplified evidentiary proceedings are useful as starting points for developing checklists for witnesses and witness examination.[5] For that reason, transcripted material is included[6] as well as other types of forms.

One of the most effective types of evidence in an ADA case can be a videotape demonstration of the plaintiff performing essential job functions. Several sections of this chapter provide forms useful in advocating or opposing that type of evidence. This section summarizes foundational issues.

Real and demonstrative evidence is admissible only after being authenticated. The concept of *authentication* refers to establishing a link between the evidence and the person, place, or thing to which it purportedly relates.[7] Federal Rule of Evidence 901 says that "[t]he requirement for authentication . . . is satisfied by evidence sufficient to support a finding that the matter in question is what its proponent claims."[8] Even though common sense suggests that writings themselves are evidence of their authors, the law of evidence traditionally has required extrinsic evidence to establish the authenticity of a writing.[9] Usually the controversy is over

---

[1] Pub. L. No. 101-336, 104 Stat. 327 (1990) (codified at 42 U.S.C. §§ 12,101–12,213 (1994); 47 U.S.C. §§ 225, 711 (1994)) [hereinafter ADA].

[2] *See* Forms 16–1 to 16–2.

[3] *See* Form 16–21.

[4] *See* Forms 16–7 to 16–8, and Forms 16–15 to 16–22.

[5] *See* Form 16–4.

[6] *See* Forms 16–5 to 16–6 and Forms 16–9 to 16–14.

[7] L. Packel & A. Poulin, Pennsylvania Evidence (1987) [hereinafter Packel & Poulin], § 901, at 672 (authentication concept); McCormick on Evidence §§ 212–214, 218–228 (3d ed. 1984).

[8] Fed. R. Evid. 901(a), (b) (giving examples of authentication of records).

[9] Packel & Poulin § 901.5, at 683 (writing itself insufficient proof of authenticity; when writing supplied by agent, proponent must establish (1) agent actually signed, (2) agent was the agent of the principal, and (3) agent acted within authority). *But see* Fed. R. Evid. 902 (self-authentication of certain documents such as certified copies of public records, newspapers). The authentication requirement originated with illiterate juries. The courts feared that such juries might give either too much weight to written evidence because they were in awe of it or too little weight because they could not understand it. Hence the authentication rule provided oral testimony on which the jury could rely.

authorship.[10] The examples given in Rule 901 focus largely on authorship.[11]

Authentication is not limited conceptually to writings. McCormick gives the example of an article of clothing found at a crime scene, which cannot be evidence against the defendant unless the defendant's ownership or other connection with the clothing is established.

Establishing the defendant connection is an authentication problem.[12] When a party in ADA litigation offers demonstrative evidence of the plaintiff's ability or inability to perform job functions, establishing a connection between the demonstration and the actual job functions is an authentication problem also.

Judge Friendly engaged in a useful review of the authentication concept in *United States v. Sliker.*[13] Most fundamentally, he observed that authentication is a logical requirement that a piece of evidence be what it claims to be.[14] "Evidence admitted as something can have no probative value unless that is what it really is."[15] He noted that the type and quantum of authentication evidence should depend on the purpose for which evidence is offered because authorship may not be the important issue. In *Sliker*, Judge Friendly found that records of criminal transactions were sufficiently connected to a sham bank regardless of who wrote them. The content and the physical location of the records were the probative authentication evidence.[16] He noted in particular, as appropriate methods of authenticating evidence, distinctive characteristics, combined with other circumstances,[17] contents, and where the evidence was found.[18] He approved the appropriateness of comparing the sound of a voice on an audiotape with the sound of a witness's voice in the trial.[19]

In the actual trial, the proponent of videotape demonstration evidence must have one or more sponsoring witnesses. One sponsor may be the plain-

---

[10] *See, e.g.,* Packel & Poulin § 901.9, at 691 (applying authentication rules for writings to telephone conversations and focusing on identity of speaker); McCormick on Evidence § 218, at 686–87 (3d ed. 1984) (using term authentication in limited sense of proof of authorship).

[11] *See, e.g.,* Fed. R. Evid. 901(b)(2) (handwriting), 901(b)(5) (voice identification), 901(b)(6) (identity of called party in telephone conversation).

[12] McCormick on Evidence § 218, at 686 (3d ed. 1984).

[13] 751 F.2d 477, 488–89 (2d Cir. 1984) (evaluating authentication of records of fraudulent transactions and audiotapes of defendant conversations in reviewing conviction for wire fraud in scheme to defraud banks).

[14] *Id.* at 499.

[15] *Id.* (approving trial judge's listening to audiotape and comparing voices before allowing jury to hear it, although jury ultimately decided fact question of authenticity).

[16] *Id.* at 489 (citing cases where physical proximity authenticated physical evidence).

[17] *Id.* at 500 (citing Fed. R. Evid. 901(b)(3), (4) advisory committee's notes).

[18] *Id.* (citing case involving letter combined with testimony).

[19] United States v. Sliker, 751 F.2d 477, 500 (2d Cir. 1984).

tiff.[20] The testimony from these witnesses must establish that the videotape accurately shows the identity of the plaintiff, the capabilities of the plaintiff, and the requirements of the job.

The ultimate question for the videotape medium is trustworthiness. If the techniques used to create the videotape are apparently reliable, the information should be admitted unless the opponent of admissibility can raise some reasonable factual question undercutting trustworthiness,[21] especially if the opponent of evidentiary use was notified, was present, and thus had an opportunity to object to aspects of the demonstration in time for them to be modified.

The larger battle usually will relate to the accuracy of the portrayal of the plaintiff's capabilities and job functions, especially the latter.

[B] Sample Forms

[1] Defendants' Motion to Exclude Expert Witness

FORM 16–1   **Sample Defendants' Motion to Exclude Expert Witness**

IN THE UNITED STATES DISTRICT COURT
FOR THE [NORTHERN] DISTRICT OF [ILLINOIS]
[EASTERN] DIVISION

U.S. EQUAL OPPORTUNITY COMMISSION
Plaintiff,   Civil Action No. [92-C-7330]
v.
[A.I.C. SECURITY INVESTIGATIONS, LTD.];
[A.I.C. INTERNATIONAL, LTD.];
and [unnamed defendant C],
Defendants.

Judge [Marvin E. Aspen]

DEFENDANTS' MOTION TO EXCLUDE EXPERT WITNESS

Defendants, [A.I.C. SECURITY INVESTIGATIONS, LTD.], [A.I.C. INTERNATIONAL, LTD.], and [defendant C], by and through their attorneys, [WESSELS & PAUTSCH, P.C.], [Charles W. Pautsch], [attorney A], and [attorney B], hereby move this Honorable Court to exclude from trial the testimony of [E. Richard B.], M.D., and state in support hereof as follows:

---

[20] *See generally* L. Packel & D.B. Spina, Trial Advocacy: A Systematic Approach 97–98 (1984) (sponsoring witnesses for real and demonstrative evidence).

[21] *See* United States v. Hutson, 821 F.2d 1015, 1020 (5th Cir. 1987) (remanding embezzlement conviction, although computer records were admissible under business records exception, despite trustworthiness challenge based on fact that defendant embezzled by altering computer files; access to files offered in evidence was restricted by special code).

1. On [November 5, 1992], the Equal Opportunity Commission ("EEOC") filed this instant action alleging that Defendants violated the Americans with Disabilities Act.

2. Shortly thereafter the Honorable [Marvin E. Aspen] placed this case on an expedited docket.

3. Subsequently, in [December] of [1992], the Plaintiff EEOC named two expert witnesses, [A], M.D., and [B], M.D.

4. On [December 2] and [14], [1992] respectively, Defendants disclosed to Plaintiffs their witnesses, Doctors [Larry S. M.] and [Peter A. L.].

5. On [December 11, 1992], Defendants deposed Dr. [A], and on [December 19, 1992], Defendants deposed Dr. [B].

6. On [January 22, 1993], discovery closed in this case. On or about [January 21], Plaintiffs cancelled their previously scheduled deposition of [Dr. L.] in [Detroit] on [January 22, 1993]. Plaintiffs made no attempts to depose [Dr. M.] during the discovery period.

7. On [January 29, 1993], all parties came before this Court on various motions, at which time Court entertained status issues regarding the progression of this case. During this hearing EEOC Attorney [B] indicated there were no expert witnesses. Defendants' counsel conveyed to the Court that Defendants intended to call their two previously identified medical experts as witnesses at trial; however, because neither witness had been deposed by Plaintiffs during the discovery period, the Court established additional time for Plaintiffs to depose Defendants' named experts.

8. Accordingly, the parties have scheduled the deposition of [Dr. Larry M.] for [February 11, 1993]; Defendants have tentatively agreed to have [Dr. Peter L.] come to [Detroit] to examine [Charles Wessel], as ordered by the Court, on [February 12, 1993], at which time he could also be deposed by Plaintiffs in [Chicago].

9. On [February 9, 1993], Plaintiff EEOC sent, via facsimile, Supplemental Responses to Defendants' First Set of Interrogatories to Plaintiff. EEOC now intends to call [E. Richard B.], M.D., as an additional expert witness at trial. (Attached hereto as Exhibit No. 1.)

10. Plaintiffs have sought no Leave of Court to name any additional expert witnesses at this point in time, long after the discovery cutoff.

11. Plaintiffs have no right to notice new expert witnesses at this extremely late date, discovery having already closed on [January 22, 1993], and only limited discovery having now been permitted by the Court solely with respect to expert witnesses identified by the Defendants long ago, back in [1992].

WHEREFORE, defendants respectfully request an Order prohibiting [E. Richard B.], M.D., from testifying at trial.

Dated this [10th] day of [February] [1993].

Respectfully submitted,

[A.I.C. SECURITY INVESTIGATIONS, LTD.];

[A.I.C. INTERNATIONAL, LTD.];

and [defendant C],

By: [attorney A]

> **[2]   Defendants' Emergency Motion to Exclude Testimony of Attorney**

FORM 16–2   Sample Defendants' Motion to Exclude Testimony of Attorney

DEFENDANTS' EMERGENCY MOTION IN LIMINE TO EXCLUDE
TESTIMONY OF ATTORNEY [MICHAEL C.]

The Defendants, [A.I.C. SECURITY INVESTIGATIONS, LTD.], [A.I.C. IN-TERNATIONAL, LTD.], and [unnamed defendant C], by and through their attorneys, [WESSELS & PAUTSCH, P.C.], by [Charles W. Pautsch], [attorney A], and [attorney B], hereby move to exclude testimony of Attorney [Michael C.] based upon the following:

1. On [February 22, 1993], the parties in the above-captioned case submitted a Final Pretrial Order to the Court.

2. Within the Final Pretrial Order is Plaintiffs' List of Witnesses (Schedule D-11).

3. In Plaintiffs' List of Witnesses, it is indicated that Plaintiffs will call [Michael C.] as a witness at trial.

4. [Michael C.] is an attorney practicing law in the [Chicago] area and, upon information and belief, is licensed to practice law in the State of [Illinois].

5. For a period of time prior to [August 1992], [Michael C.] represented and counseled Defendants [A.I.C. International, Ltd.] and [A.I.C. Security Investigations, Ltd.] in numerous matters, including employment law matters.

6. As a previous attorney for [A.I.C. International, Ltd.] and [A.I.C. Security Investigations, Ltd.], [Michael C.] cannot at trial divulge any information he obtained while acting in the capacity of attorney for Defendants.

7. In addition, Defendants in this action cannot be forced into a position of having to divulge confidential information in order to effectively cross-examine [Michael C].

8. If Defendants are forced to choose between effective cross-examination or divulgence of confidential and highly sensitive material, Defendants will be foreclosed from due process of law.

9. If [Michael C.] testifies at trial against Defendants using information he obtained through his representation of Defendants, he will violate ABA Model Code of Professional Responsibility Canon 4, Disciplinary Rule 4-101 — Preser-

vation of Confidences and Secrets of Client. (See [Ill. Rev. Stat. ch. 110A, Rule 4-101].) Moreover, if the testimony of [Michael C.] forces Defendants to use confidential information to effectively cross-examine [Michael C.], then [Michael C.] will still be in violation of [Canon 4] and [Disciplinary Rule 4-101] cited above and will have breached his common-law fiduciary duty to Defendants. *See [Financial General Bankshares, Inc. v. Metzger,* 680 F.2d 768, 771 (D.C. Cir. 1982)].

10. Defendants do not intend to waive their attorney-client privilege at trial with regard to information in the possession of [Michael C.] and, therefore, will be foreclosed from effective cross-examination of [Michael C.] and due process of law.

WHEREFORE, Defendants respectfully request that [Michael C.] be excluded from testifying at trial.

Dated this [4th] day of [March] [1993].
[A.I.C. SECURITY INVESTIGATIONS, LTD.];
[A.I.C. INTERNATIONAL, LTD.];
and [defendant C]
By: [attorney A]

[3]   Memorandum Supporting Motion to Admit Videotape Demonstration[22]

FORM 16–3   Sample Motion in Limine to Admit Videotape Demonstration

MOTION IN LIMINE TO ADMIT VIDEOTAPE DEMONSTRATION OF PLAINTIFF'S CAPABILITIES TO PERFORM JOB FUNCTIONS

Plaintiff moves the court for an order that a videotape showing the Plaintiff performing the essential functions of the job in controversy in this case is admissible into evidence and ordering the Defendant not to object to it.

Rules 403, 611, and 901 of the Federal Rules of Evidence permit demonstrative evidence to be shown to a fact-finder under certain conditions. Those conditions are satisfied in this case because the videotape shows the Plaintiff performing the

---

[22] The contents of the motion appearing in Form 16–3 could be used in support of admissibility at the time of objection at trial as well as in a motion in limine. Note that in cases involving "day in the life" videotapes, the opponent's usual claim is that the activities portrayed on the videotape are more difficult than activities undertaken in real life. In an ADA case, the person opposing a videotape demonstration would claim that the activities portrayed on the videotape are easier than the activities involved on the job, and real life. In either kind of case, however, the criteria for admissibility are the same: that the videotape accurately portrays the questions in the case (that is, that the activities portrayed are reasonably similar to the real-world activities) and that the jury is instructed and otherwise cautioned in order to minimize the risks of prejudice.

ordinary functions of the job for which Plaintiff applied, under realistic conditions. The following cases support the admissibility of such demonstrative evidence. Under the following cases, the Defendant has not and cannot show any aspect of the videotape that is unduly prejudicial or that is significantly misleading in terms of the functions of the job as the Defendant itself has defined them.

See [*Sterkel v. Fruehauf Corp.*, 975 F.2d 528, 523 (8th Cir. 1992) (affirming denial of mistrial; model of slider pens on truck trailer shown to jury was not exactly correct in its dimension but no showing that jury was misled)]; [*Roland v. Langlois*, 945 F.2d 956, 963 (7th Cir. 1991) (affirming trial court admission of life-sized model of amusement park ride component; no requirement that demonstrative evidence be completely accurate as long as jury is alerted to perceived inaccuracies in personal injury case)]; [*Petty v. Ideco*, 761 F.2d 1146, 1151 (5th Cir. 1985) (affirming admission of videotape showing the functioning of oil well equipment because of failure to object and procedure used at trial permitting stopping of videotape whenever opposing party had any objection)]; [*In re Beverly Hill Fire Litigation*, 695 F.2d 207, 222 (6th Cir. 1982) (affirming admission of model of exterior portions of a wall involved in fire in personal injury action)].

Videotape demonstrations of an ADA plaintiff's capabilities are similar in terms of evidentiary issues to videotapes or movies showing "a day in the life" of an injured plaintiff. Such videotapes regularly are admitted as long as certain conditions are satisfied. See [*Bannister v. Town of Nobel*, 812 F.2d 1265, 1268 (10th Cir. 1987) (approving admission of "day in the life" videotape because (1) tape fairly represented facts regarding impact of injuries on plaintiff's day-to-day activities and did not depict victim in unlikely circumstances or performing improbable tasks, (2) no showing of self-serving behavior because of awareness of videotaping and no showing of exaggeration of difficulty in performing tasks, (3) no showing of undue prejudice by dominating evidentiary record in jury's mind, and (4) no showing that inability to cross-examine tape prejudiced deponent; videotape depicted daily routine, including getting around school, getting into car, pumping gasoline for car, and performing different routine tasks at home)]; [*id.*, 812 F.2d 1265, 1270 (affirming admission of videotape showing car like the one involved in accident approaching an inclined ramp, becoming airborne, and landing; videotape not offered as re-creation of accident but as demonstration of certain principles; instruction given that "the film is not being introduced for the purpose of attempting to recreate the accident involved in this case")]; [*id.*, 812 F.2d 1265, 1270 (no error to permit "day in the life" videotape admitted into evidence to be shown during closing argument)]; [*United States v. Sanders*, 696 F. Supp. 334, 335 (N.D. Ill. 1988) (admitting promotional videotapes to help jury understand commodities trading, drawing analogies between them, and "day in the life" videotapes; admissible under catchall exception to hearsay rule)].

Videotape or live demonstrations of the ADA Plaintiff's capability to perform essential functions also are similar to in-court demonstration of injuries. Such evidence routinely is admitted. See [*Monk v. Doctors' Hospital*, 403 F.2d 580, 584 (D.C. Cir. 1968) (permissible for plaintiff to demonstrate injury as long as foundation is laid to prevent undue prejudice and make demonstration realistic)]; [*Lester v. Sayles*, 850 S.W.2d 858, 870 (Mo. 1993) (affirming trial court's allowance of mother's demonstration of physical therapy she performs on daughter; no showing of exaggeration of symptoms or pain)]; [*Fravel v. Burlington Northern Railroad,* 671 S.W.2d 339 (Mo. Ct. App. 1984) (affirming allowance of demonstration by plaintiff of injuries to leg by having physician manipulate leg in front of jury; defense counsel did not make record of alleged grimaces and exclamations of pain)]; [*LeMaster v. Chicago Rock Island & Pacific Railroad Co.,* 343 N.E.2d 65 (Ill. App. Ct. 1976) (affirming trial judge discretion to permit plaintiff to disrobe to bathing suit and demonstrate taking off and putting on arm and leg prostheses and to re-dress, along with a series of photographs showing essentially the same thing)]; [*Bellart v. Martell,* 137 N.W.2d 729 (Wis. 1965) (no error to permit personal injury plaintiff to display arm and leg stump to jury and to demonstrate operation and putting on prostheses)].

[4] Checklist for Voir Dire

_____ 1. Basic Juror Attitudes toward the Disabled

      _____ a. Have you ever worked with a person who had a physical or mental disability?

      _____ b. Have you ever had a supervisor with a physical or mental disability?

      [If the potential juror answers yes, explore the experience with questions such as]

      (1) How closely did you work with the disabled person?
      (2) What was the nature of the disability?
      (3) How did the disability affect the person's ability to do his or her job?
      (4) How did the disability affect relations with co-workers?
      (5) How did the disability affect relations with the employer?
      (6) Do you think the employer treated the disabled person fairly? Why or why not?

      _____ c. Does anyone in your family have a physical or mental disability?

      _____ d. Have you ever contributed to an organization that has as its goal the protection or support of persons with physical or mental disabilities?

      _____ e. If you have contributed to such an organization, does it have as its goal the placing of disabled persons in the mainstream of American life, or does it favor separating them and providing support because they do not work?

      _____ f. What is your reaction when you see wheelchair ramps on buildings and curbs of streets, and when you see special devices on buses for the handicapped?

      _____ g. Have you ever been waited on by a disabled person?

_____ 2. Attitudes toward Discrimination and Accommodation

      _____ a. What kind of disability discrimination do you think present law prohibits?

      _____ b. What kind of disability discrimination should be prohibited?

_____ c. Should a distinction be drawn between discrimination based on physical disabilities and discrimination based on mental disabilities?

_____ d. Under what circumstances do you think it is justifiable to treat persons with physical or mental disabilities differently from non-disabled persons?

_____ e. Should employers consider changing job duties and the organization of work in order to make it possible for a disabled person to perform job functions?

_____ f. What kinds of changes should be considered?

_____ g. What kinds should not be considered?

_____ 3. Attitudes toward Discrimination and Accommodation in Public Accommodations and Commercial Facilities

_____ a. Do you think that persons with physical or mental disabilities should be allowed to use facilities like movie theaters and retail stores along with everyone else?

_____ b. Should special arrangements be made to make it easier for persons with physical or mental disabilities to use such public places?

_____ c. Do you think any distinction should be drawn between persons who have mobility disabilities, such as being confined to wheelchairs or going on crutches, from those who have visual limitations like blindness or hearing limitations like deafness? What distinctions?

_____ d. Are there any circumstances under which people with physical or mental disabilities should be excluded from public facilities, including stores and places of entertainment like movie theaters?

_____ e. Suppose the disabled people wishing to use such facilities are severely deformed or make unusual noises?

_____ f. Under what circumstances should "socially acceptable behavior" be applied to exclude disabled persons from public places?

_____ g. If you were running a small dress shop, what would be your policy toward use of your shop by persons with physical or mental disabilities?

_____ h. How much trouble would you go to to make sure that disabled persons had access to your place of business?

_____ i. Would it make any difference if you were operating a video game parlor, a movie theater, or a place in which athletic activities such as tennis or ice skating were performed?[23]

---

[23] Many of the ideas for this checklist are adapted from R. B. Conlin, _Effective Voir Dire in Sex Discrimination Cases,_ Trial 23 (July 1993).

[5] Proposed Voir Dire Questions

FORM 16–4 Sample Proposed Voir Dire Questions

PLAINTIFFS' PROPOSED VOIR DIRE QUESTIONS

1. Are you acquainted with any of the parties in this case or any member of their families? The parties in this case are [names of parties].

2. To the best of your knowledge, is any member of your family or household or any close friend acquainted with any of the parties?

3. Have you or, again, any member of your family or household or any close friend ever met any of the attorneys in this case or, to your knowledge, any attorney associated in practice with one of those attorneys? The attorneys in this case are [names of attorneys].

4. Have you or any member of your family or household or any close friends ever had any business dealings with any of the parties involved in this case?

5. Have you or any member of your family or household or any close friend ever met or even heard of any person identified as a possible witness in this case? The following individuals are possible witnesses in this case: [list of witnesses].

6. Did you hear anything about this case before you came into the courtroom this morning?

7. As you look around this room, do you recognize any friends or acquaintances among the other prospective jurors?

8. What is your occupation and employer? How long have you worked there? What is your position? How long have you held that position?

9. Have you or a close friend or relative or member of your household ever been a supervisor, manager, or executive? If so, provide the details.

10. If you have ever been an owner, supervisor, manager, or executive of a business, did you ever terminate or recommend the termination of an employee? If so, provide the details.

11. If you have been an owner, supervisor, manager, or executive, did any employee under you or in your company ever raise a claim or file a lawsuit for employment discrimination or other employment-related claims? If so, provide the details.

12. Have you or a close friend or relative or member of your household had any training or employment experience in personnel or human resources?

13. Please identify the members of your immediate family and anyone else who lives with you.

14. What is the occupation, employer, and position of each member of your family?

15. Have you or a member of your family or household or any close friend ever been terminated or laid off from any job for a reason that was considered discriminatory or unfair? If so, provide details.

16. Have you or any member of your family or household or any close friend, or any business you owned or operated, ever been involved in a lawsuit of any kind? Are you now involved in a lawsuit?

17. Have you or a member of your family or household or a close friend ever made a claim of employment discrimination or other claim relating to employment?

18. Do you or does any member of your immediate family suffer from any disability? If so, does that disability interfere with the ability to work?

19. Have you or any member of your family or any close friend had cancer? Would that fact interfere with your ability to try this case fairly?

20. From what you have heard thus far about the case — the type of lawsuit, the parties, the witnesses who may testify — do you believe you or your family could possibly be affected in any way by the outcome of this case?

21. Is there anything about the nature of this case that would prevent you from being fair and impartial?

22. Is there anything else about yourself that would affect your ability to render a fair and impartial verdict based on the evidence and law?

23. Do you believe you can give both sides a fair trial?

DEFENDANTS' LIST OF PROPOSED VOIR DIRE QUESTIONS

1. Are you acquainted with any of the individual parties in this case or any member of their families? The individual parties in this case are
[Charles H. Wessel]
[defendant C]

2. Are you acquainted with any of the corporate parties in this case? The corporate parties in this case are
[A.I.C. International, Ltd.]
[A.I.C. Security Investigations, Ltd.]

3. To the best of your knowledge, is any member of your family or household or any close friend acquainted with any of the parties?

4. Have you ever filed a charge of discrimination with the Equal Employment Opportunity Commission?

5. To the best of your knowledge, has any member of your family or household or any close friend filed a charge of discrimination with the Equal Employment Opportunity Commission?

6. Have you or any member of your family or household or any close friend ever been employed by the Equal Employment Opportunity Commission?

7. Have you or, again, any member of your family or household or any close friend ever met any of the attorneys in this case, or, to your knowledge any attorney associated in practice with one of those attorneys? The attorneys and law firms in this case are
[list of attorneys and law firms]

8. Have you or any member of your family or household or any close friend ever had any business dealings with any of the parties involved in this case?

9. Have you or any member of your family or household or any close friend ever met or even heard of any person identified as a possible witness in this case? The following individuals are possible witnesses in this case:
[list of witnesses]

10. Did you hear anything about this case before you came into the courtroom this morning? If so, what did you hear?

11. As you look around this room, do you recognize any friends or acquaintances among the other prospective jurors?

12. What is your occupation and employer? How long have you worked there? What is your position? How long have you held that position?

13. Please describe the members of your immediate family and anyone else who lives with you.

14. What is the occupation, employer, and position of each member of your family?

15. Have you or any member of your family or household or any close friend ever been terminated or laid off from any job for a reason that was considered discriminatory or unfair? If so, give details.

16. Have you or any member of your family or household or any close friend, or any business you owned or operated, ever been involved in a lawsuit of any kind? Are you now involved in a lawsuit?

17. Have you or any member of your family or household or any close friend ever made a claim of employment discrimination or other claim relating to employment?

18. Do you or does any member of your immediate family suffer from any disability? If so, does that disability interfere with the ability to work?

19. Do you or any member of your family or any close friend have cancer, or has anyone close to you died from cancer in the past 15 years? Would that fact interfere with your ability to render a fair and impartial verdict in this case?

20. What do you think about women in business and their holding high positions in business?

21. [Charles Wessel] has been diagnosed as terminally ill with inoperable cancer. Will this make you unable to render a fair and impartial verdict regarding whether [Mr. Wessel] was qualified to remain in his position as Executive Director?

22. If [Charles Wessel] is hospitalized or dies before or during the course of this trial, would it affect your ability to render a fair and impartial verdict in this case?

23. Do you have any preconceived notions or opinions about cancer, brain cancer, or terminal illness that would prohibit you from rendering a fair and impartial verdict in this case?

24. From what you have heard thus far about the case—the type of lawsuit, the parties, the witnesses who may testify—do any of you believe you or your family could possibly be affected in any way by the outcome of this case?

25. Is there anything about the nature of this case that would prevent you from being fair and impartial?

26. Is there anything else about yourself that would affect your ability to render a fair and impartial verdict based on the evidence and law?

27. Do you believe you can give both sides a fair trial?

28. Would the fact that this trial involves individuals from the [name] family, as parties and potential witnesses who have been and are active in City of [Chicago] politics, affect your impartiality at all?

29. Have you read, seen, or heard any news regarding this case?

[6] **Plaintiffs' Trial Brief**

FORM 16–5 **Sample Plaintiffs' Trial Brief**

IN THE UNITED STATES DISTRICT COURT FOR THE [NORTHERN]
DISTRICT OF [ILLINOIS]
[EASTERN] DIVISION
U.S. EQUAL EMPLOYMENT OPPORTUNITY COMMISSION and
[CHARLES H. WESSEL],

Plaintiffs,

v.   Civil Action No. [92 C 7330]

[A.I.C. SECURITY INVESTIGATIONS, LTD.];
[A.I.C. INTERNATIONAL, LTD.];
and [unnamed defendant C],

Judge [Aspen]

Defendants.   Magistrate [Judge Guzman]

PLAINTIFFS' TRIAL BRIEF

Plaintiff, Equal Employment Opportunity Commission (the ["Commission"
or "EEOC"], and Intervening Plaintiff, [Charles Wessel], hereby submit this Trial
Brief in the above-captioned cause.

I. Nature of the Case

This action is brought pursuant to Title I of the Americans with Disabilities
Act of 1990, 42 U.S.C. §§ 12,101 *et seq.,* and Title I of the Civil Rights Act of
1991, 42 U.S.C. § 1981a. The EEOC and the Intervening Plaintiff, [Charles Wes-
sel], allege that the Defendants, [A.I.C. Security Investigations, Ltd. ("A.I.C.")],
[A.I.C. International, Ltd. ("A.I.C. International")], and [defendant C] discriminated against [Wessel] on the basis of his disability, terminal cancer, by discharging
him from his position as Executive Director at [A.I.C.].

II. Factual Summary

[A.I.C.] is a wholly owned subsidiary of [A.I.C. International]. [Defendant
C] became the sole shareholder of [A.I.C International] on [June 6, 1992]. Prior to
[June 6, 1992], the sole owner of [A.I.C. International] was [Victor V.]. [A.I.C.
International] and its subsidiaries have been and are now currently engaged in the
business of providing commercial security services, hardware, and investigative
services to customers in the [Chicago] area. There are two companies held by
[A.I.C. International]: [A.I.C. Security Investigations, Ltd.], the security guard division, and [A.I.C. Security Systems, Inc.], the security systems (hardware) division. In his position of Executive Director, [Charles Wessel] was the Chief Executive of [A.I.C.], responsible for the security guard company.

[Charles Wessel] was hired by [Victor V]. in [February 1986] and reported to [Victor V.] until his death on [June 6, 1992], and to [David P.], President of [A.I.C. International], until [David P.]'s termination on [July 6, 1992]. [Wessel] is a widely recognized leader in the security guard industry, having worked in the industry for approximately 30 years. He is licensed as a private detective and a private security contractor by the state of [Illinois] and the state of [Florida]. [Wessel] is also a member of, and has served on the Boards of, numerous professional associations within the security industry, including the Associated Detectives of [Illinois], the Associated Guard and Patrol Agencies, Inc., and the Special Agents Association. In addition, [Wessel] served as the principal drafter of the [Illinois] Licensing Act for private investigators and security guards.

In [June 1987], [Wessel] was diagnosed with lung cancer. Following surgery and recuperation, Wessel returned to work at [A.I.C.]. In [July 1991], [Wessel] suffered pneumothorax during a biopsy and went into respiratory arrest. Thereafter, [Wessel] was again diagnosed with lung cancer, this time affecting his right lung. Surgery was performed, and following a period of treatment and recuperation, [Wessel] again returned to work as Executive Director at [A.I.C.]. In [April 1992], [Wessel] was diagnosed with metastatic brain cancer. [Wessel]'s doctors consider his condition to be terminal. [Wessel] received radiation treatments. Some of the treatments were scheduled late in the afternoon. [Wessel] continued to work at [A.I.C.] throughout the course of the treatments and did not miss an entire day of work in [July 1992], although on the days when the radiation treatments were scheduled in the afternoon, he had to leave work at approximately [2:30 P.M.].

On [June 6, 1992], [Victor V.] died. After his death, [Victor V.]'s widow, [defendant C], became sole shareholder of [A.I.C. International] and [A.I.C.]. On or about [June 10, 1992], [defendant C] hired [Beverly K.] to work for [A.I.C.] On [July 29, 1992], [Beverly K.] had a meeting with [Wessel]. During that meeting, [Beverly K.] apprised [Wessel] that [defendant C] had decided that it was time for [Wessel] to retire. At that time, [Wessel] expressed his unwillingness to retire. On [July 30, 1992], [Beverly K.] advised [Wessel] by telephone that his employment at [A.I.C.] was terminated effective [July 31, 1992]. [Wessel] was paid through [July 31, 1992]. Prior to his termination from [A.I.C.], [Wessel] was never subject to any warnings relating to his performance or any disciplinary action. There is also no evidence to suggest that either [Victor V.] or [David P.], [Wessel]'s supervisors during most of the time he was employed at [A.I.C.], ever expressed any dissatisfaction with [Wessel]'s performance. Similarly, there is no evidence that any customer of [A.I.C.] ever expressed any dissatisfaction with [Wessel]'s performance of his duties throughout his tenure at [A.I.C.]. [Wessel] received a merit salary increase and a bonus in each year he was employed by [A.I.C.], except [1991], when no bonuses were given to any employees, and [1992], because he was not given a review prior to his termination.

III. Legal Analysis

A. Plaintiffs' Prima Facie Case

The initial burden on Plaintiffs in this case is to prove by a preponderance of the evidence that [Wessel] was a qualified individual with a disability within the meaning of the Americans with Disabilities Act ("ADA") at the time of his termination. *Disability* under the ADA is defined as a "physical or mental impairment that substantially limits one or more of the major life activities of such individual." 42 U.S.C. § 12,102(2)(A). A *physical or mental impairment* is defined as "a physiological disorder or condition, cosmetic disfigurement, or anatomical loss affecting one or more of several body systems . . . or any mental or psychological disorder . . ." 29 C.F.R. § 1630.2(h). *Major life activities* are defined as "functions such as caring for oneself, performing manual tasks, walking, seeing, hearing, speaking, breathing, learning, and working." 29 C.F.R. § 1630.2(i). The term *substantially limits* means "unable to perform a major life activity that the average person in the general population can perform or significantly restricted as to the condition, manner, or duration under which an individual can perform a particular major life activity as compared to the condition, manner, or duration under which the average person in the general population can perform that same major life activity." 29 C.F.R. § 1630.2(j). In addition, Plaintiffs must establish that at the time of his discharge, [Wessel] was otherwise qualified for the position of Executive Director at [A.I.C.]. That is, that except for his disability, [Wessel] possesses the necessary qualifications for the position, such as the requisite educational background, experience, skills, and other job-related factors.

In this instance, undisputed evidence demonstrates that [Wessel] was a qualified individual with a disability within the meaning of the ADA as a matter of law. It is undisputed that [Wessel] has been diagnosed with terminal metastatic brain cancer. It is similarly indisputable that, as a result of his cancer, [Wessel] was limited in his ability to perform strenuous physical activity as compared with the average person in the general population. Therefore, at the time of his discharge, [Wessel] was "disabled" within the meaning of the ADA, in that he had a physiological disorder, cancer, affecting his neurological and respiratory systems, which restricted the condition, manner, or duration under which he could perform the major life activities of performing manual tasks, walking, speaking, and breathing as compared with the condition, manner, or duration under which the average person in the general population could perform the same major life activities.

Plaintiffs will also be able to establish that [Wessel] was otherwise qualified for the position of Executive Director at [A.I.C.], in that he possessed the necessary education, experience, and skills to perform his job functions. In fact, the evidence will establish that [Wessel] was a recognized leader in the security industry with approximately 30 years' experience, who is licensed as a private detective and a private security contractor in the state of [Illinois] and the state of [Florida]. Similarly, the evidence will demonstrate a long history of involvement with professional associations within the industry. Finally, the evidence will establish that [Wessel] was the principal drafter of the licensing act for private investigators and security guards in the state of [Illinois], further demonstrating that, except for his disability, [Wessel] possessed the necessary skills to perform the job of Executive Director at [A.I.C.].

Plaintiffs will, thereafter, have to establish by a preponderance of the evidence that [Wessel] could perform the essential functions of the position of Executive

Director of [A.I.C.].[24] The evidence as to what tasks comprise the essential functions of the position of Executive Director at [A.I.C.] and whether [Wessel] could perform those functions is in dispute. Plaintiffs intend to prove that the essential functions of [Wessel]'s job were made up of activities associated with the overall administration and operation of the guard division. Specifically, the essential functions included supervision of day-to-day security guard operations, maintenance of profitability, decision-making and problem-solving, delegation of duties and responsibilities to mid-level management, supervision of mid-level management, discipline, policymaking, and customer contact. Deposition of [Larry J. R.] (p. 35, lines 5–22, and p. 171, lines 7–14). Plaintiffs further intend to prove that at the time of his discharge, [Wessel] was performing all of the essential functions of his job without the need for any accommodation.[25]

Finally, Plaintiffs will have to demonstrate that [Wessel]'s disability was a motivating factor in the decision to terminate his employment. Plaintiffs are not required to prove that [Wessel]'s disability was the sole motivation or primary motivation for Defendants' decision to terminate [Wessel]. Plaintiffs need only prove that [Wessel]'s disability played a part in the decision. Plaintiffs do not anticipate that the nexus between [Wessel]'s disability and the termination decision will be contested. Although Plaintiffs and Defendants disagree as to whether or not [Wessel]'s performance deteriorated in this case as a result of his cancer, Defendants have never asserted that there was some other cause of any alleged performance deterioration other than [Wessel]'s cancer. Therefore, it does not appear that Defendants are actually challenging the causal connection between [Wessel]'s cancer and his termination, despite their assertions that [Wessel] could not perform the

---

[24] Under the ADA, the definition of whether a disabled individual can perform the essential functions of the job at issue refers to a consideration of whether the individual can perform such functions with or without reasonable accommodation. However, as will be more fully discussed in the "Undue Hardship" section of this brief, there is no need for a consideration of accommodations here. At the time of his discharge, Wessel was able to perform the essential functions of the job without accommodation. In addition, there is no evidence that Wessel ever requested any accommodation from the defendants. Consequently, there is no issue of accommodation in this case, except as it may relate to a time after Wessel's discharge, for the consideration of damages.

[25] It is also anticipated that the defendants will attempt to rely on the finding of the Social Security Administration that Wessel was entitled to Social Security disability benefits after July 29, 1992, to support their argument that Wessel could not perform the essential functions of his job as Executive Director at A.I.C. Although the statements made by Wessel and his treating physicians in support of his application for disability benefits are admissible and can be considered along with other relevant evidence, the finding is not entitled to preclusive effect. Instead, as the Seventh Circuit noted in Overton v. Reilly, 977 F.2d 1190 (7th Cir. 1992), the finding of disability by the Social Security Administration "may be relevant evidence of the severity of [plaintiff]'s handicap, but it can hardly be construed as a judgment that [plaintiff] could not do his job. . . ." *Id.* at 1196. That conclusion is strengthened in this case, as it was in *Overton,* because Wessel was awarded disability benefits based on the finding that he met the criteria for a listed disability and was not working without the Social Security Administration's making an inquiry into the ability to find work within the national economy. *Id.* (citing Garfield v. Schweiker, 732 F.2d 605, 607 (7th Cir. 1984)).

essential functions of his job, that his disability could not be reasonably accommodated without undue hardship, and that his continued presence constituted a direct threat to the safety of others.[26]

B. Undue Hardship

It is anticipated that in making their argument that [Wessel] could not perform the essential functions of his job, Defendants will attempt to rely on the undue hardship defense, arguing that reasonable accommodation of [Wessel]'s disability would have created an undue hardship. However, the undue hardship defense is not at issue in this case. Plaintiffs will prove that [Wessel] could perform the essential functions of his job without *accommodation*, as that term is defined for purposes of the ADA. Therefore, there need be no lengthy consideration of accommodation and undue hardship as none was requested in this instance and, in fact, no accommodation was given or required.

C. Direct Threat

It is also anticipated that Defendants will argue that [Wessel] did not meet job-related qualification standards consistent with [A.I.C.]'s business necessity because he posed a direct threat to the health and safety of others in the workplace. In so arguing, Plaintiffs anticipate that Defendants will assert that [Wessel] posed a direct threat to the safety of others because his medical condition prevented him from safely operating a motor vehicle. That assertion is contested by Plaintiffs, because [Wessel] was not under any driving restriction by his treating physicians. However, even if it were assumed that [Wessel]'s driving created a significant risk of imminent, substantial harm, Defendants cannot prevail on a direct-threat defense. *Direct threat* is defined as "a significant risk of substantial harm to the health and safety of the individual or others that cannot be eliminated or reduced by reasonable accommodation. The determination that an individual poses a 'direct threat' shall be based on an individual assessment of the individual's present ability to safely perform the essential functions of the job." 29 C.F.R. § 1630.2(r).

Initially, and most significantly, Defendants' direct-threat defense is without merit because Defendants cannot establish that driving was an essential function of the position of Executive Director at [A.I.C.]. Therefore, any inability to drive could not serve as the basis for asserting the defense. In order to rely on a safety requirement to screen out disabled individuals, the employer must demonstrate that the requirement, as applied to the individual, satisfies the direct-threat standard under the ADA in order to show that the requirement is job-related and consistent

---

[26] The parties disagree as to whether the plaintiffs must prove that Wessel's disability was a motivating factor or the sole factor in the termination decision. However, that issue need not be resolved for purposes of this case, because each of the defendants' stated reasons for the termination — inability to perform the essential functions of the job, undue hardship, and direct threat — unquestionably relate to Wessel's disability. That is, none of the defendants' assertions in this case challenge the causal nexus between Wessel's disability and his termination.

with business necessity. 29 C.F.R. § 1630.15 and EEOC Interpretive Guidance thereto. In this instance, Defendants cannot demonstrate that driving was an essential function of [Wessel]'s job; therefore, they cannot use any existing driving restrictions as a basis for asserting the direct-threat defense in that they cannot satisfy the element of job-relatedness.

Even if Defendants were able to demonstrate that there was some driving that [Wessel] performed within the scope of his employment, Defendants cannot prevail on a direct-threat defense because they never told [Wessel] not to drive. Certainly, such an order would be required before Defendants could terminate [Wessel]'s employment. The conclusion that Defendants were required to apprise [Wessel] of their concern and to order him to stop driving (and, potentially, consider transportation accommodations for him) prior to being permitted to rely on a direct-threat defense is bolstered by the ADA's requirement that an employer engage in good-faith consideration of any accommodation that would have eliminated or reduced the threat before permitting reliance on the direct-threat defense. 29 C.F.R. § 1630.2(r).

D. Punitive Damages

Section 1981a of the Civil Rights Act of 1991 provides that a plaintiff under the Americans with Disabilities Act may recover punitive damages against a defendant if the plaintiff demonstrates that the defendant "engaged in a discriminatory practice or discriminatory practices with malice or with reckless indifference to the federally protected rights of an aggrieved individual." 42 U.S.C. § 1981a(b)(1). This standard is the same as that applied by courts under § 1981. *See, e.g.,* [*Rowlett v. AnheuserBusch, Inc.,* 832 F.2d 194 (1st Cir. 1987) ("reckless or callous indifference to the federally protected rights of others')]; [*Beauford v. Sisters of Mercy-Province of Detroit, Inc.,* 816 F.2d 1104 (6th Cir. 1987)]. In [*Rowlett*], the court also noted that Congress intended damages awards in civil rights actions to "be governed by the same principles as damage awards under the common law." The Supreme Court, as noted in [*Pacific Mutual Life Insurance Co. v. Haslip,* _____ U.S. _____, 111 S. Ct. 1032, 113 L. Ed. 2d 1 (1991)], has more than once approved the common-law method for assessing punitive damages awards:

> It is a well-established principle of the common law . . . a jury may inflict what are called exemplary, punitive or vindictive damages upon a defendant, having in view the enormity of his offense rather than the measure of compensation to the plaintiff. . . . [I]f repeated judicial decisions for more than a century are to be received as the best exposition of what the law is, the question will not admit of argument.

[*Id.* at _____ U.S. _____, _____, 113 L. Ed. 2d 1, 14].
The legislative history for § 1981a states that

> Compensatory and punitive damages will not give back to a plaintiff, in many cases, the career that they [*sic*] lost or the ability to rise further in that career. Congress doesn't have the ability to do that. It's a lasting permanent damage. I think what the increased remedies under the bill will do, however, is primarily

act as a deterrent. . . . It is the deterrent value that is so important. Allowing full compensatory and punitive damages . . . would provide a stronger incentive for employers to implement effective remedies for intervention and prevention, which I think is the real goal. Data suggests that employers do indeed implement measures to interrupt and prevent employment discrimination when they perceive that there is increased liability.

[H.R. Rep. No. 400(*l*), 102d Cong., 1st Sess., *reprinted in* 1991 U.S.C.C.A.N. 607 (quoting testimony of [Nancy E.] and [Dr. Freada K.], respectively)].

Although the statements were made with respect to gender and race discrimination, they are equally true for disability discrimination. When Congress enacted the Americans with Disabilities Act, it stated that the purpose of the Act was to "provide a clear and comprehensive national mandate for the elimination of discrimination against individuals with disabilities" and to "provide clear, strong, consistent, enforceable standards addressing discrimination against individuals with disabilities." 42 U.S.C. §§ 12,101 *et seq.* Thus, punitive damages are clearly available in this case.

The Supreme Court has previously discussed the "reckless disregard" standard under the Age Discrimination in Employment Act. In [*Trans World Airlines v. Thurston,* 469 U.S. 111 (1985)], it was stated that "a violation is 'willful' if 'the employer knew or showed reckless disregard for the matter of whether its conduct was prohibited by the ADEA.' . . . We hold that this is an acceptable way to articulate a definition of 'willful.'" A similar standard is appropriate under the Americans with Disabilities Act. The Defendants showed reckless disregard for the matter of whether its conduct was prohibited by the Americans with Disabilities Act; therefore, [Wessel]'s entitlement to punitive damages should be submitted to the jury.

IV. Conclusion

The Plaintiffs' proof will, therefore, establish that

(1) [Charles Wessel] had, at the time of his termination, a *disability*, as that term is defined in the ADA;

(2) He was "otherwise qualified" for the position he held. This element requires proof by Plaintiffs, by a preponderance of the evidence, that, except for [Wessel]'s disability, [Wessel] possesses the necessary qualifications for the position, such as educational background, experience, skills, and other job-related factors;

(3) [Wessel] was capable of performing all of the essential functions of the position, either with or without a reasonable accommodation by the employer;

(4) [Wessel]'s disability did not prevent him from performing the essential functions of the position, such that any functions he could not perform because of his disability were merely marginal functions not essential to performance of the job of Executive Director; and

(5) [Wessel]'s disability was a motivating factor in the decision to discharge him.

[7]   Defendants' Trial Brief

FORM 16–6   Sample Defendants' Trial Brief

IN THE UNITED STATES DISTRICT COURT FOR THE [NORTHERN]
DISTRICT OF [ILLINOIS]
[EASTERN] DIVISION

U.S. EQUAL EMPLOYMENT OPPORTUNITY COMMISSION
and [CHARLES H. WESSEL],

Plaintiffs,
v.   Civil Action No. [92 C 7330]
[A.I.C. SECURITY INVESTIGATIONS, LTD.];
     [A.I.C. INTERNATIONAL, LTD.];
and [unnamed defendant C],
Defendants.   Honorable [Marvin E. Aspen]

DEFENDANTS' TRIAL BRIEF

I. NATURE OF THE CASE

    This action is brought pursuant to Title I of the Americans with Disabilities
Act (ADA). 42 U.S.C. §§ 12,111 *et seq.* This law, as it pertains to Defendants
[A.I.C. SECURITY INVESTIGATIONS, LTD.], [A.I.C. INTERNATIONAL,
LTD.], and [unnamed defendant C] (hereinafter jointly "[A.I.C.]" unless otherwise specified), took effect on [July 26, 1992]. *Id.* Plaintiffs allege that Defendants unlawfully discriminated against [Charles Wessel] by discharging him on
account of his disability, cancer. Defendants assert that this action is without
merit because [Wessel] is not a qualified individual with a disability and therefore he is afforded no cause of action under ADA. Furthermore, Defendants assert that their challenged actions were for legitimate, nondiscriminatory business
reasons.

II. FACTUAL SUMMARY

    [Charles Wessel] worked as the Executive Director of [A.I.C. Security Inves-
tigations, Ltd.], the security guard division of [A.I.C. International, Ltd.], from
[February 1986] to [July 1992]. [Mr. Wessel] suffered from emphysema during the
entire course of his employment with [A.I.C.] and, for five of the six-plus years he
spent at [A.I.C.], he battled cancer in various locations in his body.
    In [1987], he first experienced cancer in his left lung, and he had approxi-
mately one-third of that lung removed through surgery. For a period of time following his surgery upon his return to work, [Wessel] was driven to and from his
home and work by an employee of [A.I.C.]. In [1991], [Wessel] experienced a
recurrence of cancer, this time in his right lung, and he had approximately one-

third of that lung removed in late [1991]. Upon his eventual return to work, [Wessel] was again offered a driver from [A.I.C.] to get him to and from work; however, he declined.

In early [April 1992], [Wessel] was diagnosed with two inoperable brain tumors that multiplied to four tumors in various parts of his brain by the end of [June 1992]. [Wessel] indicated to [A.I.C.] management that he had been instructed not to drive, yet he continued to drive to, from, and during work. [Wessel] took part in arrangements for his own replacement, interviewing candidates for his position from outside [A.I.C.] and, on [July 22, 1992], promoted [Jan D.] from within [A.I.C.] to a position as his heir apparent.

During his last year with [A.I.C.], [Wessel] was absent from work roughly 25 percent of the time due to hospitalizations, convalescence, and treatments that included periods of daily radiation treatments between [April] and [July 1992]. On [July 29, 1992], [Wessel] indicated to [Beverly K.], a managerial employee of [A.I.C.] that he reported to, that he would retire immediately if the company provided him with certain severance terms that he proposed. When his terms were subsequently accepted, [Wessel] rejected the agreement and named additional terms that would require [A.I.C.]'s disability insurance provider to pay a higher amount than [Wessel] would otherwise be entitled to under the plan.

[Wessel] was thereafter excluded from his position of Executive Director on or about [July 30, 1992]. He did not provide any medical information to [A.I.C.] when asked, nor would he or his treating physicians supply adequate information regarding his condition, including driving restrictions.

III. LEGAL ANALYSIS

At this time, there exists little or no case law specifically regarding the ADA that may provide the Court with any guidance in the instant action. However, the ADA expressly contemplates that the voluminous precedent arising out of section 504 of the Rehabilitation Act of 1973 (29 U.S.C. §§ 794 *et seq.*) may serve as guidance for determinations involving the ADA. *See* 42 U.S.C. § 12,117(b).

In these regards, case law under the Rehabilitation Act has loosely followed the shifting of burdens of proof enunciated in [*McDonnell Douglas Corp. v. Green,* 411 U.S. 792 (1973)], [*Texas Department of Community Affairs v. Burdine,* 450 U.S. 248 (1981)], and their progeny, although these cases are almost never referred to in Rehabilitation Act case law.[27] A prima facie case under the ADA, however,

---

[27] The Equal Employment Opportunity Commission [hereinafter EEOC] Rules implementing Title I, ADA §§ 101–107, 42 U.S.C. §§ 12,111–12,117 (1994) [hereinafter Title I], of the ADA suggest that the *McDonnell Douglas/Burdine* analysis "may" apply to ADA cases. 29 C.F.R. § 1630.15(a). *But see* Pushkin v. Regents of Univ. of Colo., 658 F.2d 1372, 1384–85 (10th Cir. 1981) (Rehabilitation Act of 1973 (29 U.S.C. §§ 701–709, 720–724, 730–732, 740, 741, 750, 760–764, 770–776, 780–787, 790–794 (1994) [hereinafter Rehabilitation Act of 1973]) contemplates neither a disparate treatment nor a disparate impact analysis because the law, similarly to the ADA, "sets forth its own criteria for scrutinizing claims. . . ."). *See also* Title VII of the Civil Rights Act of 1964, 42 U.S.C. §§ 2000e to 2000e-16 (1994) [hereinafter Title VII].

will necessarily differ from that of an action under Title VII of the Civil Rights Act due to the substantial differences in the two statutes.

The ADA proscribes in pertinent part discrimination "against a qualified individual with a disability because of the disability of such individual. . . ." 42 U.S.C. § 12,112(a). A *qualified individual with a disability* is defined as "an individual with a disability who, with or without reasonable accommodation, can perform the essential functions of the employment position that such individual holds or desires." 42 U.S.C. § 12,111(8).

Thus, similar to the analysis used in Rehabilitation Act cases,[28] Plaintiff has the burden of showing

(1) [Charles Wessel] is an "individual with a disability";
(2) He was "qualified" (i.e., he could perform the essential functions of his position of Executive Director for Defendants [A.I.C.]'s guard division, with or without reasonable accommodation);
(3) He was excluded from his position solely because of his disability; and
(4) Defendants are subject to the ADA.

See [*Overton v. Reilly,* 977 F.2d 1190, 1193 (7th Cir. 1992) (Rehabilitation Act Plaintiff "may not maintain an action . . . unless he is 'qualified' ")]; [*Carr v. Barr,* 59 Empl. Prac. Dec. (CCH) para. 41,651 (ex. 1) (D.D.C. 1992) (handicapped plaintiff must initially show that he is "otherwise qualified" and excluded from position solely because of that handicap, and, if this is shown, "the burden shifts to defendants to demonstrate job-related criteria and that 'reasonable accommodation' is not feasible. If defendants meet their showing, the burden would shift once again to the plaintiff, requiring him to rebut the employer's evidence by showing that the accommodation of the handicapped imposes no undue hardship upon the defendant.")].

The first and second elements of Plaintiffs' foregoing prima facie burden of proof are explicitly stated in the ADA. 42 U.S.C. § 12,111(8).[29] The parties have a divergence of opinion as to the third element listed above, since the EEOC will argue that Plaintiffs need only demonstrate that [Mr. Wessel]'s disability was a motivating factor rather than the sole factor for his exclusion from his position.

Virtually all of the cases concerning the Rehabilitation Act have held that Plaintiff must prove that his or her handicap was the sole basis for an exclusion from a position. *See* [*School Board of Nassau County v. Arline,* 480 U.S. 273, 275 (1987)]; [*Ristoff v. United States,* 839 F.2d 1242, 1244 (7th Cir. 1988)]; [*Carter v. Casa Central,* 849 F.2d 1048, 1053 (7th Cir. 1988)]; [*Pesterfield v. TVA,* 941 F.2d

---

[28] The phrase "qualified individual with a disability" from the ADA is comparable to an individual who is "otherwise qualified" under the Rehabilitation Act of 1973. *See* 29 C.F.R. § 1630.2(m) (1996). Both laws treat "qualified" in the identical terms of one who "with or without reasonable accommodation can perform the essential functions" of a particular position. *Compare* 42 U.S.C. § 12,111(8) (1994) *with* 29 C.F.R. § 1613.702(f) (1996).

[29] There remain, however, some issues under the law concerning the identification and reasonableness of accommodations, the burdens of proof, and the determination of essential functions.

437, 441 (6th Cir. 1991)]; [*Doe v. New York University,* 666 F.2d 761, 774 (2d Cir. 1981) (adopted in *Norcross v. Sneed,* 755 F.2d 113, 117–18 (8th Cir. 1985))]; [*Pushkin v. Regents of University of Colorado,* 658 F.2d 1372 (10th Cir. 1981)]; [*Treadwell v. Alexander,* 707 F.2d 473, 475 (11th Cir. 1983)].

The United States Court of Appeals for the [Eighth] Circuit articulated the underlying logic behind the necessity that handicap discrimination be shown to be Defendants' sole motive when it stated:

> Thus both the language of the statute and its interpretation by the Supreme Court indicate that [the Rehabilitation Act] was designed to prohibit discrimination within the ambit of an employment relationship in which the employee is potentially able to do the job in question.

[*Beauford v. Father Flanagan's Boys' Home,* 831 F.2d 768, 771 (8th Cir. 1987)]. This, then, represents the key distinction between a handicap or disability and those classes (race, color, religion, sex, etc.) that are protected under Title VII — the Rehabilitation Act and ADA protect only persons who are "qualified," whereas Title VII proscribes all levels of class-based differentiation.

Accordingly, individuals who are handicapped, or, for purposes of the ADA, disabled, are afforded only an equal footing to compete for jobs with others, and a plaintiff is entitled to no preferential treatment where other nondiscriminatory motives factor into the challenged action. This conclusion is supported by the congressional findings stated in § 2(q) of the ADA, 42 U.S.C. § 12,101(9), that "the continuing existence of unfair and unnecessary discrimination and prejudice denies people with disabilities the opportunity to compete on an equal basis and to pursue those opportunities for which our free society is justifiably famous. . . ."

In addition to the overwhelming case law under the Rehabilitation Act, another compelling reason for requiring Plaintiffs to prove that unlawful discrimination was the sole reason rather than a reason for Defendants' action, is that the ADA was excluded from recent federal legislation on this very issue.

The Civil Rights Act of 1991 (Pub. L. No. 102–166, 105 Stat. 1071) made sweeping amendments to civil rights laws, including the recently enacted ADA, which, at the time, in many respects had not yet become effective. Specifically, section 107 of the 1991 Civil Rights Act added subsection (m) to section 703 of Title VII. Thus, 42 U.S.C. § 2000e-2 now reads at the newly added subsection (m):

> . . . an unlawful employment practice is established when the complaining party demonstrates that race, color, religion, sex, or national origin was a motivating factor for any employment practice, even though other factors also motivated the practice.

Conspicuously absent from the amendments of the Civil Rights Act of 1991 is any similar language applicable to the ADA. Clearly, Congress did not intend to interrupt the well-reasoned and thoroughly developed body of law that existed under the Rehabilitation Act, which, again, Congress intended would apply in ADA actions.

The instant action may bring to the fore the issue of what burdens each of the parties should bear as to accommodation. Defendants submit that if [Charles

Wessel] is determined to be totally disabled under the law, then accommodation does not become an issue. *See* [*Byrne v. Board of Education, School District of West Allis,* 741 F. Supp. 167, 169 (E.D. Wis. 1990)].

As recently as [October] of [1992], however, the [Seventh] Circuit Court of Appeals declined to allocate the burden of proof regarding reasonable accommodations under the Rehabilitation Act. [*Overton v. Reilly,* 977 F.2d 1190, 1194 (7th Cir. 1992)]. Distinguishing between sections 501 and 504 of the Act (section 504 being, of course, more similar to the ADA), the court held that "section 504 . . . may require the plaintiff to show that a proposed accommodation is reasonable, although the case law on this issue is, to say the least, complex" (citations omitted). [*Id.*]

Thus, the [Seventh] Circuit Court of Appeals at least has implied some duty on the part of the plaintiff to come forward with some evidence on the issue of accommodation.

The [Eleventh] Circuit Court, in [*Treadwell v. Alexander,* 707 F.2d 473, 478 (11th Cir. 1983)], was more elaborate:

> Although the plaintiff initially has the burden of coming forward with evidence to make at least a facial showing that his handicap can be accommodated, the . . . employer has the ultimate burden of persuasion in showing an inability to accommodate.

The foregoing analysis conforms to the language of the ADA, since the Plaintiff must initially show that he is "qualified," which, by its very definition, incorporates the idea of performance "with or without reasonable accommodation." 42 U.S.C. § 12,111(8). It reasonably follows that the employer bears the shifting burden of demonstrating the unreasonableness of or any "undue hardship" involved with any proposed accommodations. 42 U.S.C. § 12,111(10).

The express language of the ADA further supports the foregoing placements of burdens. In construing the term *discriminate,* 42 U.S.C. § 12,112(b)(5)(A) states that unlawful conduct under the Act could include, *inter alia*:

> not making reasonable accommodations to the known physical or mental limitations of an otherwise qualified individual with a disability who is an applicant or employee, unless such covered entity can demonstrate that the accommodation would impose undue hardship. . . .

The foregoing language of the ADA imposes a duty to accommodate only "known" limitations, which can only be lawfully avoided by "demonstrating" undue hardship, i.e., that the accommodation is not reasonable. The burdens of the parties are self-evident from this language.[30]

To determine the overall issue of whether Plaintiff was "qualified," this Court should adhere to the Supreme Court's holding in [*Arline,* 480 U.S. 273], that in

---

[30] Moreover, punitive and compensatory damages made available by the recent Civil Rights Act of 1991 (42 U.S.C. §§ 1981a, 2000e to 2000e-17 (1994) [hereinafter Civil Rights Act of 1991]) may not be awarded unless the person with the disability "has informed the covered entity that accommodation is needed. . . ."

most cases, an "individualized inquiry" must be made under the particular circumstances of this case, giving appropriate weight to the Defendants' legitimate business concerns. [*Id.* at 287.]

B. DEFENDANTS' BURDEN OF PROOF

If Plaintiff can establish a prima facie case that he was disabled, qualified, and excluded from his former position based upon his disability, then the burden shifts to Defendants to articulate a legitimate, nondiscriminatory reason for their challenged actions, or to rebut the prima facie showing that Plaintiff is disabled or qualified.

The ADA defines a qualified individual in terms of ability to perform the "essential functions" of the position; however, the Act provides that "consideration shall be given to the employer's judgment as to what functions of a job are essential. . . ." 42 U.S.C. § 12,111(8). Thus, Defendants' burden of proof in rebuttal of Plaintiffs' prima facie case would include evidence of essential functions ignored by Plaintiff, and that Plaintiff could not perform. The employer's judgment must, by law, be considered in these regards.

Finally, a specific defense that applies to the instant action is provided for in the ADA, at 42 U.S.C. § 12,113, if an employer "den[ies] a job or benefit to an individual with a disability" because he poses "a direct threat to the health or safety of other individuals in the workplace." The EEOC guidelines for Rules, at 29 C.F.R. § 1630.2(r), interpret this provision as follows:

> An employer may require, as a qualification standard, that an individual not pose a direct threat to the health or safety of himself/herself or others.
> * * *
>
> The risk can only be considered when it poses a significant risk, i.e., high probability, of substantial harm's . . .
>
> Where accommodation is not at issue, an employer may lawfully discharge an employee who poses such a "direct threat."

[*Id.*]

C. DAMAGES RECOVERABLE UNDER ADA

Section 12,117 of the ADA provides, in subsection (A), that

> The powers, remedies, and procedures set forth in Section 705, 706, 707, 709 and 710 of the Civil Rights of 1964 (42 U.S.C. §§ 2000e-4, 2000e-5, 2000e-6, 2000e-8 and 2000e-9) shall be the powers, remedies, and procedures this title provides to the commission . . . or to any person alleging discrimination on the basis of disability in violation of any provision of this chapter, or . . . concerning employment.

Section 706(g)(1) of the Civil Rights Act, as amended in 1991, provides in pertinent part:

> If the court finds that the respondent has intentionally engaged in . . . an unlawful employment practice charged in the complaint, the court may enjoin the respondent from engaging in such unlawful employment practice, and order such affirmative action as may be appropriate, which may include, but is not limited to, reinstatement or hiring of employees, with or without back pay . . . or any other equitable relief as the court deems appropriate.
> * * *
>
> Interim earnings or amounts earnable with reasonable diligence by the person or persons discriminated against shall operate to reduce the back pay otherwise allowable.

42 U.S.C. § 2000e-5(g)(1).

Section 706(g)(2)(A) restricts the right of reinstatement and backpay with the following qualifications:

> No order of the court shall require the . . . reinstatement . . . of an individual as an employee, or the payment to him of any back pay, if such individual was suspended or discharged for any reason other than discrimination.

Subsection (B) of Section 706(g)(2) goes on to provide essentially that where the defendant demonstrates that it would have taken the same action in the absence of any impermissible motivating factor establishing by the plaintiff, the court:

> (i) may grant declaratory relief, injunctive relief (except as provided in clause (ii)), and attorneys' fees and costs demonstrated to be directly attributable only to the pursuit of a claim under Section 703(m); and
>
> (ii) shall not award damages or issue an order requiring any admission, reinstatement . . . or payment described in subparagraph (A).

Finally, subsection (k) goes on to provide:

> In any action or proceeding under this subchapter, the court, in its discretion, may allow the prevailing party, other than the commission . . . a reasonable attorney's fee (including expert fees) as part of the costs, and the commission . . . shall be liable for costs the same as a private person.

42 U.S.C. § 2000e-5(k).

The Civil Rights Act of 1991 provides (at 42 U.S.C. § 1981a(a)(2)) that if a respondent is shown to have engaged in unlawful intentional discrimination (not an employment practice that is unlawful because of its disparate impact, rather, intentional disparate treatment) violative of section 102 of the ADA (42 U.S.C. § 12,112), or committed a violation of section 102(B)(5) of the Act, against an individual, then the complaining party may potentially recover

> compensatory and punitive damages as allowed in Subsection (B), in addition to any relief authorized by Section 706(G) of the Civil Rights Act of 1964, from the respondent.

Subsection (B) goes on to provide that

(1) Punitive Damages — to recover punitive damages, the complaining party must demonstrate "that the respondent engaged in a discriminatory practice or discriminatory practices with malice or with reckless indifference to the federally protected rights of an aggrieved individual"

(2) Compensatory Damages — Compensatory damages may not include back pay, interest, or any other type of relief authorized under § 706(G) of the Civil Rights Act of 1964;

(3) Limitations — [Compensatory and punitive damages are limited, in this action, under 42 U.S.C. § 1981a(b)(3)(C) to $200,000 based upon the uncontested fact that only Defendant AIC Security Investigations, Ltd., employs any employees, and more than 200 but fewer than 501 in number].[31]

It is important to note, however, that no compensatory or punitive damages may be awarded in this action where Defendants demonstrate "good-faith efforts," in consultation with the person with the disability who has informed the covered entity that accommodation is needed, "to identify and make a reasonable accommodation that would provide such individual with an equally effective opportunity and would not cause an undue hardship on the operation of the business." 42 U.S.C. § 1981a(a)(3). This exclusion of compensatory and punitive damages is denominated in the statute as the "reasonable accommodation and good faith effort" defense, applicable in actions "where a discriminatory practice involves the provision of a reasonable accommodation." *Id.* Reasonable accommodation is involved in any action where the individual with a disability invokes some reasonable accommodation in order to meet his or her burden of demonstrating that he or she is qualified.

Finally, Defendants submit that no claim for punitive damages is at issue because no claims for such damages have been properly joined in this action. In support of this contention, Defendants submit:

(1) The Complaint of the EEOC is the only pleading properly joined in this action, and it seeks no remedy of punitive damages.
(2) Although [Charles Wessel] has filed a motion to intervene as a party Plaintiff, he never filed nor served his Complaint following the Court's Order granting his motion to intervene.[32]

---

[31] 42 U.S.C. § 1981a(4)(c)(2) (1994) provides that "the court shall not inform the jury of the limitations described in subsection (b)(3)" but shall simply cap any verdict of the jury subsequent to its decision.

[32] Charles Wessel's motion to intervene specifically sought leave of court for permission to file a complaint by attaching a "proposed" copy to the motion. The motion was granted in open court on December 20, 1992, yet no complaint was filed or served by Charles Wessel.

[8]   Plaintiff's Opening Statement (Mock Trial)

FORM 16–7   Sample Plaintiff's Opening Statement

This case presents the story of [Steve Lyons]. [Steve Lyons] worked for Defendant [Eastern Pharmaceuticals] for more than [20] years until his employment was terminated last [August]. [Steve Lyons] was a staff accountant at the time of his termination.

In the summer of [1991], [Steve Lyons] began to experience blurry vision and slurred speech. In [June] of that year, he was diagnosed as having Multiple Sclerosis ("MS"). Although diagnosed with MS, [Steve] was able to continue his work at [Eastern]. All that he needed was a magnification device for his computer and someone to answer his incoming calls.

In late [July] of last year, [Steve Lyons] suffered another, more severe MS attack. After this attack, his vision and speech were worse than they had been before and he began to have some problems walking and coordinating muscle movement. [Steve] reasonably requested that the defendant provide him with the following accommodations:

(a) a reader who would communicate written messages and computer information to him,

(b) a speaker who would communicate oral messages from him; and

(c) [Eastern]'s making the office area "handicapped friendly."

[Eastern] refused to make such reasonable accommodations, and on [August 5, 1992], [Lisa Brown], [Eastern]'s Accounting Manager, fired [Steve Lyons].

The Americans with Disabilities Act ("ADA") was promulgated to protect people like [Steve Lyons] from this type of discrimination. People with disabilities have long been excluded from normal life activities. In passing the ADA, Congress estimated that disabled people are unemployed at a rate of approximately 66 percent. Congress found that often there was not a justifiable reason for this, as many disabled people are qualified not only to work but also to participate in activities from which they are regularly excluded. Such is the case here. [Steve Lyons] is capable of performing essential job functions if [Eastern] provides him with the reasonable accommodations that he requested. They refused to do so, and terminated his employment. [Eastern] has blatantly violated the ADA.

You will hear two witnesses testify today. The first witness will be [Steve Lyons], the plaintiff. He will testify about his role as staff accountant at [Eastern Pharmaceuticals], and what transpired after his diagnosis with MS when he requested the second set of accommodations, which were denied prior to his termination.

The second testimony that you will hear will come from [Dr. Willard Allen], a neurologist with expertise in the field of Multiple Sclerosis. He will testify about the plaintiff's capabilities, general symptoms, and progression of the disease.

After you have heard all of the evidence, it will be clear that the defendant has violated the Americans with Disabilities Act by terminating the plaintiff's employment when the defendant refused to make reasonable accommodations that would not have caused undue hardship.

[9] Defendant's Opening Statement (Mock Trial)

FORM 16–8 Sample Defendant's Opening Statement

Good morning, ladies and gentlemen of the jury. My name is [John Black], and I represent the defendant in today's case, [Eastern Pharmaceuticals]. [Eastern Pharmaceuticals] is a drug manufacturing company that produces many drugs that allow us to live longer and better lives. [Eastern] was brought into court today by the plaintiff [Steve Lyons].

Obviously, [Mr. Lyons] suffers from physical ailments that limit his eyesight, his speech, and his motor skills. To protect disabled individuals from discrimination, the government has enacted the Americans with Disabilities Act (ADA), as opposing counsel has advised you.

It is true that [Mr. Lyons] is disabled. It is true that he was terminated from his position at [Eastern]. However, to sustain a cause of action under the ADA, the individual must also prove that he was discriminated against. [Mr. Lyons] will be unable to meet this burden. In fact, I will prove to you today through the testimony of the controller of [Eastern], [Mr. Henry Bell], that [Mr. Lyons] was terminated because of his subpar performance. His disability played no role whatsoever in his termination.

[Mr. Lyons], on the other hand, will claim that he was discriminated against because the accommodations that he sought were not provided by [Eastern]. However, [Arthur Smith], a partner at [Eastern]'s auditing firm — [Ernst & Young] — will show that it would have been an undue hardship to [Eastern] to provide these accommodations. The ADA permits an employer not to provide accommodations if doing so would cause the entity to suffer an undue hardship. In [Mr. Lyons]'s case, the cost difference between providing the accommodations and keeping [Mr. Lyons] on board and hiring someone else to do his job was astronomical. Also, the nature of the pharmaceutical industry is highly dependent upon reinvesting any available funds back into the company for research and development purposes. Any cut whatsoever in these funds will have an immediate impact on both the company's short-term and long-run possibilities for developing drugs, and survival for that matter. Therefore, providing [Mr. Lyons] with the accommodations he sought would cause [Eastern] to suffer an undue hardship.

Furthermore, it will be demonstrated that even if the accommodations were provided for [Mr. Lyons], he still would not be able to perform the essential functions of his job. Therefore, even with the protection of the ADA, [Lyons] has no substantial cause of action.

In conclusion, it is true that [Mr. Lyons] suffers from a disability and that he was terminated from his job at [Eastern]; however, he was not discriminated against. If [Mr. Lyons] were not disabled, he still would have been let go. [Lyons] cannot be allowed to recover under the ADA.

[10]   Testimony by Plaintiff in HIV Case[33]

FORM 16–9   Sample Plaintiff's Testimony in HIV Case

BEFORE: HONORABLE [ROBERT S. GAWTHROP III], J.

JURY TRIAL — DAY 2
[JOHN DOE] — DIRECT]

Page 188
BY [MR. EPSTEIN]:

Q.   Did he ever raise any other subject of any type as the reason for the nonre-newal of your contract at the end of the year?
A.   No.
Q.   You started to say you loved your job, you wanted to stay there. What did you resolve to do to effect that end?
A.   I wanted to work for other attorneys in the firm, just do as good a job as I could on those tasks, so that I would continue to work there at that firm.
Q.   Did you believe that at that time, that the statements of [Steven A.] were a final resolution of your employment at the [Kohn] firm?
A.   There was no indication that that was the case, no.
Q.   Why?
A.   I had not received written notice and I was still under a contract. He had told me to find a job as soon as possible, but I thought I could change people's mind by working really hard.
Q.   During the month of [January], did [Steven A.] do anything that made you feel uncomfortable?
A.   It was starting in [December] through [January].

[JOHN DOE] — DIRECT

Page 189

He stayed his distance. Our offices were two offices apart, and he would not come by, say hello. He would not talk to me. He avoided me. One point, he wouldn't use the phone. There were no phone calls in [January]. At one point, he wanted to give me an assignment. He said, I want to assign you something,

---

[33] The testimony in Form 16–9 was presented in the trial of the case of *Doe v. Kohn Nast & Graf, P.C.,* No. 93-4510 (E.D. Pa.). This testimony was presented on the second and third days of trial in Philadelphia, Pennsylvania.

but he had his secretary type the assignment up, and had the secretary come in, lay it in my office.

I did the assignment. Gave it back to him. And then he gave his secretary a note and the secretary came and laid the note in my office. No direct contact at all.

Q. Where was your office in this suite at the [Kohn] firm in connection with [Steven A.]'s office in the [Kohn] firm?
A. [Mr. A.]s office — [Steve] would probably be at the end of that jury box. My office would be at this end of this jury box.
Q. About how much distance is there between that?
A. Twenty feet maybe.
Q. Had [Steven A.] ever, before [January] of [1993], ever given you assignments where he would actually just give it to you in writing, and hand it through his secretary?

[JOHN DOE] — DIRECT

Page 193

prepared and gave to [Dianne N.] at the end of [January] of [1993]?
A. Yes, it is.
Q. Were the statements made in this memorandum truthful statements at the time that you made them?
A. Yes.
Q. Had you, on or about [January 29, 1993], had any contact with any lawyer regarding bringing an action against the firm?
A. At this time, no.
Q. On or about [January 29, 1993], had you taken any steps to complain about the firm's behavior toward you, to the organization that we have acronymed as the EEOC or the Equal Employment Opportunity Commission?
A. At this time, no.
Q. Had you complained to any state agency, and, specifically, the [Pennsylvania] Human Relations Commission, about any behavior or treatment of you at the [Kohn] firm?
Λ. No.
Q. Would you please read into the record this document, as it appears at paragraph four, starting with the word, beginning — by the way, so the record reflects, who's the memorandum to?

[JOHN DOE] — DIRECT

Page 222

hour and the jurors are reminded of my prior admonition. (Court was thereupon recessed at [3:35 P.M.] After the recess, the following proceedings were held commencing at [3:50 P.M.])

THE COURT: [Mr. Epstein], I'd ask that you avoid speaking directly to the jury.

[MR. EPSTEIN]: I wasn't aware that I did it and if I did it, I apologize to the Court, Your Honor.

THE COURT: Except for stipulations or summations.

(To the Clerk) Bring in the jury, please.

(The jury entered the courtroom.)

BY [MR. EPSTEIN]:

Q. During this same general time period in early [February 1993], did something occur that made you realize that [Steven A.] knew of your infection with the AIDS virus?
A. Yes.
Q. Can you please tell the jury what happened in the beginning of [February 1993] that led you to this conclusion?

[JOHN DOE] — DIRECT

Page 223

A. I had been asked to obtain a copy of a memorandum of understanding between Canada and France. It's a legal document. And I went to the file that was outside [Mr. A.]'s office and it wasn't there and I thought maybe [Mr. A.] had a copy of this document in his office where we routinely kept documents that weren't in the file.
I went into his office and I went to the back of his desk where he had the credenza table. I was looking through the documents of various pleadings that we were working on them were laying there and I came across a copy of my letter from [Dr. John B.] from [Johns Hopkins] and a copy of my policy.
Q. Did you give [Steven A.] any right to have either one of those documents?
A. No, I did not.
Q. Did you provide him with either copies or the original documents for him to copy at any time?
A. No, I did not.
Q. Had you authorized anyone to do that on your behalf?
A. No, I did not.
Q. Do you have any idea how [Steven A.] rightfully came into possession of those documents

[JOHN DOE] — DIRECT

Page 224

when you found them in his office?

A. I have no idea how [Mr. A.] obtained them.

Q. When you saw the two documents, the one regarding your disability policy and the one regarding the letter from [Dr. B.] in his office, what was your reaction?

A. I was angry and my heart dropped. I felt like: Oh my God. This is what it's all about. I know now that — Well, my fear was was reality. Even though I tried not to let anyone know that I was HIV-positive, the explanation for the behavior now was clear.

Q. What did you do after you discovered these documents in his office?

A. I called the AIDS Law Project in [Pennsylvania]; I contacted the Equal Employment Opportunity Commission, the [Pennsylvania] Human Relations Commission, and I sought legal counsel.

Q. The documents that you saw copies of, were the originals still in the office?

A. I believe the originals were still at my desk, yes.

Q. In your desk where you had originally told us they were before?

A. Yes.

[JOHN DOE] — DIRECT

Page 225

Q. Did you consider confronting [Steven A.] with this revelation that you had just made that he had documents from your desk drawer?

A. No. It was clear. No.

Q. After you talked to the AIDS Law Project, what did you do as a result of that conversation or in addition to that conversation?

A. I sought legal counsel in [Washington, D.C.].

Q. I'd like you again to turn to, and if it's not readily available to you, the document that has previously been marked as P-39. Is that in fact one of the documents which you found in [Mr. A.]'s office?

A. No, this not the document.

Q. P-40. Excuse me. I'll have to get a copy of that. Was it the letter from [Dr. B.] that you were talking about?

A. Yes.

Q. Was this the document that you found in [Mr. A.]'s office?

A. I saw a copy of that document laying on the table, yes.

Q. And this the document that's been marked as P-40?

[JOHN DOE] — DIRECT

Page 226

A. Yes.

Q. And in addition to that, did you also see a copy of the document relating to your disability insurance that the jury viewed earlier?

A. Yes. Mr. [A.] and I had been talking about the disability and a copy of that policy in his possession when it shouldn't have been.

Q. Getting back to what I asked you before, did you also take action beyond calling the AIDS Law Project?

A. I retained a lawyer to seek legal advice.

Q. Who was that lawyer?

A. It was [Deborah K.] of the firm of [Bernabei] and [Katz] in [Washington, D.C.].

Q. Will you please tell us how you came to choose a [Washington, D.C.] firm instead of a firm that was located in the [Philadelphia] area?

A. There were two reasons. I wanted this problem resolved by good attorneys and I wanted it outside of the [Philadelphia] community. I didn't want my career ruined.

Q. Why did you think having — going to a [Philadelphia] lawyer wouldn't resolve the problem?

A. [Pat P.] had told me in [January] and a couple times throughout this period that if I sued

* * *

[JOHN DOE] — DIRECT

Page 234

Honor, may I have it admitted into evidence?

THE COURT: Without objection it is admitted?

A. It reads: "PERSONAL CONFIDENTIAL" bold and underlined.

"[Nicole M.], Esquire, [Barnabei] and [Katz], [1773 T. Street, N.W.] [Washington, D.C]. [20009].

"Dear [Ms. M.]: I am interested in retaining [Ms. Lynne B.] to representing me in an employment discrimination case.

"I prepared the attached memorandum setting forth the facts of the situation and potential claims. I am a commercial litigator and not an attorney adept in this field so my memorandum does not profess to include all the potential claims that may be asserted.

"I have included the relevant documents to provide you further insight. After you have an opportunity to review the materials, please contact me so that we can discuss whether your firm is interested in pursuing this matter on my behalf and to arrange for a meeting.

"Thank you for your consideration

"Very truly yours."

Q. And did you send that letter out with the

[JOHN DOE — DIRECT]
* * *

Page 255

character with you as [S.]?

A. No, I wouldn't have said that.
Q. Now did you send copies of the chronological history that you prepared for your lawyers just the history not the materials but did you send a copy of the chronological materials that you sent your lawyers to anyone else?
A. Yes, I sent a copy of the narrative telling what was going on at the firm and how they were treating me to four news sources and believe it was [ABC], [CBS], [PBS], the [Front Line], and [NBC].
Q. [S.], why did you do that?
A. I did it because I wanted to the expose the law firm, what they were doing.
Q. Why?
A. Because it was wrong.
Q. Were you mad?
A. I was angry, yes.
Q. Were you angry that they were violating the law?

[MR. SWEENEY]: Objection, Your Honor.

THE COURT: I'll sustain that.

BY [MR. EPSTEIN]:

Q. Did you send to any news source any documentation regarding the allegations that you

[JOHN DOE — DIRECT]

Page 256

were making of discrimination based on your disability?

A. Can you repeat that, please?
Q. Did you send any documentation along with those letters to the news sources where you alleged that you were the victim of unlawful discrimination?
A. No. I sent a cover letter, the narrative, and an article about [Lynne B.] and [Deborah K.].
Q. In the opening statements of counsel, they alleged that you offered, and in fact I think I stated this in my opening as well, that you offered to receive money for giving them your story. Is that true?

A. No. That's incorrect. I did I think what [Mr. Sweeney] said. I asked them if they would help finance my litigation to oppose discrimination at this firm. I knew when I was at the law firm the kind of practice that they had. They would have a psychiatrist pick a jury like they did the other day; that they would have fancy computers like this.

MR. SWEENEY: Objection.

THE COURT: State your grounds.

[MR. O'BRIEN]: May we see you at side bar,
* * *

JURY TRIAL–DAY 3

[JOHN DOE] — DIRECT

and this envelope until I requested the [Kohn] firm, through the course of this litigation, to produce to me all documents, all mail, that I had received which they had not provided me. And they gave me a copy of this document.

Q. Did you ever receive a copy of this letter?
A. I never received this envelope or the ability to respond to a job at [Cohen Shapiro], because I never received this.
Q. Did you ever give them permission to return to sender mail that was directed to you?
A. No. I explicitly had given them my mail address. I knew that they had my address. They knew where I was located. I expected any mail that was personal and confidential to be forwarded to me at my home.
Q. In fact, on occasion, they did mail letters to you, did they not, so they knew where you were?
A. Yes, they did.
Q. After you were expelled from the [Kohn] firm, did you take any action to file your claim with any State or Federal agencies?
A. Yes, I contacted the EEOC and the [Pennsylvania] Human Relations Commission.
Q. On what basis did you file with these agencies,

[JOHN DOE] — DIRECT

Page _____

what was the basis of your claim, stated basis of your claim, as to why you were filing?

A. I subsequently filed other claims, other commissions, but at the time I filed these claims, I filed a claim with the EEOC and the [PHRC]. That's what we call those commissions for short, for discrimination, on the basis of my disability, being infected with the human immunodeficiency virus.

Q. Why did you go to these agencies? Did you go to the Federal agencies, the agency, the EEOC, the [Pennsylvania] Human Relations Commission, as opposed to just coming right into this Court? You're a lawyer?

A. In order to allow these matters sometimes to be investigated and conciliated peacefully among the parties, those commissions have been charged by the legislators of the Federal Government, or the state government, to try to resolve the matters. And they require me to get a letter from them giving me permission to bring the action in a Court of law.

Q. Is it a prerequisite to coming into this courtroom that you first file with both of those agencies?

MR. SWEENEY: Objection, Your Honor, leading.

[JOHN DOE] — DIRECT

THE COURT: I will sustain it.

BY MR. EPSTEIN:

Q. What are the prerequisites to coming into this courtroom and filing a claim under either the [Pennsylvania] Human Relations Act or Title 7, or the ADA, Americans with Disabilities Act?

A. In order for me to stop the discrimination and get my claims redressed, I have to get what is called a right-to-sue letter from the [PHRA], [PHRC], and the EEOC, which will permit me to file a complaint in Court, in either the [Common Pleas] Court or the United States District Court, which brought me here.

Q. Again, I ask you, does that mean that it is a prerequisite to come into this courtroom?

A. Yes, it is what we called exhaustion of our administrative remedies.

Q. Were you aware of that when you filed with those agencies?

A. Yes, I was.

Q. Did you, in fact, receive a notice of right to sue from the EEOC?

A. Yes, I did.

Q. I'm going to show you a document that has previously been marked as one of the defendant's

[JOHN DOE] — DIRECT

pendency of litigation cannot be used against someone? Somebody can confess to a murder in the middle of trial, you can hold that against them.

[MS. O'CONNELL]: It reserves all defense claims.

THE COURT: That, if anything, is helpful to your cause, is it not there?

[MS. O'CONNELL]: Yes, sir.

THE COURT: If that is an objection, I think it is overruled.

[MS. O'CONNELL]: Thank you, sir.

(Side-bar.)

BY [MR. EPSTEIN]:

Q. Would you please read to the jury, and for the record, the statements made by [Mr. K.] that are dated here [September 24, 1993]?
A. It reads, "Pursuant to paragraph twelve of the employment agreement, dated [September 17, 1991], between you and the undersigned firm, this will confirm in writing the notice, previously given to you orally by [Mr. A.], that the agreement has not been renewed for the period subsequent to [December 31, 1993].

This notice is given as a precaution only and is without prejudice to our understanding and

JOHN DOE — DIRECT

Page ____

position that no such written notice is necessary under paragraph twelve in light of your prior acts and the fact that your employment relationship with the firm ended in [March 1993]. Further, we expressly reserve the right to assert any and all defenses and claims against you under the agreement and otherwise."

BY [MR. EPSTEIN]:

Q. Does this letter confirm your understanding that, in fact, [Mr. K.] had ended your employment relationship in [March 1993]?
A. I understood this to be saying —

[MR. SWEENEY]: Objection.

THE COURT: Sustain that as leading.

BY [MR. EPSTEIN]:

Q. What did you understand [Mr. K.] to be saying about that subject?
A. I understood him to be telling me that when he threw me out —

[MR. SWEENEY]: Objection, Your Honor.

THE COURT: State your grounds.

[MR. SWEENEY]: It is a conclusion.

THE COURT: Sure it is. I think a proper one. Overruled. Proper, that is to say, under the Rules of Evidence. I comment not upon its veracity.

[JOHN DOE]–DIRECT

Page 82

THE WITNESS: I understood him to be saying that, although I threw you out of my firm on [March] of [1993], I'm giving you this notice confirming the fact that you are not a member of this firm and your contract is not being renewed for the following year there.

[MR. SWEENEY]: Move to strike, Your Honor.

THE COURT: Motion denied.

BY [MR. EPSTEIN]:

Q. You filed a lawsuit in this matter, did you not?
A. Yes, I did.
Q. Were you, at that time, represented by the law firm that you had hired in Washington, [Bernabei & Katz]?
A. No. Come [August] of [1993], I was no longer represented by them.
Q. Why?
A. By that time, I had exhausted my financial resources. And my parents were taking a second mortgage on their home, no longer had any money to help me, so I could not pay for my lawyers.
Q. What did you do in order to file this lawsuit, who filed it on your behalf?
A. I filed the lawsuit by myself, what we call pro

[JOIIN DOE] — DIRECT

se.

Q. Did you continue in that status until [March] of [1994]?
A. Yes.
Q. And, thereafter, did you continue to be pro se even after the intervention of the EEOC?
A. Yes. In [March] of [1994], the EEOC certified this case, and the Court granted them permission to intervene. But I still did not have private counsel so I continued assisting the EEOC in prosecuting this case.

Q. In the context of this lawsuit, can you tell the jury what your claims are in brief, just what the complaint states you claim under, which acts with regard to your claim of disability discrimination?

[MR. SWEENEY]: Objection, Your Honor.

THE COURT: State your grounds.

[MR. SWEENEY]: The obligation of the Court to instruct the jury on the law not the witness.

[MR. EPSTEIN]: I'm not going to ask him what the law is, merely what the five areas of claim are before he gets off the witness stand.

THE COURT: I'm going to permit him to do that. That objection is overruled.

[JOHN DOE] — DIRECT

THE WITNESS: I filed a complaint in this United States Court alleging Federal violations of my Federal rights, and also several state common law claims.

Under the Federal laws, I'm alleging that these defendants, [Harold K.], [Steven A.], and [Kohn, Nast & Graf], violated my Federal rights under the Americans with Disabilities Act. Specifically, they discharged me on the basis that I was infected with HIV, a disability, that they retaliated against me when they found out that I was going to sue the law firm. That they coerced me, interfered and intimidated with my rights to oppose a discrimination.

[MR. SWEENEY]: Objection, Your Honor.

THE COURT: State your grounds, sir.

[MR. SWEENEY]: I think we are getting into the area that we discussed at sidebar.

BY [MR. EPSTEIN]:

Q. Can you keep it broader?
A. Okay. That I brought a claim, third claim under the ADA for intimidation, interference and coercion. That I brought a fourth claim under the Americans with Disabilities Act for improper medical inquiry.

[JOHN DOE] — DIRECT

Q. Were those same claims, and those same types of claims brought under the [Pennsylvania] Human Relations Act?
A. Yes. There are parallel claims under the [Pennsylvania] Human Relations Act.

Q. Now, in addition to those claims, did you bring any claims regarding your contract of employment?
A. Well, I had also a Federal claim under the Equal — under the insurance laws of the Federal Government for discrimination, for deprivation of my right to have disability insurance.
And then I also —
Q. That is under what Act, sir?
A. We call it the ERISA Act, the Employment Retirement Insurance Act.
Q. And?
A. Employer.
Q. Security Act?
A. Security Act, thank you.
Q. Now, in addition to that, were there claims brought, pursuant to the terms of that contract, for the years 19 — the balance of the year of [1993], and the entire year of [1994]?
A. Yes, sir.
Q. How about the other common-law claims, what are

[JOHN DOE] — DIRECT

they, what other two claims do you have?

A. The present claims that I understand are pending before this Court — I don't want to misstate this.
Q. I don't want you to go into it deeply. What two categories of claim?
A. I believe I have a defamation claim and I have invasion of privacy claim.
Q. With regard to the defamation, as you were leaving the offices, you saw the reaction of the individuals who were watching you leave, did you not?
A. Yes.
Q. What was your — what was your belief, based upon their reaction to your leaving under those circumstances?

[MR. SWEENEY]: Objection, Your Honor.
THE COURT: State your grounds.
[MR. SWEENEY]: No foundation.
THE COURT: What foundation do you want? Do you want him to articulate, verbalize what their reactions were, sir?
[MR. SWEENEY]: No, sir, the basis for him having an understanding of what was inside someone else's mind.

[11] Transcript of Plaintiff Testimony[34]

A. I have limited endurance. If I'm climbing stairs, I have to stop after about two flights and rest. I'm unable to run, which means there are a number of sports

---

[34] The following testimony from Stone v. Entergy Services, Inc., Civ. A. No. 94-2669, 1995 WL 368473, at *4 (E.D. La. June 20, 1995) ("Although plaintiff cannot walk briskly, and has some trouble climbing stairs," plaintiff's "ability to walk is not substantially limited nor significantly restricted . . . ."), albeit taken at a deposition rather than at trial, is a good

that I can't participate in. I have limited motion in my body. When I go to bend over, I try to make sure that I either bend from the knees or support myself by holding on to a window sill, piece of furniture, something like that. If I'm walking in a group, if the group does not pace itself to me, I am left far behind. Certain activities I know I'm limited, so I try not to put myself in a position where balance would be a particular problem. Walking down stairs, my right foot won't really support me. I can't lift my right heel off the ground, so in handling stairs, I have to be careful to put my whole foot on the stair when I'm going up; otherwise I've got a problem.

Q. We talked about your limited endurance, you get winded after about two flights of stairs. You have trouble handling stairs in general because of your right foot?

A. That's correct.

Q. You have limited body motion which results in your needing to bend from the knees or have a support?

A. Yes.

Q. And you need to pace yourself slower than the average person when you're walking?

A. Significantly.

Q. And you do have some trouble with balance?

A. Occasionally.

Q. Not all the time?

A. Not all the time.

Q. Other than these problems, is there any other way you differ from the average person because of your polio residuals?

A. I already told you I can't do a situp. That's about it.[35]

[12] Transcript of Testimony (Mock Trial)

Q. Plaintiff calls [Steve Lyons]. Please state your name, address, and occupation for the court.

A. My name is [Steve Lyons] and I was a staff accountant at [Eastern] until I was fired on [August 5, 1992]. My address is [2222 22d Street], [Lower Merion], [Pennsylvania] [22222].

Q. Are you currently employed?

A. No, I am not.

Q. What is your educational background?

A. I have a economics degree from [Georgetown University], and I received my CPA before I started with [Eastern] on [July 7, 1972].

---

example of the direct examination of an ADA plaintiff. This case involved a plaintiff who suffered from such post-polio residuals as "muscle weakness, partial paralysis, one leg [being] longer than the other and one foot [being] longer than the other." This testimony occurred when the plaintiff was asked about his present limitations.

[35] *Id.* (emphasis added) (citation omitted). Despite the presence of such limitations, the *Stone* court concluded that plaintiff did "not have a physical impairment that substantially limits a major life activity." 1995 WL 368473, at *4.

Q. When were you first diagnosed with Multiple Sclerosis?

A. Around [June 20th] I had problems with blurry vision and slurred speech and at that time I went and talked with my normal physician, who referred me to [Dr. Allen], a neurologist. [Dr. Allen], on [June 26th], was the first to diagnose that I had Multiple Sclerosis.

Q. Excuse me. [June 26th] of which year was this?

A. [1991].

Q. Has MS affected any of your major life activities? By major life activities I mean functions which you perform every day?

A. Yes, MS has substantially limited my ability to read, speak, and walk.

Q. Thank you. When were you first hired by [Eastern]?

A. I was hired as an accounting clerk on [July 7, 1972], and since that time I had received several promotions and on [July 11, 1989], I was promoted to staff accountant and since then I have been working [20] years for the company as a loyal employee.

Q. What were your essential job functions as staff accountant?

A. My essential job functions as a staff accountant included producing financial reports using spreadsheet applications and computers, operating an adding machine to perform various mathematical functions, and maintaining the general ledger and communicating the results with outside vendors and [Eastern]'s purchasing agents regarding the fixed-asset acquisitions.

Q. What initial accommodations were made to deal with your blurry vision and slurred speech?

A. Initially, when I noticed the blurry vision and slurred speech, I approached [Ms. Lisa Brown], the Accounting Manager, and at that time my vision was not as bad as it is today and they were able to accommodate me by giving me a magnifying glass so that I could read the computer screen and other papers.

Q. What accommodation, if any, did they make to deal with your slurred speech?

A. For my slurred speech, all my incoming calls were rerouted to another employee to answer my calls.

Q. Who did you say [Lisa Brown] was?

A. She was [Eastern]'s Accounting Manager and my supervisor.

Q. Was she your supervisor during your whole time at [Eastern] or just during the time you were staff accountant?

A. During the period that I was staff accountant.

Q. When did you inform her that you suffer from MS?

A. I initially informed her after I received my diagnosis on [June 26, 1991]. After I had informed her of my MS, she made the necessary accommodations for me soon afterwards.

Q. Prior to your diagnosis with MS, had you ever received any unfavorable job evaluations?

A. No, I had not. I had always received satisfactory or above-average job performance.

Q. What was your most recent job evaluation?

A. My most recent job evaluation, which was in [1991], was that my work was satisfactory.[36]

Q. Was this prior to or after your diagnosis?

A. Prior to my most recent attack of MS.

Q. OK, but subsequent to the initial diagnosis?

A. That's correct.

Q. In [July of 1992], you suffered another MS attack?

A. Yes, I did. With this attack, my eyesight and speech deteriorated further and I had difficulty with walking and coordination of muscle movements at that time. At that time I approached [Ms. Brown] to request further accommodations, which included having a reader communicate written messages and computer information to me, having a speaker communicate oral messages from me, and having the office area of [Eastern]'s facility made "handicapped friendly." At that time, [Ms. Brown] informed me that the accommodations were unreasonable and would create undue financial hardship for [Eastern]. Soon thereafter she fired me from my job.

Q. Do you believe that you can perform the essential job functions of staff accountant if you were provided with the reasonable accommodations that you requested?

A. Yes, I believe I can. As an accountant, I believe that most of my functions relate to the mental abilities and the MS has not affected any of my mental faculties, just my vision and speech.

Q. Did [Ms. Brown] give you any indication aside from the undue financial burden as to the reason for the company terminating your employment?

A. She mentioned that I can no longer perform my essential job functions and she also suggested that there were other healthy individuals who could perform the job without the changes I have requested.

Q. As far as you know, are there any other people working for [Eastern] who suffer from Multiple Sclerosis?

A. No one else that I know of. No.

Q. Nothing further.

Cross-Examination of Plaintiff

Q. I just have a couple questions for you, [Mr. Lyons]. Do you have an employment contract with [Eastern Pharmaceuticals]?

A. No, I don't.

Q. So is it fair to say that you are an employee at will?

A. Yes, but I was given. . . .

Q. Thank you. It is "yes" or "no." OK. You said that your last evaluation was in [1991]. When exactly in [1991]?

A. Yes, that is correct. It was toward the end of the year, so it was around [December 31st]. That is when [Eastern] provides all its employees with employee evaluations.

---

[36] The witness's answer regarding the contents of the job evaluation is hearsay.

Q. So it was a full eight months between the time of your last evaluation and the time you were terminated?

A. That is correct.

Q. Since your termination from [Eastern] have you gotten another job?

A. No, I have not.

Q. Have you looked for another job?

A. Yes, I have.[37]

Q. What is happening when you look for jobs?

A. Most people I assume look at my disability and have assumed that I cannot perform the functions without the accommodations necessary and have determined that it would be an undue hardship for them.[38]

Q. They told you this, that it would be an undue hardship?

A. No, they haven't.

Q. You just have that impression?

A. That's correct. When I first go and meet with the potential employers and they first learn that I can't speak, that my speech is slurred, they react differently than if I could speak normally.

Q. Do you bring lawsuits against them for not hiring you?

A. No, I haven't.

Q. Isn't it true that at the time of your firing you were engaging in the illegal use of drugs?

A. No, that is not true.

Q. No further questions.

Redirect

Q. Did you receive any indication after your review in [December] of [1991] and prior to your termination in [August] of [1992] that either [Eastern] or [Ms. Brown] felt that your performance was subpar or that they were unhappy with anything that you were doing?

A. No. I had not gotten that impression or a verbal communication saying that to me.

Q. When did you get the impression that they were dissatisfied with your work?

A. The first indication that they felt my performance was subpar was with the actual termination.

Q. Thank you. Nothing further.

By the Court

Q. In what way did you communicate your request for accommodation just before you were terminated?

---

[37] Counsel would have been better advised not to ask the question that produced this answer.

[38] These answers are more helpful to defense counsel.

A. In what way? I verbally requested to [Ms. Brown] that the following accommodations that I mentioned earlier be made available to me: a reader, a speaker, and making it "handicapped friendly."
Q. So you didn't request this in writing?
A. No, I didn't.

Plaintiff Calls [Dr. Willard Allen]

Q. Please state your name, address, and occupation for the court.
A. My name is [Dr. Willard Allen], [3333 3d Boulevard], [Upper Merion], [PA] [33333]. I am Chief of Neurology at [Jefferson Hospital], where I have been the Chief of Neurology for five years.
Q. How long have you been a neurologist?
A. I have been a neurologist for 15 years. I graduated with a [B.S.] degree in [Biology] from the University of [Pennsylvania] and I received my medical degree from [Harvard University] Medical School. Afterwards, I was a resident at the [Massachusetts General Hospital], where I also did a fellowship in neurology.
Q. Are you licensed to practice medicine in this state?
A. Yes, I am licensed to practice medicine in [Pennsylvania], [New York], [Maryland], [New Jersey], and [Massachusetts].
Q. Have you had much contact with MS patients?
A. Yes, I have. As I stated previously, my area of specialization is neurology, and I have done extensive research on MS, and have also published many materials regarding MS, including articles on the effects of MS on patients and society's negative reaction to the disease.
Q. Have you been involved in any clinical studies of MS patients?
A. Yes. And in my published materials I used results of clinical studies that I have done on MS patients.
Q. What are the effects and common symptoms of MS?
A. MS is a chronic degenerative disease of the central nervous system in which gradual destruction of the myelin occurs throughout the brain or the spinal cord or both. Basically, myelin is a sheath that surrounds a nerve fiber that facilitates the transmission of nerve impulses. MS basically interferes with the transmission and causes muscular weakness, loss of coordination, and speech and visual disturbances. Now that doesn't mean a patient who suffers from MS has all of these symptoms, for there can be variations and some people might suffer from one or the other and the symptoms can be more severe to less severe.

And generally, MS attacks occur, remit, and then recur. The studies show it seems to happen randomly and there is no pattern that develops on how these attacks occur. Basically, the flare-ups are greatest during the first three to four years of the disease, but afterwards another attack might not happen for the next 10 to 20 years. And during typical episodes the symptoms worsen over a period of a few days to a few weeks and then remit. During the remission period, the recovery is usually rapid over a period of weeks, although at times it may extend over several months and, again, the extent of the recovery varies from person to person and the remission may be complete or it might be partial.

Q. Do you know the plaintiff in this case?

A. Yes, I do. He has been a patient of mine since [June 1991], when I diagnosed him with MS.[39]

Q. Did you know the plaintiff prior to this diagnosis?

A. No, I did not.

Q. What were the results of your initial examination of the plaintiff?

A. The initial examination showed that the plaintiff suffered a mild MS attack in which he had slurred speech and blurry vision and afterwards it remitted. He was able basically to recover all of his functionality except for a slight vision problem.

Q. Doctor, is there a known cause for MS?

A. At this time there is no cause for it. We are currently in the research area trying to determine the actual cause of it.

Q. OK. Is there a known cure for MS?

A. No. There is no actual cure for MS. There have been certain drugs that we can give to try to make the attacks less frequent, but at this time there is no effective cure for it.

Q. On average, how long does a typical MS patient live with the disease?

A. The patient lives approximately 30 years after the onset of the disease, it being the rare case where a patient may die within a few years.

Q. I believe you said before that it is possible that MS will remit and then recur randomly over the course of many years?

A. That is correct.

Q. So can one say with any scientific accuracy that the plaintiff's condition will only deteriorate with no hope of remission?[40]

A. No. I think it is the exact opposite. Scientific experience has shown that after an attack, the majority of the patients would become better before having another attack which would worsen their condition.

Q. In your expert opinion Doctor, do you believe that if the plaintiff is provided with the accommodations that he requested, he can perform the essential job functions of staff accountant?

A. Yes, he could. Again, MS basically is a disease that causes muscular weakness, loss of coordination, and speech and visual disturbances. It has nothing to do with impairment of mental capacity.

Q. Doctor, the plaintiff testified that his essential job functions as staff accountant were as follows: producing financial reports through spreadsheet applications, operating an adding machine to perform various mathematical functions, maintaining the general ledger, and communicating with outside vendors and [Eastern]'s purchasing agents regarding fixed-asset acquisitions. Assuming that

---

[39] It is more common to present a medical expert who is not the treating physician, both to protect doctor-patient privilege and to avoid any inference of bias in favor of the plaintiff by the physician. There is no reason, however, why the treating physician cannot be the only expert, if the physician qualifies as an expert.

[40] The question is leading but did no harm because of the answer.

those are his essential job functions, do you believe that the plaintiff, if provided with the accommodations that he requested, can perform those functions as staff accountant?

A. Yes. In my medical opinion, I believe that he can perform the essential job functions because, again, the disease only causes the muscular weaknesses, loss of coordination, and speech and visual disturbances. It does not affect his mental abilities which I deem as the essential function of the staff accountant position.

Q. Thank you. Nothing further.

By the Court

Q. Before you start, Counsel, do you stipulate to his qualifications as an expert?
A. Yes.

By Defense Counsel

Q. Is [Mr. Lyons] still a patient of yours, [Dr. Allen]?
A. Yes, he is.
Q. So, in other words, you have a financial stake in having him continue to be a patient of yours which is directly correlated with his employment and benefits?
A. No. That is not really true because even if he was not employed by [Eastern], he is still a patient. If he can't pay by [Eastern]'s medical coverage, then the government will pay by disability insurance.
Q. You said that the plaintiff could perform the essential job functions because they all just required no physical abilities, right?
A. Yes.
Q. But the functions, computer work and operating the adding machine, require some degree of manual dexterity, don't they?
A. I suppose so.
Q. Doctor, what are the criteria for coverage by Social Security disability?
A. I have no idea.
Q. Nothing further.

By the Court

Q. Any redirect?
A. No.[41]

---

[41] At this point, Defense moved for a judgment as a matter of law as no reasonable jury could find for the plaintiff on its claim of discrimination in violation of the ADA. The motion was denied.

DEFENDANT'S CASE-IN-CHIEF

By Defense Counsel

Defense Calls [Henry Bell]

Q. Please state your name and address for the record.
A. My name is [Henry Bell], [4444 44th Street], [Lower Radnor], [Pennsylvania] [44444].
Q. What is your position?
A. I am controller of [Eastern Pharmaceuticals].
Q. Please tell us about your background and qualifications.
A. I am 37 years old and I graduated from [Villanova] with a Bachelor's Degree in Accountancy in [May 1977]. I obtained my CPA certificate in [1979]. Right out of school I worked eight years with [Deloitte Haskins & Sells], an independent public accounting firm. Following those eight years, I obtained a position with [Eastern] in their accounting department. I served as controller for the last four years.
Q. You said you graduated from [Villanova] in [1977] and you obtained your CPA certificate in [1979]. How come there is a two-year delay?
A. There is a two-year practice requirement. You have to pass the exam and then practice as an independent public accountant for two years before you can obtain your certificate.
Q. So that is as soon as you could be qualified, two years later?
A. Yes.
Q. To the best of your knowledge, how many people work at [Eastern]?
A. [Eastern] employs approximately 300 people.
Q. Please tell us about some of the products which [Eastern] produces.
A. Major products manufactured by [Eastern] include drugs which minimize the risk of infection during organ transplant operations, such as [Governor C.]'s recent operation. We are also on the cutting edge of AIDS research, and we have a product on the market that helps prevent the risk of skin cancer.
Q. How many people use these drugs?
A. These are drugs which help many people every day.
Q. Do you supervise anyone?
A. Yes.
Q. What supervising roles do you perform as controller?
A. I have overall responsibility for the accounting department, including the staff accountants.
Q. Could you please describe the essential functions of the staff accountant at [Eastern]?
A. The essential job functions of the staff accountant include producing financial reports through spreadsheet applications, operating an adding machine to perform various mathematical functions, maintaining a computerized general ledger system, communicating with outside vendors and [Eastern] purchasing agents concerning fixed-asset acquisitions.
Q. Could [Mr. Lyons] perform these essential functions when he was terminated?

A. No.

Q. Why not?

A. We have had various problems with [Mr. Lyons], including the fact that he is unable to keep up with the hectic pace of [Eastern]'s demanding financial reporting schedule. We issue financial reports at the end of every month and for regulatory agencies at the end of every fiscal quarter and at the end of the financial year. The accounting department operates in a real nonflexible deadline-oriented atmosphere with minimal room for error. [Mr. Lyons] is not able to produce these required reports in a timely manner.

Q. In addition to the essential job functions you discussed earlier, are there any continuing education requirements which the staff accountant at [Eastern] is required to maintain?

A. To maintain his certification as a CPA in [Pennsylvania] he needs a minimum amount of continuing education each year and basically this involves keeping abreast of current financial reporting literature and also any tax requirements as they relate to his job calculating depreciation of fixed assets and things of that nature. So yes, there are various continuing education requirements.

Q. Did you have occasion to talk to [Mr. Lyons] about his compliance with the continuing education requirements?

A. Yes, I did.

Q. And what, if anything, did he say about his compliance with the continuing education requirements?[42]

A. [Mr. Lyons] told me that he had not been keeping up with his continuing education requirements.

Q. If the accommodations which [Mr. Lyons] requested were met by [Eastern], would this enable him to perform his essential job function?[43]

A. If he was provided with the accommodations, no, he couldn't perform the essential job functions.

Q. What effect would an intermediary between [Lyons] and his computer and his adding machine have on his performance?

A. Although in most instances two heads are better than one, I think accounting is unique in that aspect because any time you insert more people into a process the risk of error is greater as far as transposing a number or miscommunicating, and we are in a position where we can't afford to have any type of clerical errors in our financial data.

Q. Is it your practice to give employees who have performance difficulties warnings before you fire them for those performance difficulties?

A. Warnings, not in the sense of necessarily written evaluations because our written evaluation process is done annually, but verbally as projects are turned in and we find errors.

---

[42] This is hearsay, but it is admissible under an exception to the hearsay rule because it is an admission by a party opponent.

[43] This calls for a speculative answer by the witness. However, because this witness is the supervisor and is responsible for establishing or not establishing or, at least, policing compliance with the various job requirements, it is probably within the knowledge of this witness to answer the question, and, therefore, should be allowed.

Q. Was that done in [Mr. Lyons]'s case?

A. Yes.

Q. Why was [Lyons] terminated from his position as staff accountant at [Eastern]?

A. [Mr. Lyons] was terminated because he could not adequately perform his essential job functions. His work was illegible, we had caught some errors in his work, it was not completed in a timely manner, and we were getting some complaints from outside vendors.

Q. Did [Mr. Lyons]'s termination have anything to do with the fact that he was disabled?

A. No.

Q. Since [Mr. Lyons]'s termination has he ever sought a recommendation letter from you to help him with his job search?

A. No. He has never asked for a recommendation.

Q. Is it common for ex-employees to ask you for a recommendation letter?

A. Yes.

Q. Wouldn't it make it much more difficult for someone to get a job without a letter of recommendation from its former employer?[44]

A. I would think so.

Cross-Examination by Plaintiff Counsel

Q. Have you ever allowed any of your accountants of [Mr. Lyons]'s level to use support personnel to assist them in using their computers or adding machines?

A. Yes.

Q. Doesn't that raise the same risk of error?

A. No, because you have [Mr. Lyons] in a review function then and nothing is . . . [Mr. Lyons] is at a level where he would be the last review of financial data for the area that he covers. So anybody who did work for him, he would review for accuracy.

Q. So your testimony is that the people that you have allowed to use support personnel in conjunction with their computer and adding machine functions have been in jobs different from [Mr. Lyons]s?

A. Yes.

Q. And there is something special about [Mr. Lyons]'s position in which the introduction of such a support person would increase the risk of error — more than use of a support person at other levels?[45]

A. Yes, this is true.

Q. Do you have any reason to question [Dr. Allen]'s diagnosis of the plaintiff's condition?

A. No.

Q. Do you suspect then that possibly the illegible writing problem may be tied into the MS symptoms rather than just his incompetency or whatever it is that you said caused this?

---

[44] This question may be subject to objection as calling for speculation.

[45] It would have been better not to ask this question, because it gives the witness an opportunity to explain an otherwise obscure and possibly illogical position.

A. I have no medical background or basis to make that determination.

Q. Regarding the accommodations that he requested, you commented that he is in a special position so that having two heads will not be better than one. Isn't it possible that [Lyons] could check for accuracy the work of his accommodator so that it really would be his work, he would just be directing him or her in the various functions of operating the computer or the adding machine so that it would be the same result as if he did it himself; he just wouldn't be doing the actual typing?

A. I would say that yes, he could check the accuracy, but the problem comes in with meeting the deadlines and I don't think he could perform the job on a timely basis.

Q. How direct is your supervision on [Mr. Lyons]?

A. I am not the direct supervisor of [Mr. Lyons] — there is an intermediary between [Mr. Lyons] and myself.

Q. Aside from what [Ms. Brown] has told you, do you first-hand know anything about [Mr. Lyons] and his employment problems over the past year or year and a half?

A. Yes, I do, because as I indicated, nobody reviews [Mr. Lyons]'s work. It would come directly to me as controller.

Q. Isn't it true that his last review a year ago was nothing but favorable, or was at least satisfactory — there was no indication that he had subpar performance?

A. This is true.

Q. Switching the scope a little bit: Does [Eastern] have wheelchair access ramps, wheelchair bathrooms, or anything?

A. No.

Q. Do you realize that that may not be in compliance with the laws as they stand today?

A. I am not legal counsel.

Q. Are you aware of any continuing education accommodations that are made for people with disabilities? Obviously, if someone has trouble getting around, I would suspect that there may be some accommodations that can be made in terms of the continuing education?

A. I am not aware.

Q. But you have no reason to doubt that it is possible that there could be such an accommodation?

A. It is possible.

Q. So you testified that your company employs approximately 300 people?

A. Yes.

Q. So it is probable that there is someone or some two people at the company who have enough free time on their hands so that it wouldn't be that the company would have to hire someone to do the accommodations requested by [Mr. Lyons], there could just be some shifting around of job functions and possibly someone could move in to do that on a part-time basis and continue to do his or her other job when the accommodations are not needed.

A. I don't believe that is true. I think we are a pretty streamlined operation and everybody works eight full hours a day. So I would say no.

Q. Including the people who answer the telephones? They never have any free time as far as you know?

A.   No.

Q.   You mentioned that [Mr. Lyons] was the staff accountant. He was in the position of last review work of the accounting information?

A.   Yes.

Q.   Does that not mean that you would have to have trust and faith in his abilities such that he is the last reviewer?

A.   Yes.

Q.   You testified, sir, that it would take too long if you made the accommodations that [Mr. Lyons] requested, is that what you said?

A.   Yes.

Q.   Did you try it out? Did you try out his accommodations to see how long it would take?

A.   No, we did not.

Q.   You didn't conduct any experiments to see.

A.   No.

Q.   Do you do all your own typing?

A.   No, I do not.

Q.   Do you do all your own data entry on the computer?

A.   I do not have in my position . . . I don't have much data entry from a pure clerical standpoint.

Q.   When you get reports and documents from your subordinates — you do get such things?

A.   Yes.

Q.   Do you check the addition and the other arithmetic on all of those you saw personally?

A.   No.

Q.   So it is possible that by delegating these functions to these support personnel, that some errors could be introduced? Isn't that true? Isn't it possible?

A.   It is possible, yes.

Q.   But you have concluded that it is tolerable. That possibility of error is tolerable.

A.   Well, it is being performed from me and it's coming back to me. Yes.

Q.   Did you or anyone at [Eastern] consider possibly moving [Mr. Lyons] to another position maybe that has lesser responsibility, possibly going back to as he was as a clerk? Something so that the fact that he moves more slowly than he used to wouldn't be a problem if he had fewer things to do?

A.   He never asked that.

Q.   You never thought about doing that either?

A.   No.

Q.   OK. Nothing further. Any redirect?

By Defense Counsel

Q.   Yes. Have you noticed a change in [Mr. Lyons]'s performance between the time of his most recent evaluation eight months prior to his termination and the date of his termination?

A.   Yes, a marked decrease.

Q. Are there generally spare days each month and each quarter between the date a report is completed and the due date of that report?

A. No.

Q. So what effect would an additional step in the report-generating process have?[46]

A. We would probably have a more difficult time meeting our inflexible due dates and probably miss a couple of them.

Q. Nothing further.

Defense Calls [Arthur Smith] as an Expert Witness

Q. Please state your name for the record.

A. My name is [Arthur Smith].

Q. Please tell us about your background and qualifications, [Mr. Smith].

A. I am 45 years old. I have a Bachelor's Degree in Accountancy from [Lehigh University]. I obtained that in [May] of [1970]. I also have an MBA with concentrations in Finance and Accounting from [Wharton School of Business] at [Penn]. I obtained that in [May 1980]. I have been a CPA since [1972]. I have worked at [Ernst & Young International Accounting Tax & Consulting Firm] for 23 years, the last 12 as a partner. I specialize in manufacturing with a concentration in the pharmaceutical industry.

Q. What is your relationship with [Eastern]?

A. [Ernst & Young] has audited [Eastern] for the past 15 years and I have been the partner in charge of the audits for the past six years.

Q. Were you here when [Mr. Lyons] testified?

A. Yes.

Q. In your opinion as an expert, what would it cost in dollars for [Eastern] to meet these accommodations that [Lyons] has requested?[47]

A. About [$64,000] per year.

Q. How does that break down?

A. Well, the cost of employing [Lyons] was [$54,000] per year. He makes [$45,000] in salary and there is an extra [$9,000] in benefits that [Eastern] pays for him. The approximate cost of a reader or an intermediary to do his work would be [$25,000] per year. The cost of making the building handicapped friendly is [$250,000]. Depreciated over 10 years, this turns into an expense of [$25,000] a year. It is also important to remember the cash flow impact of that [$250,000].

On the other hand, the cost of replacing [Lyons] is [$40,000] per year, [$33,000] in salary and [$7,000] in benefits, so when you add and subtract all

---

[46] This question might be considered speculative.

[47] The Federal Rules of Evidence 703 and 705 permit an expert to testify as to the expert's conclusion without laying the factual foundation that leads to the conclusion, so this question and the anticipated answer are permissible. But if the expert should be asked on cross-examination to disclose the facts on which he bases his conclusion, Federal Rule of Evidence 705 requires that the expert disclose those facts.

those factors, [Eastern]'s annual incremental cost of accommodating [Lyons] would be [$64,000] per year.

Q. Are there any other possible expenses connected with this?

A. Yes. One other possible expense is an increase in [Eastern]'s audit fees because of the increased audit risk resulting from having an intermediary help [Lyons] with his work.

Q. You testified earlier that you and your firm have audited [Eastern]'s financial statements for the past number of years. Over the past five years, what has [Eastern]'s net income averaged?

A. Approximately [$500,000] per year.

Q. What would be the effect on net income of providing the accommodations for [Lyons]?

A. As I said earlier, net income would decline by [$64,000], which is more than a 10 percent decrease.

Q. What difference does it make if net income goes down?

A. Funds available for research and development purposes vary directly with net income. Therefore, when net income decreases, so do the funds for research and development purposes. Research and development is crucial to a pharmaceutical company's success and survival.

[Eastern] never even pays dividends because it reinvests all of its net income into research and development to maintain its market share. Again, they really have no alternative from this strategy if they wish to maintain their position and actually survive as a pharmaceutical company.

Q. So what effect would a decrease in net income of [$64,000] a year have?

A. That would have a direct dollar-for-dollar impact on [Eastern]'s budgeted research and development and would be a threat on the continuing existence of the company. A [$64,000] decrease in net income reduces funds available for research and development purposes by the sum of [$64,000].

Q. In your opinion, would you consider this to be an undue hardship to [Eastern]?

A. Certainly. It would threaten their continuing existence.

Q. Has [Lyons] ever asked you for a reference letter or to work at your firm?

A. No.

Q. What is the practice of employees at firms which you audit regarding recommendation letters?

Q. It is often typical that employees of entities that we audit ask for recommendation letters from our firm concerning their performance and even inquire about jobs working for us.

A. [Mr. Lyons] did not do this?

Q. No, he did not.

Cross-Examination

Q. You testified previously that the reasonable accommodations requested by [Mr. Lyons] were in your mind unreasonable. What accommodations do you recollect [Mr. Lyons] requesting?

A. [Mr. Lyons] requested that [Eastern] make the building handicap accessible. That [Eastern] make the building handicap accessible and also that [Eastern] provide him with an intermediary who could do reading for him and also communicate to other parties for him.

Q.   You also testified that a replacement could be brought in for [Mr. Lyons] for [$40,000]?

A.   Yes.

Q.   Isn't it possible that once people achieve a certain status of seniority, they can always be replaced with cheaper and younger help, so it is just a fact that you can bring in someone for a smaller salary? Isn't it possible that that person also lacks the expertise that [Mr. Lyons] acquired over the years working at [Eastern]?

A.   It is possible that [Lyons] has familiarity with the organization that is of some benefit, but it would not take any significant amount of time for a replacement familiar with the industry to overcome that capability of [Mr. Lyons].

Q.   You testified that it is possible that [Eastern] would suffer an increase in audit fees because of the presence of [Mr. Lyons] in the accounting department. It seems unlikely that many large companies in this country do not have hand-icapped people working in their accounting departments. I can't imagine from a policy standpoint that your firm can get away with charging people more money because they are accommodating people with disabilities by offering them employment.

A.   Our audits are risk-based audits so when there is ever an increased audit risk, no matter how that risk gets there, it is going to take us more time to do our job effectively and we can certainly justify increasing audit fees.

Q.   Suppose that there is a handicapped person working in the manufacturing plant at [Eastern] as opposed to the accounting department, so the risk is in the manufacturing of the drugs and possible lawsuits and products liability and things of that sort. How do you handle that in your audit? Do you look purely at the numbers and who is putting the numbers together for you? Are you looking at a whole picture of the company?

A.   We do look at a whole picture of the company. That wouldn't necessarily require more audit effort but it would just result in us increasing a reserve for lawsuits.

Q.   You also testified that you believe that the reasonable accommodation would cause an undue hardship based on the comparison to the net income of the company?

A.   Yes.

Q.   If you use profit at the bottom line for everything, it is conceivable that you can have a company with a billion dollars in revenue that is turning no profits. Would you say that for them to spend an extra $50,000 would also be an undue hardship?

A.   I would have to be more familiar with that, it is possible.[48]

* * *

---

[48] It is important to understand that gross income also plays a part in deciding whether something is a reasonable accommodation; therefore, the questions about gross income are pertinent for issues other than the issue of profitability.

A. I think in this industry it is all driven with cash flow.

Q. Is [Eastern] a private company or do they issue stock?

A. It is a closely held company, so they have financial reporting requirements but are not traded publicly.

Q. The investment is all internal?

A. Yes.

Q. So it may be less important to them than to a company for instance that is doing an IPO or is publicly traded, where word of the decrease in profit could drive the shares down.

A. I don't think our risk here is decrease in profits as much as a decrease in cash flow and investment.

Q. Last question: I realize auditing is done independently and is very quantitative and mathematical, but is there some human factor that comes into play here? There are millions and millions of people in the country who are disabled and from an accounting standpoint you could exclude them completely from employment because they will have an adverse effect on the balance sheets, but from the policy standpoint, it is not really possible and many laws have been enacted to actually prevent this. So do you believe that some human factor should also go into the analysis that you are doing, or is this strictly quantitative?

A. Well . . .

Q. If a qualified person in a wheelchair came to your company seeking a position, would you hire them?

A. Yes.

Q. And if that is the case, would you not also have to make the place handicap friendly to accommodate his wheelchair access?

A. Yes.

Q. Then does that not sort of invalidate your charge when you were calculating approximately [$50,000], you were looking at that cost into [Mr. Lyons] individually? Is that not sort of not correct then, you can't really charge that to [Mr. Lyons], you have to sort of make it a general company expense that you would have to do as a cost of doing business. Is that not correct?

A. Well, yes, it is a — cost of doing business that directly affects the cash flow of the company.

Q. But in a sense you cannot charge that to [Mr. Lyons] directly. It is a general company cost.

A. If [Eastern] were to have to make its building handicap friendly, it would cost [$250,000] no matter if it was [Mr. Lyons] or someone else.

Q. Besides that, has it been a practice of [Eastern] to bring in no salary replacements for its senior employees?

A. I am not familiar with that.

---

[49] In this hypothetical, drafted along with the testimony in §§ 16.01[B][13][a] and 16.01[B][13][b] by Charles Fisher, an assistant to Henry H. Perritt, Jr., on June 6, 1993, the plaintiff Mr. SDT (schizophrenic decompensating telemarketer) has been denied a job "out of hand" as a telemarketer due to the fact that he is schizophrenic and has a history of not

[13] Expert Testimony: Psychological Evaluation[49]

[a] *Expert Testimony for the Plaintiff*

Q. Please state your name, address, and occupation for the court.

A. My name is [Dr. Robert Smith], [5555 55th Street], [Upper Treddyffrin], [Pennsylvania] [55555], and I am a practicing psychiatrist.

Q. How long have you been a psychiatrist?

A. Ten years.

Q. What is your educational background?

A. I received Bachelor of Arts degrees in both psychology and prelaw from the [University of Washington] in [Seattle]. I received my M.D. from [Hahnemann School of Medicine] in [Philadelphia].

Q. Where did you do your residency?

A. I did my residency at [Hahnemann University] Hospital in [Philadelphia], specializing in the areas of psychology and psychiatric medicine.

Q. Are you licensed to practice medicine in this state?

A. Yes.

Q. Are you licensed to practice in states other than [Pennsylvania]?

A. Yes, I am licensed to practice in [Delaware], [Maryland], [New Jersey], [New York], and the [District of Columbia].

Q. What is your area of specialization?

A. I deal primarily with patients suffering from schizophrenia.

Q. Approximately how many schizophrenic patients have you treated in your career, Doctor?

A. I have diagnosed and treated over 100 schizophrenic patients over the last 10 years.

Q. Have you been involved with any clinical studies of patients suffering from schizophrenia?

A. I have been involved in no less than seven such studies.

Q. Have you published any material based on schizophrenia or schizophrenic patients?

A. Yes, I have authored several articles and two books on the subject.

Q. Are you familiar with the literature concerning schizophrenia?

A. Yes. The literature on this subject is extensive, but I stay abreast of the latest findings in order to give proper treatment to my patients.

Q. Do you know [Mr. SDT], the plaintiff, in this case?

A. Yes, I have examined [Mr. SDT].

Q. What is your clinical impression of the plaintiff?

A. The plaintiff suffers from a relatively moderate case of schizophrenia.

---

taking his medication. *Decompensation* is the term commonly used to describe a schizophrenic's progressive returns to premedication morbidity as a result of a failure either to take prescribed medication or to take the medication in the manner prescribed. Under the circumstances, liability appears relatively easy to establish, although certain employment contracting and insurance issues might arise. Sections 16.01[B][13][a] and 16.01[B][13][b] contain sample expert testimony for the plaintiff and the defendant, respectively.

Q. When you say moderate, what do you mean?

A. I mean that [Mr. SDT] is high-functioning from a cognitive standpoint and that with proper medication[50] he is capable of overcoming the debilitating effects of his condition.

Q. What does that mean in terms of [Mr. SDT], compared with someone who is not schizophrenic?

A. When [Mr. SDT] is properly medicated, his abilities are much the same as someone who does not suffer from the disorder.

Q. Could the plaintiff work the phones as a telemarketer as long as he was properly medicated?

A. Yes, I believe that [Mr. SDT] is fully capable of performing the tasks of a telemarketer when he is medicated.

Q. Are there side effects of his medication that would cause trouble with performing the duties of a telemarketer?

A. Patients often complain of excessive tiredness when they are taking medication for schizophrenia. This tiredness generally disappears after about three weeks. Patients can also experience a stiffness in the tongue, but this can be successfully treated in most cases with cogentin.

Q. What would happen if [Mr. SDT] stopped taking his medication?

A. His cognitive functioning would deteriorate and he would begin to experience symptoms of the disorder. This process is known as decompensation.

Q. What is [Mr. SDT]'s history with respect to taking his medication?

A. He has a history of not taking his medication.

Q. Wouldn't this cause problems if he were employed by the defendant?

A. If the plaintiff were not taking his medication, he would not be able to perform his job responsibilities satisfactorily.

Q. Based on the plaintiff's history, wasn't it prudent for the defendant to deny him employment?[51]

A. The plaintiff is capable of performing the required duties of the position for which he applied. He is also completely capable of understanding that taking his medication as prescribed would be a requirement of his being hired and his continued employment.

Q. What would be the effect if [Mr. SDT] were made aware by the defendant that failure to take his medication in the prescribed manner would result in his being fired?[52]

A. He would understand the meaning and gravity of such a statement.

---

[50] Because this is mock testimony, there is no reason to overcomplicate the text with a discussion of what medication the plaintiff might be taking. Haldol, prolixin, loxitane, and thorozene are all possible choices, though there are others. It should be noted that haldol and prolixin can be administered by intramuscular injection once a month rather than by daily oral ingestion and that this would greatly facilitate efforts to guarantee that the patient is taking his medication.

[51] This is a leading question, but there is no prejudice because it suggests an answer favoring the opponent.

[52] *See* § 4.09 regarding last chance agreements.

Q. Would the defendant be able to tell if [Mr. SDT] stopped taking his medication?

A. Yes, the symptoms of decompensation are very apparent.

Q. Would the defendant need to have the plaintiff's supervisor specially trained to recognize the symptoms of decompensation?

A. No. In the early stages of decompensation there would be noticeable changes in the plaintiff's mood, personality, and behavior.

Q. What type of changes would be typical?

A. The most likely red-flag changes would be that the plaintiff would become suspicious and/or withdrawn. In the later stages of decompensation, the plaintiff might begin to talk to himself (respond to internal stimuli) and would verbalize feelings of paranoia.

Q. Could these symptoms of early decompensation be due to things other than failing to take his medication?

A. Of course, [Mr. SDT] might simply not feel like talking one day and therefore appear withdrawn. But due to his special circumstances, it seems that the prudent thing to do would be to play it safe and test his blood or urine to see if he is taking his medication.

Q. Is it possible that the plaintiff could decompensate without any of these symptoms to put the defendant on notice of a problem?

A. Decompensation without notice is possible but highly unlikely with high-function schizophrenics like [Mr. SDT].

Q. Is [Mr. SDT] capable of safely and competently performing the duties of a telemarketer in the defendant's employ?

A. Yes.

[b]   Expert Testimony for the Defense

Q. Doctor, have you had an opportunity to examine [Mr. SDT]?

A. Yes.

Q. What is your clinical opinion as to the plaintiff's condition?

A. The plaintiff suffers from schizophrenia.[53]

Q. Do you believe that the plaintiff is capable of working the phones as a telemarketer?

A. No. While it is true that the plaintiff is high-functioning when properly medicated, his history indicates that when he begins to feel okay following a period of relatively normal functioning, he discontinues taking his medication and it is this medication that allows him to function with the degree of clarity and concentration that would be required for the telemarketing position.

Q. You heard [Dr. Smith] say that there would be indications that the plaintiff was not taking his medication and that his supervisor would be able to know if the plaintiff was decompensating. Do you agree?

---

[53] The testimony concerning Mr. SDT's degree of debilitation has been omitted because this hypothetical is based on a high-functioning schizophrenic.

A. While I agree that there are noticeable symptoms of decompensation in most cases, I do not believe that the plaintiff's supervisor would be able to spot the often subtle symptomatology of the early stages of decompensation. Additionally, the plaintiff's cognitive functioning, and thereby his ability to do the job, might well be affected long before any noticeable symptomatology appeared.

Q. Could the plaintiff's ability to interact effectively with potential customers be eroded before anyone knew he was not taking his medication?

A. Yes.[54]

[14] Plaintiff's Closing Argument (Mock Trial)

FORM 16–10 Sample Plaintiff's Closing Argument

Ladies and gentlemen of the jury. [Steve Lyons] is afflicted with MS. This disease substantially limits the major life activities of reading, speaking, and walking. Thus, according to the ADA, [Steve Lyons] is disabled. It has been shown that although [Steve Lyons] is disabled he would have been able to continue in his position as staff accountant at [Eastern] had they not refused to make the reasonable accommodations that he requested.

Defendant [Eastern] has failed to prove that it would constitute an undue hardship if they were required to make the reasonable accommodations requested by [Steve Lyons]. All that [Steve Lyons] requested was a reader to communicate written and computer information to him, a speaker to communicate oral messages from him, and the addition of a ramp and other things to make the building handicap friendly.

Given the size of the company, it is likely that [Eastern] could find someone already employed to serve as [Steve Lyons]'s reader and speaker. As for [Eastern]'s contention that it will cost them [$250,000] to make their building handicap friendly, they cannot place this expense squarely on the shoulders of [Steve Lyons]. [Steve Lyons] may not be the first and certainly will not be the last disabled person to work at [Eastern]. The addition of wheelchair ramps and other renovations is inevitable regardless of the outcome of this case. As the jury, you need to send a strong message to employers like [Eastern] that discrimination against qualified individuals with disabilities will no longer be tolerated.

[Steve Lyons] suffers from a mysterious disease. As [Dr. Allen] testified, little is known about what causes MS and there is no cure. What is known is that the average MS patient lives 30 years with the disease. MS affects the motor skills of the person but has no effect on the cognitive abilities and functions. [Steve Lyons] is as mentally sharp today as he was prior to his diagnosis. He simply has trouble with his eyesight, speech, and muscle coordination.

[Steve Lyons] was wrongfully terminated by [Eastern]. He was fired because he has MS. The defendant claims that [Steve Lyons] was fired for subpar job

---

[54] The testimony concerning the expert's qualifications and experience in the field of psychiatry has been omitted to avoid needless redundancy.

performance, yet [Steve Lyons] never had anything but satisfactory year-end employment reviews. To find for the defendant in this case is to give credence to the many stereotypes that are cast upon people with disabilities. Because it is apparent that [Steve Lyons] is not at all disabled mentally, it is just as apparent that he was wrongfully terminated. This is a blatant violation of the ADA. It is up to you the jury to correct this manifest injustice.

[15]   Defense's Closing Argument (Mock Trial)

FORM 16–11   Sample Defense's Closing Argument

Ladies and gentlemen of the jury, it is now time for you to make your decision in this case. As in all cases, this decision will not be an easy one. My only words of advice to you are to make this decision with your minds and not your hearts. It might make each of you feel good or even feel less guilty about the way you treated a disabled individual in the past if you were to hold in favor of [Mr. Lyons]. But the decision based on these factors will not be a just and equitable one. Rather, each of you must detach your emotions from this case and perform an analysis considering both the facts of the case which you have heard and the relevant law.

The relevant law in this case is the Americans with Disabilities Act. This law prohibits employers from discriminating against disabled workers. Applying the facts to this law, it is true that [Mr. Lyons] is disabled. It is true that [Eastern] was [Mr. Lyons]'s employer. It is also true that [Eastern] terminated [Mr. Lyons]'s employment, but it is not true that [Eastern] discriminated against [Mr. Lyons].

[Mr. Lyons] was let go because his work was subpar. His work was illegible, his work was inaccurate, and his work was late. Outside vendors lodged complaints against [Mr. Lyons] and the quality of his work.

[Mr. Lyons] on the other hand would have you believe that he was let go because [Eastern] didn't want to provide the accommodations which he sought. If this were true, [Mr. Lyons] would have a good case for himself, but there are two substantial holes in this theory.

First, as you heard [Arthur Smith] a partner at an international accounting firm testify, providing the accommodations which [Mr. Lyons] requested would have caused [Eastern] to suffer an undue hardship. The ADA does not require that an employer provide accommodations if they will thereby suffer an undue hardship. The pharmaceutical industry is ultra-dependent upon research and development. Even a minimal decrease in the funds available for R&D purposes has a monumental effect on the firm's health and ability to survive in the market. Forcing [Eastern] to provide [Mr. Lyons] with the accommodations he sought would most probably put [Eastern] out of business, taking with them the drugs which they manufacture to enable us to live longer and better lives.

Second, as you heard [Mr. Lyons]'s supervisor [Henry Bell] testify, [Mr. Lyons] would not be able to perform the essential functions of his job even if [Eastern] provided him with every accommodation he requested. The work of an accountant must be precise and exact. There is no room for error. Close enough is not good enough.

As I have demonstrated for you analytically, applying the facts of the case to the relevant law, [Mr. Lyons] cannot sustain his cause of action under the ADA because [Eastern] did not discriminate against him.

Therefore, you must find for the defendant, [Eastern Pharmaceuticals], and deny [Mr. Lyons]'s request for damages. Thank you.

[16]   Agreed Jury Instructions (EEOC)

FORM 16–12   Sample Agreed Jury Instructions

AGREED JURY INSTRUCTIONS

PRELIMINARY INSTRUCTION

AGREED INSTRUCTION 1
MEMBERS OF THE JURY:

You have now been sworn as the jury to try this case. As the jury you will decide the disputed questions of fact.

In this case there are two Plaintiffs, the Equal Employment Opportunity Commission and [Charles Wessel]. The Equal Employment Opportunity Commission (or EEOC) as many of you may know, is a government agency. [Charles Wessel] is a former Executive Director for [A.I.C. Security Investigations, Ltd.], who claims that his employer discriminated against him on the basis of his disability, cancer. In this case the EEOC's claims are the same as those of [Mr. Wessel], and [Mr. Wessel] and the EEOC will be jointly presenting the Plaintiff's case. The EEOC is participating in this lawsuit as a Plaintiff, not as an impartial government agency or an expert in disability discrimination. You should not infer that discrimination on the basis of disability has occurred because the EEOC chose to participate, nor should you attach any special significance to this case because of the EEOC's participation. The EEOC is required to meet the same burden of proof in this case as must be met by a private Plaintiff.

The Defendants in this lawsuit are [A.I.C. Security Investigations, Ltd.], [A.I.C. International, Ltd.], and [defendant C]. [A.I.C. Security Investigations, Ltd.] is a wholly owned subsidiary of [A.I.C. International, Ltd.]. [Defendant C] is the sole shareholder of [A.I.C. International Ltd.]. [A.I.C. Security Investigations, Ltd.] provides commercial security services, hardware, and investigative services to customers in the [Chicago] area.

As the judge, I will decide all questions of law and procedure. From time to time during the trial and at the end of the trial, I will instruct you on the rules of the law that you must follow in making your decision.

Soon, the lawyers for each of the parties will make what is called an opening statement. Opening statements are intended to assist you in understanding the evidence. What the lawyers say is not evidence.

After the opening statements, the Plaintiffs will call witnesses and present evidence. Then, the Defendants will have an opportunity to call witnesses and present evidence. After the parties' main case is completed, the Plaintiffs may be permitted to present rebuttal evidence. After all the evidence is completed, the lawyers will again address you to make final arguments. Then I will instruct you on the applicable law. You will then retire to deliberate on a verdict.

Keep an open mind during the trial. Do not decide any fact until you have heard all of the evidence, the closing arguments, and my instructions.

Pay close attention to the testimony and evidence. Even though the court reporter is making stenographic notes of everything that is said, a typewritten copy of the testimony will not be available for your use during deliberations. On the other hand, any exhibits received in evidence will be available to you during your deliberations.

If you would like to take notes during the trial, you may do so. If you do not take notes, be careful not to get so involved in not taking notes that you become distracted and miss part of the testimony. Your notes are to be used only as aids to your memory, and if your memory should later be different from your notes, you should rely on your memory and not on your notes. If you do not take notes, rely on your own independent memory of the testimony. Do not be unduly influenced by the notes of other jurors. A juror's notes are not entitled to any greater weight than the recollection of each juror concerning the testimony.

Until this trial is over, do not discuss this case with anyone and do not permit anyone to discuss the case in your presence. Do not discuss the case even with the other jurors until all of the jurors are in the jury room actually deliberating at the end of the case. If anyone should attempt to discuss this case or to approach you concerning the case, you should inform the Court immediately. Hold yourself completely apart from the people involved in the case — the parties, the witnesses, the attorneys, and the persons associated with them. It is important not only that you be fair and impartial but that you also appear to be fair and impartial.

Do not make any independent investigation of any fact or matter in this case. You are to be guided solely by what you see and hear in this trial. Do not learn anything about the case from any other source. In particular, do not read any newspaper account of this trial or listen to any radio or television newscast concerning it. Do not listen to any local radio or television newscast until this trial is over, or read any local newspaper unless someone else first removes any possible reference to this trial.

During the trial, it may be necessary for me to confer with the lawyers out of your hearing or to conduct a part of the trial out of your presence. I will handle these matters as briefly and as conveniently for you as I can, but you should remember that they are a necessary part of any trial.

It is now time for the opening statements.

Adapted from Pattern Jury Instructions (Civil Cases), U.S. Fifth Circuit District Judges Association (1991), Instruction 1.1.

Given:

Denied:

Given as Modified:

AGREED INSTRUCTION 2
STIPULATION OF FACT

The parties have agreed, or stipulated, to the following facts. This means that both sides agree that these are facts. You must therefore treat these facts as having been proved.

Adapted from Pattern Jury Instructions (Civil Cases), U.S. Fifth Circuit District Judges Association (1991), Instruction 2.3.

Given:

Denied:

Given as Modified:

AGREED INSTRUCTION 3
GENERAL INSTRUCTION
MEMBERS OF THE JURY:

You have heard the evidence in this case. I will now instruct you on the law that you must apply. It is your duty to follow the law as I give it to you. On the other hand, you the jury are the judges of the facts. Do not consider any statement that I have made in the course of trial or make in these instructions as an indication that I have any opinion about the facts of this case.

You have heard the closing arguments of the attorneys. Statements and arguments of the attorneys are not evidence and are not instructions on the law. They are intended only to assist the jury in understanding the evidence and parties' contentions.

Answer each question from the facts as you find them. Your answers and your verdict must be unanimous.

You must answer all questions from a preponderance of the evidence. By this I mean the greater weight and degree of credible evidence before you. In other words, a preponderance of the evidence just means the amount of evidence that persuades you that a claim is more likely so than not so. In determining whether any fact has been proved by a preponderance of the evidence in the case, you may, unless otherwise instructed, consider the testimony of all witnesses, regardless of who may have called them, and of all exhibits received in evidence, regardless of who may have produced them.

In determining the weight to give to the testimony of a witness, you should ask yourself whether there was evidence tending to prove that the witness testified falsely concerning some important fact, or whether there was evidence that at some other time the witness said or did something, or failed to say or do something, that was different from the testimony the witness gave before you during the trial.

You should keep in mind, of course, that a simple mistake by a witness does not necessarily mean that the witness was not telling the truth as he or she remembers it, because people may forget some things or remember other things inaccurately. So, if a witness has made a misstatement, you need to consider whether that misstatement was an intentional falsehood or simply an innocent lapse of memory;

and the significance of that may depend on whether it has to do with an important fact or with only an unimportant detail.

While you should consider only the evidence in this case, you are permitted to draw such reasonable inferences from the testimony and exhibits as you feel are justified in the light of common experience. In other words, you may make deductions and reach conclusions that reason and common sense lead you to draw from the facts that have been established by the testimony and evidence in the case.

The testimony of a single witness may be sufficient to prove any fact, even if a greater number of witnesses may have testified to the contrary, if, after considering all the other evidence, you believe that single witness.

There are two types of evidence that you may consider in properly finding the truth as to the facts in the case. One is direct evidence — such as testimony of an eyewitness. The other is indirect or circumstantial evidence — the proof of a chain of circumstances that indicates the existence or nonexistence of certain other facts. As a general rule, the law makes no distinction between direct and circumstantial evidence, but simply requires that you find the facts from a preponderance of all the evidence, both direct and circumstantial.

Any notes that you have taken during this trial are only aids to memory. If your memory should differ from your notes, then you should rely on your memory and not on the notes. The notes are not evidence. A juror who has not taken notes should rely on his or her independent recollection of the evidence and should not be unduly influenced by the notes of other jurors. Notes are not entitled to any greater weight than the recollection or impression of each juror about the testimony.

When you retire to the jury room to deliberate on your verdict, you may take these instructions with you as well as the stipulations of fact and the exhibits which the Court has admitted into evidence. Select your Foreperson and conduct your deliberations; follow all of the instructions that the Court has given you about your conduct during the trial. If you recess during your deliberations, follow all of the instructions that the Court has given you about/on your conduct during the trial. After you have reached your unanimous verdict, your Foreperson is to fill in on the form your answers to the questions. Do not reveal your answers until such time as you are discharged, unless otherwise directed by me. You must never disclose to anyone, not even to me, your numerical division on any question.

If you want to communicate with me at any time, please give a written message or question to the bailiff, who will bring it to me. I will then respond as promptly as possible either in writing or by having you brought into the courtroom so that I can address you orally. I will always first disclose to the attorneys your question and my response before I answer your question.

After you have reached a verdict, you are not required to talk with anyone about the case unless the Court orders otherwise.

Adapted from Pattern Jury Instructions (Civil Cases), U.S. Fifth Circuit District Judges Association (1991), Instruction 3.1.

Given:

Denied:

Given as Modified:

AGREED INSTRUCTION 4
BURDEN OF PROOF

In this case the Plaintiffs must prove every essential part of their claim by a preponderance of the evidence.

A preponderance of the evidence simply means evidence that persuades you that the Plaintiffs' claim is more likely true than not true.

In deciding whether any fact has been proved by a preponderance of the evidence, you may, unless otherwise instructed, consider the testimony of all witnesses, regardless of who may have called them, and all exhibits received in evidence, regardless of who may have produced them.

If the proof fails to establish any essential part of the Plaintiffs' claim by a preponderance of the evidence, you should find for the Defendant as to that claim.

Adapted from Pattern Jury Instructions (Civil Cases), U.S. Fifth Circuit District Judges Association (1991), Instruction 2.20.
Given:
Denied:
Given as Modified:

AGREED INSTRUCTION 5
DISABILITY — DEFINITION

Disability, as defined by the Americans with Disabilities Act, means

(1) a physical or mental impairment that substantially limits one or more major life activities;
(2) a record of such impairment; or
(3) being regarded as having such impairment.

29 C.F.R. § 1630.2(g)
Given:
Denied:
Given as Modified:

AGREED INSTRUCTION 6
MENTAL OR PHYSICAL IMPAIRMENT — DEFINITION

The term *mental or physical impairment* is defined as

(1) any physiological disorder or condition, cosmetic disfigurement, anatomical loss affecting one or more of the following body systems: neurological; neuromuscular; special sense organs; cardiovascular; reproductive; digestive; genitourinary; hemic and lymphatic; skin; and endocrine; or
(2) any mental or psychological disorder, such as mental retardation, organic brain syndrome, emotional or mental illness, and specific learning disabilities.

29 C.F.R. § 1630.2(h)
Given:
Denied:
Given as Modified:

AGREED INSTRUCTION 7
MAJOR LIFE ACTIVITY — DEFINITION

The term *major life activity* refers to basic life activities that an average person can perform with little or no difficulty, such as caring for one's self, performing manual tasks, walking, seeing, hearing, speaking, breathing, learning, working, sitting, standing, lifting and reaching.
29 C.F.R. § 1630.2(i)
Given:
Denied:
Given as Modified:

AGREED INSTRUCTION 8
SUBSTANTIALLY LIMITS — DEFINITION

A physical or mental impairment *substantially limits* one or more of a person's major life activities when it

(1) renders the individual unable to perform a major life activity that the average person in the population could perform, or
(2) significantly restricts, as to condition, manner, or duration, the individual's ability to perform a particular major life activity as compared to the condition, manner, or duration under which the average person in the general population could perform the same major life activity.

The question of whether the individual's impairment substantially limits a major life activity depends on the impairment's

(1) nature and severity;
(2) duration or expected duration;
(3) expected or actual permanent or long term impact.

29 C.F.R. § 1630.2(i).
Given:
Denied:
Given as Modified:

[17]   Plaintiffs' Proposed Jury Instructions (EEOC)

FORM 16–13   Sample Plaintiffs' Proposed Jury Instructions

PLAINTIFFS' PROPOSED JURY INSTRUCTIONS
PLAINTIFFS' PRELIMINARY INSTRUCTION 1
LIMITING INSTRUCTION

The testimony (or exhibit) being offered relates to [Mr. Wessel]'s medical condition at a time after the date on which he left his employment with Defendants. As I will instruct you at the end of the trial, this will be relevant to the amount of backpay to which [Mr. Wessel] is entitled, if your verdict is for the Plaintiffs. You may not consider the testimony with respect to the question whether [Wessel] was able to perform his job on [July 29, 1992].
Given:
Denied:
Given as Modified:

PLAINTIFFS' INSTRUCTION 2
EXPERT WITNESS

When knowledge of technical subject matter may be helpful to the jury, a person who has special training or experience in that technical field — an expert witness — is permitted to state his opinion on those technical matters. However, you are not required to accept that opinion. As with any other witness, it is up to you to decide whether to rely upon it.

In deciding whether to accept or rely upon the opinion of an expert witness, you may consider any bias of the witness, including any bias you may infer from evidence that the expert witness has been or will be paid for reviewing the case and testifying, or from evidence that he testifies regularly as an expert witness and his income from such testimony represents a significant portion of his income.

Adapted from Pattern Jury Instructions (Civil Cases), U.S. Fifth Circuit District Judges Association (1991), Instruction 3.1.
Given:
Denied:
Given as Modified:

PLAINTIFFS' INSTRUCTION 3
AMERICANS WITH DISABILITIES ACT

This is an action brought under the Americans with Disabilities Act. The purpose of the Act is to provide a clear and comprehensive national mandate for the elimination of discrimination against individuals with disabilities. The Act makes it unlawful for an employer to discriminate against a qualified individual with a disability by terminating him from his employment because of his disability.

Adapted from Americans with Disabilities Act, 42 U.S.C. § 12,101(b)(1); 42 U.S.C. § 12,112(a).
Given:
Denied:
Given as Modified:

PLAINTIFFS' INSTRUCTION 4
PARTIES' CONTENTIONS

In this case, the Plaintiffs contend that [Charles Wessel] was unlawfully terminated from his position as Executive Director at [A.I.C. Security Investigations] because of his disability, cancer.

The Defendants deny that they unjustifiably discharged [Wessel] from his employment on account of his disability. The Defendants instead contended that their request that [Wessel] remove himself from the position of Executive Director was justified because he could no longer perform the essential functions of Executive Director of [A.I.C. Security Investigations, Ltd.], with or without reasonable accommodation. Defendants also contend that the Plaintiff posed a direct threat to the health or safety of himself or others in the workplace.

Adapted from Pattern Jury Instructions (Civil Cases), U.S. Fifth Circuit District Judges Association (1983), Federal Claims Instruction No. 10 (1983).
Given:
Denied:
Given as Modified:

PLAINTIFFS' INSTRUCTION 5
PLAINTIFFS' PRIMA FACIE CASE

The Plaintiff in an Americans with Disabilities Act case has the burden of proving by a preponderance of the evidence the following elements:

(1) That he had at the time of his termination, a *disability*, as that term is defined in the ADA.
(2) That he was "otherwise qualified" for the position he held. This element requires proof by the Plaintiffs, by a preponderance of the evidence, that, except for [Wessel]'s disability, [Wessel] possesses the necessary qualifications for the position, such as educational background, experience, skills, and other job-related factors.
(3) That [Wessel] was capable of performing all of the essential functions of the position, with or without reasonable accommodation;
(4) That [Wessel]'s disability did not prevent him from performing the essential functions of the position, such that any functions he could not perform because of his disability were merely marginal functions not essential to performance of the job of Executive Director; and
(5) That [Wessel]'s disability was a motivating factor in the decision to discharge him.

The Plaintiffs are not required to prove that [Wessel]'s disability was the sole motivation or the primary motivation for the Defendants' decision. The Plaintiffs need only prove that [Wessel]'s disability played a part in the decision. In addition, the Plaintiffs are not required to produce direct evidence of unlawful motive. Intentional discrimination, if it exists, is seldom admitted but is a fact that you may infer from the existence of other facts.

Adapted from [*Chiari v. City of League City*, 920 F.2d 311, 315–18 (5th Cir. 1991)]; [*Prewitt v. United States Postal Service*, 662 F.2d 292, 309–10 (5th Cir. 1981)]; Devitt & Blackmar, Federal Jury Practice and Instructions, ch. 104.01 *et seq.*
Given:
Denied:
Given as Modified:

PLAINTIFFS' INSTRUCTION 6
OTHERWISE QUALIFIED — DEFINITION

An individual is otherwise qualified within the meaning of the Americans with Disabilities Act if he satisfies the prerequisites for the position, such as possessing the appropriate educational background, employment experience, skills, licenses, etc.

29 C.F.R. § 1630.2(m); EEOC Interpretive Guidance to Regulations at 29 C.F.R. § 1630(2)(m).
Given:
Denied:
Given as Modified:

PLAINTIFFS' INSTRUCTION 7
QUALIFIED INDIVIDUAL

The determination of whether [Wessel] was qualified, in that he was able to perform the essential functions of his position, with or without reasonable accommodation, must be made with respect to the time of the employment decision. The determination should be based on whether he was capable of performing the essential functions of his position as Executive Director at the time of the decision to terminate him, and should not be based on speculation that he might have become unable to perform the essential functions of the position in the future or might have caused increased health insurance premiums or workers' compensation costs.

Adapted from EEOC interpretive Guidance to Regulations at 29 C.F.R. § 1630(2)(m).
Given:
Denied:
Given as Modified:

PLAINTIFFS' INSTRUCTION 8
LIMITING INSTRUCTION

You will recall that during the course of this trial I have admitted certain evidence in the form of testimony and exhibits that related to [Mr. Wessel]'s medical condition at a time after he left his employment with Defendants. You may consider such evidence only for the limited purpose of determining the appropriate backpay to which [Mr. Wessel] is entitled, if your verdict is for the Plaintiffs. You may not consider such evidence for the purpose of determining whether [Wessel] was a qualified individual at the time of his discharge.

Adapted from Pattern Jury Instructions (Civil Cases), U.S. Fifth Circuit District Judges Association (1991), Federal Claims Instruction No. 2.15 (1991).
Given:
Denied:
Given as Modified:

PLAINTIFFS' INSTRUCTION 9
ESSENTIAL FUNCTIONS — DEFINITION

The term *essential functions* means the fundamental job duties of the employment position the individual with a disability holds. The term *essential functions* does not include the marginal functions of the position. Whether a particular function is essential is a factual determination that must be made on a case-by-case basis. In determining whether or not a particular function is essential, all relevant evidence should be considered.

Adapted from EEOC Regulation 29 C.F.R. § 1630.2(n); EEOC Interpretive Guidance to 29 C.F.R. § 1630.2(n).
Given:
Denied:
Given as Modified:

PLAINTIFFS' INSTRUCTION 10
SOCIAL SECURITY DISABILITY AND UNEMPLOYMENT COMPENSATION

The definition of *disability* under the Americans with Disabilities Act is not the same as the definition of *disability* in other laws, such as state workers' compensation laws or other federal or state laws that provide benefits for people with disabilities and disabled veterans. Therefore, in making your determination of whether [Charles Wessel] was disabled and/or unable to perform the essential functions of his job as Executive Director of [A.I.C. Security Investigations, Ltd.], because of his disability, you may consider the determination of the Social Security Administration that [Charles Wessel] was entitled to disability benefits as evidence to be considered in conjunction with all other relevant evidence in resolving the question; however, you cannot consider the determination of the Social Security Administration as a definitive finding that [Wessel] could or could not perform the essential functions of his job.

Similarly, the fact that the [Illinois] Department of Employment Security has found that [Wessel] is eligible for unemployment compensation, based on a finding that he is able to work and is diligently seeking employment, may be considered by you in conjunction with all other relevant evidence in determining whether he was or was not able to perform, and whether he continues to be able to perform, the essential functions of his job as Executive Director. However, you cannot consider the determination of the [Illinois] Department of Employment Security as a definitive finding that [Wessel] was able, or not, to work, and was actively seeking employment following his termination from [A.I.C. Security Investigations, Ltd.].

Adapted from EEOC Interpretive Guidance, 29 C.F.R. § 1630.2(k); EEOC Technical Assistance Manual, § 2.2; [*Overton v. Reilly,* 977 F.2d 1190, 1196 (7th Cir. 1992)]; [*Mitchell v. Humana Hospital-Shoals,* 942 F.2d 1581, 1583 n.2 (11th Cir. 1991)].
Given:
Denied:
Given as Modified:

PLAINTIFFS' INSTRUCTION 11
THREAT TO SAFETY DEFENSE

If you find that the Plaintiffs have established each of the elements of their claim, then you will consider the Defendants' defense, which the Defendants must establish by a preponderance of the evidence. It is Defendants' defense that [Charles Wessel] poses a direct threat to the health or safety of himself or others in the workplace.

You may find that [Charles Wessel] poses a direct threat only if the Defendants have proved, more likely than not, that [Charles Wessel] poses a significant risk of substantial harm to the health and safety of himself or others in the workplace that cannot be eliminated or reduced by reasonable accommodation. The threat must relate to the work environment; [Wessel]'s activities outside the work environment are irrelevant.

A significant risk is more than an elevated risk of injury on the job. A significant risk is a specific risk having a high probability of imminent, substantial harm. In determining whether [Wessel] posses a significant risk, you must consider the following factors:

(1) The duration of the risk;
(2) The nature and severity of the potential harm;
(3) The likelihood that potential harm will occur; and
(4) The imminence of the potential harm.

If an individual poses a direct threat as a result of his disability, the employer must determine whether a reasonable accommodation would either eliminate the risk or reduce it to an acceptable level.

Adapted from Americans with Disabilities Act, 42 U.S.C. §§ 12,113(b), 12,111(3); EEOC Interpretive Guidance, 29 C.F.R. § 1630.2(r); [*School Board of Nassau County v. Arline,* 480 U.S. 273 (1987)]; [*Mantolete v. Bolger,* 767 F.2d 1416 (9th Cir. 1985)]; [*Strathie v. Department of Transportation,* 716 F.2d 227 (3d Cir. 1983)]; [*New York State Ass'n for Retarded Citizens v. Carey,* 612 F.2d 644 (2d Cir. 1979)]; 56 Fed. Reg. 35, 745 (1991).

Given:
Denied:
Given as modified:

PLAINTIFFS' INSTRUCTION 12[55]
CONSIDER DAMAGES ONLY IF NECESSARY

If the Plaintiffs have proved their claim against the Defendants by a preponderance of the evidence, you must determine the damages to which [Charles Wessel] is entitled. You should not interpret the fact that I have given instructions about [Wessel]'s damages as any indication in any way that I believe that the Plaintiffs should, or should not, win this case. it is your task first to decide whether the Defendants are liable. I am instructing you on damages only so that you will have guidance in the event you decide that the Defendants are liable and that [Wessel] is entitled to recover money from the Defendants.

Adapted from Pattern Jury Instructions (Civil Cases), U.S. Fifth Circuit District Judges Association (1991), Instruction 3.1.
Given:
Denied:
Given as Modified:

---

[55] In EEOC v. A.I.C. Security Investigations, Ltd., 55 F.3d 1276 (7th Cir. 1995), the Seventh Circuit held that it was error for the district court to give this direct threat instruction, a slightly different one from either instruction originally tendered by the parties:

> [I]t is the defendant's defense that Charles Wessel posed a threat to the health and safety of himself or others in the workplace. You may find that Charles Wessel posed a direct threat only if the defendants have proven by a preponderance of the evidence that, more likely than not, Charles Wessel in the performance of an essential function of his job posed a significant threat of substantial harm to himself or others in the workplace that could not be eliminated or reduced by a reasonable accommodation.

Id. at 1283–84. The court of appeals held that the limitation of the defense to "in the performance of an essential function of his job" was error because it invited the jury to consider whether Wessel had to drive to accomplish his job, a question that should have been confined as a subset of the question of accommodation. Nevertheless, the court of appeals thought that the relatively minor error did not prejudice the jury's consideration of the case and rejected this basis for overturning the jury verdict in the plaintiff's favor. *Id.* at 1284–85.

PLAINTIFFS' INSTRUCTION 13
DEFENDANTS' LIABILITY

If you find that the Plaintiffs have proved that the Defendants discriminated against [Wessel] on the basis of his disability, the three Defendants together will be liable for any backpay, future out-of-pocket expenses, or compensatory damages that are proved.

PLAINTIFFS' INSTRUCTION 14
DAMAGES

If you find that the Defendants are liable to [Charles Wessel], then you must also determine an amount that is fair compensation for all of the injuries that he suffered because of the discrimination. The purpose of damages is to make the Plaintiff whole — that is, to compensate the Plaintiff for the damage that the Plaintiff has suffered. Under the Americans with Disabilities Act, damages include (1) lost salary and benefits, (2) future out-of-pocket expenses, and (3) compensatory damages for intangible losses. Intangible losses may include but are not limited to emotional pain, suffering, inconvenience, mental anguish, humiliation, shame, loss of self-esteem, fear, embarrassment, depression, and injury to reputation or professional standing that the plaintiff has suffered or may suffer in the future.

You may award damages only for injuries that the Plaintiffs prove were caused by the Defendants' allegedly discriminatory conduct. The damages that you award must be fair compensation for all of [Wessel]'s damages, no more and no less. Damages are not allowed as a punishment and cannot be imposed or increased to penalize the Defendants. You should not award damages for speculative injuries but only for those injuries that [Charles Wessel] has actually suffered or is reasonably likely to suffer in the future.

You must use sound discretion in fixing an award of damages, drawing reasonable inferences where you find them appropriate from the facts and circumstances in evidence.

You should consider the following elements of damages, to the extent you find them proved by a preponderance of the evidence:

Adapted from Pattern Jury Instructions (Civil Cases), U.S. Fifth Circuit District Judges Association (1991), Instruction 15.2, and 42 U.S.C. § 1981a.
Given:
Denied:
Given as Modified:

PLAINTIFFS' INSTRUCTION 15
BACKPAY AND BENEFITS

One element of the damages that you must consider is backpay and benefits. That is, as part of a damages recovery, you must award [Charles Wessel] an amount equal to the pay and benefits that he would have received from the Defendants had he not been discharged, from the time that he was discharged until the date of trial, unless you find that [Charles Wessel] became unable to perform the essential functions of the position of Executive Director with or without reasonable accommodation at some point following his discharge and prior to the date of trial. If you so find, then you should calculate backpay and benefits from the date of discharge up to the date that he became unable to perform the essential functions of the position of Executive Director. The parties have stipulated that [Wessel] would have earned [$3,893.75] per month for each month he continued to work for [A.I.C.]. The parties have stipulated that [Wessel] was receiving [$350] per month designated as a car allowance from [A.I.C.] but dispute whether he would have continued to receive it for each month that he continued to be employed by EEOC. The parties have also stipulated that Defendants would have paid [$598.84] per month in health insurance premiums and [$247.72] per quarter in life insurance premiums as long as [Wessel] had remained employed. You may include in the calculation all forms of compensation [Wessel] would have earned, including salary, car allowances, bonuses, raises, vacation pay, and health insurance benefits.

Plaintiffs are not required to prove with unrealistic precision the amount of lost earnings, if any, due [Wessel]. Any ambiguities in determining what he would have earned should be resolved against the Defendants.

If Defendants prove that [Charles Wessel] unjustifiably failed to take a new job of like kind, status, and pay that was available to him, or failed to make reasonable efforts to find a new job, you should subtract from his damages any amount he could have earned in a new job after his discharge.

Adapted from Devitt & Blackmar, Federal Jury Practice and Instruction § 106.07.
Given:
Denied:
Given as modified:

PLAINTIFFS' INSTRUCTION 16
REASONABLE ACCOMMODATION

In this case Plaintiffs do not claim that Defendants should have provided a reasonable accommodation to [Wessel] prior to his discharge. [Wessel] never requested a reasonable accommodation, and claims that he was able to perform the essential functions of his position without accommodation. However, if you determine that Plaintiffs have proved that [Wessel] was unlawfully terminated because of his disability, then you may consider the question of reasonable accommodation in determining the backpay to which [Wessel] is entitled. Backpay should include lost earnings for the period during which [Wessel] could have continued to perform the essential functions of his position, with or without reasonable accommodation.

The term *reasonable accommodation* means modification or adjustment to the work environment, or to the manner or circumstances under which a job is customarily held or performed.

Required reasonable accommodations may include making existing facilities used by employees readily accessible to and usable by individuals with disabilities; job restructuring; part-time or modified work schedules; reassignment to a vacant position; modification of examinations, training materials, or policies; the provision of qualified readers or interpreters; and other similar accommodations for individuals with disabilities. The list is not exhaustive, but is intended to provide general guidance about the reasonable accommodation concept.

42 U.S.C. § 12,111(9) (1991); 29 C.F.R. § 1630.2(o).
Given:
Denied:
Given as Modified:

PLAINTIFFS' INSTRUCTION 17
FUTURE OUT-OF-POCKET EXPENSES

If you find for Plaintiffs, you should also consider future out-of-pocket expenses. These include the reasonable expected costs for expenses such as insurance premiums and other consequential damages that will result from Defendants' discriminatory conduct.
Given:
Denied:
Given as Modified:

PLAINTIFFS' INSTRUCTION 18
COMPENSATORY DAMAGES FOR INTANGIBLE INJURY

No evidence of the monetary value of intangible things, such as mental or physical pain and suffering, has been, or need be, introduced. You are not trying to determine value, but an amount that will fairly compensate [Wessel] for the damages he has suffered. There is no exact standard for fixing the compensation to be awarded for these elements of damages. Any award that you make should be fair in light of the evidence.

If you find that [Wessel] is entitled to compensatory damages for intangible losses, you should be guided by dispassionate common sense. Computing damages may be difficult, but you must not let that difficulty lead you to engage in arbitrary guesswork. On the other hand, the law does not require that the Plaintiffs prove the amount of [Wessel]'s losses with mathematical precision, but only with as much definiteness and accuracy as the circumstances permit.

Adapted from Pattern Jury Instructions (Civil Cases), U.S. Fifth Circuit District Judges Association (1991), Instruction 15.4.
Given:
Denied:
Given as Modified:

PLAINTIFFS' INSTRUCTION 19
PUNITIVE DAMAGES

If you find that the Defendants are liable for [Wessel]'s injuries, you must award the compensatory damages Plaintiffs have proved. You also may award punitive damages, if the Plaintiffs have proved that a Defendant acted with malice or willfulness or with reckless indifference to the rights of [Wessel]. One acts willfully with respect to the rights of others if the Defendant knew or should have known that [Wessel]'s rights would be violated by the discriminatory acts proved.

Punitive damages, unlike backpay and benefits, out-of-pocket expenses, and other compensatory damages, should be considered for each Defendant separately. If you determine that a Defendant acted with malice or with reckless indifference to [Wessel]'s right as to justify an award of punitive damages, you may exercise your discretion to award those damages. In making any award of punitive damages, you should consider that the purpose of punitive damages is to punish the Defendant for malicious or reckless conduct, and to deter the Defendant and others from engaging in similar conduct in the future. The law does not require you to award punitive damages, however. If you decide to award punitive damages, you must use sound reason in setting the amount of the damages. The amount of an award of punitive damages must not reflect bias, prejudice, or sympathy toward any party. However, the amount can be as large as you believe necessary to fulfill the purposes of punitive damages. You may consider the financial resources of the Defendant in fixing the amount of punitive damages, and may impose punitive damages against one or more of the Defendants, and not others, or against more than one Defendants in different amounts.

Adapted from Pattern Jury Instructions (Civil Cases), U.S. Fifth Circuit District Judges Association (1991), Instruction 15.13, 42 U.S.C. § 1981a(b)(1)(1991).
Given:
Denied:
Given as Modified:

PLAINTIFFS' INSTRUCTION 20
VERDICT FORMS

Upon retiring to the jury room, you will select one of your number to act as Foreperson. The Foreperson will preside over your deliberations and will be your spokesperson here in Court.

Verdict forms have been prepared for your convenience.

If you find in favor of [Wessel] and against the Defendants, you should calculate damages, using the jury verdict form that reads as follows:

We the jury find that the Defendants violated the Americans with Disabilities Act by discharging [Charles Wessel] on the basis of his disability.

Having found in favor of [Wessel] and against Defendants, we further assess damages in the following amount:
_____Backpay and benefits
_____Future out-of-pocket expenses
_____Compensatory damages for intangible losses.

If you find that the Defendants violated the ADA, and you further find that the Defendants or any of them engaged in a discriminatory practice with malice or with reckless indifference to the federally protected rights of [Wessel], you may award punitive damages, using the jury verdict form that reads as follows:

We the jury find that [the Defendant] violated the Americans with Disabilities Act by discharging [Charles Wessel] on the basis of his disability.

Having found in favor of [Wessel] and having further found that [the Defendant] engaged in a discriminatory practice with malice or with reckless indifference to the federally protected rights of [Wessel], we assess punitive damages in the amount of [____].

If you find in favor of the Defendants and against [Wessel], you should use the jury verdict form that reads as follows:

We the jury find that the Defendant did not violate the Americans with Disabilities Act by discharging [Charles Wessel], and therefore find for the Defendants and against the Plaintiffs.

You will take the verdict forms to the jury room and, when you have reached unanimous agreement as to your verdict, you will have your Foreperson fill in, date, and sign the form that sets forth the verdict upon which you unanimously agree; and then return with your verdict to the courtroom.

Adapted from Devitt, Blackmar, & Wolff, Federal Jury Practice and Instruction § 74.04.
Given:
Denied:
Given as Modified:

PLAINTIFFS' VERDICT FORM (ALL DEFENDANTS)

We the jury find that the Defendants violated the Americans with Disabilities Act by discharging [Charles Wessel] on the basis of his disability.

Having found in favor of [Wessel] and against Defendants, we further assess damages in the following amounts:

____Backpay and benefits
____Future out-of-pocket expenses
____Compensatory damages for intangible losses.
[Foreperson]

PLAINTIFFS' VERDICT FORM ([A.I.C. SECURITY INVESTIGATIONS, LTD.])

We the jury find that the Defendant [A.I.C. Security Investigations, Ltd.] violated the Americans with Disabilities Act by discharging [Charles Wessel] on the basis of his disability.

Having found in favor of [Wessel] and having further found that [A.I.C. Security Investigations, Ltd.] engaged in a discriminatory practice with malice or with reckless indifference to the federally protected rights of [Wessel], we assess punitive damages in the amount of [___].
[Foreperson]

PLAINTIFFS' VERDICT FORM ([A.I.C. INTERNATIONAL, LTD.])

We the jury find that the Defendant [A.I.C. International, Ltd.] violated the Americans with Disabilities Act by discharging [Charles Wessel] on the basis of his disability.

Having found in favor of [Wessel] and having further found that [A.I.C. International, Ltd.] engaged in a discriminatory practice with malice or with reckless indifference to the federally protected rights of [Wessel], we assess punitive damages in the amount of [___].
[Foreperson]

PLAINTIFFS' VERDICT FORM (DEFENDANT C)

We the jury find that Defendant [C] violated the Americans with Disabilities Act by discharging [Charles Wessel] on the basis of his disability.

Having found in favor of [Wessel] and having further found that [Defendant C] engaged in a discriminatory practice with malice or with reckless indifference to the federally protected rights of [Wessel], we assess punitive damages in the amount of [___].
[Foreperson]

PLAINTIFFS' VERDICT FORM

We the jury find that the Defendants did not violate the Americans with Disabilities Act by discharging [Charles Wessel], and therefore find for the Defendants and against the Plaintiffs.
[Foreperson]

[18]   Defendants' Proposed Jury Instructions (EEOC)

FORM 16–14   Sample Defendants' Proposed Jury Instructions

DEFENDANTS' PROPOSED JURY INSTRUCTIONS
PRELIMINARY INSTRUCTION — PART ONE
DEFENDANTS' INSTRUCTION 1
EXPERT WITNESSES

A witness who has special knowledge, skill, experience, training, or education in a certain field may give his or her opinion as an expert regarding any matter in which he or she is skilled. in determining the weight to be given to the experts' opinions, you should consider the qualifications and reliability of the expert and the reasons given for his or her opinion. Consider how extensive each expert's educational background is in the field. You are not bound by an expert's opinion merely because he or she is an expert; you may accept or reject it, as in the case of other witnesses. Give it the weight you deem it entitled.
Given:
Denied:
Given as Modified:

DEFENDANTS' INSTRUCTION 2
AMERICANS WITH DISABILITIES ACT

This is an action brought under the Americans with Disabilities Act. The Act makes it unlawful for an employer to discriminate against a qualified individual with a disability. The Act provides no protection to an individual with a disability who is not qualified.
A qualified individual with a disability is a person who, with or without reasonable accommodation, can perform the essential functions of the employment position.

DEFENDANTS' INSTRUCTION 3
CONTENTIONS OF THE PARTIES

In this case, Plaintiffs claim that, because of [Charles H. Wessel]'s disability, he was unjustifiably discharged from his position as Executive Director at [A.I.C. Security Investigations, Ltd.].
The Defendants deny that they unjustifiably discharged [Wessel] from employment on account of his disability. The Defendants instead contend that [Wessel] was justifiably excluded from the position of Executive Director because he could no longer perform the essential functions of the position of Executive Director at [A.I.C. Security Investigations, Ltd.] with or without reasonable accommodation. Defendants also contend that [Wessel] was excluded from his position as Executive Director due to legitimate business reasons. In addition, Defendants contend that they, in good faith, offered [Charles H. Wessel] further reasonable accommodations

and provided to [Charles H. Wessel] reasonable accommodations, and that any further accommodation beyond those offered would have imposed an undue hardship upon the business of [A.I.C. Security Investigations, Ltd.]. Defendants also contend that Plaintiff posed a direct threat to the health or safety of himself or others in the workplace.

Adapted from Pattern Jury Instructions (Civil Cases), U.S. Fifth Circuit District Judges Association (1983), Federal Claims Instruction No. 10 (1983).
Given:
Denied:
Given as Modified:

DEFENDANTS' INSTRUCTION 4
PLAINTIFFS' PRIMA FACIE CASE

The Plaintiff in an Americans with Disabilities Act ("ADA") case has the burden of proving by a preponderance of the evidence all of the following elements:

(1) That [Wessel] has a *disability*, as that term is defined in the ADA;
(2) That he is "otherwise qualified" for the position he held; this element requires proof by the Plaintiffs, by a preponderance of the evidence, that, except for [Wessel]'s disability, [Wessel] possessed the necessary qualifications for the position, such as educational background, experience, skills, and other job-related factors;
(3) That [Wessel] was capable of performing all of the essential functions of the position of Executive Director either with or without reasonable accommodation by the employer;
(4) That [Wessel]'s disability did not prevent him from performing the essential functions of the position, such that any functions he could not perform because of his disability were marginal functions not essential to performance of the job of Executive Director; and
(5) That [Wessel]'s disability was the sole motivating factor in the decisions ending [Wessel]'s employment with [A.I.C. Security Investigations, Ltd.].

Adapted from [*School Board of Nassau County v. Arline*, 480 U.S. 273, 275 (1987)]; [*Ristoff v. United States*, 839 F.2d 1242 (7th Cir. 1988)].
Given:
Denied:
Given as Modified:

DEFENDANTS' INSTRUCTION 5
DEFENDANTS' REBUTTAL OF PLAINTIFF'S PRIMA FACIE CASE — INTENTIONAL
DISABILITY DISCRIMINATION

If you find that Plaintiff has shown the foregoing elements, then you should consider Defendants' explanation for its conduct toward Plaintiff.

Defendants have contended that their actions toward [Wessel] were taken for reasons unrelated to [Wessel]'s disability. Therefore, Defendants need only articulate to you a legitimate, nondiscriminatory reason for their conduct toward [Charles Wessel]. With respect to such reasons, Plaintiff, in order to prevail, must then convince you by a preponderance of the evidence either that an unlawfully discriminatory reason was the sole motivating factor for the decision or that Defendants' stated reasons were mere pretext. Pretext is shown if you find that the stated reasons are false or are unworthy of belief.

If Plaintiff has so satisfied you, you should find for Plaintiff. If not, you should find for Defendants.

Adapted from Federal Claims Instruction No. 10, Pattern Jury Instructions — Civil Cases (U.S. Fifth Circuit District Judges Ass'n 1983); [*School Board of Nassau County v. Arline*, 480 U.S. 273, 275 (1987)]; [*Ristoff v. United States*, 839 F.2d 1242 (7th Cir. 1988)]. *See* [*McDonnell Douglas Corp. v. Green*, 411 U.S. 792, 802–06 (1973)]; [*Texas Department of Community Affairs v. Burdine*, 450 U.S. 248, 256–69 (1981)].

Given:

Denied:

Given as Modified:

DEFENDANTS' INSTRUCTION 6
DEFENDANTS' REBUTTAL OF PLAINTIFF'S PRIMA FACIE CASE — REASONABLE ACCOMMODATION AND DEFENSE OF UNDUE HARDSHIP

Defendants will be excused from liability if Defendants prove by a preponderance of the evidence the following: that [Wessel]'s disability prevented him from performing essential functions of the job; and that there is no accommodation Defendants could have made without undue hardship that would enable [Wessel] to perform all essential functions of the job.

If you find that [Wessel]'s disability was the sole motivating factor in that decision, Defendants will be excused from liability if they prove by a preponderance of the evidence the following: that [Wessel]'s disability prevented him from performing any of the essential functions of the job; and that there is no further reasonable accommodation Defendants could have made without undue hardship that would enable [Wessel] to perform all essential functions of the job.

Here, this affirmative defense of Defendants' inability to make further reasonable accommodations without undue hardship that would enable [Wessel] to perform the essential functions of the job is claimed by Defendants as the basis for their employment decisions regarding [Wessel].

To determine whether Defendants have met their burden of proof on this affirmative defense as to each of these employment decisions, you must consider the following issues: the essential functions of the Executive Director job, reasonable accommodation, and undue hardship. I will explain the significance of each of these issues in turn.

42 U.S.C. §§ 12,111, 12113; 29 C.F.R. §§ 1630.2(m)–(p), 1630.9, 1630.15(b)–(d), and guidelines; [*School Board of Nassau County v. Arline*, 480 U.S. 273, 275

(1987)]; [*Chiari v. City of League City,* 920 F.2d 311, 315–19 (5th Cir. 1991)]; *Strathie v. Department of Transportation,* 716 F.2d 227, 230–31 (3d Cir. 1983)]; [*Prewitt v. United States Postal Service,* 662 F.2d 292, 307–10 (5th Cir. 1981)].
Given:
Denied:
Given as Modified:

DEFENDANTS' INSTRUCTION 7
ADA: ESSENTIAL FUNCTIONS OF THE JOB

Job functions may be considered essential for any of several reasons, such as the following:

(1) The employer's judgment as to what functions of a job are essential;
(2) The reason the position exists is to perform that function;
(3) A limited number of employees are available among whom the performance of the function may be distributed; or
(4) The function is highly specialized so that the incumbent is hired for his or her expertise or ability to perform that particular function.

Evidence of whether a particular function is essential also includes the amount of time the employee must spend performing the function; the consequences of not requiring the incumbent to perform the function; and the work experiences of incumbents in similar jobs. To the extent such evidence is before you, you may consider all of these factors in determining whether any particular function is essential to the job in question. Defendants have the burden of proving by a preponderance of the evidence that any particular function is essential to the job in question.

42 U.S.C. § 12,111(8). 29 C.F.R. § 1630.2(n)(2)(3).
Given:
Denied:
Given as Modified:

DEFENDANTS' INSTRUCTION 8
ADA: PERFORMANCE STANDARDS

It is important to note that the inquiry into essential functions is not intended to second-guess an employer's business judgment with regard to performance standards, whether qualitative or quantitative, or to require employers to lower such standards.

29 C.F.R. § 1630 (interpretive Guidance on Title I of the Americans with Disabilities Act, *id.* § 1630.2(n)).
Given:
Denied:
Given as Modified:

DEFENDANTS' INSTRUCTION 9
ADA: REASONABLE ACCOMMODATION

An accommodation is a modification or adjustment to the work environment, or to the manner or circumstances under which the position held or desired is customarily performed, that enables a qualified individual with a disability to perform the essential functions of the job. Plaintiffs bear the initial burden of coming forward with evidence that a proposed accommodation is reasonable and that such an accommodation could permit the essential functions of the job to be performed where, without such accommodation, they could not be performed.

An employer would not be required to make an accommodation if the accommodation is unreasonable. A proposed accommodation is unreasonable if it would alter the essential nature of the position or reallocate essential functions of the job to another individual. Defendants bear the burden of proving by a preponderance of the evidence whether the accommodation is reasonable. Defendants would not have to implement the accommodation if it would impose an undue hardship on the business of [A.I.C. Security Investigations, Ltd.].

[*Overton v. Reilly,* 977 F.2d 1190, 1194 (7th Cir. 1992)]; [*Treadwell v. Alexander,* 707 F.2d 473, 478 (11th Cir. 1983)]; 42 U.S.C. § 12,111(9); 29 C.F.R. § 1630.2(o) and guidelines thereto.
Given:
Denied:
Given as Modified:

DEFENDANTS' INSTRUCTION 10
ADA: UNDUE HARDSHIP

A proposed accommodation would impose an undue hardship on [A.I.C. Security Investigations, Ltd.], and Defendants would not be liable for failing to implement such an accommodation, if the accommodation would impose significant difficulty and expense on the business of [A.I.C. Security Investigations, Ltd.]. In determining whether any proposed accommodation would create an undue hardship, you may consider the following factors to the extent there is evidence of them before you:

(1) The nature and net cost of the accommodation needed, taking into consideration the availability of tax credits and deductions or outside funding;
(2) The overall financial resources of employer's facility or facilities involved in the provision of the accommodation, the number of persons employed at such facility, and the effect on the employer's expenses and resources;
(3) The overall financial resources of the employer as a whole, the overall size of the business with respect to its total number of employees, and the number, type, and location of its facilities;
(4) The type of operation or operations of employer, including the composition, structure, and functions of the workforce, and the geographic separateness and

administrative or fiscal relationship of the facility or facilities in question to the employer; and

(5) The impact of the accommodation on the operation of the facility involved, including the impact on the ability of the other employees to perform their duties and the impact on the facility's ability to conduct business.

Defendants also bear the burden of proving by a preponderance of the evidence that a proposed accommodation would create undue hardship on the business of [A.I.C. Security Investigations, Ltd.].

42 U.S.C. § 12,111(10)(b); 29 C.F.R. § 1630.2(p) and guidelines thereto.
Given:
Denied:
Given as Modified:

DEFENDANTS' INSTRUCTION 11
ADA: FAILURE TO PERFORM ESSENTIAL FUNCTION OF JOB

If Plaintiffs do not prove to your satisfaction by a preponderance of the evidence that [Wessel] could perform all of the essential functions of the job of Executive Director for [A.I.C.], even with any reasonable accommodation that would not cause an undue hardship on the business of [A.I.C.] presented in the evidence during this trial, you must find in favor of Defendants.

[*Chiari v. City of League City*, 920 F.2d 311, 318 (5th Cir. 1991)]; [*Prewitt v. United States Postal Service*, 662 F.2d 292, 308 (5th Cir. 1981)].
Given:
Denied:
Given as Modified:

DEFENDANTS' INSTRUCTION 12
ADA: LIMITATION ON DAMAGES — GOOD FAITH AND INDEPENDENT JUSTIFICATION

If your finding is that Defendants discriminated against [Wessel] by failing to provide any reasonable accommodation that [A.I.C. Security Investigations, Ltd.] could have provided without undue hardship to itself, then you will be asked to answer two further questions. First, you will be asked to determine whether the Defendants have proved by a preponderance of the evidence that they made a good-faith effort to identify and make a reasonable accommodation.

Second, you will be asked to determine whether Defendants have proved by a preponderance of the evidence that [Wessel] would not have remained employed, even in the absence of discrimination, because of [Wessel]'s disability. That is, you must also determine whether Defendants have shown by a preponderance of the evidence that disability discrimination was not the sole factor in the decision.

Your answer to these questions will have a bearing on the relief available to [Wessel], which need not concern you at this time, and about which you should not speculate.

42 U.S.C. § 1981a(a)(3).
Given:
Denied:
Given as Modified:

DEFENDANTS' INSTRUCTION 13
THREAT TO SAFETY DEFENSE

If you find that the Plaintiffs have established each of the elements of their claim, then you will consider this defense, which the Defendants must establish by a preponderance of the evidence. It is the Defendants' defense that [Charles Wessel] poses a threat to the health or safety of himself or others in the workplace.

You may find that [Charles Wessel] poses a direct threat only if the Defendants have proved, more likely than not, that [Charles Wessel] poses a significant risk to the health and safety of himself or others in the workplace that cannot be eliminated or reduced by reasonable accommodation.

If an individual poses a direct threat as a result of his disability, the employer must determine whether a reasonable accommodation would either eliminate the risk or reduce it to an acceptable level.

Adapted from Americans with Disabilities Act, 42 U.S.C. §§ 12,113(b), 12,111(3); [*School Board of Nassau County v. Arline,* 480 U.S. 273, 275 (1987)]; [*Mantolete v. Bolger,* 767 F.2d 1416 (9th Cir. 1985)]; [*Strathie v. Department of Transportation,* 716 F.2d 227 (3d Cir. 1983)].
Given:
Denied:
Given as Modified:

DEFENDANTS' SPECIAL INTERROGATORIES
FIRST SET OF SPECIAL INTERROGATORIES

(1) Do you find that Plaintiffs have proved by a preponderance of the evidence that [Charles H. Wessel] was able to perform the essential functions of the position of Executive Director with or without reasonable accommodation?
Yes [___] No [___]
If your answer to question 1 is "Yes," answer question 2.
If your answer to question 1 is "No," skip questions 2, 3, and 4.
(2) Do you find that Plaintiffs have proved by a preponderance of the evidence that Defendants discharged [Charles H. Wessel] from his position of Executive Director solely because of [Wessel]'s disability?
Yes [___] No [___]
If your answer to question 2 is "Yes," answer question 3.
If your answer to question 2 is "No," skip questions 3 and 4.
(3) Do you find that Defendants have proved by a preponderance of the evidence that there is no reasonable accommodation it could have made without undue hardship to [A.I.C. Security Investigations, Ltd.] that would have enabled [Wessel] to perform all of the essential functions of the job of Executive Director?

Yes [___] No [___]

If your answer to question 3 is "Yes," skip question 4.

If your answer to question 3 is "No," answer question 4.

(4) Do you find that Defendants have proved by a preponderance of the evidence that they would have discharged [Charles Wessel] from his position as Executive Director due to legitimate business reasons in the absence of any discrimination on the basis [Wessel]'s disability?

Yes [___] No [___]

INSTRUCTIONS TO BE FOLLOWED AFTER ANSWERING FIRST SET OF SPECIAL INTERROGATORIES

If you answered "Yes" to Interrogatories 1 and 2 above and "No" to Interrogatories 3 or 4 above, then complete Verdict Form 2, which follows. If you answered "No" to Interrogatories 1 and 2 above or "Yes" to Interrogatories 3 or 4 above, then complete Verdict Form 1, which follows. If you complete Verdict Form 2, you must answer the Second Set of Interrogatories.

VERDICT FORM 1

We the jury find that the Defendants did not violate the Americans with Disabilities Act and therefore find for the Defendants and against the Plaintiffs.
[Foreperson]

NOTE: If you answered this verdict form, then do not answer Second Set of Special Interrogatories, and return this form to the judge immediately.

VERDICT FORM 2

We the jury find that the following Defendants violated the Americans with Disabilities Act (place an "X" by each Defendant you find liable):
 [A.I.C. Security Investigations, Ltd.] [___]
 [A.I.C. International, Ltd.] [___]
 [Defendant C] [___]

[Foreperson]

NOTE: If you completed this verdict form, then answer Second Set of Special Interrogatories.

SECOND SET OF SPECIAL INTERROGATORIES

(1) Do you find that Defendants have proved by a preponderance of the evidence that they made a good-faith effort to make a reasonable accommodation to enable Plaintiff to perform the job of Executive Director?
 Yes [___] No [___]
[Foreperson]
NOTE: Now please go on to the Jury Instructions pertaining to damages.

DAMAGES
DEFENDANTS' INSTRUCTION 14
INSTRUCTION NOT TO BE TAKEN AS INDICATION OF LIABILITY: PLAIN-
TIFF MUST PROVE DAMAGES

I will now instruct you on the issue of damages. My charge to you on the law of damages must not be taken as any indication that you must decide for the Plaintiffs. It is for you to decide on the evidence presented and the rules of law I give you whether [Charles H. Wessel] is entitled to recover anything from the Defendants. If you decide that [Charles H. Wessel] is not entitled to recover, your verdict will be for the Defendants and you need not go further. Only if you decide that [Charles H. Wessel]'s rights under the Americans with Disabilities Act ("ADA") have been violated by the intentional acts of the Defendants will you then consider the measure of damages. In other words, if you find that the Plaintiffs have failed to prove any one of the elements of proof that are essential to their claim by a preponderance of the evidence, then your verdict must be against the Plaintiffs and in favor of Defendants on this claim. In this case, the Plaintiff EEOC is seeking compensatory damages for [Charles H. Wessel]. Plaintiff [Wessel] is seeking compensatory and punitive damages. It is the Plaintiffs' burden to prove that [Charles H. Wessel] actually suffered damages and that such damages were directly caused by Defendants. It is Plaintiffs' burden to prove the amount of such damages by a preponderance of the credible evidence.

[Memphis Community School District v. Stachura, 106 S. Ct. 2537 (1986)]; [Carey v. Piphus, 435 U.S. 247, 264–65 (1978)].
Given:
Denied:
Given as Modified:

DEFENDANTS' INSTRUCTION 15
COMPENSATORY DAMAGES

If you find that the Defendants are liable to [Charles H. Wessel], then you must also determine an amount that is fair compensation for his damages. The purpose of compensatory damages is to make [Wessel] whole — that is, to compensate him for the damage that he has suffered. Compensatory damages are not limited to expenses that [Wessel] may have incurred. If Defendants are found liable, Plaintiff is entitled to compensatory damages for physical injury, pain and suffering, mental anguish, shock, and discomfort that he has suffered as a direct result of Defendants' conduct.

You can award compensatory damages only for injuries that the Plaintiffs prove were the proximate result of the Defendants' allegedly wrongful conduct. The damages that you award must be full compensation for all of [Charles H. Wessel]'s damages, no more and no less. Compensatory damages are not allowed as a punishment and cannot be imposed or increased to penalize the Defendant. You should not award compensatory damages for speculative injuries, but only for those injuries that [Charles H. Wessel] has actually suffered or is reasonably likely to suffer in the future.

If you decide to award compensatory damages, you should be guided by dispassionate common sense. Computing damages may be difficult, but you must not let that difficulty lead you to engage in arbitrary guesswork. On the other hand, the law does not require that the Plaintiffs prove the amount of [Wessel]'s losses with mathematical precision, but only with as much definiteness and accuracy as the circumstances permit.

You must use sound discretion in fixing an award of damages, drawing reasonable inferences where you find them appropriate from the facts and circumstances in evidence.

Adapted from Pattern Jury Instructions (Civil Cases), U.S. Fifth Circuit District Judges Association (1991), Instruction 15.2; 42 U.S.C. § 1981a.
Given:
Denied:
Given as Modified:

DEFENDANTS' INSTRUCTION 16
BACKPAY AWARD

One element of the damages that you must consider is backpay. That is, as part of a damages recovery, you must award [Charles H. Wessel] an amount equal to the pay and benefits that he would have received from the Defendants had he not been discharged until the date of trial, unless you find that [Charles H. Wessel] became unable to perform the essential functions of the position of Executive Director with or without reasonable accommodation at some point following his discharge and prior to the date of trial. If you so find, then you should calculate backpay and benefits from the date of discharge up to the date that he became unable to perform the essential functions of the position of Executive Director. The parties have stipulated that [Wessel] would have earned [$3,893.75] per month for each month he continued to work for [A.I.C.]. The parties have also stipulated that Defendants would have paid [$598.84] per month in health insurance premiums and [$247.72] per quarter in life insurance premiums as long as he had remained employed.

There are certain deductions and offsets that must be made relative to any backpay award.

First, you must deduct from any backpay award any amount that could have been earned by [Wessel] through the exercise of reasonable diligence since the time of his layoff.

Second, all unemployment, Social Security, Supplemental Unemployment, and other benefits received by [Wessel] must be deducted from any backpay award.

Third, you may not include backpay for any period during which [Wessel] merely drew unemployment compensation and did not actively seek employment.

Adapted from Devitt & Blackmar, Federal Jury Practice and Instructions §§ 87.14 and 87.19 (Supp. 1980); 29 C.F.R. § 60.110(19); [*Peters v. Missouri Pacific Rail-*

road, 483 F.2d 490 (5th Cir.), *cert. denied,* 414 U.S. 1002 (1973)]; [*Bowe v. Colgate-Palmolive Co.,* 416 F.2d 711 (7th Cir. 1969)]; [*Dunlop v. Hawaiian Telephone Co.,* 415 F. Supp. 330 (D. Haw. 1976)]; [*Buick v. Board of Education,* 10 Empl. Prac. Dec. ¶ 10,363 (E.D.N.Y. 1975)]; [*Bradford v. Sloan Paper Co.,* 383 F. Supp. 1157 (ND. Ala. 1974)]; [*Schulz v. Hickok Manufacturing Co.,* 358 F. Supp. 1208 (ND. Ga. 1973)]; [*Doe v. Osteopathic Hospital of Wichita, Inc.,* 330 F. Supp. 1357 (D. Kan. 1971)]; [*Ainsworth v. United States,* 399 F.2d 176 (Ct. Cl. 1968)].
Given:
Denied:
Given as Modified:

DEFENDANTS' INSTRUCTION 17
EFFECT OF FAILURE TO MITIGATE DAMAGES

You are instructed that any person who claims damages as a result of alleged discrimination has a duty under the law to mitigate those damages — that is, to take advantage of any reasonable opportunity he may have had under the circumstances to reduce or minimize the loss or damage. An employee who believes he has been wrongfully dismissed has a duty to make every reasonable effort to seek and accept other employment. It was [Wessel]'s duty to earn what he could from the time he was no longer working for [A.I.C. Security Investigations, Ltd.].

So, if you should find from a preponderance of the evidence that [Wessel] failed to seek out and take advantage of employment that was reasonably available to him under all the circumstances, as shown by the evidence, then you should reduce the amount of his damages by the amount he could have reasonably realized if he had taken advantage of such an opportunity. You must not compensate [Wessel] for any portion of his damages that resulted from his failure to use ordinary care to minimize his damages and to seek other employment.

Adapted from Devitt & Blackmar, Federal Jury Practice and Instructions §§ 1, 86.06 (Supp. 1980); 42 U.S.C. § 2000e-5(g); 8 Am. Jur. Pleading and Practice Forms (Damages), Form 335 (Rev. 1969); [*Taylor v. Safeway Stores, Inc.,* 524 F.2d 263 (10th Cir. 1975)]. [*Higgins v. Lawrence PC,* 107 Mich. App. 178, 181, 309 NW.2d 194 (1981)].
Given:
Denied:
Given as Modified:

DEFENDANTS' INSTRUCTION 18
DUTY TO MITIGATE — DEFINITION

If you find that [Wessel] failed to mitigate his damages, you must reduce the sum you award to [Wessel] by the amount he could have earned. By mitigating damages I mean that [Wessel] exercised reasonable care and diligence to obtain suitable alternative employment.

If you find that [Wessel] did not make any efforts to obtain suitable alternative employment and you find that other jobs for which [Wessel] was qualified were available, [Wessel] would have failed to mitigate his damages. Any amounts that he could have earned should be deducted from his backpay award. Similarly, if you find [Wessel] refused employment or any interim jobs, then you must reduce the backpay awarded by the amount he could have earned had he not refused or voluntarily terminated employment.

[*Coleman v. City of Omaha,* 714 F.2d 804 (8th Cir. 1983)]; [*Jackson v. Shell Oil Co.,* 702 F.2d 197 (9th Cir. 1983)]; [*EEOC v. Sandia Corp.,* 639 F.2d 600 (10th Cir. 1980)]; [*Wehr v. Burroughs Corp.,* 619 F.2d 276 (3d Cir. 1980)]; [*United States v. Lee Way Motor Freight, Inc.,* 625 F.2d 918 (10th Cir. 1979)].
Given:
Denied:
Given as Modified:

DEFENDANTS' INSTRUCTION 19
CALCULATION OF FUTURE DAMAGES

If you should find that [Wessel] is reasonably certain to suffer damages in the future from his injuries, then you should award him the amount you believe would fairly compensate him for such future damages, unless you find that [Wessel] became unable to perform the essential functions of the position of Executive Director at some point following his discharge and prior to the date of trial.

If you so find, you should stop calculating damages as of that point in time. In the alternative, if you find that [Wessel] will be unable to perform the essential functions of the position of Executive Director at some point in time after trial, then you should stop calculating damages as of that date. An award of future damages requires that payment be made now for a loss that the Plaintiff will not actually suffer until some future date. If you should find that the Plaintiff is entitled to future damages, including future earnings, then you must determine the present worth in dollars of such future damages.

If you award damages for loss of future earning, you must consider two particular factors:

(1) You should reduce any award by the amount of the expenses that the Plaintiff would have incurred in making those earnings.
(2) If you make an award for future loss of earnings, you must reduce it to present value by considering the interest that the Plaintiff could earn on the amount of the award if he made a relatively risk-free investment. The reason you must make this reduction is because an award of an amount representing future loss of earnings is more valuable to the Plaintiff if he receives it today than if he received it in the future, when he would otherwise have earned it. It is more valuable because the Plaintiff can earn interest on it for the period of time between the date of the award and the date he would have earned the money. Thus, you should adjust the amount of interest that the Plaintiff can earn on that amount in the future.

If you make any award for future medical expenses, you should adjust or discount the award to present value in the same manner as with loss of future earnings.

However, you may not make any adjustment to present value for any damages you may award for future pain and suffering or future mental anguish.

Pattern Jury Instructions (Civil Cases), U.S. Fifth Circuit District Judges Association (1991), Instruction 13.3.
Given:
Denied:
Given as Modified:

DEFENDANTS' INSTRUCTION 20
PUNITIVE DAMAGES

If Defendant were found liable to [Charles H. Wessel], you must award [Wessel] the compensatory damages that Plaintiffs have proved. You also may award punitive damages, if [Wessel] has proved that Defendants acted with malice or reckless indifference to the civil rights of [Wessel]. *Malice* means conduct that is intended by the Defendants to cause injury to [Wessel] or carried on by the Defendants with a conscious disregard of the rights or safety of [Wessel] when they are aware of the probable dangerous consequences of [Wessel]'s conduct and willfully and deliberately fail to avoid those consequences.

If you determine that the Defendants acted with reckless indifference to [Wessel]'s civil rights as to justify an award of punitive damages, you may exercise your discretion to award those damages. In making any award of punitive damages, you should consider that the purpose of punitive damages is to punish a Defendant for malicious conduct, and to deter the Defendants and others from engaging in similar conduct in the future. The law does not require you to award punitive damages; however, if you decide to award punitive damages, you must use sound reason in setting the amount of damages. The amount of an award of punitive damages must not reflect bias, prejudice, or sympathy toward any party. However, the amount can be as large as you believe necessary to fulfill the purposes of punitive damages. You may consider the financial resources of the Defendants in fixing the amount of punitive damages.

Pattern Jury Instructions (Civil Cases), U.S. Fifth Circuit District Judges Association (1991), Instruction 15.13; 42 U.S.C. § 1981a.
Given:
Denied:
Given as Modified:

VERDICT FORMS

Upon retiring to the jury room, you will select one of your members to act as foreperson. The foreperson will preside over your deliberations and will be your spokesperson here in Court.

Verdict forms have been prepared for your convenience.

If you find in favor of [Wessel] and against the Defendants you should calculate damages, using the jury verdict form that reads as follows:

VERDICT FORM 1

We the jury find that the Defendants violated the Americans with Disabilities Act by discharging [Charles Wessel] on the basis of his disability.

Having found in favor of [Wessel] and against the Defendant, we award [Wessel] backpay in the following amount: [_____].

We would enter the above award of backpay against the following Defendants in the following amounts:

NOTE: You are to apportion the above award of backpay among the Defendants.
    [A.I.C. International, Ltd.] [_____]
    [A.I.C. Security Investigations, Ltd.] [_____]
    [defendant C] [_____]
[Foreperson]

If you find that the Defendants violated the ADA, and you further find that Defendants did not prove that they demonstrated good-faith efforts to reasonably accommodate [Charles Wessel]'s disability, then you should use jury Verdict Form 2 instead of jury Verdict Form 1. Jury Verdict Form 2 reads as follows:

VERDICT FORM 2

We the jury find that the Defendants violated the Americans with Disabilities Act by discharging [Charles Wessel] on the basis of his disability.

Having found in favor of [Wessel] and having further found that Defendants did not prove that they demonstrated good-faith efforts to reasonably accommodate [Charles Wessel]'s disability, we assess damages as follows:
    Backpay [_____]

We would enter the above backpay award against the following Defendants:

NOTE: You are to apportion the above award of backpay among the Defendants.
[A.I.C. International, Ltd.] [_____]
[A.I.C. Security Investigations, Ltd.] [_____]
[defendant C] [_____]

Compensatory damages [_____]
[Foreperson]

If you find that the Defendants violated the ADA, and you further find that

(a) Defendants did not prove that they demonstrated good-faith efforts to reasonably accommodate [Charles Wessel]'s disability; and
(b) Defendants engaged in a discriminatory practice with malice or with reckless indifference to the federally protected rights of [Wessel],

you should use Jury Verdict Form 3 instead of either Jury Verdict Form 1 or 2.

Jury Verdict Form 3 reads as follows:

VERDICT FORM 3

We the jury find that the Defendants violated the Americans with Disabilities Act by discharging [Charles Wessel] on the basis of his disability.

Having further found that Defendants did not prove that they demonstrated good-faith efforts to reasonably accommodate [Charles Wessel]'s disability and that the Defendant engaged in a discriminatory practice with malice or with reckless indifference to the federally protected rights of [Wessel], we assess damages as follows:

Backpay [_____]

We would enter the above backpay award against the following Defendants:

NOTE: You are to apportion the above award of backpay among the Defendants.
[A.I.C. International, Ltd.] [_____]
[A.I.C. Security Investigations, Ltd.] [_____]
[defendant C] [_____]

Compensatory damages [_____]
Punitive damages [_____]
[Foreperson]

You will take the verdict forms to the jury room and, when you have reached unanimous agreement as to your verdict, you will have your foreperson fill in the date, sign the form that sets forth the verdict upon which you unanimously agree, and then return with your verdict to the courtroom.

Adapted from Devitt & Blackmar, Federal Jury Practice and Instruction § 74.04 (_____).
Given:
Denied:
Given as Modified:

[19]   Plaintiff's Jury Instructions (Mock Trial)

FORM 16–15   Sample Plaintiff's Jury Instructions: Economic Burden

PROPOSED JURY INSTRUCTIONS ON ECONOMIC BURDEN
(PLAINTIFF'S REQUEST

The Plaintiff claims that the Defendant discriminated against him by terminating his employment due to his disability. Specifically, the Plaintiff claims that after the onset of multiple sclerosis ("MS"), he requested certain accommodations from the Defendant employer. Minor accommodations were made initially after the Plaintiff's diagnosis, but once the Plaintiff's vision and speech worsened, the Plaintiff's second request for accommodations was denied. Shortly thereafter, his employment with the Defendant was terminated.

The Defendant denies that the Plaintiff was terminated due to his disability but rather asserts that the subpar job performance of the Plaintiff was the reason for the termination. The Defendant also claims that it would be an undue hardship on the company to provide the accommodations requested by the Plaintiff.

In order to prevail in this case, the Plaintiff must prove by a preponderance of the evidence each of the following:

(1) that the Plaintiff is an individual with a "disability," for his ailment substantially limits major life activities,

(2) that the Plaintiff is a "qualified individual with a disability," and therefore can perform his essential job functions with or without the Defendant's providing "reasonable accommodations," and

(3) that the Defendant is an *employer*, *covered entity*, *person*, and engaged in an *industry affecting commerce* as defined by the ADA.

The Defendant has admitted that it is an *employer*, etc., as defined by the ADA. The Defendant has not admitted, however, that the Plaintiff has a "disability," nor has it admitted that the Plaintiff is a "qualified individual with a disability." The Plaintiff has presented two witnesses that have testified as to these matters. If you find that the Plaintiff has established these two elements, you must find for the Plaintiff, unless you believe the undue hardship defense asserted by the Defendant.

The Defendant asserts that to provide the accommodations requested by the Plaintiff would cause the company an undue hardship, both financially and competitively. The Defendant's expert witness has testified to this. The ADA allows the undue hardship defense only when the cost of the accommodation to the employer is disproportionate to the overall financial resources, size, and type of operation of the defendant employer. The ADA was written so that the undue hardship defense would be applicable only in limited circumstances. The burden of proof for establishing economic hardship is on the Defendant. Absent conclusive evidence by the Defendant that an undue hardship exists, you cannot allow this defense, and must find in favor of the Plaintiff. Even if you believe that the accommodations requested by the Plaintiff would cause a burden on the Defendant, and if you believe that the burden would not be severe, then you must find in favor of the Plaintiff, so long as the Plaintiff has met his burden of proof.

FORM 16–16   Sample Jury Instructions: Qualified Individual with a Disability

PROPOSED JURY INSTRUCTIONS ON "QUALIFIED INDIVIDUAL WITH A DISABILITY"
(PLAINTIFF'S REQUEST)

The Plaintiff claims that the Defendant discriminated against him by terminating his employment due to his disability. Specifically, the Plaintiff claims that after the onset of multiple sclerosis ("MS"), he requested certain accommodations from the Defendant employer. Minor accommodations were made initially after the

Plaintiff's diagnosis, but once the Plaintiff's vision and speech worsened, the Plaintiff's second request for accommodations was denied. Shortly thereafter, his employment with the Defendant was terminated.

The Defendant denies that the Plaintiff was terminated due to his disability but rather asserts that the subpar job performance of the Plaintiff was the reason for the termination.

Under the ADA, a *qualified individual with a disability* is one who suffers from a disability but is able, either with or without reasonable accommodations, to perform the essential job functions of the employment position.

In this case, the Plaintiff was a staff accountant at the time of his termination. Both parties agree that the essential job functions of the Plaintiff were as follows: (i) producing financial reports through spreadsheet applications, (ii) operating an adding machine to perform various mathematical functions, (iii) maintaining the general ledger, and (iv) communicating with outside vendors and [Eastern]'s purchasing agents regarding fixed-asset acquisition.

It is up to you to decide whether, based on the testimony, the Plaintiff is capable of performing the essential job functions, either with or without the accommodations requested. If you answer in the affirmative, then you will find the Plaintiff to be a "qualified individual with a disability."[56]

[20] Defendant's Jury Instructions: Establishing Plaintiff as a Qualified Individual with a Disability (Mock Trial)

FORM 16–17 **Sample Defendant's Jury Instructions: Establishing Plaintiff as Qualified Individual with a Disability**

In this case, the Plaintiff must prove that he is a *qualified individual with a disability* within the meaning of the Americans with Disabilities Act.

To find that the Plaintiff is a qualified individual with a disability, the Plaintiff must prove by a preponderance of the evidence that

(1) the Plaintiff has a disability, and
(2) the Plaintiff can, with or without the accommodations he requested, perform the essential functions of the staff accountant position that he formerly held.

If you find that the Plaintiff is not a qualified individual with a disability, then your verdict should be for the Defendant.

[21] Defendant's Jury Instructions: Business Necessity

In *Belk v. Southwestern Bell Telephone Co.,* 194 F.3d 946 (8th Cir. 1999), the court of appeals reversed the district court for refusing to give

---

[56] The jury instructions in both Forms 16–15 and 16–16 were drafted on July 14, 1993, by Brian Sopinsky and Marc Lisker, former assistants to Henry H. Perritt, Jr.

this instruction on a business necessity defense, justifying its agility tests for an employee with a full leg brace who sought a job as a pole climber:

Southwestern Bell Telephone also contends that plaintiff Ricky Belk was not qualified for the position he sought because he did not pass the physical performance test. Southwestern Bell Telephone Company contends that all applicants for the position for which Belk applied, excluding those applicants who have satisfactory past job experience, are required to take this test. An employer may use the qualification of standards, employment tests, or other selection criteria that screen out or tend to screen out an individual with a disability or a class of individuals with disabilities, on the basis of disability, as long as the standard, test, or other selection criterion, as used by the employer is job related for the position in question, is consistent with business necessity, and performance cannot be accomplished by reasonable accommodation.

[22]   Approved Jury Instructions in Title II Case[57]

FORM 16–18   Sample Approved Jury Instructions for Title II Case

Now, the law also requires, however, that a nursing home facility such as [Fair Acres] make reasonable accommodations to the known physical and mental limitations of an otherwise-qualified handicapped person. But they [*sic*] are not required to make fundamental or substantial modifications to their program. In other words, they are not required to become something other than what they purport to be; that is, a skilled long-term nursing home with certain admission criteria which they believe they are entitled to use and determine who should be admitted and who should not be admitted. The accommodation that the law requires them to make must be reasonable; it can't be unreasonable. This is just an analogy, it may not be applicable in this case, but they cannot make a nursing home — turn it into a burn center or a psychiatric institution or something like that, because that would require substantial or fundamental modification of the program which they have in existence. But on the other hand, if their program would accommodate [Mrs. Wagner] with only inconsequential or nonsubstantial changes, then under the law they are required to do that. So that if you find that a fundamental or substantial modification is necessary in order to accommodate the plaintiff, the Rehabilitation Act does not apply. On the other hand, if they can accommodate her with reasonable changes in their program, then of course the Act does apply.[58]

---

[57] The instruction in Form 16–18 was approved as appropriate in an ADA Title II case involving the rejection of a nursing home applicant because of the behavioral manifestations of the applicant's Alzheimer's disease.

[58] Wagner v. Fair Acres Geriatric Ctr., 49 F.3d 1002, 1019 n.19 (3d Cir. 1995) (remanding for consideration of decision to allow new trial).

[23]   Jury Instructions: Expert's Basis for Opinion (Mock Trial)

FORM 16–19   Sample Jury Instructions: Expert's Basis for Opinion

You have heard the Defendant's expert testify as to whether providing the accommodations sought by the Plaintiff would cause an undue hardship on the Defendant. His opinion is based on his personal knowledge of the Defendant's financial condition. In general, the opinion of an expert has value only when you accept the facts upon which it is based. This is true whether the facts are assumed hypothetically by the expert, come from his personal knowledge of the Defendant, from some other proper source, or from a combination of these.[59]

[24]   Establishing Undue Hardship (Mock Trial)

FORM 16–20   Sample Jury Instructions: Establishing Undue Hardship

In its defense, the Defendant claims that even if you should find that the Plaintiff has proved all the necessary elements of his claim, the Defendant has not violated the ADA by refusing to provide reasonable accommodations because providing such accommodations would cause the Defendant undue hardship.

To determine whether the reasonable accommodations requested by the Plaintiff would cause undue hardship, you must determine that the accommodations require significant difficulty or expense in light of

(1) the overall financial resources of the Defendant;

(2) the number of persons employed by the Defendant;

(3) the effect on expenses and resources, or the impact otherwise of such accommodation upon the Defendant's operations;

(4) the nature and cost of the accommodation needed by the Defendant; and

(5) the type of operation of the covered entity, including the composition, structure, and functions of the Defendant's workforce.

If you find that providing the reasonable accommodations suggested by the Plaintiff would cause the Defendant undue hardship, then your verdict should be for the Defendant.

---

[59] *See* Gordon v. State Farm Life Ins. Co., 203 A.2d 320 (Pa. 1964) (quoting Jackson v. United States Pipe Line Co., 191 A. 165 (Pa. 1937)); Pennsylvania Bar Inst., Pennsylvania Suggested Standard Jury Instructions (Civil) para. 5.31 (1984).

[25]   Proving Essential Function

FORM 16-21   Sample Jury Instructions: Proving Essential Function

The defendants have the burden of proving by a preponderance of the evidence that the ability to perform all of the duties of a firefighter is an essential function of the assistant fire chief's position. In this case, the burden of proving whether firefighting, with all of its responsibilities, is an essential function is on the defendants.

Hamlin v. Charter Township of Flint, 165 F.3d 426, 431 (6th Cir. 1999) (approving jury instruction is not placing overall burden of persuasion on defendant; affirming in material part judgment for plaintiff on jury verdict).

[26]   Jury Instructions in Title II Zoning Case

In a suit claiming that a village refused to grant a zoning variance to permit a front driveway to accommodate the plaintiff's disability, the court of appeals approved the following jury instructions:

The Fair Housing Act and the Americans with Disabilities Act also prohibit Wilmette from making a permit decision, "because of" a citizen's handicap unless Wilmette can prove that resident, because of his or her handicap, poses a legitimate threat to the health and safety of others.

The court also instructed:

In order to prevail on [the intentional discrimination] claim, Plaintiffs must establish that the Defendant's refusal to grant a front driveway permit was based upon a discriminatory motive. As applied to this case, Plaintiffs must establish that Astrid Dadian was a person who was physically disabled or handicapped, and that the Village took that into consideration in denying the permit.

For purposes of this determination, you may consider the Village's defense that Mrs. Dadian was not qualified to operate a vehicle using a front driveway and that the refusal was not based upon discrimination but rather on safety concerns. As to this defense, the burden of proof is on the Village to prove by a preponderance of the evidence that Astrid Dadian's use of a front driveway posed a legitimate safety risk.[60]

[27]   Plaintiff's Proposed Findings (Mock Trial)

FORM 16–22   Sample Plaintiff's Proposed Findings

UNITED STATES DISTRICT COURT FOR THE [EASTERN] DISTRICT OF [PENNSYLVANIA]

---

[60] *Dadian,* _____ F.3d at _____.

[Steve Lyons],
Plaintiff
v.   Civil Action No. [820130]
[Eastern Pharmaceuticals, Incorporated],
Defendant.

PROPOSED FINDINGS OF FACT

The Plaintiff requests that the court make the following findings of fact in this action:

1. The Plaintiff is afflicted with multiple sclerosis ("MS").

2. MS substantially limits the Plaintiff in the major life activities of reading, speaking, and walking, and therefore the Plaintiff has a *disability* as defined by the ADA.

3. The Plaintiff, with the reasonable accommodations of (i) having a reader communicate written and computer information to him, (ii) having a speaker communicate oral messages from him, and (iii) having the office area of [Eastern] made "handicapped friendly," can perform the essential functions of his job as staff accountant in [Eastern]'s finance department.

4. Because the Plaintiff can perform his essential job function with the reasonable accommodations, he is a *qualified individual with a disability* as defined by the ADA.

5. The Plaintiff was diagnosed with MS on [June 26, 1991].

6. At the time of the diagnosis of MS, the Plaintiff suffered from blurry vision and slurred speech.

7. Immediately after the Plaintiff's diagnosis of MS on [June 26, 1991], he informed his supervisor, [Lisa Brown], [Eastern]'s Accounting Manager, of his condition.

8. On [July 28, 1992], the Plaintiff suffered another MS attack. After this attack, the Plaintiff's eyesight and speech deteriorated further and he began having difficulty walking and coordinating muscle movement.

9. After the second MS attack, the plaintiff requested the following reasonable accommodations: (i) a reader to communicate written messages and computer information to him, (ii) a speaker to communicate oral messages from him, and (iii) having the office area of [Eastern]'s facility made "handicapped friendly."

10. [Ms. Brown] refused to make the reasonable accommodations requested by the plaintiff for his disability, and she terminated him on [August 5, 1992].

11. The decisions made and the actions taken by [Ms. Brown] in refusing the request for accommodations and terminating the Plaintiff were within the course and scope of her employment.

Dated: [Philadelphia], [Pennsylvania]
[July 14, 1993]
Signed: [_____]
[Louis Watt]
Attorney for the Plaintiff

301

[1234 Main Street]
[Villanova], [Pennsylvania] [19085]
[(215) 555-1212]

[28]   Defendant's Proposed Findings (Mock Trial)

FORM 16–23   **Sample Defendant's Proposed Findings**

UNITED STATES DISTRICT COURT FOR THE [EASTERN] DISTRICT OF [PENNSYLVANIA]

[Steven Lyons],
Plaintiff
v.   Civil Action, File Number [820130]
[Eastern Pharmaceuticals, Incorporated],
Defendant.

PROPOSED FINDINGS OF FACT AND CONCLUSIONS OF LAW

The following findings of fact and conclusions of law have been organized such that each cardinal number represented by an arabic symbol (e.g., "1.") states a proposed conclusion of law and each indented letter of the Roman alphabet (e.g., "a.") states a proposed finding of fact. Each proposed finding of fact supports the conclusion of law preceding it. The final conclusion of law is supported by each of the preceding conclusions of law.

1. [Eastern] did not provide reasonable accommodations for [Lyons].
   a. [Lyons] requested that [Eastern] (1) provide him with a reader to communicate written messages and computer information to him, (2) provide him with a speaker to communicate oral messages from him, and (3) make the office area of [Eastern]'s facility "handicapped friendly."
   b. [Lyons]'s request that [Eastern] (1) provide him with a reader to communicate written messages and computer information to him, (2) provide him with a speaker to communicate oral messages from him, and (3) make the office area of Eastern's facility "handicapped friendly" was a request for reasonable accommodations.[61]
   c. [Eastern] did not (1) provide [Lyons] with a reader to communicate written messages and computer information to him, (2) provide Lyons with a speaker to communicate oral messages from him, or (3) make the office area of [Eastern]'s facility "handicapped friendly."

2. [Eastern] knew that [Lyons] had a physical limitation.

---

[61] This fact would have been proved by submission into evidence of the EEOC's determination letter.

a. Multiple sclerosis ("MS") is a physical limitation.
b. [Lyons] suffers from MS.
c. [Lyons] has a physical limitation.
d. [Lisa Brown] was [Lyons]'s supervisor at [Eastern].
e. [Lyons] informed [Lisa Brown] that he had MS.
f. [Lyons] informed [Eastern] that he had MS.

3. [Lyons] is an individual with a disability.
a. MS is a physical impairment.
b. [Lyons] has MS.
c. [Lyons] has a physical impairment.
d. MS substantially limits [Lyons]'s ability to read, speak, and walk.
e. Reading, speaking, and walking are major life activities of [Lyons].
f. MS substantially limits some of [Lyons]'s major life activities.

4. [Lyons] is not a qualified individual with a disability.
a. The essential job functions of the staff accountant at [Eastern] are (1) producing financial reports through spreadsheet applications, (2) operating an adding machine to perform various mathematical functions, (3) maintaining the general ledger, and (4) communicating with outside vendors and [Eastern]'s purchasing agents regarding fixed-asset acquisitions.
b. [Lyons] was staff accountant at [Eastern].
c. [Lyons]'s essential job functions were (1) producing financial reports through spreadsheet applications, (2) operating an adding machine to perform various mathematical functions, (3) maintaining the general ledger, and (4) communicating with outside vendors and [Eastern]'s purchasing agents regarding fixed-asset acquisitions.
d. [Lyons] requested reasonable accommodations to perform his essential job functions.
e. With the reasonable accommodations, [Lyons] would not have been able to perform his essential job functions.

5. Providing [Lyons] with the reasonable accommodations he requested would have been an undue burden to [Eastern].
a. Providing the reasonable accommodations would have cost [Eastern] [$64,000] per year.
b. Spending [$64,000] per year would cause a dollar-for-dollar decrease in net income.
c. A [$64,000]-per-year decrease in net income would negatively impact monies available for research and development purposes.
d. Providing the reasonable accommodations would have negatively impacted monies available for research and development purposes.
e. Pharmaceutical companies must, at a minimum, maintain at a constant level monies available for research and development purposes in order to survive.
f. Providing the reasonable accommodations would negatively affect [Eastern]'s ability to survive.

6. [Eastern] did not discriminate against [Lyons] because of his known physical limitation and disability by not providing him with the reasonable accommodations he sought, because he is not a qualified individual with a disability and/or providing [Lyons] with the reasonable accommodations he requested would have caused an undue burden to [Eastern].

[John Black], Attorney for Defendant
[1111 Cherry Street]
[Philadelphia], [Pennsylvania] [19105]

[29]   Actual Jury Verdict Form (EEOC)

FORM 16–24   Sample Actual Jury Verdict Form

We the jury find the following Defendants violated the Americans with Disabilities Act. [Place an "X" by each Defendant you find liable]
  [A.I.C. Security Investigations, Ltd.] [X]
  [defendant C] [X]
  Having found in favor of [Wessel] and against Defendants, we further assess damages in the following amounts.
  Backpay and Benefits [$22,000]
  Compensatory Damages [$50,000]
[signatures of seven jury members]
  We the jury find, as to punitive damages, for the Plaintiff and against the Defendants in the following amounts as to each Defendant individually.
  [A.I.C. Security Investigations, Ltd.] [$250,000]
  [defendant C] [$250,000]
[signatures of seven jury members]

[30]   Jury Interrogatories[62]

FORM 16-25   Sample Jury Interrogatories

Do you find from a preponderance of the evidence that the Plaintiff was a qualified person with a disability at the time the Plaintiff was terminated from his employment with the Defendant?

Do you find from a preponderance of evidence that the Plaintiff was intentionally discriminated against because the Defendant knew or perceived him to have a disability?

---

[62] In *Farley v. Nationwide Mutual Insurance Co.*, 197 F.3d 1322 (11th Cir. 1999), the court of appeals found that the following jury interrogatories and verdict forms were not plain error.

Past lost earnings	$_____
Future lost earnings, reduced to present value	$_____
Emotional pain and suffering, inconvenience, and mental anguish	$_____
Total Damages	$_____

If you find that the Defendant intentionally discriminated against the Plaintiff because of his disability, . . . [y]ou may award compensatory damages, based on the evidence introduced at trial, for future pecuniary losses, emotional pain and suffering, inconvenience, and mental anguish.

It is unlawful for an employer to intentionally discriminate against a qualified individual with a disability because of that person's disability. In this case, the Plaintiff claims that the Defendant intentionally discriminated against him because he had a disability. . . . In order for the Plaintiff to establish his claim of intentional discrimination by the Defendant, he has the burden of proving the following essential elements by a preponderance of the evidence that

1. He is a qualified person with a disability, as the term is defined in these instructions;
2. The Defendant intentionally discriminated against the Plaintiff, that is, the fact that the Plaintiff was a qualified person with a disability was a motivating factor in the Defendant's decision to terminate the Plaintiff.
3. As a direct result of the Defendant's intentional discrimination, the Plaintiff sustained damages.

CHAPTER 17

REMEDIES

§ 17.01 INTRODUCTION

[A] Overview

This chapter contains material relating to remedies in Americans with Disabilities Act (ADA)[1] cases. It considers not only posttrial relief in the form of judgments[2] and decrees, but also judicial relief available without trial — consent judgments[3] and decrees,[4] interlocutory relief, particularly preliminary injunctions,[5] the implementation of judicial orders through the contempt process,[6] and judgment-related motions[7] and documents, including an ADA judgment notice for employees.[8]

[B] Sample Forms

[1] Preliminary Injunction Order to Show Cause

FORM 17–1   **Sample Preliminary Injunction Order to Show Cause**

UNITED STATES DISTRICT COURT

[judicial district] OF [state]

[name]
Plaintiff,
v.

Civ. No. [case number]

[state] BOARD OF LAW EXAMINERS,
Defendant.

ORDER TO SHOW CAUSE

Upon the affidavit of [plaintiff], sworn to [date], the affidavit of [Hobart L.], M.D., sworn to [date], and the Summons and Complaint herein,

LET THE DEFENDANT SHOW CAUSE before the Honorable [name], United States Courthouse, [address] on [date] at [time] in the forenoon of that day,

---

[1] Pub. L. No. 101-336, 104 Stat. 327 (1990) (codified at 42 U.S.C. §§ 12,101–12,213 (1994); 47 U.S.C. §§ 225, 711 (1994)) [hereinafter ADA].

[2] *See* Form 17-14.

[3] *See* Forms 17-4 and 17-5.

[4] *See* Forms 17-6 and 17-7.

[5] *See* Forms 17-1 through 17-3.

[6] *See* Forms 17-8 through 17-10.

[7] *See* Forms 17-11 through 17-13.

[8] *See* Form 17-17.

or as soon thereafter as counsel may be heard, as to why an Order should not be entered herein pursuant to the Americans with Disabilities Act (ADA), 42 U.S.C. §§ 12,101 *et seq.,* granting a preliminary injunction directing the [state] Board of Law Examiners to allow Plaintiff to take the [state] Bar Examination, which is scheduled to commence on [date], with certain accommodations. Under the requested preliminary injunction, the Plaintiff would be allowed:

a. To take the examination in a separate room, isolated from other Bar candidates;

b. To hand mark answers as opposed to filling in the computer-scored answer sheet with respect to multiple-choice questions;

c. To be provided with a large-print exam and to be allowed to use a straight-edge ruler; and

d. To be allotted time to take the examination over a four-day period, with approximately five hours of testing each day, plus 15-minute breaks on the hour, if needed, and a lunch break.

SUFFICIENT CAUSE APPEARING THEREFOR, let service of a conformed copy of this Order to Show Cause and the papers upon which it is granted upon the [state] Board of Law Examiners be deemed good and sufficient service thereof if made by personal delivery thereof to the Office of the [state] Board of Law Examiners not later than [date], and by sending a copy thereof by certified mail, return receipt requested to the [state] Board of Law Examiners at [address], not later than [date].

[2]   Preliminary Injunctions in Title I Cases

Preliminary injunctions in ADA Title I[9] cases present some special problems. These problems are the same ones encountered in Title VII[10] litigation.[11] The first question is whether such relief is available to a private party before the party has exhausted Equal Employment Opportunity Commission (EEOC) procedures. The answer is yes.[12] The second question refers to the procedures to be followed. Federal Rule of Civil Procedure 65 provides the answer. The third question is how irreparable injury can be established.[13] Irreparable injury can be established when a preliminary injunction is sought against altering or removing records,[14] hiring or promoting third

---

[9] ADA §§ 101–107, 42 U.S.C. §§ 12,111–12,117 (1994) [hereinafter Title I].

[10] 42 U.S.C. §§ 2000e to 2000e-16 (1994) [hereinafter Title VII].

[11] ADA § 107(a), 42 U.S.C. § 12,117(a) (1994) (incorporating by reference remedial provisions of Title VII). *See generally* Henry H. Perritt, Jr., Labor Injunctions (John Wiley & Sons 1986) [hereinafter Perritt], § 14.3.

[12] Hicks v. Dothan City Bd. of Educ., 814 F. Supp. 1044, 1049 (M.D. Ala. 1993) (EEOC procedures not being exhausted, plaintiff must show irreparable harm if preliminary injunction is not granted).

[13] White v. Carlucci, 862 F.2d 1209 (5th Cir. 1989) (establishing irreparable injury as matter of fact in Title VII cases).

[14] EEOC v. Recruit USA, Inc., 939 F.2d 746 (9th Cir. 1991).

parties when that might foreclose meaningful relief for plaintiffs,[15] retaliating against the plaintiff for asserting ADA rights,[16] and preventing psychic injury that could not be compensated by a later injunction or a money judgment.[17]

[3]   Memorandum Opposing Preliminary Injunction

FORM 17–2   Sample Memorandum Opposing Preliminary Injunction

UNITED STATES DISTRICT COURT

[judicial district] OF [state]

[name],
Plaintiff,
v.   [case number]
[state] BOARD OF LAW EXAMINERS,
Defendant.

DEFENDANT'S MEMORANDUM OF LAW

PRELIMINARY STATEMENT

The plaintiff herein, [name] (hereafter "Plaintiff"), has commenced this action pursuant to the Americans with Disabilities Act (42 U.S.C. §§ 12,101 *et seq.;* hereinafter "the ADA"). The essential allegations are that Plaintiff is a law school graduate with a severe visual impairment and that the defendant has not made the [state] Bar Examination, scheduled for [date], accessible to Plaintiff, as required by the ADA. The defendant [state] Board of Law Examiners (hereinafter "the Board") has been ordered to show cause why a preliminary injunction should not issue that would require the Board to make a number of special accommodations to Plaintiff with reference to this examination.

FACTS

Plaintiff suffers from a long-standing, severe, and uncorrectable visual impairment (*see* Affidavit of [plaintiff], ¶¶ 3–5; Affidavit of [Hobart A. L.], M.D., ¶¶ 3–5). This impairment lengthens the amount of time Plaintiff requires to read

---

[15] Black Fire Fighters Ass'n v. City of Dallas, 905 F.2d 63, 66 (5th Cir. 1990) (affirming denial of preliminary injunction but accepting general proposition stated in text).

[16] Baker v. Buckeye Cellulose Corp., 856 F.2d 167 (11th Cir. 1988) (reversing denial of preliminary injunction and requiring evidentiary hearing on retaliation allegations).

[17] Gutierrez v. Municipal Court, 838 F.2d 1031, 1045 (9th Cir. 1988) (approving preliminary injunction against enforcement of English-only rule).

testing materials, and requires her to rest her eyes more frequently in order to reduce eye fatigue ([plaintiff] Affidavit, Exhibit H).

In anticipation of Plaintiff's graduating from the [name] Law School in [month, year], Plaintiff applied in [month] of that year to take the [month, year] [state] Bar Examination ([plaintiff] Affidavit, ¶¶ 13, 14). Plaintiff, supported by documentation from her ophthalmologist, requested that the Board grant her a number of accommodations, including time and one-half to take the exam ([plaintiff] Affidavit, ¶ 16, Exhibit D). All these accommodations were granted by the Board, with the exception of the color of the paper available to her during the exam[18] ([plaintiff] Affidavit, Exhibit E).

Following the exam, but prior to the publication of the test results, Plaintiff wrote a letter to [James T. F.], Executive Secretary to the Board. In Plaintiff's letter, Plaintiff complained at considerable length about the conduct of the exam proctor and another candidate taking the test (*see* Affidavit of [James T. F.], Exhibit A). However, at no time did Plaintiff claim that, despite the accommodations made, she had been denied adequate time to complete the exam. Quite the contrary, Plaintiff explicitly stated:

"In fact, I am extremely grateful. I honestly feel that the special conditions, especially the large-print exam and the additional time were necessary for me to be able to take and complete the exam." ([James T. F.] Affidavit, Exhibit A, p. 3).

Pointedly, Plaintiff requested that, should she have to retake the exam, the same accommodations be extended to her:

"Second, if I did not pass the exam and am not waived in, I should have the same testing accommodations [*sic*] as I had for the [month] exam, with the extra time and the large-print exam." ([James T. F.] Affidavit, Exhibit A, p. 3).

Similarly, Plaintiff made no complaints of a lack of adequate time in her contacts with other members of the Board's staff (*see* Affidavit of [Mary G.]).

Further evidence of a lack of time pressure during the [month] examination is provided by an analysis of Plaintiff's exam booklets (*see* [James T. F.] Affidavit, ¶ 10). Plaintiff apparently completed each of the essay questions, writing a considerable amount in response to each of the questions and even adding an unnecessary "end of question" at the end of each response ([James T. F.] Affidavit, ¶ 10). Additionally, Plaintiff completed all of the short-answer questions in the exam, and there is no evidence that Plaintiff lacked sufficient time to do so ([James T. F.] Affidavit, ¶ 10).

It was only after Plaintiff was notified that she had failed the [month] bar examination that Plaintiff asserted for the first time that she did not have adequate time to complete the examination. In applying to retake the exam in [month, year], in addition to the other accommodations requested, Plaintiff added a request that she be permitted to take the exam over a four-day period, with only five hours of testing per day ([Dr. L.] Affidavit, ¶ 13).[19]

---

[18] The color of the paper is apparently no longer at issue, and the plaintiff does not address this request in her motion for a preliminary injunction.

[19] In point of fact, the plaintiff's actual request for accommodation for the examination only asks for "extra time (for rest and for work)." *See* [James T. F.] Affidavit, Exhibit B. The plaintiff's ophthalmologist, [Dr. Hobart L.], made the specific request for a four-day examination.

The Board reviewed Plaintiff's application for accommodations and considered all relevant factors, including the requirements of the ADA, the Board's prior experience in accommodating blind and visually handicapped candidates, the availability of aural compensatory aids such as audiotapes and readers/writers, the importance of the time element of the examination in the determination of minimal competence and the comparability of examination results, considerations of examination security, the fact that Plaintiff had apparently completed the [month] examination within the time allotted, and the fact that the medical documentation submitted by Plaintiff did not indicate any change in her medical condition. On [date], the Board advised Plaintiff that all of her requests, with the exception of the four-day extension, had been granted ([James T. F.] Affidavit, Exhibit D). Specifically, the Board made the following accommodations:

1. A separate testing room with enhanced lighting. Plaintiff would be free to bring any additional lighting she wished.
2. A large-print copy of the exam.
3. Plaintiff would be permitted to use a ruler to assist in reading.
4. Plaintiff would be permitted to write the answers to the multiple-choice and Multi-State Bar Examination questions in the question books, to be transcribed onto computer sheets by Board staff.

Although the Board declined to grant Plaintiff a four-day examination, it took the unprecedented step of offering Plaintiff the option of specifying the hours that she wished to take the exam during the two days during which it was being conducted ([James T. F.] Affidavit, Exhibit D, ¶ [5]). In addition, although not requested by Plaintiff, the Board offered to make available an audiotaped copy of the examination and an amanuensis to serve as a reader/writer.

Plaintiff thereafter petitioned the Board for reconsideration of her request for a four-day examination ([James T. F.] Affidavit, Exhibit D, ¶ [2]). The Board reconsidered Plaintiff's situation and concluded that the extensive accommodations made by it were reasonable and sufficient to compensate for Plaintiff's vision deficit. Accordingly, Plaintiff's petition was denied ([James T. F.] Affidavit, Exhibit F). This action was subsequently commenced by Plaintiff. .

DISCUSSION

Plaintiff bears a "heavy burden" of demonstrating a "clear entitlement" to an injunction ([*New York v. Nuclear Regulatory Commission,* 550 F.2d 745, 755 (2d Cir. 1977)]). The Board respectfully submits that Plaintiff has failed to carry her burden of demonstrating her entitlement to a preliminary injunction, which, as the Court of Appeals for this Circuit has observed, is a broad and potentially drastic remedy (*see* [*General Fireproofing Co. v. Wyman,* 444 F.2d 391, 393 (2d Cir. 1971)]).

It is well settled in this Circuit that a party seeking injunctive relief must establish (a) that the injunction is necessary to prevent irreparable harm and (b) either that (i) it is likely to succeed on the merits on the underlying claim or (ii) there are sufficiently serious questions going to the merits of the claim as to make them a fair ground for litigation, together with a balance of hardships tipping decidedly in favor toward the movant ([*Abdul Wali v. Coughlin,* 754 F.2d 1015, 1025 (2d Cir. 1985)]). An application of this standard to the facts before the Court amply demonstrates Plaintiff's lack of entitlement to a preliminary injunction.

A. An Injunction Is Not Necessary to Prevent "Irreparable Harm"

Clearly, the Court's intervention is not necessary in order to provide Plaintiff with the first three accommodations she seeks in the Order to Show Cause (*see* Order to Show Cause, dated [date], subparagraphs a, b, and c). As it did prior to Plaintiff's taking the [month, year] examination, the Board has unequivocally and irrevocably offered Plaintiff the opportunity to take the upcoming examination in a separate room, to hand mark her answers as opposed to marking a computer-scored answer sheet, to be provided a large-print exam, and to utilize a straight-edge ruler (*see* [Plaintiff] Affidavit, Exhibits E and I; [James T. F.] Affidavit, Exhibit D; Affidavit of [Charles T. B., Jr., Esq.]).[20] Thus, there is no necessity to invoke the drastic injunctive power of the court with reference to these three accommodations.

With reference to Plaintiff's remaining request to take the examination for five hours per day for four days, an examination of the proofs submitted to the Court indicates serious doubt as to the likelihood of "irreparable injury" as well as the necessity for the unusual accommodations Plaintiff seeks.

Plaintiff's argument that she will suffer "irreparable injury" is premised upon two contentions: first, that without the four-day schedule Plaintiff will be unable to pass the exam, and, second, that such a failure constitutes an irreparable injury. Both of these assumptions lack merit.

A review of Plaintiff's [month] exam reveals that she was apparently under no time pressure to complete the examination and did, in fact, complete all portions (*see* [James T. F.] Affidavit, ¶ 10). More compelling proof, however, comes from Plaintiff. First, Plaintiff made no request for a four-day exam prior to the [month, year] examination and made no objection to the Board's offer that she be allowed time and one-half to take the exam. Although Plaintiff now proffers the excuse that she believed that this was the maximum amount of time allowed by the Board, this is unpersuasive. If Plaintiff believed that she required four days and that the ADA mandated such an accommodation, Plaintiff could have commenced an action under the ADA or a special proceeding under [statute] to compel such an accommodation. Indeed, that is precisely what Plaintiff has done now, and offers no excuse as to why she did not do so previously if she felt aggrieved. More critically, perhaps, is the fact that Plaintiff never complained about the time given to complete the examination until after she was advised that she had failed. In Plaintiff's [date] letter to the Board (approximately nine weeks after the [month, year] exam but prior to the publication of the results), Plaintiff complained at considerable length about

---

[20] Indeed, the Board had already voluntarily offered the plaintiff more accommodations than she requested in the order to show cause (that is, a tape-recorded copy of the examination and an amanuensis to serve as a reader/writer).

the conduct of the exam proctor and another candidate taking the test. However, at no time did Plaintiff claim that, despite the accommodations made for her, she had been denied adequate time to complete the exam. Quite the contrary, Plaintiff thanked the Board for the accommodations it extended, specifically noting the additional time Plaintiff had been given. Critically, Plaintiff stated in her letter that, if she failed, she wanted the same accommodations on the next exam. Not only is the Board prepared to give Plaintiff those accommodations that she found so satisfactory, it is willing to accommodate Plaintiff even further with a schedule to be designed by her, a tape-recorded copy of the exam, and/or an amanuensis to read any or all of the exam to Plaintiff and record her responses. Given Plaintiff's previous unsolicited expression of satisfaction with the [month] accommodations, her present assertion that additional accommodations are necessary to prevent irreparable injury rings particularly hollow.

A similar problem exists with reference to the assertions now made by Plaintiff's ophthalmologist. Although [Dr. L.] now states that Plaintiff requires four days, prior to the [month, year] examination [Dr. L.] stated that ". . . she needs more time to take an exam — possibly half again as much time." ([plaintiff] Affidavit, Exhibit D). At no time prior to Plaintiff's taking the first bar exam did [Dr. L.] state or even imply that Plaintiff required four days to take the exam.

We submit that Plaintiff will not suffer any injury should the court refrain from issuing an injunction that would in effect grant Plaintiff most, if not all, the relief she seeks in the underlying action. As noted above, the Board has offered Plaintiff virtually all the accommodations sought by her, plus several others Plaintiff has not even requested. Because Plaintiff expends much time and effort in reading, Plaintiff may avail herself of an amanuensis to read some or all of the questions to her, and record any or all of her answers. The Board has taken the unprecedented step of offering Plaintiff the opportunity to set her own schedule for the exam, which Plaintiff may take at any time during the two-day period within which it is given. Thus, we submit that the court's intervention is not required to prevent any alleged injury to plaintiff.

However, even assuming, arguendo, that Plaintiff might be detrimentally affected by the Board's determination, Plaintiff's assertion that she is entitled to an injunction remains without merit. In order for an injunction to issue, the alleged injury must be actual and imminent, as opposed to remote or speculative ([*New York v. Nuclear Regulatory Commission*, 550 F.2d 745, 755 (2d Cir. 1977)], *quoted at* [*Jackson Dairy, Inc. v. HY Hood & Sons, Inc.*, 596 F.2d 70, 72 (2d Cir. 1979)]). Whether Plaintiff will fail the exam unless given a four-day schedule, as opposed to the alternative schedule and additional accommodations offered by the Board, is indeed speculative, especially in view of the fact that Plaintiff was apparently able to complete the [month] exam without any difficulties with the time factor. Second, the harm that may be visited upon Plaintiff is not the type that justifies the issuance of an injunction. Thus, Plaintiff's possible inability to be admitted to practice law involves issues relating to employment and Plaintiff's ability to secure an income. As the Court of Appeals for this Circuit has observed, loss of income and the concomitant loss of reputation "is not the sort of irreparable harm which is an essential predicate to the issuance of injunctive relief." ([*Curtin v. Henderson*, 514 F. Supp. 16, 19 (E.D.N.Y. 1980) (citing [*New York v. Nuclear Regulatory Commission*, 550 F.2d 745, 755 (2d Cir. 1977))].

Based upon the following, we respectfully submit that Plaintiff has failed to demonstrate that an injunction is necessary to prevent irreparable injury to her.

B. The Plaintiff Is Unlikely to Succeed on the Merits

Plaintiff's case rests upon her assertion that Defendant has violated Titles II and III of the ADA. An examination of the relevant law as applied to the facts of this case lends no support to this claim.

Plaintiff's Title III claim is premised upon 42 U.S.C. § 12,189, which provides that:

> Any person that offers examinations or courses related to applications, licensing, certification, or credentialing for secondary or postsecondary education, professional, or trade purposes shall offer such examinations or courses in a place and manner accessible to persons with disabilities or offer alternative accessible arrangements for such individuals.

An examination of the implementing regulations make it clear that this title is inapplicable to the case at bar. As set forth in 28 C.F.R. § 36.101:

> Purpose. The purpose of this part is to implement title III of the Americans with Disabilities Act of 1990, 42 U.S.C. § 12181, which prohibits discrimination on the basis of disability by public accommodations and requires places of public accommodation and commercial facilities to be designed, constructed, and altered in compliance with the accessibility standards established by this part.

Although Plaintiff selectively quotes from 28 C.F.R. § 36.309 in support of her contention that Title III applies to the Board, a review of the full contents of that section reveals its obvious inapplicability to governmental agencies:

> (a) General. Any private entity that offers examinations or courses related to applications, licensing, certification, or credentialing for secondary or postsecondary education, professional, or trade purposes shall offer such examinations or courses in a place and manner accessible to person with disabilities or offer alternative accessible arrangements for such individuals.

The subsections that apply this general standard all specify their applicability to private entities only (*see* 28 C.F.R. § 36.309(b)(1), (3), and (c)(1), (3)).

Critically, the United States Department of Justice, Civil Rights Division, Office on the Americans with Disabilities Act, which is the agency given the mandate of ensuring compliance with the ADA, has specifically recognized the inapplicability of Title III to governmental entities (*see* The Americans with Disabilities Act, Title III Technical Assistance Manual, annexed hereto).

The reed to which Plaintiff clings in this regard is an obviously ambiguous reference to bar examinations in Appendix B to 28 C.F.R. § 36.309, which states: "Examinations covered by this section would include a bar exam or the Scholastic Aptitude Test prepared by the Educational Testing Service."

Any attempt to shoehorn this language into the facts of this case runs afoul of the clear language of the section itself, which, as the Department of Justice has asserted, specifies its applicability only to private entities. More critically, it also runs afoul of subsection (a) of Appendix B, § 36.309, which also specifies that the section applies only to private entities. The only reasonable interpretation of the subsection relied upon by Plaintiff is that the drafters believed that the bar exam was prepared by the [Educational Testing Service], as is the [Scholastic Aptitude] test. No other interpretation comports with the clear language of the regulation, which renders Title III inapplicable to governmental entities.

Plaintiff fares no better under Title II, which does apply to governmental entities (*see* 42 U.S.C. § 12,131(I)(B)). Pursuant to that section and § 12,132, the Board must make "reasonable modification" to its policies and provide auxiliary aids and services to disabled individuals such as Plaintiff. We respectfully submit a review of the Board's actions demonstrates that it has been more than reasonable in its efforts to accommodate Plaintiff. In response to Plaintiff's requests, the Board has allowed Plaintiff to take the exam in a separate testing room, enjoying an absence from distractions not provided to other candidates. Not only will the room have enhanced lighting, Plaintiff will be able to bring whatever additional illumination she desires. Plaintiff will be provided a large-print copy of the exam and allowed to bring a ruler to assist her in following the print. Plaintiff will be permitted to make her answers to multiple-choice and Multi-State Bar Examination questions in a separate book, to be transcribed by Board staff following the exam. In short, the only accommodation not granted by the Board is Plaintiff's request for a four-day exam, based upon legitimate concerns for the validity of the testing process and the security of the examination. However, as a compromise, and despite the questionable necessity for such accommodations in light of Plaintiff's previous bar exam experience, the Board has offered Plaintiff a tape-recorded copy of the examination, an amanuensis to read any or all of the exam to her and record her answers, and the unprecedented opportunity to make her own schedule for the two days of the examination so as to allow Plaintiff to take as much time as she wished with the exam, interspersed with whatever rest times Plaintiff desired. Plaintiff has apparently rejected all these proposed accommodations. Given the legitimate concerns of the Board and their statutory mandate to ensure the admission of qualified applicants to the bar, we submit their proposed accommodations are more than reasonable and amply satisfy the mandates of Title II.

C. The "Balancing of the Hardships"

Even if one were to assume that there exist sufficiently serious questions going to the merits of the claim as to make them a fair ground for litigation, in order to be entitled to an injunction, Plaintiff must still prove that the equities of the situation tip "decidedly" in her favor ([*Abdul Wali v. Coughlin,* 754 F.2d 1015 (2d Cir. 1985)]).

Unquestionably, Plaintiff paints a sympathetic picture of her situation. Plaintiff has obviously struggled throughout her life to overcome her disability and achieve the lofty goals she has set for herself. Plaintiff asserts that the only remaining obstacle to passing the bar exam is this one accommodation and that "neither the Law Examiners nor the bar examination will be harmed by allowing the requested accommodation" (Plaintiff's Memorandum of Law, p. 13). As tempted as one might be to be swayed by this argument, it must be rejected.

The Board of Law examiners bears the burden of assuring that all attorneys admitted to practice in [state] are competent to serve the public who seeks their services. To this end, the Board has established the bar examination to ensure minimal competence. While the Board has the legal obligation to "level the playing field" for all examination candidates with disabilities, it has a concomitant obligation to ensure that no candidate, whether disabled or not, has an advantage over any other. The Board, upon a detailed consideration of Plaintiff's condition and the alternatives available to her, has determined that the accommodations offered to Plaintiff will provide her with a fair opportunity to demonstrate her knowledge and abilities within the time constraints that the practice of law mandates. We respectfully submit that should this Court substitute its judgment for that of the Board, it will not have leveled the playing field but, rather, tipped it in favor of Plaintiff. To do so would possibly result in the admission of an unqualified candidate.[21] Given the potential harm that such an admission could cause both to the public and Plaintiff herself, we submit that the equities of this situation hardly tip "decidedly" in favor of Plaintiff.

CONCLUSION

Plaintiff has failed to carry her heavy burden of demonstrating her entitlement to a preliminary injunction; consequently, Plaintiff's application should be denied.

[4]　Affidavit Opposing Preliminary Injunction

FORM 17–3　　　　**Sample Affidavit Opposing Preliminary Injunction**

UNITED STATES DISTRICT COURT

[judicial district] OF [state]

[name]
Plaintiff,
v.
[state] BOARD OF LAW EXAMINERS,
Defendant.

---

[21] This is especially true because, as noted previously, the plaintiff failed her previous bar exam when the evidence suggests that she had sufficient time to complete the exam.

AFFIDAVIT OF [CHARLES T. B.]

IN OPPOSITION TO MOTION FOR PRELIMINARY INJUNCTION

STATE OF [state]

COUNTY OF [name]

[Charles T. B.], being duly sworn deposes and says:

1. I am a member of the [state] Board of Law Examiners ("Board"), and I submit this affidavit in response to the application made on Plaintiff's behalf for an order directing that, in addition to the extensive accommodations the Board has granted to Plaintiff in taking the bar examination on [dates], Plaintiff be given four full days to complete the examination instead of the two days normally prescribed for candidates. The Board has agreed to provide Plaintiff with (1) a separate testing room with enhanced lighting; (2) a large-print copy of the examination, and, if requested, a taped copy of the examination and the services of an amanuensis to serve as a reader/writer; (3) a ruler; (4) freedom to write the answers to short-answer questions on the question books themselves; and (5) as much time as the candidate wishes to spend during the two days when the exam is to be regularly administered. The only requested accommodation denied by the Board was the administration of the exam over four days instead of the regular two days.

2. In brief summary, the position of the Board in defense of this action, and the essential thrust of this affidavit, is that the Board, having been entrusted pursuant to the [state] Judiciary Law with the responsibility for composing and administering the bar examination, has a duty to make judgments about the accommodations to be extended to applicants who seek special accommodations to account for physical or mental disabilities and not simply to defer to medical conclusions about the extent of such accommodations. The practice of law, as the Court is well aware, is largely time driven: court deadlines must be met, work must be done and decisions must be made promptly to protect clients' interests, and legal fees must usually be based on time spent. The bar examination thus reflects the need to absorb, analyze, and resolve issues within a limited time. In determining whether accommodations requested in respect of a disability are reasonable, the Board must consider the need to preserve the essential purpose and integrity of the bar examination process as a fair measurement of minimum competence to practice law. In carrying out that duty, the Board believes that neither the Americans with Disabilities Act nor the Board's other legal responsibilities call for it to abdicate to the medical profession the making of judgments about how much accommodation each disabled individual should be accorded. While the Board is not competent to make medical judgments, neither is the medical profession competent to judge how much variation from regular examination procedures can be granted without compromising the objective of administering examinations on fair and equal terms to all candidates. Thus, while a medical doctor may be fully qualified to diagnose the nature and extent of a disability, the Board cannot leave it to the diagnosing doctor to determine how much time and other accommodations may be appropriate.

In this case, in full recognition of the medial diagnosis, the Board has concluded that granting additional time, beyond the two days prescribed for all candidates who have no disabilities, would not be a reasonable accommodation of Plaintiff's disability.

3. Although not required by law, the membership of the Board has always been made up of practicing lawyers. The Board, appointed by the Court of Appeals, has established a set of rules for administering the examination and procedures for composing the so-called [state] portion of the exam (which consists of all the essay questions and 50 short-answer questions, excluding the Multi-State portion, which consists of 200 short-answer questions composed under the auspices of the National Conference of Bar Examiners). The Board must make judgments about the kinds of conditions under which the examinations are given, the scheduling of the examination, and the amount of time allowed. In composing the examination, the Board must be conscious of the number of issues projected and the amount of time required of candidates to read and understand the questions, and, in the case of essay questions, to write complete answers dealing with all the issues.

4. The members of the Board must exercise their judgment of what is required to demonstrate minimum competence to practice law. As practicing attorneys, their background and experience provide a basis for the judgments they must make. The background and experience of the present Board are as follows:

[List names and qualifications of Board attorneys.]

5. The letters and affidavits from physicians submitted on [plaintiff's] behalf unquestionably demonstrate a substantial visual disability that has rendered Plaintiff unable to read at a normal pace for extended periods of time and requires Plaintiff to rest at intervals. The Board does not dispute Plaintiff's demonstration of disability. It does, however, question the conclusion of Plaintiff's doctors that she requires four days to take the bar examination. The doctors' analyses of Plaintiff's condition nowhere support that specific conclusion. They might as easily have said that Plaintiff requires six or eight days. Nor do the physicians address the relief from eyestrain that can be afforded by the provision of an audiotape of the examination text or a reader/writer. The Board has offered to extend such accommodations, which have been utilized successfully in the past by blind and other severely visually impaired bar examination candidates, to Plaintiff. And, of course, the doctors, understandably, nowhere purport to make a judgment about whether or not the allowance of four days for the taking of the examination would maintain the fairness and integrity of the examination process.

6. Notably a number of applicants who are completely blind have over the years successfully completed the examination, and many have done so without having been given additional time. Some have used a braille or a taped version of the examination or used an amanuensis. Blind or other visually impaired persons have been granted special accommodations for many years, long predating the adoption of the Americans with Disabilities Act. The Board has determined that [plaintiff] may use a taped version of the examination and an amanuensis who will be permitted to read the examination questions to her and, if Plaintiff wishes,

transcribe her answers, both to the short-answer and essay questions, so that Plaintiff need not consume undue amounts of time reading the questions.

7. During the two days on which the examination is regularly administered, Plaintiff will be allowed as much time as she wishes. Plaintiff's doctor suggests that this only aggravates Plaintiff's problems because extended hours only add to her fatigue. However, there is no apparent reason why Plaintiff cannot allocate her time between work on the examination and rest. The whole purpose of allowing as much time as a candidate may wish on a single day is not to impose an intolerable burden of continuous work over 10 or 15 hours or more, but rather to enable the candidate to use the time effectively with appropriate rest periods.

8. The security and integrity of the examination process are of vital concern to the Board, and that is the primary reason why the Board cannot readily accede to requests for time exceeding the two days when the exam is regularly administered. It is no reflection upon Plaintiff's character to note that administration of the exam over four days affords opportunities for compromising the examination that cannot be effectively controlled. Obviously, the Board cannot make individual judgments about whether each candidate can be trusted to observe the constraints against giving help to or obtaining help from others in completing the examination.

9. From the time the Board of Law Examiners came into existence, it has granted four days for completion of the examination in only five instances. In all of those cases, extreme and extraordinary health conditions were demonstrated that, in the view of the Board, warranted the unusual accommodation. In one case, the applicant was, functionally, a quadriplegic and could write only with the use of a stick held in his mouth. In another case, the applicant was allowed to take the examination in a room close to his hospital where medication could be administered, if necessary. In two other cases, accommodations were provided pursuant to stipulations in the context of expedited litigation, without prejudice in future litigation. In one or more of those instances, it might have been argued that too much time was given or alternatively that enough time was accorded, but the Board exercised its best judgment in light of all of the medical information before it and the need to maintain fairness in the examination process.

10. The difficulty that now faces the Board, particularly under the Americans with Disabilities Act, is the tendency for more and more applicants to seek what they know to be the maximum amount of additional time the Board has ever allowed to obtain a medical recommendation that coincides exactly with that maximum time. Unless the Board is to wholly abdicate its responsibility to make judgments about the extent of accommodation to be granted, it cannot simply accept at face value a medical judgment, however well intended, that states that four days are needed, and thereupon to grant that accommodation in every case. The Board does not believe that the Americans with Disabilities Act or other applicable law compels the Board to subordinate its judgment concerning time requirements to whatever medical authority may be submitted.

[Charles T. B.]

[5] Consent Judgment

FORM 17–4   **Sample Consent Judgment**

IN THE [type] COURT OF [location]

[John Jones],
Plaintiff,

v.   No. [case number]

[XYZ, Inc.],
Defendant.

JUDGMENT BY CONSENT

Upon consideration of the attached agreement [not included herein], hereby incorporated by reference, between Plaintiff, [John Jones], and Defendant, [XYZ, Inc.], to settle this case, it is ordered that judgment is entered for Plaintiff against Defendant in the amount of [$10,000].

Judge [name]

Dated [date]

[6] Consent Judgment Memorandum

FORM 17–5   **Sample Consent Judgment Memorandum**

I. Facts

On [July 5, 1992], [John Jones], then an employee of [XYZ, Inc. ("XYZ")], requested reasonable accommodations from [XYZ]'s management to accommodate [Jones]'s recent loss of vision. [XYZ] refused to grant [Jones]'s request and fired him. In response to the firing, [Jones] sued [XYZ] in federal court under the Americans with Disabilities Act ("ADA"). Shortly thereafter, [Jones] and [XYZ] agreed to a consent judgment. Under the terms of the consent judgment, [XYZ] agreed to pay [Jones] [$10,000] in consideration for Jones's promise to forfeit all legal claims related to [XYZ]'s refusal to provide reasonable accommodations.

II. Discussion

A consent judgment is a method for settling disputes after a lawsuit has been filed.[22] A consent judgment incorporates features of a contract and a judgment. The

---

[22] This memorandum discusses only consent judgments. Due to the procedural merger of law and equity in the federal and most state courts, the term "judgment" now includes the

first half of this memorandum describes the common attributes of consent judgments. The second half of this memorandum discusses construing and enforcing a consent judgment and related issues attributable to the instrument's dual character as a contract and a judgment.

A. Consent Judgments in General

A *consent judgment* is a contract to end a lawsuit in which the relief to be provided by the judgment and the wording to effectuate that relief are agreed to by the parties.[23] Consent judgments are a desirable means of settling a dispute when parties can agree upon the terms of the settlement but want their agreement to have the force of a judgment. A consent judgment serves this unique purpose because of its dual character. Not only is a consent judgment a contract settling the underlying dispute and providing for the entry of judgment in a pending or contemplated action,[24] but also it is a judgment.[25] As a contract, a consent judgment embodies the intent of the parties. Accordingly, consent judgments vary greatly depending upon the needs of the parties in a particular situation. However, no matter how complex the underlying agreement, the court has no duty to inquire into the wisdom of the parties entering the bargain.[26]

B. Construction and Enforcement of Consent Judgments

The scope of a consent judgment's effect depends upon how a court construes the judgment and to what extent the judgment is binding. Ordinarily, consent judgments are enforceable in the same manner as other judgments. However, because the underlying agreement is the product of the parties and not the court, construing the judgment may become a crucial prelude to enforcing it. Since the court's construction of the agreement ultimately determines the effect of the consent judgment, parties should carefully consider contract principles when drafting the agreement underlying the consent judgment.

---

term "decree." Fed. R. Civ. P. 54(a). However, consent judgments and consent decrees must be distinguished. A *consent judgment* incorporates features of a contract and a judgment, but a *consent decree* incorporates features of a contract and an injunction. The distinction between a judgment and an injunction is in the method of enforcement. Once a court issues a judgment, the parties to the original lawsuit control the execution process. Perritt at 16. Conversely, when a court issues an injunction, the court retains authority to enforce the injunction, primarily through the court's inherent contempt powers.

[23] Interspace, Inc. v. Morris, 650 F. Supp. 107, 109 (S.D.N.Y. 1986).

[24] James Fleming, Jr., *Consent Judgments as Collateral Estoppel,* 108 U. Pa. L. Rev. 173, 175 (1959).

[25] Consent judgments are distinguishable from confession of judgments. A *confession of judgment* involves the unilateral concession by the defendant that the plaintiff's cause is right. In contrast, a consent judgment is in the nature of a bilateral contract as to how the underlying dispute should be resolved. National Hygienics, Inc. v. Southern Farm Bureau Ins. Co., 707 F.2d 183 (5th Cir. 1983).

[26] Risk v. Director of Ins., 3 N.W.2d 922 (Neb. 1942).

In addition to its contractual qualities, a consent judgment represents a final decision on the merits. Therefore, it has res judicata effect.[27] A more debated issue is the extent to which consent judgments may be subject to collateral attack. Strict application of the doctrine of collateral estoppel suggests that no issues should be barred from subsequent collateral attack because no issues in a consent judgment have been litigated.[28] Two fact scenarios seem to bring this proposition into question. The first contemplates the parties to the underlying agreement requesting that the court determine the propriety of the agreement prior to entering judgment. Regardless of whether the court ultimately concludes on the correctness of the agreement, no issues have been litigated, so collateral estoppel does not apply. The second scenario exists when the parties have stipulated the existence or nonexistence of certain facts and the judgment expressly or impliedly recites these facts. Although once again none of these facts was litigated, authority exists supporting the proposition that the doctrine of collateral estoppel requires that these issues be given binding effect.[29] Regardless of the doctrine of collateral estoppel, contract law ordinarily ensures that these issues are binding if a court finds that it was the parties' intention to be bound.

In summary, a consent judgment provides an alternative to litigation when the parties to the dispute can successfully negotiate their own settlement but want their contract to have the status of a judgment issued by the court.

[7] Consent Decree

FORM 17–6 **Sample Consent Decree**

IN THE [type] COURT OF [location]

[John Jones],
Plaintiff,

v.   No. [case number]

[XYZ, Inc.],
Defendant.

DECREE

Defendant, [XYZ, Inc.], is hereby ordered to comply with the terms of the attached agreement [not included herein] by immediately hiring [Robert Jones], son of Plaintiff, [John Jones], as a management trainee in Defendant's corporate man-

---

[27] Assuming, of course, that the other essential requirements of res judicata exist. Epic Metals Corp. v. H.H. Robertson Co., 870 F.2d 1574, 1576 (Fed. Cir. 1989) (for res judicata purposes, consent judgments have the same force and effect as judgments entered after a trial on the merits).

[28] United States v. International Bldg. Co., 345 U.S. 502, 505 (1953). *See* 18 C. Wright, A. Miller, & E. Cooper, Federal Practice & Procedure § 4443 (1981).

[29] *See* Restatement (Second) of Judgments § 27 cmt. e (1982).

agement training program. In addition, Defendant must continue to employ [Robert Jones] until at least [July 5, 1998], provided that [Robert Jones]'s job performance in the Defendant's management training program does not fall below the level of *fully as expected*, as defined in the Defendant's employee handbook currently in force.

Judge [name]

Dated [date]

[8]   Consent Decree Memorandum

FORM 17–7   Sample Consent Decree Memorandum

I. Facts

On [July 5, 1992], [John Jones], then an employee of [XYZ, Inc. ("XYZ")], requested reasonable accommodations from [XYZ]'s management to accommodate Jones's recent loss of vision. [XYZ] refused to grant [Jones]'s request and fired him. In response to the firing, [Jones] sued [XYZ] in federal court under the Americans with Disabilities Act ("ADA"). Shortly thereafter [Jones] and [XYZ] agreed to settle their lawsuit via a consent decree. Under the terms of the agreement, [XYZ] agreed to hire [Jones]'s 23-year-old son, [Robert], as a management trainee in [XYZ]'s corporate management training program. Further, [XYZ] promised [Jones] that [XYZ] would continue to employ [Robert] at least until [July 5, 1998], provided that [Robert]'s job performance did not fall below the level of "fully as expected."[30] As consideration for [XYZ]'s promise, [Jones] promised to waive all legal claims related to [XYZ]'s refusal to provide him with reasonable accommodations for his blindness.

II. Discussion

A consent decree is a method for settling disputes, after a lawsuit has been filed, that has attributes of a contract and an injunction.[31] This memorandum discusses the general nature of a consent decree, construction and enforcement of consent decrees, and the validity of consent decrees under the ADA.

A *consent decree* is an agreement of the parties in settlement of litigation that the court approves and embodies in an order.[32] Although the terms of the agreement are the product of the parties' negotiations, the trial court must approve the agree-

---

[30] "Fully as expected" is the phrase used in XYZ's employee handbook to describe an average performer.

[31] *See* Local No. 93, Int'l Ass'n of Firefighters v. City of Cleveland, 478 U.S. 501, 519 (1986).

[32] Lloyd C. Anderson, *Implementation of Consent Decrees in Structural Reform Litigation,* 1986 U. Ill. L. Rev. 727.

ment. In deciding whether to approve or deny the issuance of a consent decree, the court has the duty to decide whether the decree is fair, adequate, and reasonable.[33] However, as long as the agreement is otherwise reasonable, a court need not require that the agreement serve the best interests of the public.[34] Thus, a court's review of a consent decree is more than a rubber stamping. After court approval, the agreement takes on the status of a consent decree. Inherent in this status is the trial court's retention of authority to modify or enforce its decree even without a provision in the decree stating that the court shall retain jurisdiction over the matter to ensure compliance.[35] Accordingly, a consent decree might be best characterized as a judgment subject to continued judicial proceeding.[36]

Despite this characterization, a consent decree is principally an agreement between the parties that will be construed as a contract and interpreted to give effect to what the parties agreed to, as reflected in the decree itself or in the documents incorporated in the decree by reference.[37] Accordingly, the parties to the lawsuit should always heed contract principles when drafting the agreement.

As a judicial act, though, a consent decree is considered a final judgment on the merits.[38] A consent decree is also given res judicata effect.[39] Concerning collateral estoppel, a consent decree is similar to a consent judgment in that no issues have been litigated. Accordingly, a consent decree should be barred from collateral attack only when the parties intend for their agreement to have this effect.

One final issue peculiar to consent decrees in settlement of ADA claims arises because the ADA incorporates by reference the enforcement provisions of the Civil Rights Act of 1964.[40] The question arises as to whether consent decrees are valid in the context of litigation under the Civil Rights Act, given the Act's prohibition against court orders requiring an employer to give relief to an employee who suffers adverse job action if such action was taken for any reason other than discrimination.[41] The Supreme Court has held that consent decrees are not included among these prohibited court orders.[42] Accordingly, consent orders are also a permissible mode of settlement for lawsuits brought under the ADA.

---

[33] United States v. Colorado, 937 F.2d 505, 509 (10th Cir. 1991).

[34] United States v. Oregon, 913 F.2d 576, 581 (9th Cir. 1990).

[35] Picon v. Morris, 933 F.2d 660, 662 (8th Cir. 1991).

[36] United States v. Oregon, 913 F.2d 576, 580 (9th Cir. 1990).

[37] SEC v. Levine, 881 F.2d 1165, 1178–79 (2d Cir. 1989).

[38] Vanguards of Cleveland v. City of Cleveland, 753 F.2d 479, 484 (6th Cir. 1985), *aff'd,* 478 U.S. 501 (1986).

[39] United States v. Fisher, 864 F.2d 434, 439 (7th Cir. 1988).

[40] ADA § 107(a), 42 U.S.C. § 12,117(a) (1994). *See also* Civil Rights Act of 1964, 42 U.S.C. ch. 21 (1994) [hereinafter Civil Rights Act of 1964].

[41] 42 U.S.C. § 2000e-5(g) (1994).

[42] Local No. 93, Int'l Ass'n of Firefighters v. City of Cleveland, 478 U.S. 501, 523 (1986).

[9]   Contempt Motion

FORM 17–8   Sample Contempt Motion

UNITED STATES DISTRICT COURT FOR THE [EASTERN] DISTRICT OF
[PENNSYLVANIA]

[John Jones]   .
Plaintiff,
v.

Civil Action No. [case number]

[XYZ, Inc.]
Defendant

MOTION FOR ORDER TO SHOW CAUSE WHY EMPLOYER IN ADA
ACTION SHOULD NOT BE PUNISHED FOR CONTEMPT

Mr. [John Jones], by his undersigned counsel, respectfully moves this Court
for an Order requiring the Defendant to show cause why this Court should not hold
the Defendant in contempt for failing to comply with this Court's Order of [January
2, 1993]. As grounds for this motion, [Mr. Jones] shows the Court:

1. On [January 2, 1993], this Court entered an Order requiring that, within
15 days of the Order, the Defendant reinstate [Mr. Jones] as a telemarketing assistant and make reasonable accommodations for [Mr. Jones]'s disability by changing
his job requirements.
2. As of [January 30, 1993], the Defendant has failed to reinstate [Mr. Jones]
and otherwise comply with this Court's Order of [January 2, 1993].

Accordingly, [Mr. Jones] respectfully requests that this Court issue an Order
directing the Defendants to show cause why this Court should not hold them in
contempt for failing to comply with this Court's Order of [January 2, 1993].

Respectfully submitted,

[attorney for plaintiff]

[10]   Memorandum of Law Supporting Contempt Motion

**FORM 17–9   Sample Memorandum of Law Supporting Contempt
                Motion**

I. FACTS

From [January 1987] through [July 5, 1992], [XYZ, Inc. ("XYZ")], employed
[John Jones] as a telemarketing assistant. On [July 4, 1992], [Jones] injured himself

during a backyard barbecue, rendering himself completely and permanently blind. On [July 5, 1992], when [Jones] informed [XYZ] of his misfortune, [XYZ] terminated him. At the time of his termination, [Jones] had a good work record that showed above average performance in his position. In response to [XYZ]'s actions, [Jones] filed suit under the Americans with Disabilities Act ("ADA") in federal court, alleging that [XYZ] terminated him because of his disability, therefore discriminating against him.[43] [Jones] sought a permanent injunction requiring [XYZ] to reinstate him in the telemarketing position he formerly held.

On [January 2, 1993], the Court granted [Jones]'s request and issued an order requiring that [XYZ] reinstate [Jones] in his former position within 15 days and provide reasonable accommodations for [Jones]'s disability by changing his job requirements. As of [January 30, 1993], [XYZ] had not complied with the Court's order. Accordingly, [Jones] petitioned the Court for an order to show cause why the Court should not hold [XYZ] in contempt.

II. DISCUSSION

This memorandum discusses contempt proceedings as they relate to the ADA. The first part of the memorandum describes the general nature of contempt by distinguishing between civil and criminal contempt, the two types of contempt. The second part of the memorandum discusses judicial procedure peculiar to civil and criminal contempt. Although civil contempt proceedings are more relevant than criminal contempt proceedings in ADA cases in which the employer refuses to comply with a court order, both are discussed in detail. Finally, this memorandum concludes with a discussion of impossibility, a complete defense to civil contempt.

A. The Nature of Contempt

Courts may use their contempt powers to ensure that an employer honors an injunction issued as a result of an ADA lawsuit.[44] Although the ADA does not specifically discuss the use of contempt to enforce injunctions,[45] contempt is a remedy available for violation of an ADA-related injunction.[46]

An employer may be charged with civil or criminal contempt when it refuses or fails to obey an ADA injunction. The purpose and character of the potential punishment distinguishes civil from criminal contempt.[47] Whether a particular contumacious act is classified as civil or criminal contempt is important because the procedural protections are much greater for one accused of criminal contempt.[48]

---

[43] See ADA § 102(b)(1), 42 U.S.C. § 12,112(b)(1) (1994).

[44] Bessette v. W.B. Conkey Co., 194 U.S. 324, 327 (1904).

[45] The ADA enforcement provisions — at ADA § 107, 42 U.S.C. § 12,117 (1994); ADA § 203, 42 U.S.C. § 12,133 (1994); and ADA § 308, 42 U.S.C. § 12,188 (1994) — make no mention of contempt.

[46] Perritt at 445 (contempt is remedy available for violation of any court order). Because the ADA authorizes injunctive relief, a court presented with an ADA case could issue an order that, if violated, would be punishable by contempt.

[47] Gompers v. Bucks Stove & Range Co., 221 U.S. 418, 441 (1911).

[48] Id. at 446. Criminal contempt would be involved only if a prosecutor exercised the discretion to prosecute for contempt. It is far more likely that a victim of an ADA violation would seek civil contempt.

Civil contempt punishes to enforce the rights of a litigant,[49] and the nature of the punishment is to force future compliance with the injunction.[50] In addition, a private litigant prosecutes civil contempt proceedings, and the proceedings usually result either in the imposition of money penalties payable to the private complainant, or in the incarceration of the defendant for an indefinite period pending compliance with the court order.[51] Penalties for civil contempt are considered conditional because the contemnor can avoid remission of a monetary penalty or secure release from custody by complying with the terms of the court order.[52]

In contrast with civil contempt, criminal contempt punishes to vindicate public authority.[53] In addition, criminal contempt punishes the offender for past contempt, is punitive, and cannot be ended by any act of the contemnor.[54] Punishment for criminal contempt may include incarceration and a fine payable to the United States, which serves as the prosecutor in criminal contempt proceedings in federal court.

Moreover, contempt is subdivided into direct and indirect contempt. This distinction is important because direct contempt may be punished summarily by the judge in whose presence the contumacious acts occurred. Indirect contempt may be punished only through a fact-finding process that determines whether or not out-of-court conduct was contumacious.[55] Direct contempt covers acts committed under the eye and within the hearing of the court.[56] In a summary proceeding to punish such direct contempt, a court need not hear evidence on contempt committed within its sight or hearing before punishing the contemnor.[57] Given this distinction between direct and indirect contempt, an employer's refusal to obey an ADA-related court order would almost always be treated as indirect contempt when the refusal occurred away from the courthouse. The only ADA context in which direct contempt could plausibly arise is if a witness refused an order to testify at a trial or hearing.

Despite the different classifications of contempt and the possibility that contempt related to an ADA injunction could be classified as either direct or indirect contempt, the most likely classification in ADA cases is civil contempt. The purpose and character of the punishment test confirms this conclusion because the private plaintiff in this proceeding seeks future compliance with the injunction.

---

[49] Penfield Co. v. SEC, 330 U.S. 585, 590 (1947).

[50] Perritt at 446.

[51] Gompers v. Bucks Stove & Range Co., 221 U.S. 418, 418 (1911).

[52] *Id.* In *UMWA v. Bagwell*, ___ U.S. ___, 114 S. Ct. 2552 (1994), the Supreme Court made this analytical framework less certain. It reversed the Virginia Supreme Court and held that, under the facts of that case, contempt penalties announced in advance and assessed only after further noncompliance occurred were criminal rather than civil. 114 S. Ct. at 2562. The Court suggested that coercive penalties are likely to be found to be criminal in nature unless they have a compensatory purpose.

[53] Carbon Fuel Co. v. UMWA, 517 F.2d 1348, 1349 (4th Cir. 1975).

[54] *Id.*

[55] *In re* Heathcock, 696 F.2d 1362, 1365 (11th Cir. 1983).

[56] United States v. Marshall, 451 F.2d 372, 374 (9th Cir. 1971).

[57] United States v. Vague, 697 F.2d 805, 808 (7th Cir. 1983).

Most contempt proceedings related to an employer's refusal to obey a court order resulting from an ADA lawsuit should be characterized as civil contempt.[58]

B. Proceedings to Punish Contempt

1. Criminal Contempt Proceedings

Federal Rule of Criminal Procedure 42 governs criminal contempt proceedings. Subsection (a) of Rule 42 states that criminal contempt may be punished summarily if the judge certifies that the judge saw or heard the conduct constituting the contempt, and that it was committed in the actual presence of the court.[59] Subsection (a) addresses only direct criminal contempt.

Subsection (b) addresses all other criminal contempt and requires three procedural stages:

1. Proper notice of the criminal nature of the contempt citation;
2. Trial by jury when "an act of Congress so provides";
3. Trial before an impartial (nondisqualified) judge.[60]

Commencing criminal contempt proceedings under Rule 42(b) requires only notice.[61] Although criminal contempt proceedings have been commenced by indictment or information, this is not required.[62] For the notice to be adequate, it must state the time and place of hearing and allow reasonable time for preparation of a defense.[63] Further, the notice must state the essential facts constituting the criminal contempt charged and describe it as such.[64] A jury trial is required in a criminal contempt proceeding only when the contempt is considered a serious offense.[65] Criminal contempt is a serious offense when it is punishable by more than six months in prison.[66] Thus, an employer is entitled to a jury trial in all ADA criminal contempt cases in which conviction would result in a sentence greater than six months.

The final procedural requirement of an impartial judge arises when the contempt involved disrespect to, or criticism of, a judge.[67] In these instances, the alleged contemnor is entitled to a full hearing before a different judge.[68]

---

[58] In addition to civil contempt proceedings, the court may institute criminal proceedings against the defendant based on the same conduct. United States v. UMWA, 330 U.S. 258, 303 (1947).

[59] Fed. R. Crim. P. 42(a).

[60] *Id.* 42(b); Perritt at 614.

[61] Fed. R. Crim. P. 42(b).

[62] United States v. Mensik, 440 F.2d 1232, 1234 (4th Cir. 1971).

[63] Fed. R. Crim. P. 42(b).

[64] *Id.*

[65] Codispoti v. Pennsylvania, 418 U.S. 506, 511 (1974).

[66] *Id.*

[67] *See* United States v. Prugh, 479 F.2d 611, 613 (8th Cir. 1973).

[68] United States v. Meyer, 462 F.2d 827, 842 (D.C. Cir. 1972).

Distinct from the procedural requirements of a criminal contempt proceeding are the mechanics for initiating those proceedings. Criminal contempt proceedings may be initiated in three ways:

1. The court may bring charges on its own motion;
2. A private party may petition the court to prosecute another for criminal contempt[69]; or
3. The local United States Attorney may initiate the criminal contempt proceeding.

A court usually brings charges on its own motion only in summary proceedings pursuant to Rule 42(a). The court may bring contempt charges at the time of the contumacious act or at some later time.[70] Local prosecuting authorities usually initiate contempt proceedings for indirect criminal contempt. A private party may ask the U.S. Attorney to prosecute another for criminal contempt. Similarly, the local prosecuting authority may initiate criminal contempt proceedings in accordance with local criminal procedure.

2. Civil Contempt Proceedings

Notice and the opportunity to be heard are the essential characteristics of civil contempt proceedings.[71] The requirements for notice vary based upon the rules of procedure used by the court in which the litigant initiates the contempt proceedings. The rules of procedure used in the contempt proceedings should be the same ones used in the lawsuit that originally gave rise to the court order in dispute. This is because courts consider a proceeding for contempt to enforce a remedy in a civil action a proceeding in that original civil action.[72] Because the contempt proceeding involves new issues, the alleged contemnor is entitled to notice of the facts alleged in the contempt proceeding. Nevertheless, a new civil action is not involved. Rather, the first step in initiating civil contempt proceedings is to file a motion or "order to show cause," depending on local practice, with the clerk of the court with jurisdiction over the main action. The adequacy of the contents of this initial document will, of course, be determined by the rules of civil procedure used by the court in which the complaint is filed. Because lawsuits under the ADA involve

---

[69] *See* Charles B. Blackmar, West's Federal Forms § 7766 (1971) (example of a Petition for Prosecution of Criminal Contempt).

[70] United States v. Schiffer, 351 F.2d 91, 94–95 (6th Cir. 1965).

[71] Perritt at 448. This discussion assumes that the employer was the defendant in the initial ADA lawsuit and is also charged with contempt. Accordingly, no new process is required when the employer is already subject to the jurisdiction of the court, because the contempt proceeding is considered a continuation of the original proceeding. C.A. Wright & A.R. Miller, Federal Practice and Procedure § 2960 (1973) [hereinafter Wright & Miller], at 589.

[72] Gompers v. Bucks Stove & Range Co., 221 U.S. 418, 444–45 (1947). This makes sense because a litigant commences proceedings for civil contempt to enforce rights which that litigant has gained as a result of a prior legal action.

federal subject matter jurisdiction,[73] this memorandum addresses only the form and content of the motion for an order to show cause under the Federal Rules of Civil Procedure.[74]

Under the Federal Rules of Civil Procedure, a motion to the court for an order to show cause why an employer in an ADA action should not be punished for contempt must

1. Be made in writing;
2. State with particularity the grounds therefor; and
3. Set forth the relief or order sought.[75]

No difficulties exist with the requirements of a writing or the relief or order sought. The purpose of the particularity requirement is to provide the defendant with notice of the grounds upon which the motion is based and the relief sought. Further, the movant must provide the defendant with adequate information for the defendant to process the motion correctly.[76]

Once the plaintiff has filed its motion, and the motion's contents comply with the appropriate court's standards, formal civil contempt procedure commences. As stated earlier, the essential attributes of these proceedings are notice and the opportunity to be heard.

The proper or permissible form of notice varies with the local practice[77] and should comport with the appropriate federal or state rule of civil procedure governing pleadings or motions, as appropriate.

The appropriate form of the requisite hearing in a civil contempt proceeding is flexible. The opportunity to be heard contemplates that the person have an opportunity to present argument and evidence on possible defenses.[78] Form varies with the issues.[79] Regardless of the desirability and expediency of summary proceedings, they must always comport with the requirements of due process.[80]

---

[73] The plaintiff may always obtain federal question jurisdiction in a lawsuit filed under the ADA. 28 U.S.C. § 1331 (1994). In contrast, if the plaintiff brings the initial action in state court, whether the lawsuit eventually ends up in federal court depends upon the defendant's success in removing the lawsuit. *Id.* § 1441.

[74] See the applicable state rules of procedure for ADA injunctions issued by state courts.

[75] Fed. R. Civ. P. 7(b)(1).

[76] Registration Control Sys., Inc. v. Compusystems, Inc., 922 F.2d 805 (Fed. Cir. 1990).

[77] Wright & Miller at 588.

[78] *See* Washington Metro. Area Transit Auth. v. Transit Union, 531 F.2d 617, 621–22 (D.C. Cir. 1976) (reversing contempt for failure to consider defenses adequately).

[79] Wright & Miller at 590.

[80] Shillitani v. United States, 384 U.S. 364, 371 (1966).

C. Impossibility

Impossibility is a defense to civil contempt for violation of an injunction.[81] Impossibility occupies a unique position in an ADA-related civil contempt proceeding because it not only serves as a potential defense to contempt charges but also may be used in the original ADA lawsuit when an employer attempts to establish undue hardship. For example, in attempting to establish undue hardship an employer might attempt to show that financial constraints prevent it from providing reasonable accommodations. If a court rejects this argument and fails to find undue hardship, the question arises whether the employer may relitigate this issue when he asserts the defense of impossibility in the contempt proceedings. In *Maggio v. Zeitz*,[82] the Supreme Court ruled that it is not permissible to relitigate the legal or factual basis of the order alleged to have been disobeyed.[83] However, the Court stated that if the two disputes may be characterized as asking the same question (i.e., the employer's financial capability to provide reasonable accommodations) at two different points in time, then the latter issue must be tried just as any other issue.

Another, related, issue concerns burdens of proof in establishing undue hardship and impossibility. The structure of ADA section 102(b)(5) and the ADA's legislative history make it clear that the employer has the burden of establishing undue hardship.[84] Similarly, in establishing the defense of impossibility, the initial burden of production lies with the alleged contemnor. However, the burden of persuasion shifts back to the party seeking the contempt order when the contemnor has satisfied its burden of production of evidence establishing his present inability to comply. As applied to an ADA lawsuit, this means that the employer has a greater evidentiary burden in establishing undue hardship in the original lawsuit than in establishing impossibility in the contempt proceedings. Although strategically an employer might be tempted to relitigate the burdensomeness of making accommodation in the civil contempt proceeding, the law-of-the-case doctrine is likely to prevent relitigation of this issue if it was decided in the context of an undue burden defense in establishing liability or in proceedings on a preliminary injunction.[85]

---

[81] United States v. Rylander, 460 U.S. 752, 757, *reh'g denied,* 462 U.S. 1112 (1983) (contempt for failure to produce records pursuant to an IRS subpoena).

[82] 333 U.S. 56, 69 (1948).

[83] *Id.* at 74.

[84] *See* § 4.10[B].

[85] Maggio v. Zeitz, 333 U.S. 56, 68 (1948) (original proceeding is separate from contempt proceeding; when original proceeding terminates in final order, it becomes res judicata and not subject to collateral attack in contempt proceedings). Res judicata would not, of course, preclude relitigation in a subsequent criminal contempt proceeding because the burden of proof is more demanding in the criminal context.

[11]   Motion to Reduce Coercive Civil Contempt Fines to a Judgment

FORM 17–10   Sample Motion to Reduce Fines to a Judgment

In the [type] Court of [location]

[John Jones],
Plaintiff,
v.   No. [case number]
[XYZ, Inc.],
Defendant.

Plaintiff, [John Jones], by his undersigned counsel, respectfully moves the court for further relief in the above-referenced cause. As grounds for this motion, Plaintiff shows the court the following:

1. On [February 1, 1993], this court found the defendant, [XYZ, Inc. ("XYZ")], in contempt for failing to comply with this court's [January 2, 1993], order requiring that the Defendant reinstate the Plaintiff in his former position as a telemarketing assistant with [XYZ].

2. In its [February 1, 1993], order, this court ordered [XYZ] fined prospectively [$1,000] per day for each day after [February 1, 1993], that [XYZ] failed to reinstate [John Jones] as a telemarketing assistant at [XYZ]. In the same order this court also stated that the purpose of this fine was to coerce [XYZ] to comply with this court's [January 2, 1993], order.

3. Plaintiff now advises the court that as of the date of this motion, the defendant has not yet reinstated [Jones] to his position as a telemarketing assistant.

Plaintiffs respectfully pray

a. That the court issue an order directing the defendant to show cause why it should not be fined [$10,000] pursuant to the prospective fine schedule included in this court's [February 1, 1993], order;

b. That this court hold an assessment hearing to assess fines in the amount of [$10,000] against the defendant; and

c. That, upon conclusion of the assessment hearing, this court enter a judgment in favor of the plaintiff for [10,000].

Respectfully submitted,

[attorney for the plaintiff]

[address]

§ 17.02   ASSESSMENT AND COLLECTION OF CIVIL CONTEMPT FINES

[A]   Generally

A court assesses coercive civil contempt fines when an employer fails to comply with a contempt order whose terms expressly provide for such fines. This section discusses not only the procedure for assessing and collecting coercive contempt fines but also the arguments used to avoid paying coercive contempt fincs.

Understanding how an employee gets to the point of collecting coercive civil contempt fines requires some knowledge of the events preceding the assessment of those fines. This series of events consists of three distinct stages. In the first stage, the court issues an injunction as a result of an ADA lawsuit. In the second stage, the employer violates the injunction and the court issues a contempt order that specifies prospective monetary penalties or "fines" if the employer violates the contempt order. In the third stage, the employer violates the contempt order, the related fines accrue pursuant to the fine provision in the order, and the employee tries to collect the fines.

The first stage in assessing coercive civil contempt fines is for a court to issue an injunction. A court must issue either an injunction to compel or to prohibit certain conduct by the employer.

The second stage of the assessment process begins when the employer fails to comply with the terms of the injunction. To force compliance with the injunction, courts use their civil contempt powers. In a civil proceeding, a private plaintiff must invoke these powers. Accordingly, the employee commences civil contempt proceedings by filing a "show cause" motion with the court. Provided that the court finds the contents of this motion adequate, the court then issues a "show cause" order. This order commands the defendant to appear at a hearing to defend himself against the contempt charges. If the employer is unsuccessful in defending himself against these charges, the court issues a contempt order. Although the circumstances of each case determine the contents of the contempt order, at a minimum, the order should reiterate the terms of the original injunction and order future compliance with the injunction. If the defendant's previous noncompliance has injured the employee, the court may order compensatory fines.[86] In any event, the court uses the threat of fines to coerce compliance, and thus

---

[86] Compensatory actions are essentially backward-looking, seeking to compensate the employee through the payment of money for damages caused by the employer's past acts of disobedience of the court's order. Latrine Steel Co. v. United Steelworkers, 545 F.2d 1336, 1344 (3d Cir. 1976) (coercive contempt order could not survive invalidation of underlying injunction and, thus, was subject to being vacated).

includes a provision in the order mandating that the employer be fined for each day or occurrence of future noncompliance.[87]

The final stage of the assessment process begins when the employer violates the contempt order. When the employee has evidence of the employer's prohibited conduct, the employee may move the court to assess fines pursuant to the prospective fine schedule set forth in the contempt order. This motion should describe both the violation and the relief sought by the employee. The court then orders the employer to appear before the court and defend itself against these new contempt allegations. If the court finds the employer in contempt, the court enters a judgment in favor of the employee for the amount of the accrued fines and issues a new order with provisions similar to, or more stringent than, the first contempt order. Having a judgment in hand, the employee then executes the judgment to collect the fines.[88]

In order to avoid paying the fines, counsel for the employer may make either or both of two arguments. First, the employer might characterize coercive fines as a criminal sanction by asserting that courts assess coercive fines because of past contumacy and that the court failed to provide the employer with the usual criminal procedure safeguards. Because a court cannot impose criminal sanctions without providing the employer with all the procedural safeguards owed a criminal defendant, this argument leads to the conclusion that the fines must be revoked because the employer was denied due process. The employee's counsel can refute this argument by asserting that the fine was prospective at the time the employer received notice of it[89] and that the purpose of the fine was to coerce compliance with the injunction, thereby making it civil in nature.

Second, the employer might argue that even if the fines are civil, they become moot after the employer complies with the injunction because compliance was the ultimate goal of initially assessing the fines. Accepting this

---

[87] Coercive sanctions, in contrast to compensatory sanctions, look to the future and are designed to aid the plaintiff by bringing a defiant party into compliance with the court order or by ensuring that a potentially contumacious party adheres to an injunction by setting forth in advance the penalties the court will impose if the party deviates from the path of obedience. *Id.* The court order may also include a provision mandating that the employer be incarcerated either until the employer complies or for future noncompliance.

[88] *But see id.* at 1346 (describing coercive contempt fines as payable into court or public treasury and not to complainant). In UMWA v. Bagwell, ___ U.S. ___, 114 S. Ct. 2552 (1994), the Supreme Court made this analytical framework less certain. It reversed the Virginia Supreme Court and held that, under the facts of that case, contempt penalties announced in advance and assessed only after further noncompliance occurred were criminal rather than civil. 114 S. Ct. at 2562. The Court suggested that coercive penalties are likely to be found to be criminal in nature unless they have a compensatory purpose.

[89] If the employer had complied with the injunction upon receiving notice of it, the court would not have fined the employer.

argument means that any employer subject to coercive contempt fines could avoid payment of the fines by postponing actual collection until after the employer complied with the injunction. Such a rule provides no incentive for compliance with the court order, and courts reject it as undermining public respect for the judiciary.[90]

[B] Sample Forms

[1] Plaintiffs' Motion for Entry of Judgment (EEOC)

FORM 17–11   **Sample Plaintiff's Motion for Entry of Judgment**

IN THE UNITED STATES DISTRICT COURT FOR THE [NORTHERN] DISTRICT OF [ILLINOIS] [EASTERN] DIVISION

U.S. EQUAL EMPLOYMENT OPPORTUNITY COMMISSION and [CHARLES H. WESSEL],

Plaintiffs,
v.   Civil Action No. [92 C 7330]
[A.I.C. SECURITY INVESTIGATIONS LTD.];
[A.I.C. INTERNATIONAL, LTD.];
and [unnamed defendant C],
Defendants.

Magistrate Judge [Guzman]

PLAINTIFFS' MOTION FOR ENTRY OF JUDGMENT

Plaintiffs, Equal Employment Opportunity Commission and [Charles H. Wessel], respectfully move the Court, pursuant to Rule 58 of the Federal Rules of Civil Procedure, for entry of judgment on the verdicts rendered on [March 19, 1993], and for equitable relief. A draft judgment, incorporating the claims for relief of each Plaintiff, is attached.

[certificate of service]

[draft judgment]

---

[90] Bagwell v. UMWA, 423 S.E.2d 349, 357 (Va. 1992), *rev'd*, ___ U.S. ___, 114 S. Ct. 2552 (1994).

[2]   Motion in Opposition to Judgment for Damages

FORM 17–12   Sample Motion in Opposition to Judgment for Damages

IN THE UNITED STATES DISTRICT COURT FOR THE [NORTHERN]
DISTRICT OF [ILLINOIS]
[EASTERN] DIVISION

U.S. EQUAL EMPLOYMENT OPPORTUNITY COMMISSION,

Plaintiff,

v.   Civil Action No. [92 C 7330]

[A.I.C. SECURITY INVESTIGATIONS, LTD.];
[A.I.C. INTERNATIONAL, LTD.];
and [unnamed defendant C],
Defendants.

Honorable [Marvin E. Aspen]

Magistrate Judge [Ronald A. Guzman]

DEFENDANTS' MOTION IN OPPOSITION TO PLAINTIFFS' PROPOSED
JUDGMENT FOR DAMAGES

The Defendants, [A.I.C. SECURITY INVESTIGATIONS, LTD. (hereinafter
"A.I.C.")] and [defendant C], by and through their attorneys, [WESSELS &
PAUTSCH, P.C.], by [Charles W. Pautsch], [attorney A], and [attorney B], upon
order of the Court hereby move in opposition to the draft judgment submitted by
Plaintiffs and move that the jury verdict on damages be effected in the final judg-
ment[91] as follows:

1. The jury verdict of [$50,000] in compensatory damages is speculative and
excessive and goes against the weight of the evidence at trial.

2. The jury verdict of [$250,000] in punitive damages against [A.I.C.], and
[$250,000] in punitive damages against [defendant C], is excessive and goes against
the weight of the evidence at trial.

3. Pursuant to 42 U.S.C. § 1981a(b)(3), the Court is charged to reduce the
sum of compensatory and punitive damages Plaintiffs may recover not to exceed
the statutory maximum of [$200,000] based upon the parties' stipulation in the
pretrial order that [A.I.C.] employs more than 200 but less than 500 employees.

---

[91] The defendants are submitting this motion on the limited issue of damages pursuant to
the court's express request that such issues be addressed prior to its entry of judgment in
this action. The defendants reserve the right to bring any postjudgment motions on these or
any other issues deemed appropriate.

WHEREFORE, Defendants [A.I.C. SECURITY INVESTIGATIONS, LTD.] and [defendant C] request, without waiver of their rights to file any postjudgment motions as provided for in the Federal Rules of Civil Procedure, that the Court first apply the statutory cap of [$200,000] to the total compensatory and punitive damages awarded by the jury, and second, that the Court exercise its discretion in further reducing the jury's award of compensatory and punitive damages on the basis of the record at trial and the guidance afforded by other case law cited in the accompanying memorandum.

Dated this [26th] day of [March 1993].

[A.I.C. SECURITY INVESTIGATIONS, LTD.] and [defendant C]

By:

[attorney A]

[3]   Objections to Entry of Judgment

FORM 17–13   Sample Objections to Entry of Judgment

IN THE UNITED STATES DISTRICT COURT FOR THE [NORTHERN]
DISTRICT OF [ILLINOIS]
[EASTERN] DIVISION

U.S. EQUAL EMPLOYMENT OPPORTUNITY COMMISSION,

Plaintiff,
v.   Civil Action No. [92 C 7330]
[A.I.C. SECURITY INVESTIGATIONS, LTD.];
[A.I.C. INTERNATIONAL, LTD.];
and [unnamed defendant C],   Honorable [Marvin E. Aspen]
Defendants.   Magistrate Judge [Guzman]

DEFENDANTS' OBJECTIONS TO PLAINTIFFS' MOTION FOR
ENTRY OF JUDGMENT

Defendants, [A.I.C. SECURITY INVESTIGATIONS, LTD.] and [defendant C], by and through their attorneys, [WESSELS & PAUTSCH, P.C.], by [Charles W. Pautsch], [attorney A], and [attorney B], hereby object to the Plaintiffs' Motion for Entry of Judgment in the above-captioned action based upon the following:

1. Defendants object to paragraph two (2) of Plaintiffs' draft judgment because the jury award of [$50,000] in compensatory damages is excessive and goes against the weight of the evidence at trial.[92]

2. Defendants further object to paragraph two (2) of Plaintiffs' draft judgment because it impermissibly fails to aggregate "the sum of the amount of compensatory damages awarded . . . and the amount of punitive damages awarded" for purposes of the statutory caps on such damages. *See* 42 U.S.C. § 1981a(b)(3).

3. Defendants object to paragraphs three (3) and four (4) of Plaintiffs' draft judgment because they fail to aggregate "the sum of the amount of compensatory damages awarded . . . and the amount of punitive damages awarded" for purposes of the statutory caps on such damages. 42 U.S.C. § 1981a(b)(3).

4. Defendants further object to paragraph four (4) of Plaintiffs' draft judgment because it wholly ignores 42 U.S.C. § 1981a(b)(3) in that total compensatory and punitive damages recoverable by [Wessel] "shall not exceed" [$200,000] because the parties have stipulated in the Pretrial Order that this is a case of a Respondent who has more than 200 but fewer than 500 employees; as detailed in the accompanying memorandum, Plaintiffs' apparent position that the Civil Rights Act of 1991 places no cap on the compensatory or punitive damages [Wessel] may recover from [defendant C] is contrary to the law.

5. Defendants further object to paragraphs three (3) and four (4) of Plaintiffs' draft judgment because the jury award of [$250,000] in punitive damages against [A.I.C.] and [defendant C], each, is excessive and goes against the weight of the evidence at trial.

6. Defendants object to paragraphs five (5) through ten (10) of the Plaintiffs' draft judgment because the requested injunctive relief would be punitive in its effect and would not serve any principles of equity since no one other than [Wessel] has complained against Defendants, Defendants remain subject to the law under the ADA regardless of any equitable relief, and the peculiar circumstances of this case do not justify the broad injunctive remedies sought by Plaintiffs.

7. Defendants further object to paragraphs (5) through ten (10) of the Plaintiffs' draft judgment because they seek punitive measures such as postings at the property of its clients, which is intrusive to such parties and would effectively cause the loss of many such clients, and further any notices, posted or hand-delivered to employees, would serve no equitable purpose in light of the massive media attention and publicity given to this action since its inception.

8. Defendants further object to paragraphs five (5) through (10) of the Plaintiffs' draft judgment because the three-year period Plaintiffs seek for any injunctive relief is excessive and punitive, especially under these circumstances, where the jury in effect determined that [Wessel] was not qualified and was not entitled to backpay beyond [November] and thus could have been permissibly discharged after [November], but not [July], of [1992].

---

[92] This position is argued more fully in Defendants' accompanying memorandum of law on damages, which Defendants are submitting pursuant to the court's request. Defendants' submission of said memorandum does not constitute a waiver of their right to submit any postjudgment motions they may deem appropriate.

9. Defendants object to paragraph six (6) of Plaintiffs' draft judgment because, in addition to the foregoing objections, Plaintiffs seek injunctive relief that is nonsensical in that it would apply to "any person" filing a charge, opposing an unlawful practice under the ADA, etc.; Defendants are already prohibited by law from retaliating against their employees or applicants, 42 U.S.C. § 2000e-3, and the proposed judgment of the Plaintiffs is impracticable and unnecessary.

Respectfully submitted on this [26th] day of [March] [1993].

[4] Judgment

FORM 17–14   Sample Judgment

IN THE UNITED STATES DISTRICT COURT FOR THE [NORTHERN]
DISTRICT OF [ILLINOIS]
[EASTERN] DIVISION

U.S. EQUAL EMPLOYMENT OPPORTUNITY COMMISSION,

Plaintiff,
v.   Civil Action No. [92 C 7330]
[A.I.C. SECURITY INVESTIGATIONS, LTD.];
[A.I.C. INTERNATIONAL, LTD.];
and [unnamed defendant C],
Defendants.   Magistrate Judge [Guzman]

JUDGMENT

The Court hereby enters judgment upon the verdicts of the jury, rendered [March 18, 1993], in favor of Plaintiff Equal Employment Opportunity Commission ("EEOC") and Intervening Plaintiff [Charles H. Wessel ("Wessel")] and against Defendants [A.I.C. Security Investigations, Ltd. ("A.I.C.")] and [defendant C]. Pursuant to the Court's ruling of [March 17, 1993], Defendant [A.I.C. International, Ltd.] is dismissed as a Defendant.

The Court orders that judgment be entered in favor of EEOC and [Wessel] and against the Defendants as follows:

1. [A.I.C.] shall pay [Wessel] the sum of [$22,000] as backpay based on the jury award, plus interest at the rate of [six percent (6%)], compounded annually, to the date of judgment, in accordance with 42 U.S.C. § 2000e-5, incorporated by reference into the Americans with Disabilities Act ("ADA"), 42 U.S.C. § 12,117.

2. [A.I.C.] and [defendant C], jointly and severally, shall pay [Wessel] the sum of [$50,000] as compensatory damages, based upon the jury award, in accordance with 42 U.S.C. § 1981a(b).

The Court further orders that judgment be entered in favor of [Wessel] and against the Defendants as follows:

3. [A.I.C.] and [defendant C], jointly and severally, shall pay [Wessel] the sum of [$150,000] as punitive damages, reduced from the jury award of [$500,000] in accordance with 42 U.S.C. § 1981a(b).

The Court further orders, pursuant to 42 U.S.C. § 2000e-5, incorporated by reference into the ADA, 42 U.S.C. § 12,117, equitable relief in favor of the Equal Employment Opportunity Commission and against Defendants [A.I.C.] and [defendant C] as follows:

4. [A.I.C.], its officers, agents, employees, successors, and all those in active concert or participation with them, or any of them and [defendant C], are enjoined from engaging in any employment practice that discriminates against any qualified individual on the basis of disability, including but not limited to discharging any qualified employee because of his or her disability.

5. [A.I.C.], its officers, agents, employees, successors, and all those in active concert or participation with them, or any of them, and [defendant C], shall not engage in retaliation or reprisal of any kind against any person because of such person's opposition to any practice made unlawful under the ADA; because of such person's filing a charge, testifying, or participating in any manner in any investigation, proceeding, or hearing under the ADA; because such person was identified as a potential witness for the EEOC in this action, or in the investigation giving rise to this action, or because such person asserts any right under this Judgment.

6. Within seven (7) days of the entry of this Judgment, [A.I.C.] and [defendant C] shall provide a copy of the Notice attached as Exhibit A to every employee of [A.I.C.]. In addition, [A.I.C.] and [defendant C] shall post a copy of the Notice on the premises of [A.I.C.] in a conspicuous location. Further, all new employees of [A.I.C.] are to be given a copy of this notice in [A.I.C.]'s Employee Handbook or Training Manual.

7. [A.I.C.] and [defendant C] shall maintain, and keep available for inspection and copying by the EEOC, records providing the following information with respect to any employee who is disabled within the meaning of the ADA: name, address, telephone number, Social Security number, date of hire, date of disciplinary action, if applicable, date of discharge, if applicable, and reason for any adverse employment action.

8. Every six (6) months for the duration of this Judgment, [A.I.C.] and [defendant C] shall provide to the EEOC a report including the information set forth in the records described in Paragraph 7.

9. For the purposes of paragraphs four (4) through eight (8) above, this judgment shall remain in effect for a period of three years from the date of entry.[93]

---

[93] EEOC v. A.I.C. Sec. Investigations, Ltd., 823 F. Supp. 571, 581 (N.D Ill. 1993) (judgment), *aff'd in part, rev'd in part,* 55 F.3d 1276 (7th Cir. 1995) (affirming compensatory damages award of $50,000 and punitive damages award of $150,000 against corporation, but reversing award against individual).

[5]   Preliminary Injunction

FORM 17–15[94]   **Sample Preliminary Injunction**

ORDER

On [February 1, 1994], the Court held a consolidated trial and hearing pursuant to Fed. R. Civ. P. 65(a)(2) on plaintiff's application for a preliminary injunction in the above-styled matter.

Consistent with the contemporaneously filed Memorandum, the Court hereby GRANTS [Miss Thomas]'s application for preliminary injunction. Accordingly, a preliminary injunction is ENTERED PROHIBITING defendant [Davidson Academy] from enforcing the decision to expel [Miss Thomas] or otherwise to interfere with her continued enrollment at [Davidson Academy]; and PROHIBITING [Davidson Academy] and its officials and employees from retaliating, coercing, intimidating, threatening, or interfering with [Miss Thomas] in the exercise and enjoyment of her rights as granted under the Americans with Disabilities Act of 1990 and the Rehabilitation Act of 1973. The Court waives any requirement for security under Fed. R. Civ. P. 65(c). Furthermore, the Court retains jurisdiction of this case through the remainder of the [1993–1994] academic calendar.

[6]   Temporary Restraining Order in Title II Case

FORM 17–16[95]   **Sample Temporary Restraining Order in Title II Case**

TEMPORARY RESTRAINING ORDER

WHEREAS, pursuant to Fed. R. Civ. P. 65(b), the court finds that the exceptions to the ban on open burning found in [Ordinance 105.05] of the [City of Mallard] pose a threat of irreparable harm to the life and health of plaintiff [Heather K.] in violation of Title II of the Americans with Disabilities Act, 42 U.S.C. §§ 12,131 *et seq.,* the following sections of [City of Mallard] [Ordinance 105.05] are, for the [10] days following issuance of this order, hereby temporarily restrained and enjoined upon the terms stated.

1. [Ordinance 105.05], [subparagraph 1.], which permits *recreational fires*, defined as open fires for cooking, heating, recreation, and ceremonies, provided

---

[94] Form 17-15 represents the text of a typical injunction granted under the ADA. This order was issued as part of the proceedings in Thomas v. Davidson Academy, 846 F. Supp. 611, 620 (M.D. Tenn. 1994) (preliminary injunction based on failure to exercise leniency with respect to student's outburst caused by fear of bleeding associated with blood disorder).

[95] Form 17-16 represents a temporary restraining order from an actual ADA Title II, ADA §§ 201–246, 42 U.S.C. §§ 12,131–12,165 (1994) [hereinafter Title II], case. The source of this restraining order is Heather K. v. City of Mallard, 887 F. Supp. 1249 (N.D. Iowa 1995).

they comply with the limits for emissions of visible air contaminants established by the State Department of Natural Resources, . . . is temporarily restrained and enjoined, with the exception that recreational fires pursuant to this subparagraph shall be permitted on [Sunday], [May 28, 1995], and [Monday], [May 29, 1995], in observance of the National Holiday of Memorial Day. Nothing in this court's order shall be construed as restraining or enjoining the ordinary use of outdoor cooking appliances such as charcoal or gas grills, barbecues, or hibachis, and like outdoor cooking fire receptacles at any time during the effective period of this temporary restraining order.

2. [Ordinance 105.05], [subparagraph 2.], which permits *backyard burning*, defined as backyard burning of residential waste at dwellings of four-family units or less, . . . is temporarily restrained and enjoined in its entirety for the duration of this temporary restraining order.

3. [Ordinance 105.05], [subparagraph 3.], which permits *training fires*, defined as fires set for the purpose of bona fide training of public or industrial employees in *fire*fighting methods, provided that the Executive Director receives notice in writing at least one week before such action commences, . . . is temporarily restrained and enjoined only to the extent that the [City of Mallard] shall provide notice by personal service to plaintiffs herein of the occurrence of any such training fires not less than 24 hours before any such fires are scheduled to commence.

4. [Ordinance 105.05], [subparagraph 4.], which permits any "variance" in the following terms — "any person wishing to conduct open burning of materials not permitted herein may make application for a variance to the Executive Director" — . . . is temporarily restrained and enjoined only to the extent that the [City of Mallard] shall provide notice by personal service to plaintiffs herein of the occurrence of any such variance fires not less than 24 hours before any such fires are scheduled to commence.

This temporary restraining order shall be binding upon the parties to this action, their officers, agents, servants, employees, and attorneys, and upon those persons in active concert or participation with them who receive actual notice of the order.

The [City of Mallard], [Iowa], shall provide notice of this temporary restraining order by posting notice copies of this temporary restraining order in such public places as are reasonably calculated to give reasonable notice to the citizens of [Mallard] of the existence and terms of the temporary restraining order not later than 24 hours following the date and time on which this order is signed and filed with the Clerk of Court for the [Northern] District of [Iowa].

IT IS SO ORDERED.

[7] Notice to Employees

FORM 17–17   Sample Notice to Employees

IN THE UNITED STATES DISTRICT COURT FOR THE [NORTHERN]
DISTRICT OF [ILLINOIS]
[EASTERN] DIVISION

U.S. EQUAL EMPLOYMENT OPPORTUNITY COMMISSION,
Plaintiff,
v.   Civil Action No. [92 C 7330]
[A.I.C. SECURITY INVESTIGATIONS, LTD.];
[A.I.C. INTERNATIONAL, LTD.];
and [unnamed defendant C],
Defendants.   Magistrate Judge [Guzman]

NOTICE TO ALL EMPLOYEES OF [A.I.C.]

This Notice is being posted by order of the Court in a lawsuit brought against [A.I.C. SECURITY INVESTIGATIONS, LTD. ("A.I.C.")] and [defendant C] by the Equal Employment Opportunity Commission ("EEOC") and [Charles H. Wessel]. In the suit a federal jury has determined that [A.I.C.] and [defendant C] violated the Americans with Disabilities Act ("ADA") by discharging [Charles H. Wessel] from his position as Executive Director of [A.I.C.] because of his disability. [A.I.C.] and defendants have been ordered by the Court to pay to [Charles H. Wessel] backpay, compensatory damages, including damages for mental distress, and punitive damages.

Under the Court's Judgment, [A.I.C.] and [defendant C] have been ordered not to discriminate against any qualified employee or applicant for employment because of his or her disability. The Court has also ordered [A.I.C.] and [defendant C] not to retaliate against any person who participated in the EEOC's investigation or trial of the case, or who exercises his or her rights under this Notice.

Should you have any complaints of discrimination on the basis of disability, you can contact the EEOC at [536 South Clark Street], [Room 982], [Chicago], [Illinois] [60605]. The EEOC charges no fee for their services and has employees that speak languages other than English. The EEOC's offices are accessible to the disabled.

THIS IS AN OFFICIAL NOTICE AND MUST
NOT BE DEFACED BY ANYONE

This Notice must remain posted for three (3) years from the date shown above and must not be altered, defaced, or covered by any other material. Any questions

345

concerning this Notice or compliance with its provisions should be directed to the EEOC, at the address shown above.[96]

---

[96] EEOC v. A.I.C. Sec. Investigations, Ltd., 823 F. Supp. 571, 582 (N.D. Ill. 1993), *aff'd in part, rev'd in part,* 55 F.3d 1276 (7th Cir. 1995) (affirming compensatory damages award of $50,000 and punitive damages award of $150,000 against corporation, but reversing award against individual).

CHAPTER 18

PREVENTIVE MATERIALS

§ 18.01 INTRODUCTION AND OVERVIEW

The purpose of the Americans with Disabilities Act (ADA)[1] is not to increase the number of lawsuits brought by disabled persons but to change behavior by public and private institutions to increase the opportunities available to the disabled. Accordingly, as important as the legal theories and the institutional procedures analyzed in other parts of this book are, the practical steps that can be taken by employers, government entities, and places of public accommodation to improve opportunities for the disabled are equally important. This chapter outlines some of those practical steps. Following these steps not only will increase opportunities for the disabled but also will reduce the likelihood of being sued and losing.

Section 18.02 suggests some matters of general philosophy that apply to all kinds of entities covered by the ADA. The chapter then provides materials that employers, government entities, and places of public accommodation can use to avoid the need for the rest of the materials in this book. The chapter provides a significant amount of strategic and tactical analysis in terms of how personnel procedures and employee handbooks should be written, in addition to actual language that can be adapted to particular employer circumstances.[2] In addition to substantive rules, employer commitments, and policy statements,[3] this chapter also provides language by which employers can avoid legal liability based on breach of contract, model procedures for handling claims of disability discrimination, and requests for accommodation of disabilities.

§ 18.02 MATTERS OF GENERAL PHILOSOPHY

Compliance with the spirit of the ADA requires adherence to the following principles:

1. To accept the proposition that the majority of physically and mentally disabled persons can participate meaningfully in employment and other kinds of activities and programs from which they historically were excluded;
2. To identify specific barriers to meaningful participation by physically and mentally disabled persons;
3. To evaluate the necessity of these barriers to the essential nature of the activity;

---

[1] Pub. L. No. 101-336, 104 Stat. 327 (1990) (codified at 42 U.S.C. §§ 12,101–12,213 (1994); 47 U.S.C. §§ 225, 711 (1994)) [hereinafter ADA].

[2] *See* Forms 18–6, 18–7, 18–18, and 18–19, and Forms 18–21 through 18–23.

[3] *See* Form 18–2.

4. To be willing to remove nonessential barriers when that can be done at reasonable costs;

5. To engage in a dialogue with disabled persons and their representatives to understand the kinds of barrier removal and other accommodation that might improve opportunities for the disabled without imposing great costs on institutions.

§ 18.03 OVERVIEW OF EMPLOYER ATTITUDES AND ACTION

The first step is to understand the basics of the ADA, as explained in earlier chapters. The core employment requirements of the ADA are

1. Not disqualifying disabled applicants or employees because of their inability to perform marginal or nonessential job functions

2. Requiring employers to demonstrate the job-relatedness and business necessity of the requirements or selection criteria that tend to screen out disabled applicants

3. Requiring employers to make reasonable accommodations to assist disabled applicants or employees in meeting legitimate criteria.[4]

Employers who seek to develop an implementation plan can use the following basic approach:[5]

1. Employers should identify barriers to equal employment opportunities for disabled applicants and employees;

2. Employers should identify possible accommodations;

3. Employers should assess the reasonableness of each accommodation;

4. Employers should implement the accommodation that is most reasonable for both the employer and the employee.[6]

This four-step process should be applied with respect to each stage of the employment relationship, beginning with the recruitment process.

---

[4] H.R. Rep. No. 485, 101st Cong., 2d Sess., pt. 2 (1990) [hereinafter House Labor Report], at 71.

[5] *Id.* at 66; S. Rep. No. 116, 101st Cong., 1st Sess. (1989) [hereinafter Senate Report], at 35.

[6] House Labor Report at 66; Senate Report at 35. Section 18.07 elaborates on the suggestion by Congress and the Equal Employment Opportunity Commission [hereinafter EEOC] that the process of reasonable accommodation should be an interactive one involving both the employer and the disabled employee.

§ 18.04 EMPLOYMENT CONTACTS

[A] Generally

Employers should review the major types of communication they initiate with the outside world in connection with employment. The types of communication are described below.

[B] Sample Forms

[1] Policy Statement on Disability Discrimination in Employment[7]

FORM 18–1   Sample Disability Discrimination Policy Statement

The employer takes its obligations under the Americans with Disabilities Act and applicable state disability and handicap discrimination statutes seriously. Accordingly, it does not refuse to hire, dismiss from employment, or discriminate in compensation or other terms of employment because of an otherwise qualified employee's or applicant's mental or physical disability.

Employees must, however, be able to perform the essential functions of their jobs. It is not illegal discrimination to require that all employees, including those with disabilities, be able to perform the essential functions of their jobs or jobs for which they apply.

It is the employer's responsibility and prerogative to define job functions.

[Include this paragraph only if the reasonable accommodation policy statement in § 18.04[B][3] and the reasonable accommodation procedure in § 18.07 are also included.] If you as an employee believe that job functions have been defined in a way that is inconsistent with the essential character of the job or believe that you have been the victim of discrimination in violation of this policy statement, you may request reasonable accommodation as explained in [§ 18.07] of this policy.

[2] Disability Discrimination and Harassment Policy Statement

FORM 18–2   Sample Disability Discrimination and Harassment Policy Statement

[Company name] has adopted a policy that forbids disability discrimination, including harassment in either a business or personal context. The policy applies to all workplace relationships, not solely to persons in a management or supervisory capacity. Thus, it also applies to people in the same job grade or department. The

---

[7] The statement in Form 18–1 is suited for publication as an internal personnel policy direction to personnel specialists and supervisors. It also could be included in employee handbooks.

behavior could relate to physical actions or verbal or visual communications. It could be open or subtle. But if it is offensive to another, it is forbidden. Violations of the policy subject an employee to the full range of the [company]'s disciplinary policies.

It is the policy of [company] to maintain an employment atmosphere free of any pressures on employees relating to mental or physical disability. Consistent with applicable federal and state laws, [company] endorses the objective that employees be free of situations where disability forms the basis for business decisions.

Disability discrimination or harassment will not be tolerated at [company], and employees who engage in such conduct are subject to the full range of [company]'s disciplinary policies.

[3]   Reasonable Accommodation Policy Statement

FORM 18–3[8]   Sample Reasonable Accommodation Policy Statement

The employer takes seriously its obligations under the Americans with Disabilities Act and applicable state disability and handicap discrimination laws to provide reasonable accommodation to the mental and physical disabilities of employees and applicants for employment. Accordingly, when an employee or applicant requests reasonable accommodation, the employer gives serious consideration to the possibility of special arrangements such as modified work schedules, allowing the employee to use employee-provided special equipment, and modification in job responsibilities. Each request for reasonable accommodation must be considered on its own merits, in light of the particular job, of other related jobs, of the capabilities of the particular employee, and of the specific accommodation requested.

When the employer makes accommodation to the needs of a particular employee, the employer does not make any commitment that these special arrangements are permanent or that they automatically will be extended to any other employee. Rather, the employer must retain its flexibility to reorganize work and to redefine job requirements in light of the overall needs of its business.

[Include the following language only if the reasonable accommodation procedure provided in § 18.07 is included.] These case-by-case evaluations are made under the procedure described in [§ 18.07] of this policy statement (handbook), which is commenced by an individual employee's request for accommodation.

[4]   Employment Advertisements

Advertisements for positions should state that the employer does not discriminate based on disability.[9] A more specific statement like the following should also be considered:

---

[8] The language in Form 18–3 is suitable for inclusion either in a statement of personnel policies for internal use by personnel specialists and supervisors or in an employee handbook.

[9] *See* Form 18–4.

The employer will not refuse to hire a disabled applicant who is capable of performing the essential requirements of the job with reasonable accommodation.

[5] Job Advertisement Language

FORM 18–4   **Sample Job Advertisement Language**

The [name] company does not discriminate based on physical or mental disability and makes reasonable accommodation to permit disabled persons to perform essential job functions.

[6] Job Applications

Employment application forms should repeat the same nondiscrimination notice selected by the employer for advertisements. In addition, the application should invite applicants to identify any disability for which the applicant seeks accommodation.

Requesting information about disabilities on applications is tricky. The request must be framed so as to avoid violating the ADA's limitations on requiring information.[10] Nevertheless, inviting voluntary disclosure puts both the employer and the applicant in a better practical position to assess the feasibility of accommodating disabilities. It also may put the employer in a better position to defend the claim of disability discrimination by an employee who failed to disclose the disability.

Language like the following should be considered:

You are not required to disclose information about physical or mental limitations that you believe will not interfere with your capability to do the job. On the other hand, if you want the employer to consider special arrangements to accommodate a physical or mental impairment, you may identify that impairment in the space provided and suggest the kind of accommodation that you believe would be appropriate.

Permitting the employee to suggest the kind of accommodation the employee believes to be appropriate is responsive to the language in the ADA's legislative history on the best way to begin a dialogue about reasonable accommodation.[11]

Title I,[12] the employment title, of the ADA forces employers to design job application procedures differently than most employers have designed

---

[10] *See* Chapter 4.

[11] House Labor Report at 65–66 (suggesting problem-solving approach involving affected employee).

[12] ADA §§ 101–108, 42 U.S.C. §§ 12,111–12,117 (1994) [hereinafter Title I].

them in the past. The ADA requires the elimination of all potential sources of discrimination against disabled individuals during job application procedures.[13] This requirement certainly extends to questions asked in job applications.

Employers have traditionally asked applicants about their physical and mental well-being in job applications. Under the ADA, however, employers can no longer ask applicants about their health or medical history.[14] These restrictions are designed to make employers base their selection decisions solely on the qualifications of the applicants. The intent of the ADA requirements is, therefore, to try to ensure that employers will hire the most qualified applicant, the applicant who is able to perform the essential job functions, with or without reasonable accommodations, for all vacant positions.

To adhere to the ADA requirements and thereby minimize the risk of discrimination claims by disabled individuals, employers must be attentive to what must be excluded from job applications rather than to what is included in them. Employers must eliminate all inquiries in job applications that could possibly be interpreted as seeking information about disabilities suffered by the applicants. Furthermore, an application may not ask whether the applicant will need reasonable accommodations to perform the essential job functions because a disabled applicant could perceive this information as discriminatory.[15]

Only after an employer offers a position to an applicant should the applicant's need for reasonable accommodations be brought up. At this point, the employer will have already selected the most qualified applicant for the job, and reasonable accommodations must be made for that applicant to perform the essential job functions as long as providing the accommodations does not cause an undue hardship to the entity.

A goal of the ADA is to prevent a job applicant's disability from being a source of discrimination against the applicant by a potential employer. The

---

[13] ADA § 102(a)–(b), 42 U.S.C. § 12,112(a)–(b) (1994). *See* Form 18–5.

[14] ADA § 102(c)(1)(A), 42 U.S.C. § 12,112(c)(1)(A) (1994). The entity can, however, inquire about an applicant's ability to perform job-related functions. ADA § 102(c)(1)(B), 42 U.S.C. § 12,112(c)(1)(B) (1994). Nonetheless, an applicant can be excluded from consideration for a position only if the applicant will not be able to perform the essential job functions after reasonable accommodations have been made for the applicant's disability.

[15] An example of an acceptable job application inquiry is: "Can you lift a 50-pound box with or without reasonable accommodations for any disability from which you may suffer (answer "yes" or "no" only)?" It is important to note that this question does not require an individual to disclose whether he or she is disabled. A disabled individual who can perform the essential job function only after reasonable accommodations have been made for that individual's disability will answer this question with the same response ("yes") as a non-disabled individual who requires no accommodations. Therefore, the employer has no way of telling whether the applicant is disabled.

ADA does not require that employers give preference to disabled job applicants. However, it does require that employers give them the same opportunities for employment as are given to nondisabled applicants. The best way of ensuring that employers treat all applicants equally is to eliminate all possible sources of discrimination against disabled individuals. Because job applications are one of the first and most important communications between a job applicant and an employer, it is imperative that the employer adhere to the antidiscrimination requirements of the ADA when drafting job applications. The possible repercussions of a discrimination claim against an employer far outweigh any benefits from the additional knowledge an employer may gain through even borderline discriminatory questions in a job application.

[7] Interviews and Disability Checklist[16]

Interviews are inherently harder to manage than applications and advertisement because there is a greater risk of conflicting post hoc testimony regarding what went on in the interview. Employers should consider supplying explicit guidelines to all persons conducting employment interviews, with strict instructions not to deviate from those guidelines on the subject of disabilities.

The following checklist is a starting point:

_____ Do not ask about mental or physical impairments unless the employee brings up the subject explicitly or unless the employee has disclosed a disability on the employment application.

_____ State emphatically the employer's commitment to provide a discrimination-free workplace for disabled applicants and employees, including the making of reasonable accommodation to disabilities, as soon as the subject of disability comes up.

_____ Limit preemployment inquiries to asking whether an applicant can perform particular job functions. EEOC and Department of Justice Questions and Answers (Q&A) say that employers should not make preemployment inquiries on application forms or in interviews regarding whether individuals are disabled. "If the applicant has a disability known to the employer, the employer may ask how he or she can perform job functions that the em-

---

[16] Interviewers should not only be trained and rehearsed in the use of these do's and don'ts but should also have copies readily available for reference during the interviewing process.

ployer considers difficult or impossible to perform because of the disability, and whether an accommodation would be needed."[17]

_____ Emphasize that the only purpose for discussing a mental or physical impairment is to ascertain the employee's view on how the disability does not interfere with the performance of essential job functions and the nature of accommodation by the employer that should be considered.[18]

The specific requirements of the job should be discussed and, to the extent the applicant is willing to do so, compared with the applicant's capabilities. If the applicant is rejected for the position, a statement should be given to the applicant explaining how the disability influenced the decision not to hire. This statement should be reviewed with counsel.

The advantage of this approach is that it builds a specific documentation base showing rational consideration of the employer's obligation not to discriminate based on disability. There are major disadvantages, however. For example, the guidelines governing verbal conduct also serve to establish the employer's awareness and consideration of the disability. A determined applicant almost certainly can fashion an argument on how a discriminatory inference can be drawn from the conversation at the interview or from any statement of reasons for rejection.

Employers, therefore, should consider an alternate approach under which the regular interviewers are instructed not to discuss mental or physical impairments under any circumstance. This strategy would instruct the regular interviewers to refer an applicant wishing to discuss the impact of a disability to specialized equal employment counselors. The advantage of this approach is that training on the appropriate treatment of disabled applicants can be focused on a smaller number of personnel. There are, however, two obvious disadvantages: (1) only a large employer can afford specialized personnel; and (2) requiring disabled applicants to undergo a more demanding interview protocol arguably is discriminatory because it represents an additional barrier to employment.

---

[17] U.S. Dep't of Justice, Questions and Answers (rev. Sept. 1992) [hereinafter Q&A], at 5.

[18] If this guideline is subsequently challenged, the employer can point to the language in the ADA's legislative history encouraging such a dialogue. *See* House Labor Report at 65–66.

[8] Job Description[19]

FORM 18–5   Sample Job Description

Secretary
  Supports senior lawyer in all functions.
  Transcribes dictation.
  Uses word processing hardware and software to process 75 words per minute.
  Makes appointments using the telephone.
  Keeps schedule and provides attorney with copies daily.
  Welcomes visitors and makes them feel comfortable.
  Keeps track of deadlines and due dates error-free, advising attorney in advance when actions must be taken.
  Records attorney time.

§ 18.05   PREVIOUS EMPLOYMENT REFERENCES

Policies and procedures should be developed for checking references and other background investigation inquiries on disabled (and nondisabled) applicants. Those making inquiries on behalf of the employer should be instructed not to discuss mental or physical impairments, except strictly according to the following guidelines. Inquiries relating to a disability may be directed to specialized equal employment personnel.

1. The inquiry about the applicant's disability should begin with an emphatic restatement of the employer's commitment to provide equal opportunity for disabled applicants, and should explain that the only reason for asking about the disability is to facilitate making reasonable accommodation;

2. The inquiry should determine as specifically as possible the requirements of the previous job, and any overlap between those requirements and the applicant's impairments;

3. The inquiry should determine as specifically as possible what changes in job duties or assignments were made in order to accommodate the applicant's disability;

4. The inquiry should ascertain as specifically as possible the applicant's previous performance and conduct without regard to the disability, and aspects of performance or conduct on which the disability may have had some influence.

---

[19] Form 18–5 is a good example of a carefully worded job description. It is worded so as to permit auxiliary aids and equipment to accommodate disabilities, and states performance expectations (for example, words per minute and making visitors comfortable).

§ 18.06   EMPLOYMENT TESTING

[A]   Generally

The categories of employment testing covered in the following sections should be undertaken only in conjunction with a clear statement as to the legitimate business need for the testing procedure. This statement need not be disclosed to employees, but it should be available, and it should be in force prior to the filing of any discrimination claim.

[B]   Medical Tests

Medical testing should not be undertaken unless it can be justified on one of the following grounds:

1. It is a preemployment examination that focuses on the ability to perform essential job functions, not on the disabilities of employees or applicants;
2. It is an employment entrance examination uniformly required of all employees, and it produces information that is maintained in confidence to inform supervisors, first aid and safety personnel, and government enforcement personnel about the implications of disabilities;
3. It is another type of medical examination or inquiry and is part of a voluntary employee wellness program, or is aimed solely at determining the ability to perform job-related functions, and can be shown to be job-related and consistent with business necessity.[20]

[C]   Blood Tests

When blood testing or medical testing is justified for drug abuse prevention reasons, the employer should be able to justify the particular procedures used, based on the case law relating to drug testing under federal constitutional constraints and collective bargaining agreements.

Human immunodeficiency virus (HIV) testing for AIDS is particularly difficult to justify. The risk of the invasion of privacy due to inappropriate or inadvertent disclosure is enormous and, because the condition is neither very contagious nor curable, the affirmative reasons for testing are difficult to discover.

[D]   Skill Testing

Skill testing should be undertaken only if the employer has detailed justification for each aspect of the test and can relate each aspect to an

---

[20] *See* ADA § 102(c), 42 U.S.C. § 12,112(c) (1994).

essential function of the job for which an employee/applicant is being tested. Skill tests should be adaptable in order to respond appropriately both to any job requirement identified by the applicant as nonessential and subject to modification as a part of the employer's duty reasonably to accommodate, and to any functions, the performance of which is called into question by the applicant's limitations.

§ 18.07   EMPLOYEE HANDBOOKS AND POLICY STATEMENTS

[A]   Generally

Whenever an employer decides to maintain written employment policies and to give written information to employees in the form of handbooks, the employer and its counsel must navigate among conflicting forces. The purpose of having the written documents is to communicate. Good communication requires clarity and precision, two qualities that are difficult to achieve at the same time. Moreover, especially when the intended audience is the workforce in general, the objective of communicating will be limited by the desire not to stir up problems. For example, a handbook might explain disability discrimination most clearly and precisely by outlining, in some detail, the steps to file a charge with the EEOC or a state agency and then to file suit after a right-to-sue letter is received. It also might explain the different theories of disability discrimination that might be asserted.

Very few employers would want to do this, however. Such detailed explanation of litigation might have the effect of encouraging employees to litigate over borderline cases rather than working them out through internal employer procedures. Indeed, any reference to the rights granted by the ADA might tend to increase litigation beyond what it would be if the employees were wholly ignorant of their rights. Nevertheless, few employers would take the position that disability and other forms of discrimination should never be mentioned in materials prepared for employee consumption.

Striking a balance between these extremes cannot be accomplished mechanically or with a single solution fitting all employers and all situations. Rather, in the end, the language of an employee handbook must feel right to the employer and its counsel. The material presented in this chapter generally strikes a compromise between broad generalities such as "We treat everyone fairly," and extensive detail similar to the terms of a statute, administrative regulation, or formal contract. When major alternatives clearly exist with respect to specificity, the chapter points them out.

There is another matter regarding style. Precision can be the enemy of simplicity and clarity. A good, airtight contract does not necessarily make a good employee handbook, although there is a growing recognition in the legal profession that clarity is clarity regardless of whether legal or ordinary writing is involved and that plain language is a desirable goal in all kinds of writing. The drafter of handbook language must be conscious of writing for a general audience, frequently with limited education and reading comprehension.

The inherent tensions are less with respect to personnel policy statements and manuals intended for internal use by personnel specialists and supervisors. This audience's economic interests and legal claims do not diverge from those of the employer as an entity, so the risk of putting ideas into people's heads is not a significant concern. Also, these audiences usually have somewhat more formal education than the general workforce and can comprehend more complex language and legal explanations.

Still, there is not much point in having separate personnel policy documents that reiterate statutes, administrative regulations, and contracts. The purpose of such separate documents is to simplify, explain, interpret, and define institutional positions.[21] When the details of a legal document are important, it is usually better to quote just the applicable excerpt than to paraphrase the actual document.

If an employer has both an internal personnel policy statement designed for use by personnel specialists and supervisors, and an employee handbook distributed to the workforce in general, the relationship between the two must be considered. In most cases, it is desirable to include the actual, verbatim language of the employee handbook in the personnel policy statement, followed or preceded by additional explanation intended for the policy statement only. Such an approach ensures that the employer is saying the same thing to the general workforce and to supervisors and personnel specialists. It is also more efficient for supervisors and personnel specialists, who need not be inconvenienced by referring to two different documents whenever an issue comes up. Even if the style of the policy statement is more technical and more sophisticated, the pertinent language from the employee handbook can be excerpted and quoted in the policy statement.

[B]   Sample Forms

[1]   Reasonable Accommodation Language[22]

FORM 18–6   **Sample Reasonable Accommodation Language**

If you believe that you have been the victim of discrimination in hiring, compensation, or with respect to other terms of employment, or if you believe that

---

[21] *See* Forms 18–8 through 18–15.

[22] The language in Form 18–6 regarding reasonable accommodation is suitable for inclusion in either a statement of personnel policies for internal use by personnel specialists and supervisors or an employee handbook.

you are about to be laid off or terminated because of a mental or physical disability despite the fact that you are otherwise qualified, you may request review by the [personnel department/human resources department/person to whom your supervisor reports/office of the president].

Also, if you believe that specific accommodation of your mental or physical disability would permit you to perform the essential functions of the job, you may request accommodation through the same procedures.

If you use these procedures, it is your responsibility to identify the specific decision or decisions that you think discriminate against you and/or to suggest the specific changes in work organization or job requirements that would permit you to perform the essential functions of the job despite your disability.

[2] Post-Complaint/Request Procedure Language[23]

FORM 18–7   Sample Post-Complaint/Request Procedure Language

Whenever a complaint of disability discrimination or a request for accommodation is received, it must be forwarded immediately to [the entity or person responsible for coordinating ADA compliance]. The employee should be contacted promptly and a meeting arranged to discuss the complaint or request.

If intentional discrimination is alleged, it may be desirable to schedule an initial meeting without the participation of any supervisor involved in the alleged discrimination. Otherwise, and in all cases when accommodation is requested, the immediate supervisor should participate in the initial meeting. The initial meeting has the following purposes:

(1) To clarify the employee's complaint or request;
(2) To identify any difficulties in remedying the alleged discrimination or in making the requested accommodation;
(3) To discuss other feasible alternatives presenting fewer difficulties for the employer;
(4) To establish an action plan for follow-up, with specific responsibilities assigned to the participants.

Ordinarily, it is desirable to list any matters agreed to and any follow-up steps at the end of the meeting and have the employee initial the summary. It is not necessary, and probably better, that the list not be typed and formalized.

The participants should not commit themselves in this meeting to the existence of discrimination or to specific changes in work organization or job requirements until further review can be done after the meeting.

---

[23] The language in Form 18–7 is appropriate for a personnel policy statement designed for internal use by personnel specialists and supervisors. It is not, however, as suitable for an employee handbook.

[3]   Disability Discrimination or Harassment Complaint Procedure

FORM 18–8   Sample Disability Discrimination or Harassment
               Complaint Procedure

Procedure for the Filing and Disposition of Complaints of
Disability Discrimination or Harassment

I. Introduction

[Name] University has issued a policy statement condemning disability discrimination as violative of its own standards and those of applicable federal and
state law. This procedure provides the structure for the filing and resolution of
complaints of disability discrimination relating to the employment life of its employees and educational experience of its students. All allegations of disability
discrimination that occur subsequent to the date on which the underlying policy is
adopted by the board of trustees shall be subject to this procedure, except where
neither complainant nor respondent has any role as an evaluator one of the other.
In cases covered by this exception, the procedure set forth in the University's
student handbook or applicable "Code of Conduct" shall apply.

II. Established Resources and Considerations

Confidentiality is essential in any effort to investigate and resolve allegations
of disability discrimination. The interests of both the complainant and the respondent must be protected as information is gathered and evaluated. Therefore, only
persons who have a "need to know" within the investigation and resolution of
complaints and appropriate senior administrative officials are entitled to information
in the application of this procedure. University employees or students who disclose
to persons not in the "need to know" chain information that is obtained within the
informal or formal steps of this procedure will be subject to disciplinary action.

The president shall make a standing appointment of one or more members of
the faculty, administration, or staff to serve as the complaint officer. This person is
responsible to determine at the first formal step if alleged disability discrimination
may have occurred. As provided in this procedure, the complaint officer also is
responsible to convene the review board and to provide such administrative assistance as the board may request. However, it is the expectation that the officer would
not attend the proceedings of the board.

A review board may be established as provided in this procedure. The board's
function is to review referrals from the complaint officer and also any appeals of
the decisions of the complaint officer as provided for in this procedure. The review
board comprises three members: one is appointed by the complainant, one is appointed by the respondent, and the third person to serve as chairperson is appointed
by the complaint officer. The board is empowered to convene appropriate hearings
and to keep its own records in a format determined for each respective case. The
board's procedures may include by example, but are not limited to, such approaches

as open or closed hearings, individual interviews, and the examination of written documentation.

However, the board is not bound by rules of judicial or administrative hearing procedures or by formal rules of evidence.

III. Informal Procedure

The university encourages its members to attempt informal resolution of complaints of disability discrimination. The university has many offices and individuals who may be able to provide counseling on a confidential basis for a person who believes that he or she is the victim of disability discrimination. The departments of [names of departments] are staffed with caring and experienced human resources and development specialists who may be able to help resolve concerns on an ad hoc and confidential basis.

IV. Formal Procedure

When a person is unable to resolve a problem of disability discrimination informally, the following procedure may be invoked for the formal examination of the allegation:

1. A formal, written complaint, utilizing the university's standard form, shall be submitted to the university complaint officer. The purpose of the complaint form is to assist the complainant in formulating a concise statement of his/her concern and to assist the complaint officer to see the basic facts of the allegation, along with the complainant's requested remedy. The complaint must be filed no later than [six months] from the date on which the subject conduct allegedly occurred.

2. The complaint officer shall review the charges made in the complaint with the complainant, shall provide guidance and counseling as to the complainant's options and available procedures, and shall make such investigation of the charges as the officer may deem appropriate. In order to achieve a complete review of the case, the officer shall notify the respondent of the complaint and confer as necessary with the respondent. With the approval of both the complainant and the respondent, the complaint officer may attempt private mediation in an effort to resolve the alleged problem without the need for additional proceedings.

3. Within [20] business days of receiving the complaint, the complaint officer shall issue a written report on the case to the complainant and respondent.

(a) If the complaint officer finds that the case cannot reasonably be construed to constitute disability discrimination or that there is insufficient information to conclude that disability discrimination may have occurred, the complaint officer shall file a report closing the case and stating the reasons why the complaint should be dismissed. The complaint officer shall also advise the complainant in the written report that the decision may be appealed to the review board. The complainant must notify the complaint officer of his/her desire to appeal the decision within [five] business days of the officer's decision.

(b) If the complaint officer decides that the case can reasonably be construed to have constituted disability discrimination, the complaint officer shall convene a review board.

4. The complainant and the respondent will each designate his/her board member, and the complaint officer will designate the chairperson of the board, all within [15] business days of the issuance of the complaint officer's report. Within [10] business days of the appointment of the board, the board shall begin its proceedings.

In appearances before the board, the complainant and the respondent may each be accompanied by an adviser of their own choosing who is a member of the university community (current faculty member, administrator, staff member, or student).

The board will render its conclusions in a written report no later than [20] business days from the date of the board's initiation of the proceedings. The board's report shall be limited to findings of fact and the conclusions of whether or not disability discrimination occurred. The report shall be delivered to the complaint officer and to the vice president responsible for the area in which the respondent employee is assigned, or to the judicial affairs officer if the respondent is a student and the complainant is not.

The vice president and/or the judicial affairs officer shall communicate the board's conclusions to the complainant and the respondent. It is the sole responsibility of the vice president or judicial affairs officer to determine and take any disciplinary action based on the report provided by the board.

5. When the vice president or judicial affairs officer takes disciplinary action against the respondent, the respondent may utilize the existing applicable university grievance procedure to dispute the discipline.

[4]   Disability Discrimination Complaint Form

FORM 18–9   Sample Disability Discrimination Complaint Form

[Name] University Complaint of Disability Discrimination

INFORMATION ON COMPLAINANT:
Name: [_____]
Campus Department/Campus/Home: [_____]
Home Address: [_____]
Telephone: [_____]

INFORMATION ON RESPONDENT:
Name: [_____]
Campus: [_____]
Department Address: [_____]
Explain the actions, events, or other factors and the dates and times of such occurrences that lead you to make this complaint: [_____]
State the action requested to resolve this problem: [_____]
Date: [_____]
Received by: [_____]

Date: [_____]
Signed: [_____]

[5] Internal Report of Accommodation Request

FORM 18–10 **Sample Internal Report of Accommodation Request**

**[Name] Corporation Americans with Disabilities Act
Accommodation Consideration**

Name [_____] Employee No. [_____]
Dept. [_____] Craft [_____] Location [_____]
Description of Disability: [_____]
Description of Essential Job Functions: [_____]
Nature of Impact of Disability on Essential Function Performance: [_____]
Has the employee requested an accommodation? If so, explain and comment:
[_____]
Please Return to: [_____]
　　　　　[address]
　　　(If there is not adequate space, use reverse side or attach other documentation.)

[6] Post-Complaint/Request Procedure

After the initial meeting, the personnel specialist, the supervisor, and other management and human resources or position control and compensation personnel should consider the differences between the job requirements or work organization as it existed up to that point and the work organization or job requirements suggested by the employee or applicant. The following questions must be addressed:

1. Should accommodation be made only for this individual, or is it appropriate to redefine the work organization or job requirements permanently in order to reduce the likelihood of future problems?
2. What are the costs of making the requested accommodation, both in quantitative dollar terms and in other less quantifiable terms?
3. Are there other ways to accommodate the particular disability at lower cost?
4. What is the possibility of significant ripple effects if the request for alternative accommodation is made? (Will it destabilize the compensation structure? Will it make position descriptions in general and job titles incoherent?)
5. What are the estimates of the likely costs of not providing accommodations when there are major costs associated with the requested

accommodation?[24] More precise estimates may require assistance of counsel.

When there are major conflicts between the accommodation that appears necessary to prevent major ADA claim costs and other needs of the entity with respect to compensation and position control policy, the conflicts should be explained in writing, the major alternatives should be identified, and a recommendation should be made to the lowest level authority in the employing entity that has authority over both of the conflicting functions. For example, if the conflict is between the compensation policy and the management of employee discrimination claim risks, the matter should be referred up the chain of command until an officer is reached who has authority over both the compensation policy and employee claims risk management functions.

[7]   Handbook on Requests for Accommodation

FORM 18–11   **Sample Handbook on Requests for Accommodation**

A GUIDE FOR [corporation name] EMPLOYEES:
UNDERSTANDING TITLE I OF THE AMERICANS WITH
DISABILITIES ACT
EFFECTIVE: JULY 26, 2002
RESOURCE DEVELOPMENT
JULY 2002
[name] CORPORATION
EQUAL EMPLOYMENT OPPORTUNITY

It has always been the policy of [name] Corporation to afford equal employment opportunity to all qualified individuals regardless of race, sex, age, national origin, religion, sexual orientation, and disability. It is also the policy of the Corporation to make reasonable accommodation for otherwise qualified individuals with disabilities.

It is critical to [corporation] success that it values employees who desire to be productive partners in helping the Corporation attain its goals. Accordingly, and in keeping with our obligation under the Americans with Disabilities Act, we will support our employees and those candidates for employment who are affected by physical or mental impairments that may limit their opportunities to be productive. As appropriate, we will work to eliminate artificial or real barriers to productive employment and to afford qualified individuals with opportunities to pursue available employment to the full extent of their abilities and talents.

ALL EMPLOYEES are expected to cooperate and to support actively the efforts to ensure that this policy will be effective. Employees with questions about

---

[24] When precise cost estimates are needed, the assistance of counsel may be required.

the policy or its interpretation and implications should not hesitate to contact their supervisors/managers, the field personnel staff of the Labor Relations Department, and members of the Human Resources and Health Services sections of the Resource Development Department.

[name]
CHAIRMAN, PRESIDENT, & C.E.O.
INTRODUCTION TO THE AMERICANS WITH DISABILITIES ACT

On July 26, 1990, President Bush signed into law the Americans with Disabilities Act ("ADA"). The implications of this law are immense, and it can be considered the most important civil rights statute enacted since the Civil Rights Act of 1964. There are five sections included in the Act:

Title I — Employment
Title II — Public Services and Transportation
Title III — Public Accommodations/Commercial Facilities
Title IV — Telecommunications
Title V — Miscellaneous

While each of these sections may affect [corporation] and its employees, Titles I and III have the most significant impact. Title III covers buildings and facilities that are accessible to the public, and Title I establishes provisions for equitable dealing with employees or candidates for employment. Title I will be the principal focus of these guidelines.

Title I makes it unlawful to discriminate in all aspects of employment against a qualified individual with a disability, as long as that individual can perform the ESSENTIAL FUNCTIONS of the job. This includes an obligation for employers to provide REASONABLE ACCOMMODATION for individuals with disabilities unless doing so would cause an UNDUE HARDSHIP on the operation of the business.

All employees need to understand the Americans with Disabilities Act and how it affects them at work. The following section defines a number of the critical terms included in Title I.

DEFINITIONS

Qualified Individual with a Disability: A qualified individual with a disability is a person who can perform those functions/tasks that are essential to the job, with or without reasonable accommodation, and who can satisfy job requirements such as education, experience, skills, licenses, and any other job-related qualification standards.

Disability: A disability is a physical or mental impairment that substantially limits one or more major life activities.

• Examples of physical or mental impairments include
  Orthopedic Impairments

369

>   Visual Impairments
>   Speech Impairments
>   HIV Infection
>   Cancer
>   Heart Disease
>   Hearing Impairments
>   Cerebral Palsy
>   Muscular Dystrophy
>   Multiple Sclerosis
>   Specific Learning Disabilities
>   Diabetes
>   Mental Retardation
>   Emotional Illness
>   Alcoholism
>   Epilepsy

*   Major life activities include hearing, seeing, walking, speaking, breathing, performing manual tasks, caring for oneself, learning, and working.

Essential Functions: Essential functions are those job functions that the individual who holds the position must be able to perform unaided or with a reasonable accommodation.

*   Factors in considering whether a job function is essential:
    _____ Employer's established job description.
    _____ Actual work experience of other incumbents of the same position.
    _____ Amount of time spent performing the function.
    _____ Consequences of not requiring employee to perform the function.

Reasonable Accommodation: A reasonable accommodation is any modification or adjustment to the work environment or to the manner in which a job is customarily performed that enables a qualified individual with a disability to perform the essential functions of the job.

*   Reasonable accommodation need not be made if it would impose an undue hardship on the employer:
    _____ Undue hardship means more than a minimal expense or inconvenience.
    _____ Difficulty or expense must be significant not to be reasonable.

*   An accommodation need not be the best or most expensive one available, so long as it is effective.

*   An employer is not required to provide an accommodation that is primarily for personal use.

MORE INFORMATION ABOUT THE DISABLED AND THE ADA

According to U.S. government statistics, there are 43 million Americans with disabilities, and, of these, approximately 30 percent are of working age. Almost 70 percent of that group are unemployed, but, as a group, they may be the best-educated group of unemployed people. When the disabled have been employed, they have generally established better attendance, productivity, and accident records, and have less turnover, than those employees who are not disabled.

Here are some questions and answers that may help you understand how the ADA affects [corporation] and its employees:

Q. Is [corporation] required to hire a certain number of people with disabilities?

A. No. There are no quotas, minimum hiring standards, or special reporting requirements. However, [corporation] is required to make hiring decisions based on an individual's abilities, not his/her disabilities.

Q. Does the ADA affect only the hiring process?

A. No. It affects all aspects of employment, including testing, evaluation, discipline, training, promotion, medical examinations, termination, leaves of absence, benefits, compensation, and layoff/furlough.

Q. If an employee is returning from layoff/furlough with restrictions/disabilities, does [corporation] have to employ them?

A. Yes, if the employee can perform the essential functions of the job, with or without accommodation. The ADA applies to employees returning to active service just as it applies to candidates for employment.

Q. Doesn't the ADA increase litigation and [corporation]'s liability?

A. Because of the way the law is written (not all regulations and remedies are clearly defined), some litigation is inevitable. The most effective protection is complete and voluntary compliance with the ADA.

Q. What kind of steps have to be taken to comply with the ADA?

A. There are too many steps to outline all of them in this booklet, but some of the more critical steps are

_____ Establish job descriptions that differentiate between essential and marginal functions for each job or group of jobs.

_____ Provide procedures for determining whether an accommodation is appropriate and reasonable.

_____ Train employees to focus on a person's abilities and not on his/her disabilities.

_____ Change certain medical examination processes.

_____ Establish a resource which supervisors and employees can contact for clarification and advice on ADA requirements.

Q. How should job descriptions be developed, and what are the specific uses for which they are used?

A. Job descriptions are developed for each unique job or group of jobs using a panel of job function "experts." The Association of [name] has a computer database and application program developed to assist [member businesses] in this effort.

Once a job description is finalized, it is available to aid in the determination of whether an employee can perform the essential functions of the position with or without reasonable accommodations. The job description also can be used in assisting in the determination of whether a reasonable accommodation can be made in the duties of the job and will be helpful to our Health Services personnel in the areas of rehabilitation and job-oriented physical examinations.

DO'S AND DON'TS WHEN INTERVIEWING

The ADA imposes certain responsibilities, and prohibits certain areas of discussion, in regard to preemployment interviews and examinations. Every employee whose duties involve any participation in a selection process must be familiar with these requirements and prohibitions. It should be noted that these provisions apply to all selection processes, whether they involve new hirings or existing employees.

An employer may not make any preemployment inquiries regarding disability but may ask questions about the ability to perform specific job functions and may, with certain limitations, ask individuals with a disability to describe or demonstrate how they would perform those functions.

Some examples of questions that may be asked are

_____ DO inquire about an individual's ability to perform specific (both essential and marginal) job functions, tasks, or duties, as long as these questions are not phrased in terms of a disability.

_____ DO ask, "Are you able to perform these tasks with or without an accommodation?" If the individual indicates that the tasks can be performed with an accommodation, then you may ask, "How would you perform the tasks, and with what accommodation(s)?"

_____ DO describe or demonstrate a particular job function and inquire whether the individual can perform that function with or without a reasonable accommodation.

_____ DO say, "Our business hours are 9:00 A.M. to 5:00 P.M. Will you be able to work those hours?"

_____ DO say, "These are the tasks of the job. How would you complete each task?"

_____ DO ask, "Is there any reason you cannot perform the requirements of the job?"

_____ DO ask, "Can you lift 50 pounds (or 100 pounds) without difficulty?" (But only ask this question if those lifting requirements are an essential function of the job.)

The following questions and similar questions are not to be used:

_____ DON'T make an inquiry about a disability, or about the nature or severity of a disability. (Such an inquiry must not be done directly, in writing, or in background or reference checks.)

_____ DON'T ask about the condition causing the disability.

_____ DON'T ask, "Do you have any physical defects that preclude you from performing certain kinds of work?"

_____ DON'T ask, "Do you have any disabilities or impairments that may affect your performance in the position for which you are applying?"

_____ DON'T ask, "Are you taking any prescribed drugs?"

_____ DON'T ask, "Have you ever been treated for drug addiction or alcoholism?"

_____ DON'T make any medical inquiry or give a preemployment medical examination prior to making a conditional offer of employment.

_____ DON'T ask whether an individual has a disability.

_____ DON'T ask how a particular individual became disabled or the prognosis of the individual's disability.

_____ DON'T ask, "Have you ever been hospitalized? If so, for what condition?"

_____ DON'T ask, "Have you ever been treated by a psychiatrist or psychologist? if so, for what condition?"

_____ DON'T ask, "Is there any health-related reason you may not be able to perform the job for which you are applying?"

_____ DON'T ask, "Do you expect to go to the doctor frequently?"

_____ DON'T ask, "Have you ever submitted a claim for Workers' Compensation?"

_____ DON'T ask, "How many days were you absent from work because of illness last year?"

_____ DON'T ask, "Do you have a disability that would prevent you from doing the job?"

_____ DON'T ask, "Do you have a bad back that would prevent you from doing heavy lifting?"

If an individual has a known disability that might interfere or prevent performance of job functions, they may, however, be asked to describe or demonstrate how these functions will be performed, with or without an accommodation.

If a known disability would not interfere with performance of job functions, an individual may be required to describe or demonstrate how they will perform a job only if this is required of all applicants for the position.

THE REASONABLE ACCOMMODATION PROCESS

REASONABLE ACCOMMODATIONS

An employer must provide a reasonable accommodation to the known physical or mental limitations of a qualified applicant or employee with a disability, unless it can show that the accommodation would cause an undue hardship on the operation of its business.

The reasonable accommodation process will require the close cooperation between the hiring department, human resources, and health services.

WORKING THROUGH THE REASONABLE ACCOMMODATION PROCESS

Once it is acknowledged/understood that an accommodation must be considered, the following steps should be taken:

_____ Analyze the particular job and determine its essential functions.

_____ Confer with the individual with a disability and ascertain

- The job-related limitations; and

- How a reasonable accommodation would lessen those limitations.

_____ Identify possible accommodations and assess the cost and effectiveness of each.

_____ Allow and invite the individuals to suggest specific accommodations.

_____ Determine which reasonable accommodations would not create an undue hardship.

_____ Ask the individual with a disability about his or her preference for a reasonable accommodation.

_____ Select the accommodation that is most appropriate for both the employer and the disabled applicant or employee. It is the employer's privilege to select among alternative accommodations, but the preference of the qualified individual with a disability should be weighed carefully.

EXAMPLES OF REASONABLE ACCOMMODATIONS

_____ Making facilities readily accessible to, and usable by, an individual with a disability.

_____ Restructuring a job by reallocating or redistributing marginal job functions.

_____ Altering when or how an essential job function is performed.

_____ Establishing part-time or modified work schedules.

_____ Obtaining or modifying equipment or devices.

_____ Modifying examinations, training materials, or policies.

_____ Providing qualified readers or interpreters.

_____ Reassigning the individual to a vacant position.

_____ Permitting use of accrued paid leave or unpaid leave for necessary treatment.

_____ Providing reserved parking for a person with a mobility impairment.

_____ Allowing an employee to utilize equipment or devices that an employer is not required to provide.

EXAMPLES OF FACILITY ACCOMMODATIONS

_____ Installation of ramps.

_____ Removal of raised thresholds.

_____ Rearranging office furniture and equipment.

_____ Making accessible, and providing accessible "path of travel" to, equipment and facilities used by an employee, such as to copying machines, meeting rooms, washrooms, lunchrooms, and lounges.

EXAMPLES OF EQUIPMENT ACCOMMODATIONS

_____ TDDs (Telecommunications Devices for the Deaf) make it possible for people with hearing and/or speech impairments to communicate over the telephone.

_____ Telephone amplifiers are useful for people with hearing impairments.

_____ Special software for standard computers and other equipment can enlarge print or convert print documents to spoken words for people with vision and/or reading disabilities.

_____ Desks or work stations can be modified to accommodate specific physical impairments.

[Corporation]'S INTERNAL DISCRIMINATION COMPLAINT PROCEDURE

[Corporation], since its inception, has fostered the underlying principles of Equal Employment Opportunity and does not condone any acts of discrimination because of age, race, sex, religion, national origin, sexual orientation, or physical or mental disability. Neither does it condone any forms of sexual harassment. In looking toward the future, [corporation] is committed to valuing people for their abilities and contributions.

However, it is recognized that from time to time, there are occurrences that may cause some of us to believe that we are being treated unfairly because of age, sex, race, national origin, sexual orientation, or disability. Each employee has the right and the obligation to bring these occurrences to the attention of the company. [Corporation]'s Administrative Instruction [AI-26], "International Resolution of Discrimination Complaints," provides a method for any employee to have a complaint investigated and, if justified, have the basis for the complaint corrected.

Based on where employees are located, individuals who believe they have a well-founded complaint may file such a complaint with the Personnel Manager at [city, state] or [city, state] or the Manager — Equal Employment, [city, state]. [Corporation] will conduct a confidential investigation of the complaint and advise of a finding on the complaint within [45] days. If individuals wish to appeal the findings, they may appeal to the Assistant Vice President — Human Resources.

This procedure is not intended to diminish or replace other courses of action available to the individual. Rather, it is an attempt to allow [corporation] to ensure that its commitment to valuing employees and complying with the Law is diligently pursued throughout the Corporation.

For further information and guidance, please contact the office of the Assistant Vice President — Human Resources.

The information from the Accommodation Consideration Form[25] is reviewed by an ADA Accommodation Panel made up of representatives from the Law, Safety, Medical, Claims, and Human Resources (part of Resource Development) departments, and a departmental expert/coordinator from each department where an accommodation is requested.

---

[25] *See* § 18.07[B][2].

[8]   Employer Guidelines: Requests for Reasonable Accommodations

FORM 18–12   Sample Employer Guidelines: Reqeusts for Reasonable Accommodations

TABLE OF CONTENTS
SECTIONS

FORMS
REQUEST FOR REASONABLE ACCOMMODATIONS: [FORM 6]

§ 1. Scope

These sections govern the procedure applicable to a request by a disabled individual for reasonable accommodations due to his or her disability. These sections cover both current employees and individuals who have been extended offers of employment (Hirees). These sections are based on the provisions of the employment title of the Americans with Disabilities Act of 1990 (ADA).

§ 2. How Requests for Reasonable Accommodations Are Made

A request for reasonable accommodations by a disabled individual must be made by submitting a Request for Reasonable Accommodations Form [(Form RRA. 1)] to the employer's or prospective employer's personnel department. A Hiree may submit a [Form RRA. 1] to his or her interviewer. The interviewer is considered an authorized representative of the prospective employer's personnel department.

§ 3. When Requests for Reasonable Accommodations Must Be Made

A request for reasonable accommodations by a disabled individual to his or her employer or prospective employer must be made as soon as reasonably possible. The personnel department must provide every applicant for employment with a [Form RRA. 1] along with an application for employment. The personnel department must inform the applicant that the [Form RRA. 1] is to be submitted to the entity only if the applicant receives an offer of employment.

A memorandum on the personnel department bulletin board shall notify all employees of the availability of [Form RRA. 1] in the personnel department. The disabled employee may pick up this form from the personnel department, or can request that the personnel department mail him or her the form. If an employee's direct supervisor has reason to know that an employee has become disabled and has not yet returned to work, the supervisor may forward a copy of the form to the employee by mail. The disabled individual must return the [Form RRA. 1] to the personnel department within a reasonable time after the disability has been incurred.

§ 4. Receipt of [Form RRA. 1] by Personnel Department

Upon receipt of [Form RRA. 1], the personnel department shall perform four functions. First, the personnel department shall mail an acknowledgment of the receipt of the [Form RRA. 1] to the disabled individual. Second, the personnel department shall forward a copy of the [Form RRA. 1] to the review team. Third, the personnel department shall enter the relevant data from the [Form RRA. 1] with the relevant data from all other such forms in the log designated for this purpose. The log shall be updated periodically to reflect the status and/or disposition of all requests for reasonable accommodations. Fourth, the personnel department shall permanently maintain the original [Form RRA. 1] in the disabled individual's personnel file.

§ 5. Composition of Review Team

The review team comprises [five (5)] members. There are [three (3)] permanent members and [two (2)] temporary members. The permanent members are the human resources manager, the corporate controller, and the building engineer. The two temporary members are selected from volunteers from within the entity. The temporary members are selected randomly from the pool of volunteers. Each temporary member serves a term of [three] years on the review team. After a term on the review team, the temporary member must wait [three] years before volunteering to be a temporary member of the review team again.

§ 6. Guidelines for Review Team Determinations

The review team shall approve a request by a disabled individual for reasonable accommodations if three requirements are met. First, the reasonable accommodations must be required due to the individual's disability. Second, the reasonable accommodations must enable the individual to perform his or her essential job functions. And third, the reasonable accommodations must not impose an undue hardship upon the operations of the entity. The review team may request from the disabled individual, or acquire by other means, any evidence that the review team deems necessary to make its determination. The review team may also call any witness it deems necessary. Evidence obtained by the review team regarding both the disabled individual's ability to perform the essential job functions after reasonable accommodations have been made and the potential undue hardship that the entity will suffer must be recorded. The criteria in the written job description, so long as they are job-related and consistent with business necessity, shall be the sole basis for determining the essential job functions. The review team determination must be based exclusively on the evidence considered.

§ 7. Communication of Review Team Determination to Disabled Individual

The review team shall notify the disabled individual by mail that a decision has been reached regarding his or her request for reasonable accommodations. The notification must inform the disabled individual that he or she must schedule a meeting with the review team to learn the status of his or her request. If the disabled individual does not request a meeting with the review team within [thirty (30)] days of the mailing of the notification, the review team shall send a notification by certified mail to the disabled individual, stating that he or she has [thirty (30)] more days in which to schedule a meeting or else his or her request will be considered abandoned.

At the meeting, the review team shall communicate its determination to the disabled individual both orally and through a written memorandum. The communications must include the findings of fact and the reasons for the decision. If the review team rejects the request for reasonable accommodations, the communications must inform the disabled individual of his or her rights as provided in § 9. The review team shall also forward a copy of the determination to the personnel department for inclusion in the disabled individual's personnel file.

§ 8. Actions Taken after Approval of Reasonable Accommodations by Review Team

The review team is authorized to request the approved reasonable accommodations for the disabled individual through the entity's prescribed means for such requests.

§ 9. Rights of the Disabled Individual after Rejection of Request for Reasonable Accommodations

The disabled individual has the right to review all evidence considered by the review team. The disabled individual may seek a hearing with the review team to refute the evidence considered by the review team or to submit additional material evidence. The disabled individual must notify the review team within [thirty (30)] days of the determination meeting if he or she desires a hearing. The review team, upon a showing of excusable neglect or good cause, may extend the time for notification by the disabled individual upon a request by him or her received not later than [sixty (60)] days after the determination meeting. If the disabled individual requests a hearing, the review team must hold the hearing as soon as reasonably possible. The review team shall base its final decision on the same guidelines as provided in § 6. Within two weeks of the hearing, the view team shall issue a final determination through the same process as provided in § 7 based on any new evidence. If the disabled individual's request for reasonable accommodations is rejected for a second time, his or her sole recourse shall be through the courts.

FORM 18–13   Sample Request for Reasonable Accommodations Form

REQUEST FOR REASONABLE ACCOMMODATIONS FORM ([FORM RRA.1])

   (1)   Date: [_____]

   (2)   Name of employee or applicant for employment: [_____]

   (3)   Department: [_____]

   (4)   Current position: [_____]

   (5)   Position applied for: [_____]

   (6)   Nature of disability: [_____]

   (7)   Accommodations sought — check all that apply:

      ()   Alterations to existing facilities.

      ()   Job restructuring.

      ()   Part-time or modified work schedule.

      ()   Reassignment to a vacant position.

      ()   Acquisition or modification of equipment or devices.

      ()   Adjustment or modification of examinations, training materials, or policies.

      ()   Provision of qualified readers or interpreters.

      ()   Other.

   (8)   For each item checked in (7), please provide a detailed description of the exact accommodations sought: [_____]

   (9)   Are you currently engaging in the illegal use of drugs? () yes () no

Signature: [_____]

[9]   Requests for Reasonable Accommodation

Inherent in a request for reasonable accommodations by a disabled individual are two competing interests: (1) the interests of the disabled individual to work to the individual's full potential, and (2) the interests of the entity to minimize expenses and maximize profits. Title I, the ADA's employment title, favors the interests of the individual over those of the entity.[26] The ADA requires the entity to make reasonable accommodations[27] for the individual's disability as long as the individual will thereby be able

---

[26] *See* ADA § 102(a), 42 U.S.C. § 12,112(a) (1994).

[27] ADA § 101(9), 42 U.S.C. § 12,111(9) (1994).

to perform his or her essential job functions without causing an undue hardship[28] to the entity.[29]

The procedural guidelines in Forms 18–12 to 18–14 are designed to facilitate the goals of the ADA. As with any other set of guidelines, cost-benefit judgments play an important part in their development. Even though there are no due process issues involved with such internal procedures, a procedural fairness evaluation[30] is useful in appraising the guidelines. Judge Friendly's list of procedural elements[31] serves as a useful tool in analyzing the procedural provisions in the request for reasonable accommodations guidelines. Under the analytical framework set forth in *Manhews v. Eldridge,*[32] each procedural element is evaluated in the following terms:

1. The marginal utility in the fact-finding accuracy that the element affords;
2. The seriousness of the deprivation to the disabled individual if a factual error is made;
3. The burden to the entity that results from providing the procedural element.

The seriousness of the deprivation to the disabled individual is a constant in requests for reasonable accommodations. The effect of fact-finding accuracy and the burden to the entity vary depending on the procedural element and how that element is implemented. The following procedural elements should be considered:

1. An unbiased tribunal;
2. A notice of the proposed action and the grounds asserted;
3. A reason why the proposed action should not be taken;
4. A right to present evidence, including the right to call witnesses;
5. A right to know opposing evidence and to cross-examine adverse witnesses;
6. A decision based exclusively on the evidence considered;
7. A right to counsel;
8. A record of the evidence considered by the tribunal;
9. A right to the tribunal's written findings of fact and reasons for its decision;
10. An appellate review.

---

[28] ADA § 101(10), 42 U.S.C. § 12,111(10); ADA § 102, 42 U.S.C. § 12,112 (1994).

[29] ADA § 101(10), 42 U.S.C. § 12,111(10); ADA § 102, 42 U.S.C. § 12,112 (1994).

[30] For a similar analysis, see Henry H. Perritt, Jr., Employee Dismissal Law and Practice § 8.13 (John Wiley & Sons, 4th ed. 1997) (procedural fairness evaluation of employer dismissal procedures) [hereinafter Employee Dismissal Law and Practice].

[31] *See* Friendly, *Some Kind of Hearing,* 123 U. Pa. L. Rev. 1267 (1973).

[32] 424 U.S. 319 (1976).

An unbiased tribunal. An unbiased tribunal is an essential element of accurate fact-finding. The review team is designed to constitute an unbiased tribunal. The three management-level review team members should not be biased toward either the individual or the immediate supervision because they are employed midway between the entity's hierarchical extremes. The review team is in direct contact with neither the average employee nor the top management. Even if the disabled individual does not perceive the permanent team members as completely unbiased, that disabled individual cannot plausibly question the motives of the two randomly selected members of the review team. Also, the additional diversity that the temporary review team members provide serves to dispel further any possible perceived biases.

The entity will suffer a burden by having at least three of its key personnel take time from their normal duties to perform review team functions. However, the burden and expense the entity would suffer by employing an outside tribunal to evaluate requests for reasonable accommodations would be far greater. Therefore, the review team accomplishes the essential requirement of an unbiased tribunal through a minimum of burden to the entity.

A notice of the proposed action and the grounds asserted. The disabled individual sets the reasonable accommodations evaluation process in motion by submitting a request for reasonable accommodations form. The form itself provides a notice of what information is material to the subsequent decisions of the request.

A reason why the proposed action should not be taken. The disabled individual is the party initiating the evaluation process and thus provides the reasons on the form.

A right to present evidence, including the right to call witnesses. The guidelines do not permit the disabled individual to present any evidence or call any witnesses prior to the review team's determination. Rather, the review team determines which evidence it will consider. It is empowered to call any witnesses and request any evidence, from the disabled individual or others, that it deems necessary.

The fact that the review team, not the disabled individual, determines what evidence and which witnesses are to be considered does not impair fact-finding accuracy. The review team is an unbiased investigatory tribunal and has no reason either not to request relevant evidence or not to call relevant witnesses the disabled individual would have presented or called. Therefore, the same information is considered in the review team's determination, just as if the disabled individual had submitted it.

The burden to the entity of allowing the disabled individual to present evidence and call witnesses would be substantial. The determination process would be converted from an efficient fact-finding mechanism into a quasi-trial. This quasi-trial could continue for days, keeping some of the entity's key employees from their daily, "profitable" tasks and duties.

A right to know opposing evidence and to cross-examine adverse witnesses. As explained previously, neither the disabled individual nor the entity presents any evidence. Rather, the review team acquires the evidence it deems necessary to make its determination. Therefore, there is no true opposing evidence, only relevant evidence. Allowing the disabled individual to know the relevant evidence to be considered by the review team prior to its determination would provide no improvements to fact-finding accuracy.

Based on the same reasoning, the cross-examination of adverse witnesses is also not required.

A decision based exclusively on the evidence considered. A decision based exclusively on the evidence considered is a fundamental requirement of procedural fairness because it enhances accurate fact-finding. Any burden, if there is one, of providing this procedure pales in comparison to its utility.

A right to counsel. The guidelines do not authorize a disabled individual to have the assistance of counsel because the determination process is generally neither technical nor complex. Therefore, the right to counsel does not promote fact-finding accuracy. If the disabled individual were allowed representation by counsel, the determination process could be converted from a mechanism for making decisions into a quasi-trial, dramatically increasing the burden to the entity.

A record of the evidence considered by the tribunal. The preparation of a record of the considered evidence is essential to the appellate review procedure provided for by the guidelines. Absent this record, the disabled individual would not be able to refute the evidence considered by the review team in making its determination. Furthermore, the burden to the entity of maintaining this record is so minimal that even if appellate review were not permitted, the record should be maintained to assist future review team determinations.

A right to the tribunal's written findings of fact and reasons for its decision. This requirement also facilitates appellate review by the disabled individual. The benefits to fact-finding accuracy and the burden to the entity of providing this procedure are similar to those relating to the decision based on the record.

An appellate review. The guidelines provide for automatic appellate review if the disabled individual desires it. Appellate review gives the disabled individual the opportunity to refute any evidence considered by the review team and/or to submit any additional relevant evidence the review team did not consider. Therefore, it greatly enhances fact-finding accuracy. This procedure makes up for any possible shortcomings of procedural fairness at the initial stages of the determination process by providing for them at the end of the process. Even though automatic appellate review imposes a substantial burden upon the entity, the possible repercussions of an erroneous determination warrant its implementation.[33]

[10]   Requests for Reemployment

FORM 18–14   Sample Employer Guidelines: Requests for Reemployment

TABLE OF CONTENTS
SECTIONS

FORMS
REQUEST FOR REEMPLOYMENT FORM

§ 101. Scope

These sections govern requests for reemployment by an individual who suffered an injury covered by workers' compensation statutes. These sections cover requests both by individuals who have fully recovered from their injuries and by those who continue to suffer disabilities.

§ 102. How Requests for Reemployment Are Made

An individual who was injured must submit a Request for Reemployment Form ([Form WCRR.1]) to the entity's personnel department to be considered for reemployment.

---

[33] The material in this section was developed with the help of Brian Sopinsky, assistant to Henry H. Perritt, Jr.

§ 103. When Requests for Reemployment Must Be Made

The personnel department shall forward [Form WCRR.1] to the injured employee as soon as reasonably possible after the entity becomes aware of the employee's work-related injury. The personnel department shall also forward a Request for Reasonable Accommodations Form ([Form RRA.1]) to the injured individual at the same time as the [Form WCRR.1]. The entity may transmit the forms to the employee by mail.

The individual seeking reemployment may submit [Form WCRR.1] as soon as he or she is capable of performing the essential duties of the position requested.

§ 104. How Requests for Reemployment Are Treated by the Entity

The entity shall treat a request for reemployment by a fully recovered individual in the same manner as any other request for employment. A request for reemployment by a fully recovered individual is not to be afforded any better or worse treatment than other requests for employment. If a position is available, the entity must award it to the most qualified applicant.

The entity shall grant all requests for reemployment by disabled individuals. The entity shall also provide all reasonable accommodations requested by the individual due to his or her disability, provided that such accommodations do not cause an undue hardship to the entity (*see* Employer Guidelines: Requests for Reasonable Accommodations § 6).

§ 105. When Requested Position Is Unavailable but Alternate Position Is Available

The entity shall utilize its pool of reemployment requests to fill all employment openings. The entity shall use an employment request to fill the job requested as well as all vacant positions at or below the level of the requested position. Alternate positions are awarded based on the same criteria as requested positions (*see* § 102). The provision of an alternate position may be considered a reasonable accommodation for a disabled individual.

§ 106. Status of Rejected Requests for Reemployment

All individuals who request reemployment but are not awarded positions shall have their requests for reemployment retained by the entity for [six (6)] months. The entity shall use the requests for reemployment to fill future vacant positions as provided in § § 102 and 103. The entity shall notify the individual requesting reemployment of this procedure.

The entity shall also provide all individuals requesting reemployment with a list of available positions at other entities. The list shall be based on the physical capabilities and skills of the applicant.

FORM 18–15   Sample Request for Reemployment Form

REQUEST FOR REEMPLOYMENT FORM

> [FORM WCRR.1]
> (1) Date [_____]
> (2) Name [_____]
> (3) Department (prior to injury) [_____]
> (4) Position (prior to injury) [_____]
> (5) Position requested [_____]
> (6) If you will require reasonable accommodation to perform the position requested, please complete the enclosed Request for Reasonable Accommodations Form ([Form RRA.1]). [_____]
>
> Signature [_____]

§ 18.08   NEGLIGENT HIRING

Employers should be alert to the possibility that stretching to accommodate an employee's disability may open up possible liability for negligent hiring. For example, if an employer hires someone with limited dexterity to perform a job that requires considerable dexterity in order to avoid risks of injury to other employees, an accident involving that employee almost certainly will result in a claim that the employer breached a duty to other employees when it hired the disabled employee. Similarly, if an employee with a mental impairment engages in conduct that injures other employees, customers, or suppliers, the same kind of allegation can be made.

The best way to address this conflict is to identify specifically what risks may exist to other personnel, and to evaluate how to protect against these risks.

The ADA, as discussed in Chapter 4, permits excluding disabled employees and applicants in order to prevent injury to others.[34]

§ 18.09   PRIVACY OF PERSONNEL FILES

Any source of information about physical or mental impairments, including employment applications, results of interviews or investigations, or test procedures should be carefully controlled by the employer to minimize

---

[34] *See generally* Lutz v. Cybularz, 607 A.2d 1089 (Pa. Super. Ct. 1992) (affirming summary judgment for newspaper distributor on negligent hiring claim based in part on the physical disabilities of truck driver who was determined to be independent contractor.) *Cf.* Crabtree v. Montana State Library, 665 P.2d 231 (Mont. 1983) (refusing to validate state statute affording public employment preference to veterans and disabled civilians notwithstanding potential risk of negligent hiring lawsuits).

the potential for inappropriate disclosure. Any records pertaining to treatment for alcohol or drug abuse must be kept strictly confidential to prevent discrimination as a by-product of seeking help for personal problems.[35]

The EEOC permits employers to supply medical information to workers' compensation offices under sections of the ADA relating to the confidentiality of information obtained from a medical examination or inquiry.[36] The EEOC also prohibits questions about an applicant's history of workers' compensation claims in the EEOC's Interpretive Guidance for 29 C.F.R. § 1630.13(a) of the regulations concerning preemployment medical examinations and inquiries.[37] Such an inquiry is prohibited even though arguably job-related and consistent with business necessity.[38]

§ 18.10 RULES OF CONDUCT

The employer should have counsel review its rules of conduct to identify any rules that may have an unjustifiable adverse impact on disabled applicants or employees.

§ 18.11 PERFORMANCE STANDARDS

Employers should review the existing performance standards for each major job classification to determine those standards that may have an unjustifiable adverse impact on disabled applicants or employees.

§ 18.12 COUNSELING AND PERIODIC EVALUATION

Employers should supplement their regular counseling and periodic evaluation practices to ensure that no evaluator or counselor makes remarks that might be construed as discriminatory based on disabilities. Conversely, the employers should inquire of any employee already known to be disabled as to whether the employee believes that the disability is being accommodated reasonably.

---

[35] *Cf. In re* Collester, 599 A.2d 1275 (N.J. 1992).

[36] *Id. See* ADA § 102(c)(3)(B), 42 U.S.C. § 12,112(c)(3)(B) (1994) (information of medical condition or history treated as confidential medical record).

[37] 56 Fed. Reg. 35,750 (July 26, 1991) (codified at 29 C.F.R. pt. 1630 app. § 1630(a) (1996)). *See* ADA § 102(c)(2)(A), 42 U.S.C. § 12,112(c)(2)(A) (1994) (prohibition against medical examination or inquiry relating to disability status).

[38] 56 Fed. Reg. 35,732 (July 26, 1991) (preamble to final EEOC regulations explaining changes to 29 C.F.R. § 1630.13 (1996)). *See* ADA § 102(c)(2)(B), 42 U.S.C. § 12,112(c)(2)(B) (1994) (preemployment inquiry permitted regarding ability to perform job-related function).

§ 18.13 PROGRESSIVE DISCIPLINE

Employers should consider implementing or expanding existing progressive discipline procedures. Under these progressive procedures, the employees whose disciplinary problems are associated with physical or mental impairments covered by the ADA are given appropriate opportunities to conform their conduct to what the employer reasonably may require, and the employer is given reasonable opportunity to consider steps toward the reasonable accommodation the employee may wish to suggest. The progressive discipline may include "last chance agreements."

§ 18.14 CHANGES IN ORGANIZATION OF WORK

After a request for accommodation is made, employers should consult with the disabled individual to decide on the appropriate accommodations.[39] In addition, the Senate Report suggests taking the following four informal steps:

1. Identify the barriers to equal opportunity, distinguishing between essential and nonessential job tasks, and both the abilities and the limitations of the disabled individual;
2. Identify possible accommodations, by consulting the disabled individual, the state and federal agencies, and other opportunities;
3. Assess the reasonableness of each possible accommodation in terms of effectiveness and equal opportunity;
4. Implement the accommodation that is most appropriate for the employee and the employer and does not impose an undue hardship on the employer's operation; or permit the employee to provide his or her own accommodation if it does not impose an undue hardship.[40]

The expressed choice of the applicant should be given primary consideration "unless another effective accommodation exists that would provide a meaningful equal opportunity or that the accommodation requested would pose an undue hardship."[41]

§ 18.15 INTERACTIVE PROBLEM SOLVING

The EEOC guidelines suggest an interactive approach, involving the disabled employee/applicant in exploring the possibilities for accommodating the disability.[42] This interactive approach considers the following factors:

---

[39] Senate Report at 34.

[40] *Id.* at 35.

[41] *Id.*

[42] 29 C.F.R. pt. 1630 app. § 1630.9 (1996) (process of determining the appropriate reasonable accommodation).

1. Analysis of the particular job, determining both the purpose and the essential functions;
2. Consultation with the disabled individual not only to ascertain the precise job-related limitations imposed by the disability but also to determine how the limitations could be overcome with reasonable accommodation;
3. Identification of potential accommodations in consultation with the disabled employee and assessment of the effectiveness each would have in enabling performance of the essential functions of the position;
4. Consideration of the preference of the disabled employee and selection of the accommodation that is most appropriate for both the employee and the employer.[43]

The EEOC guidelines proceed to give a concrete illustration of the interactive determination of reasonable accommodation. The illustration involves a consultation between a sack handler, who handles 50-pound sacks but has a back problem, and an employer. The consultation results in a conclusion that the essential job requirement is not the mere lifting and carrying of the sacks but the requirement that the job holder move the sacks from the loading dock to the storage room. The illustration describes the employer's and employee's considering the various kinds of vehicles that could carry the sacks, the particular function the employee cannot perform, and the exclusion of a cart as one possibility because no suitable carts are available. This discussion is followed by the ultimate agreement that a dolly is an appropriate reasonable accommodation.[44]

§ 18.16   AFFIRMATIVE ACTION

The approach suggested by this chapter encourages employers to take affirmative action in complying with ADA requirements. Employers may also wish to consider outreach efforts to communities or facilities for the disabled. This may be particularly appropriate and serve employer self-interest well when labor shortages are encountered.

§ 18.17   ADVISORY COMMITTEE

Large employers who employ a significant numbers of disabled employees, or who anticipate employing significant numbers of disabled applicants, should consider establishing a disability accommodation advisory

---

[43] *Id.*

[44] 29 C.F.R. pt. 1630 app. § 1630.9 (1996) (reasonable accommodation process illustrated).

committee. If carefully selected, such committees can provide useful practical information to employers both on the limitations likely to be associated with different types of disabilities and on cost-effective ways of accommodating these limitations.[45] In addition, an advisory committee can play a useful role in reviewing particular cases, either encouraging the employer to change its decision or encouraging employees to accept the outcome of employer decisions.

§ 18.18 ECONOMIC IMPACT

The Preliminary Regulatory Impact Analysis (PRIA) contained in the preamble to the EEOC's proposed regulations justifies the requirements of Title I through the use of economic analysis. The PRIA indicates that failure to implement the ADA's provisions mandating nondiscrimination against disabled persons in employment could result in lost benefits to the economy of approximately $400 million.[46] The proposed regulations (and, by implication, the substantially similar final regulations) were not expected to impact significantly the economic viability of smaller entities.[47] Economists studying discrimination in the workplace have variously concluded that discriminatory employment practices result in suboptimal human capital investments that reduce overall societal productivity and increase economic costs to employers and taxpayers.[48] Economic analysis suggests that continued discrimination against individuals with disabilities in employment lowers the competitiveness of the potential workforce pool by reducing the number of available workers, drains the public purse through entitlements and support payments, and allocates inefficiently the costs of reasonable accommodations for disabled persons.[49]

---

[45] *See generally* House Labor Report at 66 (suggesting consultation with disabled employee or applicant and establishing governmental advisory groups).

[46] 56 Fed. Reg. 8579 (1991). The $400 million figure is composed of estimated reasonable accommodation expenses of $16 million, productivity gains of more than $164 million, and decreased support payments and increased tax revenues totaling about $222 million. *Id.* The PRIA was not revised when the final regulations were issued. Rather, comments were solicited in preparation for a January 1, 1992, revision. 56 Fed. Reg. at 35,734 (1991) (preamble to final EEOC regulations).

[47] 56 Fed. Reg. 8579 (1991). Not only are smaller entities less likely to be required to make reasonable accommodations, but also a combination of factors, including the two-year exemption period, the availability of tax credits, and the lack of reporting requirements, ensures that disadvantageous economic effects to such entities should be minimal. *Id.*

[48] *Id.* at 8581. Economic rationales for the efficacy of nondiscrimination policies include the theory of discrimination coefficients, the theory of short-run profit maximizing (based on marginal productivity), the theory of imperfect market information, and a characterization of the problem as one of internalizing the costs of externalities. *See id.* at 8580–81.

[49] *Id.* at 8580. Becker's analysis indicates that discriminatory employment practices result in suboptimal hiring practices because individuals who are potentially more qualified are excluded from consideration for positions, thus suggesting that the resulting workforce is

§ 18.19　　DISCLAIMERS

[A]　Generally

Under the common law of contracts in virtually every state, unilaterally adopted employer policy statements may be contractually enforceable.[50] The same theories that lead to enforcement also permit employers to negate contractual status for such statements by including prominent disclaimers[51] in any statement or employee handbook or manual.[52] In many cases, an employee's breach of contract claim is premised not on a written communication but on oral statements from lower-level employees. Disclaimers can eliminate the apparent authority of lower-level employees to make such promises.

To be effective, a statement similar to the following samples from *Employee Dismissal Law and Practice* should be included in employment applications or other written documents communicated to employees when they first enter service.

[B]　Sample Forms

[1]　Sample Disclaimers

FORM 18–16　　Sample Disclaimer #1

I understand that no store manager or representative of the company, other than the president or vice president of the Company, has any authority to enter into any agreement for employment for any specified period of time, or to make any agreement contrary to the foregoing (reservation of employment at-will).[53]

---

less efficient than it would be with the more qualified, but excluded, individuals. *Id.* Clearly, attaining higher levels of employment of individuals with disabilities would result in lower welfare and unemployment payments to such individuals because they would be more capable of financially supporting themselves. *Id.* Finally, because employers are more likely to be able to afford the cost of making reasonable accommodations in the workplace, such accommodations are more likely to be made, and because an employer may be able to reuse the benefit of the reasonable accommodation expense for another employee as well, the net cost of the accommodation is reduced commensurately. *Id.*

[50] *See* Henry H. Perritt, Jr., Employee Dismissal Law and Practice ch. 6 (4th ed. 1997) (contract theories for wrongful dismissal).

[51] *See* Forms 18–16 and 18–17.

[52] *See* Swanson v. Liquid Air Corp., 826 P.2d 664, 673 (Wash. 1992) (analytical framework for disclaimer assessment; allowing jury to decide if disclaimer on page six of 200-page handbook was effectively communicated to employee).

[53] *Id.*

FORM 18–17   Sample Disclaimer #2

I agree my employment and compensation can be terminated, with or without cause, and with or without notice, at any time I understand that no representative of your company has any authority to enter into any other agreement with me . . . .[54]

§ 18.20   LIMITING RELIEF TO INTERNAL REMEDIES

[A] Generally

Employers also may wish to limit employees to internal procedures, regardless of whether these procedures are contractual entitlements. The general principles of contract construction are consistent with literal enforcement of the following sample language from *Employee Dismissal Law and Practice.*

[B] Sample Forms

[1] Sample Language Limiting Relief

FORM 18–18   Sample Language Limiting Relief

In consideration of my employment, I understand and accept that "cause" for my termination will be determined to exist or not to exist within the sole discretion of my employer. I waive any rights I may have to obtain court determination or review of an employer's finding that there is cause for my dismissal.[55]

FORM 18–19   Sample Language Limiting Employee's Right to Relitigate

In consideration of my employer's affording me certain rights to obtain higher-level review of supervisory actions adverse to me, including a possible de-

---

[54] *Id.* As an example, in Shelby v. Zayre Corp., 474 So. 2d 1069, 1071 (Ala. 1985), an employee claimed that the assistant manager who hired her had promised that she would have permanent employment, knowing that the representation of permanent employment was false. The employee had quit her previous job in reliance on that representation. The Supreme Court of Alabama affirmed judgment for the employer, finding that any reliance on the supervisor's statement was unreasonable because the plaintiff admitted reading and understanding the quoted provision of the employment application. The language limiting authority was outcome-determinative.

[55] Employee Dismissal Law and Practice § 8.9, at 167. If an employer elects either to require pretermination exhaustion of certain procedures or to afford an internal complaint procedure, the employer may wish to limit an employee's right to relitigate the dismissal in the courts. This can be accomplished by the inclusion of language similar to the language in Form 18–19.

cision to terminate my employment, and decisions on reasonable accommodation of disabilities, I waive any rights I may have to obtain court review of the appropriateness of such adverse action, and will utilize the internal company procedures as the exclusive means of protesting adverse supervisory action, including discharge and refusal of accommodation. The internal procedures provide an adequate opportunity for the true facts to be determined and for me to present my side of any controversy. I will accept the determination resulting from such internal procedures as final and binding, and waive any right I may have to protest such a determination or to obtain review of it in any proceeding outside the company.[56]

Thus, as a result of this language, the employees are required to exhaust internal remedies as a matter of basic contract doctrine.

§ 18.21   ARBITRATION AGREEMENT

[A]   Generally

If the internal procedures terminate in arbitration,[57] an employee's agreement to be bound by the arbitration should be enforceable in any jurisdiction that has adopted the Uniform Arbitration Act[58] under a trend in the federal cases. In *Gilmer v. Interstate/Johnson Lane Corp.,*[59] the United States Supreme Court approved the enforcement of an individual employee contract provision sending controversies regarding the legitimacy of termination to arbitration even though such controversies required the application of statutory law. Under the Employee Polygraph Protection Act,[60] the Ninth Circuit reached a similar result.[61] The Seventh Circuit held, however, that conditioning the use of internal procedures on refraining from filing an Age Discrimination in Employment Act charge with the EEOC constitutes retaliation for asserting rights under the ADA.[62] This raises questions on any

---

[56] *Id.*

[57] *See* Form 18–20.

[58] Unif. Arb. Act § 1–25.

[59] 500 U.S. 20 (1991).

[60] 29 U.S.C. §§ 2001–2009 (1994).

[61] *See* Saari v. Smith Barney, Harris Upham & Co., 968 F.2d 877, 881–82 (9th Cir. 1992) (vacating district court refusal to order arbitration of federal Polygraph Protection Act claim under broker-dealer agreement arbitration clause). *But see* Hillding v. McDonnell Douglas Helicopter Co., 59 Fair Empl. Prac. Cas. (BNA) 869 (D. Ariz. 1992) (denying res judicata effect to binding decision of employee grievance committee under Alexander v. Gardner-Denver Co., 415 U.S. 36 (1974); distinguishing *Gilmer,* but granting summary judgment on Title VII (42 U.S.C. §§ 2000e to 2000e-16 (1994) [hereinafter Title VII]) and contract claims on other grounds).

[62] 29 U.S.C. §§ 621–634 (1994) [hereinafter ADEA]; EEOC v. Board of Governors, 957 F.2d 424, 431 (7th Cir. 1992) (reversing summary judgment; grievance processing was suspended when employee filed ADEA claim).

contractual election-of-remedies provision when federal nondiscrimination rights are involved.

Even if a purported waiver is found to be legally ineffective in subsequent litigation, any arbitration award in the employer's favor should be entitled to some evidentiary weight in a wrongful dismissal lawsuit.[63] Accordingly, waiver language also should be included prominently on forms used to commence an internal review of an adverse employment action and on any settlement document. Failure to follow the recommendations of internal review entities can produce liability.[64]

The procedural model developed under the Employee Retirement Income Security Act (ERISA)[65] for handling claims for employee benefits is useful for a broader range of employment disputes. The model requires that employees be given notice of adverse determinations with sufficient specificity to allow the employee to make pertinent arguments or to present pertinent data as to why the determination should be changed. ERISA, however, does not require any particular mode or formality for the notice or associated procedures.[66]

The American Arbitration Association (AAA) makes it easy to write arbitration agreements that are enforceable without specifying great detail about the arbitration process.[67] The AAA recommends that the language in Form 18–21 be included in employment contracts, personnel manuals or policy statements, employment applications, or "other agreements."[68]

---

[63] See Barrentine v. Arkansas-Best Freight Sys., Inc., 450 U.S. 728, 743 n.22 (1981) (quoting Alexander v. Gardner-Denver, 415 U.S. 36, 59 n.21 (1974), to same effect); Darden v. Illinois Bell Tel. Co., 797 F.2d 497, 504 (7th Cir. 1986) (approving "great weight" given to arbitration award by district judge in deciding to dismiss Title VII claim; arbitrator fully considered race discrimination under collective agreement prohibiting discrimination); Gonzalez v. Southern Pac. Transp. Co., 773 F.2d 637, 645 (5th Cir. 1985) (on rehearing) (Railway Labor Act (45 U.S.C. §§ 151–185 (1994) arbitrator's award deciding outcome-determinative facts entitled to preclusive effect in suit for retaliation under federal railroad liability act).

[64] See Mace v. Charleston Area Med. Ctr. Found., 422 S.E.2d 624, 632 (W. Va. 1992) (failure to follow recommendation of internal grievance committee was single piece of evidence most supportive of $230,000 jury verdict finding retaliation for asserting veterans' reemployment rights).

[65] 29 U.S.C. § 1133 (1994). See also Employee Retirement Income Security Act, 29 U.S.C. §§ 1001–1461 (1994) [hereinafter ERISA].

[66] Halpin v. W.W. Grainger, Inc., 962 F.2d 685, 693–94 (7th Cir. 1992) (ERISA required reversal of denial of long-term disability benefits because plan's procedure was arbitrary and capricious and violated regulatory requirements for notice of appeal rights, including specific reasons for initial denial).

[67] See AAA, Resolving Employment Disputes: A Manual on Drafting Procedures (1993) (available from AAA Headquarters, 140 West 51st St., New York, NY 10020-1203; (212) 484-4000; (fax) (212) 307-4387); AAA, 1993 Employment Dispute Resolution Rules (Jan. 1, 1993) (including mediation and arbitration rules).

[68] AAA, 1993 Employment Dispute Resolution Rules 3–4 (Jan. 1, 1993).

[B]   Sample Forms

[1]   Sample Arbitration Agreement

FORM 18–20   Sample Arbitration Agreement

1. Under this agreement, the employee and employer agree to use the dispute resolution procedure specified in this agreement as the exclusive means of resolving disputes over employee rights and employer obligations under the Americans with Disabilities Act (ADA). The employee understands that, absent this agreement, the employee would be entitled to assert ADA rights by filing charges with the Equal Employment Opportunity Commission (EEOC) or state or local human rights agencies and ultimately to file a lawsuit in state or federal court or both. Understanding these rights, the employee elects to waive them and prefers the machinery described in this agreement.

2. This agreement and the arbitration procedure described in it apply to any and all claims connected with mental or physical disability and the impact of such disabilities on the employee's qualification to perform job duties, and any and all accommodation that might be requested by the employee or undertaken by the employer. It specifically covers refusals of promotion, pay increase, transfer, change in job duties, or termination of employment because of limitations on performance of job duties, or termination of employment because of limitations on performance of job functions due to mental or physical disabilities.

3. Procedure. If the employee or employer wishes to present a dispute or assert a claim under this agreement, the claim or dispute must be presented under the following steps. Any dispute over compliance with these procedures shall be resolved by the arbitrators appointed under paragraph 5.

Step 1. The employee informs either his immediate supervisor or the designated ADA officer in the human resources department of the employee's claim or dispute. This may be done orally, in which case the supervisor or ADA officer will make a brief written record. If the employer wishes to present a dispute, the first step necessitates informing the employee in writing.

Step 2. If the complaint or dispute is resolved by informal discussion between employer representative and employee, the resolution shall be recorded in writing and signed by the employee and either the supervisor or the designated ADA officer.

Step 3. If the dispute or claim is not resolved informally in steps 1 and 2, it may be presented by either party to the employer's ADA compliance committee.

Step 4. If the ADA compliance committee resolves the claim or dispute on terms acceptable to both employee and employer, the resolution shall be recorded in writing and signed by the employee and the chairperson of the employer ADA compliance committee.

Step 5. If the claim or dispute is not resolved in the preceding steps, either employee or employer may present the claim in writing for final and binding arbitration selected in accordance with this agreement.

4. Claim Form. The following form shall be used for presenting claims and disputes:

Name of employee: [_____]
Type of disability: [_____]
Accommodation requested: [_____]
Means by which accommodation was requested: [_____]

Accommodation offered by employer: [_____]
Remedy desired by person presenting claim or dispute: [_____]

5. Methodology for Selecting Arbitrator. The employee or employer may suggest a particular individual to serve as arbitrator. If the other party agrees on that person and the person agrees to serve, that person shall be the arbitrator. If there is no agreement on a specific individual, either employee or employer may request the appointment of an arbitrator by the American Arbitration Association in New York, and the parties agree to use and be bound by the decisions of an arbitrator appointed by that association. If these methods for selecting an arbitrator fail, the parties agree that a state or federal court may appoint an arbitrator under the provisions of the Federal Arbitration Act or any version of the Uniform Arbitration Act in the state of employment.

6. Both employee and employer may be represented by counsel or other representatives.

7. Costs. An employee requesting arbitration shall pay [$100], unless the arbitrator finds that payment of such amount would represent undue hardship for the employee. The employer shall pay any remaining costs. If the arbitrator finds that frivolous claims or bad-faith conduct have been presented in the arbitration proceeding, the arbitrator may allocate the cost differently from the allocation provided in this section.

8. Scope of Arbitrator Authority. The arbitrator may resolve any questions of jurisdiction and any procedural issues. The arbitrator shall make a final and binding decision on the claim or dispute as it was presented.

9. The arbitrator may determine remedies to be applied, but if reorganization of work or change in job duties is part of the remedy selected by the arbitrator, the arbitrator shall give the employer an election to pay a monetary sum instead of making the changes.

10. The arbitrator may not impose monetary compensation in excess of [five (5)] years' compensation.

11. Procedures. Burdens of proof shall be those applied under the ADA. The employee has the burden of establishing a disability and qualifications to perform essential functions of the desired position; the employer has the burden of establishing undue hardship in making the requested accommodation.

12. Both employee and employer may be present throughout the hearing. Both employer and employee shall be allowed a brief opening statement.

13. Both employee and employer may present witnesses indicated on witness lists submitted at the commencement of the hearing, except that the arbitrator may exclude repetitive or cumulative testimony. The employer shall make available any employee witnesses at no loss in pay as directed by the arbitrator.

14. Both employer and employee may examine and cross-examine witnesses.

15. Both employer and employee may present documentary and demonstrative evidence as appropriate to the issues.

16. The rules of evidence shall not be applied strictly, but the arbitrator may give little or no weight to hearsay.

17. Both employee and employer may make brief closing statements.

18. The arbitrator shall issue a written decision, making specific findings of fact and conclusions, within [ninety (90)] days after the conclusion of the hearing.

19. Judgment may be entered on the arbitration award in any court.

FORM 18–21   Sample Language Requiring Arbitration

Any controversy or claim arising out of or relating to this contract, or the breach thereof, shall be settled by arbitration in accordance with the employment dispute resolution rules of the American Arbitration Association, and judgment on the award rendered by the arbitrators may be entered in any court having jurisdiction thereof.[69]

The AAA recommends the language in Form 18–22 for the arbitration of existing disputes.

FORM 18–22   Sample Language: Arbitration of Existing Disputes

We, the undersigned parties, hereby agree to submit to arbitration under the Employment Dispute Resolution Rules of the American Arbitration Association the following controversy: [cite briefly].

We further agree that the above controversy be submitted to [one (1)]/[three (3)] arbitrators selected from the panels of arbitrators of the American Arbitration Association. We further agree that we will faithfully observe this agreement and the rules, and that we will abide by and perform any award rendered by the arbitrators and that a judgment of the court having jurisdiction may be entered on the award.[70]

FORM 18–23[71]   Sample Discovery Provisions: Option #1

The parties shall cooperate in the voluntary exchange of such documents and information as will serve to expedite the adjudication. Discovery shall be conducted in the most expeditious and cost-effective manner possible and shall be limited to that which is relevant and for which each party has a substantial, demonstrable need. Upon request, the employee shall be entitled to a true copy of his or her

---

[69] *Id.* at 4.

[70] *Id.* The pamphlet does not explain why the existing-agreement language goes further in specifying who the arbitrators are and expressly commits to observe the agreement, the rules, and the award, because other suggested language for future claims does not have these provisions.

[71] The AAA suggests the options in Forms 18–23 through 18–25 as alternative language if the parties desire discovery in arbitration.

personnel records kept in the ordinary course of business and at least one deposition of an employer representative designated by the employee.[72]

FORM 18–24   Sample Discovery Provisions: Option #2

Each party shall have the right to take the deposition of one individual and any expert witness designated by another party. Each party also shall have the right to propound requests for production of documents to any party. Additional discovery may be had only when the arbitrator so orders, upon a showing of substantial need.[73]

FORM 18–25   Sample Discovery Provisions: Option #3

In preparation for the arbitration hearing, each party may utilize all methods of discovery authorized by the procedural rules and statutes of this state, and may enforce the right to such discovery in the manner provided by said rules and statutes and/or by the arbitration law of this state.[74]

§ 18.22   RELEASES

[A]   Generally

Disclaimers are preventive in character; they attempt to preclude the possibility that a legal right to employment security will arise in the first place. An *employee release* is a contract in which a discharged employee abandons claims against a former employer after they have arisen in exchange for benefits such as severance pay or continuation of salary and benefits for a period of time.[75] Employee releases generally are effective in barring implied-in-fact contract claims against employers but may not be as effective in barring statutory claims.[76]

---

[72] AAA, Resolving Employment Disputes: A Manual on Drafting Procedures 11–12 (1993).

[73] *Id.* at 12.

[74] *Id.*

[75] *See* Forms 18–26 and 18–27.

[76] Stroman v. West Coast Grocery Co., 884 F.2d 458, 462 (9th Cir. 1989) (reversing district court and finding that release waived Title VII claims despite lack of explicit reference to Title VII and absence of attorneys; based on employee understanding); Riley v. American Family Mut. Ins. Co., 881 F.2d 368, 373 (7th Cir. 1989) (affirming district court conclusion that release negotiated in connection with settlement of state law claim barred Title VII claim because knowing and voluntary; extensive review of cases and different standards); Myers v. Health Specialists, S.C., 587 N.E.2d 494, 499 (Ill. App. Ct. 1992) (reversing summary judgment; release, properly construed as "general release," did not bar claim for failure to buy malpractice insurance; generally analyzing principles for construing releases).

The scope of employee releases is limited to the intentions of the parties as set forth on the face of the agreement. The mere acceptance of termination payments does not necessarily show that the employee intends to give up rights to litigate the validity of the termination. Similarly, the acceptance of one kind of accommodation to a disability does not necessarily waive the right to assert ADA claims with respect to the refusal of other kinds of accommodation.

Note that the introductory paragraph of Form 18-26 makes it clear that the agreement is a waiver and that it is intended to extinguish rights. This sort of preamble buttresses agreement validity against a subsequent challenge that a signatory did not know that he or she was waiving rights by signing the agreement.

Paragraph 2 is extremely broad and might be subject to the defense that it does not call to the signatory's attention particular kinds of employment law claims. For example, an age discrimination claim probably would not be waived by this paragraph.[77] In comparison, paragraph 3 specifically refers to the ADA, and if its recitation that counsel was consulted is true, it is much more likely to be given effect regarding an ADA claim.

Paragraph 4 strengthens the agreement against any attack that it is not supported by consideration or is not fair. Paragraph 5 is useful to reduce the likelihood of "fraud in the inducement" claims.

[B]   Sample Forms

   [1]   Release Agreement

FORM 18–26   Sample Release Agreement

THIS AGREEMENT, made this [date], by and between [employer name] (hereinafter "Employer") and [employee name] (hereinafter "Employee"), is intended by the parties to be a settlement and release whereby [employer] and [employee] extinguish their respective rights and claims against one another as hereinafter enumerated.

FOR VALUABLE CONSIDERATION, receipt of which is hereby acknowledged, Employee agrees as follows:

1. Employee agrees upon the execution of this Agreement to surrender to legal counsel for Employer all [employer] information in whatever form it is possessed by Employee, including but not limited to computer printouts, index cards, mailing labels, floppy disk(s), or other methods of computer storage, and photostatic, typewritten, and handwritten copies of the same.

---

[77] *See* Employee Dismissal Law and Practice §§ 2.6, 8.10.

2. Employee releases and discharges Employer, its successors and assigns, directors, officers, shareholders, and employees, from all rights, claims, and causes of action that Employee now has, or may hereafter have, that arose, arise, or may arise out of any action, contract, conduct, or course of conduct whatsoever at any time prior to the date of the signing of this Agreement, specifically, but not limited to, any and all claims and causes of action arising out of or pertaining to Employee's employment by Employer and its termination.

3. Employee specifically releases and discharges Employer, its successors and assigns, directors, officers, shareholders and employees, from all rights, claims, and causes of action that Employee now has, or may hereafter have, that arose, arise, or may arise out of any action, contract, conduct, or course of conduct whatsoever at any time prior to the date of the signing of this Agreement, pertaining to any physical or mental disability Employee may have had during employment or any steps taken by the employer to accommodate such disabilities or refusal to accommodate such disabilities. Employee subscribes to this paragraph after having consulted legal counsel about applicable rights under the Americans with Disabilities Act and state and local law protecting disabled employees.

4. In consideration of the foregoing promises of Employee and notwithstanding any other provision of the Agreement, Employer agrees that Employee may retain the [number] clients listed on the two handwritten pages attached hereto, collectively designated Exhibit B, and incorporated herein by reference.

5. The parties, in executing this Agreement, do not rely on any inducements, promises, or representations made by any other party, or a party's agents or attorneys, other than those expressed herein. The parties have read this Agreement, consisting of [_] pages and have had the consequences explained by their respective attorneys. In executing this Agreement the parties intended to be legally bound.

By: [_____]

[2] Refusal to Accommodate Release

FORM 18–27 Sample Release for Refusal to Accommodate

Release from Liability for Employer's Refusal to Provide Reasonable Accommodations

In consideration of [amount] paid by [Employer] on [date], the receipt of which is hereby acknowledged, I, [Employee], my heirs, legal representatives, successors, and assigns, release [Employer] from all lawsuits arising out of [Employer's] refusal to provide reasonable accommodations, as defined by the Americans with Disabilities Act ("ADA"), for my blindness. This release includes all lawsuits I ever had, presently have, or may have in the future pertaining to [Employer's] refusal to provide reasonable accommodations. In addition, this release includes, but is not limited to, lawsuits potentially arising under the ADA, all state or federal statutes governing discrimination against handicapped individuals, and all wrongful termination claims, whether based on tort or contract theories of recovery.

I understand the terms of this release and have executed it voluntarily. In witness whereof, I execute this release on [date], at [city, state].

[Signature of Releasor]

[3] Hypothetical Release and Commentary

Hypothetical. On July 5, 1992, John Jones, then an employee of XYZ, Inc. ("XYZ"), requested reasonable accommodations from XYZ's management to accommodate Jones's recent lost of vision. XYZ refused to grant Jones's request and fired him. In response to the firing, Jones threatened to sue XYZ under the Americans with Disabilities Act ("ADA"). In turn, XYZ offered Jones $10,000 in exchange for a signed statement by Jones releasing XYZ from all liability related to their refusal to provide reasonable accommodations for him. Jones accepted XYZ's offer and signed a release drafted by XYZ's counsel.[78]

Commentary. A release[79] is a contract an employer uses to protect itself from pending or potential lawsuits arising from the employer's past conduct. This section discusses the essential elements of an ADA claim release and suggests additional provisions that practitioners might want to include in their releases.

To be valid, a release must be supported by consideration and release only those claims the law permits parties to release. In addition, the releasor must voluntarily and knowingly enter into the release.

Because a release is a contract, the release must meet all requirements of a contract, including the requirement of consideration. Furthermore, the parties must determine what consideration is adequate given the legal remedies forfeited by the employee. In addition, it is prudent for the parties to

---

[78] *See* § 18.08[7].

[79] This memorandum makes no distinction between a release and a covenant not to sue. Although both documents are contracts, a *release* is a covenant that surrenders a right of action, while a *covenant not to sue* is an agreement not to enforce a right of action. W. Prosser & P. Keeton, Prosser and Keeton on Torts § 49, at 332–36 (5th ed. 1984) [hereinafter Prosser & Keeton]. In jurisdictions that distinguish between the two documents, the distinction is important as a matter of procedure and when joint tortfeasors are involved. As a matter of procedure, a release is an affirmative defense, Fed. R. Civ. P. 8(c), but a breach of a covenant not to sue would not affect the lawsuit brought in violation of the covenant. Instead, the amount recovered in a lawsuit brought in violation of a covenant not to sue would be used to compute damages in a subsequent lawsuit based on the employee's breach of that covenant not to sue. Prosser & Keeton at 334. When joint tortfeasors are the defendants in a lawsuit, the distinction between a release and a covenant not to sue has import in determining which of the tortfeasors the document legally releases. Jurisdictions have varied views concerning the distinction between and related legal effect of releases and covenants not to sue. *See id.* at 332–36.

state that the release is supported by consideration and specify the consideration for the release.[80]

Besides the contractual requirements, waivers of certain claims may be limited by law.[81] For example, an employee cannot waive claims under the Fair Labor Standards Act[82] except in settlements supervised by the Wage and Hour Administration of the Department of Labor.[83] In the case of claim releases under the ADA, such a statutory limitation is not at issue because the ADA does not expressly prohibit the use of releases. Moreover, the Civil Rights Act of 1964,[84] whose enforcement powers, remedies, and procedures are the enforcement powers, remedies, and procedures available to plaintiffs under the ADA,[85] permits the use of releases.[86]

Related to the requirement that the law must permit the release is the idea that the substantive terms of the release should not conflict with any other agreement to which the employer is bound. An example of such agreements includes any labor contract, such as a collective bargaining agreement.[87]

Finally, in addition to the requirements and limitations concerning the substantive terms of the contract, the employee must knowingly and voluntarily agree to the terms of the release.[88]

The more carefully a release is drafted, the more likely it is that the document will have the effect intended by the parties.[89] Depending upon the

---

[80] One practitioner suggests that the recital of consideration should also include statements that the consideration is "good and valuable" and that the consideration is "hereby received and acknowledged." Such a statement would support the argument that the consideration is adequate and help enforce a release signed by and delivered to an employee who might try to renege on the release by returning the settlement check. J.H. Carey, *A Checklist for Drafting Employee Releases,* Prac. Law. 21, 27 (Apr. 1989). It is dubious that such formal boilerplate makes much difference, except psychologically in discouraging suit.

[81] In addition, the release must not be contrary to public policy or unconscionable. *See* Bartel Dental Books Co. v. Schultz, 786 F.2d 486, 488 (2d Cir.), *cert. denied,* 478 U.S. 1006 (1986).

[82] 29 U.S.C. §§ 201–219 (1994).

[83] J.H. Carey, *A Checklist for Drafting Employee Releases,* Prac. Law. 21–24 (Apr. 1989) (citing D.A. Schulte, Inc. v. Gangi, 328 U.S. 108, 114–15 (1946)).

[84] 42 U.S.C. ch. 21 (1994) [hereinafter Civil Rights Act of 1964].

[85] ADA § 107(a), 42 U.S.C. § 12,117(a) (1994).

[86] Wright v. Southwestern Bell Tel. Co., 925 F.2d 1288, 1292 (10th Cir. 1991) (Title VII claims may be waived by agreement, but the waiver must be knowing and voluntary).

[87] *See* W.R. Grace & Co. v. Local Union 759, Int'l Union of United Rubber Workers of Am., 461 U.S. 757 (1983) (employer entered into a conciliation agreement with the EEOC that conflicted with the seniority provisions of the employer's existing collective bargaining agreement with the union).

[88] Wright v. Southwestern Bell Tel. Co., 925 F.2d 1288, 1292 (10th Cir. 1991).

[89] Bartel Dental Books Co. v. Schultz, 786 F.2d 486, 488 (2d Cir. 1986) (stating that contract principles apply to interpretation of releases).

needs and complexity of a particular release, counsel should consider including in their releases provisions addressing some or all of the following concerns:

1. A recital of facts that led to the release;
2. The specific legal identity of parties released;
3. The purpose of the document;
4. The specific claims released by the employee;
5. A confidentiality clause;[90]
6. A clause in which the employer specifies that entering into the agreement is not an admission of fault;
7. An amicable resolution of disputed claims statement, supporting an argument that the release is an offer of settlement inadmissible in any other legal proceedings;
8. A statement that if any terms of the agreement are inoperative, for any reason, those provisions are severable and the remaining provisions retain full effect;
9. An integration clause stating that the release constitutes the entire agreement between the parties;
10. The presence of choice of law and forum clauses;
11. Any other additional commitments.[91]

§ 18.23   TITLE III MATERIALS

Title III[92] involves relationships that are less formal than employer-employee relationships. Accordingly, there is less opportunity for internal governance documentation to reduce the exposure to ADA liability. There are, however, certain kinds of documents that promote Title III compliance, as presented in § § 18.24 and 18.26.

§ 18.24   STRATEGIES FOR PRIVATE PLACES OF PUBLIC ACCOMMODATION

[A]   Existing Facilities

Private places of public accommodation can fulfill the duties under Title III of the ADA by developing a basic compliance strategy that includes actions with respect both to existing facilities and services, and to new facilities.

---

[90] Such a clause is useful if the employer does not want other employees to know how much the employer paid the employee to execute the release.

[91] See J.H. Carey, *A Checklist for Drafting Employee Releases,* Prac. Law. 21, 26–30 (Apr. 1989), for a more detailed discussion of these clauses and additional suggestions.

[92] ADA §§ 301–310, 42 U.S.C. §§ 12,181–12,189 (1994) [hereinafter Title III].

With respect to existing facilities and services, the enterprise should do at least the following:

1. Erect signs indicating the enterprise's commitment to afford access to the disabled and instructing how someone should request assistance or accommodation;
2. Train all employees about how to handle requests for assistance or accommodation;
3. Establish a procedure for handling complaints that accommodation has not been forthcoming, and make sure that all employees know this procedure;
4. Work with trade associations and organizations for the disabled to establish local or regional help desks and conciliation programs to work out problems between the disabled and individual merchants;
5. Evaluate existing facilities against Department of Justice (DOJ) and Architectural and Transportation Barriers Compliance Board (ATBCB) guidelines (considered in Chapter 6) and make necessary modifications, especially in parking lots, stairways, and restrooms.

[B] New Facilities

Whenever a private place of public accommodation plans a new facility or an addition to an existing facility, one of the first subjects in interviewing architects should be compliance with the ADA. The architects should be knowledgeable about the requirements of the ATBCB guidelines and creative in identifying alternative ways to meet those requirements. It almost certainly will be cheaper to build a new facility to provide for disabled access than to modify the facility after it has been built.

When particular accommodations are ruled out in the design stages, the cost implications of the rejected alternatives should be documented carefully with an eye toward sustaining an unreasonableness or undue hardship defense as discussed in § 6.04.

§ 18.25 PUBLIC ACCOMMODATION AND COMMERCIAL FACILITY NOTICE

[A] Generally

The notice in Form 18–28 does not add to the obligations imposed by the ADA itself. It can build goodwill and channel complaints or requests for accommodation to the management rather than to a lawyer. The only significant disadvantage would occur if a notice like this were posted and if the person handling inquiries were unavailable or unresponsive. Any such notice should be coupled with appropriate instructions to employees, like those presented in Form 18–29. Employees of entities covered by Title III should be instructed about their obligations under the ADA lest, out of ignorance, they act in a way that causes liability for the entity.

[B] Sample Forms

[1] Sample Public Accommodation and Commercial Facility Notice

FORM 18–28   **Sample Public Accommodation and Commercial Facility Notice**

We take our obligations under the Americans with Disabilities Act seriously. We do not discriminate based on physical or mental disability, and we strive to make our facility accessible to the disabled. If you are disabled and have a specific request or suggestion, please contact [name].

[2] Directions to Employees Regarding Disabled Customers

FORM 18–29   **Sample Directions to Employees Regarding Disabled Customers**

The Americans with Disabilities Act and similar state statutes and local ordinances obligate us to make our facilities accessible to persons with physical and mental disabilities. We take these obligations seriously and have caused notices to be posted on the premises informing the public that we do. An important part of your job responsibility is to be sensitive and responsive to persons with disabilities. Sometimes accessibility to the disabled can be improved by physical changes in design and layout of the premises. To some extent we have made those design and layout changes.

In other instances, the most effective way to ensure accessibility is to provide special personal assistance.

You may be requested to provide such assistance either by a disabled customer or by your supervisor. In either event, you must take such a request seriously. You must be considerate and you must not act so as to cause undue commotion or embarrassment to the disabled customer.

In many instances, suggestion by the disabled person is the best guide as to how to be helpful. You should not override a request with your own judgment about what is "best" for the disabled customer.

In many instances, the simplest and best response to a request is to do what the customer asks. An easy example is helping someone in a wheelchair over a curb or through a doorway.

Occasionally, however, you may receive a request from a customer that seems to you as though it would create a risk to other customers, to yourself, or to employees, or would interfere with your performance of your other job responsibilities in a major way. You should not take it upon yourself to refuse the request. Instead, you should make every effort to obtain instructions of advice from your supervisor or from the designated ADA compliance officer.

§ 18.26   PRIVATE DISPUTE RESOLUTION

Section 513 of the ADA[93] provides for the use of alternative means of dispute resolution, including settlement negotiations, conciliation, facilitation, mediation, fact-finding, minitrials, and arbitration. In the House Judiciary Report,[94] the House and Senate Conference Committee adopted language in the House Conference Report[95] noting that "the use of these alternative dispute resolution procedures is completely voluntary. Under no condition would an arbitration clause in a collective bargaining agreement or employment contract prevent an individual from pursuing their rights under the ADA."[96]

The range of internal dispute resolution procedures that may be useful to employers in avoiding the high costs of court litigation is considered in the book *Employee Dismissal Law and Practice.*[97] Such procedures are particularly appropriate for potential claims of disability discrimination because they offer an opportunity for the employer and employee to work things out through the employer's reasonable accommodation or the employee's better understanding of essential job functions. Employers should consider new internal dispute resolution procedures, including mediation, advisory committees, and arbitration, as they prepare to conform to the ADA.

Alternative dispute resolution is not limited to employment disputes; it also may be used for disputes arising over governmental service and access to places of public accommodation. In the governmental setting, alternative dispute resolution merges with the reform of administrative procedures. In this setting, however, agencies should consider the value of mediation and arbitration, compared with traditional agency hearings.[98]

In the Title III context, most requests for accommodation are addressed informally. It might be helpful, however, for trade associations and chambers of commerce to consider developing alternative dispute resolution programs in conjunction with organizations for the disabled. Such programs must provide a well-publicized point of intervention to which a complaint may be referred when a disabled person believes that a merchant is not accommodating a disability appropriately. Then representatives from trade asso-

---

[93] 42 U.S.C. § 12,213 (1994).

[94] H.R. Rep. No. 485, 101st Cong., 2d Sess., pt. 3 (1990).

[95] H.R. Conf. Rep. No. 596, 101st Cong., 2d Sess., *reprinted in* 136 Cong. Rec. H4582 (daily ed. July 12, 1990), para. 81.

[96] *Id.*

[97] Employee Dismissal Law and Practice ch. 9.

[98] *See* Administrative Conference of the United States, Recommendation 95–7, 60 Fed. Reg. 43,108 (1995) (recommending agency use of mediation for ADA disputes).

ciations and organizations for the disabled can become involved to conciliate a resolution.

Such a program could be combined with a "help line" or "help desk" for those disabled persons seeking accommodation in places of public accommodation.

AMERICANS WITH DISABILITIES ACT

Enacted by the Congress July 26, 1990, as amended through July 17, 2002

Titles I, III, and V are compared with the House Bill and the Senate Bill by footnotes to the final provisions noting differing House and Senate language.

42 U.S.C. sec. 12101

Chapter 26

Equal Opportunity for Individuals with Disabilities

An Act to establish a clear and comprehensive prohibition of discrimination on the basis of disability.

SECTION 1. SHORT TITLE: TABLE OF CONTENTS

(a) SHORT TITLE. — This Act may be cited as the "Americans with Disabilities Act of 1990."

(b) TABLE OF CONTENTS. — The table of contents is as follows:

TITLE III — PUBLIC ACCOMMODATIONS AND SERVICES OPERATED BY PRIVATE ENTITIES

TITLE IV — TELECOMMUNICATIONS RELAY SERVICES

TITLE V — MISCELLANEOUS PROVISIONS

SEC. 2. [42 U.S.C. sec. 12101] FINDINGS AND PURPOSES

(a) FINDINGS —

The Congress finds that —

(1) some 43,000,000 Americans have one or more physical or mental disabilities, and this number is increasing as the population as a whole is growing older;

(2) historically, society has tended to isolate and segregate individuals with disabilities, and, despite some improvements, such forms of discrimination against individuals with disabilities continue to be a serious and pervasive social problem;

(3) discrimination against individuals with disabilities persists in such critical areas as employment, housing, public accommodations, education, transportation, communication, recreation, institutionalization, health services, voting, and access to public services;

(4) unlike individuals who have experienced discrimination on the basis of race, color,[1] sex, national origin, religion, or age, individuals who have experienced discrimination on the basis of disability have often had no legal recourse to redress such discrimination;

(5) individuals with disabilities continually encounter various forms of discrimination, including outright intentional exclusion, the discriminatory effects of architectural, transportation, and communication barriers, overprotective rules and policies, failure to make modifications to existing facilities and practices, exclusionary qualification standards and criteria, segregation, and relegation to lesser services, programs, activities, benefits, jobs, or other opportunities;

(6) census data, national polls, and other studies have documented that people with disabilities, as a group, occupy an inferior status in our society, and are severely disadvantaged socially, vocationally, economically, and educationally;

(7) individuals with disabilities are a discrete and insular minority who have been faced with restrictions and limitations, subjected to a history of purposeful unequal treatment, and relegated to a position of political power-

---

[1] The word "color" was not in the Senate-passed bill.

lessness in our society, based on characteristics that are beyond the control of such individuals and resulting from stereotypic assumptions not truly indicative of the individual ability of such individuals to participate in, and contribute to, society;

(8) the Nation's proper goals regarding individuals with disabilities are to assure equality of opportunity, full participation, independent living, and economic self-sufficiency for such individuals; and

(9) the continuing existence of unfair and unnecessary discrimination and prejudice denies people with disabilities the opportunity to compete on an equal basis and to pursue those opportunities for which our free society is justifiably famous, and costs the United States billions of dollars in unnecessary expenses resulting from dependency and nonproductivity.

(b) PURPOSE —

It is the purpose of this Act —

(1) to provide a clear and comprehensive national mandate for the elimination of discrimination against individuals with disabilities;

(2) to provide clear, strong, consistent, enforceable standards addressing discrimination against individuals with disabilities;

(3) to ensure that the Federal Government plays a central role in enforcing the standards established in this Act on behalf of individuals with disabilities; and

(4) to invoke the sweep of congressional authority, including the[2] power to enforce the fourteenth amendment and to regulate commerce, in order to address the major areas of discrimination faced day-to-day by people with disabilities.

SEC. 3. [42 U.S.C. sec. 12102] DEFINITIONS

As used in this Act:

(1) AUXILIARY AIDS AND SERVICES —

The term "auxiliary aids and services" includes —

---

[2] The Senate-passed bill used the word "its" instead of the word "the."

(A) qualified interpreters or other effective methods of making aurally delivered materials available to individuals with hearing impairments;

(B) qualified readers, taped texts, or other effective methods of making visually delivered materials available to individuals with visual impairments;

(C) acquisition or modification of equipment or devices; and

(D) other similar services and actions.

(2) DISABILITY —

The term "disability" means, with respect to an individual —

(A) a physical or mental impairment that substantially limits one or more of the major life activities of such individual;

(B) a record of such an impairment; or

(C) being regarded as having such an impairment.

(3) STATE —

The term "State" means each of the several States, the District of Columbia, the Commonwealth of Puerto Rico, Guam, American Samoa, the Virgin Islands, the Trust Territory of the Pacific Islands, and the Commonwealth of the Northern Mariana Islands.

TITLE I [Subchapter I] — EMPLOYMENT

SEC. 101. [42 U.S.C. sec. 12111] DEFINITIONS

As used in this title:

(1) COMMISSION —

The term "Commission" means the Equal Employment Opportunity Commission established by section 705 of the Civil Rights Act of 1964 (42 U.S.C. 2000e-4).

(2) COVERED ENTITY —

The term "covered entity" means an employer, employment agency, labor organization, or joint labor-management committee.

(3) DIRECT THREAT —

The term "direct threat" means a significant risk to the health or safety of others that cannot be eliminated by reasonable accommodation.[3]

(4) EMPLOYEE —

The term "employee" means an individual employed by an employer. With respect to employment in a foreign country such term includes an individual who is a citizen of the United States.

(5) EMPLOYER —

(A) IN GENERAL —

The term "employer" means a person engaged in an industry affecting commerce who has 15 or more employees for each working day in each of 20 or more calendar weeks in the current or preceding calendar year, and any agent of such person, except that, for two years following the effective date of this title, an employer means a person engaged in an industry affecting commerce who has 25 or more employees for each working day in each of 20 or more calendar weeks in the current or preceding year, and any agent of such person.

(B) EXCEPTIONS —

The term "employer" does not include —

(i) the United States, a corporation wholly owned by the government of the United States, or an Indian tribe; or

(ii) a bona fide private membership club (other than a labor organization) that is exempt from taxation under section 501(c) of the Internal Revenue Code of 1986.

(6) Illegal use of drugs —

(A) IN GENERAL —

The term "illegal use of drugs" means the use of drugs, the possession or distribution of which is unlawful under the Controlled Substances Act (21

---

[3] The Senate-passed bill did not contain a definition of *direct threat*, and thus the paragraphs from this point on were numbered differently.

U.S.C. 812). Such term does not include the use of a drug taken under supervision by a licensed health care professional, or other uses authorized by the Controlled Substances Act or other provisions of Federal law.

(B) DRUGS —

The term "drug" means a controlled substance, as defined in schedules I through V of section 202 of the Controlled Substances Act.[4]

(7) PERSON, ETC. —

The terms "person," "labor organization," "employment agency," "commerce," and "industry affecting commerce," shall have the same meaning given such terms in section 701 of the Civil Rights Act of 1964 (42 U.S.C. 2000e).

(8) QUALIFIED INDIVIDUAL WITH A DISABILITY —

The term "qualified individual with a disability" means an individual with a disability who, with or without reasonable accommodation, can perform the essential functions of the employment position that such individual holds or desires. For the purposes of this title, consideration shall be given to the employer's judgment as to what functions of a job are essential, and if an employer has prepared a written description before advertising or interviewing applicants for the job, this description shall be considered evidence of the essential functions of the job.[5]

(9) REASONABLE ACCOMMODATION —

The term "reasonable accommodation" may include —

(A) making existing facilities used by employees readily accessible to and usable by individuals with disabilities; and

(B) job restructuring, part-time or modified work schedules, reassignment to a vacant position, acquisition or modification of equipment or devices, appropriate adjustment or modifications of examinations, training materials or policies, the provision of qualified readers or interpreters, and other similar accommodations for individuals with disabilities.

---

[4] The Senate-passed bill defined *illegal drug* instead of illegal use of drugs.

[5] The Senate-passed bill did not contain the sentence beginning, "For purposes of this title, consideration . . . ."

(10) UNDUE HARDSHIP —

(A) IN GENERAL —

The term "undue hardship" means an action requiring significant difficulty or expense, when considered in light of the factors set forth in subparagraph (B).

(B) FACTORS TO BE CONSIDERED —

In determining whether an accommodation would impose an undue hardship on a covered entity, factors to be considered include —

(i) the nature and cost of the accommodation needed under this Act;

(ii) the overall financial resources of the facility or facilities involved in the provision of the reasonable accommodation; the number of persons employed at such facility; the effect on expenses and resources, or the impact otherwise of such accommodation upon the operation of the facility;

(iii) the overall financial resources of the covered entity; the overall size of the business of a covered entity with respect to the number of its employees; the number, type, and location of its facilities; and

(iv) the type of operation or operations of the covered entity, including the composition, structure, and functions of the workforce of such entity; the geographic separateness, administrative, or fiscal relationship of the facility or facilities in question to the covered entity.[6]

---

[6] The Senate-passed bill read as follows:

(9) Undue Hardship —
(A) In General — The term "undue hardship" means an action requiring significant difficulty or expense.
(B) Determination — In determining whether an accommodation would impose an undue hardship on a covered entity, factors to be considered include —
(i) the overall size of the business of a covered entity with respect to the number of employees, number and type of facilities, and the size of the budget;
(ii) the type of operation maintained by the covered entity, including the composition and structure of the workforce of such entity; and

SEC. 102. [42 U.S.C. sec. 12112] DISCRIMINATION

(a) GENERAL RULE —

No covered entity shall discriminate against a qualified individual with a disability because of the disability of such individual in regard to job application procedures, the hiring, advancement, or discharge of employees, employee compensation,[7] job training, and other terms, conditions, and privileges of employment.

(b) CONSTRUCTION —

As used in subsection (a), the term "discriminate"[8] includes —

(1) limiting, segregating, or classifying a job applicant or employee in a way that adversely affects the opportunities or status of such applicant or employee because of the disability of such applicant or employee;

(2) participating in a contractual or other arrangement or relationship that has the effect of subjecting a covered entity's[9] qualified applicant or employee with a disability to the discrimination prohibited by this title (such relationship includes a relationship with an employment or referral agency, labor union, an organization providing fringe benefits to an employee of the covered entity, or an organization providing training and apprenticeship programs);

(3) utilizing standards, criteria, or methods of administration —

(A) that have the effect of discrimination on the basis of disability; or

(B) that perpetuate the discrimination of others who are subject to common administrative control;

(4) excluding or otherwise denying equal jobs or benefits to a qualified individual because of the known disability of an individual with whom the qualified individual is known to have a relationship or association;

---

[7] In the Senate-passed bill, the word "advancement" appeared after "compensation," rather than after "hiring."

[8] The Senate-passed bill used the word "discrimination."

[9] The Senate-passed bill did not contain the phrase "covered entity's."

(5)(A)[10] not making reasonable accommodations to the known physical or mental limitations of an otherwise qualified[11] individual with a disability[12] who is an applicant or employee, unless such covered entity can demonstrate that the accommodation would impose an undue hardship on the operation of the business of such covered entity; or

(B) denying employment opportunities to a job applicant or employee who is an otherwise qualified individual with a disability,[13] if such denial is based on the need of such covered entity to make reasonable accommodation to the physical or mental impairments of the employee or applicant;

(6) using qualification standards,[14] employment tests or other selection criteria that screen out or tend to screen out an individual with a disability or a class of individuals with disabilities unless the standard,[15] test or other selection criteria, as used by the covered entity, is shown to be job-related for the position in question and is consistent with business necessity; and

(7) failing to select and administer tests concerning employment in the most effective manner to ensure that, when such test is administered to a job applicant or employee who has a disability that impairs sensory, manual, or speaking skills, such test results accurately reflect the skills, aptitude, or whatever other factor of such applicant or employee that such test purports to measure, rather than reflecting the impaired sensory, manual, or speaking skills of such employee or applicant (except where such skills are the factors that the test purports to measure).

(c) Covered entities in foreign countries

(1) In general

It shall not be unlawful under this section for a covered entity to take any action that constitutes discrimination under this section with respect to an employee in a workplace in a foreign country if compliance with this section would cause such covered entity to violate the law of the foreign country in which such workplace is located.

---

[10] The Senate-passed bill was structured slightly differently, having no subparagraph (A) and numbering subparagraph (B) of this paragraph as paragraph (6).

[11] The Senate-passed bill did not contain the phrase "an otherwise."

[12] The Senate-passed bill did not contain the phrase "with a disability."

[13] The Senate-passed bill used the phrase "a qualified individual" rather than the phrase "an otherwise qualified individual."

[14] The Senate-passed bill did not contain the phrase "qualification standards."

[15] The Senate-passed bill did not contain the word "standard."

(2) Control of corporation

(A) Presumption

If an employer controls a corporation whose place of incorporation is a foreign country, any practice that constitutes discrimination under this section and is engaged in by such corporation shall be presumed to be engaged in by such employer.

(B) Exception

This section shall not apply with respect to the foreign operations of an employer that is a foreign person not controlled by an American employer.

(C) Determination

For purposes of this paragraph, the determination of whether an employer controls a corporation shall be based on —

(i) the interrelation of operations;

(ii) the common management;

(iii) the centralized control of labor relations; and

(iv) the common ownership or financial control, of the employer and the corporation.

(d) MEDICAL EXAMINATIONS AND INQUIRIES —

(1) IN GENERAL —

The prohibition against discrimination as referred to in subsection (a) shall include medical examinations and inquiries.

(2) PREEMPLOYMENT —

(A) PROHIBITED EXAMINATION OR INQUIRY —

Except as provided in paragraph (3), a covered entity shall not conduct a medical examination or make inquiries of a job applicant[16] as to whether

---

[16] The Senate-passed bill contained the phrase "or employee."

such applicant[17] is an individual with a disability or as to the nature or severity of such disability.

(B) ACCEPTABLE INQUIRY —

A covered entity may make preemployment inquiries into the ability of an applicant to perform job-related functions.

(3) EMPLOYMENT ENTRANCE EXAMINATION —

A covered entity may require a medical examination after an offer of employment has been made to a job applicant and prior to the commencement of the employment duties of such applicant, and may condition an offer of employment on the results of such examination, if —

(A) all entering employees are subjected to such an examination regardless of disability;

(B) information obtained regarding the medical condition or history of the applicant is collected and maintained on separate forms and in separate medical files and is treated as a confidential medical record, except that —

(i) supervisors and managers may be informed regarding necessary restrictions on the work or duties of the employee and necessary accommodations;

(ii) first aid and safety personnel may be informed, when appropriate, if the disability might require emergency treatment; and

(iii) government officials investigating compliance with this Act shall be provided relevant information on request; and

(C) the results of such[18] examination are used only in accordance with this title.

(4) EXAMINATION AND INQUIRY —

(A) PROHIBITED EXAMINATIONS AND INQUIRIES —

A covered entity shall not require[19] a medical examination and shall not make inquiries of an employee as to whether such employee is an individual

---

[17] The Senate-passed bill contained the phrase "or employee."
[18] The Senate-passed bill contained the word "physical."
[19] The Senate-passed bill used the phrase "conduct or require" rather than "require."

with a disability or as to the nature or severity of the disability, unless such examination or inquiry is shown to be job-related and consistent with business necessity.

(B) ACCEPTABLE EXAMINATIONS AND INQUIRIES — [20]

A covered entity may conduct voluntary medical examinations, including voluntary medical histories, which are part of an employee health program available to employees at that work site.[21] A covered entity may make inquiries into the ability of an employee to perform job-related functions.

(C) REQUIREMENT —

Information obtained under subparagraph (B) regarding the medical condition or history of any employee are subject to the requirements of subparagraphs (B) and (C) of paragraph (3).[22]

SEC. 103. [42 U.S.C. sec. 12113] DEFENSES

(a) IN GENERAL —

It may be a defense to a charge of discrimination under this Act that an alleged application of qualification standards, tests, or selection criteria that screen out or tend to screen out or otherwise deny a job or benefit to an individual with a disability has been shown to be job-related and consistent with business necessity, and such performance cannot be accomplished by reasonable accommodation, as required under this title.[23]

(b) QUALIFICATION STANDARDS —

The term "qualification standards" may include a requirement that an individual[24] shall not pose a direct threat to the health or safety of other individuals in the workplace.

---

[20] The Senate-passed bill used the title "Acceptable Inquiries."

[21] The Senate-passed bill did not contain the first sentence.

[22] The Senate-passed bill did not contain this subparagraph (C).

[23] The Senate-passed bill did not contain the phrase "as required under this title."

[24] The Senate-passed bill contained the phrase "with a currently contagious disease or infection" at this point.

(c) RELIGIOUS ENTITIES —

(1) IN GENERAL —

This title shall not prohibit a religious corporation, association, educational institution, or society from giving preference in employment to individuals of a particular religion to perform work connected with the carrying on by such corporation, association, educational institution, or society of its activities.

(2) RELIGIOUS TENETS REQUIREMENT — [25]

Under this title, a religious organization may require[26] that all applicants and employees conform to the religious tenets of such organization.

(d) List of Infectious and Communicable Diseases. — [27]

(1) In General — The Secretary of Health and Human Services, not later than 6 months after the date of enactment of this Act, shall —

(A) review all infectious and communicable disease which may be transmitted through handling the food supply;

(B) publish a list of infectious and communicable diseases which are transmitted through handling the food supply;

(C) publish the methods by which such diseases are transmitted; and

(D) widely disseminate such information regarding the list of diseases and their modes of transmissibility to the general public.

---

[25] The Senate-passed bill used the paragraph caption, "Qualification Standard."

[26] The Senate-passed bill contained the phrase "as a qualification standard to employment," at this point.

[27] Subsection (d) was added by conferees after the Senate sent the conference report back to the conferees with instructions to add this subsection, on July 11, 1990. The first conference report deleted the following subsection (d) that was contained in the House-passed bill:

> (d) FOOD HANDLING JOBS —
> It shall not be a violation of this Act for an employer to refuse to assign or continue to assign any employee with an infectious or communicable disease of public health significance to a job involving food handling, provided that the employer shall make reasonable accommodation that would offer an alternative employment opportunity for which the employee is qualified and for which the employee would sustain no economic damage.

Such list shall be updated annually.

(2) Applications —

In any case in which an individual has an infectious or communicable disease that is transmitted to others through the handling of food, that is included on the list developed by the Secretary of Health and Human Services under paragraph (1), and which cannot be eliminated by reasonable accommodation, a covered entity may refuse to assign or continue to assign such individual to a job involving food handling.

(3) Construction —

Nothing in this Act shall be construed to preempt, modify, or amend any State, county, or local law, ordinance, or regulation applicable to food handling which is designed to protect the public health from individuals who pose a significant risk to the health or safety of others, which cannot be eliminated by reasonable accommodation, pursuant to the list infectious or communicable diseases and the modes of transmissibility published by the Secretary Health and Human Services.

SEC. 104. [42 U.S.C. sec. 12114] ILLEGAL USE OF DRUGS AND ALCOHOL[28]

(a) QUALIFIED INDIVIDUAL WITH A DISABILITY —

For purposes of this title, the term "qualified individual with a disability" shall not include any employee or applicant who is currently engaging in the illegal use of drugs, when the covered entity acts on the basis of such use.

(b) RULES OF CONSTRUCTION —

Nothing in subsection (a) shall be construed to exclude as a qualified individual with a disability an individual who —

(1) has successfully completed a supervised drug rehabilitation program and is no longer engaging in the illegal use of drugs, or has otherwise been rehabilitated successfully and is no longer engaging in such use;

---

[28] The Senate-passed bill used the section title, "Illegal Drugs and Alcohol." The Senate-passed bill language for this section was significantly different from the final language, as discussed in Chs. 2 and 4.

(2) is participating in a supervised rehabilitation program and is no longer engaging in such use; or

(3) is erroneously regarded as engaging in such use, but is not engaging in such use; except that it shall not be a violation of this Act for a covered entity to adopt or administer reasonable policies or procedures, including but not limited to drug testing, designed to ensure that an individual described in paragraph (1) or (2) is no longer engaging in the illegal use of drugs.

(c) AUTHORITY OF COVERED ENTITY —

A covered entity —

(1) may prohibit the illegal use of drugs and the use of alcohol at the workplace by all employees;

(2) may require that employees shall not be under the influence of alcohol or be engaging in the illegal use of drugs at the workplace;

(3) may require that employees behave in conformance with the requirements established under the Drug-Free Workplace Act of 1988 (41 U.S.C. 701 *et seq.*);

(4) may hold an employee who engages in the illegal use of drugs or who is an alcoholic to the same qualification standards for employment or job performance and behavior that such entity holds other employees, even if any unsatisfactory performance or behavior is related to the drug use or alcoholism of such employee; and

(5) may, with respect to Federal regulations regarding alcohol and the illegal use of drugs, require that —

(A) employees comply with the standards established in such regulations of the Department of Defense, if the employees of the covered entity are employed in an industry subject to such regulations, including complying with regulations (if any) that apply to employment in sensitive positions in such an industry, in the case of employees of the covered entity who are employed in such positions (as defined in the regulations of the Department of Defense);

(B) employees comply with the standards established in such regulations of the Nuclear Regulatory Commission, if the employees of the covered entity are employed in an industry subject to such regulations, including complying with regulations (if any) that apply to employment in sensitive positions in such an industry, in the case of employees of the covered entity who are employed in such positions (as defined in the regulations of the Nuclear Regulatory Commission); and

(C) employees comply with the standards established in such regulations of the Department of Transportation, if the employees of the covered entity are employed in a transportation industry subject to such regulations, including complying with such regulations (if any) that apply to employment in sensitive positions in such an industry, in the case of employees of the covered entity who are employed in such positions (as defined in the regulations of the Department of Transportation).

(d) DRUG TESTING —

(1) IN GENERAL —

For purposes of this title, a test to determine the illegal use of drugs shall not be considered a medical examination.

(2) CONSTRUCTION —

Nothing in this title shall be construed to encourage, prohibit, or authorize the conducting of drug testing for the illegal use of drugs by job applicants or employees or making employment decisions based on such test results.

(e) TRANSPORTATION EMPLOYEES — [29]

Nothing in this title shall be construed to encourage, prohibit, restrict, or authorize the otherwise lawful exercise by entities subject to the jurisdiction of the Department of Transportation[30] of authority to —

(1) test employees of such entities[31] in, and applicants for, positions involving safety-sensitive duties[32] for the illegal use of drugs and for on-duty impairment by alcohol; and

---

[29] The House-passed bill entitled subsection (e), "Rail Employees." The Senate-passed bill had no subsection (e).

[30] The conference report substituted "entities subject to the jurisdiction of the Department of Transportation" for "railroad" in the House-passed bill.

[31] The conference report substituted "employees of such entities" for "railroad employees" in the House-passed bill.

[32] The conferees deleted the phrase "as determined by the Secretary of Transportation," contained in the House passed bill.

(2) remove such persons who test positive for illegal use of drugs and on-duty impairment by alcohol[33] pursuant to paragraph (1) from safety-sensitive duties in implementing subsection (c).

SEC. 105. [42 U.S.C. sec. 12115] POSTING NOTICES

Every employer, employment agency, labor organization, or joint labor-management committee covered under this title shall post notices in an accessible format to applicants, employees, and members describing the applicable provisions of this Act, in the manner prescribed by section 711 of the Civil Rights Act of 1964 (42 U.S.C. 2000e-10).

SEC. 106. [42 U.S.C. sec. 12116] REGULATIONS

Not later than 1 year after the date of enactment of this Act, the Commission shall issue regulations in an accessible format to carry out this title in accordance with subchapter II of chapter 5 of title 5, United States Code.

SEC. 107. [42 U.S.C. sec. 121117] ENFORCEMENT

(a) POWERS, REMEDIES, AND PROCEDURES —

The powers,[34] remedies, and procedures set forth in sections 705,[35] 706, 707, 709, and 710 of the Civil Rights Act of 1964 (42 U.S.C. 2000e-4,[36] 2000e-5, 2000e-6, 2000e-8, and 2000e-9) shall be the powers, remedies, and procedures this title provides to[37] the Commission, to the Attorney General,[38] or to any person alleging[39] discrimination on the basis of disability in violation of any provision of this Act, or regulations promulgated under section 106, concerning employment.

(b) COORDINATION —

The agencies with enforcement authority for actions which allege employment discrimination under this title and under the Rehabilitation Act of 1973

---

[33] The conference report inserted the phrase "for illegal use of drugs and on- duty impairment by alcohol" at this point.

[34] The Senate-passed bill did not contain the word "powers."

[35] The Senate-passed bill did not contain the reference to § 705.

[36] The Senate-passed bill did not contain the reference to § 2000e-4.

[37] The Senate-passed bill used the phrase "shall be available, with respect to" rather than the language "shall be the powers . . . provides to."

[38] The Senate-passed bill did not contain "to the Attorney General."

[39] The Senate-passed bill used the phrase "individual who believes that he or she is being subjected to" rather than the language "person . . . subjected to."

shall develop procedures to ensure that administrative complaints filed under this title and under the Rehabilitation Act of 1973 are dealt with in a manner that avoids duplication of effort and prevents imposition of inconsistent or conflicting standards for the same requirements under this title and the Rehabilitation Act of 1973. The Commission, the Attorney General, and the Office of Federal Contract Compliance Programs[40] shall establish such coordinating mechanisms (similar to provisions contained in the joint regulations promulgated by the Commission and the Attorney General at part 42 of title 28 and part 1691 of title 29, Code of Federal Regulations, and the Memorandum of Understanding between the Commission and the Office of Federal Contract Compliance Programs dated January 16, 1981 (46 Fed. Reg. 7435, January 23, 1981)) in regulations implementing this title and Rehabilitation Act of 1973 not later than 18 months after the date of enactment of this Act.[41]

SEC. 108. [42 U.S.C. sec. 12117] EFFECTIVE DATE

This title shall become effective 24 months after the date of enactment.

TITLE II-[Subchapter II] PUBLIC SERVICES

SUBTITLE A-[Division A] PROHIBITION AGAINST DISCRIMINATION AND OTHER GENERALLY APPLICABLE PROVISIONS

SEC. 201. [42 U.S.C. sec. 12131] DEFINITION

As used in this title:

(1) PUBLIC ENTITY —

The term "public entity" means —

(A) any State or local government;

(B) any department, agency, special purpose district, or other instrumentality of a State or States or local government; and

---

[40] The conference report substituted the phrase "The Commission, the Attorney General, and the Office of Federal Contract Compliance Programs" for the phrase "Such agencies" in the House-passed bill.

[41] The conferees added the cross-reference following the "similar to the provisions" language and the deadline to the House-passed bill. The Senate-passed bill did not contain a coordination subsection.

(C) the National Railroad Passenger Corporation, and any commuter authority (as defined in section 103(8) of the Rail Passenger Service Act).

(2) QUALIFIED INDIVIDUAL WITH A DISABILITY —

The term "qualified individual with a disability" means an individual with a disability who, with or without reasonable modifications to rules, policies, or practices, the removal of architectural, communication, or transportation barriers, or the provision of auxiliary aids and services, meets the essential eligibility requirements for the receipt of services or the participation in programs or activities provided by a public entity.

SEC. 202. [42 U.S.C. sec. 12132] DISCRIMINATION

Subject to the provisions of this title, no qualified individual with a disability shall, by reason of such disability, be excluded from participation in or be denied the benefits of the services, programs, or activities of a public entity, or be subjected to discrimination by any such entity.

SEC. 203. [42 U.S.C. sec. 12133] ENFORCEMENT

The remedies, procedures, and rights set forth in section 505 of the Rehabilitation Act of 1973 (29 U.S.C. 794a) shall be the remedies, procedures and rights this title provides to any person alleging discrimination on the basis of disability in violation of section 202.

SEC. 204. [42 U.S.C. sec. 12134] REGULATIONS

(a) IN GENERAL —

Not later than 1 year after the date of enactment of this Act, the Attorney General shall promulgate regulations in an accessible format that implement this subtitle. Such regulations shall not include any matter within the scope of the authority of the Secretary of Transportation under section 223, 229, or 244.

(b) RELATIONSHIP TO OTHER REGULATIONS —

Except for "program accessibility, existing facilities," and "communications," regulations under subsection (a) shall be consistent with this Act and with the coordination regulations under part 41 of title 28, Code of Federal Regulations (as promulgated by the Department of Health, Education, and Welfare on January 13, 1978), applicable to recipients of Federal financial assistance under section 504 of the Rehabilitation Act of 1973 (29 U.S.C.

794). With respect to "program accessibility, existing facilities," and "communications," such regulations shall be consistent with regulations and analysis as in part 39 of title 28 of the Code of Federal Regulations, applicable to federally conducted activities under such section 504.

(c) STANDARDS —

Regulations under subsection (a) shall include standards applicable to facilities and vehicles covered by this subtitle, other than facilities, stations, rail passenger cars, and vehicles covered by subtitle B. Such standards shall be consistent with the minimum guidelines and requirements issued by the Architectural and Transportation Barriers Compliance Board in accordance with section 504(a) of this Act.

SEC. 205. [42 U.S.C. sec. 12134] EFFECTIVE DATE

(a) GENERAL RULE —

Except as provided in subsection (b), this subtitle shall become effective 18 months after the date of enactment of this Act.

(b) EXCEPTION —

Section 204 shall become effective on the date of enactment of this Act.

SUBTITLE B — [Division B] ACTIONS APPLICABLE TO PUBLIC TRANSPORTATION PROVIDED BY PUBLIC ENTITIES CONSIDERED DISCRIMINATORY[42]

PART I — PUBLIC TRANSPORTATION OTHER THAN BY AIRCRAFT OR CERTAIN RAIL OPERATIONS

SEC. 221. [42 U.S.C. sec. 12141] DEFINITIONS

As used in this part:

(1) DEMAND RESPONSIVE SYSTEM —

The term "demand responsive system" means any system of providing designated public transportation which is not a fixed route system.

---

[42] Subtitle B was not in the Senate-passed bill.

(2) DESIGNATED PUBLIC TRANSPORTATION —

The term "designated public transportation" means transportation (other than public school transportation) by bus, rail, or any other conveyance (other than transportation by aircraft or intercity or commuter rail transportation (as defined in section 241)) that provides the general public with general or special service (including charter service) on a regular and continuing basis.

(3) FIXED ROUTE SYSTEM —

The term "fixed route system" means a system of providing designated public transportation on which a vehicle is operated along a prescribed route according to a fixed schedule.

(4) OPERATES —

The term "operates," as used with respect to a fixed route system or demand responsive system, includes operation of such system by a person under a contractual or other arrangement or relationship with a public entity.

(5) PUBLIC SCHOOL TRANSPORTATION —

The term "public school transportation" means transportation by schoolbus vehicles of schoolchildren, personnel, and equipment to and from a public elementary or secondary school and school-related activities.

(6) SECRETARY —

The term "Secretary" means the Secretary of Transportation.

SEC. 222. [42 U.S.C. scc. 12142] PUBLIC ENTITIES OPERATING FIXED ROUTE SYSTEMS

(a) PURCHASE AND LEASE OF NEW VEHICLES —

It shall be considered discrimination for purposes of section 202 of this Act and section 504 of the Rehabilitation Act of 1973 (29 U.S.C. 794) for a public entity which operates a fixed route system to purchase or lease a new bus, a new rapid rail vehicle, a new light rail vehicle, or any other new vehicle to be used on such system, if the solicitation for such purchase or lease is made after the 30th day following the effective date of this subsection and if such bus, rail vehicle, or other vehicle is not readily accessible to and usable by individuals with disabilities, including individuals who use wheelchairs.

(b) PURCHASE AND LEASE OF USED VEHICLES —

Subject to subsection (c)(1), it shall be considered discrimination for purposes of section 202 of this Act and section 504 of the Rehabilitation Act of 1973 (29 U.S.C. 794) for a public entity which operates a fixed route system to purchase or lease, after the 30th day following the effective date of this subsection, a used vehicle for use on such system unless such entity makes demonstrated good faith efforts to purchase or lease a used vehicle for use on such system that is readily accessible to and usable by individuals with disabilities, including individuals who use wheelchairs.

(c) REMANUFACTURED VEHICLES —

(1) GENERAL RULE —

Except as provided in paragraph (2), it shall be considered discrimination for purposes of section 202 of this Act and section 504 of the Rehabilitation Act of 1973 (29 U.S.C. 794) for a public entity which operates a fixed route system —

(A) to remanufacture a vehicle for use on such system so as to extend its usable life for 5 years or more, which remanufacture begins (or for which the solicitation is made) after the 30th day following the effective date of this subsection; or

(B) to purchase or lease for use on such system a remanufactured vehicle which has been remanufactured so as to extend its usable life for 5 years or more, which purchase or lease occurs after such 30th day and during the period in which the usable life is extended; unless, after remanufacture, the vehicle is, to the maximum extent feasible, readily accessible to and usable by individuals with disabilities, including individuals who use wheelchairs.

(2) EXCEPTION FOR HISTORIC VEHICLES —

(A) GENERAL RULE —

If a public entity operates a fixed route system any segment of which is included on the National Register of Historic Places and if making a vehicle of historic character to be used solely on such segment readily accessible to and usable by individuals with disabilities would significantly alter the historic character of such vehicle, the public entity only has to make (or to purchase or lease a remanufactured vehicle with) those modifications which are necessary to meet the requirements of paragraph (1) and which do not significantly alter the historic character of such vehicle.

(B) VEHICLES OF HISTORIC CHARACTER DEFINED BY REGULATIONS —

For purposes of this paragraph and section 228(b), a vehicle of historic character shall be defined by the regulations issued by the Secretary to carry out this subsection.

SEC. 223. [42 U.S.C. sec. 12143] PARATRANSIT AS A COMPLEMENT TO FIXED ROUTE SERVICE

(a) GENERAL RULE —

It shall be considered discrimination for purposes of section 202 of this Act and section 504 of the Rehabilitation Act of 1973 (29 U.S.C. 794) for a public entity which operates a fixed route system (other than a system which provides solely commuter bus service) to fail to provide with respect to the operations of its fixed route system, in accordance with this section, paratransit and other special transportation services to individuals with disabilities, including individuals who use wheelchairs, that are sufficient to provide to such individuals a level of service (1) which is comparable to the level of designated public transportation services provided to individuals without disabilities using such system; or (2) in the case of response time, which is comparable, to the extent practicable, to the level of designated public transportation services provided to individuals without disabilities using such system.

(b) ISSUANCE OF REGULATIONS —

Not later than 1 year after the effective date of this subsection, the Secretary shall issue final regulations to carry out this section.

(c) REQUIRED CONTENTS OF REGULATIONS —

(1) ELIGIBLE RECIPIENTS OF SERVICE —

The regulations issued under this section shall require each public entity which operates a fixed route system to provide the paratransit and other special transportation services required under this section —

(A)(i) to any individual with a disability who is unable, as a result of a physical or mental impairment (including a vision impairment) and without the assistance of another individual (except an operator of a wheelchair lift or other boarding assistance device), to board, ride, or disembark from any vehicle on the system which is readily accessible to and usable by individuals with disabilities;

(ii) to any individual with a disability who needs the assistance of a wheelchair lift or other boarding assistance device (and is able with such assistance) to board, ride, and disembark from any vehicle which is readily accessible to and usable by individuals with disabilities if the individual wants to travel on a route on the system during the hours of operation of the system at a time (or within a reasonable period of such time) when such a vehicle is not being used to provide designated public transportation on the route; and

(iii) to any individual with a disability who has a specific impairment-related condition which prevents such individual from traveling to a boarding location or from a disembarking location on such system;

(B) to 1 other individual accompanying the individual with the disability; and

(C) to other individuals, in addition to the one individual described in subparagraph (B), accompanying the individual with a disability provided that space for these additional individuals is available on the paratransit vehicle carrying the individual with a disability and that the transportation of such additional individuals will not result in a denial of service to individuals with disabilities.[43]

For purposes of clauses (i) and (ii) of subparagraph (A), boarding or disembarking from a vehicle does not include travel to the boarding location or from the disembarking location.

(2) SERVICE AREA —

The regulations issued under this section shall require the provision of paratransit and special transportation services required under this section in the service area of each public entity which operates a fixed route system, other

---

[43] The conferees deleted "and" and added the phrase "; and (C) to other individuals, in addition to the one individual described in subparagraph (B), accompanying the individual with a disability provided that space for these additional individuals is available on the paratransit vehicle carrying the individual with a disability and that the transportation of such additional individuals will not result in a denial of service to individuals with disabilities."

than any portion of the service area in which the public entity solely provides commuter bus service.

(3) SERVICE CRITERIA —

Subject to paragraphs (1) and (2), the regulations issued under this section shall establish minimum service criteria for determining the level of services to be required under this section.

(4) UNDUE FINANCIAL BURDEN LIMITATION —

The regulations issued under this section shall provide that, if the public entity is able to demonstrate to the satisfaction of the Secretary that the provision of paratransit and other special transportation services otherwise required under this section would impose an undue financial burden on the public entity, the public entity, notwithstanding any other provision of this section (other than paragraph (5)), shall only be required to provide such services to the extent that providing such services would not impose such a burden.

(5) ADDITIONAL SERVICES —

The regulations issued under this section shall establish circumstances under which the Secretary may require a public entity to provide, notwithstanding paragraph (4), paratransit and other special transportation services under this section beyond the level of paratransit and other special transportation services which would otherwise be required under paragraph (4).

(6) PUBLIC PARTICIPATION —

The regulations issued under this section shall require that each public entity which operates a fixed route system hold a public hearing, provide an opportunity for public comment, and consult with individuals with disabilities in preparing its plan under paragraph (7).

(7) PLANS —

The regulations issued under this section shall require that each public entity which operates a fixed route system —

(A) within 18 months after the effective date of this subsection, submit to the Secretary, and commence implementation of, a plan for providing paratransit and other special transportation services which meets the requirements of this section; and

(B) on an annual basis thereafter, submit to the Secretary, and commence implementation of, a plan for providing such services.

(8) PROVISION OF SERVICES BY OTHERS —

The regulations issued under this section shall —

(A) require that a public entity submitting a plan to the Secretary under this section identify in the plan any person or other public entity which is providing a paratransit or other special transportation service for individuals with disabilities in the service area to which the plan applies; and

(B) provide that the public entity submitting the plan does not have to provide under the plan such service for individuals with disabilities.

(9) OTHER PROVISIONS —

The regulations issued under this section shall include such other provisions and requirements as the Secretary determines are necessary to carry out the objectives of this section.

(d) REVIEW OF PLAN —

(1) GENERAL RULE —

The Secretary shall review a plan submitted under this section for the purpose of determining whether or not such plan meets the requirements of this section, including the regulations issued under this section.

(2) DISAPPROVAL —

If the Secretary determines that a plan reviewed under this subsection fails to meet the requirements of this section, the Secretary shall disapprove the plan and notify the public entity which submitted the plan of such disapproval and the reasons therefor.

(3) MODIFICATION OF DISAPPROVED PLAN —

Not later than 90 days after the date of disapproval of a plan under this subsection, the public entity which submitted the plan shall modify the plan to meet the requirements of this section and shall submit to the Secretary, and commence implementation of, such modified plan.

(e) DISCRIMINATION DEFINED —

As used in subsection (a), the term "discrimination" includes —

(1) a failure of a public entity to which the regulations issued under this section apply to submit, or commence implementation of, a plan in accordance with subsections (c)(6) and (c)(7);

(2) a failure of such entity to submit, or commence implementation of, a modified plan in accordance with subsection (d)(3);

(3) submission to the Secretary of a modified plan under subsection (d)(3) which does not meet the requirements of this section; or

(4) a failure of such entity to provide paratransit or other special transportation services in accordance with the plan or modified plan the public entity submitted to the Secretary under this section.

(f) STATUTORY CONSTRUCTION —

Nothing in this section shall be construed as preventing a public entity —

(1) from providing paratransit or other special transportation services at a level which is greater than the level of such services which are required by this section,

(2) from providing paratransit or other special transportation services in addition to those paratransit and special transportation services required by this section, or

(3) from providing such services to individuals in addition to those individuals to whom such services are required to be provided by this section.

SEC. 224. [42 U.S.C. sec. 12144] PUBLIC ENTITY OPERATING A DEMAND RESPONSIVE SYSTEM

If a public entity operates a demand responsive system, it shall be considered discrimination, for purposes of section 202 of this Act and section 504 of the Rehabilitation Act of 1973 (29 U.S.C. 794), for such entity to purchase or lease a new vehicle for use on such system, for which a solicitation is made after the 30th day following the effective date of this section, that is not readily accessible to and usable by individuals with disabilities, including individuals who use wheelchairs, unless such system, when viewed in its entirety, provides a level of service to such individuals equivalent to the level of service such system provides to individuals without disabilities.

SEC. 225. [42 U.S.C. sec. 12145] TEMPORARY RELIEF WHERE LIFTS ARE UNAVAILABLE

(a) GRANTING —

With respect to the purchase of new buses, a public entity may apply for, and the Secretary may temporarily relieve such public entity from the obligation under section 222(a) or 224 to purchase new buses that are readily accessible to and usable by individuals with disabilities if such public entity demonstrates to the satisfaction of the Secretary —

(1) that the initial solicitation for new buses made by the public entity specified that all new buses were to be lift-equipped and were to be otherwise accessible to and usable by individuals with disabilities;

(2) the unavailability from any qualified manufacturer of hydraulic, electromechanical, or other lifts for such new buses;

(3) that the public entity seeking temporary relief has made good faith efforts to locate a qualified manufacturer to supply the lifts to the manufacturer of such buses in sufficient time to comply with such solicitation; and

(4) that any further delay in purchasing new buses necessary to obtain such lifts would significantly impair transportation services in the community served by the public entity.

(b) DURATION AND NOTICE TO CONGRESS —

Any relief granted under subsection (a) shall be limited in duration by a specified date, and the appropriate committees of Congress shall be notified of any such relief granted.

(c) FRAUDULENT APPLICATION —

If, at any time, the Secretary has reasonable cause to believe that any relief granted under subsection (a) was fraudulently applied for, the Secretary shall —

(1) cancel such relief if such relief is still in effect; and

(2) take such other action as the Secretary considers appropriate.

Sec. 226. [42 U.S.C. sec. 12146] NEW FACILITIES

For purposes of section 202 of this Act and section 504 of the Rehabilitation Act of 1973 (29 U.S.C. 794), it shall be considered discrimination for a public entity to construct a new facility to be used in the provision of designated public transportation services unless such facility is readily accessible to and usable by individuals with disabilities, including individuals who use wheelchairs.

SEC. 227. [42 U.S.C. sec. 12147] ALTERATIONS OF EXISTING FACILITIES

(a) GENERAL RULE —

With respect to alterations of an existing facility or part thereof used in the provision of designated public transportation services that affect or could affect the usability of the facility or part thereof, it shall be considered discrimination, for purposes of section 202 of this Act and section 504 of the Rehabilitation Act of 1973 (29 U.S.C. 794), for a public entity to fail to make such alterations (or to ensure that the alterations are made) in such a manner that, to the maximum extent feasible, the altered portions of the facility are readily accessible to and usable by individuals with disabilities, including individuals who use wheelchairs, upon the completion of such alterations. Where the public entity is undertaking an alteration that affects or could affect usability of or access to an area of the facility containing a primary function, the entity shall also make the alterations in such a manner that, to the maximum extent feasible, the path of travel to the altered area and the bathrooms, telephones, and drinking fountains serving the altered area, are readily accessible to and usable by individuals with disabilities, including individuals who use wheelchairs, upon completion of such alterations, where such alterations to the path of travel or the bathrooms, telephones, and drinking fountains serving the altered area are not disproportionate to the overall alterations in terms of cost and scope (as determined under criteria established by the Attorney General).

(b) SPECIAL RULE FOR STATIONS —

(1) GENERAL RULE —

For purposes of section 202 of this Act and section 504 of the Rehabilitation Act of 1973 (29 U.S.C. 794), it shall be considered discrimination for a public entity that provides designated public transportation to fail, in accordance with the provisions of this subsection, to make key stations (as determined under criteria established by the Secretary by regulation) in rapid rail and light rail systems readily accessible to and usable by individuals with disabilities, including individuals who use wheelchairs.

(2) RAPID RAIL AND LIGHT RAIL KEY STATIONS —

(A) ACCESSIBILITY —

Except as otherwise provided in this paragraph, all key stations (as determined under criteria established by the Secretary by regulation) in rapid rail and light rail systems shall be made readily accessible to and usable by individuals with disabilities, including individuals who use wheelchairs, as soon as practicable but in no event later than the last day of the 3-year period beginning on the effective date of this paragraph.

(B) EXTENSION FOR EXTRAORDINARILY EXPENSIVE STRUCTURAL CHANGES —

The Secretary may extend the 3-year period under subparagraph (A) up to a 30-year period for key stations in a rapid rail or light rail system which stations need extraordinarily expensive structural changes to, or replacement of, existing facilities; except that by the last day of the 20th year following the date of the enactment of this Act at least 2/3 of such key stations must be readily accessible to and usable by individuals with disabilities.

(3) PLANS AND MILESTONES —

The Secretary shall require the appropriate public entity to develop and submit to the Secretary a plan for compliance with this subsection —

(A) that reflects consultation with individuals with disabilities affected by such plan and the results of a public hearing and public comments on such plan, and

(B) that establishes milestones for achievement of the requirements of this subsection.

SEC. 228. [42 U.S.C. sec. 12148] PUBLIC TRANSPORTATION PROGRAMS AND ACTIVITIES IN EXISTING FACILITIES AND ONE CAR PER TRAIN RULE

(a) PUBLIC TRANSPORTATION PROGRAMS AND ACTIVITIES IN EXISTING FACILITIES —

(1) IN GENERAL —

With respect to existing facilities used in the provision of designated public transportation services, it shall be considered discrimination, for purposes of section 202 of this Act and section 504 of the Rehabilitation Act of 1973 (29 U.S.C. 794), for a public entity to fail to operate a designated public transportation program or activity conducted in such facilities so that, when viewed in the entirety, the program or activity is readily accessible to and usable by individuals with disabilities.

(2) EXCEPTION — [44]

Paragraph (1) shall not require a public entity to make structural changes to existing facilities in order to make such facilities accessible to individuals who use wheelchairs, unless and to the extent required by section 227(a) (relating to alterations) or section 227(b) (relating to key stations).

(3) UTILIZATION —

Paragraph (1) shall not require a public entity to which paragraph (2) applies, to provide to individuals who use wheelchairs services made available to the general public at such facilities when such individuals could not utilize or benefit from such services provided at such facilities.[45]

---

[44] The conference report substituted "EXCEPTION" for "KEY STATIONS" in the paragraph title.

[45] The conference report substituted the language

> "require a public entity to make structural changes to existing facilities in order to make such facilities accessible to individuals who use wheelchairs, unless and to the extent required by section 227(a) (relating to alterations) or section 227(b) (relating to key stations).
> (3) UTILIZATION —
> Paragraph (1) shall not require a public entity to which paragraph (2) applies, to provide to individuals who use wheelchairs services made available to the general public at such facilities when such individuals could not utilize or benefit from such services provided at such facilities."

for the language "apply to a key station if the portion of such station providing access to the vehicle boarding or disembarking location has not been made readily accessible to and usable by individuals with disabilities who use wheelchairs at that station." in the House-passed bill.

(b) ONE CAR PER TRAIN RULE —

(1) GENERAL RULE —

Subject to paragraph (2), with respect to 2 or more vehicles operated as a train by a light or rapid rail system, for purposes of section 202 of this Act and section 504 of the Rehabilitation Act of 1973 (29 U.S.C. 794), it shall be considered discrimination for a public entity to fail to have at least 1 vehicle per train that is accessible to individuals with disabilities, including individuals who use wheelchairs, as soon as practicable but in no event later than the last day of the 5-year period beginning on the effective date of this section.

(2) HISTORIC TRAINS —

In order to comply with paragraph (1) with respect to the remanufacture of a vehicle of historic character which is to be used on a segment of a light or rapid rail system which is included on the National Register of Historic Places, if making such vehicle readily accessible to and usable by individuals with disabilities would significantly alter the historic character of such vehicle, the public entity which operates such system only has to make (or to purchase or lease a remanufactured vehicle with) those modifications which are necessary to meet the requirements of section 222(c)(1) and which do not significantly alter the historic character of such vehicle.

SEC. 229. [42 U.S.C. sec. 12149] REGULATIONS

(a) IN GENERAL —

Not later than 1 year after the date of enactment of this Act, the Secretary of Transportation shall issue regulations, in an accessible format, necessary for carrying out this part (other than section 223).

(b) STANDARDS —

The regulations issued under this section and section 223 shall include standards applicable to facilities and vehicles covered by this subtitle. The standards shall be consistent with the minimum guidelines and requirements issued by the Architectural and Transportation Barriers Compliance Board in accordance with section 504 of this Act.

SEC. 230. [42 U.S.C. sec. 12150] INTERIM ACCESSIBILITY REQUIRE-MENTS

If final regulations have not been issued pursuant to section 229, for new construction or alterations for which a valid and appropriate State or local building permit is obtained prior to the issuance of final regulations under such section, and for which the construction or alteration authorized by such permit begins within one year of the receipt of such permit and is completed under the terms of such permit, compliance with the Uniform Federal Accessibility Standards in effect at the time the building permit is issued shall suffice to satisfy the requirement that facilities be readily accessible to and usable by persons with disabilities as required under sections 226 and 227, except that, if such final regulations have not been issued one year after the Architectural and Transportation Barriers Compliance Board has issued the supplemental minimum guidelines required under section 504(a) of this Act, compliance with such supplemental minimum guidelines shall be necessary to satisfy the requirement that facilities be readily accessible to and usable by persons with disabilities prior to issuance of the final regulations.

SEC. 231. [42 U.S.C. sec. 12150] EFFECTIVE DATE

(a) GENERAL RULE —

Except as provided in subsection (b), this part shall become effective 18 months after the date of enactment of this Act.

(b) EXCEPTION —

Sections 222, 223 (other than subsection (a)), 224, 225, 227(b), 228(b), and 229 shall become effective on the date of enactment of this Act.

PART II-PUBLIC TRANSPORTATION BY INTERCITY AND COM-MUTER RAIL

SEC. 241. [42 U.S.C. sec. 12161] DEFINITIONS

As used in this part:

(1) COMMUTER AUTHORITY —

The term "commuter authority" has the meaning given such term in section 103(8) of the Rail Passenger Service Act (45 U.S.C 502(8)).

(2) COMMUTER RAIL TRANSPORTATION —

The term "commuter rail transportation" has the meaning given the term "commuter rail passenger transportation" in section 103(9) of the Rail Passenger Service Act (45 U.S.C 502(9)).

(3) INTERCITY RAIL TRANSPORTATION —

The term "intercity rail transportation" means transportation provided by the National Railroad Passenger Corporation.

(4) RAIL PASSENGER CAR —

The term "rail passenger car" means, with respect to intercity rail transportation, single-level and bi-level coach cars, single- level and bi-level dining cars, single-level and bi-level sleeping cars, single-level and bi-level lounge cars, and food service cars.

(5) RESPONSIBLE PERSON —

The term "responsible person" means —

(A) in the case of a station more than 50 percent of which is owned by a public entity, such public entity;

(B) in the case of a station more than 50 percent of which is owned by a private party, the persons providing intercity or commuter rail transportation to such station, as allocated on an equitable basis by regulation by the Secretary of Transportation; and

(C) in a case where no party owns more than 50 percent of a station, the persons providing intercity or commuter rail transportation to such station and the owners of the station, other than private party owners, as allocated on an equitable basis by regulation by the Secretary of Transportation.

(6) STATION —

The term "station" means the portion of a property located appurtenant to a right-of-way on which intercity or commuter rail transportation is operated, where such portion is used by the general public and is related to the provision of such transportation, including passenger platforms, designated waiting areas, ticketing areas, restrooms, and, where a public entity providing rail transportation owns the property, concession areas, to the extent that such public entity exercises control over the selection, design, construction, or alteration of the property, but such term does not include flag stops.

SEC. 242. [42 U.S.C. sec. 12162] INTERCITY AND COMMUTER RAIL ACTIONS CONSIDERED DISCRIMINATORY

(a) INTERCITY RAIL TRANSPORTATION —

(1) ONE CAR PER TRAIN RULE —

It shall be considered discrimination for purposes of section 202 of this Act and section 504 of the Rehabilitation Act of 1973 (29 U.S.C. 794) for a person who provides intercity rail transportation to fail to have at least one passenger car per train that is readily accessible to and usable by individuals with disabilities, including individuals who use wheelchairs, in accordance with regulations issued under section 244, as soon as practicable, but in no event later than 5 years after the date of enactment of this Act.

(2) NEW INTERCITY CARS —

(A) GENERAL RULE —

Except as otherwise provided in this subsection with respect to individuals who use wheelchairs, it shall be considered discrimination for purposes of section 202 of this Act and section 504 of the Rehabilitation Act of 1973 (29 U.S.C. 794) for a person to purchase or lease any new rail passenger cars for use in intercity rail transportation, and for which a solicitation is made later than 30 days after the effective date of this section, unless all such rail cars are readily accessible to and usable by individuals with disabilities, including individuals who use wheelchairs, as prescribed by the Secretary of Transportation in regulations issued under section 244.

(B) SPECIAL RULE FOR SINGLE-LEVEL PASSENGER COACHES FOR INDIVIDUALS WHO USE WHEELCHAIRS —

Single-level passenger coaches shall be required to —

(i) be able to be entered by an individual who uses a wheelchair;

(ii) have space to park and secure a wheelchair;

(iii) have a seat to which a passenger in a wheelchair can transfer, and a space to fold and store such passenger's wheelchair; and

(iv) have a restroom usable by an individual who uses a wheelchair, only to the extent provided in paragraph (3).

(C) SPECIAL RULE FOR SINGLE-LEVEL DINING CARS FOR INDIVIDUALS WHO USE WHEELCHAIRS —

Single-level dining cars shall not be required to —

(i) be able to be entered from the station platform by an individual who uses a wheelchair; or

(ii) have a restroom usable by an individual who uses a wheelchair if no restroom is provided in such car for any passenger.

(D) SPECIAL RULE FOR BI-LEVEL DINING CARS FOR INDIVIDUALS WHO USE WHEELCHAIRS —

Bi-level dining cars shall not be required to —

(i) be able to be entered by an individual who uses a wheelchair;

(ii) have space to park and secure a wheelchair;

(iii) have a seat to which a passenger in a wheelchair can transfer, or a space to fold and store such passenger's wheelchair; or

(iv) have a restroom usable by an individual who uses a wheelchair.

(3) ACCESSIBILITY OF SINGLE-LEVEL COACHES —

(A) GENERAL RULE —

It shall be considered discrimination for purposes of section 202 of this Act and section 504 of the Rehabilitation Act of 1973 (29 U.S.C. 794) for a person who provides intercity rail transportation to fail to have on each train which includes one or more single-level rail passenger coaches —

(i) a number of spaces —

(I) to park and secure wheelchairs (to accommodate individuals who wish to remain in their wheelchairs) equal to not less than one-half of the number of single-level rail passenger coaches in such train; and

(II) to fold and store wheelchairs (to accommodate individuals who wish to transfer to coach seats) equal to not less than one-half of the number of single-level rail passenger coaches in such train, as soon as practicable, but in no event later than 5 years after the date of enactment of this Act; and

(ii) a number of spaces —

(I) to park and secure wheelchairs (to accommodate individuals who wish to remain in their wheelchairs) equal to not less than the total number of single-level rail passenger coaches in such train; and

(II) to fold and store wheelchairs (to accommodate individuals who wish to transfer to coach seats) equal to not less than the total number of single-level rail passenger coaches in such train, as soon as practicable, but in no event later than 10 years after the date of enactment of this Act.

(B) LOCATION —

Spaces required by subparagraph (A) shall be located in single-level rail passenger coaches or food service cars.

(C) LIMITATION —

Of the number of spaces required on a train by subparagraph (A), not more than two spaces to park and secure wheelchairs nor more than two spaces to fold and store wheelchairs shall be located in any one coach or food service car.

(D) OTHER ACCESSIBILITY FEATURES —

Single-level rail passenger coaches and food service cars on which the spaces required by subparagraph (A) are located shall have a restroom usable by an individual who uses a wheelchair and shall be able to be entered from the station platform by an individual who uses a wheelchair.

(4) FOOD SERVICE —

(A) SINGLE-LEVEL DINING CARS —

On any train in which a single-level dining car is used to provide food service —

(i) if such single-level dining car was purchased after the date of enactment of this Act, table service in such car shall be provided to a passenger who uses a wheelchair if —

(I) the car adjacent to the end of the dining car through which a wheelchair may enter is itself accessible to a wheelchair;

(II) such passenger can exit to the platform from the car such passenger occupies, move down the platform, and enter the adjacent accessible car described in subclause (I) without the necessity of the train being moved within the station; and

(III) space to park and secure a wheelchair is available in the dining car at the time such passenger wishes to eat (if such passenger wishes to remain in a wheelchair), or space to store and fold a wheelchair is available in the dining car at the time such passenger wishes to eat (if such passenger wishes to transfer to a dining car seat); and

(ii) appropriate auxiliary aids and services, including a hard surface on which to eat, shall be provided to ensure that other equivalent food service is available to individuals with disabilities, including individuals who use wheelchairs, and to passengers traveling with such individuals.

Unless not practicable, a person providing intercity rail transportation shall place an accessible car adjacent to the end of a dining car described in clause (i) through which an individual who uses a wheelchair may enter.

(B) BI-LEVEL DINING CARS —

On any train in which a bi-level dining car is used to provide food service —

(i) if such train includes a bi-level lounge car purchased after the date of enactment of this Act, table service in such lounge car shall be provided to individuals who use wheelchairs and to other passengers; and

(ii) appropriate auxiliary aids and services, including a hard surface on which to eat, shall be provided to ensure that other equivalent food service is available to individuals with disabilities, including individuals who use wheelchairs, and to passengers traveling with such individuals.

(b) COMMUTER RAIL TRANSPORTATION —

(1) ONE CAR PER TRAIN RULE —

It shall be considered discrimination for purposes of section 202 of this Act and section 504 of the Rehabilitation Act of 1973 (29 U.S.C. 794) for a person who provides commuter rail transportation to fail to have at least one passenger car per train that is readily accessible to and usable by individuals with disabilities, including individuals who use wheelchairs, in accordance with regulations issued under section 244, as soon as practicable, but in no event later than 5 years after the date of enactment of this Act.

(2) NEW COMMUTER RAIL CARS —

(A) GENERAL RULE —

It shall be considered discrimination for purposes of section 202 of this Act and section 504 of the Rehabilitation Act of 1973 (29 U.S.C. 794) for a person to purchase or lease any new rail passenger cars for use in commuter rail transportation, and for which a solicitation is made later than 30 days after the effective date of this section, unless all such rail cars are readily accessible to and usable by individuals with disabilities, including individuals who use wheelchairs, as prescribed by the Secretary of Transportation in regulations issued under section 244.

(B) ACCESSIBILITY —

For purposes of section 202 of this Act and section 504 of the Rehabilitation Act of 1973 (29 U.S.C. 794), a requirement that a rail passenger car used in commuter rail transportation be accessible to or readily accessible to and usable by individuals with disabilities, including individuals who use wheelchairs, shall not be construed to require —

(i) a restroom usable by an individual who uses a wheelchair if no restroom is provided in such car for any passenger;

(ii) space to fold and store a wheelchair; or

(iii) a seat to which a passenger who uses a wheelchair can transfer.

(c) USED RAIL CARS —

It shall be considered discrimination for purposes of section 202 of this Act and section 504 of the Rehabilitation Act of 1973 (29 U.S.C. 794) for a person to purchase or lease a used rail passenger car for use in intercity or commuter rail transportation, unless such person makes demonstrated good faith efforts to purchase or lease a used rail car that is readily accessible to and usable by individuals with disabilities, including individuals who use wheelchairs, as prescribed by the Secretary of Transportation in regulations issued under section 244.

(d) REMANUFACTURED RAIL CARS —

(1) REMANUFACTURING —

It shall be considered discrimination for purposes of section 202 of this Act and section 504 of the Rehabilitation Act of 1973 (29 U.S.C. 794) for a person to remanufacture a rail passenger car for use in intercity or commuter rail transportation so as to extend its usable life for 10 years or more, unless the rail car, to the maximum extent feasible, is made readily accessible to and usable by individuals with disabilities, including individuals who use wheelchairs, as prescribed by the Secretary of Transportation in regulations issued under section 244.

(2) PURCHASE OR LEASE —

It shall be considered discrimination for purposes of section 202 of this Act and section 504 of the Rehabilitation Act of 1973 (29 U.S.C. 794) for a person to purchase or lease a remanufactured rail passenger car for use in intercity or commuter rail transportation unless such car was remanufactured in accordance with paragraph (1).

(e) STATIONS —

(1) NEW STATIONS —

It shall be considered discrimination for purposes of section 202 of this Act and section 504 of the Rehabilitation Act of 1973 (29 U.S.C. 794) for a person to build a new station for use in intercity or commuter rail transportation that is not readily accessible to and usable by individuals with disabilities, including individuals who use wheelchairs, as prescribed by the Secretary of Transportation in regulations issued under section 244.

(2) EXISTING STATIONS —

(A) FAILURE TO MAKE READILY ACCESSIBLE —

(i) GENERAL RULE —

It shall be considered discrimination for purposes of section 202 of this Act and section 504 of the Rehabilitation Act of 1973 (29 U.S.C. 794) for a responsible person to fail to make existing stations in the intercity rail transportation system, and existing key stations in commuter rail transportation systems, readily accessible to and usable by individuals with disabilities, including individuals who use wheelchairs, as prescribed by the Secretary of Transportation in regulations issued under section 244.

(ii) PERIOD FOR COMPLIANCE —

(I) INTERCITY RAIL —

All stations in the intercity rail transportation system shall be made readily accessible to and usable by individuals with disabilities, including individuals who use wheelchairs, as soon as practicable, but in no event later than 20 years after the date of enactment of this Act.

(II) COMMUTER RAIL —

Key stations in commuter rail transportation systems shall be made readily accessible to and usable by individuals with disabilities, including individuals who use wheelchairs, as soon as practicable but in no event later than 3 years after the date of enactment of this Act, except that the time limit may be extended by the Secretary of Transportation up to 20 years after the date of enactment of this Act in a case where the raising of the entire passenger platform is the only means available of attaining accessibility or where other extraordinarily expensive structural changes are necessary to attain accessibility.

(iii) DESIGNATION OF KEY STATIONS —

Each commuter authority shall designate the key stations in its commuter rail transportation system, in consultation with individuals with disabilities and organizations representing such individuals, taking into consideration such factors as high ridership and whether such station serves as a transfer or feeder station. Before the final designation of key stations under this clause, a commuter authority shall hold a public hearing.

(iv) PLANS AND MILESTONES —

The Secretary of Transportation shall require the appropriate person to develop a plan for carrying out this subparagraph that reflects consultation with individuals with disabilities affected by such plan and that establishes milestones for achievement of the requirements of this subparagraph.

(B) REQUIREMENT WHEN MAKING ALTERATIONS —

(i) GENERAL RULE —

It shall be considered discrimination, for purposes of section 202 of this Act and section 504 of the Rehabilitation Act of 1973 (29 U.S.C. 794), with respect to alterations of an existing station or part thereof in the intercity or commuter rail transportation systems that affect or could affect the usability of the station or part thereof, for the responsible person, owner, or person in control of the station to fail to make the alterations in such a manner that, to the maximum extent feasible, the altered portions of the station are readily accessible to and usable by individuals with disabilities, including individuals who use wheelchairs, upon completion of such alterations.

(ii) ALTERATIONS TO A PRIMARY FUNCTION AREA —

It shall be considered discrimination, for purposes of section 202 of this Act and section 504 of the Rehabilitation Act of 1973 (29 U.S.C. 794), with respect to alterations that affect or could affect the usability of or access to an area of the station containing a primary function, for the responsible person, owner, or person in control of the station to fail to make the alterations in such a manner that, to the maximum extent feasible, the path of travel to the altered area, and the bathrooms, telephones, and drinking fountains serving the altered area, are readily accessible to and usable by individuals with disabilities, including individuals who use wheelchairs, upon completion of such alterations, where such alterations to the path of travel or the bathrooms, telephones, and drinking fountains serving the altered area are not disproportionate to the overall alterations in terms of cost and scope (as determined under criteria established by the Attorney General).

(C) REQUIRED COOPERATION —

It shall be considered discrimination for purposes of section 202 of this Act and section 504 of the Rehabilitation Act of 1973 (29 U.S.C. 794) for an owner, or person in control, of a station governed by subparagraph (A) or (B) to fail to provide reasonable cooperation to a responsible person with respect to such station in that responsible person's efforts to comply with such subparagraph. An owner, or person in control, of a station shall be liable to a responsible person for any failure to provide reasonable cooperation as required by this subparagraph. Failure to receive reasonable cooperation required by this subparagraph shall not be a defense to a claim of discrimination under this Act.

SEC. 243. [42 U.S.C. sec. 12163] CONFORMANCE OF ACCESSIBILITY STANDARDS

Accessibility standards included in regulations issued under this part shall be consistent with the minimum guidelines issued by the Architectural and Transportation Barriers Compliance Board under section 504(a) of this Act.

SEC. 244. [42 U.S.C. sec. 12164] REGULATIONS

Not later than 1 year after the date of enactment of this Act, the Secretary of Transportation shall issue regulations, in an accessible format, necessary for carrying out this part.

SEC. 245. [42 U.S.C. sec. 12165] INTERIM ACCESSIBILITY REQUIRE-MENTS

(a) STATIONS —

If final regulations have not been issued pursuant to section 244, for new construction or alterations for which a valid and appropriate State or local building permit is obtained prior to the issuance of final regulations under such section, and for which the construction or alteration authorized by such permit begins within one year of the receipt of such permit and is completed under the terms of such permit, compliance with the Uniform Federal Accessibility Standards in effect at the time the building permit is issued shall suffice to satisfy the requirement that stations be readily accessible to and usable by persons with disabilities as required under section 242(e), except that, if such final regulations have not been issued one year after the Architectural and Transportation Barriers Compliance Board has issued the supplemental minimum guidelines required under section 504(a) of this Act, compliance with such supplemental minimum guidelines shall be necessary to satisfy the requirement that stations be readily accessible to and usable by persons with disabilities prior to issuance of the final regulations.

(b) RAIL PASSENGER CARS —

If final regulations have not been issued pursuant to section 244, a person shall be considered to have complied with the requirements of section 242(a) through (d) that a rail passenger car be readily accessible to and usable by individuals with disabilities, if the design for such car complies with the laws and regulations (including the Minimum Guidelines and Requirements for Accessible Design and such supplemental minimum guidelines as are issued under section 504(a) of this Act) governing accessibility of such cars, to the extent that such laws and regulations are not inconsistent with this part and are in effect at the time such design is substantially completed.

SEC. 246. [42 U.S.C. sec. 12165] EFFECTIVE DATE

(a) GENERAL RULE —

Except as provided in subsection (b), this part shall become effective 18 months after the date of enactment of this Act.

(b) EXCEPTION —

Sections 242 and 244 shall become effective on the date of enactment of this Act.

TITLE III — PUBLIC ACCOMMODATIONS AND SERVICES OPERATED BY PRIVATE ENTITIES

Sec. 301. [42 U.S.C. sec. 12181] DEFINITIONS

As used in this title:

(1) COMMERCE —

The term "commerce" means travel, trade, traffic, commerce, transportation, or communication —

(A) among the several States;

(B) between any foreign country or any territory or possession and any State; or

(C) between points in the same State but through another State or foreign country.

(2) COMMERCIAL FACILITIES —[46]

The term "commercial facilities" means facilities —

(A) that are intended for nonresidential use; and

(B) whose operations will affect commerce.

---

[46] The Senate-passed bill used the term "potential places of employment" instead of the term "commercial facilities."

Such term shall not include railroad locomotives, railroad freight cars, railroad cabooses, railroad cars described in section 242 or covered under this title, railroad rights-of-way,[47] or facilities that are covered or expressly exempted from coverage under the Fair Housing Act of 1968 (42 U.S.C. 3601 *et seq.*).

(3) DEMAND RESPONSIVE SYSTEM — [48]

The term "demand responsive system" means any system of providing transportation of individuals by a vehicle, other than a system which is a fixed route system.

(4) FIXED ROUTE SYSTEM —

The term "fixed route system" means a system of providing transportation of individuals (other than by aircraft) on which a vehicle is operated along a prescribed route according to a fixed schedule.

(5) OVER-THE-ROAD BUS —

The term "over-the-road bus" means a bus characterized by an elevated passenger deck located over a baggage compartment.

(6) PRIVATE ENTITY —

The term "private entity" means any entity other than a public entity (as defined in section 201(1)).

(7) PUBLIC ACCOMMODATION —

The following private[49] entities are considered public accommodations for purposes of this title, if the operations of such entities affect commerce —

(A) an inn, hotel, motel, or other[50] place of lodging, except for an establishment located within a building that contains not more than five rooms for rent or hire and that is actually occupied by the proprietor of such establishment as the residence of such proprietor;

---

[47] The Senate-passed bill had no reference to railroad equipment.

[48] The Senate-passed bill did not address demand responsive systems, fixed route systems or over-the-road buses, covered by the present paragraphs 3, 4, and 5.

[49] The Senate-passed bill used the term "privately operated entities."

[50] The Senate-passed bill had the word "similar" at this point.

(B) a restaurant, bar, or other establishment serving food or drink;

(C) a motion picture house, theater, concert hall, stadium, or other place of exhibition or entertainment;

(D) an auditorium, convention center, lecture hall, or other place of public gathering;[51]

(E) a bakery, grocery store, clothing store, hardware store, shopping center, or other[52] sales or rental[53] establishment;

(F) a laundromat, dry-cleaner, bank, barber shop, beauty shop, travel service, shoe repair service, funeral parlor, gas station, office of an accountant or lawyer, pharmacy, insurance office, professional office of a health care pro-vider, hospital, or other[54] service establishment;

(G) a terminal, depot, or other station[55] used for specified public transpor-tation;

(H) a museum, library, gallery, or[56] other[57] place of public display or collection;

(I) a park, zoo, amusement park, or other place of recreation;[58]

(J) a nursery, elementary, secondary, undergraduate, or postgraduate private school, or other place of education;[59]

(K) a day care center, senior citizen center, homeless shelter, food bank, adoption agency,[60] or other[61] social service center establishment;[62] and

---

[51] The Senate-passed bill did not include a reference to "other place of public gathering."
[52] The Senate-passed bill had the words "similar retail" at this point.
[53] The Senate-passed bill did not refer to rental establishments.
[54] The Senate-passed bill had the word "similar" at this point.
[55] The Senate-passed bill did not say "depot, or other station."
[56] The Senate-passed bill said "and."
[57] The Senate-passed bill had the word "similar" at this point.
[58] The Senate-passed bill concluded with the word "zoo."
[59] The Senate-passed bill did not say "or other place of education."
[60] The Senate-passed bill used the term "adoption program" instead of "adoption agency."
[61] The Senate-passed bill had the word "similar" at this point.
[62] The Senate-passed bill did not have the word "establishment."

(L) a gymnasium, health spa, bowling alley, golf course, or other place of exercise or recreation.

(8) RAIL AND RAILROAD — [63]

The terms "rail" and "railroad" have the meaning given the term "railroad" in section 202(e) of the Federal Railroad Safety Act of 1970 (45 U.S.C. 431(e)).

(9) READILY ACHIEVABLE — [64]

The term "readily achievable" means easily accomplishable and able to be carried out without much difficulty or expense. In determining whether an action is readily achievable, factors to be considered include —

(A) the nature and cost of the action needed under this Act;[65]

(B) the overall financial resources of the facility or facilities involved in the action; the number of persons employed at such facility; the effect on expenses and resources, or the impact otherwise of such action upon the operation of the facility;

(C) the overall financial resources of the covered entity; the overall size of the business of a covered entity with respect to the number of its employees; the number, type, and location of its facilities; and

(D) the type of operation or operations of the covered entity, including the composition, structure, and functions of the workforce of such entity; the geographic separateness, administrative or fiscal relationship of the facility or facilities in question to the covered entity.[66]

(10) SPECIFIED PUBLIC TRANSPORTATION — [67]

The term "specified public transportation" means transportation by bus, rail, or any other conveyance (other than by aircraft) that provides the general

---

[63] The Senate-passed bill defined "public transportation" but not "rail or railroad."

[64] The Senate-passed bill was structured into an "in general" part (A), and a "determination" Part (B).

[65] This factor was included but as the third item in the Senate-passed bill.

[66] Instead of the factors now appearing at subparagraphs (B), (C), and (D), the Senate-passed bill said "(i) the overall size of the covered entity with respect to number of employees, number and type of facilities, and size of budget; (ii) the type of operation including the composition and structure of the entity."

[67] The Senate-passed did not contain a definition for this term.

public with general or special service (including charter service) on a regular and continuing basis.

(11) VEHICLE — [68]

The term "vehicle" does not include a rail passenger car, railroad locomotive, railroad freight car, railroad caboose, or a railroad car described in section 242 or covered under this title.

SEC. 302. [42 U.S.C. sec. 12182] PROHIBITION OF DISCRIMINATION BY PUBLIC ACCOMMODATIONS

(a) GENERAL RULE —

No individual shall be discriminated against on the basis of disability in the full and equal enjoyment of the goods, services, facilities, privileges, advantages, or[69] accommodations of any place of public accommodation by any person who owns, leases (or leases to), or operates a place of public accommodation.[70]

(b) CONSTRUCTION —

(1) GENERAL PROHIBITION —

(A) ACTIVITIES —

(i) DENIAL OF PARTICIPATION —

It shall be discriminatory to subject an individual or class of individuals on the basis of a disability or disabilities of such individual or class, directly, or through contractual, licensing, or other arrangements, to a denial of the opportunity of the individual or class to participate in or benefit from the goods, services, facilities, privileges, advantages, or[71] accommodations of an entity.

---

[68] The Senate-passed did not contain a definition for this term.

[69] The Senate-passed bill said "and."

[70] The Senate-passed bill did not have the language "by any person who owns, leases (or leases to), or operates."

[71] The Senate-passed bill said "and."

(ii) PARTICIPATION IN UNEQUAL BENEFIT —

It shall be discriminatory to afford an individual or class of individuals, on the basis of a disability or disabilities of such individual or class, directly, or through contractual, licensing, or other arrangements with the opportunity to participate in or benefit from a good, service, facility, privilege, advantage, or[72] accommodation that is not equal to that afforded to other individuals.

(iii) SEPARATE BENEFIT —

It shall be discriminatory to provide an individual or class of individuals, on the basis of a disability or disabilities of such individual or class, directly, or through contractual, licensing, or other arrangements with a good, service, facility, privilege, advantage, or accommodation that is different or separate from that provided to other individuals, unless such action is necessary to provide the individual or class of individuals with a good, service, facility, privilege, advantage, or accommodation, or other opportunity that is as effective as that provided to others.

(iv) INDIVIDUAL OR CLASS OF INDIVIDUALS —

For purposes of clauses (i) through (iii) of this subparagraph, the term "individual or class of individuals" refers to the clients or customers of the covered public accommodation that enters into the contractual, licensing or other arrangement.[73]

(B) INTEGRATED SETTINGS —

Goods, services,[74] facilities, privileges, advantages, and accommodations shall be afforded to an individual with a disability in the most integrated setting appropriate to the needs of the individual.

(C) OPPORTUNITY TO PARTICIPATE —

Notwithstanding the existence of separate or different programs or activities provided in accordance with this section, an individual with a disability shall not be denied the opportunity to participate in such programs or activities that are not separate or different.

---

[72] The Senate-passed bill used "and."
[73] The Senate-passed bill did not contain a provision equivalent to subparagraph (iv).
[74] The Senate-passed bill included "services" at the end of the list.

(D) ADMINISTRATIVE METHODS —

An individual or entity shall not, directly or through contractual or other arrangements, utilize standards or criteria or methods of administration —

(i) that have the effect of discriminating on the basis of disability; or

(ii) that perpetuate the discrimination of others who are subject to common administrative control.

(E) ASSOCIATION —

It shall be discriminatory to exclude or otherwise deny equal goods, services, facilities, privileges, advantages,[75] accommodations, or other opportunities to an individual or entity because of the known disability of an individual with whom the individual or entity is known to have a relationship or association.

(2) SPECIFIC PROHIBITIONS —

(A) DISCRIMINATION —

For purposes of[76] subsection (a), discrimination[77] includes[78] —

(i) the imposition or application of eligibility criteria that screen out or tend to screen out an individual with a disability or any class of individuals with disabilities from fully and equally enjoying any goods, services, facilities, privileges, advantages, or[79] accommodations, unless such criteria can be shown to be necessary for the provision of the goods, services, facilities, privileges, advantages, or accommodations being offered;

(ii) a failure to make reasonable modifications in policies, practices, or procedures, when such modifications are necessary to afford such goods, services, facilities, privileges, advantages, or[80] accommodations to individuals with disabilities, unless the entity can demonstrate that making such modifications would fundamentally alter the nature of such goods, services, facilities, privileges, advantages, or accommodations;

---

[75] The Senate-passed bill had "and" at this point.
[76] The Senate-passed bill said "As used in" instead of "For purposes of."
[77] The Senate-passed bill said "the term discrimination . . . ."
[78] The Senate-passed bill said "shall include."
[79] The Senate-passed bill used "and."
[80] The Senate-passed bill used "and."

(iii) a failure to take such steps as may be necessary to ensure that no individual with a disability is excluded, denied services, segregated or otherwise treated differently than other individuals because of the absence of auxiliary aids and services, unless the entity can demonstrate that taking such steps would fundamentally alter the nature of the good, service, facility, privilege, advantage, or accommodation being offered or would result in an undue burden;

(iv) a failure to remove architectural barriers, and communication barriers that are structural in nature, in existing facilities, and transportation barriers in existing vehicles and rail passenger cars[81] used by an establishment for transporting individuals (not including barriers that can only be removed through the retrofitting of vehicles or rail passenger cars[82] by the installation of a hydraulic or other lift), where such removal is readily achievable; and

(v) where an entity can demonstrate that the removal of a barrier under clause (iv) is not readily achievable, a failure to make such goods, services, facilities, privileges, advantages, or[83] accommodations available through alternative methods if such methods are readily achievable.[84]

---

[81] The Senate-passed bill omitted "and rail passenger cars."

[82] The Senate-passed bill omitted "or rail passenger cars."

[83] The Senate-passed bill used "and."

[84] The Senate-passed bill had a subparagraph (vi) reading:

> (vi) with respect to a facility or part thereof that is altered by, on behalf of, or for the use of an establishment in a manner that affects or could affect the usability of the facility or part thereof, a failure to make alterations in such a manner that, to the maximum extent feasible, the altered portions of the facility are readily accessible to and usable by individuals with disabilities, including individuals who use wheelchairs, and where the entity is undertaking major structural alterations that affect or could affect the usability of the facility (as defined under criteria established by the Attorney General), the entity shall also make the alterations in such a manner that, to the maximum extent feasible, the path of travel to the altered area and the bathrooms, telephones, and drinking fountains serving the remodeled area, are readily accessible to and usable by individuals with disabilities, except that this paragraph shall not be construed to require the installation of an elevator for facilities that are less than three stories or that have less than 3,000 square feet per story unless the building is a shopping center, a shopping mall, or the professional office of a health care provider or unless the Attorney General determines that a particular category of such facilities requires the installation of elevators based on the usage of such facilities.

(B) FIXED ROUTE SYSTEM —

(i) ACCESSIBILITY —

It shall be considered discrimination for a private entity which[85] operates[86] a fixed route system and[87] which is not subject to section 304 to purchase or lease a vehicle[88] with a seating capacity in excess of 16 passengers (including the driver) for use on such system, for which a solicitation is made after the 30th day following the effective date of this subparagraph,[89] that is not readily accessible to and usable by individuals with disabilities, including individuals who use wheelchairs.[90]

(ii) EQUIVALENT SERVICE —

If a private entity[91] which operates a fixed route system and which is not subject to section 304 purchases or leases a vehicle with a seating capacity of 16 passengers or less (including the driver) for use on such system after the effective date of this subparagraph that is not readily accessible to or usable by individuals with disabilities, it shall be considered discrimination for such entity to fail to operate such system so that, when viewed in its entirety, such system ensures a level of service to individuals with disabilities, including individuals who use wheelchairs, equivalent to the level of service provided to individuals without disabilities.[92]

(C) DEMAND RESPONSIVE SYSTEM — [93]

For purposes of subsection (a), discrimination includes —

(i) a failure of a private entity which operates a demand responsive system and which is not subject to section 304 to operate such system so that, when

---

[85] The Senate-passed bill said "for an entity that . . . ."

[86] The Senate-passed bill said "used a vehicle for . . . ."

[87] The Senate-passed bill had additional language at this point: "to transport individuals not covered under section 203 or 304," instead of "which is not subject to section 304."

[88] The Senate-passed bill referred to "a bus or vehicle that is capable of carrying in excess of 16 passengers."

[89] The Senate-passed bill referred to the effective date of this Act.

[90] The Senate-passed bill contained the proviso: "except that over-the-road buses shall be subject to section 304(b)(4) and section 305."

[91] The Senate-passed bill referred to "such entity" without the restriction of not being subject to section 304.

[92] The Senate-passed bill version of this subparagraph did not refer to "such" system.

[93] The Senate-passed bill's version of this paragraph (C) referred to entities not subject to §§ 203 or 304, and had significant differences in wording and structure.

viewed in its entirety, such system ensures a level of service to individuals with disabilities, including individuals who use wheelchairs, equivalent to the level of service provided to individuals without disabilities; and

(ii) the purchase or lease by such entity for use on such system of a vehicle with a seating capacity in excess of 16 passengers (including the driver), for which solicitations are made after the 30th day following the effective date of this subparagraph, that is not readily accessible to and usable by individuals with disabilities (including individuals who use wheelchairs) unless such entity can demonstrate that such system, when viewed in its entirety, provides a level of service to individuals with disabilities equivalent to that provided to individuals without disabilities.

(D) OVER-THE-ROAD BUSES — [94]

(i) LIMITATION ON APPLICABILITY —

Subparagraphs (B) and (C) do not apply to over-the-road buses.

(ii) ACCESSIBILITY REQUIREMENTS —

For purposes of subsection (a), discrimination includes (I) the purchase or lease of an over-the-road bus which does not comply with the regulations issued under section 306(a)(2) by a private entity which provides transportation of individuals and which is not primarily engaged in the business of transporting people, and (II) any other failure of such entity to comply with such regulations.

(3) SPECIFIC CONSTRUCTION —

Nothing in this title shall require an entity to permit an individual to participate in or benefit from the goods, services, facilities, privileges, advantages and accommodations of such entity where such individual poses a direct threat to the health or safety of others. The term "direct threat" means a significant risk to the health or safety of others that cannot be eliminated by a modification of policies, practices, or procedures or by the provision of auxiliary aids or services.

---

[94] The Senate-passed bill treated over-the-road buses differently.

SEC. 303. [42 U.S.C. sec. 12183] NEW CONSTRUCTION AND ALTERATIONS IN PUBLIC ACCOMMODATIONS AND COMMERCIAL FACILITIES[95]

(a) APPLICATION OF TERM — [96]

Except as provided in subsection (b), as applied to public accommodations and commercial facilities, discrimination for purposes of section 302(a) includes —

(1) a failure to design and construct facilities for first occupancy later than 30 months after the date of enactment of this Act that are readily accessible to and usable by individuals with disabilities, except where an entity can demonstrate that it is structurally impracticable to meet the requirements of such subsection in accordance with standards set forth or incorporated by reference in regulations issued under this title; and

(2) with respect to a facility or part thereof that is altered by, on behalf of, or for the use of an establishment in a manner that affects or could affect the usability of the facility or part thereof, a failure to make alterations in such a manner that, to the maximum extent feasible, the altered portions of the facility are readily accessible to and usable by individuals with disabilities, including individuals who use wheelchairs. Where the entity is undertaking an alteration that affects or could affect usability of or access to an area of the facility containing a primary function, the entity shall also make the alterations in such a manner that, to the maximum extent feasible, the path of travel to the altered area and the bathrooms, telephones, and drinking fountains serving the altered area, are readily accessible to and usable by individuals with disabilities where such alterations to the path of travel or the bathrooms, telephones, and drinking fountains serving the altered area are not disproportionate to the overall alterations in terms of cost and scope (as determined under criteria established by the Attorney General).[97]

(b) ELEVATOR —

Subsection (a) shall not be construed to require the installation of an elevator for facilities that are less than three stories or have less than 3,000 square

---

[95] The title of the Senate-passed bill's § 303 was, "New construction in public accommodation and potential places of employment."

[96] The Senate-passed bill's subsection (a) applied to public accommodation and potential places of employment rather than to public accommodation and commercial facilities.

[97] The Senate-passed bill did not contain this subparagraph, covering the subject matter elsewhere.

feet per story unless the building is a shopping center, a shopping mall, or the professional office of a health care provider or unless the Attorney General determines that a particular category of such facilities requires the installation of elevators based on the usage of such facilities.

SEC. 304. [42 U.S.C. sec. 12184] PROHIBITION OF DISCRIMINATION IN SPECIFIED[98] PUBLIC TRANSPORTATION SERVICES PROVIDED BY PRIVATE ENTITIES

(a) GENERAL RULE —

No individual shall be discriminated against on the basis of disability in the full and equal enjoyment of specified[99] public transportation services provided by a private[100] entity that is primarily engaged in the business of transporting people[101] and whose operations affect commerce.

(b) CONSTRUCTION —

For purposes of subsection (a), discrimination includes —

(1) the imposition or application by a entity described in subsection (a)[102] of eligibility criteria that screen out or tend to screen out an individual with a disability or any class of individuals with disabilities from fully enjoying the specified[103] public transportation services provided by the entity, unless such criteria can be shown to be necessary for the provision of the services being offered;[104]

(2) the failure of such[105] entity to —

(A) make reasonable modifications consistent with those required under section 302(b)(2)(A)(ii);

(B) provide auxiliary aids and services consistent with the requirements of section 302(b)(2)(A)(iii); and

---

[98] The Senate-passed bill omitted "specified."

[99] The Senate-passed bill omitted "specified."

[100] The Senate-passed bill said "privately operated."

[101] The Senate-passed bill said "but is not in the principal business of providing air transportation," at this point.

[102] The Senate-passed bill omitted "described in subsection (a)."

[103] The Senate-passed bill omitted "specified."

[104] The Senate-passed bill omitted the proviso beginning "unless."

[105] The Senate-passed bill did not say "such entity."

(C) remove barriers consistent with the requirements of section 302(b)(2)(A) and with the requirements of section 303(a)(2);[106]

(3) the purchase or lease by such entity[107] of a new vehicle (other than an automobile, a van with a seating capacity of less than 8 passengers,[108] including the driver, or an over-the-road bus) which is to be used to provide specified public transportation and for which a solicitation is made after the 30th day following the effective date of this section,[109] that is not readily accessible to and usable by individuals with disabilities, including individuals who use wheelchairs; except that the new vehicle need not be readily accessible to and usable by such individuals if the new vehicle is to be used solely in a demand responsive system and if the entity can demonstrate that such system, when viewed in its entirety, provides a level of service to such individuals equivalent to the level of service provided to the general public;[110]

(4)(A) the purchase or lease by such entity of an over-the-road bus which does not comply with the regulations issued under section 306(a)(2); and

(B) any other failure of such entity to comply with such regulations; and[111]

(5) the purchase or lease by such entity of a new van with a seating capacity of less than 8 passengers, including the driver, which is to be used to provide specified public transportation and for which a solicitation is made after the 30th day following the effective date of this section that is not readily accessible to or usable by individuals with disabilities, including individuals who use wheelchairs; except that the new van need not be readily accessible to and usable by such individuals if the entity can demonstrate that the system for which the van is being purchased or leased, when viewed in its entirety, provides a level of service to such individuals equivalent to the level of service provided to the general public;[112]

(6) the purchase or lease by such entity of a new rail passenger car that is to be used to provide specified public transportation, and for which a solic-

---

[106] The Senate-passed bill referred only to §§ 302(b)(2)(A)(iv), (v), and (vi), and did not refer to § 303(a)(2).

[107] The Senate-passed bill did not say "by such entity."

[108] The Senate-passed bill did not refer to vans.

[109] The Senate-passed bill wording was somewhat different in the operative portion of this subparagraph.

[110] The Senate-passed bill did not contain the proviso beginning "except."

[111] The Senate-passed bill did not contain subparagraph (4).

[112] The Senate-passed bill had no subparagraph (5).

itation is made later than 30 days after the effective date of this paragraph, that is not readily accessible to and usable by individuals with disabilities, including individuals who use wheelchairs; and[113]

(7) the remanufacture by such entity of a rail passenger car that is to be used to provide specified public transportation so as to extend its usable life for 10 years or more, or the purchase or lease by such entity of such a rail car, unless the rail car, to the maximum extent feasible, is made readily accessible to and usable by individuals with disabilities, including individuals who use wheelchairs.[114]

(c) HISTORICAL OR ANTIQUATED CARS — [115]

(1) EXCEPTION —

To the extent that compliance with subsection (b)(2)(C) or (b)(7) would significantly alter the historic or antiquated character of a historical or antiquated rail passenger car, or a rail station served exclusively by such cars, or would result in violation of any rule, regulation, standard, or order issued by the Secretary of Transportation under the Federal Railroad Safety Act of 1970, such compliance shall not be required.

(2) DEFINITION —

As used in this subsection, the term "historical or antiquated rail passenger car" means a rail passenger car —

(A) which is not less than 30 years old at the time of its use for transporting individuals;

(B) the manufacturer of which is no longer in the business of manufacturing rail passenger cars; and

(C) which —

(i) has a consequential association with events or persons significant to the past; or

---

[113] The Senate-passed bill had no subparagraph (6).
[114] The Senate-passed bill had no subparagraph (7).
[115] The Senate-passed bill did not have a subsection on historical or antiquated cars.

(ii) embodies, or is being restored to embody, the distinctive characteristics of a type of rail passenger car used in the past, or to represent a time period which has passed.

SEC. 305. [42 U.S.C. sec. 12185] STUDY[116]

(a) PURPOSES —

The Office of Technology Assessment shall undertake a study to determine —

(1) the access needs of individuals with disabilities to over-the-road buses and over-the-road bus service; and

(2) the most cost-effective methods for providing access to over-the-road buses and over-the-road bus service to individuals with disabilities, particularly individuals who use wheelchairs, through all forms of boarding options.

(b) CONTENTS —

The study shall include, at a minimum, an analysis of the following:

(1) The anticipated demand by individuals with disabilities for accessible over-the-road buses and over-the-road bus service.

(2) The degree to which such buses and service, including any service required under sections 304(b)(4) and 306(a)(2), are readily accessible to and usable by individuals with disabilities.

(3) The effectiveness of various methods of providing accessibility to such buses and service to individuals with disabilities.

(4) The cost of providing accessible over-the-road buses and bus service to individuals with disabilities, including consideration of recent technological and cost saving developments in equipment and devices.

(5) Possible design changes in over-the-road buses that could enhance accessibility, including the installation of accessible restrooms which do not result in a loss of seating capacity.

---

[116] The Senate-passed bill study provision was worded differently.

(6) The impact of accessibility requirements on the continuation of over-the-road bus service, with particular consideration of the impact of such requirements on such service to rural communities.

(c) ADVISORY COMMITTEE —

In conducting the study required by subsection (a), the Office of Technology Assessment shall establish an advisory committee, which shall consist of —

(1) members selected from among private operators and manufacturers of over-the-road buses;

(2) members selected from among individuals with disabilities, particularly individuals who use wheelchairs, who are potential riders of such buses; and

(3) members selected for their technical expertise on issues included in the study, including manufacturers of boarding assistance equipment and devices.

The number of members selected under each of paragraphs (1) and (2) shall be equal, and the total number of members selected under paragraphs (1) and (2) shall exceed the number of members selected under paragraph (3).

(d) DEADLINE —

The study required by subsection (a), along with recommendations by the Office of Technology Assessment, including any policy options for legislative action, shall be submitted to the President and Congress within 36 months after the date of the enactment of this Act. If the President determines that compliance with the regulations issued pursuant to section 306(a)(2)(B) on or before the applicable deadlines specified in section 306(a)(2)(B) will result in a significant reduction in intercity over-the-road bus service, the President shall extend each such deadline by 1 year.

(e) REVIEW —

In developing the study required by subsection (a), the Office of Technology Assessment shall provide a preliminary draft of such study to the Architectural and Transportation Barriers Compliance Board established under section 502 of the Rehabilitation Act of 1973 (29 U.S.C. 792). The Board shall have an opportunity to comment on such draft study, and any such comments by the Board made in writing within 120 days after the Board's receipt of the draft study shall be incorporated as part of the final study required to be submitted under subsection (d).

SEC. 306. [42 U.S.C. sec. 12186] REGULATIONS

(a) TRANSPORTATION PROVISIONS —[117]

(1) GENERAL RULE —

Not later than 1 year after the date of the enactment of this Act, the Secretary of Transportation shall issue regulations in an accessible format to carry out[118] sections 302(b)(2)(B) and (C) and to carry out section 304 (other than subsection (b)(4)).

(2) SPECIAL RULES FOR PROVIDING ACCESS TO OVER-THE-ROAD BUSES —

(A) INTERIM REQUIREMENTS —

(i) ISSUANCE —

Not later than 1 year after the date of the enactment of this Act, the Secretary of Transportation shall issue regulations in an accessible format to carry out sections 304(b)(4) and 302(b)(2)(D)(ii) that require each private entity which uses an over-the-road bus to provide transportation of individuals to provide accessibility to such bus; except that such regulations shall not require any structural changes in over-the-road buses in order to provide access to individuals who use wheelchairs during the effective period of such regulations and shall not require the purchase of boarding assistance devices to provide access to such individuals.

(ii) EFFECTIVE PERIOD —

The regulations issued pursuant to this subparagraph shall be effective until the effective date of the regulations issued under subparagraph (B).

(B) FINAL REQUIREMENT —

(i) REVIEW OF STUDY AND INTERIM REQUIREMENTS —

The Secretary shall review the study submitted under section 305 and the regulations issued pursuant to subparagraph (A).

---

[117] The Senate-passed bill referred to "accessibility standards," and contained much less detail.

[118] The Senate-passed bill said "that shall include standards applicable to facilities and vehicles covered under" instead of "to carry out."

(ii) ISSUANCE —

Not later than 1 year after the date of the submission of the study under section 305, the Secretary shall issue in an accessible format new regulations to carry out sections 304(b)(4) and 302(b)(2)(D)(ii) that require, taking into account the purposes of the study under section 305 and any recommendations resulting from such study, each private entity which uses an over-the-road bus to provide transportation to individuals to provide accessibility to such bus to individuals with disabilities, including individuals who use wheelchairs.

(iii) EFFECTIVE PERIOD —

Subject to section 305(d), the regulations issued pursuant to this subparagraph shall take effect —

(I) with respect to small providers of transportation (as defined by the Secretary), 7 years after July 26, 1990; and

(II) with respect to other providers of transportation, 6 years after July 26, 1990.

(C) LIMITATION ON REQUIRING INSTALLATION OF ACCESSIBLE RESTROOMS —

The regulations issued pursuant to this paragraph shall not require the installation of accessible restrooms in over-the-road buses if such installation would result in a loss of seating capacity.

(3) STANDARDS —

The regulations issued pursuant to this subsection shall include standards applicable to facilities and vehicles covered by sections 302(b)(2) and 304.

(b) OTHER PROVISIONS —

Not later than 1 year after the date of the enactment of this Act, the Attorney General shall issue regulations in an accessible format to carry out the provisions of this title not referred to in subsection (a) that include standards applicable to facilities and vehicles covered under section 302.

(c) CONSISTENCY WITH ATBCB GUIDELINES —

Standards included in regulations issued under subsections (a) and (b) shall be consistent with the minimum guidelines and requirements issued by the

Architectural and Transportation Barriers Compliance Board in accordance with section 504 of this Act.

(d) INTERIM ACCESSIBILITY STANDARDS — [119]

(1) FACILITIES —

If final regulations have not been issued pursuant to this section, for new construction or alterations for which a valid and appropriate State or local building permit is obtained prior to the issuance of final regulations under this section, and for which the construction or alteration authorized by such permit begins within one year of the receipt of such permit and is completed under the terms of such permit, compliance with the Uniform Federal Accessibility Standards in effect at the time the building permit is issued shall suffice to satisfy the requirement that facilities be readily accessible to and usable by persons with disabilities as required under section 303, except that, if such final regulations have not been issued one year after the Architectural and Transportation Barriers Compliance Board has issued the supplemental minimum guidelines required under section 504(a) of this Act, compliance with such supplemental minimum guidelines shall be necessary to satisfy the requirement that facilities be readily accessible to and usable by persons with disabilities prior to issuance of the final regulations.

(2) VEHICLES AND RAIL PASSENGER CARS —

If final regulations have not been issued pursuant to this section, a private entity shall be considered to have complied with the requirements of this title, if any, that a vehicle or rail passenger car be readily accessible to and usable by individuals with disabilities, if the design for such vehicle or car complies with the laws and regulations (including the Minimum Guidelines and Requirements for Accessible Design and such supplemental minimum guidelines as are issued under section 504(a) of this Act) governing accessibility of such vehicles or cars, to the extent that such laws and regulations are not inconsistent with this title and are in effect at the time such design is substantially completed.

SEC. 307. [42 U.S.C. sec. 12187] EXEMPTIONS FOR PRIVATE CLUBS AND RELIGIOUS ORGANIZATIONS

The provisions of this title shall not apply to private clubs or establishments exempted from coverage under title II of the Civil Rights Act of 1964 (42

---

[119] The Senate-passed bill had no subsection (d).

U.S.C. 2000-a(e)) or to religious organizations or entities controlled by religious organizations, including places of worship.

SEC. 308. [42 U.S.C. sec. 12188] ENFORCEMENT

(a) IN GENERAL —

(1) AVAILABILITY OF REMEDIES AND PROCEDURES —

The remedies and procedures set forth in section 204(a) of the Civil Rights Act of 1964 (42 U.S.C. 2000a-3(a)) are the remedies and procedures this title provides to any person who is being subjected to discrimination[120] on the basis of disability in violation of this title or who has reasonable grounds for believing that such person is about to be subjected to discrimination in violation of section 303.[121] Nothing in this section shall require a person with a disability to engage in a futile gesture if such person has actual notice that a person or organization covered by this title does not intend to comply with its provisions.[122]

(2) INJUNCTIVE RELIEF —

In the case of violations of sections 302(b)(2)(A)(iv)[123] and section 303(a), injunctive relief shall include an order to alter facilities to make such facilities readily accessible to and usable by individuals with disabilities to the extent required by this title. Where appropriate, injunctive relief shall also include requiring the provision of an auxiliary aid or service, modification of a policy, or provision of alternative methods, to the extent required by this title.

(b) ENFORCEMENT BY THE ATTORNEY GENERAL —

(1) DENIAL OF RIGHTS —

(A) DUTY TO INVESTIGATE —[124]

---

[120] The Senate-passed bill said "shall be available to any individual who is being or is about to be subjected to discrimination."

[121] The Senate-passed bill omitted the clause "or who has reasonable grounds . . . ."

[122] The Senate-passed bill did not contain the futile gesture sentence.

[123] The Senate-passed bill also referred to subparagraph (vi).

[124] The Senate-passed bill version of this paragraph was structured differently, omitting the certification concept and enumerating powers differently.

(i) IN GENERAL —

The Attorney General shall investigate alleged violations of this title, and shall undertake[125] periodic reviews of compliance of covered entities under this title.

(ii) ATTORNEY GENERAL CERTIFICATION —

On the application of a State or local government, the Attorney General may, in consultation with the Architectural and Transportation Barriers Compliance Board, and after prior notice and a public hearing at which persons, including individuals with disabilities, are provided an opportunity to testify against such certification, certify that a State law or local building code or similar ordinance that establishes accessibility requirements meets or exceeds the minimum requirements of this Act for the accessibility and usability of covered facilities under this title. At any enforcement proceeding under this section, such certification by the Attorney General shall be rebuttable evidence that such State law or local ordinance does meet or exceed the minimum requirements of this Act.

(B) POTENTIAL VIOLATION —[126]

If the Attorney General has reasonable cause to believe that —

(i) any person or group of persons is engaged in a pattern or practice of discrimination under this title; or

(ii) any person or group of persons has been discriminated against under this title and such discrimination raises an issue of general public importance,

the Attorney General may commence a civil action in any appropriate United States district court.

(2) AUTHORITY OF COURT —

In a civil action under paragraph (1)(B), the court —

---

[125] The Senate-passed bill said "which shall include undertaking."
[126] The Senate-passed bill used different language to describe pattern-and-practice and other discrimination.

(A) may grant any equitable relief that such court considers to be appropriate, including, to the extent required by this title —[127]

(i) granting temporary, preliminary, or permanent relief;

(ii) providing an auxiliary aid or service, modification of policy, practice, or procedure,[128] or alternative method; and

(iii) making facilities readily accessible to and usable by individuals with disabilities;[129]

(B) may award such other relief as the court considers to be appropriate, including monetary damages to persons aggrieved when requested by the Attorney General; and

(C) may, to vindicate the public interest, assess a civil penalty against the entity in an amount —

(i) not exceeding $50,000 for a first violation; and

(ii) not exceeding $100,000 for any subsequent violation.

(3) SINGLE VIOLATION — [130]

For purposes of paragraph (2)(C), in determining whether a first or subsequent violation has occurred, a determination in a single action, by judgment or settlement, that the covered entity has engaged in more than one discriminatory act shall be counted as a single violation.

(4) PUNITIVE DAMAGES — [131]

For purposes of subsection (b)(2)(B), the term "monetary damages" and "such other relief" does not include punitive damages.

(5) JUDICIAL CONSIDERATION —

In a civil action under paragraph (1)(B),[132] the court, when considering what amount of civil penalty, if any, is appropriate, shall give consideration to

---

[127] The Senate-passed bill omitted "to the extent required by this title."
[128] The Senate-passed bill omitted "practice, or procedure."
[129] The Senate-passed bill said "to the extent required by this title."
[130] The Senate-passed bill omitted explicit reference to single violation.
[131] The Senate-passed bill omitted specific reference to punitive damages.
[132] The Senate-passed bill referred to paragraph (1).

any good faith effort or attempt to comply with this Act by the entity. In evaluating good faith, the court shall consider, among other factors it deems relevant, whether the entity could have reasonably anticipated the need for an appropriate type of auxiliary aid needed to accommodate the unique needs of a particular individual with a disability.[133]

SEC. 309. [42 U.S.C. sec. 12189] EXAMINATIONS AND COURSES[134]

Any person that offers examinations or courses related to applications, licensing, certification, or credentialing for secondary or postsecondary education, professional, or trade purposes shall offer such examinations or courses in a place and manner accessible to persons with disabilities or offer alternative accessible arrangements for such individuals.

SEC. 310. [42 U.S.C. sec. 12181 note, 12182, 12188 note] EFFECTIVE DATE[135]

(a) GENERAL RULE —

Except as provided in subsections (b), and (c), this title shall become effective 18 months after the date of the enactment of this Act.

(b) CIVIL ACTIONS —

Except for any civil action brought for a violation of section 303, no civil action shall be brought for any act or omission described in section 302 which occurs — [136]

(1) during the first 6 months after the effective date, against businesses that employ 25 or fewer employees and have gross receipts of $1,000,000 or less; and

(2) during the first year after the effective date, against businesses that employ 10 or fewer employees and have gross receipts of $500,000 or less.

---

[133] The Senate-passed bill omitted the last sentence.

[134] The Senate-passed bill did not refer to examinations and courses.

[135] The Senate-passed bill said simply, "This title shall become effective 18 months after the date of enactment of this Act."

[136] The conference report inserted the language "for any act or omission described in section 302 which occurs-" to the House-passed bill.

(c) EXCEPTION —

Sections 302(a) for purposes of section 302(b)(2)(B) and (C) only, 304(a) for purposes of section 304(b)(3) only, 304(b)(3), 305, and 306 shall take effect on the date of the enactment of this Act.

TITLE IV — TELECOMMUNICATIONS

SEC. 401. TELECOMMUNICATIONS RELAY SERVICES FOR HEARING-IMPAIRED AND SPEECH-IMPAIRED INDIVIDUALS

(a) TELECOMMUNICATIONS —

Title II of the Communications Act of 1934 (47 U.S.C. 201 *et seq.*) is amended by adding at the end thereof the following new section:

"SEC. 225. TELECOMMUNICATIONS SERVICES FOR HEARING-IMPAIRED AND SPEECH-IMPAIRED INDIVIDUALS

"(a) DEFINITIONS —

As used in this section —

"(1) COMMON CARRIER OR CARRIER —

The term 'common carrier' or 'carrier' includes any common carrier engaged in interstate communication by wire or radio as defined in section 3(h) and any common carrier engaged in intrastate communication by wire or radio, notwithstanding sections 2(b) and 221(b).

"(2) TDD —

The term 'TDD' means a Telecommunications Device for the Deaf, which is a machine that employs graphic communication in the transmission of coded signals through a wire or radio communication system.

"(3) TELECOMMUNICATIONS RELAY SERVICES —

The term 'telecommunications relay services' means telephone transmission services that provide the ability for an individual who has a hearing impairment or speech impairment to engage in communication by wire or radio with a hearing individual in a manner that is functionally equivalent to the ability of an individual who does not have a hearing impairment or speech impairment to communicate using voice communication services by wire or radio. Such term includes services that enable two-way communication between an individual who uses a TDD or other nonvoice terminal device and an individual who does not use such a device.

"(b) AVAILABILITY OF TELECOMMUNICATIONS RELAY SERVICES —

"(1) IN GENERAL —

In order to carry out the purposes established under section 1, to make available to all individuals in the United States a rapid, efficient nationwide communication service, and to increase the utility of the telephone system of the Nation, the Commission shall ensure that interstate and intrastate telecommunications relay services are available, to the extent possible and in the most efficient manner, to hearing-impaired and speech- impaired individuals in the United States.

"(2) USE OF GENERAL AUTHORITY AND REMEDIES —

For the purposes of administering and enforcing the provisions of this section and the regulations prescribed thereunder, the Commission shall have the same authority, power, and functions with respect to common carriers engaged in intrastate communication as the Commission has in administering and enforcing the provisions of this title with respect to any common carrier engaged in interstate communication. Any violation of this section by any common carrier engaged in intrastate communication shall be subject to the same remedies, penalties, and procedures as are applicable to a violation of this Act by a common carrier engaged in interstate communication.

"(c) PROVISION OF SERVICES —

Each common carrier providing telephone voice transmission services shall, not later than 3 years after the date of enactment of this section, provide in compliance with the regulations prescribed under this section, throughout[137] the area in which it offers service, telecommunications relay services, individually, through designees, through a competitively selected vendor, or in concert with other carriers. A common carrier shall be considered to be in compliance with such regulations —

"(1) with respect to intrastate telecommunications relay services in any State that does not have a certified program under subsection (f) and with respect

---

[137] The conference report substituted "throughout" for "within" in the House-passed bill.

to interstate telecommunications relay services, if such common carrier (or other entity through which the carrier is providing such relay services) is in compliance with the Commission's regulations under subsection (d); or

"(2) with respect to intrastate telecommunications relay services in any State that has a certified program under subsection (f) for such State, if such common carrier (or other entity through which the carrier is providing such relay services) is in compliance with the program certified under subsection (f) for such State.

"(d) REGULATIONS —

"(1) IN GENERAL —

The Commission shall, not later than 1 year after the date of enactment of this section, prescribe regulations to implement this section, including regulations that —

"(A) establish functional requirements, guidelines, and operations procedures for telecommunications relay services;

"(B) establish minimum standards that shall be met in carrying out subsection (c);

"(C) require that telecommunications relay services operate every day for 24 hours per day;

"(D) require that users of telecommunications relay services pay rates no greater than the rates paid for functionally equivalent voice communication services with respect to such factors as the duration of the call, the time of day, and the distance from point of origination to point of termination;

"(E) prohibit relay operators from failing to fulfill the obligations of common carriers by refusing calls or limiting the length of calls that use telecommunications relay services;

"(F) prohibit relay operators from disclosing the content of any relayed conversation and from keeping records of the content of any such conversation beyond the duration of the call; and

"(G) prohibit relay operators from intentionally altering a relayed conversation.

"(2) TECHNOLOGY —

The Commission shall ensure that regulations prescribed to implement this section encourage, consistent with section 7(a) of this Act, the use of existing technology and do not discourage or impair the development of improved technology.

"(3) JURISDICTIONAL SEPARATION OF COSTS —

"(A) IN GENERAL —

Consistent with the provisions of section 410 of this Act, the Commission shall prescribe regulations governing the jurisdictional separation of costs for the services provided pursuant to this section.

"(B) RECOVERING COSTS —

Such regulations shall generally provide that costs caused by interstate telecommunications relay services shall be recovered from all subscribers for every interstate service and costs caused by intrastate telecommunications relay services shall be recovered from the intrastate jurisdiction. In a State that has a certified program under subsection (f), a State commission shall permit a common carrier to recover the costs incurred in providing intrastate telecommunications relay services by a method consistent with the requirements of this section.

"(e) ENFORCEMENT —

"(1) IN GENERAL —

Subject to subsections (f) and (g), the Commission shall enforce this section.

"(2) COMPLAINT —

The Commission shall resolve, by final order, a complaint alleging a violation of this section within 180 days after the date such complaint is filed.

"(f) CERTIFICATION —

"(1) STATE DOCUMENTATION —

Any State desiring to establish a State program under this section shall submit documentation to the Commission that describes the program of such State for implementing intrastate telecommunications relay services and the procedures and remedies available for enforcing any requirements imposed by the State program.

"(2) REQUIREMENTS FOR CERTIFICATION —

After review of such documentation, the Commission shall certify the State program if the Commission determines that —

"(A) the program makes available to hearing-impaired and speech-impaired individuals, either directly, through designees, through a competitively selected vendor, or through regulation of intrastate common carriers, intrastate telecommunications relay services in such State in a manner that meets or exceeds the requirements of regulations prescribed by the Commission under subsection (d); and

"(B) the program makes available adequate procedures and remedies for enforcing the requirements of the State program.

"(3) METHOD OF FUNDING —

Except as provided in subsection (d), the Commission shall not refuse to certify a State program based solely on the method such State will implement for funding intrastate telecommunication relay services.

"(4) SUSPENSION OR REVOCATION OF CERTIFICATION —

The Commission may suspend or revoke such certification if, after notice and opportunity for hearing, the Commission determines that such certification is no longer warranted. In a State whose program has been suspended or revoked, the Commission shall take such steps as may be necessary, consistent with this section, to ensure continuity of telecommunications relay services.

"(g) COMPLAINT —

"(1) REFERRAL OF COMPLAINT —

If a complaint to the Commission alleges a violation of this section with respect to intrastate telecommunications relay services within a State and certification of the program of such State under subsection (f) is in effect, the Commission shall refer such complaint to such State.

"(2) JURISDICTION OF COMMISSION —

After referring a complaint to a State under paragraph (1), the Commission shall exercise jurisdiction over such complaint only if —

"(A) final action under such State program has not been taken on such complaint by such State —

"(i) within 180 days after the complaint is filed with such State; or

"(ii) within a shorter period as prescribed by the regulations of such State; or

"(B) the Commission determines that such State program is no longer qualified for certification under subsection (f)."

(b) CONFORMING AMENDMENTS —

The Communications Act of 1934 (47 U.S.C. 151 *et seq.*) is amended —

(1) in section 2(b) (47 U.S.C. 152(b)), by striking "section 224" and inserting "sections 224 and 225;" and

(2) in section 221(b) (47 U.S.C. 221(b)), by striking "section 301" and inserting "sections 225 and 301."

SEC. 402. CLOSED-CAPTIONING OF PUBLIC SERVICE ANNOUNCEMENTS

Section 711 of the Communications Act of 1934 is amended to read as follows:

"SEC. 711. CLOSED-CAPTIONING OF PUBLIC SERVICE ANNOUNCEMENTS

"Any television public service announcement that is produced or funded in whole or in part by any agency or instrumentality of Federal government shall include closed captioning of the verbal content of such announcement. A television broadcast station licensee —

"(1) shall not be required to supply closed captioning for any such announcement that fails to include it; and

"(2) shall not be liable for broadcasting any such announcement without transmitting a closed caption unless the licensee intentionally fails to transmit the closed caption that was included with the announcement."

TITLE V — [Subchapter IV] MISCELLANEOUS PROVISIONS

SEC. 501. [42 U.S.C. sec. 12201] CONSTRUCTION

(a) IN GENERAL —

Except as otherwise provided in this Act,[138] nothing in this Act shall be construed to apply a lesser standard[139] than[140] the standards applied under title V of the Rehabilitation Act of 1973 (29 U.S.C. 790 *et seq.*) or the regulations issued by Federal agencies pursuant to such title.

(b) RELATIONSHIP TO OTHER LAWS — [141]

Nothing in this Act shall be construed to invalidate or limit the remedies, rights, and procedures[142] of any[143] Federal law or law of any State or political subdivision of any State or jurisdiction that provides greater or equal protection for the rights of individuals with disabilities than are afforded by this Act. Nothing in this Act shall be construed to preclude the prohibition of, or the imposition of restrictions on, smoking in places of employment covered by title I, in transportation covered by title II or III, or in places of public accommodation covered by title III.[144]

(c) INSURANCE —

Titles I through IV of this Act shall not be construed to prohibit or restrict —

(1) an insurer, hospital or medical service company, health maintenance organization, or any agent, or entity that administers benefit plans, or similar organizations from underwriting risks, classifying risks, or administering such risks that are based on or not inconsistent with State law; or

---

[138] The Senate-passed bill did not contain this phrase.

[139] The Senate-passed bill read, "to reduce the scope of coverage or apply a lesser standard . . . ."

[140] The Senate-passed bill had the phrase "the coverage required or" at this point.

[141] The Senate-passed bill had the caption "Other Laws."

[142] The Senate-passed bill did not have the phrase "the remedies, rights, and procedures."

[143] The Senate-passed bill had the word "other" at this point.

[144] The last sentence, beginning with "Nothing" was not in the Senate-passed bill.

(2) a person or organization covered by this Act from establishing, sponsoring, observing or administering the terms of a bona fide benefit plan that are based on underwriting risks, classifying risks, or administering such risks that are based on or not inconsistent with State law; or

(3) a person or organization covered by this Act from establishing, sponsoring, observing or administering the terms of a bona fide benefit plan that is not subject to State laws that regulate insurance.

Paragraphs (1), (2), and (3) shall not be used as a subterfuge to evade the purposes of title I and III.

(d) ACCOMMODATIONS AND SERVICES —

Nothing in this Act shall be construed to require an individual with a disability to accept an accommodation, aid, service, opportunity, or benefit which such individual chooses not to accept.[145]

SEC. 502. [42 U.S.C. sec. 12202] STATE IMMUNITY[146]

A State shall not be immune under the eleventh amendment to the Constitution of the United States from an action in Federal or State court of competent[147] jurisdiction for a violation of this Act. In any action against a State for a violation of the requirements of this Act, remedies (including remedies both at law and in equity) are available for such a violation to the same extent as such remedies are available for such a violation in an action against any public or private entity other than a State.

SEC. 503. [42 U.S.C. sec. 12203] PROHIBITION AGAINST RETALIATION AND COERCION[148]

(a) RETALIATION —

No person[149] shall discriminate against any[150] individual because such[151] individual has opposed any act or practice made unlawful by this Act or

---

[145] Subsection (d) was not in the Senate-passed bill.

[146] The state immunity section was numbered § 503 in the Senate-passed bill.

[147] The Senate-passed bill did not refer to state courts.

[148] This section was numbered as § 502 in the Senate-passed bill.

[149] The Senate-passed bill said "No individual."

[150] The Senate-passed bill said "any other individual."

[151] The Senate-passed bill said "such other individual."

because such[152] individual made a charge, testified, assisted, or participated in any manner in an investigation, proceeding, or hearing under this Act.

(b) INTERFERENCE, COERCION, OR INTIMIDATION —

It shall be unlawful to coerce, intimidate, threaten, or interfere with any individual[153] in the exercise or enjoyment of, or on account of his or her having exercised or enjoyed, or on account of his or her having aided or encouraged any other individual[154] in the exercise or enjoyment of, any right granted or protected by this Act.

(c) REMEDIES AND PROCEDURES —

The remedies and procedures available under sections 107, 203,[155] and 308 of this Act shall be available to aggrieved persons for violations of subsections (a) and (b), with respect to title I, title II and title III, respectively.[156]

SEC. 504. [42 U.S.C. sec. 12204] REGULATIONS BY THE ARCHITECTURAL AND TRANSPORTATION BARRIERS COMPLIANCE BOARD

(a) ISSUANCE OF GUIDELINES —

Not later than 9 months[157] after the date of enactment of this Act, the Architectural and Transportation Barriers Compliance Board shall issue minimum guidelines that shall supplement the existing Minimum Guidelines and Requirements for Accessible Design for purposes of titles II and III of this Act.[158]

(b) CONTENTS OF GUIDELINES —

The supplemental[159] guidelines issued under subsection (a) shall establish additional requirements, consistent with this Act, to ensure that buildings, facilities, rail passenger cars,[160] and vehicles are accessible, in terms of ar-

---

[152] The Senate-passed bill said "such other individual."
[153] The Senate-passed bill said "any person."
[154] The Senate-passed bill said "any other person."
[155] The Senate-passed bill referred to § 205.
[156] The Senate-passed bill did not contain the concluding reference to titles I, II, and III.
[157] The Senate-passed bill had a deadline of 6 months.
[158] The Senate-passed bill did not contain the phase "of this Act."
[159] The Senate-passed bill did not contain the word "supplemental."
[160] The Senate-passed bill did not include "rail passenger cars."

chitecture and design, transportation, and communication, to individuals with disabilities.

(c) QUALIFIED HISTORIC PROPERTIES —

(1) IN GENERAL —

The supplemental guidelines issued under subsection (a) shall include procedures and requirements for alterations that will threaten or destroy the historic significance of qualified historic buildings and facilities as defined in 4.1.7(1)(a) of the Uniform Federal Accessibility Standards.

(2) SITES ELIGIBLE FOR LISTING IN NATIONAL REGISTER —

With respect to alterations of buildings or facilities that are eligible for listing in the National Register of Historic Places under the National Historic Preservation Act (16 U.S.C. 470 *et seq.*), the guidelines described in paragraph (1) shall, at a minimum, maintain the procedures and requirements established in 4.1.7(1) and (2) of the Uniform Federal Accessibility Standards.

(3) OTHER SITES —

With respect to alterations of buildings or facilities designated as historic under State or local law, the guidelines described in paragraph (1) shall establish procedures equivalent to those established by 4.1.7(1)(b) and (c) of the Uniform Federal Accessibility Standards, and shall require, at a minimum, compliance with the requirements established in 4.1.7(2) of such standards.[161]

SEC. 505. [42 U.S.C. sec. 12205] ATTORNEY'S FEES

In any action or administrative proceeding commenced pursuant to this Act, the court or agency, in its discretion, may allow the prevailing party, other than the United States, a reasonable attorney's fee, including litigation expenses, and costs, and the United States shall be liable for the foregoing the same as a private individual.

---

[161] The Senate-passed bill did not contain subsection (c) regarding Historic Properties.

SEC. 506. [42 U.S.C. sec. 12206] TECHNICAL ASSISTANCE

(a) PLAN FOR ASSISTANCE —

(1) IN GENERAL —

Not later than 180 days after the date of enactment of this Act, the Attorney General, in consultation with the Chair of the Equal Employment Opportunity Commission, the Secretary of Transportation,[162] the Chair of the Architectural and Transportation Barriers Compliance Board, and the Chairman of the Federal Communications Commission, shall develop a plan to assist entities covered under this Act, and[163] other Federal[164] agencies,[165] in understanding the responsibility of such entities and agencies[166] under this Act.

(2) PUBLICATION OF PLAN —

The Attorney General shall publish the plan referred to in paragraph (1) for public comment in accordance with subchapter II of chapter 5 of title 5, United States Code (commonly known as the Administrative Procedure Act).[167]

(b) AGENCY AND PUBLIC ASSISTANCE —

The Attorney General may[168] obtain the assistance of other Federal agencies in carrying out subsection (a), including the National Council on Disability, the President's Committee on Employment of People with Disabilities, the Small Business Administration, and the Department of Commerce.

(c) IMPLEMENTATION —

(1) RENDERING ASSISTANCE — [169]

Each Federal agency[170] that has responsibility under paragraph (2) for implementing this Act may render technical assistance to individuals and in-

---

[162] The Senate-passed bill included the National Council on Disability.
[163] The Senate-passed bill used "along with" instead of "and."
[164] The Senate-passed bill used "executive" instead of "Federal."
[165] The Senate-passed bill added "and commissions."
[166] The Senate-passed bill added "and commissions."
[167] The Senate-passed bill cited the Administrative Procedure Act differently.
[168] The Senate-passed bill used the phrase "is authorized to" instead of "may."
[169] The Senate-passed bill entitled this paragraph, "Authority to Contract."
[170] The Senate-passed bill said, "Each department or agency."

stitutions that have rights or duties under the respective title or titles for which such agency has responsibility.[171]

(2) IMPLEMENTATION OF TITLES —

(A) TITLE I —

The Equal Employment Opportunity Commission and the Attorney General shall implement the plan for assistance developed under[172] subsection (a), for title I.

(B) TITLE II —

(i) SUBTITLE A —

The Attorney General shall implement such plan for assistance for subtitle A of title II.

(ii) SUBTITLE B —

The Secretary of Transportation shall implement such plan for assistance for subtitle B of title II.

(C) TITLE III —

The Attorney General, in coordination with the Secretary of Transportation and the Chair of the Architectural Transportation Barriers Compliance Board, shall implement such plan for assistance for title III, except for section 304, the plan for assistance for which shall be implemented by the Secretary of Transportation.[173]

(D) TITLE IV —

The Chairman of the Federal Communications Commission, in coordination with the Attorney General, shall implement such plan for assistance for title IV.

---

[171] The Senate-passed bill said "rights or responsibilities under this Act."

[172] The Senate-passed bill said "as described in" instead of "developed under."

[173] The Senate-passed bill did not have the exception for § 304.

(3) TECHNICAL ASSISTANCE MANUALS —

Each Federal agency that has responsibility under paragraph (2) for implementing this Act shall, as part of its implementation responsibilities, ensure the availability and provision of appropriate technical assistance manuals to individuals or entities with rights or duties under this Act no later than six months after applicable final regulations are published under titles I, II, III, and IV.[174]

(d) GRANTS AND CONTRACTS —

(1) IN GENERAL —

Each Federal agency[175] that has responsibility under subsection (c)(2)[176] for implementing this Act may make grants or award[177] contracts[178] to effectuate the purposes of this section, subject to the availability of appropriations. Such grants and contracts may be awarded to individuals, institutions not organized for profit and no part of the net earnings of which inures to the benefit of any private shareholder or individual (including educational institutions), and associations representing individuals who have rights or duties under this Act. Contracts may be awarded to entities organized for profit, but such entities may not be the recipients of grants described in this paragraph.

(2) DISSEMINATION OF INFORMATION —

Such grants and contracts, among other uses, may be designed to ensure wide dissemination of information about the rights and duties established by this Act and to provide information and technical assistance about techniques for effective compliance with this Act.

---

[174] The Senate-passed bill did not have a subparagraph referring to technical assistance manuals.

[175] The Senate-passed bill used the phrase "department and agency."

[176] The Senate-passed bill did not contain the phrase "under subsection (c)(2)."

[177] The Senate-passed bill used the phrase "enter into."

[178] At this point, the Senate-passed bill read, "may make grants or enter into contracts with individuals, profit institutions, and nonprofit institutions, including educational institutions and groups or associations representing individuals who have rights or duties under this Act, ..."

(e) FAILURE TO RECEIVE ASSISTANCE —

An employer, public accommodation, or other entity covered under this Act shall not be excused from compliance with[179] the requirements of this Act because of any failure to receive technical assistance under this section, including any failure in the development or dissemination of any technical assistance manual authorized by this section.[180]

SEC. 507. [42 U.S.C. sec. 12207] FEDERAL WILDERNESS AREAS

(a) STUDY —

The National Council on Disability shall conduct a study and report on the effect that wilderness designations and wilderness land management practices have on the ability of individuals with disabilities to use and enjoy the National Wilderness Preservation System as established under the Wilderness Act (16 U.S.C. 1131 *et seq.*).

(b) SUBMISSION OF REPORT —

Not later than 1 year after the enactment of this Act, the National Council on Disability shall submit the report required under subsection (a) to Congress.

(c) SPECIFIC WILDERNESS ACCESS — [181]

(1) IN GENERAL —

Congress reaffirms that nothing in the Wilderness Act is to be construed as prohibiting the use of a wheelchair in a wilderness area by an individual whose disability requires use of a wheelchair, and consistent with the Wilderness Act[182] no agency is required to provide any form of special treatment or accommodation, or to construct any facilities or modify any conditions of lands within a wilderness area in order to facilitate such use.

---

[179] The Senate-passed bill used the word "meeting" instead of the phrase "compliance with."

[180] The Senate-passed bill did not have the explicit reference to manuals beginning, "including any failure . . . ."

[181] The conference report restructured this subsection into two paragraphs, adding paragraph (2) to the House-passed version.

[182] The conference report deleted "but" and added "and consistent with the Wilderness Act" to the House-passed bill.

(2) DEFINITION —

For purposes of paragraph (1), the term "wheelchair" means a device designed solely for use by a mobility-impaired person for locomotion, that is suitable for use in an indoor pedestrian area.[183]

SEC. 508. [42 U.S.C. sec. 12208] TRANSVESTITES

For the purposes of this Act, the term "disabled" or "disability" shall not apply to an individual solely because that individual is a transvestite.

SEC. 509. [42 U.S.C. sec. 12209] INSTRUMENTALITIES OF THE CONGRESS

The General Accounting Office, the Government Printing Office, and the Library of Congress shall be covered as follows:

(1) In General —

The rights and protections under this chapter shall, subject to paragraph (2), apply with respect to the conduct of each instrumentality of the Congress.

(2) Establishment of Remedies and Procedures by Instrumentalities

The chief official of each instrumentality of the Congress shall establish remedies and procedures to be utilized with respect to the rights and protections provided pursuant to paragraph (1).

(3) Report to Congress —

The chief official of each instrumentality of the Congress shall, after establishing remedies and procedures for purposes of paragraph (2), submit to the Congress a report describing the remedies and procedures.

(4) Definition of Instrumentality —

For purposes of this section, the term "instrumentality of the Congress" means the following: General Accounting Office, the Government Printing Office, and the Library of Congress.

---

[183] The Senate-passed bill had no subsection (c).

(5) Enforcement of employment rights —

The rememdies and procedures set forth in section 2000e-16 of this title shall be available to any employee of an instrumentality of the Congress who alleges a violation of the rights and protections under sections 12112 through 12114 of this title that are made applicable by this section, except that the authorities of the Equal Employment Opportunity Commission shall be exercised by the chief official of the instrumentality of the Congress.

(6) Enforcement of rights to public services and accommodations —

The remedies and procedures set forth in section 2000e-16 of this title shall be available to any qualified person with a disability who is a visitor, guest, or patron of an instrumentality of Congress and who alleges a violation of the rights and protections under sections 12131 through 12150 or section 12182 or 12183 of this title that are made applicable by this section, except that the authorities of the Equal Employment Opportunity Commission shall be exercised by the chief official of the instrumentality of the Congress.

(7) Construction —

Nothing in this section shall alter the enforcement procedures for individuals with disabilities provided in the General Accounting Office Personnel Act of 1980 and regulations promulgated pursuant to that Act.

The Congressional Accountability Act of 1995, Pub. L. No. 104-1, 109 Stat 3, January 23, 1995, codified at 2 U.S.C. secs. 1203-1224, 1301-1443, made the ADA applicable to employees of the Senate and House of Representatives, with specialized procedures, institutions and remedies available for violations.

SEC. 510. [42 U.S.C. sec. 12210] ILLEGAL USE OF DRUGS[184]

(a) IN GENERAL —

For purposes of this Act, the term "individual with a disability" does not include an individual who is currently engaging in the illegal use of drugs, when the covered entity acts on the basis of such use.

---

[184] The language in this section was reworked in the House and the Conference to such an extent as to make a detailed comparison with Senate-passed language impracticable.

(b) RULES OF CONSTRUCTION —

Nothing in subsection (a) shall be construed to exclude as an individual with a disability an individual who —

(1) has successfully completed a supervised drug rehabilitation program and is no longer engaging in the illegal use of drugs, or has otherwise been rehabilitated successfully and is no longer engaging in such use;

(2) is participating in a supervised rehabilitation program and is no longer engaging in such use; or

(3) is erroneously regarded as engaging in such use, but is not engaging in such use; except that it shall not be a violation of this Act for a covered entity to adopt or administer reasonable policies or procedures, including but not limited to drug testing, designed to ensure that an individual described in paragraph (1) or (2) is no longer engaging in the illegal use of drugs; however, nothing in this section shall be construed to encourage, prohibit, restrict, or authorize the conducting of testing for the illegal use of drugs.

(c) HEALTH AND OTHER SERVICES —

Notwithstanding subsection (a) and section 511(b)(3), an individual shall not be denied health services, or services provided in connection with drug rehabilitation, on the basis of the current illegal use of drugs if the individual is otherwise entitled to such services.

(d) DEFINITION OF ILLEGAL USE OF DRUGS —

(1) IN GENERAL —

The term "illegal use of drugs" means the use of drugs, the possession or distribution of which is unlawful under the Controlled Substances Act (21 U.S.C. 812). Such term does not include the use of a drug taken under supervision by a licensed health care professional, or other uses authorized by the Controlled Substances Act or other provisions of Federal law.

(2) DRUGS —

The term "drug" means a controlled substance, as defined in schedules I through V of section 202 of the Controlled Substances Act.

SEC. 511. [42 U.S.C. sec. 12211] DEFINITIONS

(a) HOMOSEXUALITY AND BISEXUALITY —

For purposes of the definition of "disability" in section 3(2), homosexuality and bisexuality are not impairments and as such are not disabilities under this Act.[185]

(b) CERTAIN CONDITIONS —

Under this Act, the term "disability" shall not include —

(1) transvestism, transsexualism, pedophilia, exhibitionism, voyeurism, gender identity disorders not resulting from physical impairments, or other sexual behavior disorders;

(2) compulsive gambling, kleptomania, or pyromania; or

(3) psychoactive substance use disorders resulting from current illegal use of drugs.[186]

SEC. 512. [29 U.S.C. sec. 706] AMENDMENTS TO THE REHABILITATION ACT[187]

(a) DEFINITION OF HANDICAPPED INDIVIDUAL —

Section 7(8) of the Rehabilitation Act of 1973 (29 U.S.C. 706(8)) is amended by redesignating subparagraph (C) as subparagraph (D), and by inserting after subparagraph (B) the following subparagraph:

"(C)(i) For purposes of title V, the term 'individual with handicaps' does not include an individual who is currently engaging in the illegal use of drugs, when a covered entity acts on the basis of such use.

"(ii) Nothing in clause (i) shall be construed to exclude as an individual with handicaps an individual who —

---

[185] The Senate-passed bill simply listed homosexuality and bisexuality in the list of conditions now contained in subsection (b).

[186] The Senate-passed bill did not separate paragraphs (1), (2), and (3).

[187] The Senate-passed bill contained significantly different language in this section.

"(I) has successfully completed a supervised drug rehabilitation program and is no longer engaging in the illegal use of drugs, or has otherwise been rehabilitated successfully and is no longer engaging in such use;

"(II) is participating in a supervised rehabilitation program and is no longer engaging in such use; or

"(III) is erroneously regarded as engaging in such use, but is not engaging in such use; except that it shall not be a violation of this Act for a covered entity to adopt or administer reasonable policies or procedures, including but not limited to drug testing, designed to ensure that an individual described in subclause (I) or (II) is no longer engaging in the illegal use of drugs.

"(iii) Notwithstanding clause (i), for purposes of programs and activities providing health services and services provided under title I, II and III, an individual shall not be excluded from the benefits of such programs or activities on the basis of his or her current illegal use of drugs if he or she is otherwise entitled to such services.

"(iv) For purposes of programs and activities providing educational services, local educational agencies may take disciplinary action pertaining to the use or possession of illegal drugs or alcohol against any handicapped student who currently is engaging in the illegal use of drugs or in the use of alcohol to the same extent that such disciplinary action is taken against nonhandicapped students. Furthermore, the due process procedures at 34 CFR 104.36 shall not apply to such disciplinary actions.

"(v) For purposes of sections 503 and 504 as such sections relate to employment, the term 'individual with handicaps' does not include any individual who is an alcoholic whose current use of alcohol prevents such individual from performing the duties of the job in question or whose employment, by reason of such current alcohol abuse, would constitute a direct threat to property or the safety of others."

(b) DEFINITION OF ILLEGAL DRUGS —

Section 7 of the Rehabilitation Act of 1973 (29 U.S.C. 706) is amended by adding at the end the following new paragraph:

"(22)(A) The term 'drug' means a controlled substance, as defined in schedules I through V of section 202 of the Controlled Substances Act (21 U.S.C. 812).

"(B) The term 'illegal use of drugs' means the use of drugs, the possession or distribution of which is unlawful under the Controlled Substances Act. Such term does not include the use of a drug taken under supervision by a licensed health care professional, or other uses authorized by the Controlled Substances Act or other provisions of Federal law."

(c) CONFORMING AMENDMENTS —

Section 7(8)(B) of the Rehabilitation Act of 1973 (29 U.S.C. 706(8)(B)) is amended —

(1) in the first sentence, by striking "Subject to the second sentence of this subparagraph," and inserting "Subject to subparagraphs (C) and (D),"; and

(2) by striking the second sentence.

SEC. 513. [42 U.S.C. sec. 12212] ALTERNATIVE MEANS OF DISPUTE RESOLUTION[188]

Where appropriate and to the extent authorized by law, the use of alternative means of dispute resolution, including settlement negotiations, conciliation, facilitation, mediation, factfinding, minitrials, and arbitration, is encouraged to resolve disputes arising under this Act.

SEC. 514. [42 U.S.C. sec. 12213] SEVERABILITY

Should any provision in this Act be found to be unconstitutional by a court of law, such provision shall be severed from the remainder of the Act, and such action shall not affect the enforceability of the remaining provisions of the Act.

---

[188] The Senate-passed bill did not contain this section.

EEOC REGULATIONS FOR ADA TITLE I — CODE OF FEDERAL REGULATIONS, TITLE 29 PART 1630

§ 1630.1 Purpose, applicability, and construction.

(a) Purpose. The purpose of this part is to implement title I of the Americans with Disabilities Act (42 U.S.C. 12101, *et seq.*) (ADA), requiring equal employment opportunities for qualified individuals with disabilities, and sections 3(2), 3(3), 501, 503, 506(e), 508, 510, and 511 of the ADA as those sections pertain to the employment of qualified individuals with disabilities.

(b) Applicability. This part applies to "covered entities" as defined at § 1630.2(b).

(c) Construction —

(1) In general. Except as otherwise provided in this part, this part does not apply a lesser standard than the standards applied under title V of the Rehabilitation Act of 1973 (29 U.S.C. 790–794a), or the regulations issued by Federal agencies pursuant to that title.

(2) Relationship to other laws. This part does not invalidate or limit the remedies, rights, and procedures of any Federal law or law of any State or political subdivision of any State or jurisdiction that provides greater or equal protection for the rights of individuals with disabilities than are afforded by this part.

§ 1630.2 Definitions.

(a) Commission means the Equal Employment Opportunity Commission established by section 705 of the Civil Rights Act of 1964 (42 U.S.C. 2000e-4).

(b) Covered Entity means an employer, employment agency, labor organization, or joint labor management committee.

(c) Person, labor organization, employment agency, commerce and industry affecting commerce shall have the same meaning given those terms in section 701 of the Civil Rights Act of 1964 (42 U.S.C. 2000e).

(d) State means each of the several States, the District of Columbia, the Commonwealth of Puerto Rico, Guam, American Samoa, the Virgin

Islands, the Trust Territory of the Pacific Islands, and the Commonwealth of the Northern Mariana Islands.

(e) Employer —

(1) In general. The term employer means a person engaged in an industry affecting commerce who has 15 or more employees for each working day in each of 20 or more calendar weeks in the current or preceding calendar year, and any agent of such person, except that, from July 26, 1992 through July 25, 1994, an employer means a person engaged in an industry affecting commerce who has 25 or more employees for each working day in each of 20 or more calendar weeks in the current or preceding year and any agent of such person.

(2) Exceptions. The term employer does not include —

(i) The United States, a corporation wholly owned by the government of the United States, or an Indian tribe; or

(ii) A bona fide private membership club (other than a labor organization) that is exempt from taxation under section 501(c) of the Internal Revenue Code of 1986.

(f) Employee means an individual employed by an employer.

(g) Disability means, with respect to an individual —

(1) A physical or mental impairment that substantially limits one or more of the major life activities of such individual;

(2) A record of such an impairment; or

(3) being regarded as having such an impairment.

(See § 1630.3 for exceptions to this definition).

(h) Physical or mental impairment means:

(1) Any physiological disorder, or condition, cosmetic disfigurement, or anatomical loss affecting one or more of the following body systems: neurological, musculoskeletal, special sense organs, respiratory (including speech organs), cardiovascular, reproductive, digestive, genito-urinary, hemic and lymphatic, skin, and endocrine; or

(2) Any mental or psychological disorder, such as mental retardation, organic brain syndrome, emotional or mental illness, and specific learning disabilities.

(i) Major Life Activities means functions such as caring for oneself, performing manual tasks, walking, seeing, hearing, speaking, breathing, learning, and working.

(j) Substantially limits —

(1) The term substantially limits means:

(i) Unable to perform a major life activity that the average person in the general population can perform; or

(ii) Significantly restricted as to the condition, manner or duration under which an individual can perform a particular major life activity as compared to the condition, manner, or duration under which the average person in the general population can perform that same major life activity.

(2) The following factors should be considered in determining whether an individual is substantially limited in a major life activity:

(i) The nature and severity of the impairment;

(ii) The duration or expected duration of the impairment; and

(iii) The permanent or long term impact, or the expected permanent or long term impact of or resulting from the impairment.

(3) With respect to the major life activity of working —

(i) The term substantially limits means significantly restricted in the ability to perform either a class of jobs or a broad range of jobs in various classes as compared to the average person having comparable training, skills and abilities. The inability to perform a single, particular job does not constitute a substantial limitation in the major life activity of working.

(ii) In addition to the factors listed in paragraph (j)(2) of this section, the following factors may be considered in determining whether an individual is substantially limited in the major life activity of "working":

(A) The geographical area to which the individual has reasonable access;

(B) The job from which the individual has been disqualified because of an impairment, and the number and types of jobs utilizing similar training, knowledge, skills or abilities, within that geographical area, from which the individual is also disqualified because of the impairment (class of jobs); and/or

(C) The job from which the individual has been disqualified because of an impairment, and the number and types of other jobs not utilizing similar training, knowledge, skills or abilities, within that geographical area, from which the individual is also disqualified because of the impairment (broad range of jobs in various classes).

(k) Has a record of such impairment means has a history of, or has been misclassified as having, a mental or physical impairment that substantially limits one or more major life activities.

(l) Is regarded as having such an impairment means:

(1) Has a physical or mental impairment that does not substantially limit major life activities but is treated by a covered entity as constituting such limitation;

(2) Has a physical or mental impairment that substantially limits major life activities only as a result of the attitudes of others toward such impairment; or

(3) Has none of the impairments defined in paragraphs (h) (1) or (2) of this section but is treated by a covered entity as having a substantially limiting impairment.

(m) Qualified individual with a disability means an individual with a disability who satisfies the requisite skill, experience, education and other job-related requirements of the employment position such individual holds or desires, and who, with or without reasonable accommodation, can perform the essential functions of such position. (See § 1630.3 for exceptions to this definition).

(n) Essential functions —

(1) In general. The term essential functions means the fundamental job duties of the employment position the individual with a disability holds or desires. The term "essential functions" does not include the marginal functions of the position.

(2) A job function may be considered essential for any of several reasons, including but not limited to the following:

(i) The function may be essential because the reason the position exists is to perform that function;

(ii) The function may be essential because of the limited number of employees available among whom the performance of that job function can be distributed; and/or

(iii) The function may be highly specialized so that the incumbent in the position is hired for his or her expertise or ability to perform the particular function.

(3) Evidence of whether a particular function is essential includes, but is not limited to:

(i) The employer's judgment as to which functions are essential;

(ii) Written job descriptions prepared before advertising or interviewing applicants for the job;

(iii) The amount of time spent on the job performing the function;

(iv) The consequences of not requiring the incumbent to perform the function;

(v) The terms of a collective bargaining agreement;

(vi) The work experience of past incumbents in the job; and/or

(vii) The current work experience of incumbents in similar jobs.

(o) Reasonable accommodation.

(1) The term reasonable accommodation means:

(i) Modifications or adjustments to a job application process that enable a qualified applicant with a disability to be considered for the position such qualified applicant desires; or

(ii) Modifications or adjustments to the work environment, or to the manner or circumstances under which the position held or desired is customarily performed, that enable a qualified individual with a disability to perform the essential functions of that position; or

(iii) Modifications or adjustments that enable a covered entity's employee with a disability to enjoy equal benefits and privileges of employment as are enjoyed by its other similarly situated employees without disabilities.

(2) Reasonable accommodation may include but is not limited to:

(i) Making existing facilities used by employees readily accessible to and usable by individuals with disabilities; and

(ii) Job restructuring; part-time or modified work schedules; reassignment to a vacant position; acquisition or modifications of equipment or devices; appropriate adjustment or modifications of examinations, training materials, or policies; the provision of qualified readers or interpreters; and other similar accommodations for individuals with disabilities.

(3) To determine the appropriate reasonable accommodation it may be necessary for the covered entity to initiate an informal, interactive process with the qualified individual with a disability in need of the accommodation. This process should identify the precise limitations resulting from the disability and potential reasonable accommodations that could overcome those limitations.

(p) Undue hardship —

(1) In general. Undue hardship means, with respect to the provision of an accommodation, significant difficulty or expense incurred by a covered entity, when considered in light of the factors set forth in paragraph (p)(2) of this section.

(2) Factors to be considered. In determining whether an accommodation would impose an undue hardship on a covered entity, factors to be considered include:

(i) The nature and net cost of the accommodation needed under this part, taking into consideration the availability of tax credits and deductions, and/or outside funding;

(ii) The overall financial resources of the facility or facilities involved in the provision of the reasonable accommodation, the number of persons employed at such facility, and the effect on expenses and resources;

(iii) The overall financial resources of the covered entity, the overall size of the business of the covered entity with respect to the number of its employees, and the number, type and location of its facilities;

(iv) The type of operation or operations of the covered entity, including the composition, structure and functions of the workforce of such entity, and the geographic separateness and administrative or fiscal relationship of the facility or facilities in question to the covered entity; and

(v) The impact of the accommodation upon the operation of the facility, including the impact on the ability of other employees to perform their duties and the impact on the facility's ability to conduct business.

(q) Qualification standards means the personal and professional attributes including the skill, experience, education, physical, medical, safety and other requirements established by a covered entity as requirements which an individual must meet in order to be eligible for the position held or desired.

(r) Direct Threat means a significant risk of substantial harm to the health or safety of the individual or others that cannot be eliminated or reduced by reasonable accommodation. The determination that an individual poses a "direct threat" shall be based on an individualized assessment of the individual's present ability to safely perform the essential functions of the job. This assessment shall be based on a reasonable medical judgment

499

that relies on the most current medical knowledge and/or on the best available objective evidence. In determining whether an individual would pose a direct threat, the factors to be considered include:

(1) The duration of the risk;

(2) The nature and severity of the potential harm;

(3) The likelihood that the potential harm will occur; and

(4) The imminence of the potential harm.

§ 1630.3 Exceptions to the definitions of "Disability" and "Qualified Individual with a Disability."

(a) The terms disability and qualified individual with a disability do not include individuals currently engaging in the illegal use of drugs, when the covered entity acts on the basis of such use.

(1) Drug means a controlled substance, as defined in schedules I through V of Section 202 of the Controlled Substances Act (21 U.S.C. 812)

(2) Illegal use of drugs means the use of drugs the possession or distribution of which is unlawful under the Controlled Substances Act, as periodically updated by the Food and Drug Administration. This term does not include the use of a drug taken under the supervision of a licensed health care professional, or other uses authorized by the Controlled Substances Act or other provisions of Federal law.

(b) However, the terms disability and qualified individual with a disability may not exclude an individual who:

(1) Has successfully completed a supervised drug rehabilitation program and is no longer engaging in the illegal use of drugs, or has otherwise been rehabilitated successfully and is no longer engaging in the illegal use of drugs; or

(2) Is participating in a supervised rehabilitation program and is no longer engaging in such use; or

(3) Is erroneously regarded as engaging in such use, but is not engaging in such use.

(c) It shall not be a violation of this part for a covered entity to adopt or administer reasonable policies or procedures, including but not limited to drug testing, designed to ensure that an individual described in paragraph (b) (1) or (2) of this section is no longer engaging in the illegal use of drugs. (See § 1630.16(c) Drug testing).

(d) Disability does not include:

(1) Transvestism, transsexualism, pedophilia, exhibitionism, voyeurism, gender identity disorders not resulting from physical impairments, or other sexual behavior disorders;

(2) Compulsive gambling, kleptomania, or pyromania; or

(3) Psychoactive substance use disorders resulting from current illegal use of drugs.

(e) Homosexuality and bisexuality are not impairments and so are not disabilities as defined in this part.

§ 1630.4 Discrimination prohibited.

It is unlawful for a covered entity to discriminate on the basis of disability against a qualified individual with a disability in regard to:

(a) Recruitment, advertising, and job application procedures;

(b) Hiring, upgrading, promotion, award of tenure, demotion, transfer, layoff, termination, right of return from layoff, and rehiring;

(c) Rates of pay or any other form of compensation and changes in compensation;

(d) Job assignments, job classifications, organizational structures, position descriptions, lines of progression, and seniority lists;

(e) Leaves of absence, sick leave, or any other leave;

(f) Fringe benefits available by virtue of employment, whether or not administered by the covered entity;

(g) Selection and financial support for training, including: apprenticeships, professional meetings, conferences and other related activities, and selection for leaves of absence to pursue training;

(h) Activities sponsored by a covered entity including social and recreational programs; and

(i) Any other term, condition, or privilege of employment.

The term discrimination includes, but is not limited to, the acts described in §§ 1630.5 through 1630.13 of this part.

§ 1630.5 Limiting segregating, and classifying.

It is unlawful for a covered entity to limit, segregate, or classify a job applicant or employee in a way that adversely affects his or her employment opportunities or status on the basis of disability.

§ 1630.6 Contractual or other arrangements.

(a) In general. It is unlawful for a covered entity to participate in a contractual or other arrangement or relationship that has the effect of subjecting the covered entity's own qualified applicant or employee with a disability to the discrimination prohibited by this part.

(b) Contractual or other arrangement defined. The phrase contractual or other arrangement or relationship includes, but is not limited to, a relationship with an employment or referral agency; labor union, including collective bargaining agreements; an organization providing fringe benefits to an employee of the covered entity; or an organization providing training and apprenticeship programs.

(c) Application. This section applies to a covered entity, with respect to its own applicants or employees, whether the entity offered the contract or initiated the relationship, or whether the entity accepted the contract or acceded to the relationship. A covered entity is not liable for the actions of the other party or parties to the contract which only affect that other party's employees or applicants.

§ 1630.7 Standards, criteria, or methods of administration.

It is unlawful for a covered entity to use standards, criteria, or methods of administration, which are not job-related and consistent with business necessity, and:

(a) That have the effect of discriminating on the basis of disability; or

(b) That perpetuate the discrimination of others who are subject to common administrative control.

§ 1630.8 Relationship or association with an individual with a disability.

It is unlawful for a covered entity to exclude or deny equal jobs or benefits to, or otherwise discriminate against, a qualified individual because of the known disability of an individual with whom the qualified individual is known to have a family, business, social or other relationship or association.

§ 1630.9 Not making reasonable accommodation.

(a) It is unlawful for a covered entity not to make reasonable accommodation to the known physical or mental limitations of an otherwise qualified applicant or employee with a disability, unless such covered entity can demonstrate that the accommodation would impose an undue hardship on the operation of its business.

(b) It is unlawful for a covered entity to deny employment opportunities to an otherwise qualified job applicant or employee with a disability based on the need of such covered entity to make reasonable accommodation to such individual's physical or mental impairments.

(c) A covered entity shall not be excused from the requirements of this part because of any failure to receive technical assistance authorized by section 506 of the ADA, including any failure in the development or dissemination of any technical assistance manual authorized by that Act.

(d) A qualified individual with a disability is not required to accept an accommodation, aid, service, opportunity or benefit which such qualified individual chooses not to accept. However, if such individual rejects a reasonable accommodation, aid, service, opportunity or benefit that is necessary to enable the individual to perform the essential functions of the position held or desired, and cannot, as a result of that rejection, perform the essential functions of the position, the individual will not be considered a qualified individual with a disability.

§ 1630.10 Qualification standards, tests, and other selection criteria.

It is unlawful for a covered entity to use qualification standards, employment tests or other selection criteria that screen out or tend to screen out an individual with a disability or a class of individuals with disabilities, on the basis of disability, unless the standard, test or other selection criteria, as used by the covered entity, is shown to be job-related for the position in question and is consistent with business necessity.

§ 1630.11 Administration of tests.

It is unlawful for a covered entity to fail to select and administer tests concerning employment in the most effective manner to ensure that, when a test is administered to a job applicant or employee who has a disability that impairs sensory, manual or speaking skills, the test results accurately reflect the skills, aptitude, or whatever other factor of the applicant or employee that the test purports to measure, rather than reflecting the impaired sensory, manual, or speaking skills of such employee or applicant (except where such skills are the factors that the test purports to measure).

§ 1630.12 Retaliation and coercion.

(a) Retaliation. It is unlawful to discriminate against any individual because that individual has opposed any act or practice made unlawful by this part or because that individual made a charge, testified, assisted, or participated in any manner in an investigation, proceeding, or hearing to enforce any provision contained in this part.

(b) Coercion, interference or intimidation. It is unlawful to coerce, intimidate, threaten, harass or interfere with any individual in the exercise or enjoyment of, or because that individual aided or encouraged any other individual in the exercise of, any right granted or protected by this part.

§ 1630.13 Prohibited medical examinations and inquiries.

(a) Pre-employment examination or inquiry. Except as permitted by § 1630.14, it is unlawful for a covered entity to conduct a medical examination of an applicant or to make inquiries as to whether an applicant is an individual with a disability or as to the nature or severity of such disability.

(b) Examination or inquiry of employees. Except as permitted by § 1630.14, it is unlawful for a covered entity to require a medical examination of an employee or to make inquiries as to whether an employee is an individual with a disability or as to the nature or severity of such disability.

§ 1630.14 Medical examinations and inquiries specifically permitted.

(a) Acceptable pre-employment inquiry. A covered entity may make pre-employment inquiries into the ability of an applicant to perform job-related functions, and/or may ask an applicant to describe or to demonstrate how, with or without reasonable accommodation, the applicant will be able to perform job-related functions.

(b) Employment entrance examination. A covered entity may require a medical examination (and/or inquiry) after making an offer of employment to a job applicant and before the applicant begins his or her employment duties, and may condition an offer of employment on the results of such examination (and/or inquiry), if all entering employees in the same job category are subjected to such an examination (and/or inquiry) regardless of disability.

(1) Information obtained under paragraph (b) of this section regarding the medical condition or history of the applicant shall be collected and maintained on separate forms and in separate medical files and be treated as a confidential medical record, except that:

(i) Supervisors and managers may be informed regarding necessary restrictions on the work or duties of the employee and necessary accommodations;

(ii) First aid and safety personnel may be informed, when appropriate, if the disability might require emergency treatment; and

(iii) Government officials investigating compliance with this part shall be provided relevant information on request.

(2) The results of such examination shall not be used for any purpose inconsistent with this part.

(3) Medical examinations conducted in accordance with this section do not have to be job-related and consistent with business necessity. However, if certain criteria are used to screen out an employee or employees with disabilities as a result of such an examination or inquiry, the exclusionary criteria must be job-related and consistent with business necessity, and performance of the essential job functions cannot be accomplished with reasonable accommodation as required in this part. (See § 1630.15(b) Defenses to charges of discriminatory application of selection criteria.)

(c) Examination of employees. A covered entity may require a medical examination (and/or inquiry) of an employee that is job-related and consistent with business necessity. A covered entity may make inquiries into the ability of an employee to perform job-related functions.

(1) Information obtained under paragraph (c) of this section regarding the medical condition or history of any employee shall be collected and maintained on separate forms and in separate medical files and be treated as a confidential medical record, except that:

(i) Supervisors and managers may be informed regarding necessary restrictions on the work or duties of the employee and necessary accommodations;

(ii) First aid and safety personnel may be informed, when appropriate, if the disability might require emergency treatment; and

(iii) Government officials investigating compliance with this part shall be provided relevant information on request.

(2) Information obtained under paragraph (c) of this section regarding the medical condition or history of any employee shall not be used for any purpose inconsistent with this part.

(d) Other acceptable examinations and inquiries. A covered entity may conduct voluntary medical examinations and activities, including voluntary medical histories, which are part of an employee health program available to employees at the work site.

(1) Information obtained under paragraph (d) of this section regarding the medical condition or history of any employee shall be collected and maintained on separate forms and in separate medical files and be treated as a confidential medical record, except that:

(i) Supervisors and managers may be informed regarding necessary restrictions on the work or duties of the employee and necessary accommodations;

(ii) First aid and safety personnel may be informed, when appropriate, if the disability might require emergency treatment; and

(iii) Government officials investigating compliance with this part shall be provided relevant information on request.

(2) Information obtained under paragraph (d) of this section regarding the medical condition or history of any employee shall not be used for any purpose inconsistent with this part.

§ 1630.15 Defenses.

Defenses to an allegation of discrimination under this part may include, but are not limited to, the following:

(a) Disparate treatment charges. It may be a defense to a charge of disparate treatment brought under §§ 1630.4 through 1630.8 and 1630.11 through 1630.12 that the challenged action is justified by a legitimate, non-discriminatory reason.

(b) Charges of discriminatory application of selection criteria —

(1) In general. It may be a defense to a charge of discrimination, as described in § 1630.10, that an alleged application of qualification standards, tests, or selection criteria that screens out or tends to screen out or otherwise denies a job or benefit to an individual with a disability has been shown to be job-related and consistent with business necessity, and such performance cannot be accomplished with reasonable accommodation, as required in this part.

(2) Direct threat as a qualification standard. The term "qualification standard" may include a requirement that an individual shall not pose a direct threat to the health or safety of the individual or others in the workplace. (See § 1630.2(r) defining direct threat.)

(c) Other disparate impact charges. It may be a defense to a charge of discrimination brought under this part that a uniformly applied standard, criterion, or policy has a disparate impact on an individual with a disability or a class of individuals with disabilities that the challenged standard, criterion or policy has been shown to be job-related and consistent with business necessity, and such performance cannot be accomplished with reasonable accommodation, as required in this part.

(d) Charges of not making reasonable accommodation. It may be a defense to a charge of discrimination, as described in § 1630.9, that a requested or necessary accommodation would impose an undue hardship on the operation of the covered entity's business.

(e) Conflict with other federal laws. It may be a defense to a charge of discrimination under this part that a challenged action is required or necessitated by another Federal law or regulation, or that another Federal law or regulation prohibits an action (including the provision of a particular reasonable accommodation) that would otherwise be required by this part.

(f) Additional defenses. It may be a defense to a charge of discrimination under this part that the alleged discriminatory action is specifically permitted by §§ 1630.14 or 1630.16.

§ 1630.16 Specific activities permitted.

(a) Religious entities. A religious corporation, association, educational institution, or society is permitted to give preference in employment to individuals of a particular religion to perform work connected with the carrying on by that corporation, association, educational institution, or society of its activities. A religious entity may require that all applicants and employees conform to the religious tenets of such organization. However, a religious entity may not discriminate against a qualified individual, who satisfies the permitted religious criteria, because of his or her disability.

(b) Regulation of alcohol and drugs. A covered entity:

(1) May prohibit the illegal use of drugs and the use of alcohol at the workplace by all employees;

(2) May require that employees not be under the influence of alcohol or be engaging in the illegal use of drugs at the workplace;

(3) May require that all employees behave in conformance with the requirements established under the Drug-Free Workplace Act of 1988 (41 U.S.C. 701 *et seq.*);

(4) May hold an employee who engages in the illegal use of drugs or who is an alcoholic to the same qualification standards for employment or job performance and behavior to which the entity holds its other employees, even if any unsatisfactory performance or behavior is related to the employee's drug use or alcoholism;

(5) May require that its employees employed in an industry subject to such regulations comply with the standards established in the regulations (if any) of the Departments of Defense and Transportation, and of the Nuclear Regulatory Commission, regarding alcohol and the illegal use of drugs; and

(6) May require that employees employed in sensitive positions comply with the regulations (if any) of the Departments of Defense and Transportation and of the Nuclear Regulatory Commission that apply to employment in sensitive positions subject to such regulations.

(c) Drug testing —

(1) General policy. For purposes of this part, a test to determine the illegal use of drugs is not considered a medical examination. Thus, the

administration of such drug tests by a covered entity to its job applicants or employees is not a violation of § 1630.13 of this part. However, this part does not encourage, prohibit, or authorize a covered entity to conduct drug tests of job applicants or employees to determine the illegal use of drugs or to make employment decisions based on such test results.

(2) Transportation Employees. This part does not encourage, prohibit, or authorize the otherwise lawful exercise by entities subject to the jurisdiction of the Department of Transportation of authority to:

(i) Test employees of entities in, and applicants for, positions involving safety sensitive duties for the illegal use of drugs or for on-duty impairment by alcohol; and

(ii) Remove from safety-sensitive positions persons who test positive for illegal use of drugs or on-duty impairment by alcohol pursuant to paragraph (c)(2)(i) of this section.

(3) Confidentiality. Any information regarding the medical condition or history of any employee or applicant obtained from a test to determine the illegal use of drugs, except information regarding the illegal use of drugs, is subject to the requirements of §§ 1630.14(b) (2) and (3) of this part.

(d) Regulation of smoking. A covered entity may prohibit or impose restrictions on smoking in places of employment. Such restrictions do not violate any provision of this part.

(e) Infectious and communicable diseases; food handling jobs —

(1) In general. Under title I of the ADA, section 103(d)(1), the Secretary of Health and Human Services is to prepare a list, to be updated annually, of infectious and communicable diseases which are transmitted through the handling of food. (Copies may be obtained from Center for Infectious Diseases, Centers for Disease Control, 1600 Clifton Road, NE., Mailstop C09, Atlanta, GA 30333.) If an individual with a disability is disabled by one of the infectious or communicable diseases included on this list, and if the risk of transmitting the disease associated with the handling of food cannot be eliminated by reasonable accommodation, a covered entity may refuse to assign or continue to assign such individual to a job involving food handling. However, if the individual with a disability is a current employee, the employer must consider whether he or she can be accommodated by reassignment to a vacant position not involving food handling.

(2) Effect on state or other laws. This part does not preempt, modify, or amend any State, county, or local law, ordinance or regulation applicable to food handling which:

(i) Is in accordance with the list, referred to in paragraph (e)(1) of this section, of infectious or communicable diseases and the modes of transmissibility published by the Secretary of Health and Human Services; and

(ii) Is designed to protect the public health from individuals who pose a significant risk to the health or safety of others, where that risk cannot be eliminated by reasonable accommodation.

(f) Health insurance, life insurance, and other benefit plans —

(1) An insurer, hospital, or medical service company, health maintenance organization, or any agent or entity that administers benefit plans, or similar organizations may underwrite risks, classify risks, or administer such risks that are based on or not inconsistent with State law.

(2) A covered entity may establish, sponsor, observe or administer the terms of a bona fide benefit plan that are based on underwriting risks, classifying risks, or administering such risks that are based on or not inconsistent with State law.

(3) A covered entity may establish, sponsor, observe, or administer the terms of a bona fide benefit plan that is not subject to State laws that regulate insurance.

(4) The activities described in paragraphs (f) (1), (2), and (3) of this section are permitted unless these activities are being used as a subterfuge to evade the purposes of this part.

APPENDIX TO PART 1630 — INTERPRETIVE GUIDANCE ON TITLE I OF THE AMERICANS WITH DISABILITIES ACT

TITLE 29, Code of Federal Regulations
PART 1630 — REGULATIONS TO IMPLEMENT THE
EQUAL EMPLOYMENT PROVISIONS OF THE AMERICANS
WITH DISABILITIES ACT

Appendix to Part 1630 — Interpretive Guidance on Title I of the
Americans with Disabilities Act [as amended through 17 June 2002]

Background

The ADA is a Federal antidiscrimination statute designed to remove barriers which prevent qualified individuals with disabilities from enjoying the same employment opportunities that are available to persons without disabilities.

Like the Civil Rights Act of 1964 that prohibits discrimination on the bases of race, color, religion, national origin, and sex, the ADA seeks to ensure access to equal employment opportunities based on merit. It does not guarantee equal results, establish quotas, or require preferences favoring individuals with disabilities over those without disabilities.

However, while the Civil Rights Act of 1964 prohibits any consideration of personal characteristics such as race or national origin, the ADA necessarily takes a different approach. When an individual's disability creates a barrier to employment opportunities, the ADA requires employers to consider whether reasonable accommodation could remove the barrier.

The ADA thus establishes a process in which the employer must assess a disabled individual's ability to perform the essential functions of the specific job held or desired. While the ADA focuses on eradicating barriers, the ADA does not relieve a disabled employee or applicant from the obligation to perform the essential functions of the job. To the contrary, the ADA is intended to enable disabled persons to compete in the workplace based on the same performance standards and requirements that employers expect of persons who are not disabled.

However, where that individual's functional limitation impedes such job performance, an employer must take steps to reasonably accommodate, and thus help overcome the particular impediment, unless to do so would impose an undue hardship. Such accommodations usually take the form of adjustments to the way a job customarily is performed, or to the work environment itself.

This process of identifying whether, and to what extent, a reasonable accommodation is required should be flexible and involve both the employer and the individual with a disability. Of course, the determination of whether an individual is qualified for a particular position must necessarily be made on a case-by-case basis. No specific form of accommodation is guaranteed for all individuals with a particular disability. Rather, an accommodation must be tailored to match the needs of the disabled individual with the needs of the job's essential functions.

This case-by-case approach is essential if qualified individuals of varying abilities are to receive equal opportunities to compete for an infinitely diverse range of jobs. For this reason, neither the ADA nor this part can supply the "correct" answer in advance for each employment decision concerning an individual with a disability. Instead, the ADA simply establishes parameters to guide employers in how to consider, and take into account, the disabling condition involved.

Introduction

The Equal Employment Opportunity Commission (the Commission or EEOC) is responsible for enforcement of title I of the Americans with Disabilities Act (ADA), 42 U.S.C. 12101 et seq. (1990), which prohibits employment discrimination on the basis of disability. The Commission believes that it is essential to issue interpretive guidance concurrently with the issuance of this part in order to ensure that qualified individuals with disabilities understand their rights under this part and to facilitate and encourage compliance by covered entities. This appendix represents the Commission's interpretation of the issues discussed, and the Commission will be guided by it when resolving charges of employment discrimination. The appendix addresses the major provisions of this part and explains the major concepts of disability rights.

The terms "employer" or "employer or other covered entity" are used interchangeably throughout the appendix to refer to all covered entities subject to the employment provisions of the ADA.

Section 1630.1 Purpose, Applicability and Construction

Section 1630.1(a) Purpose

The Americans with Disabilities Act was signed into law on July 26, 1990. It is an antidiscrimination statute that requires that individuals with disabilities be given the same consideration for employment that individuals without disabilities are given. An individual who is qualified for an employment opportunity cannot be denied that opportunity because of the fact that the individual is disabled. The purpose of title I and this part is to ensure that qualified individuals with disabilities are protected from discrimination on the basis of disability.

The ADA uses the term "disabilities" rather than the term "handicaps" used in the Rehabilitation Act of 1973, 29 U.S.C. 701-796. Substantively, these terms are equivalent. As noted by the House Committee on the Judiciary, "[t]he use of the term 'disabilities' instead of the term 'handicaps' reflects the desire of the Committee to use the most current terminology. It reflects the preference of persons with disabilities to use that term rather than 'handicapped' as used in previous laws, such as the Rehabilitation Act of 1973 * * *." H.R. Rep. No. 485 part 3, 101st Cong., 2d Sess. 26-27 (1990) (hereinafter House Judiciary Report); see also S. Rep. No. 116, 101st Cong., 1st Sess. 21 (1989) (hereinafter Senate Report); H.R. Rep. No. 485 part 2, 101st Cong., 2d Sess. 50-51 (1990) [hereinafter House Labor Report].

The use of the term "Americans" in the title of the ADA is not intended to imply that the Act only applies to United States citizens. Rather, the ADA protects all qualified individuals with disabilities, regardless of their citizenship status or nationality.

Section 1630.1(b) and (c) Applicability and Construction

Unless expressly stated otherwise, the standards applied in the ADA are not intended to be lesser than the standards applied under the Rehabilitation Act of 1973.

The ADA does not preempt any Federal law, or any State or local law, that grants to individuals with disabilities protection greater than or equivalent to that provided by the ADA. This means that the existence of a lesser standard of protection to individuals with disabilities under the ADA will not provide a defense to failing to meet a higher standard under another law. Thus, for example, title I of the ADA would not be a defense to failing to collect information required to satisfy the affirmative action requirements of section 503 of the Rehabilitation Act. On the other hand, the existence of a lesser standard under another law will not provide a defense to failing to meet a higher standard under the ADA. See House Labor Report at 135; House Judiciary Report at 69-70.

This also means that an individual with a disability could choose to pursue claims under a State discrimination or tort law that does not confer greater substantive rights, or even confers fewer substantive rights, if the potential available remedies would be greater than those available under the ADA and this part. The ADA does not restrict an individual with a disability from pursuing such claims in addition to charges brought under this part. House Judiciary at 69-70.

The ADA does not automatically preempt medical standards or safety requirements established by Federal law or regulations. It does not preempt State, county, or local laws, ordinances or regulations that are consistent with this part, and are designed to protect the public health from individuals who pose a direct threat, that cannot be eliminated or reduced by reasonable accommodation, to the health or safety of others. However, the ADA does preempt inconsistent requirements established by State or local law for safety or security sensitive positions. See Senate Report at 27; House Labor Report at 57.

An employer allegedly in violation of this part cannot successfully defend its actions by relying on the obligation to comply with the require-ments of any State or local law that imposes prohibitions or limitations on the eligibility of qualified individuals with disabilities to practice any oc-cupation or profession. For example, suppose a municipality has an ordi-nance that prohibits individuals with tuberculosis from teaching school chil-dren. If an individual with dormant tuberculosis challenges a private school's refusal to hire him or her because of the tuberculosis, the private school would not be able to rely on the city ordinance as a defense under the ADA.

Sections 1630.2(a)-(f) Commission, Covered Entity, etc.

The definitions section of part 1630 includes several terms that are identical, or almost identical, to the terms found in title VII of the Civil Rights Act of 1964. Among these terms are 'Commission," "Person," "State," and "Employer." These terms are to be given the same meaning under the ADA that they are given under title VII.

In general, the term "employee" has the same meaning that it is given under title VII. However, the ADA's definition of "employee" does not contain an exception, as does title VII, for elected officials and their personal staffs. It should be further noted that all State and local governments are covered by title II of the ADA whether or not they are also covered by this part. Title II, which is enforced by the Department of Justice, becomes effective on January 26, 1992. See 28 CFR part 35.

The term "covered entity" is not found in title VII. However, the title VII definitions of the entities included in the term "covered entity" (e.g., employer, employment agency, etc.) are applicable to the ADA.

Section 1630.2(g) Disability

In addition to the term "covered entity," there are several other terms that are unique to the ADA. The first of these is the term "disability." Congress adopted the definition of this term from the Rehabilitation Act definition of the term "individual with handicaps." By so doing, Congress intended that the relevant caselaw developed under the Rehabilitation Act be generally applicable to the term "disability" as used in the ADA. Senate Report at 21; House Labor Report at 50; House Judiciary Report at 27.

The definition of the term "disability" is divided into three parts. An individual must satisfy at least one of these parts in order to be considered an individual with a disability for purposes of this part. An individual is considered to have a "disability" if that individual either (1) has a physical or mental impairment which substantially limits one or more of that person's major life activities, (2) has a record of such an impairment, or, (3) is regarded by the covered entity as having such an impairment. To understand the meaning of the term "disability," it is necessary to understand, as a preliminary matter, what is meant by the terms "physical or mental impairment," "major life activity," and "substantially limits." Each of these terms is discussed below.

Section 1630.2(h) Physical or Mental Impairment

This term adopts the definition of the term "physical or mental impairment" found in the regulations implementing section 504 of the Rehabilitation Act at 34 CFR part 104. It defines physical or mental impairment as any physiological disorder or condition, cosmetic disfigurement, or anatomical loss affecting one or more of several body systems, or any mental or psychological disorder.

It is important to distinguish between conditions that are impairments and physical, psychological, environmental, cultural and economic characteristics that are not impairments. The definition of the term "impairment" does not include physical characteristics such as eye color, hair color, left-handedness, or height, weight or muscle tone that are within "normal" range and are not the result of a physiological disorder. The definition, likewise, does not include characteristic predisposition to illness or disease. Other conditions, such as pregnancy, that are not the result of a physiological disorder are also not impairments. Similarly, the definition does not include common personality traits such as poor judgment or a quick temper where these are not symptoms of a mental or psychological disorder. Environmental, cultural, or economic disadvantages such as poverty, lack of education or a prison record are not impairments. Advanced age, in and of itself, is also not an impairment. However, various medical conditions commonly associated with age, such as hearing loss, osteoporosis, or arthritis would constitute impairments within the meaning of this part. See Senate Report at 22-23; House Labor Report at 51-52; House Judiciary Report at 28-29.

Section 1630.2(i) Major Life Activities

This term adopts the definition of the term "major life activities" found in the regulations implementing section 504 of the Rehabilitation Act at 34 CFR part 104. "Major life activities" are those basic activities that the average person in the general population can perform with little or no difficulty. Major life activities include caring for oneself, performing manual tasks, walking, seeing, hearing, speaking, breathing, learning, and working. This list is not exhaustive. For example, other major life activities include, but are not limited to, sitting, standing, lifting, reaching. See Senate Report at 22; House Labor Report at 52; House Judiciary Report at 28.

Section 1630.2(j) Substantially Limits

Determining whether a physical or mental impairment exists is only the first step in determining whether or not an individual is disabled. Many impairments do not impact an individual's life to the degree that they constitute disabling impairments. An impairment rises to the level of disability if the impairment substantially limits one or more of the individual's major life activities. Multiple impairments that combine to substantially limit one or more of an individual's major life activities also constitute a disability.

The ADA and this part, like the Rehabilitation Act of 1973, do not attempt a "laundry list" of impairments that are "disabilities." The determination of whether an individual has a disability is not necessarily based on the name or diagnosis of the impairment the person has, but rather on the effect of that impairment on the life of the individual. Some impairments may be disabling for particular individuals but not for others, depending on the stage of the disease or disorder, the presence of other impairments that combine to make the impairment disabling or any number of other factors.

Other impairments, however, such as HIV infection, are inherently substantially limiting.

On the other hand, temporary, non-chronic impairments of short duration, with little or no long term or permanent impact, are usually not disabilities. Such impairments may include, but are not limited to, broken limbs, sprained joints, concussions, appendicitis, and influenza. Similarly, except in rare circumstances, obesity is not considered a disabling impairment.

An impairment that prevents an individual from performing a major life activity substantially limits that major life activity. For example, an individual whose legs are paralyzed is substantially limited in the major life activity of walking because he or she is unable, due to the impairment, to perform that major life activity.

Alternatively, an impairment is substantially limiting if it significantly restricts the duration, manner or condition under which an individual can perform a particular major life activity as compared to the average person in the general population's ability to perform that same major life activity. Thus, for example, an individual who, because of an impairment, can only walk for very brief periods of time would be substantially limited in the major life activity of walking.

Part 1630 notes several factors that should be considered in making the determination of whether an impairment is substantially limiting. These factors are (1) the nature and severity of the impairment, (2) the duration or expected duration of the impairment, and (3) the permanent or long term impact, or the expected permanent or long term impact of, or resulting from, the impairment. The term "duration," as used in this context, refers to the length of time an impairment persists, while the term "impact" refers to the residual effects of an impairment. Thus, for example, a broken leg that takes eight weeks to heal is an impairment of fairly brief duration. However, if the broken leg heals improperly, the "impact" of the impairment would be the resulting permanent limp. Likewise, the effect on cognitive functions resulting from traumatic head injury would be the "impact" of that impairment.

The determination of whether an individual is substantially limited in a major life activity must be made on a case by case basis. An individual is not substantially limited in a major life activity if the limitation, when viewed in light of the factors noted above, does not amount to a significant restriction when compared with the abilities of the average person. For example, an individual who had once been able to walk at an extraordinary speed would not be substantially limited in the major life activity of walking if, as a result of a physical impairment, he or she were only able to walk at an average speed, or even at moderately below average speed.

It is important to remember that the restriction on the performance of the major life activity must be the result of a condition that is an impairment. As noted earlier, advanced age, physical or personality characteristics, and environmental, cultural, and economic disadvantages are not impairments. Consequently, even if such factors substantially limit an individual's ability to perform a major life activity, this limitation will not constitute a disability. For example, an individual who is unable to read because he or she was never taught to read would not be an individual with a disability because lack of education is not an impairment. However, an individual who is unable to read because of dyslexia would be an individual with a disability because dyslexia, a learning disability, is an impairment.

If an individual is not substantially limited with respect to any other major life activity, the individual's ability to perform the major life activity of working should be considered. If an individual is substantially limited in any other major life activity, no determination should be made as to whether the individual is substantially limited in working. For example, if an individual is blind, i.e., substantially limited in the major life activity of seeing, there is no need to determine whether the individual is also substantially limited in the major life activity of working. The determination of whether an individual is substantially limited in working must also be made on a case by case basis.

This part lists specific factors that may be used in making the determination of whether the limitation in working is "substantial." These factors are:

(1) The geographical area to which the individual has reasonable access;

(2) The job from which the individual has been disqualified because of an impairment, and the number and types of jobs utilizing similar training, knowledge, skills or abilities, within that geographical area, from which the individual is also disqualified because of the impairment (class of jobs); and/or

(3) The job from which the individual has been disqualified because of an impairment, and the number and types of other jobs not utilizing similar training, knowledge, skills or abilities, within that geographical area, from which the individual is also disqualified because of the impairment (broad range of jobs in various classes).

Thus, an individual is not substantially limited in working just because he or she is unable to perform a particular job for one employer, or because he or she is unable to perform a specialized job or profession requiring extraordinary skill, prowess or talent. For example, an individual who cannot be a commercial airline pilot because of a minor vision impairment, but who can be a commercial airline co-pilot or a pilot for a courier service, would not be substantially limited in the major life activity of working. Nor would a professional baseball pitcher who develops a bad elbow and can no longer throw a baseball be considered substantially limited in the major life activity of working. In both of these examples, the individuals are not substantially limited in the ability to perform any other major life activity and, with regard to the major life activity of working, are only unable to perform either a particular specialized job or a narrow range of jobs. See Forrisi v. Bowen, 794 F.2d 931 (4th Cir. 1986); Jasany v. U.S. Postal Service, 755 F.2d 1244 (6th Cir. 1985); E.E Black, Ltd. v. Marshall, 497 F. Supp. 1088 (D. Hawaii 1980).

On the other hand, an individual does not have to be totally unable to work in order to be considered substantially limited in the major life activity of working. An individual is substantially limited in working if the individual is significantly restricted in the ability to perform a class of jobs or a broad range of jobs in various classes, when compared with the ability of the average person with comparable qualifications to perform those same jobs. For example, an individual who has a back condition that prevents the individual from performing any heavy labor job would be substantially limited in the major life activity of working because the individual's impairment eliminates his or her ability to perform a class of jobs. This would be so even if the individual were able to perform jobs in another class, e.g., the class of semi-skilled jobs. Similarly, suppose an individual has an allergy to a substance found in most high rise office buildings, but seldom found elsewhere, that makes breathing extremely difficult. Since this individual would be substantially limited in the ability to perform the broad range of jobs in various classes that are conducted in high rise office buildings within the geographical area to which he or she has reasonable access, he or she would be substantially limited in working.

The terms "number and types of jobs" and "number and types of other jobs," as used in the factors discussed above, are not intended to require an onerous evidentiary showing. Rather, the terms only require the presentation of evidence of general employment demographics and/or of recognized occupational classifications that indicate the approximate number of jobs (e.g., "few," "many," "most") from which an individual would be excluded because of an impairment.

If an individual has a "mental or physical impairment" that "substantially limits" his or her ability to perform one or more "major life activities," that individual will satisfy the first part of the regulatory definition of "disability" and will be considered an individual with a disability. An individual who satisfies this first part of the definition of the term "disability" is not required to demonstrate that he or she satisfies either of the other parts of the definition. However, if an individual is unable to satisfy this part of the definition, he or she may be able to satisfy one of the other parts of the definition.

Section 1630.2(k) Record of a Substantially Limiting Condition

The second part of the definition provides that an individual with a record of an impairment that substantially limits a major life activity is an individual with a disability. The intent of this provision, in part, is to ensure that people are not discriminated against because of a history of disability. For example, this provision protects former cancer patients from discrimination based on their prior medical history. This provision also ensures that individuals are not discriminated against because they have been misclassified as disabled. For example, individuals misclassified as learning disabled are protected from discrimination on the basis of that erroneous classification. Senate Report at 23; House Labor Report at 52-53; House Judiciary Report at 29.

This part of the definition is satisfied if a record relied on by an employer indicates that the individual has or has had a substantially limiting impairment. The impairment indicated in the record must be an impairment that would substantially limit one or more of the individual's major life activities. There are many types of records that could potentially contain this information, including but not limited to, education, medical, or employment records.

The fact that an individual has a record of being a disabled veteran, or of disability retirement, or is classified as disabled for other purposes does not guarantee that the individual will satisfy the definition of "disability" under part 1630. Other statutes, regulations and programs may have a definition of "disability" that is not the same as the definition set forth in the ADA and contained in part 1630. Accordingly, in order for an individual who has been classified in a record as "disabled" for some other purpose to be considered disabled for purposes of part 1630, the impairment indicated in the record must be a physical or mental impairment that substantially limits one or more of the individual's major life activities.

Section 1630.2(l) Regarded as Substantially Limited in a Major Life Activity

If an individual cannot satisfy either the first part of the definition of "disability" or the second "record of" part of the definition, he or she may be able to satisfy the third part of the definition. The third part of the definition provides that an individual who is regarded by an employer or other covered entity as having an impairment that substantially limits a major life activity is an individual with a disability.

There are three different ways in which an individual may satisfy the definition of "being regarded as having a disability":

(1) The individual may have an impairment which is not substantially limiting but is perceived by the employer or other covered entity as constituting a substantially limiting impairment;

(2) The individual may have an impairment which is only substantially limiting because of the attitudes of others toward the impairment; or

(3) The individual may have no impairment at all but is regarded by the employer or other covered entity as having a substantially limiting impairment.

Senate Report at 23; House Labor Report at 53; House Judiciary Report at 29.

An individual satisfies the first part of this definition if the individual has an impairment that is not substantially limiting, but the covered entity perceives the impairment as being substantially limiting. For example, suppose an employee has controlled high blood pressure that is not substantially limiting. If an employer reassigns the individual to less strenuous work because of unsubstantiated fears that the individual will suffer a heart attack if he or she continues to perform strenuous work, the employer would be regarding the individual as disabled.

An individual satisfies the second part of the "regarded as" definition if the individual has an impairment that is only substantially limiting because of the attitudes of others toward the condition. For example, an individual may have a prominent facial scar or disfigurement, or may have a condition that periodically causes an involuntary jerk of the head but does not limit the individual's major life activities. If an employer discriminates against such an individual because of the negative reactions of customers, the employer would be regarding the individual as disabled and acting on the basis of that perceived disability. See Senate Report at 24; House Labor Report at 53; House Judiciary Report at 30-31.

An individual satisfies the third part of the "regarded as" definition of "disability" if the employer or other covered entity erroneously believes the individual has a substantially limiting impairment that the individual actually does not have. This situation could occur, for example, if an employer discharged an employee in response to a rumor that the employee is infected with Human Immunodeficiency Virus (HIV). Even though the rumor is totally unfounded and the individual has no impairment at all, the individual is considered an individual with a disability because the employer perceived of this individual as being disabled. Thus, in this example, the employer, by discharging this employee, is discriminating on the basis of disability.

The rationale for the "regarded as" part of the definition of disability was articulated by the Supreme Court in the context of the Rehabilitation Act of 1973 in School Board of Nassau County v. Arline, 480 U.S. 273 (1987). The Court noted that, although an individual may have an impairment that does not in fact substantially limit a major life activity, the reaction of others may prove just as disabling. "Such an impairment might not diminish a person's physical or mental capabilities, but could nevertheless substantially limit that person's ability to work as a result of the negative reactions of others to the impairment." 480 U.S. at 283. The Court concluded that by including "regarded as" in the Rehabilitation Act's definition, "Congress acknowledged that society's accumulated myths and fears about disability and diseases are as handicapping as are the physical limitations that flow from actual impairment." 480 U.S. at 284.

An individual rejected from a job because of the "myths, fears and stereotypes" associated with disabilities would be covered under this part of the definition of disability, whether or not the employer's or other covered entity's perception were shared by others in the field and whether or not the individual's actual physical or mental condition would be considered a disability under the first or second part of this definition. As the legislative history notes, sociologists have identified common attitudinal barriers that frequently result in employers excluding individuals with disabilities. These include concerns regarding productivity, safety, insurance, liability, attendance, cost of accommodation and accessibility, workers' compensation costs, and acceptance by coworkers and customers.

Therefore, if an individual can show that an employer or other covered entity made an employment decision because of a perception of disability based on "myth, fear or stereotype," the individual will satisfy the "regarded as" part of the definition of disability. If the employer cannot articulate a non-discriminatory reason for the employment action, an inference that the employer is acting on the basis of "myth, fear or stereotype" can be drawn.

Section 1630.2(m) Qualified Individual with a Disability

The ADA prohibits discrimination on the basis of disability against qualified individuals with disabilities. The determination of whether an individual with a disability is "qualified" should be made in two steps. The first step is to determine if the individual satisfies the prerequisites for the position, such as possessing the appropriate educational background, employment experience, skills, licenses, etc. For example, the first step in determining whether an accountant who is paraplegic is qualified for a certified public accountant (CPA) position is to examine the individual's credentials to determine whether the individual is a licensed CPA. This is sometimes referred to in the Rehabilitation Act caselaw as determining whether the individual is "otherwise qualified" for the position. See Senate Report at 33; House Labor Report at 64-65. (See Sec. 1630.9 Not Making Reasonable Accommodation).

The second step is to determine whether or not the individual can perform the essential functions of the position held or desired, with or without reasonable accommodation. The purpose of this second step is to ensure that individuals with disabilities who can perform the essential functions of the position held or desired are not denied employment opportunities because they are not able to perform marginal functions of the position. House Labor Report at 55.

The determination of whether an individual with a disability is qualified is to be made at the time of the employment decision. This determination should be based on the capabilities of the individual with a disability at the time of the employment decision, and should not be based on speculation that the employee may become unable in the future or may cause increased health insurance premiums or workers' compensation costs.

Section 1630.2(n) Essential Functions

The determination of which functions are essential may be critical to the determination of whether or not the individual with a disability is qualified. The essential functions are those functions that the individual who holds the position must be able to perform unaided or with the assistance of a reasonable accommodation.

The inquiry into whether a particular function is essential initially focuses on whether the employer actually requires employees in the position to perform the functions that the employer asserts are essential. For example, an employer may state that typing is an essential function of a position. If, in fact, the employer has never required any employee in that particular position to type, this will be evidence that typing is not actually an essential function of the position.

If the individual who holds the position is actually required to perform the function the employer asserts is an essential function, the inquiry will then center around whether removing the function would fundamentally alter that position. This determination of whether or not a particular function is essential will generally include one or more of the following factors listed in part 1630.

The first factor is whether the position exists to perform a particular function. For example, an individual may be hired to proofread documents. The ability to proofread the documents would then be an essential function, since this is the only reason the position exists.

The second factor in determining whether a function is essential is the number of other employees available to perform that job function or among whom the performance of that job function can be distributed. This may be a factor either because the total number of available employees is low, or because of the fluctuating demands of the business operation. For example, if an employer has a relatively small number of available employees for the volume of work to be performed, it may be necessary that each employee perform a multitude of different functions. Therefore, the performance of those functions by each employee becomes more critical and the options for reorganizing the work become more limited. In such a situation, functions that might not be essential if there were a larger staff may become essential because the staff size is small compared to the volume of work that has to be done. See Treadwell v. Alexander, 707 F.2d 473 (11th Cir. 1983).

A similar situation might occur in a larger work force if the workflow follows a cycle of heavy demand for labor intensive work followed by low demand periods. This type of workflow might also make the performance of each function during the peak periods more critical and might limit the employer's flexibility in reorganizing operating procedures. See Dexler v. Tisch, 660 F. Supp. 1418 (D. Conn. 1987).

The third factor is the degree of expertise or skill required to perform the function. In certain professions and highly skilled positions the employee is hired for his or her expertise or ability to perform the particular function. In such a situation, the performance of that specialized task would be an essential function.

Whether a particular function is essential is a factual determination that must be made on a case by case basis. In determining whether or not a particular function is essential, all relevant evidence should be considered. Part 1630 lists various types of evidence, such as an established job description, that should be considered in determining whether a particular function is essential. Since the list is not exhaustive, other relevant evidence may also be presented. Greater weight will not be granted to the types of evidence included on the list than to the types of evidence not listed.

Although part 1630 does not require employers to develop or maintain job descriptions, written job descriptions prepared before advertising or interviewing applicants for the job, as well as the employer's judgment as to what functions are essential are among the relevant evidence to be considered in determining whether a particular function is essential. The terms of a collective bargaining agreement are also relevant to the determination of whether a particular function is essential. The work experience of past employees in the job or of current employees in similar jobs is likewise relevant to the determination of whether a particular function is essential. See H.R. Conf. Rep. No. 101-596, 101st Cong., 2d Sess. 58 (1990) [hereinafter Conference Report]; House Judiciary Report at 33-34. See also Hall v. U.S. Postal Service, 857 F.2d 1073 (6th Cir. 1988).

The time spent performing the particular function may also be an indicator of whether that function is essential. For example, if an employee spends the vast majority of his or her time working at a cash register, this would be evidence that operating the cash register is an essential function. The consequences of failing to require the employee to perform the function may be another indicator of whether a particular function is essential. For example, although a firefighter may not regularly have to carry an unconscious adult out of a burning building, the consequence of failing to require the firefighter to be able to perform this function would be serious.

It is important to note that the inquiry into essential functions is not intended to second guess an employer's business judgment with regard to production standards, whether qualitative or quantitative, nor to require employers to lower such standards. (See Sec. 1630.10 Qualification Standards, Tests and Other Selection Criteria). If an employer requires its typists to be able to accurately type 75 words per minute, it will not be called upon to explain why an inaccurate work product, or a typing speed of 65 words per minute, would not be adequate. Similarly, if a hotel requires its service workers to thoroughly clean 16 rooms per day, it will not have to explain why it requires thorough cleaning, or why it chose a 16 room rather than a 10 room requirement. However, if an employer does require accurate 75 word per minute typing or the thorough cleaning of 16 rooms, it will have to show that it actually imposes such requirements on its employees in fact, and not simply on paper. It should also be noted that, if it is alleged that the employer intentionally selected the particular level of production to exclude individuals with disabilities, the employer may have to offer a legitimate, nondiscriminatory reason for its selection.

Section 1630.2(o) Reasonable Accommodation

An individual is considered a "qualified individual with a disability" if the individual can perform the essential functions of the position held or desired with or without reasonable accommodation. In general, an accommodation is any change in the work environment or in the way things are customarily done that enables an individual with a disability to enjoy equal employment opportunities. There are three categories of reasonable accommodation. These are (1) accommodations that are required to ensure equal opportunity in the application process; (2) accommodations that enable the employer's employees with disabilities to perform the essential functions of the position held or desired; and (3) accommodations that enable the employer's employees with disabilities to enjoy equal benefits and privileges of employment as are enjoyed by employees without disabilities. It should be noted that nothing in this part prohibits employers or other covered entities from providing accommodations beyond those required by this part.

Part 1630 lists the examples, specified in title I of the ADA, of the most common types of accommodation that an employer or other covered entity may be required to provide. There are any number of other specific accommodations that may be appropriate for particular situations but are not specifically mentioned in this listing. This listing is not intended to be exhaustive of accommodation possibilities. For example, other accommodations could include permitting the use of accrued paid leave or providing additional unpaid leave for necessary treatment, making employer provided transportation accessible, and providing reserved parking spaces. Providing personal assistants, such as a page turner for an employee with no hands or a travel attendant to act as a sighted guide to assist a blind employee on occasional business trips, may also be a reasonable accommodation. Senate Report at 31; House Labor Report at 62; House Judiciary Report at 39.

It may also be a reasonable accommodation to permit an individual with a disability the opportunity to provide and utilize equipment, aids or services that an employer is not required to provide as a reasonable accommodation. For example, it would be a reasonable accommodation for an employer to permit an individual who is blind to use a guide dog at work, even though the employer would not be required to provide a guide dog for the employee.

The accommodations included on the list of reasonable accommodations are generally self explanatory. However, there are a few that require further explanation. One of these is the accommodation of making existing facilities used by employees readily accessible to, and usable by, individuals with disabilities. This accommodation includes both those areas that must be accessible for the employee to perform essential job functions, as well as non-work areas used by the employer's employees for other purposes. For example, accessible break rooms, lunch rooms, training rooms, rest-rooms, etc., may be required as reasonable accommodations.

Another of the potential accommodations listed is "job restructuring." An employer or other covered entity may restructure a job by reallocating or redistributing nonessential, marginal job functions. For example, an employer may have two jobs, each of which entails the performance of a number of marginal functions. The employer hires a qualified individual with a disability who is able to perform some of the marginal functions of each job but not all of the marginal functions of either job. As an accommodation, the employer may redistribute the marginal functions so that all of the marginal functions that the qualified individual with a disability can perform are made a part of the position to be filled by the qualified individual with a disability. The remaining marginal functions that the individual with a disability cannot perform would then be transferred to the other position. See Senate Report at 31; House Labor Report at 62.

An employer or other covered entity is not required to reallocate essential functions. The essential functions are by definition those that the individual who holds the jobwould have to perform, with or without reasonable accommodation, in order to be considered qualified for the position. For example, suppose a security guard position requires the individual who holds the job to inspect identification cards. An employer would not have to provide an individual who is legally blind with an assistant to look at the identification cards for the legally blind employee. In this situation the assistant would be performing the job for the individual with a disability rather than assisting the individual to perform the job. See Coleman v. Darden, 595 F.2d 533 (10th Cir. 1979).

An employer or other covered entity may also restructure a job by altering when and/or how an essential function is performed. For example, an essential function customarily performed in the early morning hours may be rescheduled until later in the day as a reasonable accommodation to a disability that precludes performance of the function at the customary hour. Likewise, as a reasonable accommodation, an employee with a disability that inhibits the ability to write, may be permitted to computerize records that were customarily maintained manually.

Reassignment to a vacant position is also listed as a potential reasonable accommodation. In general, reassignment should be considered only when accommodation within the individual's current position would pose an undue hardship. Reassignment is not available to applicants. An applicant for a position must be qualified for, and be able to perform the essential functions of, the position sought with or without reasonable accommodation.

Reassignment may not be used to limit, segregate, or otherwise discriminate against employees with disabilities by forcing reassignments to undesirable positions or to designated offices or facilities. Employers should reassign the individual to an equivalent position, in terms of pay, status, etc., if the individual is qualified, and if the position is vacant within a reasonable amount of time. A "reasonable amount of time" should be determined in light of the totality of the circumstances. As an example, suppose there is no vacant position available at the time that an individual with a disability requests reassignment as a reasonable accommodation. The employer, however, knows that an equivalent position for which the individual is qualified, will become vacant next week. Under these circumstances, the employer should reassign the individual to the position when it becomes available.

An employer may reassign an individual to a lower graded position if there are no accommodations that would enable the employee to remain in the current position and there are no vacant equivalent positions for which the individual is qualified with or without reasonable accommodation. An employer, however, is not required to maintain the reassigned individual with a disability at the salary of the higher graded position if it does not so maintain reassigned employees who are not disabled. It should also be noted that an employer is not required to promote an individual with a disability as an accommodation. See Senate Report at 31-32; House Labor Report at 63.

The determination of which accommodation is appropriate in a particular situation involves a process in which the employer and employee identify the precise limitations imposed by the disability and explore potential accommodations that would overcome those limitations. This process is discussed more fully in Sec. 1630.9 Not Making Reasonable Accommodation.

Section 1630.2(p) Undue Hardship

An employer or other covered entity is not required to provide an accommodation that will impose an undue hardship on the operation of the employer's or other covered entity's business. The term "undue hardship" means significant difficulty or expense in, or resulting from, the provision of the accommodation. The "undue hardship" provision takes into account the financial realities of the particular employer or other covered entity. However, the concept of undue hardship is not limited to financial difficulty. "Undue hardship" refers to any accommodation that would be unduly costly, extensive, substantial, or disruptive, or that would fundamentally alter the nature or operation of the business. See Senate Report at 35; House Labor Report at 67.

For example, suppose an individual with a disabling visual impairment that makes it extremely difficult to see in dim lighting applies for a position as a waiter in a nightclub and requests that the club be brightly lit as a reasonable accommodation. Although the individual may be able to perform the job in bright lighting, the nightclub will probably be able to demonstrate that that particular accommodation, though inexpensive, would impose an undue hardship if the bright lighting would destroy the ambience of the nightclub and/or make it difficult for the customers to see the stage show. The fact that that particular accommodation poses an undue hardship, however, only means that the employer is not required to provide that accommodation. If there is another accommodation that will not create an undue hardship, the employer would be required to provide the alternative accommodation.

An employer's claim that the cost of a particular accommodation will impose an undue hardship will be analyzed in light of the factors outlined in part 1630. In part, this analysis requires a determination of whose financial resources should be considered in deciding whether the accommodation is unduly costly. In some cases the financial resources of the employer or other covered entity in its entirety should be considered in determining whether the cost of an accommodation poses an undue hardship. In other cases, consideration of the financial resources of the employer or other covered entity as a whole may be inappropriate because it may not give an accurate picture of the financial resources available to the particular facility that will actually be required to provide the accommodation. See House Labor Report at 68-69; House Judiciary Report at 40-41; see also Conference Report at 56-57.

If the employer or other covered entity asserts that only the financial resources of the facility where the individual will be employed should be considered, part 1630 requires a factual determination of the relationship between the employer or other covered entity and the facility that will provide the accommodation. As an example, suppose that an independently owned fast food franchise that receives no money from the franchisor refuses to hire an individual with a hearing impairment because it asserts that it would be an undue hardship to provide an interpreter to enable the individual to participate in monthly staff meetings. Since the financial relationship between the franchisor and the franchise is limited to payment of an annual franchise fee, only the financial resources of the franchise would be considered in determining whether or not providing the accommodation would be an undue hardship. See House Labor Report at 68; House Judiciary Report at 40.

If the employer or other covered entity can show that the cost of the accommodation would impose an undue hardship, it would still be required to provide the accommodation if the funding is available from another source, e.g., a State vocational rehabilitation agency, or if Federal, State or local tax deductions or tax credits are available to offset the cost of the accommodation. If the employer or other covered entity receives, or is eligible to receive, monies from an external source that would pay the entire cost of the accommodation, it cannot claim cost as an undue hardship. In the absence of such funding, the individual with a disability requesting the accommodation should be given the option of providing the accommodation or of paying that portion of the cost which constitutes the undue hardship on the operation of the business. To the extent that such monies pay or would pay for only part of the cost of the accommodation, only that portion of the cost of the accommodation that could not be recovered — the final net cost to the entity — may be considered in determining undue hardship. (See Sec. 1630.9 Not Making Reasonable Accommodation). See Senate Report at 36; House Labor Report at 69.

Section 1630.2(r) Direct Threat

An employer may require, as a qualification standard, that an individual not pose a direct threat to the health or safety of himself/herself or others. Like any other qualification standard, such a standard must apply to all applicants or employees and not just to individuals with disabilities. If, however, an individual poses a direct threat as a result of a disability, the employer must determine whether a reasonable accommodation would either eliminate the risk or reduce it to an acceptable level. If no accommodation exists that would either eliminate or reduce the risk, the employer may refuse to hire an applicant or may discharge an employee who poses a direct threat.

An employer, however, is not permitted to deny an employment opportunity to an individual with a disability merely because of a slightly increased risk. The risk can only be considered when it poses a significant risk, i.e., high probability, of substantial harm; a speculative or remote risk is insufficient. See Senate Report at 27; House Report Labor Report at 56-57; House Judiciary Report at 45.

Determining whether an individual poses a significant risk of substantial harm to others must be made on a case by case basis. The employer should identify the specific risk posed by the individual. For individuals with mental or emotional disabilities, the employer must identify the specific behavior on the part of the individual that would pose the direct threat. For individuals with physical disabilities, the employer must identify the aspect of the disability that would pose the direct threat. The employer should then consider the four factors listed in part 1630:

(1) The duration of the risk;
(2) The nature and severity of the potential harm;
(3) The likelihood that the potential harm will occur; and
(4) The imminence of the potential harm.

Such consideration must rely on objective, factual evidence — not on subjective perceptions, irrational fears, patronizing attitudes, or stereotypes — about the nature or effect of a particular disability, or of disability generally. See Senate Report at 27; House Labor Report at 56-57; House Judiciary Report at 45-46. See also Strathie v. Department of Transportation, 716 F.2d 227 (3d Cir. 1983). Relevant evidence may include input from the individual with a disability, the experience of the individual with a disability in previous similar positions, and opinions of medical doctors, rehabilitation counselors, or physical therapists who have expertise in the disability involved and/or direct knowledge of the individual with the disability.

An employer is also permitted to require that an individual not pose a direct threat of harm to his or her own safety or health. If performing the particular functions of a job would result in a high probability of substantial harm to the individual, the employer could reject or discharge the individual unless a reasonable accommodation that would not cause an undue hardship would avert the harm. For example, an employer would not be required to hire an individual, disabled by narcolepsy, who frequently and unexpectedly loses consciousness for a carpentry job the essential functions of which require the use of power saws and other dangerous equipment, where no accommodation exists that will reduce or eliminate the risk.

The assessment that there exists a high probability of substantial harm to the individual, like the assessment that there exists a high probability of substantial harm to others, must be strictly based on valid medical analyses and/or on other objective evidence. This determination must be based on individualized factual data, using the factors discussed above, rather than on stereotypic or patronizing assumptions and must consider potential reasonable accommodations. Generalized fears about risks from the employment environment, such as exacerbation of the disability caused by stress, cannot be used by an employer to disqualify an individual with a disability. For example, a law firm could not reject an applicant with a history of disabling mental illness based on a generalized fear that the stress of trying to make partner might trigger a relapse of the individual's mental illness. Nor can generalized fears about risks to individuals with disabilities in the event of an evacuation or other emergency be used by an employer to disqualify an individual with a disability. See Senate Report at 56; House Labor Report at 73-74; House Judiciary Report at 45. See also Mantolete v. Bolger, 767 F.2d 1416 (9th Cir. 1985); Bentivegna v. U.S. Department of Labor, 694 F.2d 619 (9th Cir.1982).

Section 1630.3 Exceptions to the Definitions of "Disability" and "Qualified Individual with a Disability"

Section 1630.3 (a) through (c) Illegal Use of Drugs

Part 1630 provides that an individual currently engaging in the illegal use of drugs is not an individual with a disability for purposes of this part when the employer or other covered entity acts on the basis of such use. Illegal use of drugs refers both to the use of unlawful drugs, such as cocaine, and to the unlawful use of prescription drugs.

Employers, for example, may discharge or deny employment to persons who illegally use drugs, on the basis of such use, without fear of being held liable for discrimination. The term "currently engaging" is not intended to be limited to the use of drugs on the day of, or within a matter of days or weeks before, the employment action in question. Rather, the provision is intended to apply to the illegal use of drugs that has occurred recently enough to indicate that the individual is actively engaged in such conduct. See Conference Report at 64.

Individuals who are erroneously perceived as engaging in the illegal use of drugs, but are not in fact illegally using drugs are not excluded from the definitions of the terms "disability" and "qualified individual with a disability." Individuals who are no longer illegally using drugs and who have either been rehabilitated successfully or are in the process of completing a rehabilitation program are, likewise, not excluded from the definitions of those terms. The term "rehabilitation program" refers to both in-patient and out-patient programs, as well as to appropriate employee assistance programs, professionally recognized self-help programs, such as Narcotics Anonymous, or other programs that provide professional (not necessarily medical) assistance and counseling for individuals who illegally use drugs. See Conference Report at 64; see also House Labor Report at 77; House Judiciary Report at 47.

It should be noted that this provision simply provides that certain individuals are not excluded from the definitions of "disability" and "qualified individual with a disability." Consequently, such individuals are still required to establish that they satisfy the requirements of these definitions in order to be protected by the ADA and this part. An individual erroneously regarded as illegally using drugs, for example, would have to show that he or she was regarded as a drug addict in order to demonstrate that he or she meets the definition of "disability" as defined in this part.

Employers are entitled to seek reasonable assurances that no illegal use of drugs is occurring or has occurred recently enough so that continuing use is a real and ongoing problem. The reasonable assurances that employers may ask applicants or employees to provide include evidence that the individual is participating in a drug treatment program and/or evidence, such as drug test results, to show that the individual is not currently engaging in the illegal use of drugs. An employer, such as a law enforcement agency, may also be able to impose a qualification standard that excludes individuals with a history of illegal use of drugs if it can show that the standard is job-related and consistent with business necessity. (See Sec. 1630.10 Qualification Standards, Tests and Other Selection Criteria) See Conference Report at 64.

Section 1630.4 Discrimination Prohibited

This provision prohibits discrimination against a qualified individual with a disability in all aspects of the employment relationship. The range of employment decisions covered by this nondiscrimination mandate is to be construed in a manner consistent with the regulations implementing section 504 of the Rehabilitation Act of 1973.

Part 1630 is not intended to limit the ability of covered entities to choose and maintain a qualified workforce. Employers can continue to use job-related criteria to select qualified employees, and can continue to hire employees who can perform the essential functions of the job.

Section 1630.5 Limiting, Segregating, and Classifying

This provision and the several provisions that follow describe various specific forms of discrimination that are included within the general prohibition of Sec. 1630.4. Covered entities are prohibited from restricting the employment opportunities of qualified individuals with disabilities on the basis of stereotypes and myths about the individual's disability. Rather, the capabilities of qualified individuals with disabilities must be determined on an individualized, case by case basis. Covered entities are also prohibited from segregating qualified employees with disabilities into separate work areas or into separate lines of advancement.

Thus, for example, it would be a violation of this part for an employer to limit the duties of an employee with a disability based on a presumption of what is best for an individual with such a disability, or on a presumption about the abilities of an individual with such a disability. It would be a violation of this part for an employer to adopt a separate track of job promotion or progression for employees with disabilities based on a presumption that employees with disabilities are uninterested in, or incapable of, performing particular jobs. Similarly, it would be a violation for an employer to assign or reassign (as a reasonable accommodation) employees with disabilities to one particular office or installation, or to require that employees with disabilities only use particular employer provided non-work facilities such as segregated break-rooms, lunch rooms, or lounges. It would also be a violation of this part to deny employment to an applicant or employee with a disability based on generalized fears about the safety of an individual with such a disability, or based on generalized assumptions about the absenteeism rate of an individual with such a disability.

In addition, it should also be noted that this part is intended to require that employees with disabilities be accorded equal access to whatever health insurance coverage the employer provides to other employees. This part does not, however, affect pre-existing condition clauses included in health insurance policies offered by employers. Consequently, employers may continue to offer policies that contain such clauses, even if they adversely affect individuals with disabilities, so long as the clauses are not used as a subterfuge to evade the purposes of this part.

So, for example, it would be permissible for an employer to offer an insurance policy that limits coverage for certain procedures or treatments to a specified number per year. Thus, if a health insurance plan provided coverage for five blood transfusions a year to all covered employees, it would not be discriminatory to offer this plan simply because a hemophiliac employee may require more than five blood transfusions annually. However, it would not be permissible to limit or deny the hemophiliac employee coverage for other procedures, such as heart surgery or the setting of a broken leg, even though the plan would not have to provide coverage for the additional blood transfusions that may be involved in these procedures. Likewise, limits may be placed on reimbursements for certain procedures or on the types of drugs or procedures covered (e.g. limits on the number of permitted X-rays or non-coverage of experimental drugs or procedures), but that limitation must be applied equally to individuals with and without disabilities. See Senate Report at 28-29; House Labor Report at 58-59; House Judiciary Report at 36.

Leave policies or benefit plans that are uniformly applied do not violate this part simply because they do not address the special needs of every individual with a disability. Thus, for example, an employer that reduces the number of paid sick leave days that it will provide to all employees, or reduces the amount of medical insurance coverage that it will provide to all employees, is not in violation of this part, even if the benefits reduction has an impact on employees with disabilities in need of greater sick leave and medical coverage. Benefits reductions adopted for discriminatory reasons are in violation of this part. See Alexander v. Choate, 469 U.S. 287 (1985). See Senate Report at 85; House Labor Report at 137. (See also, the discussion at Sec. 1630.16(f) Health Insurance, Life Insurance, and Other Benefit Plans).

Section 1630.6 Contractual or Other Arrangements

An employer or other covered entity may not do through a contractual or other relationship what it is prohibited from doing directly. This provision does not affect the determination of whether or not one is a "covered entity" or "employer" as defined in Sec. 1630.2.

This provision only applies to situations where an employer or other covered entity has entered into a contractual relationship that has the effect of discriminating against its own employees or applicants with disabilities. Accordingly, it would be a violation for an employer to participate in a contractual relationship that results in discrimination against the employer's employees with disabilities in hiring, training, promotion, or in any other aspect of the employment relationship. This provision applies whether or not the employer or other covered entity intended for the contractual relationship to have the discriminatory effect.

Part 1630 notes that this provision applies to parties on either side of the contractual or other relationship. This is intended to highlight that an employer whose employees provide services to others, like an employer whose employees receive services, must ensure that those employees are not discriminated against on the basis of disability. For example, a copier company whose service representative is a dwarf could be required to provide a stepstool, as a reasonable accommodation, to enable him to perform the necessary repairs. However, the employer would not be required, as a reasonable accommodation, to make structural changes to its customer's inaccessible premises.

The existence of the contractual relationship adds no new obligations under part 1630. The employer, therefore, is not liable through the contractual arrangement for any discrimination by the contractor against the contractors own employees or applicants, although the contractor, as an employer, may be liable for such discrimination.

An employer or other covered entity, on the other hand, cannot evade the obligations imposed by this part by engaging in a contractual or other relationship. For example, an employer cannot avoid its responsibility to make reasonable accommodation subject to the undue hardship limitation through a contractual arrangement. See Conference Report at 59; House Labor Report at 59-61; House Judiciary Report at 36-37.

To illustrate, assume that an employer is seeking to contract with a company to provide training for its employees. Any responsibilities of reasonable accommodation applicable to the employer in providing the training remain with that employer even if it contracts with another company for this service. Thus, if the training company were planning to conduct the training at an inaccessible location, thereby making it impossible for an employee who uses a wheelchair to attend, the employer would have a duty to make reasonable accommodation unless to do so would impose an undue hardship. Under these circumstances, appropriate accommodations might include (1) having the training company identify accessible training sites and relocate the training program; (2) having the training company make the training site accessible; (3) directly making the training site accessible or providing the training company with the means by which to make the site accessible; (4) identifying and contracting with another training company that uses accessible sites; or (5) any other accommodation that would result in making the training available to the employee.

As another illustration, assume that instead of contracting with a training company, the employer contracts with a hotel to host a conference for its employees. The employer will have a duty to ascertain and ensure the accessibility of the hotel and its conference facilities. To fulfill this obligation the employer could, for example, inspect the hotel first-hand or ask a local disability group to inspect the hotel. Alternatively, the employer could ensure that the contract with the hotel specifies it will provide accessible guest rooms for those who need them and that all rooms to be used for the conference, including exhibit and meeting rooms, are accessible. If the hotel breaches this accessibility provision, the hotel may be liable to the employer, under a non-ADA breach of contract theory, for the cost of any accommodation needed to provide access to the hotel and conference, and for any other costs accrued by the employer. (In addition, the hotel may also be independently liable under title III of the ADA). However, this would not relieve the employer of its responsibility under this part nor shield it from charges of discrimination by its own employees. See House Labor Report at 40; House Judiciary Report at 37.

Section 1630.8 Relationship or Association with an Individual with a Disability

This provision is intended to protect any qualified individual, whether or not that individual has a disability, from discrimination because that person is known to have an association or relationship with an individual who has a known disability. This protection is not limited to those who have a familial relationship with an individual with a disability.

To illustrate the scope of this provision, assume that a qualified applicant without a disability applies for a job and discloses to the employer that his or her spouse has a disability. The employer thereupon declines to hire the applicant because the employer believes that the applicant would have to miss work or frequently leave work early in order to care for the spouse. Such a refusal to hire would be prohibited by this provision. Similarly, this provision would prohibit an employer from discharging an employee because the employee does volunteer work with people who have AIDS, and the employer fears that the employee may contract the disease.

This provision also applies to other benefits and privileges of employment. For example, an employer that provides health insurance benefits to its employees for their dependents may not reduce the level of those benefits to an employee simply because that employee has a dependent with a disability. This is true even if the provision of such benefits would result in increased health insurance costs for the employer.

It should be noted, however, that an employer need not provide the applicant or employee without a disability with a reasonable accommodation because that duty only applies to qualified applicants or employees with disabilities. Thus, for example, an employee would not be entitled to a modified work schedule as an accommodation to enable the employee to care for a spouse with a disability. See Senate Report at 30; House Labor Report at 61-62; House Judiciary Report at 38-39.

Section 1630.9 Not Making Reasonable Accommodation

The obligation to make reasonable accommodation is a form of non-discrimination. It applies to all employment decisions and to the job application process. This obligation does not extend to the provision of adjustments or modifications that are primarily for the personal benefit of the individual with a disability. Thus, if an adjustment or modification is job-related, e.g., specifically assists the individual in performing the duties of a particular job, it will be considered a type of reasonable accommodation. On the other hand, if an adjustment or modification assists the individual throughout his or her daily activities, on and off the job, it will be considered a personal item that the employer is not required to provide. Accordingly, an employer would generally not be required to provide an employee with a disability with a prosthetic limb, wheelchair, or eyeglasses. Nor would an employer have to provide as an accommodation any amenity or convenience that is not job-related, such as a private hot plate, hot pot or refrigerator that is not provided to employees without disabilities. See Senate Report at 31; House Labor Report at 62.

It should be noted, however, that the provision of such items may be required as a reasonable accommodation where such items are specifically designed or required to meet job-related rather than personal needs. An employer, for example, may have to provide an individual with a disabling visual impairment with eyeglasses specifically designed to enable the individual to use the office computer monitors, but that are not otherwise needed by the individual outside of the office.

The term "supported employment," which has been applied to a wide variety of programs to assist individuals with severe disabilities in both competitive and non-competitive employment, is not synonymous with reasonable accommodation. Examples of supported employment include modified training materials, restructuring essential functions to enable an individual to perform a job, or hiring an outside professional ("job coach") to assist in job training. Whether a particular form of assistance would be required as a reasonable accommodation must be determined on an individualized, case by case basis without regard to whether that assistance is referred to as "supported employment." For example, an employer, under certain circumstances, may be required to provide modified training materials or a temporary "job coach" to assist in the training of a qualified individual with a disability as a reasonable accommodation. However, an employer would not be required to restructure the essential functions of a position to fit the skills of an individual with a disability who is not otherwise qualified to perform the position, as is done in certain supported employment programs. See 34 CFR part 363. It should be noted that it would not be a violation of this part for an employer to provide any of these personal modifications or adjustments, or to engage in supported employment or similar rehabilitative programs.

The obligation to make reasonable accommodation applies to all services and programs provided in connection with employment, and to all non-work facilities provided or maintained by an employer for use by its employees. Accordingly, the obligation to accommodate is applicable to employer sponsored placement or counseling services, and to employer provided cafeterias, lounges, gymnasiums, auditoriums, transportation and the like.

The reasonable accommodation requirement is best understood as a means by which barriers to the equal employment opportunity of an individual with a disability are removed or alleviated. These barriers may, for example, be physical or structural obstacles that inhibit or prevent the access of an individual with a disability to job sites, facilities or equipment. Or they may be rigid work schedules that permit no flexibility as to when work is performed or when breaks may be taken, or inflexible job procedures that unduly limit the modes of communication that are used on the job, or the way in which particular tasks are accomplished.

The term "otherwise qualified" is intended to make clear that the obligation to make reasonable accommodation is owed only to an individual with a disability who is qualified within the meaning of Sec. 1630.2(m) in that he or she satisfies all the skill, experience, education and other job-related selection criteria. An individual with a disability is "otherwise qualified," in other words, if he or she is qualified for a job, except that, because of the disability, he or she needs a reasonable accommodation to be able to perform the job's essential functions.

For example, if a law firm requires that all incoming lawyers have graduated from an accredited law school and have passed the bar examination, the law firm need not provide an accommodation to an individual with a visual impairment who has not met these selection criteria. That individual is not entitled to a reasonable accommodation because the individual is not "otherwise qualified" for the position.

On the other hand, if the individual has graduated from an accredited law school and passed the bar examination, the individual would be "otherwise qualified." The law firm would thus be required to provide a reasonable accommodation, such as a machine that magnifies print, to enable the individual to perform the essential functions of the attorney position, unless the necessary accommodation would impose an undue hardship on the law firm. See Senate Report at 33-34; House Labor Report at 64-65.

The reasonable accommodation that is required by this part should provide the qualified individual with a disability with an equal employment opportunity. Equal employment opportunity means an opportunity to attain the same level of performance, or to enjoy the same level of benefits and privileges of employment as are available to the average similarly situated employee without a disability. Thus, for example, an accommodation made to assist an employee with a disability in the performance of his or her job must be adequate to enable the individual to perform the essential functions of the relevant position. The accommodation, however, does not have to be the "best" accommodation possible, so long as it is sufficient to meet the job-related needs of the individual being accommodated. Accordingly, an employer would not have to provide an employee disabled by a back impairment with a state-of-the art mechanical lifting device if it provided the employee with a less expensive or more readily available device that enabled the employee to perform the essential functions of the job. See Senate Report at 35; House Labor Report at 66; see also Carter v. Bennett, 840 F.2d 63 (D.C. Cir. 1988).

Employers are obligated to make reasonable accommodation only to the physical or mental limitations resulting from the disability of a qualified individual with a disability that is known to the employer. Thus, an employer would not be expected to accommodate disabilities of which it is unaware. If an employee with a known disability is having difficulty performing his or her job, an employer may inquire whether the employee is in need of a reasonable accommodation. In general, however, it is the responsibility of the individual with a disability to inform the employer that an accommodation is needed. When the need for an accommodation is not obvious, an employer, before providing a reasonable accommodation, may require that the individual with a disability provide documentation of the need for accommodation.

See Senate Report at 34; House Labor Report at 65.

Process of Determining the Appropriate Reasonable Accommodation

Once a qualified individual with a disability has requested provision of a reasonable accommodation, the employer must make a reasonable effort to determine the appropriate accommodation. The appropriate reasonable accommodation is best determined through a flexible, interactive process that involves both the employer and the qualified individual with a disability. Although this process is described below in terms of accommodations that enable the individual with a disability to perform the essential functions of the position held or desired, it is equally applicable to accommodations involving the job application process, and to accommodations that enable the individual with a disability to enjoy equal benefits and privileges of employment. See Senate Report at 34-35; House Labor Report at 65-67.

When a qualified individual with a disability has requested a reasonable accommodation to assist in the performance of a job, the employer, using a problem solving approach, should:

(1) Analyze the particular job involved and determine its purpose and essential functions;

(2) Consult with the individual with a disability to ascertain the precise job-related limitations imposed by the individual's disability and how those limitations could be overcome with a reasonable accommodation;

(3) In consultation with the individual to be accommodated, identify potential accommodations and assess the effectiveness each would have in enabling the individual to perform the essential functions of the position; and

(4) Consider the preference of the individual to be accommodated and select and implement the accommodation that is most appropriate for both the employee and the employer.

In many instances, the appropriate reasonable accommodation may be so obvious to either or both the employer and the qualified individual with a disability that it may not be necessary to proceed in this step-by-step fashion. For example, if an employee who uses a wheelchair requests that his or her desk be placed on blocks to elevate the desktop above the arms of the wheelchair and the employer complies, an appropriate accommodation has been requested, identified, and provided without either the employee or employer being aware of having engaged in any sort of "reasonable accommodation process."

However, in some instances neither the individual requesting the accommodation nor the employer can readily identify the appropriate accommodation. For example, the individual needing the accommodation may not know enough about the equipment used by the employer or the exact nature of the work site to suggest an appropriate accommodation. Likewise, the employer may not know enough about the individual's disability or the limitations that disability would impose on the performance of the job to suggest an appropriate accommodation. Under such circumstances, it may be necessary for the employer to initiate a more defined problem solving process, such as the step-by-step process described above, as part of its reasonable effort to identify the appropriate reasonable accommodation.

This process requires the individual assessment of both the particular job at issue, and the specific physical or mental limitations of the particular individual in need of reasonable accommodation. With regard to assessment of the job, "individual assessment" means analyzing the actual job duties and determining the true purpose or object of the job. Such an assessment is necessary to ascertain which job functions are the essential functions that an accommodation must enable an individual with a disability to perform.

After assessing the relevant job, the employer, in consultation with the individual requesting the accommodation, should make an assessment of the specific limitations imposed by the disability on the individual's performance of the job's essential functions. This assessment will make it possible to ascertain the precise barrier to the employment opportunity which, in turn, will make it possible to determine the accommodation(s) that could alleviate or remove that barrier.

If consultation with the individual in need of the accommodation still does not reveal potential appropriate accommodations, then the employer, as part of this process, may find that technical assistance is helpful in determining how to accommodate the particular individual in the specific situation. Such assistance could be sought from the Commission, from State or local rehabilitation agencies, or from disability constituent organizations. It should be noted, however, that, as provided in Sec. 1630.9(c) of this part, the failure to obtain or receive technical assistance from the Federal agencies that administer the ADA will not excuse the employer from its reasonable accommodation obligation.

Once potential accommodations have been identified, the employer should assess the effectiveness of each potential accommodation in assisting the individual in need of the accommodation in the performance of the essential functions of the position. If more than one of these accommodations will enable the individual to perform the essential functions or if the individual would prefer to provide his or her own accommodation, the preference of the individual with a disability should be given primary consideration. However, the employer providing the accommodation has the ultimate discretion to choose between effective accommodations, and may choose the less expensive accommodation or the accommodation that is easier for it to provide. It should also be noted that the individual's willingness to provide his or her own accommodation does not relieve the employer of the duty to provide the accommodation should the individual for any reason be unable or unwilling to continue to provide the accommodation.

Reasonable Accommodation Process Illustrated

The following example illustrates the informal reasonable accommodation process. Suppose a Sack Handler position requires that the employee pick up fifty pound sacks and carry them from the company loading dock to the storage room, and that a sack handler who is disabled by a back impairment requests a reasonable accommodation. Upon receiving the request, the employer analyzes the Sack Handler job and determines that the essential function and purpose of the job is not the requirement that the job holder physically lift and carry the sacks, but the requirement that the job holder cause the sack to move from the loading dock to the storage room.

The employer then meets with the sack handler to ascertain precisely the barrier posed by the individual's specific disability to the performance of the job's essential function of relocating the sacks. At this meeting the employer learns that the individual can, in fact, lift the sacks to waist level, but is prevented by his or her disability from carrying the sacks from the loading dock to the storage room. The employer and the individual agree that any of a number of potential accommodations, such as the provision of a dolly, hand truck, or cart, could enable the individual to transport the sacks that he or she has lifted.

Upon further consideration, however, it is determined that the provision of a cart is not a feasible effective option. No carts are currently available at the company, and those that can be purchased by the company are the wrong shape to hold many of the bulky and irregularly shaped sacks that must be moved. Both the dolly and the hand truck, on the other hand, appear to be effective options. Both are readily available to the company, and either will enable the individual to relocate the sacks that he or she has lifted. The sack handler indicates his or her preference for the dolly. In consideration of this expressed preference, and because the employer feels that the dolly will allow the individual to move more sacks at a time and so be more efficient than would a hand truck, the employer ultimately provides the sack handler with a dolly in fulfillment of the obligation to make reasonable accommodation.

Section 1630.9(b)

This provision states that an employer or other covered entity cannot prefer or select a qualified individual without a disability over an equally qualified individual with a disability merely because the individual with a disability will require a reasonable accommodation. In other words, an individual's need for an accommodation cannot enter into the employer's or other covered entity's decision regarding hiring, discharge, promotion, or other similar employment decisions, unless the accommodation would impose an undue hardship on the employer. See House Labor Report at 70.

Section 1630.9(d)

The purpose of this provision is to clarify that an employer or other covered entity may not compel a qualified individual with a disability to accept an accommodation, where that accommodation is neither requested nor needed by the individual. However, if a necessary reasonable accommodation is refused, the individual may not be considered qualified. For example, an individual with a visual impairment that restricts his or her field of vision but who is able to read unaided would not be required to accept a reader as an accommodation. However, if the individual were not able to read unaided and reading was an essential function of the job, the individual would not be qualified for the job if he or she refused a reasonable accommodation that would enable him or her to read. See Senate Report at 34; House Labor Report at 65; House Judiciary Report at 71-72.

Section 1630.10 Qualification Standards, Tests, and Other Selection Criteria

The purpose of this provision is to ensure that individuals with disabilities are not excluded from job opportunities unless they are actually unable to do the job. It is to ensure that there is a fit between job criteria and an applicant's (or employee's) actual ability to do the job. Accordingly, job criteria that even unintentionally screen out, or tend to screen out, an individual with a disability or a class of individuals with disabilities because of their disability may not be used unless the employer demonstrates that that criteria, as used by the employer, are job-related to the position to which they are being applied and are consistent with business necessity. The concept of "business necessity" has the same meaning as the concept of "business necessity" under section 504 of the Rehabilitation Act of 1973.

Selection criteria that exclude, or tend to exclude, an individual with a disability or a class of individuals with disabilities because of their disability but do not concern an essential function of the job would not be consistent with business necessity.

The use of selection criteria that are related to an essential function of the job may be consistent with business necessity. However, selection criteria that are related to an essential function of the job may not be used to exclude an individual with a disability if that individual could satisfy the criteria with the provision of a reasonable accommodation. Experience under a similar provision of the regulations implementing section 504 of the Rehabilitation Act indicates that challenges to selection criteria are, in fact, most often resolved by reasonable accommodation. It is therefore anticipated that challenges to selection criteria brought under this part will generally be resolved in a like manner.

This provision is applicable to all types of selection criteria, including safety requirements, vision or hearing requirements, walking requirements, lifting requirements, and employment tests. See Senate Report at 37-39; House Labor Report at 70-72; House Judiciary Report at 42. As previously noted, however, it is not the intent of this part to second guess an employer's business judgment with regard to production standards. (See section 1630.2(n) Essential Functions). Consequently, production standards will generally not be subject to a challenge under this provision.

The Uniform Guidelines on Employee Selection Procedures (UGESP) 29 CFR part 1607 do not apply to the Rehabilitation Act and are similarly inapplicable to this part.

Section 1630.11 Administration of Tests

The intent of this provision is to further emphasize that individuals with disabilities are not to be excluded from jobs that they can actually perform merely because a disability prevents them from taking a test, or negatively influences the results of a test, that is a prerequisite to the job. Read together with the reasonable accommodation requirement of section 1630.9, this provision requires that employment tests be administered to eligible applicants or employees with disabilities that impair sensory, manual, or speaking skills in formats that do not require the use of the impaired skill.

The employer or other covered entity is, generally, only required to provide such reasonable accommodation if it knows, prior to the administration of the test, that the individual is disabled and that the disability impairs sensory, manual or speaking skills. Thus, for example, it would be unlawful to administer a written employment test to an individual who has informed the employer, prior to the administration of the test, that he is disabled with dyslexia and unable to read. In such a case, as a reasonable accommodation and in accordance with this provision, an alternative oral test should be administered to that individual. By the same token, a written test may need to be substituted for an oral test if the applicant taking the test is an individual with a disability that impairs speaking skills or impairs the processing of auditory information.

Occasionally, an individual with a disability may not realize, prior to the administration of a test, that he or she will need an accommodation to take that particular test. In such a situation, the individual with a disability, upon becoming aware of the need for an accommodation, must so inform the employer or other covered entity. For example, suppose an individual with a disabling visual impairment does not request an accommodation for a written examination because he or she is usually able to take written tests with the aid of his or her own specially designed lens. When the test is distributed, the individual with a disability discovers that the lens is insufficient to distinguish the words of the test because of the unusually low color contrast between the paper and the ink, the individual would be entitled, at that point, to request an accommodation. The employer or other covered entity would, thereupon, have to provide a test with higher contrast, schedule a retest, or provide any other effective accommodation unless to do so would impose an undue hardship.

Other alternative or accessible test modes or formats include the administration of tests in large print or braille, or via a reader or sign interpreter. Where it is not possible to test in an alternative format, the employer may be required, as a reasonable accommodation, to evaluate the skill to be tested in another manner (e.g., through an interview, or through education license, or work experience requirements). An employer may also be required, as a reasonable accommodation, to allow more time to complete the test. In addition, the employer's obligation to make reasonable accommodation extends to ensuring that the test site is accessible. (See Sec. 1630.9 Not Making Reasonable Accommodation) See Senate Report at 37-38; House Labor Report at 70-72; House Judiciary Report at 42; see also Stutts v. Freeman, 694 F.2d 666 (11th Cir. 1983); Crane v. Dole, 617 F. Supp. 156 (D.D.C. 1985).

This provision does not require that an employer offer every applicant his or her choice of test format. Rather, this provision only requires that an employer provide, upon advance request, alternative, accessible tests to individuals with disabilities that impair sensory, manual, or speaking skills needed to take the test.

This provision does not apply to employment tests that require the use of sensory, manual, or speaking skills where the tests are intended to measure those skills. Thus, an employer could require that an applicant with dyslexia take a written test for a particular position if the ability to read is the skill the test is designed to measure. Similarly, an employer could require that an applicant complete a test within established time frames if speed were one of the skills for which the applicant was being tested. However, the results of such a test could not be used to exclude an individual with a disability unless the skill was necessary to perform an essential function of the position and no reasonable accommodation was available to enable the individual to perform that function, or the necessary accommodation would impose an undue hardship.

Section 1630.13 Prohibited Medical Examinations and Inquiries

Section 1630.13(a) Pre-Employment Examination or Inquiry

This provision makes clear that an employer cannot inquire as to whether an individual has a disability at the pre-offer stage of the selection process. Nor can an employer inquire at the pre-offer stage about an applicant's workers' compensation history.

Employers may ask questions that relate to the applicant's ability to perform job-related functions. However, these questions should not be phrased in terms of disability. An employer, for example, may ask whether the applicant has a driver's license, if driving is a job function, but may not ask whether the applicant has a visual disability. Employers may ask about an applicant's ability to perform both essential and marginal job functions. Employers, though, may not refuse to hire an applicant with a disability because the applicant's disability prevents him or her from performing marginal functions. See Senate Report at 39; House Labor Report at 72-73; House Judiciary Report at 42-43.

Section 1630.13(b) Examination or Inquiry of Employees

The purpose of this provision is to prevent the administration to employees of medical tests or inquiries that do not serve a legitimate business purpose. For example, if an employee suddenly starts to use increased amounts of sick leave or starts to appear sickly, an employer could not require that employee to be tested for AIDS, HIV infection, or cancer unless the employer can demonstrate that such testing is job-related and consistent with business necessity. See Senate Report at 39; House Labor Report at 75; House Judiciary Report at 44.

Section 1630.14 Medical Examinations and Inquiries Specifically Permitted

Section 1630.14(a) Pre-Employment Inquiry

Employers are permitted to make pre-employment inquiries into the ability of an applicant to perform job-related functions. This inquiry must be narrowly tailored. The employer may describe or demonstrate the job function and inquire whether or not the applicant can perform that function with or without reasonable accommodation. For example, an employer may explain that the job requires assembling small parts and ask if the individual will be able to perform that function, with or without reasonable accommodation. See Senate Report at 39; House Labor Report at 73; House Judiciary Report at 43.

An employer may also ask an applicant to describe or to demonstrate how, with or without reasonable accommodation, the applicant will be able to perform job-related functions. Such a request may be made of all applicants in the same job category regardless of disability. Such a request may also be made of an applicant whose known disability may interfere with or prevent the performance of a job-related function, whether or not the employer routinely makes such a request of all applicants in the job category. For example, an employer may ask an individual with one leg who applies for a position as a home washing machine repairman to demonstrate or to explain how, with or without reasonable accommodation, he would be able to transport himself and his tools down basement stairs. However, the employer may not inquire as to the nature or severity of the disability. Therefore, for example, the employer cannot ask how the individual lost the leg or whether the loss of the leg is indicative of an underlying impairment.

On the other hand, if the known disability of an applicant will not interfere with or prevent the performance of a job-related function, the employer may only request a description or demonstration by the applicant if it routinely makes such a request of all applicants in the same job category. So, for example, it would not be permitted for an employer to request that an applicant with one leg demonstrate his ability to assemble small parts while seated at a table, if the employer does not routinely request that all applicants provide such a demonstration.

An employer that requires an applicant with a disability to demonstrate how he or she will perform a job-related function must either provide the reasonable accommodation the applicant needs to perform the function or permit the applicant to explain how, with the accommodation, he or she will perform the function. If the job-related function is not an essential function, the employer may not exclude the applicant with a disability because of the applicant's inability to perform that function. Rather, the employer must, as a reasonable accommodation, either provide an accommodation that will enable the individual to perform the function, transfer the function to another position, or exchange the function for one the applicant is able to perform.

An employer may not use an application form that lists a number of potentially disabling impairments and ask the applicant to check any of the impairments he or she may have. In addition, as noted above, an employer may not ask how a particular individual became disabled or the prognosis of the individual's disability. The employer is also prohibited from asking how often the individual will require leave for treatment or use leave as a result of incapacitation because of the disability. However, the employer may state the attendance requirements of the job and inquire whether the applicant can meet them.

An employer is permitted to ask, on a test announcement or application form, that individuals with disabilities who will require a reasonable accommodation in order to take the test so inform the employer within a reasonable established time period prior to the administration of the test. The employer may also request that documentation of the need for the accommodation accompany the request. Requested accommodations may include accessible testing sites, modified testing conditions and accessible test formats. (See Sec. 1630.11 Administration of Tests).

Physical agility tests are not medical examinations and so may be given at any point in the application or employment process. Such tests must be given to all similarly situated applicants or employees regardless of disability. If such tests screen out or tend to screen out an individual with a disability or a class of individuals with disabilities, the employer would have to demonstrate that the test is job-related and consistent with business necessity and that performance cannot be achieved with reasonable accommodation. (See Sec. 1630.9 Not Making Reasonable Accommodation: Process of Determining the Appropriate Reasonable Accommodation).

As previously noted, collecting information and inviting individuals to identify themselves as individuals with disabilities as required to satisfy the affirmative action requirements of section 503 of the Rehabilitation Act is not restricted by this part. (See Sec. 1630.1 (b) and (c) Applicability and Construction).

Section 1630.14(b) Employment Entrance Examination

An employer is permitted to require post-offer medical examinations before the employee actually starts working. The employer may condition the offer of employment on the results of the examination, provided that all entering employees in the same job category are subjected to such an examination, regardless of disability, and that the confidentiality requirements specified in this part are met.

This provision recognizes that in many industries, such as air transportation or construction, applicants for certain positions are chosen on the basis of many factors including physical and psychological criteria, some of which may be identified as a result of post-offer medical examinations given prior to entry on duty. Only those employees who meet the employer's physical and psychological criteria for the job, with or without reasonable accommodation, will be qualified to receive confirmed offers of employment and begin working.

Medical examinations permitted by this section are not required to be job-related and consistent with business necessity. However, if an employer withdraws an offer of employment because the medical examination reveals that the employee does not satisfy certain employment criteria, either the exclusionary criteria must not screen out or tend to screen out an individual with a disability or a class of individuals with disabilities, or they must be job-related and consistent with business necessity. As part of the showing that an exclusionary criteria is job-related and consistent with business necessity, the employer must also demonstrate that there is no reasonable accommodation that will enable the individual with a disability to perform the essential functions of the job. See Conference Report at 59-60; Senate Report at 39; House Labor Report at 73-74; House Judiciary Report at 43.

As an example, suppose an employer makes a conditional offer of employment to an applicant, and it is an essential function of the job that the incumbent be available to work every day for the next three months. An employment entrance examination then reveals that the applicant has a disabling impairment that, according to reasonable medical judgment that relies on the most current medical knowledge, will require treatment that will render the applicant unable to work for a portion of the three month period. Under these circumstances, the employer would be able to withdraw the employment offer without violating this part.

The information obtained in the course of a permitted entrance examination or inquiry is to be treated as a confidential medical record and may only be used in a manner not inconsistent with this part. State workers' compensation laws are not preempted by the ADA or this part. These laws require the collection of information from individuals for State administrative purposes that do not conflict with the ADA or this part. Consequently, employers or other covered entities may submit information to State workers' compensation offices or second injury funds in accordance with State workers' compensation laws without violating this part.

Consistent with this section and with Sec. 1630.16(f) of this part, information obtained in the course of a permitted entrance examination or inquiry may be used for insurance purposes described in Sec. 1630.16(f).

Section 1630.14(c) Examination of Employees

This provision permits employers to make inquiries or require medical examinations (fitness for duty exams) when there is a need to determine whether an employee is still able to perform the essential functions of his or her job. The provision permits employers or other covered entities to make inquiries or require medical examinations necessary to the reasonable accommodation process described in this part. This provision also permits periodic physicals to determine fitness for duty or other medical monitoring if such physicals or monitoring are required by medical standards or requirements established by Federal, State, or local law that are consistent with the ADA and this part (or in the case of a Federal standard, with section 504 of the Rehabilitation Act) in that they are job-related and consistent with business necessity.

Such standards may include Federal safety regulations that regulate bus and truck driver qualifications, as well as laws establishing medical requirements for pilots or other air transportation personnel. These standards also include health standards promulgated pursuant to the Occupational Safety and Health Act of 1970, the Federal Coal Mine Health and Safety Act of 1969, or other similar statutes that require that employees exposed to certain toxic and hazardous substances be medically monitored at specific intervals. See House Labor Report at 74-75.

The information obtained in the course of such examination or inquiries is to be treated as a confidential medical record and may only be used in a manner not inconsistent with this part.

Section 1630.14(d) Other Acceptable Examinations and Inquiries

Part 1630 permits voluntary medical examinations, including voluntary medical histories, as part of employee health programs. These programs often include, for example, medical screening for high blood pressure, weight control counseling, and cancer detection. Voluntary activities, such as blood pressure monitoring and the administering of prescription drugs, such as insulin, are also permitted. It should be noted, however, that the medical records developed in the course of such activities must be maintained in the confidential manner required by this part and must not be used for any purpose in violation of this part, such as limiting health insurance eligibility. House Labor Report at 75; House Judiciary Report at 43-44.

Section 1630.15 Defenses

The section on defenses in part 1630 is not intended to be exhaustive. However, it is intended to inform employers of some of the potential defenses available to a charge of discrimination under the ADA and this part.

Section 1630.15(a) Disparate Treatment Defenses

The "traditional" defense to a charge of disparate treatment under title VII, as expressed in McDonnell Douglas Corp. v. Green, 411 U.S. 792 (1973), Texas Department of Community Affairs v. Burdine, 450 U.S. 248 (1981), and their progeny, may be applicable to charges of disparate treatment brought under the ADA. See Prewitt v. U.S. Postal Service, 662 F.2d 292 (5th Cir. 1981). Disparate treatment means, with respect to title I of the ADA, that an individual was treated differently on the basis of his or her disability. For example, disparate treatment has occurred where an employer excludes an employee with a severe facial disfigurement from staff meetings because the employer does not like to look at the employee. The individual is being treated differently because of the employer's attitude towards his or her perceived disability. Disparate treatment has also occurred where an employer has a policy of not hiring individuals with AIDS regardless of the individuals' qualifications.

The crux of the defense to this type of charge is that the individual was treated differently not because of his or her disability but for a legitimate nondiscriminatory reason such as poor performance unrelated to the individual's disability. The fact that the individual's disability is not covered by the employer's current insurance plan or would cause the employer's insurance premiums or workers' compensation costs to increase, would not be a legitimate nondiscriminatory reason justifying disparate treatment of an individual with a disability. Senate Report at 85; House Labor Report at 136 and House Judiciary Report at 70. The defense of a legitimate nondiscriminatory reason is rebutted if the alleged nondiscriminatory reason is shown to be pretextual.

Section 1630.15 (b) and (c) Disparate Impact Defenses

Disparate impact means, with respect to title I of the ADA and this part, that uniformly applied criteria have an adverse impact on an individual with a disability or a disproportionately negative impact on a class of individuals with disabilities. Section 1630.15(b) clarifies that an employer may use selection criteria that have such a disparate impact, i.e., that screen out or tend to screen out an individual with a disability or a class of individuals with disabilities only when they are job-related and consistent with business necessity.

For example, an employer interviews two candidates for a position, one of whom is blind. Both are equally qualified. The employer decides that while it is not essential to the job it would be convenient to have an employee who has a driver's license and so could occasionally be asked to run errands by car. The employer hires the individual who is sighted because this individual has a driver's license. This is an example of a uniformly applied criterion, having a driver's permit, that screens out an individual who has a disability that makes it impossible to obtain a driver's permit. The employer would, thus, have to show that this criterion is job-related and consistent with business necessity. See House Labor Report at 55.

However, even if the criterion is job-related and consistent with business necessity, an employer could not exclude an individual with a disability if the criterion could be met or job performance accomplished with a reasonable accommodation. For example, suppose an employer requires, as part of its application process, an interview that is job-related and consistent with business necessity. The employer would not be able to refuse to hire a hearing impaired applicant because he or she could not be interviewed. This is so because an interpreter could be provided as a reasonable accommodation that would allow the individual to be interviewed, and thus satisfy the selection criterion.

With regard to safety requirements that screen out or tend to screen out an individual with a disability or a class of individuals with disabilities, an employer must demonstrate that the requirement, as applied to the individual, satisfies the "direct threat" standard in Sec. 1630.2(r) in order to show that the requirement is job-related and consistent with business necessity.

Section 1630.15(c) clarifies that there may be uniformly applied standards, criteria and policies not relating to selection that may also screen out or tend to screen out an individual with a disability or a class of individuals with disabilities. Like selection criteria that have a disparate impact, non-selection criteria having such an impact may also have to be job-related and consistent with business necessity, subject to consideration of reasonable accommodation.

It should be noted, however, that some uniformly applied employment policies or practices, such as leave policies, are not subject to challenge under the adverse impact theory. "No-leave" policies (e.g., no leave during the first six months of employment) are likewise not subject to challenge under the adverse impact theory. However, an employer, in spite of its "no-leave" policy, may, in appropriate circumstances, have to consider the provision of leave to an employee with a disability as a reasonable accommodation, unless the provision of leave would impose an undue hardship. See discussion at Sec. 1630.5 Limiting, Segregating and Classifying, and Sec. 1630.10 Qualification Standards, Tests, and Other Selection Criteria.

Section 1630.15(d) Defense to Not Making Reasonable Accommodation

An employer or other covered entity alleged to have discriminated because it did not make a reasonable accommodation, as required by this part, may offer as a defense that it would have been an undue hardship to make the accommodation.

It should be noted, however, that an employer cannot simply assert that a needed accommodation will cause it undue hardship, as defined in Sec. 1630.2(p), and thereupon be relieved of the duty to provide accommodation. Rather, an employer will have to present evidence and demonstrate that the accommodation will, in fact, cause it undue hardship. Whether a particular accommodation will impose an undue hardship for a particular employer is determined on a case by case basis. Consequently, an accommodation that poses an undue hardship for one employer at a particular time may not pose an undue hardship for another employer, or even for the same employer at another time. Likewise, an accommodation that poses an undue hardship for one employer in a particular job setting, such as a temporary construction worksite, may not pose an undue hardship for another employer, or even for the same employer at a permanent worksite. See House Judiciary Report at 42.

The concept of undue hardship that has evolved under section 504 of the Rehabilitation Act and is embodied in this part is unlike the "undue hardship" defense associated with the provision of religious accommodation under title VII of the Civil Rights Act of 1964. To demonstrate undue hardship pursuant to the ADA and this part, an employer must show substantially more difficulty or expense than would be needed to satisfy the "de minimis" title VII standard of undue hardship. For example, to demonstrate that the cost of an accommodation poses an undue hardship, an employer would have to show that the cost is undue as compared to the employer's budget. Simply comparing the cost of the accommodation to the salary of the individual with a disability in need of the accommodation will not suffice. Moreover, even if it is determined that the cost of an accommodation would unduly burden an employer, the employer cannot avoid making the accommodation if the individual with a disability can arrange to cover that portion of the cost that rises to the undue hardship level, or can otherwise arrange to provide the accommodation. Under such circumstances, the necessary accommodation would no longer pose an undue hardship. See Senate Report at 36; House Labor Report at 68-69; House Judiciary Report at 40-41.

Excessive cost is only one of several possible bases upon which an employer might be able to demonstrate undue hardship. Alternatively, for example, an employer could demonstrate that the provision of a particular accommodation would be unduly disruptive to its other employees or to the functioning of its business. The terms of a collective bargaining agreement may be relevant to this determination. By way of illustration, an employer would likely be able to show undue hardship if the employer could show that the requested accommodation of the upward adjustment of the business' thermostat would result in it becoming unduly hot for its other employees, or for its patrons or customers. The employer would thus not have to provide this accommodation. However, if there were an alternate accommodation that would not result in undue hardship, the employer would have to provide that accommodation.

It should be noted, moreover, that the employer would not be able to show undue hardship if the disruption to its employees were the result of those employees fears or prejudices toward the individual's disability and not the result of the provision of the accommodation. Nor would the employer be able to demonstrate undue hardship by showing that the provision of the accommodation has a negative impact on the morale of its other employees but not on the ability of these employees to perform their jobs.

Section 1630.15(e) Defense — Conflicting Federal Laws and Regulations

There are several Federal laws and regulations that address medical standards and safety requirements. If the alleged discriminatory action was taken in compliance with another Federal law or regulation, the employer may offer its obligation to comply with the conflicting standard as a defense. The employer's defense of a conflicting Federal requirement or regulation may be rebutted by a showing of pretext, or by showing that the Federal standard did not require the discriminatory action, or that there was a nonexclusionary means to comply with the standard that would not conflict with this part. See House Labor Report at 74.

Section 1630.16 Specific Activities Permitted

Section 1630.16(a) Religious Entities

Religious organizations are not exempt from title I of the ADA or this part. A religious corporation, association, educational institution, or society may give a preference in employment to individuals of the particular religion, and may require that applicants and employees conform to the religious tenets of the organization. However, a religious organization may not discriminate against an individual who satisfies the permitted religious criteria because that individual is disabled. The religious entity, in other words, is required to consider qualified individuals with disabilities who satisfy the permitted religious criteria on an equal basis with qualified individuals without disabilities who similarly satisfy the religious criteria. See Senate Report at 42; House Labor Report at 76-77; House Judiciary Report at 46.

Section 1630.16(b) Regulation of Alcohol and Drugs

This provision permits employers to establish or comply with certain standards regulating the use of drugs and alcohol in the workplace. It also allows employers to hold alcoholics and persons who engage in the illegal use of drugs to the same performance and conduct standards to which it holds all of its other employees. Individuals disabled by alcoholism are entitled to the same protections accorded other individuals with disabilities under this part. As noted above, individuals currently engaging in the illegal use of drugs are not individuals with disabilities for purposes of part 1630 when the employer acts on the basis of such use.

Section 1630.16(c) Drug Testing

This provision reflects title I's neutrality toward testing for the illegal use of drugs. Such drug tests are neither encouraged, authorized nor prohibited. The results of such drug tests may be used as a basis for disciplinary action. Tests for the illegal use of drugs are not considered medical examinations for purposes of this part. If the results reveal information about an individual's medical condition beyond whether the individual is currently engaging in the illegal use of drugs, this additional information is to be treated as a confidential medical record. For example, if a test for the illegal use of drugs reveals the presence of a controlled substance that has been lawfully prescribed for a particular medical condition, this information is to be treated as a confidential medical record. See House Labor Report at 79; House Judiciary Report at 47.

Section 1630.16(e) Infectious and Communicable Diseases; Food Handling Jobs

This provision addressing food handling jobs applies the "direct threat" analysis to the particular situation of accommodating individuals with infectious or communicable diseases that are transmitted through the handling of food. The Department of Health and Human Services is to prepare a list of infectious and communicable diseases that are transmitted through the handling of food. If an individual with a disability has one of the listed diseases and works in or applies for a position in food handling, the employer must determine whether there is a reasonable accommodation that will eliminate the risk of transmitting the disease through the handling of food. If there is an accommodation that will not pose an undue hardship, and that will prevent the transmission of the disease through the handling of food, the employer must provide the accommodation to the individual. The employer, under these circumstances, would not be permitted to discriminate against the individual because of the need to provide the reasonable accommodation and would be required to maintain the individual in the food handling job.

If no such reasonable accommodation is possible, the employer may refuse to assign, or to continue to assign the individual to a position involving food handling. This means that if such an individual is an applicant for a food handling position the employer is not required to hire the individual. However, if the individual is a current employee, the employer would be required to consider the accommodation of reassignment to a vacant position not involving food handling for which the individual is qualified. Conference Report at 61-63. (See Sec. 1630.2(r) Direct Threat).

Section 1630.16(f) Health Insurance, Life Insurance, and Other Benefit Plans

This provision is a limited exemption that is only applicable to those who establish, sponsor, observe or administer benefit plans, such as health and life insurance plans. It does not apply to those who establish, sponsor, observe or administer plans not involving benefits, such as liability insurance plans.

The purpose of this provision is to permit the development and administration of benefit plans in accordance with accepted principles of risk assessment. This provision is not intended to disrupt the current regulatory structure for self-insured employers. These employers may establish, sponsor, observe, or administer the terms of a bona fide benefit plan not subject to State laws that regulate insurance. This provision is also not intended to disrupt the current nature of insurance underwriting, or current insurance industry practices in sales, underwriting, pricing, administrative and other services, claims and similar insurance related activities based on classification of risks as regulated by the States.

The activities permitted by this provision do not violate part 1630 even if they result in limitations on individuals with disabilities, provided that these activities are not used as a subterfuge to evade the purposes of this part. Whether or not these activities are being used as a subterfuge is to be determined without regard to the date the insurance plan or employee benefit plan was adopted.

However, an employer or other covered entity cannot deny a qualified individual with a disability equal access to insurance or subject a qualified individual with a disability to different terms or conditions of insurance based on disability alone, if the disability does not pose increased risks. Part 1630 requires that decisions not based on risk classification be made in conformity with non-discrimination requirements. See Senate Report at 84-86; House Labor Report at 136-138; House Judiciary Report at 70-71. See the discussion of Sec. 1630.5 Limiting, Segregating and Classifying.

[56 FR 35734, July 26, 1991, as amended at 65 FR 36327, June 8, 2000]

APPENDIX D

DEPARTMENT OF TRANSPORTATION REGULATIONS

TITLE 49, CODE OF FEDERAL REGULATIONS

PART 25 — (RESERVED)

PART 27 — NONDISCRIMINATION ON THE BASIS OF HANDICAP IN PROGRAMS AND ACTIVITIES RECEIVING OR BENEFITTING FROM FEDERAL FINANCIAL ASSISTANCE

Subpart A — General

Subpart B — Program Accessibility Requirements in Specific Operating Administration Programs: Airports, Railroads, and Highways

Subpart C — Enforcement

27.125 Compliance procedure.
27.127 Hearings.
27.129 Decisions and notices.

AUTHORITY: Sec. 504 of the Rehabilitation Act of 1973, as amended (29 U.S.C. 794); secs. 16(a) and 16(d) of the Urban Mass Transportation Act of 1964, as amended (49 U.S.C. 16(a) and 16(d); sec. 165(b) of the Federal-aid Highway Act of 1973 (49 U.S.C. 142 nt.); the Americans with Disabilities Act of 1990 (42 U.S.C. 12101–12213; and 49 U.S.C. 322).

SOURCE: 44 FR 31468, May 31, 1979, unless otherwise noted.

Subpart A — General

§ 27.1 Purpose.

The purpose of this part is to carry out the intent of section 504 of the Rehabilitation Act of 1973 (29 U.S.C. 794) as amended, to the end that no otherwise qualified handicapped individual in the United States shall, solely by reason of his or her handicap, be excluded from the participation in, be denied the benefits of, or be subjected to discrimination under any program or activity receiving Federal financial assistance.

§ 27.3 Applicability.

(a) This part applies to each recipient of Federal financial assistance from the Department of Transportation and to each program or activity that receives or benefits from such assistance.

(b) Design, construction, or alteration of buildings or other fixed facilities by public entities subject to part 37 of this title shall be in conformance with appendix A to part 37 of this title. All other entities subject to section 504 shall design, construct or alter a building, or other fixed facilities shall be in conformance with either appendix A to part 37 of this title or the Uniform Federal Accessibility Standards, 41 CFR part 101–19 subpart 101–19.6, appendix A.

[44 FR 31468, May 31, 1979, as amended at 56 FR 45621, Sept. 6, 1991]

§ 27.5 Definitions.

As used in this part:

Act means the Rehabilitation Act of 1973, Public Law 93–112, as amended.

Air Carrier Airport means an airport serviced by a certificated air carrier unless such airport is served solely by an air carrier which provides: (1)

Passenger service at that airport in aircraft having a maximum passenger capacity of less than 56 passengers, or (2) cargo service in air transportation at that airport solely with aircraft having a maximum payload capacity of less than 18,000 pounds; provided, however, that if at any such airport, Federal funds are made available for terminal facilities, it shall be deemed to be an air carrier airport.

Applicant means one who submits an application, request, or plan to be approved by a Departmental official or by a primary recipient as a condition to eligibility for Federal financial assistance, and *application* means such an application, request, or plan.

Department means the Department of Transportation.

Discrimination means denying handicapped persons the opportunity to participate in or benefit from any program or activity receiving Federal financial assistance.

Facility means all or any portion of buildings, structures, vehicles, equipment, roads, walks, parking lots, or other real or personal property or interest in such property.

Federal financial assistance means any grant, loan, contract (other than a procurement contract or a contract of insurance or guaranty), or any other arrangement by which the Department provides or otherwise makes available assistance in the form of:

(a) Funds;

(b) Services of Federal personnel; or

(c) Real or personal property or any interest in, or use of such property, including:

(1) Transfers or leases of such property for less than fair market value or for reduced consideration; and

(2) Proceeds from a subsequent transfer or lease of such property if the Federal share of its fair market value is not returned to the Federal Government.

Handicapped person means (1) any person who (a) has a physical or mental impairment that substantially limits one or more major life activities, (b) has a record of such an impairment, or (c) is regarded as having such an impairment. (2) As used in this definition, the phrase:

(a) *Physical or mental impairment* means (i) any physiological disorder or condition, cosmetic disfigurement, or anatomical loss affecting one or more of the following body systems: neurological; musculoskeletal; special sense organs; respiratory, including speech organs; cardiovascular, reproductive; digestive; genito-urinary; hemic and lymphatic; skin; and endocrine; or (ii) any mental or psychological disorder, such as mental retardation, organic brain syndrome, emotional or mental illness, and specific learning disabilities. The term *physical or mental impairment* includes, but is not limited to, such diseases and conditions as orthopedic, visual, speech, and hearing impairments; cerebral palsy; epilepsy; muscular dystrophy; multiple sclerosis; cancer; heart disease; mental retardation; emotional illness; drug addiction; and alcoholism.

(b) *Major life activities* means functions such as caring for one's self, performing manual tasks, walking, seeing, hearing, speaking, breathing, learning, and working.

(c) *Has a record of such an impairment* means has a history of, or has been classified, or misclassified, as having a mental or physical impairment that substantially limits one or more major life activities.

(d) *Is regarded as having an impairment* means:

(1) Has a physical or mental impairment that does not substantially limit major life activities but that is treated by a recipient as constituting such a limitation;

(2) Has a physical or mental impairment that substantially limits major life activity only as a result of the attitudes of others toward such an impairment; or

(3) Has none of the impairments set forth in paragraph (1) of this definition, but is treated by a recipient as having such an impairment.

Head of Operating Administration means the head of an operating administration within the Department (U.S. Coast Guard, Federal Highway Administration, Federal Aviation Administration, Federal Railroad Administration, National Highway Traffic Safety Administration, Federal Transit Administration, and Research and Special Programs Administration) providing Federal financial assistance to the recipient.

Primary recipient means any recipient that is authorized or required to extend Federal financial assistance from the Department to another recipient for the purpose of carrying out a program.

Qualified handicapped person means:

(1) With respect to employment, a handicapped person who, with reasonable accommodation and within normal safety requirements, can perform the essential functions of the job in question, but the term does not include any individual who is an alcoholic or drug abuser whose current use of alcohol or drugs prevents such person from performing the duties of the job in question or whose employment, by reason of such current alcohol or drug abuse, would constitute a direct threat to property or the safety of others; and

(2) With respect to other activities, a handicapped person who meets the essential eligibility requirements for the receipt of such services.

Recipient means any State, territory, possession, the District of Columbia, or Puerto Rico, or any political subdivision thereof, or instrumentality thereof, any public or private agency, institution, organization, or other entity, or any individual in any State, territory, possession, the District of Columbia, or Puerto Rico, to whom Federal financial assistance from the Department is extended directly or through another recipient, for any Federal program, including any successor, assignee, or transferee thereof, but such term does not include any ultimate beneficiary under any such program.

Secretary means the Secretary of Transportation.

Section 504 means section 504 of the Act.

Special service system means a transportation system specifically designed to serve the needs of persons who, by reason of handicap, are physically unable to use bus systems designed for use by the general public. Special service is characterized by the use of vehicles smaller than a standard transit bus which are usable by handicapped persons, demand-responsive service, point of origin to point of destination service, and flexible routing and scheduling.

[44 FR 31468, May 31, 1979, as amended by Amdt. 1, 46 FR 37492, July 20, 1981; Amdt. 27–3, 51 FR 19017, May 23, 1986; 56 FR 45621, Sept. 6, 1991]

§ 27.7 Discrimination prohibited.

(a) *General.* No qualified handicapped person shall, solely by reason of his handicap, be excluded from participation in, be denied the benefits of, or otherwise be subjected to discrimination under any program or activity that receives or benefits from Federal financial assistance administered by the Department of Transportation.

(b) *Discriminatory actions prohibited.* (1) A recipient, in providing any aid, benefit, or service, may not, directly or through contractual, licensing, or other arrangements, on the basis of handicap:

(i) Deny a qualified handicapped person the opportunity to participate in or benefit from the aid, benefit, or service;

(ii) Afford a qualified handicapped person an opportunity to participate in or benefit from the aid, benefit, or service that is not substantially equal to that afforded persons who are not handicapped;

(iii) Provide a qualified handicapped person with an aid, benefit, or service that is not as effective in affording equal opportunity to obtain the same result, to gain the same benefit, or to reach the same level of achievement as persons who are not handicapped;

(iv) Provide different or separate aid, benefits, or services to handicapped persons or to any class of handicapped persons unless such action is necessary to provide qualified handicapped persons with aid, benefits or services that are as effective as those provided to persons who are not handicapped;

(v) Aid or perpetuate discrimination against a qualified handicapped person by providing financial or other assistance to an agency, organization, or person that discriminates on the basis of handicap in providing any aid, benefit, or service to beneficiaries of the recipient's program;

(vi) Deny a qualified handicapped person the opportunity to participate in conferences, in planning or advising recipients, applicants or would-be applicants, or

(vii) Otherwise limit a qualified handicapped person in the enjoyment of any right, privilege, advantage, or opportunity enjoyed by others receiving an aid, benefit, or service.

(2) For purposes of this part, aids, benefits, and services, to be equally effective, are not required to produce the identical result or level of achievement for handicapped and nonhandicapped persons, but must afford handicapped persons equal opportunity to obtain the same result, to gain the same benefit, or to reach the same level of achievement, in the most integrated setting that is reasonably achievable.

(3) Even if separate or different programs or activities are available to handicapped persons, a recipient may not deny a qualified handicapped person the opportunity to participate in the programs or activities that are not separate or different.

(4) A recipient may not, directly or through contractual or other arrangements, utilize criteria or methods of administration:

(i) That have the effect of subjecting qualified handicapped persons to discrimination on the basis of handicap,

(ii) That have the purpose or effect of defeating or substantially reducing the likelihood that handicapped persons can benefit by the objectives of the recipient's program, or

(iii) That yield or perpetuate discrimination against another recipient if both recipients are subject to common administrative control or are agencies of the same State.

(5) In determining the site or location of a facility, an applicant or a recipient may not make selections:

(i) That have the effect of excluding handicapped persons from, denying them the benefits of, or otherwise subjecting them to discrimination under any program or activity that receives or benefits from Federal financial assistance, or

(ii) That have the purpose or effect of defeating or substantially impairing the accomplishment of the objectives of the program or activity with respect to handicapped persons.

(6) As used in this section, the aid benefit, or service provided under a program or activity receiving or benefitting from Federal financial assistance includes any aid, benefit, or service provided in or through a facility that has been constructed, expanded, altered, leased or rented, or otherwise acquired, in whole or in part, with Federal financial assistance.

(c) *Communications.* Recipients shall take appropriate steps to ensure that communications with their applicants, employees, and beneficiaries are available to persons with impaired vision and hearing.

(d) *Programs limited by Federal law.* In programs authorized by Federal statute or executive order that are designed especially for the handicapped, or for a particular class of handicapped persons, the exclusion of nonhandicapped or other classes of handicapped persons is not prohibited by this part.

§ 27.9 Assurance required.

(a) *General.* Each application for Federal financial assistance to carry out a program to which this part applies, and each application to provide a facility, shall, as a condition to approval or extension of any Federal financial assistance pursuant to the application, contain, or be accompanied by, written assurance that the program will be conducted or the facility operated in compliance with all the requirements imposed by or pursuant to this part. An applicant may incorporate these assurances by reference in subsequent applications to the Department.

(b) *Future effect of assurances.* Recipients of Federal financial assistance, and transferees of property obtained by a recipient with the participation of Federal financial assistance, are bound by the recipient's assurance under the following circumstances:

(1) When Federal financial assistance is provided in the form of a conveyance of real property or an interest in real property from the Department of Transportation to a recipient, the instrument of conveyance shall include a convenant running with the land binding the recipient and subsequent transferees to comply with the requirements of this part for so long as the property is used for the purpose for which the Federal financial assistance was provided or for a similar purpose.

(2) When Federal financial assistance is used by a recipient to purchase or improve real property, the assurance provided by the recipient shall obligate the recipient to comply with the requirements of this part and require any subsequent transferee of the property, who is using the property for the purpose for which the Federal financial assistance was provided, to agree in writing to comply with the requirements of this part. The obligations of the recipient and transferees under this part shall continue in effect for as long as the property is used for the purpose for which Federal financial assistance was provided or for a similar purpose.

(3) When Federal financial assistance is provided to the recipient in the form of, or is used by the recipient to obtain, personal property, the assurance provided by the recipient shall obligate the recipient to comply with the requirements of this part for the period it retains ownership or possession of the property or the property is used by a transferee for purposes directly related to the operations of the recipient.

(4) When Federal financial assistance is used by a recipient for purposes other than to obtain property, the assurance provided shall obligate the recipient to comply with the requirements of this part for the period during which the Federal financial assistance is extended to the program.

§ 27.11 Remedial action, voluntary action and compliance planning.

(a) *Remedial action.* (1) If the responsible Departmental official finds that a qualified handicapped person has been excluded from participation in, denied the benefits of, or otherwise subjected to discrimination under, any program or activity in violation of this part, the recipient shall take such remedial action as the responsible Departmental official deems necessary to overcome the effects of the violation.

(2) Where a recipient is found to have violated this part, and where another recipient exercises control over the recipient that has violated this part, the responsible Departmental official, where appropriate, may require either or both recipients to take remedial action.

(3) The responsible Departmental official may, where necessary to overcome the effects of a violation of this part, require a recipient to take remedial action:

(i) With respect to handicapped persons who are no longer participants in the recipient's program but who were participants in the program when such discrimination occurred, and

(ii) With respect to handicapped persons who would have been participants in the program had the discrimination not occurred.

(b) *Voluntary action.* A recipient may take steps, in addition to any action that is required by this part, to assure the full participation in the recipient's program or activity by qualified handicapped persons.

(c) *Compliance planning.* (1) A recipient shall, within 90 days from the effective date of this part, designate and forward to the head of any operating administration providing financial assistance, with a copy to the responsible Departmental official the names, addresses, and telephone numbers of the persons responsible for evaluating the recipient's compliance with this part.

(2) A recipient shall, within 180 days from the effective date of this part, after consultation at each step in paragraphs (c)(2) (i)–(iii) of this section with interested persons, including handicapped persons and organizations representing the handicapped:

(i) Evaluate its current policies and practices for implementing these regulations, and notify the head of the operating administration of the completion of this evaluation;

(ii) Identify shortcomings in compliance and describe the methods used to remedy them;

(iii) Begin to modify, with official approval of recipient's management, any policies or practices that do not meet the requirements of this part according to a schedule or sequence that includes milestones or measures of achievement. These modifications shall be completed within one year from the effective date of this part;

(iv) Take appropriate remedial steps to eliminate the effects of any discrimination that resulted from previous policies and practices; and

(v) Establish a system for periodically reviewing and updating the evaluation.

(3) A recipient shall, for at least three years following completion of the evaluation required under paragraph (c)(2) of this section, maintain on file, make available for public inspection, and furnish upon request to the head of the operating administration:

(i) A list of the interested persons consulted;

(ii) A description of areas examined and any problems indentified; and

(iii) A description of any modifications made and of any remedial steps taken.

§ 27.13 Designation of responsible employee and adoption of grievance procedures.

(a) *Designation of responsible employee.* Each recipient that employs fifteen or more persons shall, within 90 days of the effective date of this regulation, forward to the head of the operating administration that provides financial assistance to the recipient, with a copy to the responsible Departmental official, the name, address, and telephone number of at least one person designated to coordinate its efforts to comply with this part. Each such recipient shall inform the head of the operating administration of any subsequent change.

(b) *Adoption of complaint procedures.* A recipient that employs fifteen or more persons shall, within 180 days, adopt and file with the head of the operating administration procedures that incorporate appropriate due process standards and provide for the prompt and equitable resolution of complaints alleging any action prohibited by this part.

§ 27.15 Notice.

(a) A recipient shall take appropriate initial and continuing steps to notify participants, beneficiaries, applicants, and employees, including those with impaired vision or hearing, and unions or professional organizations holding collective bargaining or professional agreements with the recipient, that it does not discriminate on the basis of handicap. The notification shall state, where appropriate, that the recipient does not discriminate in admission or access to, or treatment or employment in, its programs or activities. The notification shall also include an identification of the responsible employee designated pursuant to § 27.13(a). A recipient shall make the initial notification required by this section within 90 days of the effective date of this part. Methods of initial and continuing notification may include the posting of notices, publication in newspapers and magazines, placement of notices in recipients' publications and distribution of memoranda or other written communications.

(b) If a recipient publishes or uses recruitment materials or publications containing general information that it makes available to participants, beneficiaries, applicants, or employees, it shall include in those materials or publications a statement of the policy described in paragraph (a) of this section. A recipient may meet the requirement of this paragraph either by including appropriate inserts in existing materials and publications or by revising and reprinting the materials and publications. In either case, the addition or revision must be specially noted.

§ 27.17 Effect of State or local law.

The obligation to comply with this part is not obviated or affected by any State or local law.

§ 27.19 Compliance with Americans with Disabilities Act requirements and FTA policy.

(a) Recipients subject to this part (whether public or private entities as defined in 49 CFR part 37) shall comply with all applicable requirements of the Americans with Disabilities Act (ADA) of 1990 (42 U.S.C. 12101–12213) including the Department's ADA regulations (49 CFR parts 37 and 38), the regulations of the Department of Justice implementing titles II and III of the ADA (28 CFR parts 35 and 36), and the regulations of the Equal Employment Opportunity Commission (EEOC) implementing title I of the ADA (29 CFR part 1630). Compliance with the EEOC title I regulations is required as a condition of compliance with section 504 for DOT recipients even for organizations which, because they have fewer than 25 or 15 employees, would not be subject to the EEOC regulation in its own right. Compliance with all these regulations is a condition of receiving Federal financial assistance from the Department of Transportation. Any recipient not in compliance with this requirement shall be subject to enforcement action under subpart F of this part.

(b) Consistent with FTA policy, any recipient of Federal financial assistance from the Federal Transit Administration whose solicitation was made before August 26, 1990, and is for one or more inaccessible vehicles, shall provide written notice to the Secretary (e.g., in the case of a solicitation made in the past under which the recipient can order additional new buses after the effective date of this section). The Secretary shall review each case individually, and determine whether the Department will continue to participate in the Federal grant, consistent with the provisions in the grant agreement between the Department and the recipient.

[55 FR 40763, Oct. 4, 1990, as amended at 56 FR 45621, Sept. 6, 1991]

Subpart B — Program Accessibility Requirements in Specific Operating Administration Programs: Airports, Railroads, and Highways

§ 27.71 Federal Aviation Administration — airports.

(a) *Fixed facilities; new terminals.* (1) Terminal facilities designed and constructed by or for the use of a recipient of Federal financial assistance on or after the effective date of this part, the intended use of which will require it to be accessible to the public or may result in the employment therein of physically handicapped persons, shall be designed or constructed in accordance with the accessibility standards referenced in § 27.3(b) of this part. Where there is apparent ambiguity or contradiction between the definitions and the standards referenced in § 27.3(b) and the definitions and standards used in paragraph (a)(2) of this section, the terms in the standards referenced in § 27.3(b) should be interpreted in a manner that will make them consistent with the standards in paragraph (a)(2) of this section. If this cannot be done, the standards in paragraph (a)(2) of this section prevail.

(2) In addition to the accessibility standards referenced in § 27.3(b) of this part, the following standards apply to new airport terminal facilities:

(i) *Airport terminal circulation and flow.* The basic terminal design shall permit efficient entrance and movement of handicapped persons while at the same time giving consideration to their convenience, comfort, and safety. It is also essential that the design, especially concerning the location of elevators, escalators, and similar devices, minimize any extra distance that wheel chair users must travel compared to nonhandicapped persons, to reach ticket counters, waiting areas, baggage handling areas, and boarding locations.

(ii) *International accessibility symbol.* The international accessibility symbol shall be displayed at accessible entrances to buildings that meet the ANSI standards.

(iii) *Ticketing.* The ticketing system shall be designed to provide handicapped persons with the opportunity to use the primary fare collection area to obtain ticket issuance and make fare payment.

(iv) *Baggage check-in and retrieval.* Baggage areas shall be accessible to handicapped persons. The facility shall be designed to provide for efficient handling and retrieval of baggage by all persons.

(v) *Boarding.* Each operator at an airport receiving any Federal financial assistance shall assure that adequate assistance is provided for enplaning and deplaning handicapped persons. Boarding by level entry boarding platforms and by passenger lounges are the preferred methods for movement of handicapped persons between terminal buildings and aircraft at air carrier airports; however, where this is not practicable, operators at air carrier airport terminals shall assure that there are lifts, ramps, or other suitable devices not normally used for movement of freight that are available for enplaning and deplaning wheelchair users.

(vi) *Telephones.* Wherever there are public telephone centers in terminals, at least one clearly marked telephone shall be equipped with a volume control or sound booster device and with a device available to handicapped persons that makes telephone communication possible for persons wearing hearing aids.

(vii) *Teletypewriter.* Each airport shall ensure that there is sufficient teletypewriter (TTY) service to permit hearing-impaired persons to communicate readily with airline ticket agents and other personnel.

(viii) *Vehicular loading and unloading areas.* Several spaces adjacent to the terminal building entrance, separated from the main flow of traffic, and clearly marked, shall be made available for the loading and unloading of handicapped passengers from motor vehicles. The spaces shall allow individuals in wheelchairs or with braces or crutches to get in and out of automobiles onto a level surface suitable for wheeling and walking.

(ix) *Parking.* In addition to the requirements in the accessibility standards referenced in § 27.3(b) of this part the following requirements shall be met:

(A) Curb cuts or ramps with grades not exceeding 8.33 percent shall be provided at crosswalks between park areas and the terminal;

(B) Where multi-level parking is provided, ample and clearly marked space shall be reserved for ambulatory and semi-ambulatory handicapped persons on the level nearest the ticketing and boarding portion of the terminal facilities, and

(C) In multi-level parking areas, elevators, ramps, or other devices that can accommodate wheelchair users shall be easily available.

(x) *Waiting area/public space.* As the major public area of the airport terminal facility, the environment in the waiting area/public space should give the handicapped person confidence and security in using the facility. The space shall be designed to accommodate the handicapped providing clear direction about how to use all passenger facilities.

(xi) *Airport terminal information.* Airport terminal information systems shall take into consideration the needs of handicapped persons. The primary information mode shall be visual words and letters, or symbols, using lighting and color coding. Airport terminals shall also have facilities providing information orally.

(xii) *Public services.* Public service facilities such as public toilets, drinking fountains, telephones, travelers aid and first aid medical facilities shall be designed in accordance with accessibility standards referenced in § 27.3(b) of this part.

(b) *Fixed facilities; existing terminals* — (1) *Structural changes.* Where structural changes are necessary to make existing air carrier terminals which are owned and operated by recipients of Federal financial assistance accessible to and usable by handicapped persons, such changes shall be made in accordance with the ANSI standards as soon as practicable, but in no event later than three years after the effective date of this part.

(2) *Ongoing renovation.* In terminals that are undergoing structural changes involving entrances, exits, interior doors, elevators, stairs, baggage areas, drinking fountains, toilets, telephones, eating places, curbs, and parking areas, recipients shall begin immediately to incorporate accessibility features.

(3) *Transition.* Where extensive structural changes to existing facilities are necessary to meet accessibility requirements, recipients shall develop a transition plan in accordance with § 27.65(d) and submit it to the Federal Aviation Administration (FAA). Transition plans are reviewed and approved or disapproved by the FAA as expeditiously as possible after they are received.

(4) *Boarding.* Each operator at an airport receiving any Federal financial assistance shall assure that adequate assistance is provided incident to enplaning and deplaning handicapped persons. Within three years from the effective date of this part, recipients operating terminals at air carrier airports that are not equipped with jetways or passenger lounges for boarding and unboarding shall assure that there are lifts, ramps, or other suitable devices, not normally used for movement of freight, are available for enplaning and deplaning wheelchair users.

(5) *Passenger services.* Recipients operating terminals at air carrier airports shall assure that there are provisions for assisting handicapped passengers upon request in movement into, out of, and within the terminal, and in the use of terminal facilities, including baggage handling.

(6) *Guide dogs.* Seeing eye and hearing guide dogs shall be permitted to accompany their owners and shall be accorded all the privileges of the passengers whom they accompany in regard to access to terminals and facilities.

[44 FR 31468, May 31, 1979, as amended by Amdt. 27–3, 51 FR 19017, May 23, 1986. Redesignated at 56 FR 45621, Sept. 6, 1991]

§ 27.75 Federal Highway Administration — highways.

(a) *New facilities* — (1) *Highway rest area facilities.* All such facilities that will be constructed with Federal financial assistance shall be designed and constructed in accordance with the accessibility standards referenced in § 27.3(b) of this part.

(2) *Curb cuts.* All pedestrian cross-walks constructed with Federal financial assistance shall have curb cuts or ramps to accommodate persons in wheelchairs, pursuant to section 228 of the Federal-Aid Highway Act of 1973 (23 U.S.C. 402(b)(1)(F)).

(3) *Pedestrian over-passes, under-passes and ramps.* Pedestrian over-passes, under-passes and ramps, constructed with Federal financial assistance, shall be accessible to handicapped persons, including having gradients no steeper than 10 percent, unless:

(i) Alternate safe means are provided to enable mobility-limited persons to cross the roadway at that location; or

(ii) It would be infeasible for mobility-limited persons to reach the over-passes, under-passes or ramps because of unusual topographical or architectural obstacles unrelated to the federally assisted facility.

(b) *Existing facilities — Rest area facilities.* Rest area facilities on Interstate highways shall be made accessible to handicapped persons, including wheelchair users, within a three-year period after the effective date of this part. Other rest area facilities shall be made accessible when Federal financial assistance is used to improve the rest area, or when the roadway adjacent to or in the near vicinity of the rest area is constructed, reconstructed or otherwise altered with Federal financial assistance.

[44 FR 31468, May 31, 1979, as amended by Amdt. 27–3, 51 FR 19017, May 23, 1986. Redesignated at 56 FR 45621, Sept. 6, 1991]

Subpart C — Enforcement

SOURCE: 44 FR 31468, May 31, 1979. Redesignated at 56 FR 45621, Sept. 6, 1991.

§ 27.121 Compliance information.

(a) *Cooperation and assistance.* The responsible Departmental official, to the fullest extent practicable, seeks the cooperation of recipients in securing compliance with this part and provides assistance and guidance to recipients to help them comply with this part.

(b) *Compliance reports.* Each recipient shall keep on file for one year all complaints of noncompliance received. A record of all such complaints, which may be in summary form, shall be kept for five years. Each recipient shall keep such other records and submit to the responsible Departmental official or his/her designee timely, complete, and accurate compliance reports at such times, and in such form, and containing such information as the responsible Department official may prescribe. In the case of any program under which a primary recipient extends Federal financial assistance to any other recipient, the other recipient shall also submit compliance reports to the primary recipient so as to enable the primary recipient to prepare its report.

(c) *Access to sources of information.* Each recipient shall permit access by the responsible Departmental official or his/her designee during normal business hours to books, records, accounts, and other sources of information, and to facilities that are pertinent to compliance with this part. Where required information is in the exclusive possession of another agency or person who fails or refuses to furnish the information, the recipient shall so certify in its report and describe the efforts made to obtain the information. Considerations of privacy or confidentiality do not bar the Department from evaluating or seeking to enforce compliance with this part. Information of a confidential nature obtained in connection with compliance evaluation or enforcement is not disclosed by the Department, except in formal enforcement proceedings, where necessary, or where otherwise required by law.

(d) *Information to beneficiaries and participants.* Each recipient shall make available to participants, beneficiaries, and other interested persons such information regarding the provisions of this regulation and its application to the program for which the recipient receives Federal financial assistance, and make such information available to them in such manner, as the responsible Departmental official finds necessary to apprise them of the protections against discrimination provided by the Act and this part.

§ 27.123 Conduct of investigations.

(a) *Periodic compliance reviews.* The responsible Departmental official or his/her designee, from time to time, reviews the practices of recipients to determine whether they are complying with this part.

(b) *Complaints.* Any person who believes himself/herself or any specific class of individuals to be harmed by failure to comply with this part may, personally or through a representative, file a written complaint with the responsible Departmental official. A Complaint must be filed not later than 180 days from the date of the alleged discrimination, unless the time for filing is extended by the responsible Departmental official or his/her designee.

(c) *Investigations.* The responsible Departmental official or his/her designee makes a prompt investigation whenever a compliance review, report, complaint, or any other information indicates a possible failure to comply with this part. The investigation includes, where appropriate, a review of the pertinent practices and policies of the recipient, and the circumstances under which the possible noncompliance with this part occurred.

(d) *Resolution of matters.* (1) If, after an investigation pursuant to paragraph (c) of this section, the responsible Departmental official finds reasonable cause to believe that there is a failure to comply with this part, the responsible Departmental official will inform the recipient. The matter is resolved by informal means whenever possible. If the responsible Departmental official determines that the matter cannot be resolved by informal means, action is taken as provided in § 27.125.

(2) If an investigation does not warrant action pursuant to paragraph (d)(1) of this section, the responsible Departmental official or his/her designee so informs the recipient and the complainant, if any, in writing.

(e) *Intimidating and retaliatory acts prohibited.* No employee or contractor of a recipient shall intimidate, threaten, coerce, or discriminate against any individual for the purpose of interfering with any right or privilege secured by section 504 of the Act or this part, or because the individual has made a complaint, testified, assisted, or participated in any manner in an investigation, hearing, or proceeding, under this part. The identity of complainants is kept confidential at their election during the conduct of any investigation, hearing or proceeding under this part. However, when such confidentiality is likely to hinder the investigation, the complainant will be advised for the purpose of waiving the privilege.

§ 27.125 Compliance procedure.

(a) *General.* If there is reasonable cause for the responsible Departmental official to believe that there is a failure to comply with any provision of this part that cannot be corrected by informal means, the responsible Departmental official may recommend suspension or termination of, or refusal to grant or to continue Federal financial assistance, or take any other steps authorized by law. Such other steps may include, but are not limited to:

(1) A referral to the Department of Justice with a recommendation that appropriate proceedings be brought to enforce any rights of the United States under any law of the United States (including other titles of the Act), or any assurance or other contractural undertaking; and

(2) Any applicable proceeding under State or local law.

(b) *Refusal of Federal financial assistance.* (1) No order suspending, terminating, or refusing to grant or continue Federal financial assistance becomes effective until:

(i) The responsible Departmental official has advised the applicant or recipient of its failure to comply and has determined that compliance cannot be secured by voluntary means; and

(ii) There has been an express finding by the Secretary on the record, after opportunity for hearing, of a failure by the applicant or recipient to comply with a requirement imposed by or pursuant to this part.

(2) Any action to suspend, terminate, or refuse to grant or to continue Federal financial assistance is limited to the particular recipient who has failed to comply, and is limited in its effect to the particular program, or part thereof, in which noncompliance has been found.

(c) *Other means authorized by law.* No other action is taken until:

(1) The responsible Departmental official has determined that compliance cannot be secured by voluntary means;

(2) The recipient or other person has been notified by the responsible Departmental official of its failure to comply and of the proposed action;

(3) The expiration of at least 10 days from the mailing of such notice to the recipient or other person. During this period, additional efforts are made to persuade the recipient or other person to comply with the regulations and to take such corrective action as may be appropriate.

§ 27.127 Hearings.

(a) *Opportunity for hearing.* Whenever an opportunity for a hearing is required by § 27.125(b), reasonable notice is given by the responsible Departmental official by registered or certified mail, return receipt requested, to the affected applicant or recipient. This notice advises the applicant or recipient of the action proposed to be taken, the specific provision under which the proposed action is to be taken, and the matters of fact or law asserted as the basis for this action, and either:

(1) Fixes a date not less than 20 days after the date of such notice within which the applicant or recipient may request a hearing; or

(2) Advises the applicant or recipient that the matter in question has been set for hearing at a stated place and time.

The time and place shall be reasonable and subject to change for cause. The complainant, if any, also is advised of the time and place of the hearing. An applicant or recipient may waive a hearing and submit written information and argument for the record. The failure of an applicant or recipient to request a hearing constitutes a waiver of the right to a hearing under section 504 of the Act and § 27.125(b), and consent to the making of a decision on the basis of such information as may be part of the record.

(b) If the applicant or recipient waives its opportunity for a hearing, the responsible Departmental official shall notify the applicant or recipient that it has the opportunity to submit written information and argument for the record. The responsible Departmental official may also place written information and argument into the record.

(c) *Time and place of hearing.* Hearings are held at the office of the Department in Washington, DC, at a time fixed by the responsible Departmental official unless he/she determines that the convenience of the applicant or recipient or of the Department requires that another place be selected. Hearings are held before an Administrative Law Judge designated in accordance with 5 U.S.C. 3105 and 3344 (section 11 of the Administrative Procedure Act).

(d) *Right to counsel.* In all proceedings under this section, the applicant or recipient and the responsible Departmental official have the right to be represented by counsel.

(e) *Procedures, evidence and record.* (1) The hearing, decision, and any administrative review thereof are conducted in conformity with sections

554 through 557 of title 5 of the United States Code, and in accordance with such rules of procedure as are proper (and not inconsistent with this section) relating to the conduct of the hearing, giving notice subsequent to those provided for in paragraph (a) of this section, taking testimony, exhibits, arguments and briefs, requests for findings, and other related matters. The responsible Departmental official and the applicant or recipient are entitled to introduce all relevant evidence on the issues as stated in the notice for hearing or as determined by the officer conducting the hearing. Any person (other than a government employee considered to be on official business) who, having been invited or requested to appear and testify as a witness on the government's behalf, attends at a time and place scheduled for a hearing provided for by this part may be reimbursed for his/her travel and actual expenses in an amount not to exceed the amount payable under the standardized travel regulations applicable to a government employee traveling on official business.

(2) Technical rules of evidence do not apply to hearings conducted pursuant to this part, but rules or principles designed to assure production of the most credible evidence available and to subject testimony to cross examination are applied where reasonably necessary by the Administrative Law Judge conducting the hearing. The Administrative Law Judge may exclude irrelevant, immaterial, or unduly repetitious evidence. All documents and other evidence offered or taken for the record are open to examination by the parties and opportunity is given to refute facts and arguments advanced by either side. A transcript is made of the oral evidence except to the extent the substance thereof is stipulated for the record. All decisions are based on the hearing record and written findings shall be made.

(f) *Consolidation or joint hearings.* In cases in which the same or related facts are asserted to constitute noncompliance with this regulation with respect to two or more programs to which this part applies, or noncompliance with this part and the regulations of one or more other Federal departments or agencies issued under section 504 of the Act, the responsible Departmental official may, in agreement with such other departments or agencies, where applicable, provide for consolidated or joint hearings. Final decisions in such cases, insofar as this regulation is concerned, are made in accordance with § 27.129.

§ 27.129 Decisions and notices.

(a) *Decisions by Administrative Law Judge.* After the hearing, the Administrative Law Judge certifies the entire record including his recommended findings and proposed decision to the Secretary for a final decision. A copy of the certification is mailed to the applicant or recipient and to the complainant, if any. The responsible Departmental official and the applicant or recipient may submit written arguments to the Secretary concerning the Administrative Law Judge's recommended findings and proposed decision.

(b) *Final decision by the Secretary.* When the record is certified to the Secretary by the Administrative Law Judge, the Secretary reviews the record and accepts, rejects, or modifies the Administrative Law Judge's recommended findings and proposed decision, stating the reasons therefore.

(c) *Decisions if hearing is waived.* Whenever a hearing pursuant to § 27.125(b) is waived, the Secretary makes his/her final decision on the record, stating the reasons therefor.

(d) *Rulings required.* Each decision of the Administrative Law Judge or the Secretary contains a ruling on each finding or conclusion presented and specifies any failures to comply with this part.

(e) *Content of orders.* The final decision may provide for suspension or termination, or refusal to grant or continue Federal financial assistance, in whole or in part, under the program involved. The decision may contain such terms, conditions, and other provisions as are consistent with and will effectuate the purposes of the Act and this part, including provisions designed to assure that no Federal financial assistance will thereafter be extended unless and until the recipient corrects its noncompliance and satisfies the Secretary that it will fully comply with this part.

(f) *Subsequent proceedings.* (1) An applicant or recipient adversely affected by an order issued under paragraph (e) of this section is restored to full eligibility to receive Federal financial assistance if it satisfies the terms and conditions of that order or if it brings itself into compliance with this part and provides reasonable assurance that it will fully comply with this part.

(2) Any applicant or recipient adversely affected by an order entered pursuant to paragraph (e) of this section may, at any time, request the responsible Departmental official to restore its eligibility, to receive Federal financial assistance. Any request must be supported by information showing that the applicant or recipient has met the requirements of paragraph (f)(1) of this section. If the responsible Departmental official determines that those requirements have been satisfied, he/she may restore such eligibility, subject to the approval of the Secretary.

(3) If the responsible Departmental official denies any such request, the applicant or recipient may submit a request, in writing, for a hearing specifying why it believes the responsible Departmental official should restore it to full eligibility. It is thereupon given a prompt hearing, with a decision on the record. The applicant or recipient is restored to eligibility if it demonstrates to the satisfaction of the Secretary at the hearing that it satisfied the requirements of paragraph (f)(1) of this section.

(4) The hearing procedures of § 27.127(b) through (c) and paragraphs (a) through (d) of this section apply to hearings held under paragraph (f)(3) of this section.

(5) While proceedings under this paragraph are pending, the sanctions imposed by the order issued under paragraph (e) of this section shall remain in effect.

PART 37 — TRANSPORTATION SERVICES FOR INDIVIDUALS WITH DISABILITIES (ADA)

Subpart A — General

Subpart B — Applicability

Subpart C — Transportation Facilities

Subpart D — Acquisition of Accessible Vehicles by Public Entities

37.71 Purchase or lease of new non-rail vehicles by public entities operating fixed route systems.

37.73 Purchase or lease of used non-rail vehicles by public entities operating fixed route systems.

37.75 Remanufacture of non-rail vehicles and purchase or lease of remanufactured non-rail vehicles by public entities operating fixed route systems.

37.77 Purchase or lease of new non-rail vehicles by public entities operating demand responsive systems for the general public.

37.79 Purchase or lease of new rail vehicles by public entities operating rapid or light rail systems.

37.81 Purchase or lease of used rail vehicles by public entities operating rapid or light rail systems.

37.83 Remanufacture of rail vehicles and purchase or lease of remanufactured rail vehicles by public entities operating rapid or light rail systems.

37.85 Purchase or lease of new intercity and commuter rail cars.

37.87 Purchase or lease of used intercity and commuter rail cars.

37.89 Remanufacture of intercity and commuter rail cars and purchase or lease of remanufactured intercity and commuter rail cars.

37.91 Wheelchair locations and food service on intercity rail trains.

37.93 One car per train rule.

37.95 Ferries and other passenger vessels operated by public entities. [Reserved]

37.97 — 37.99 [Reserved]

Subpart E — Acquisition of Accessible Vehicles by Private Entities

37.101 Purchase or lease of vehicles by private entities not primarily engaged in the business of transporting people.

37.103 Purchase or lease of new non-rail vehicles by private entities primarily engaged in the business of transporting people.

37.105 Equivalent service standard.

37.107 Acquisition of passenger rail cars by private entities primarily engaged in the business of transporting people.

37.109 Ferries and other passenger vessels operated by private entities. [Reserved]

37.111 — 37.119 [Reserved]

Subpart F — Paratransit as a Complement to Fixed Route Service

37.121 Requirement for comparable complementary paratransit service.

37.123 ADA paratransit eligibility: Standards.

37.125 ADA paratransit eligibility: Process.

Subpart G — Provision of Service

AUTHORITY: Americans with Disabilities Act of 1990 (42 U.S.C. 12101–12213); 49 U.S.C. 322.

SOURCE: 56 FR 45621, Sept. 6, 1991, unless otherwise noted.

EDITORIAL NOTE: Nomenclature changes to part 37 appear at 58 FR 63101, Nov. 30, 1993.

Subpart A — General

§ 37.1 Purpose.

The purpose of this part is to implement the transportation and related provisions of titles II and III of the Americans with Disabilities Act of 1990.

§ 37.3 Definitions.

As used in this part:

Accessible means, with respect to vehicles and facilities, complying with the accessibility requirements of parts 37 and 38 of this title.

The Act or *ADA* means the Americans with Disabilities Act of 1990 (Pub. L. 101–336, 104 Stat. 327, 42 U.S.C. 12101–12213 and 47 U.S.C. 225 and 611), as it may be amended from time to time.

Administrator means Administrator of the Federal Transit Administration, or his or her designee.

Alteration means a change to an existing facility, including, but not limited to, remodeling, renovation, rehabilitation, reconstruction, historic restoration, changes or rearrangement in structural parts or elements, and changes or rearrangement in the plan configuration of walls and full-height partitions. Normal maintenance, reroofing, painting or wallpapering, asbestos removal, or changes to mechanical or electrical systems are not alterations unless they affect the usability of the building or facility.

Automated guideway transit system or *AGT* means a fixed-guideway transit system which operates with automated (driverless) individual vehicles or multi-car trains. Service may be on a fixed schedule or in response to a passenger-activated call button.

Auxiliary aids and services includes:

(1) Qualified interpreters, notetakers, transcription services, written materials, telephone headset amplifiers, assistive listening devices, assistive listening systems, telephones compatible with hearing aids, closed caption decoders, closed and open captioning, text telephones (also known as telephone devices for the deaf, or TDDs), videotext displays, or other effective methods of making aurally delivered materials available to individuals with hearing impairments;

(2) Qualified readers, taped texts, audio recordings, Brailled materials, large print materials, or other effective methods of making visually delivered materials available to individuals with visual impairments;

(3) Acquisition or modification of equipment or devices; or

(4) Other similar services or actions.

Bus means any of several types of self-propelled vehicles, generally rubber-tired, intended for use on city streets, highways, and busways, including but not limited to minibuses, forty- and thirty-foot buses, articulated buses, double-deck buses, and electrically powered trolley buses, used by public entities to provide designated public transportation service and by private entities to provide transportation service including, but not limited to, specified public transportation services. Self-propelled, rubber-tired vehicles designed to look like antique or vintage trolleys are considered buses.

Commerce means travel, trade, transportation, or communication among the several states, between any foreign country or any territory or possession and any state, or between points in the same state but through another state or foreign country.

Commuter authority means any state, local, regional authority, corporation, or other entity established for purposes of providing commuter rail transportation (including, but not necessarily limited to, the New York Metropolitan Transportation Authority, the Connecticut Department of Transportation, the Maryland Department of Transportation, the Southeastern Pennsylvania Transportation Authority, the New Jersey Transit Corporation, the Massachusetts Bay Transportation Authority, the Port Authority Trans-Hudson Corporation, and any successor agencies) and any entity created by one or more such agencies for the purposes of operating, or contracting for the operation of, commuter rail transportation.

Commuter bus service means fixed route bus service, characterized by service predominantly in one direction during peak periods, limited stops, use of multi-ride tickets, and routes of extended length, usually between the central business district and outlying suburbs. Commuter bus service may also include other service, characterized by a limited route structure, limited stops, and a coordinated relationship to another mode of transportation.

Commuter rail car means a rail passenger car obtained by a commuter authority for use in commuter rail transportation.

Commuter rail transportation means short-haul rail passenger service operating in metropolitan and suburban areas, whether within or across the geographical boundaries of a state, usually characterized by reduced fare, multiple ride, and commutation tickets and by morning and evening peak period operations. This term does not include light or rapid rail transportation.

Demand responsive system means any system of transporting individuals, including the provision of designated public transportation service by public entities and the provision of transportation service by private entities, including but not limited to specified public transportation service, which is not a fixed route system.

Designated public transportation means transportation provided by a public entity (other than public school transportation) by bus, rail, or other conveyance (other than transportation by aircraft or intercity or commuter rail transportation) that provides the general public with general or special service, including charter service, on a regular and containing basis.

Disability means, with respect to an individual, a physical or mental impairment that substantially limits one or more of the major life activities of such individual; a record of such an impairment; or being regarded as having such an impairment.

(1) The phrase *physical or mental impairment* means —

(i) Any physiological disorder or condition, cosmetic disfigurement, or anatomical loss affecting one or more of the following body systems: neurological, musculoskeletal, special sense organs, respiratory including speech organs, cardiovascular, reproductive, digestive, genito-urinary, hemic and lymphatic, skin, and endocrine;

(ii) Any mental or psychological disorder, such as mental retardation, organic brain syndrome, emotional or mental illness, and specific learning disabilities;

(iii) The term *physical or mental impairment* includes, but is not limited to, such contagious or noncontagious diseases and conditions as orthopedic, visual, speech, and hearing impairments; cerebral palsy, epilepsy, muscular dystrophy, multiple sclerosis, cancer, heart disease, diabetes, mental retardation, emotional illness, specific learning disabilities, HIV disease, tuberculosis, drug addiction and alcoholism;

(iv) The phrase *physical or mental impairment* does not include homosexuality or bisexuality.

(2) The phrase *major life activities* means functions such as caring for one's self, performing manual tasks, walking, seeing, hearing, speaking, breathing, learning, and work.

(3) The phrase *has a record of such an impairment* means has a history of, or has been misclassified as having, a mental or physical impairment that substantially limits one or more major life activities.

(4) The phrase *is regarded as having such an impairment* means —
(i) Has a physical or mental impairment that does not substantially limit major life activities, but which is treated by a public or private entity as constituting such a limitation;

(ii) Has a physical or mental impairment that substantially limits a major life activity only as a result of the attitudes of others toward such an impairment; or

(iii) Has none of the impairments defined in paragraph (1) of this definition but is treated by a public or private entity as having such an impairment.

(5) The term *disability* does not include —

(i) Transvestism, transsexualism, pedophilia, exhibitionism, voyeurism, gender identity disorders not resulting from physical impairments, or other sexual behavior disorders;

(ii) Compulsive gambling, kleptomania, or pyromania;

(iii) Psychoactive substance abuse disorders resulting from the current illegal use of drugs.

Facility means all or any portion of buildings, structures, sites, complexes, equipment, roads, walks, passageways, parking lots, or other real or personal property, including the site where the building, property, structure, or equipment is located.

Fixed route system means a system of transporting individuals (other than by aircraft), including the provision of designated public transportation service by public entities and the provision of transportation service by private entities, including, but not limited to, specified public transportation service, on which a vehicle is operated along a prescribed route according to a fixed schedule.

FT Act means the Federal Transit Act of 1964, as amended (49 U.S.C. App. 1601 *et seq.*).

High speed rail means a rail service having the characteristics of intercity rail service which operates primarily on a dedicated guideway or track not used, for the most part, by freight, including, but not limited to, trains on welded rail, magnetically levitated (maglev) vehicles on a special guideway, or other advanced technology vehicles, designed to travel at speeds in excess of those possible on other types of railroads.

Individual with a disability means a person who has a disability, but does not include an individual who is currently engaging in the illegal use of drugs, when a public or private entity acts on the basis of such use.

Intercity rail passenger car means a rail car, intended for use by revenue passengers, obtained by the National Railroad Passenger Corporation (Amtrak) for use in intercity rail transportation.

Intercity rail transportation means transportation provided by Amtrak.

Light rail means a streetcar-type vehicle operated on city streets, semi-exclusive rights of way, or exclusive rights of way. Service may be provided by step-entry vehicles or by level boarding.

New vehicle means a vehicle which is offered for sale or lease after manufacture without any prior use.

Operates includes, with respect to a fixed route or demand responsive system, the provision of transportation service by a public or private entity itself or by a person under a contractual or other arrangement or relationship with the entity.

Over-the-road bus means a bus characterized by an elevated passenger deck located over a baggage compartment.

Paratransit means comparable transportation service required by the ADA for individuals with disabilities who are unable to use fixed route transportation systems.

Private entity means any entity other than a public entity.

Public entity means:

(1) Any state or local government;

(2) Any department, agency, special purpose district, or other instrumentality of one or more state or local governments; and

(3) The National Railroad Passenger Corporation (Amtrak) and any commuter authority.

Purchase or lease, with respect to vehicles, means the time at which an entity is legally obligated to obtain the vehicles, such as the time of contract execution.

Public school transportation means transportation by schoolbus vehicles of schoolchildren, personnel, and equipment to and from a public elementary or secondary school and school-related activities.

Rapid rail means a subway-type transit vehicle railway operated on exclusive private rights of way with high level platform stations. Rapid rail also may operate on elevated or at grade level track separated from other traffic.

Remanufactured vehicle means a vehicle which has been structurally restored and has had new or rebuilt major components installed to extend its service life.

Secretary means the Secretary of Transportation or his/her designee.

Section 504 means section 504 of the Rehabilitation Act of 1973 (Pub. L. 93–112, 87 Stat. 394, 29 U.S.C. 794), as amended.

Service animal means any guide dog, signal dog, or other animal individually trained to work or perform tasks for an individual with a disability, including, but not limited to, guiding individuals with impaired vision, alerting individuals with impaired hearing to intruders or sounds, providing minimal protection or rescue work, pulling a wheelchair, or fetching dropped items.

Solicitation means the closing date for the submission of bids or offers in a procurement.

Specified public transportation means transportation by bus, rail, or any other conveyance (other than aircraft) provided by a private entity to the general public, with general or special service (including charter service) on a regular and continuing basis.

Station means, with respect to intercity and commuter rail transportation, the portion of a property located appurtenant to a right of way on which intercity or commuter rail transportation is operated, where such portion is used by the general public and is related to the provision of such transportation, including passenger platforms, designated waiting areas, restrooms, and, where a public entity providing rail transportation owns the property, concession areas, to the extent that such public entity exercises control over the selection, design, construction, or alteration of the property, but this term does not include flag stops (i.e., stations which are not regularly scheduled stops but at which trains will stop to board or detrain passengers only on signal or advance notice).

Transit facility means, for purposes of determining the number of text telephones needed consistent with section 10.3.1(12) of appendix A to this part, a physical structure the primary function of which is to facilitate access to and from a transportation system which has scheduled stops at the structure. The term does not include an open structure or a physical structure the primary purpose of which is other than providing transportation services.

Used vehicle means a vehicle with prior use.

Vanpool means a voluntary commuter ridesharing arrangement, using vans with a seating capacity greater than 7 persons (including the driver) or buses, which provides transportation to a group of individuals traveling directly from their homes to their regular places of work within the same geographical area, and in which the commuter/driver does not receive compensation beyond reimbursement for his or her costs of providing the service.

Vehicle, as the term is applied to private entities, does not include a rail passenger car, railroad locomotive, railroad freight car, or railroad caboose, or other rail rolling stock described in section 242 of title III of the Act.

Wheelchair means a mobility aid belonging to any class of three or four-wheeled devices, usable indoors, designed for and used by individuals with mobility impairments, whether operated manually or powered. A "common wheelchair" is such a device which does not exceed 30 inches in width and 48 inches in length measured two inches above the ground, and does not weigh more than 600 pounds when occupied.

[56 FR 45621, Sept. 6, 1991, as amended at 58 FR 63101, Nov. 30, 1993]

§ 37.5 Nondiscrimination.

(a) No entity shall discriminate against an individual with a disability in connection with the provision of transportation service.

(b) Notwithstanding the provision of any special transportation service to individuals with disabilities, an entity shall not, on the basis of disability, deny to any individual with a disability the opportunity to use the entity's transportation service for the general public, if the individual is capable of using that service.

(c) An entity shall not require an individual with a disability to use designated priority seats, if the individual does not choose to use these seats.

(d) An entity shall not impose special charges, not authorized by this part, on individuals with disabilities, including individuals who use wheelchairs, for providing services required by this part or otherwise necessary to accommodate them.

(e) An entity shall not require that an individual with disabilities be accompanied by an attendant.

(f) Private entities that are primarily engaged in the business of transporting people and whose operations affect commerce shall not discriminate against any individual on the basis of disability in the full and equal enjoyment of specified transportation services. This obligation includes, with respect to the provision of transportation services, compliance with the requirements of the rules of the Department of Justice concerning eligibility criteria, making reasonable modifications, providing auxiliary aids and services, and removing barriers (28 CFR 36.301 — 36.306).

(g) An entity shall not refuse to serve an individual with a disability or require anything contrary to this part because its insurance company conditions coverage or rates on the absence of individuals with disabilities or requirements contrary to this part.

(h) It is not discrimination under this part for an entity to refuse to provide service to an individual with disabilities because that individual engages in violent, seriously disruptive, or illegal conduct. However, an entity shall not refuse to provide service to an individual with disabilities solely because the individual's disability results in appearance or involuntary behavior that may offend, annoy, or inconvenience employees of the entity or other persons.

§ 37.7 Standards for accessible vehicles.

(a) For purposes of this part, a vehicle shall be considered to be readily accessible to and usable by individuals with disabilities if it meets the requirements of this part and the standards set forth in part 38 of this title.

(b)(1) For purposes of implementing the equivalent facilitation provision in § 38.2 of this subtitle, the following parties may submit to the Administrator of the applicable operating administration a request for a determination of equivalent facilitation:

(i) A public or private entity that provides transportation services and is subject to the provisions of subpart D or subpart E this part; or

(ii) The manufacturer of a vehicle or a vehicle component or subsystem to be used by such entity to comply with this part.

(2) The requesting party shall provide the following information with its request:

(i) Entity name, address, contact person and telephone;

(ii) Specific provision of part 38 of this subtitle with which the entity is unable to comply;

(iii) Reasons for inability to comply;

(iv) Alternative method of compliance, with demonstration of how the alternative meets or exceeds the level of accessibility or usability of the vehicle provided in part 38 of this subtitle; and

(v) Documentation of the public participation used in developing an alternative method of compliance.

(3) In the case of a request by a public entity that provides transportation services subject to the provisions of subpart D of this part, the required public participation shall include the following:

(i) The entity shall contact individuals with disabilities and groups representing them in the community. Consultation with these individuals and groups shall take place at all stages of the development of the request for equivalent facilitation. All documents and other information concerning the request shall be available, upon request, to members of the public.

(ii) The entity shall make its proposed request available for public comment before the request is made final or transmitted to DOT. In making the request available for public review, the entity shall ensure that it is available, upon request, in accessible formats.

(iii) The entity shall sponsor at least one public hearing on the request and shall provide adequate notice of the hearing, including advertisement in appropriate media, such as newspapers of general and special interest circulation and radio announcements.

(4) In the case of a request by a private entity that provides transportation services subject to the provisions of subpart E of this part or a manufacturer, the private entity or manufacturer shall consult, in person, in writing, or by other appropriate means, with representatives of national and local organizations representing people with those disabilities who would be affected by the request.

(5) A determination of compliance will be made by the Administrator of the concerned operating administration on a case-by-case basis, with the concurrence of the Assistant Secretary for Policy and International Affairs.

(6) Determinations of equivalent facilitation are made only with respect to vehicles or vehicle components used in the provision of transportation services covered by subpart D or subpart E of this part, and pertain only to the specific situation concerning which the determination is made. Entities shall not cite these determinations as indicating that a product or method constitute equivalent facilitations in situations other than those to which the determinations specifically pertain. Entities shall not claim that a determination of equivalent facilitation indicates approval or endorsement of any product or method by the Federal government, the Department of Transportation, or any of its operating administrations.

(c) Over-the-road buses acquired by public entities (or by a contractor to a public entity as provided in § 37.23 of this part) shall comply with § 38.23 and subpart G of part 38 of this title.

[56 FR 45621, Sept. 6, 1991, as amended at 58 FR 63101, Nov. 30, 1993]

§ 37.9 Standards for accessible transportation facilities.

(a) For purposes of this part, a transportation facility shall be considered to be readily accessible to and usable by individuals with disabilities if it meets the requirements of this part and the standards set forth in appendix A to this part.

(b) Facility alterations begun before January 26, 1992, in a good faith effort to make a facility accessible to individuals with disabilities may be used to meet the key station requirements set forth in §§ 37.47 and 37.51 of this part, even if these alterations are not consistent with the standards set forth in appendix A to this part, if the modifications complied with the Uniform Federal Accessibility Standard (UFAS) (41 CFR part 101–19, subpart 101–19.6) or ANSI A117.1(1980) (American National Standards Specification for Making Buildings and Facilities Accessible to and Usable by, the Physically Handicapped). This paragraph applies only to alterations of individual elements and spaces and only to the extent that provisions covering those elements or spaces are contained in UFAS or ANSI A117.1, as applicable.

(c) Public entities shall ensure the construction of new bus stop pads are in compliance with section 10.2.1.(1) of appendix A to this part, to the extent construction specifications are within their control.

(d)(1) For purposes of implementing the equivalent facilitation provision in section 2.2 of appendix A to this part, the following parties may submit to the Administrator of the applicable operating administration a request for a determination of equivalent facilitation:

(i)(A) A public or private entity that provides transportation facilities subject to the provisions of subpart C this part, or other appropriate party with the concurrence of the Administrator;

(B) With respect to airport facilities, an entity that is an airport operator subject to the requirements of 49 CFR part 27 or regulations implementing the Americans with Disabilities Act, an air carrier subject to the requirements of 14 CFR part 382, or other appropriate party with the concurrence of the Administrator.

(ii) The manufacturer of a product or accessibility feature to be used in the facility of such entity to comply with this part.

(2) The requesting party shall provide the following information with its request:

(i) Entity name, address, contact person and telephone;

(ii) Specific provision of appendix A to this part with which the entity is unable to comply;

(iii) Reasons for inability to comply;

(iv) Alternative method of compliance, with demonstration of how the alternative meets or exceeds the level of accessibility or usability of the vehicle provided in appendix A to this part; and

(v) Documentation of the public participation used in developing an alternative method of compliance.

(3) In the case of a request by a public entity that provides transportation facilities (including an airport operator), or a request by an air carrier with respect to airport facilities, the required public participation shall include the following:

(i) The entity shall contact individuals with disabilities and groups representing them in the community. Consultation with these individuals and groups shall take place at all stages of the development of the request for equivalent facilitation. All documents and other information concerning the request shall be available, upon request, to members of the public.

(ii) The entity shall make its proposed request available for public comment before the request is made final or transmitted to DOT. In making the request available for public review, the entity shall ensure that it is available, upon request, in accessible formats.

(iii) The entity shall sponsor at least one public hearing on the request and shall provide adequate notice of the hearing, including advertisement in appropriate media, such as newspapers of general and special interest circulation and radio announcements.

(4) In the case of a request by a manufacturer or a private entity other than an air carrier, the manufacturer or private entity shall consult, in person, in writing, or by other appropriate means, with representatives of national and local organizations representing people with those disabilities who would be affected by the request.

(5) A determination of compliance will be made by the Administrator of the concerned operating administration on a case-by-case basis, with the concurrence of the Assistant Secretary for Policy and International Affairs.

(6) Determinations of equivalent facilitation are made only with respect to transportation facilities, and pertain only to the specific situation concerning which the determination is made. Entities shall not cite these determinations as indicating that a products or methods constitute equivalent facilitations in situations other than those to which the determinations specifically pertain. Entities shall not claim that a determination of equivalent facilitation indicates approval or endorsement of any product or method by the Federal government, the Department of Transportation, or any of its operating administrations.

[56 FR 45621, Sept. 6, 1991, as amended at 58 FR 63102, Nov. 30, 1993; 59 FR 46703, Sept. 9, 1994]

§ 37.11 Administrative enforcement.

(a) Recipients of Federal financial assistance from the Department of Transportation are subject to administrative enforcement of the requirements of this part under the provisions of 49 CFR part 27, subpart F.

(b) Public entities, whether or not they receive Federal financial assistance, also are subject to enforcement action as provided by the Department of Justice.

(c) Private entities, whether or not they receive Federal financial assistance, are also subject to enforcement action as provided in the regulations of the Department of Justice implementing title III of the ADA (28 CFR part 36).

§ 37.13 Effective date for certain vehicle specifications.

(a) The vehicle lift specifications identified in §§ 38.23(b)(6), 38.83(b)(6), 38.95(b)(6), and 38.125(b)(6) of this title apply to solicitations for vehicles under this part after January 25, 1992.

(b) The vehicle door height requirements for vehicles over 22 feet identified in § 38.25(c) of this title apply to solicitations for vehicles under this part after January 25, 1992.

[56 FR 64215, Dec. 9, 1991]

§ 37.15 Temporary suspension of certain detectable warning requirements.

The requirements contained in sections 4.7.7, 4.29.5, and 4.29.6 of appendix A to this part are suspended temporarily until July 26, 1996.

[59 FR 17446, Apr. 12, 1994]

§§ 37.16 — 37.19 [Reserved]

Subpart B — Applicability

§ 37.21 Applicability: General.

(a) This part applies to the following entities, whether or not they receive Federal financial assistance from the Department of Transportation:

(1) Any public entity that provides designated public transportation or intercity or commuter rail transportation;

(2) Any private entity that provides specified public transportation; and

(3) Any private entity that is not primarily engaged in the business of transporting people but operates a demand responsive or fixed route system.

(b) For entities receiving Federal financial assistance from the Department of Transportation, compliance with applicable requirements of this part is a condition of compliance with section 504 of the Rehabilitation Act of 1973 and of receiving financial assistance.

(c) Entities to which this part applies also may be subject to ADA regulations of the Department of Justice (28 CFR parts 35 or 36, as applicable). The provisions of this part shall be interpreted in a manner that will make them consistent with applicable Department of Justice regulations. In any case of apparent inconsistency, the provisions of this part shall prevail.

§ 37.23 Service under contract.

(a) When a public entity enters into a contractual or other arrangement or relationship with a private entity to operate fixed route or demand responsive service, the public entity shall ensure that the private entity meets the requirements of this part that would apply to the public entity if the public entity itself provided the service.

(b) A private entity which purchases or leases new, used, or remanufactured vehicles, or remanufactures vehicles, for use, or in contemplation of use, in fixed route or demand responsive service under contract or other arrangement or relationship with a public entity, shall acquire accessible vehicles in all situations in which the public entity itself would be required to do so by this part.

(c) A public entity which enters into a contractual or other arrangement or relationship with a private entity to provide fixed route service shall ensure that the percentage of accessible vehicles operated by the public entity in its overall fixed route or demand responsive fleet is not diminished as a result.

(d) A private entity that provides fixed route or demand responsive transportation service under contract or other arrangement with another private entity shall be governed, for purposes of the transportation service involved, by the provisions of this part applicable to the other entity.

§ 37.25 University transportation systems.

(a) Transportation services operated by private institutions of higher education are subject to the provisions of this part governing private entities not primarily engaged in the business of transporting people.

(b) Transportation systems operated by public institutions of higher education are subject to the provisions of this part governing public entities. If a public institution of higher education operates a fixed route system, the requirements of this part governing commuter bus service apply to that system.

§ 37.27 Transportation for elementary and secondary education systems.

(a) The requirements of this part do not apply to public school transportation.

(b) The requirements of this part do not apply to the transportation of school children to and from a private elementary or secondary school, and its school-related activities, if the school is a recipient of Federal financial assistance, subject to the provisions of section 504 of the Rehabilitation Act of 1973, and is providing transportation service to students with disabilities equivalent to that provided to students without disabilities. The test of equivalence is the same as that provided in § 37.105. If the school does not meet the criteria of this paragraph for exemption from the requirements of this part, it is subject to the requirements of this part for private entities not primarily engaged in transporting people.

§ 37.29 Private entities providing taxi service.

(a) Providers of taxi service are subject to the requirements of this part for private entities primarily engaged in the business of transporting people which provide demand responsive service.

(b) Providers of taxi service are not required to purchase or lease accessible automobiles. When a provider of taxi service purchases or leases a vehicle other than an automobile, the vehicle is required to be accessible unless the provider demonstrates equivalency as provided in § 37.105 of this part. A provider of taxi service is not required to purchase vehicles other than automobiles in order to have a number of accessible vehicles in its fleet.

(c) Private entities providing taxi service shall not discriminate against individuals with disabilities by actions including, but not limited to, refusing to provide service to individuals with disabilities who can use taxi vehicles, refusing to assist with the stowing of mobility devices, and charging higher fares or fees for carrying individuals with disabilities and their equipment than are charged to other persons.

§ 37.31 Vanpools.

Vanpool systems which are operated by public entities, or in which public entities own or purchase or lease the vehicles, are subject to the requirements of this part for demand responsive service for the general public operated by public entities. A vanpool system in this category is deemed to be providing equivalent service to individuals with disabilities if a vehicle that an individual with disabilities can use is made available to and used by a vanpool in which such an individual chooses to participate.

§ 37.33 Airport transportation systems.

(a) Transportation systems operated by public airport operators, which provide designated public transportation and connect parking lots and terminals or provide transportation among terminals, are subject to the requirements of this part for fixed route or demand responsive systems, as applicable, operated by public entities. Public airports which operate fixed route transportation systems are subject to the requirements of this part for commuter bus service operated by public entities. The provision by an airport of additional accommodations (e.g., parking spaces in a close-in lot) is not a substitute for meeting the requirements of this part.

(b) Fixed-route transportation systems operated by public airport operators between the airport and a limited number of destinations in the area it serves are subject to the provisions of this part for commuter bus systems operated by public entities.

(c) Private jitney or shuttle services that provide transportation between an airport and destinations in the area it serves in a route-deviation or other variable mode are subject to the requirements of this part for private entities primarily engaged in the business of transporting people which provide demand responsive service. They may meet equivalency requirements by such means as sharing or pooling accessible vehicles among operators, in a way that ensures the provision of equivalent service.

§ 37.35 Supplemental service for other transportation modes.

(a) Transportation service provided by bus or other vehicle by an intercity commuter or rail operator, as an extension of or supplement to its rail service, and which connects an intercity rail station and limited other points, is subject to the requirements of this part for fixed route commuter bus service operated by a public entity.

(b) Dedicated bus service to commuter rail systems, with through ticketing arrangements and which is available only to users of the commuter rail system, is subject to the requirements of this part for fixed route commuter bus service operated by a public entity.

§ 37.37 Other applications.

(a) A private entity does not become subject to the requirements of this part for public entities, because it receives an operating subsidy from, is regulated by, or is granted a franchise or permit to operate by a public entity.

(b) Shuttle systems and other transportation services operated by privately-owned hotels, car rental agencies, historical or theme parks, and other public accommodations are subject to the requirements of this part for private entities not primarily engaged in the business of transporting people. Either the requirements for demand responsive or fixed route service may apply, depending upon the characteristics of each individual system of transportation.

(c) Conveyances used by members of the public primarily for recreational purposes rather than for transportation (e.g., amusement park rides, ski lifts, or historic rail cars or trolleys operated in museum settings) are not subject to the requirements of this part. Such conveyances are subject to Department of Justice regulations implementing title II or title III of the ADA (28 CFR part 35 or 36), as applicable.

(d) Transportation services provided by an employer solely for its own employees are not subject to the requirements of this part. Such services are subject to the regulations of the Equal Employment Opportunity Commission under title I of the ADA (29 CFR part 1630) and, with respect to public entities, the regulations of the Department of Justice under title II of the ADA (28 CFR part 35).

(e) Transportation systems operated by private clubs or establishments exempted from coverage under title II of the Civil Rights Act of 1964 (42 U.S.C. 2000–a(e)) or religious organizations or entities controlled by religious organizations are not subject to the requirements of this part.

(f) If a parent private company is not primarily engaged in the business of transporting people, or is not a place of public accommodation, but a subsidiary company or an operationally distinct segment of the company is primarily engaged in the business of transporting people, the transportation service provided by the subsidiary or segment is subject to the requirements of this part for private entities primarily engaged in the business of transporting people.

(g) High-speed rail systems operated by public entities are subject to the requirements of this part governing intercity rail systems.

(h) Private rail systems providing fixed route or specified public transportation service are subject to the requirements of § 37.107 with respect to the acquisition of rail passenger cars. Such systems are subject to the requirements of the regulations of the Department of Justice implementing title III of the ADA (28 CFR part 36) with respect to stations and other facilities.

§ 37.39 [Reserved]

Subpart C — Transportation Facilities

§ 37.41 Construction of transportation facilities by public entities.

A public entity shall construct any new facility to be used in providing designated public transportation services so that the facility is readily accessible to and usable by individuals with disabilities, including individuals who use wheelchairs. This requirement also applies to the construction of a new station for use in intercity or commuter rail transportation. For purposes of this section, a facility or station is "new" if its construction begins (i.e., issuance of notice to proceed) after January 25, 1992, or, in the case of intercity or commuter rail stations, after October 7, 1991.

§ 37.43 Alteration of transportation facilities by public entities.

(a) (1) When a public entity alters an existing facility or a part of an existing facility used in providing designated public transportation services in a way that affects or could affect the usability of the facility or part of the facility, the entity shall make the alterations (or ensure that the alterations are made) in such a manner, to the maximum extent feasible, that the altered portions of the facility are readily accessible to and usable by individuals with disabilities, including individuals who use wheelchairs, upon the completion of such alterations.

(2) When a public entity undertakes an alteration that affects or could affect the usability of or access to an area of a facility containing a primary function, the entity shall make the alteration in such a manner that, to the maximum extent feasible, the path of travel to the altered area and the bathrooms, telephones, and drinking fountains serving the altered area are readily accessible to and usable by individuals with disabilities, including individuals who use wheelchairs, upon completion of the alterations. *Provided,* that alterations to the path of travel, drinking fountains, telephones and bathrooms are not required to be made readily accessible to and usable by individuals with disabilities, including individuals who use wheelchairs, if the cost and scope of doing so would be disproportionate.

(3) The requirements of this paragraph also apply to the alteration of existing intercity or commuter rail stations by the responsible person for, owner of, or person in control of the station.

(4) The requirements of this section apply to any alteration which begins (i.e., issuance of notice to proceed or work order, as applicable) after January 25, 1992, or, in the case of intercity and commuter rail stations, after October 7, 1991.

(b) As used in this section, the phrase *to the maximum extent feasible* applies to the occasional case where the nature of an existing facility makes it impossible to comply fully with applicable accessibility standards through a planned alteration. In these circumstances, the entity shall provide the maximum physical accessibility feasible. Any altered features of the facility or portion of the facility that can be made accessible shall be made accessible. If providing accessibility to certain individuals with disabilities (e.g., those who use wheelchairs) would not be feasible, the facility shall be made accessible to individuals with other types of disabilities (e.g., those who use crutches, those who have impaired vision or hearing, or those who have other impairments).

(c) As used in this section, a *primary function* is a major activity for which the facility is intended. Areas of transportation facilities that involve primary functions include, but are not necessarily limited to, ticket purchase and collection areas, passenger waiting areas, train or bus platforms, baggage checking and return areas and employment areas (except those involving non-occupiable spaces accessed only by ladders, catwalks, crawl spaces, very narrow passageways, or freight (non-passenger) elevators which are frequented only by repair personnel).

(d) As used in this section, a "path of travel" includes a continuous, unobstructed way of pedestrian passage by means of which the altered area may be approached, entered, and exited, and which connects the altered area with an exterior approach (including side-walks, parking areas, and streets), an entrance to the facility, and other parts of the facility. The term also includes the restrooms, telephones, and drinking fountains serving the altered area. An accessible path of travel may include walks and sidewalks, curb ramps and other interior or exterior pedestrian ramps, clear floor paths through corridors, waiting areas, concourses, and other improved areas, parking access aisles, elevators and lifts, bridges, tunnels, or other passageways between platforms, or a combination of these and other elements.

(e) (1) Alterations made to provide an accessible path of travel to the altered area will be deemed disproportionate to the overall alteration when the cost exceeds 20 percent of the cost of the alteration to the primary function area (without regard to the costs of accessibility modifications).

(2) Costs that may be counted as expenditures required to provide an accessible path of travel include:

(i) Costs associated with providing an accessible entrance and an accessible route to the altered area (e.g., widening doorways and installing ramps);

(ii) Costs associated with making restrooms accessible (e.g., grab bars, enlarged toilet stalls, accessible faucet controls);

(iii) Costs associated with providing accessible telephones (e.g., relocation of phones to an accessible height, installation of amplification devices or TDDs);

(iv) Costs associated with relocating an inaccessible drinking fountain.

(f) (1) When the cost of alterations necessary to make a path of travel to the altered area fully accessible is disproportionate to the cost of the overall alteration, then such areas shall be made accessible to the maximum extent without resulting in disproportionate costs;

(2) In this situation, the public entity should give priority to accessible elements that will provide the greatest access, in the following order:

(i) An accessible entrance;

(ii) An accessible route to the altered area;

(iii) At least one accessible restroom for each sex or a single unisex restroom (where there are one or more restrooms);

(iv) Accessible telephones;

(v) Accessible drinking fountains;

(vi) When possible, other accessible elements (e.g., parking, storage, alarms).

(g) If a public entity performs a series of small alterations to the area served by a single path of travel rather than making the alterations as part of a single undertaking, it shall nonetheless be responsible for providing an accessible path of travel.

(h)(1) If an area containing a primary function has been altered without providing an accessible path of travel to that area, and subsequent alterations of that area, or a different area on the same path of travel, are undertaken within three years of the original alteration, the total cost of alteration to the primary function areas on that path of travel during the preceding three year period shall be considered in determining whether the cost of making that path of travel is disproportionate;

(2) For the first three years after January 26, 1992, only alterations undertaken between that date and the date of the alteration at issue shall be considered in determining if the cost of providing accessible features is disproportionate to the overall cost of the alteration.

(3) Only alterations undertaken after January 26, 1992, shall be considered in determining if the cost of providing an accessible path of travel is disproportionate to the overall cost of the alteration.

§ 37.45 Construction and alteration of transportation facilities by private entities.

In constructing and altering transit facilities, private entities shall comply with the regulations of the Department of Justice implementing Title III of the ADA (28 CFR part 36).

§ 37.47 Key stations in light and rapid rail systems.

(a) Each public entity that provides designated public transportation by means of a light or rapid rail system shall make key stations on its system readily accessible to and usable by individuals with disabilities, including individuals who use wheelchairs. This requirement is separate from and in addition to requirements set forth in § 37.43 of this part.

(b) Each public entity shall determine which stations on its system are key stations. The entity shall identify key stations, using the planning and public participation process set forth in paragraph (d) of this section, and taking into consideration the following criteria:

(1) Stations where passenger boardings exceed average station passenger boardings on the rail system by at least fifteen percent, unless such a station is close to another accessible station;

(2) Transfer stations on a rail line or between rail lines;

(3) Major interchange points with other transportation modes, including stations connecting with major parking facilities, bus terminals, intercity or commuter rail stations, passenger vessel terminals, or airports;

(4) End stations, unless an end station is close to another accessible station; and

(5) Stations serving major activity centers, such as employment or government centers, institutions of higher education, hospitals or other major health care facilities, or other facilities that are major trip generators for individuals with disabilities.

(c)(1) Unless an entity receives an extension under paragraph (c)(2) of this section, the public entity shall achieve accessibility of key stations as soon as possible, but in no case later than July 26, 1993, except that an entity is not required to complete installation of detectable warnings required by section 10.3.2(2) of appendix A to this part until July 26, 1994.

(2) The FTA Administrator may grant an extension of this completion date for key station accessibility for a period up to July 26, 2020, provided that two-thirds of key stations are made accessible by July 26, 2010. Extensions may be granted as provided in paragraph (e) of this section.

(d) The public entity shall develop a plan for compliance for this section. The plan shall be submitted to the appropriate FTA regional office by July 26, 1992. (See appendix B to this part for list.)

(1) The public entity shall consult with individuals with disabilities affected by the plan. The public entity also shall hold at least one public hearing on the plan and solicit comments on it. The plan submitted to FTA shall document this public participation, including summaries of the consultation with individuals with disabilities and the comments received at the hearing and during the comment period. The plan also shall summarize the public entity's responses to the comments and consultation.

(2) The plan shall establish milestones for the achievement of required accessibility of key stations, consistent with the requirements of this section.

(e) A public entity wishing to apply for an extension of the July 26, 1993, deadline for key station accessibility shall include a request for an extension with its plan submitted to FTA under paragraph (d) of this section. Extensions may be granted only with respect to key stations which need extraordinarily expensive structural changes to, or replacement of, existing facilities (e.g., installations of elevators, raising the entire passenger platform, or alterations of similar magnitude and cost). Requests for extensions shall provide for completion of key station accessibility within the time limits set forth in paragraph (c) of this section. The FTA Administrator may approve, approve with conditions, modify, or disapprove any request for an extension.

[56 FR 45621, Sept. 6, 1991, as amended at 58 FR 63102, Nov. 30, 1993]

§ 37.49 Designation of responsible person(s) for intercity and commuter rail stations.

(a) The responsible person(s) designated in accordance with this section shall bear the legal and financial responsibility for making a key station accessible in the same proportion as determined under this section.

(b) In the case of a station more than fifty percent of which is owned by a public entity, the public entity is the responsible party.

(c) In the case of a station more than fifty percent of which is owned by a private entity the persons providing commuter or intercity rail service to the station are the responsible parties, in a proportion equal to the percentage of all passenger boardings at the station attributable to the service of each, over the entire period during which the station is made accessible.

(d) In the case of a station of which no entity owns more than fifty percent, the owners of the station (other than private entity owners) and persons providing intercity or commuter rail service to the station are the responsible persons.

(1) Half the responsibility for the station shall be assumed by the owner(s) of the station. The owners shall share this responsibility in proportion to their ownership interest in the station, over the period during which the station is made accessible.

(2) The person(s) providing commuter or intercity rail service to the station shall assume the other half of the responsibility. These persons shall share this responsibility. These persons shall share this responsibility for the station in a proportion equal to the percentage of all passenger boardings at the station attributable to the service of each, over the period during which the station is made accessible.

(e) Persons who must share responsibility for station accessibility under paragraphs (c) and (d) of this section may, by agreement, allocate their responsibility in a manner different from that provided in this section.

§ 37.51 Key stations in commuter rail systems.

(a) The responsible person(s) shall make key stations on its system readily accessible to and usable by individuals with disabilities, including individuals who use wheelchairs. This requirement is separate from and in addition to requirements set forth in § 37.43 of this part.

(b) Each commuter authority shall determine which stations on its system are key stations. The commuter authority shall identify key stations, using the planning and public participation process set forth in paragraph (d) of this section, and taking into consideration the following criteria:

(1) Stations where passenger boardings exceed average station passenger boardings on the rail system by at least fifteen percent, unless such a station is close to another accessible station;

(2) Transfer stations on a rail line or between rail lines;

(3) Major interchange points with other transportation modes, including stations connecting with major parking facilities, bus terminals, intercity or commuter rail stations, passenger vessel terminals, or airports;

(4) End stations, unless an end station is close to another accessible station; and

(5) Stations serving major activity centers, such as employment or government centers, institutions of higher education, hospitals or other major

health care facilities, or other facilities that are major trip generators for individuals with disabilities.

(c)(1) Except as provided in this paragraph, the responsible person(s) shall achieve accessibility of key stations as soon as possible, but in no case later than July 26, 1993, except that an entity is not required to complete installation of detectable warnings required by section 10.3.2(2) of appendix A to this part until July 26, 1994.

(2) The FTA Administrator may grant an extension of this deadline for key station accessibility for a period up to July 26, 2010. Extensions may be granted as provided in paragraph (e) of this section.

(d) The commuter authority and responsible person(s) for stations involved shall develop a plan for compliance for this section. This plan shall be completed and submitted to FTA by July 26, 1992.

(1) The commuter authority and responsible person(s) shall consult with individuals with disabilities affected by the plan. The commuter authority and responsible person(s) also shall hold at least one public hearing on the plan and solicit comments on it. The plan shall document this public participation, including summaries of the consultation with individuals with disabilities and the comments received at the hearing and during the comment period. The plan also shall summarize the responsible person(s) responses to the comments and consultation.

(2) The plan shall establish milestones for the achievement of required accessibility of key stations, consistent with the requirements of this section.

(3) The commuter authority and responsible person(s) of each key station identified in the plan shall, by mutual agreement, designate a project manager for the purpose of undertaking the work of making the key station accessible.

(e) Any commuter authority and/or responsible person(s) wishing to apply for an extension of the July 26, 1993, deadline for key station accessibility shall include a request for extension with its plan submitted to under paragraph (d) of this section. Extensions may be granted only in a case where raising the entire passenger platform is the only means available of attaining accessibility or where other extraordinarily expensive structural changes (e.g., installations of elevators, or alterations of magnitude and cost similar to installing an elevator or raising the entire passenger platform) are necessary to attain accessibility. Requests for extensions shall provide for completion of key station accessibility within the time limits set forth in paragraph (c) of this section. The FTA Administrator may approve, approve with conditions, modify, or disapprove any request for an extension.

[56 FR 45621, Sept. 6, 1991, as amended at 58 FR 63102, Nov. 30, 1993]

§ 37.53 Exception for New York and Philadelphia.

(a) The following agreements entered into in New York, New York, and Philadelphia, Pennsylvania, contain lists of key stations for the public entities that are a party to those agreements for those service lines identified in the agreements. The identification of key stations under these agreements is deemed to be in compliance with the requirements of this Subpart.

(1) Settlement Agreement by and among Eastern Paralyzed Veterans Association, Inc., James J. Peters, Terrance Moakley, and Denise Figueroa, individually and as representatives of the class of all persons similarly situated (collectively, "the EPVA class representatives"); and Metropolitan Transportation Authority, New York City Transit Authority, and Manhattan and Bronx Surface Transit Operating Authority (October 4, 1984).

(2) Settlement Agreement by and between Eastern Paralyzed Veterans Association of Pennsylvania, Inc., and James J. Peters, individually; and Dudley R. Sykes, as Commissioner of the Philadelphia Department of Public Property, and his successors in office and the City of Philadelphia (collectively "the City") and Southeastern Pennsylvania Transportation Authority (June 28, 1989).

(b) To comply with §§ 37.47 (b) and (d) or 37.51 (b) and (d) of this part, the entities named in the agreements are required to use their public participation and planning processes only to develop and submit to the FTA Administrator plans for timely completion of key station accessibility, as provided in this subpart.

(c) In making accessible the key stations identified under the agreements cited in this section, the entities named in the agreements are subject to the requirements of § 37.9 of this part.

§ 37.55 Intercity rail station accessibility.

All intercity rail stations shall be made readily accessible to and usable by individuals with disabilities, including individuals who use wheelchairs, as soon as practicable, but in no event later than July 26, 2010. This requirement is separate from and in addition to requirements set forth in § 37.43 of this part.

§ 37.57 Required cooperation.

An owner or person in control of an intercity or commuter rail station shall provide reasonable cooperation to the responsible person(s) for that station with respect to the efforts of the responsible person to comply with the requirements of this subpart.

§ 37.59 Differences in accessibility completion dates.

Where different completion dates for accessible stations are established under this part for a station or portions of a station (e.g., extensions of different periods of time for a station which serves both rapid and commuter rail systems), accessibility to the following elements of the station shall be achieved by the earlier of the completion dates involved:

(a) Common elements of the station;

(b) Portions of the facility directly serving the rail system with the earlier completion date; and

(c) An accessible path from common elements of the station to portions of the facility directly serving the rail system with the earlier completion date.

§ 37.61 Public transportation programs and activities in existing facilities.

(a) A public entity shall operate a designated public transportation program or activity conducted in an existing facility so that, when viewed in its entirety, the program or activity is readily accessible to and usable by individuals with disabilities.

(b) This section does not require a public entity to make structural changes to existing facilities in order to make the facilities accessible by individuals who use wheelchairs, unless and to the extent required by § 37.43 (with respect to alterations) or §§ 37.47 or 37.51 of this part (with respect to key stations). Entities shall comply with other applicable accessibility requirements for such facilities.

(c) Public entities, with respect to facilities that, as provided in paragraph (b) of this section, are not required to be made accessible to individuals who use wheelchairs, are not required to provide to such individuals services made available to the general public at such facilities when the individuals could not utilize or benefit from the services.

§§ 37.63 — 37.69 [Reserved]

Subpart D — Acquisition of Accessible Vehicles By Public Entities

§ 37.71 Purchase or lease of new non-rail vehicles by public entities operating fixed route systems.

(a) Except as provided elsewhere in this section, each public entity operating a fixed route system making a solicitation after August 25, 1990, to purchase or lease a new bus or other new vehicle for use on the system, shall ensure that the vehicle is readily accessible to and usable by individuals with disabilities, including individuals who use wheelchairs.

(b) A public entity may purchase or lease a new bus that is not readily accessible to and usable by individuals with disabilities, including individuals who use wheelchairs, if it applies for, and the FTA Administrator grants, a waiver as provided for in this section.

(c) Before submitting a request for such a waiver, the public entity shall hold at least one public hearing concerning the proposed request.

(d) The FTA Administrator may grant a request for such a waiver if the public entity demonstrates to the FTA Administrator's satisfaction that —

(1) The initial solicitation for new buses made by the public entity specified that all new buses were to be lift-equipped and were to be otherwise accessible to and usable by individuals with disabilities;

(2) Hydraulic, electromechanical, or other lifts for such new buses could not be provided by any qualified lift manufacturer to the manufacturer of such new buses in sufficient time to comply with the solicitation; and

(3) Any further delay in purchasing new buses equipped with such necessary lifts would significantly impair transportation services in the community served by the public entity.

(e) The public entity shall include with its waiver request a copy of the initial solicitation and written documentation from the bus manufacturer of its good faith efforts to obtain lifts in time to comply with the solicitation, and a full justification for the assertion that the delay in bus procurement needed to obtain a lift-equipped bus would significantly impair transportation services in the community. This documentation shall include a specific date at which the lifts could be supplied, copies of advertisements in trade publications and inquiries to trade associations seeking lifts, and documentation of the public hearing.

(f) Any waiver granted by the FTA Administrator under this section shall be subject to the following conditions:

(1) The waiver shall apply only to the particular bus delivery to which the waiver request pertains;

(2) The waiver shall include a termination date, which will be based on information concerning when lifts will become available for installation on the new buses the public entity is purchasing. Buses delivered after this date, even though procured under a solicitation to which a waiver applied, shall be equipped with lifts;

(3) Any bus obtained subject to the waiver shall be capable of accepting a lift, and the public entity shall install a lift as soon as one becomes available;

(4) Such other terms and conditions as the FTA Administrator may impose.

(g)(1) When the FTA Administrator grants a waiver under this section, he/she shall promptly notify the appropriate committees of Congress.

(2) If the FTA Administrator has reasonable cause to believe that a public entity fraudulently applied for a waiver under this section, the FTA Administrator shall:

(i) Cancel the waiver if it is still in effect; and

(ii) Take other appropriate action.

§ 37.73 Purchase or lease of used non-rail vehicles by public entities operating fixed route systems.

(a) Except as provided elsewhere in this section, each public entity operating a fixed route system purchasing or leasing, after August 25, 1990, a used bus or other used vehicle for use on the system, shall ensure that the vehicle is readily accessible to and usable by individuals with disabilities, including individuals who use wheelchairs.

(b) A public entity may purchase or lease a used vehicle for use on its fixed route system that is not readily accessible to and usable by individuals with disabilities if, after making demonstrated good faith efforts to obtain an accessible vehicle, it is unable to do so.

(c) Good faith efforts shall include at least the following steps:

(1) An initial solicitation for used vehicles specifying that all used vehicles are to be lift-equipped and otherwise accessible to and usable by individuals with disabilities, or, if an initial solicitation is not used, a documented communication so stating;

(2) A nationwide search for accessible vehicles, involving specific inquiries to used vehicle dealers and other transit providers; and

(3) Advertising in trade publications and contacting trade associations.

(d) Each public entity purchasing or leasing used vehicles that are not readily accessible to and usable by individuals with disabilities shall retain documentation of the specific good faith efforts it made for three years from the date the vehicles were purchased. These records shall be made available, on request, to the FTA Administrator and the public.

§ 37.75 Remanufacture of non-rail vehicles and purchase or lease of remanufactured non-rail vehicles by public entities operating fixed route systems.

(a) This section applies to any public entity operating a fixed route system which takes one of the following actions:

(1) After August 25, 1990, remanufactures a bus or other vehicle so as to extend its useful life for five years or more or makes a solicitation for such remanufacturing; or

(2) Purchases or leases a bus or other vehicle which has been remanufactured so as to extend its useful life for five years or more, where the

purchase or lease occurs after August 25, 1990, and during the period in which the useful life of the vehicle is extended.

(b) Vehicles acquired through the actions listed in paragraph (a) of this section shall, to the maximum extent feasible, be readily accessible to and usable by individuals with disabilities, including individuals who use wheelchairs.

(c) For purposes of this section, it shall be considered feasible to re-manufacture a bus or other motor vehicle so as to be readily accessible to and usable by individuals with disabilities, including individuals who use wheelchairs, unless an engineering analysis demonstrates that including accessibility features required by this part would have a significant adverse effect on the structural integrity of the vehicle.

(d) If a public entity operates a fixed route system, any segment of which is included on the National Register of Historic Places, and if making a vehicle of historic character used solely on such segment readily accessible to and usable by individuals with disabilities would significantly alter the historic character of such vehicle, the public entity has only to make (or purchase or lease a remanufactured vehicle with) those modifications to make the vehicle accessible which do not alter the historic character of such vehicle, in consultation with the National Register of Historic Places.

(e) A public entity operating a fixed route system as described in paragraph (d) of this section may apply in writing to the FTA Administrator for a determination of the historic character of the vehicle. The FTA Administrator shall refer such requests to the National Register of Historic Places, and shall rely on its advice in making determinations of the historic character of the vehicle.

§ 37.77 Purchase or lease of new non-rail vehicles by public entities operating a demand responsive system for the general public.

(a) Except as provided in this section, a public entity operating a demand responsive system for the general public making a solicitation after August 25, 1990, to purchase or lease a new bus or other new vehicle for use on the system, shall ensure that the vehicle is readily accessible to and usable by individuals with disabilities, including individuals who use wheelchairs.

(b) If the system, when viewed in its entirety, provides a level of service to individuals with disabilities, including individuals who use wheelchairs, equivalent to the level of service it provides to individuals without disabilities, it may purchase new vehicles that are not readily accessible to and usable by individuals with disabilities.

(c) For purposes of this section, a demand responsive system, when viewed in its entirety, shall be deemed to provide equivalent service if the service available to individuals with disabilities, including individuals who use wheelchairs, is provided in the most integrated setting appropriate to the needs of the individual and is equivalent to the service provided other individuals with respect to the following service characteristics:

(1) Response time;

(2) Fares;

(3) Geographic area of service;

(4) Hours and days of service;

(5) Restrictions or priorities based on trip purpose;

(6) Availability of information and reservations capability; and

(7) Any constraints on capacity or service availability.

(d) A public entity receiving FTA funds under section 18 or a public entity in a small urbanized area which receives FTA funds under Section 9 from a state administering agency rather than directly from FTA, which determines that its service to individuals with disabilities is equivalent to that provided other persons shall, before any procurement of an inaccessible vehicle, file with the appropriate state program office a certificate that it provides equivalent service meeting the standards of paragraph (c) of this section. Public entities operating demand responsive service receiving funds under any other section of the FT Act shall file the certificate with the appropriate FTA regional office. A public entity which does not receive FTA funds shall make such a certificate and retain it in its files, subject to inspection on request of FTA. All certificates under this paragraph may be made and filed in connection with a particular procurement or in advance of a procurement; however, no certificate shall be valid for more than one year. A copy of the required certificate is found in appendix C to this part.

(e) The waiver mechanism set forth in § 37.71(b)–(g) (unavailability of lifts) of this subpart shall also be available to public entities operating a demand responsive system for the general public.

§ 37.79 Purchase or lease of new rail vehicles by public entities operating rapid or light rail systems.

Each public entity operating a rapid or light rail system making a solicitation after August 25, 1990, to purchase or lease a new rapid or light rail vehicle for use on the system shall ensure that the vehicle is readily accessible to and usable by individuals with disabilities, including individuals who use wheelchairs.

§ 37.81 Purchase or lease of used rail vehicles by public entities operating rapid or light rail systems.

(a) Except as provided elsewhere in this section, each public entity operating a rapid or light rail system which, after August 25, 1990, purchases or leases a used rapid or light rail vehicle for use on the system shall ensure that the vehicle is readily accessible to and usable by individuals with disabilities, including individuals who use wheelchairs.

(b) A public entity may purchase or lease a used rapid or light rail vehicle for use on its rapid or light rail system that is not readily accessible to and usable by individuals if, after making demonstrated good faith efforts to obtain an accessible vehicle, it is unable to do so.

(c) Good faith efforts shall include at least the following steps:

(1) The initial solicitation for used vehicles made by the public entity specifying that all used vehicles were to be accessible to and usable by individuals with disabilities, or, if a solicitation is not used, a documented communication so stating;

(2) A nationwide search for accessible vehicles, involving specific inquiries to manufacturers and other transit providers; and

(3) Advertising in trade publications and contacting trade associations.

(d) Each public entity purchasing or leasing used rapid or light rail vehicles that are not readily accessible to and usable by individuals with disabilities shall retain documentation of the specific good faith efforts it made for three years from the date the vehicles were purchased. These records shall be made available, on request, to the FTA Administrator and the public.

§ 37.83 Remanufacture of rail vehicles and purchase or lease of remanufactured rail vehicles by public entities operating rapid or light rail systems.

(a) This section applies to any public entity operating a rapid or light rail system which takes one of the following actions:

(1) After August 25, 1990, remanufactures a light or rapid rail vehicle so as to extend its useful life for five years or more or makes a solicitation for such remanufacturing;

(2) Purchases or leases a light or rapid rail vehicle which has been remanufactured so as to extend its useful life for five years or more, where the purchase or lease occurs after August 25, 1990, and during the period in which the useful life of the vehicle is extended.

(b) Vehicles acquired through the actions listed in paragraph (a) of this section shall, to the maximum extent feasible, be readily accessible to and usable by individuals with disabilities, including individuals who use wheelchairs.

(c) For purposes of this section, it shall be considered feasible to remanufacture a rapid or light rail vehicle so as to be readily accessible to and usable by individuals with disabilities, including individuals who use wheelchairs, unless an engineering analysis demonstrates that doing so would have a significant adverse effect on the structural integrity of the vehicle.

(d) If a public entity operates a rapid or light rail system any segment of which is included on the National Register of Historic Places and if making a rapid or light rail vehicle of historic character used solely on such segment readily accessible to and usable by individuals with disabilities would significantly alter the historic character of such vehicle, the public entity need only make (or purchase or lease a remanufactured vehicle with) those modifications that do not alter the historic character of such vehicle.

(e) A public entity operating a fixed route system as described in paragraph (d) of this section may apply in writing to the FTA Administrator for a determination of the historic character of the vehicle. The FTA Administrator shall refer such requests to the National Register of Historic Places and shall rely on its advice in making a determination of the historic character of the vehicle.

§ 37.85 Purchase or lease of new intercity and commuter rail cars.

Amtrak or a commuter authority making a solicitation after August 25, 1990, to purchase or lease a new intercity or commuter rail car for use on the system shall ensure that the vehicle is readily accessible to and usable by individuals with disabilities, including individuals who use wheelchairs.

§ 37.87 Purchase or lease of used intercity and commuter rail cars.

(a) Except as provided elsewhere in this section, Amtrak or a commuter authority purchasing or leasing a used intercity or commuter rail car after August 25, 1990, shall ensure that the car is readily accessible to and usable by individuals with disabilities, including individuals who use wheelchairs.

(b) Amtrak or a commuter authority may purchase or lease a used intercity or commuter rail car that is not readily accessible to and usable by individuals if, after making demonstrated good faith efforts to obtain an accessible vehicle, it is unable to do so.

(c) Good faith efforts shall include at least the following steps:

(1) An initial solicitation for used vehicles specifying that all used vehicles accessible to and usable by individuals with disabilities;

(2) A nationwide search for accessible vehicles, involving specific inquiries to used vehicle dealers and other transit providers; and

(3) Advertising in trade publications and contacting trade associations.

(d) When Amtrak or a commuter authority leases a used intercity or commuter rail car for a period of seven days or less, Amtrak or the commuter authority may make and document good faith efforts as provided in this paragraph instead of in the ways provided in paragraph (c) of this section:

(1) By having and implementing, in its agreement with any intercity railroad or commuter authority that serves as a source of used intercity or

commuter rail cars for a lease of seven days or less, a provision requiring that the lessor provide all available accessible rail cars before providing any inaccessible rail cars.

(2) By documenting that, when there is more than one source of intercity or commuter rail cars for a lease of seven days or less, the lessee has obtained all available accessible intercity or commuter rail cars from all sources before obtaining inaccessible intercity or commuter rail cars from any source.

(e) Amtrak and commuter authorities purchasing or leasing used intercity or commuter rail cars that are not readily accessible to and usable by individuals with disabilities shall retain documentation of the specific good faith efforts that were made for three years from the date the cars were purchased. These records shall be made available, on request, to the Federal Railroad Administration or FTA Administrator, as applicable. These records shall be made available to the public, on request.

[56 FR 45621, Sept. 6, 1991, as amended at 58 FR 63102, Nov. 30, 1993]

§ 37.89 Remanufacture of intercity and commuter rail cars and purchase or lease of remanufactured intercity and commuter rail cars.

(a) This section applies to Amtrak or a commuter authority which takes one of the following actions:

(1) Remanufactures an intercity or commuter rail car so as to extend its useful life for ten years or more;

(2) Purchases or leases an intercity or commuter rail car which has been remanufactured so as to extend its useful life for ten years or more.

(b) Intercity and commuter rail cars listed in paragraph (a) of this section shall, to the maximum extent feasible, be readily accessible to and usable by individuals with disabilities, including individuals who use wheelchairs.

(c) For purposes of this section, it shall be considered feasible to remanufacture an intercity or commuter rail car so as to be readily accessible to and usable by individuals with disabilities, including individuals who use wheelchairs, unless an engineering analysis demonstrates that remanufacturing the car to be accessible would have a significant adverse effect on the structural integrity of the car.

§ 37.91 Wheelchair locations and food service on intercity rail trains.

(a) As soon as practicable, but in no event later than July 26, 1995, each person providing intercity rail service shall provide on each train a number of spaces —

(1) To park wheelchairs (to accommodate individuals who wish to remain in their wheelchairs) equal to not less than one half of the number of single level rail passenger coaches in the train; and

(2) To fold and store wheelchairs (to accommodate individuals who wish to transfer to coach seats) equal to not less than one half the number of single level rail passenger coaches in the train.

(b) As soon as practicable, but in no event later than July 26, 2000, each person providing intercity rail service shall provide on each train a number of spaces —

(1) To park wheelchairs (to accommodate individuals who wish to remain in their wheelchairs) equal to not less than the total number of single level rail passenger coaches in the train; and

(2) To fold and store wheelchairs (to accommodate individuals who wish to transfer to coach seats) equal to not less than the total number of single level rail passenger coaches in the train.

(c) In complying with paragraphs (a) and (b) of this section, a person providing intercity rail service may not provide more than two spaces to park wheelchairs nor more than two spaces to fold and store wheelchairs in any one coach or food service car.

(d) Unless not practicable, a person providing intercity rail transportation shall place an accessible car adjacent to the end of a single level dining car through which an individual who uses a wheelchair may enter.

(e) On any train in which either a single level or bi-level dining car is used to provide food service, a person providing intercity rail service shall provide appropriate aids and services to ensure that equivalent food service is available to individuals with disabilities, including individuals who use wheelchairs, and to passengers traveling with such individuals. Appropriate auxiliary aids and services include providing a hard surface on which to eat.

(f) This section does not require the provision of securement devices on intercity rail cars.

§ 37.93 One car per train rule.

(a) The definition of accessible for purposes of meeting the one car per train rule is spelled out in the applicable subpart for each transportation system type in part 38 of this title.

(b) Each person providing intercity rail service and each commuter rail authority shall ensure that, as soon as practicable, but in no event later than July 26, 1995, that each train has one car that is readily accessible to and usable by individuals with disabilities, including individuals who use wheelchairs.

(c) Each public entity providing light or rapid rail service shall ensure that each train, consisting of two or more vehicles, includes at least one car that is readily accessible to and usable by individuals with disabilities, including individuals who use wheelchairs, as soon as practicable but in no case later than July 25, 1995.

§ 37.95 Ferries and other passenger vessels operated by public entities. [Reserved]

§§ 37.97 — 37.99 [Reserved]

Subpart E — Acquisition of Accessible Vehicles By Private Entities

§ 37.101 Purchase or lease of vehicles by private entities not primarily engaged in the business of transporting people.

(a) *Application.* This section applies to all purchases or leases of vehicles by private entities which are not primarily engaged in the business of transporting people, in which a solicitation for the vehicle is made after August 25, 1990.

(b) *Fixed Route System. Vehicle Capacity Over 16.* If the entity operates a fixed route system and purchases or leases a vehicle with a seating capacity of over 16 passengers (including the driver) for use on the system, it shall ensure that the vehicle is readily accessible to and usable by individuals with disabilities, including individuals who use wheelchairs.

(c) *Fixed Route System. Vehicle Capacity of 16 or Fewer.* If the entity operates a fixed route system and purchases or leases a vehicle with a seating capacity of 16 or fewer passengers (including the driver) for use on the system, it shall ensure that the vehicle is readily accessible to and usable by individuals with disabilities, including individuals who use wheelchairs, unless the system, when viewed in its entirety, meets the standard for equivalent service of § 37.105 of this part.

(d) *Demand Responsive System, Vehicle Capacity Over 16.* If the entity operates a demand responsive system, and purchases or leases a vehicle with a seating capacity of over 16 passengers (including the driver) for use on the system, it shall ensure that the vehicle is readily accessible to and usable by individuals with disabilities, including individuals who use wheelchairs, unless the system, when viewed in its entirety, meets the standard for equivalent service of § 37.105 of this part.

§ 37.103 Purchase or lease of new non-rail vehicles by private entities primarily engaged in the business of transporting people.

(a) *Application.* This section applies to all acquisitions of new vehicles by private entities which are primarily engaged in the business of transporting people and whose operations affect commerce, in which a solicitation for the vehicle is made (except as provided in paragraph (d) of this section) after August 25, 1990.

(b) *Fixed route systems.* If the entity operates a fixed route system, and purchases or leases a new vehicle other than an automobile, a van with a seating capacity of less than eight persons (including the driver), or an over-the-road bus, it shall ensure that the vehicle is readily accessible to and usable by individuals with disabilities, including individuals who use wheelchairs.

(c) *Demand responsive systems.* If the entity operates a demand responsive system, and purchases or leases a new vehicle other than an automobile, a van with a seating capacity of less than eight persons (including the driver), or an over-the-road bus, it shall ensure that the vehicle is readily accessible to and usable by individuals with disabilities, including individuals who use wheelchairs, unless the system, when viewed in its entirety, meets the standard for equivalent service of § 37.105 of this part.

(d) *Vans with a capacity of fewer than 8 persons.* If the entity operates either a fixed route or demand responsive system, and purchases or leases a new van with a seating capacity of fewer than eight persons including the driver (the solicitation for the vehicle being made after February 25, 1992), the entity shall ensure that the vehicle is readily accessible to and usable by individuals with disabilities, including individuals who use wheelchairs, unless the system, when viewed in its entirety, meets the standard for equivalent service of § 37.105 of this part.

§ 37.105 Equivalent service standard.

For purposes of §§ 37.101 and 37.103 of this part, a fixed route system or demand responsive system, when viewed in its entirety, shall be deemed to provide equivalent service if the service available to individuals with disabilities, including individuals who use wheelchairs, is provided in the most integrated setting appropriate to the needs of the individual and is equivalent to the service provided other individuals with respect to the following service characteristics:

(a) (1) Schedules/headways (if the system is fixed route);

(2) Response time (if the system is demand responsive);

(b) Fares;

(c) Geographic area of service;

(d) Hours and days of service;

(e) Availability of information;

(f) Reservations capability (if the system is demand responsive);

(g) Any constraints on capacity or service availability;

(h) Restrictions priorities based on trip purpose (if the system is demand responsive).

§ 37.107 Acquisition of passenger rail cars by private entities primarily engaged in the business of transporting people.

(a) A private entity which is primarily engaged in the business of transporting people and whose operations affect commerce, which makes a solicitation after February 25, 1992, to purchase or lease a new rail passenger car to be used in providing specified public transportation, shall ensure that the car is readily accessible to, and usable by, individuals with disabilities, including individuals who use wheelchairs. The accessibility standards in part 38 of this title which apply depend upon the type of service in which the car will be used.

(b) Except as provided in paragraph (c) of this section, a private entity which is primarily engaged in transporting people and whose operations affect commerce, which remanufactures a rail passenger car to be used in providing specified public transportation to extend its useful life for ten years or more, or purchases or leases such a remanufactured rail car, shall ensure that the rail car, to the maximum extent feasible, is made readily accessible to and usable by individuals with disabilities, including individuals who use wheelchairs. For purposes of this paragraph, it shall be considered feasible to remanufacture a rail passenger car to be readily accessible to and usable by individuals with disabilities, including individuals who use wheelchairs, unless an engineering analysis demonstrates that doing so would have a significant adverse effect on the structural integrity of the car.

(c) Compliance with paragraph (b) of this section is not required to the extent that it would significantly alter the historic or antiquated character of a historic or antiquated rail passenger car, or a rail station served exclusively by such cars, or would result in the violation of any rule, regulation, standard or order issued by the Secretary under the Federal Railroad Safety Act of 1970. For purposes of this section, a historic or antiquated rail passenger car means a rail passenger car —

(1) Which is not less than 30 years old at the time of its use for transporting individuals;

(2) The manufacturer of which is no longer in the business of manufacturing rail passenger cars; and

(3) Which —

(i) Has a consequential association with events or persons significant to the past; or

(ii) Embodies, or is being restored to embody, the distinctive characteristics of a type of rail passenger car used in the past, or to represent a time period which has passed.

§ 37.109 Ferries and other passenger vessels operated by private entities. [Reserved]

§§ 37.111 — 37.119 [Reserved]

Subpart F — Paratransit as a Complement to Fixed Route Service

§ 37.121 Requirement for comparable complementary paratransit service.

(a) Except as provided in paragraph (c) of this section, each public entity operating a fixed route system shall provide paratransit or other special service to individuals with disabilities that is comparable to the level of service provided to individuals without disabilities who use the fixed route system.

(b) To be deemed comparable to fixed route service, a complementary paratransit system shall meet the requirements of §§ 37.123–37.133 of this subpart. The requirement to comply with § 37.131 may be modified in accordance with the provisions of this subpart relating to undue financial burden.

(c) Requirements for complementary paratransit do not apply to commuter bus, commuter rail, or intercity rail systems.

§ 37.123 ADA paratransit eligibility: Standards.

(a) Public entities required by § 37.121 of this subpart to provide complementary paratransit service shall provide the service to the ADA paratransit eligible individuals described in paragraph (e) of this section.

(b) If an individual meets the eligibility criteria of this section with respect to some trips but not others, the individual shall be ADA paratransit eligible only for those trips for which he or she meets the criteria.

(c) Individuals may be ADA paratransit eligible on the basis of a permanent or temporary disability.

(d) Public entities may provide complementary paratransit service to persons other than ADA paratransit eligible individuals. However, only the cost of service to ADA paratransit eligible individuals may be considered in a public entity's request for an undue financial burden waiver under §§ 37.151–37.155 of this part.

(e) The following individuals are ADA paratransit eligible:

(1) Any individual with a disability who is unable, as the result of a physical or mental impairment (including a vision impairment), and without the assistance of another individual (except the operator of a wheelchair lift or other boarding assistance device), to board, ride, or disembark from any vehicle on the system which is readily accessible to and usable individuals with disabilities.

(2) Any individual with a disability who needs the assistance of a wheelchair lift or other boarding assistance device and is able, with such

assistance, to board, ride and disembark from any vehicle which is readily accessible to and usable by individuals with disabilities if the individual wants to travel on a route on the system during the hours of operation of the system at a time, or within a reasonable period of such time, when such a vehicle is not being used to provide designated public transportation on the route.

(i) An individual is eligible under this paragraph with respect to travel on an otherwise accessible route on which the boarding or disembarking location which the individual would use is one at which boarding or disembarking from the vehicle is precluded as provided in § 37.167(g) of this part.

(ii) An individual using a common wheelchair is eligible under this paragraph if the individual's wheelchair cannot be accommodated on an existing vehicle (e.g., because the vehicle's lift does not meet the standards of part 38 of this title), even if that vehicle is accessible to other individuals with disabilities and their mobility wheelchairs.

(iii) With respect to rail systems, an individual is eligible under this paragraph if the individual could use an accessible rail system, but —

(A) there is not yet one accessible car per train on the system; or

(B) key stations have not yet been made accessible.

(3) Any individual with a disability who has a specific impairment-related condition which prevents such individual from traveling to a boarding location or from a disembarking location on such system.

(i) Only a specific impairment-related condition which prevents the individual from traveling to a boarding location or from a disembarking location is a basis for eligibility under this paragraph. A condition which makes traveling to boarding location or from a disembarking location more difficult for a person with a specific impairment-related condition than for an individual who does not have the condition, but does not prevent the travel, is not a basis for eligibility under this paragraph.

(ii) Architectural barriers not under the control of the public entity providing fixed route service and environmental barriers (e.g., distance, terrain, weather) do not, standing alone, form a basis for eligibility under this paragraph. The interaction of such barriers with an individual's specific impairment-related condition may form a basis for eligibility under this paragraph, if the effect is to prevent the individual from traveling to a boarding location or from a disembarking location.

(f) Individuals accompanying an ADA paratransit eligible individual shall be provided service as follows:

(1) One other individual accompanying the ADA paratransit eligible individual shall be provided service —

(i) If the ADA paratransit eligible individual is traveling with a personal care attendant, the entity shall provide service to one other individual in addition to the attendant who is accompanying the eligible individual;

(ii) A family member or friend is regarded as a person accompanying the eligible individual, and not as a personal care attendant, unless the family member or friend registered is acting in the capacity of a personal care attendant;

(2) Additional individuals accompanying the ADA paratransit eligible individual shall be provided service, provided that space is available for them on the paratransit vehicle carrying the ADA paratransit eligible individual and that transportation of the additional individuals will not result in a denial of service to ADA paratransit eligible individuals;

(3) In order to be considered as "accompanying" the eligible individual for purposes of this paragraph (f), the other individual(s) shall have the same origin and destination as the eligible individual.

§ 37.125 ADA paratransit eligibility: Process.

Each public entity required to provide complementary paratransit service by § 37.121 of this part shall establish a process for determining ADA paratransit eligibility.

(a) The process shall strictly limit ADA paratransit eligibility to individuals specified in § 37.123 of this part.

(b) All information about the process, materials necessary to apply for eligibility, and notices and determinations concerning eligibility shall be made available in accessible formats, upon request.

(c) If, by a date 21 days following the submission of a complete application, the entity has not made a determination of eligibility, the applicant shall be treated as eligible and provided service until and unless the entity denies the application.

(d) The entity's determination concerning eligibility shall be in writing. If the determination is that the individual is ineligible, the determination shall state the reasons for the finding.

(e) The public entity shall provide documentation to each eligible individual stating that he or she is "ADA Paratransit Eligible." The documentation shall include the name of the eligible individual, the name of the transit provider, the telephone number of the entity's paratransit coordinator, an expiration date for eligibility, and any conditions or limitations on the individual's eligibility including the use of a personal care attendant.

(f) The entity may require recertification of the eligibility of ADA paratransit eligible individuals at reasonable intervals.

(g) The entity shall establish an administrative appeal process through which individuals who are denied eligibility can obtain review of the denial.

(1) The entity may require that an appeal be filed within 60 days of the denial of an individual's application.

(2) The process shall include an opportunity to be heard and to present information and arguments, separation of functions (i.e., a decision by a

person not involved with the initial decision to deny eligibility), and written notification of the decision, and the reasons for it.

(3) The entity is not required to provide paratransit service to the individual pending the determination on appeal. However, if the entity has not made a decision within 30 days of the completion of the appeal process, the entity shall provide paratransit service from that time until and unless a decision to deny the appeal is issued.

(h) The entity may establish an administrative process to suspend, for a reasonable period of time, the provision of complementary paratransit service to ADA eligible individuals who establish a pattern or practice of missing scheduled trips.

(1) Trips missed by the individual for reasons beyond his or her control (including, but not limited to, trips which are missed due to operator error) shall not be a basis for determining that such a pattern or practice exists.

(2) Before suspending service, the entity shall take the following steps:

(i) Notify the individual in writing that the entity proposes to suspend service, citing with specificity the basis of the proposed suspension and setting forth the proposed sanction.

(ii) Provide the individual an opportunity to be heard and to present information and arguments;

(iii) Provide the individual with written notification of the decision and the reasons for it.

(3) The appeals process of paragraph (g) of this section is available to an individual on whom sanctions have been imposed under this paragraph. The sanction is stayed pending the outcome of the appeal.

(i) In applications for ADA paratransit eligibility, the entity may require the applicant to indicate whether or not he or she travels with a personal care attendant.

§ 37.127 Complementary paratransit service for visitors.

(a) Each public entity required to provide complementary paratransit service under § 37.121 of this part shall make the service available to visitors as provided in this section.

(b) For purposes of this section, a visitor is an individual with disabilities who does not reside in the jurisdiction(s) served by the public entity or other entities with which the public entity provides coordinated complementary paratransit service within a region.

(c) Each public entity shall treat as eligible for its complementary paratransit service all visitors who present documentation that they are ADA paratransit eligible, under the criteria of § 37.125 of this part, in the jurisdiction in which they reside.

(d) With respect to visitors with disabilities who do not present such documentation, the public entity may require the documentation of the individual's place of residence and, if the individual's disability is not apparent, of his or her disability. The entity shall provide paratransit service to individuals with disabilities who qualify as visitors under paragraph (b) of this section. The entity shall accept a certification by such individuals that they are unable to use fixed route transit.

(e) A public entity is not required to provide service to a visitor for more than 21 days from the date of the first paratransit trip used by the visitor. The entity may require that such an individual, in order to receive service beyond this period, apply for eligibility under the process provided for in § 37.125 of this part.

§ 37.129 Types of service.

(a) Except as provided in this section, complementary paratransit service for ADA paratransit eligible persons shall be origin-to-destination service.

(b) Complementary paratransit service for ADA paratransit eligible persons described in § 37.123(e)(2) of this part may also be provided by on-call bus service or paratransit feeder service to an accessible fixed route, where such service enables the individual to use the fixed route bus system for his or her trip.

(c) Complementary paratransit service for ADA eligible persons described in § 37.123(e)(3) of this part also may be provided by paratransit feeder service to and/or from an accessible fixed route.

§ 37.131 Service criteria for complementary paratransit.

The following service criteria apply to complementary paratransit required by § 37.121 of this part.

(a) *Service Area* — (1) *Bus.* (i) The entity shall provide complementary paratransit service to origins and destinations within corridors with a width of three-fourths of a mile on each side of each fixed route. The corridor shall include an area with a three-fourths of a mile radius at the ends of each fixed route.

(ii) Within the core service area, the entity also shall provide service to small areas not inside any of the corridors but which are surrounded by corridors.

(iii) Outside the core service area, the entity may designate corridors with widths from three-fourths of a mile up to one and one half miles on each side of a fixed route, based on local circumstances.

(iv) For purposes of this paragraph, the core service area is that area in which corridors with a width of three-fourths of a mile on each side of each fixed route merge together such that, with few and small exceptions, all origins and destinations within the area would be served.

(2) *Rail.* (i) For rail systems, the service area shall consist of a circle with a radius of 3/4 of a mile around each station.

(ii) At end stations and other stations in outlying areas, the entity may designate circles with radii of up to $1\frac{1}{2}$ miles as part of its service area, based on local circumstances.

(3) *Jurisdictional boundaries.* Notwithstanding any other provision of this paragraph, an entity is not required to provide paratransit service in an area outside the boundaries of the jurisdiction(s) in which it operates, if the entity does not have legal authority to operate in that area. The entity shall take all practicable steps to provide paratransit service to any part of its service area.

(b) *Response time.* The entity shall schedule and provide paratransit service to any ADA paratransit eligible person at any requested time on a particular day in response to a request for service made the previous day. Reservations may be taken by reservation agents or by mechanical means.

(1) The entity shall make reservation service available during at least all normal business hours of the entity's administrative offices, as well as during times, comparable to normal business hours, on a day when the entity's offices are not open before a service day.

(2) The entity may negotiate pickup times with the individual, but the entity shall not require an ADA paratransit eligible individual to schedule a trip to begin more than one hour before or after the individual's desired departure time.

(3) The entity may use real-time scheduling in providing complementary paratransit service.

(4) The entity shall permit advance reservations to be made up to 14 days in advance of an ADA paratransit eligible individual's desired trip.

(c) *Fares.* The fare for a trip charged to an ADA paratransit eligible user of the complementary paratransit service shall not exceed twice the fare that would be charged to an individual paying full fare (i.e., without regard to discounts) for a trip of similar length, at a similar time of day, on the entity's fixed route system.

(1) In calculating the full fare that would be paid by an individual using the fixed route system, the entity may include transfer and premium charges applicable to a trip of similar length, at a similar time of day, on the fixed route system.

(2) The fares for individuals accompanying ADA paratransit eligible individuals, who are provided service under § 37.123 (f) of this part, shall be the same as for the ADA paratransit eligible individuals they are accompanying.

(3) A personal care attendant shall not be charged for complementary paratransit service.

(4) The entity may charge a fare higher than otherwise permitted by this paragraph to a social service agency or other organization for agency trips (i.e., trips guaranteed to the organization).

(d) *Trip purpose restrictions.* The entity shall not impose restrictions or priorities based on trip purpose.

(e) *Hours and days of service.* The complementary paratransit service shall be available throughout the same hours and days as the entity's fixed route service.

(f) *Capacity constraints.* The entity shall not limit the availability of complementary paratransit service to ADA paratransit eligible individuals by any of the following:

(1) Restrictions on the number of trips an individual will be provided;

(2) Waiting lists for access to the service; or

(3) Any operational pattern or practice that significantly limits the availability of service to ADA paratransit eligible persons.

(i) Such patterns or practices include, but are not limited to, the following:

(A) Substantial numbers of significantly untimely pickups for initial or return trips;

(B) Substantial numbers of trip denials or missed trips;

(C) Substantial numbers of trips with excessive trip lengths.

(ii) Operational problems attributable to causes beyond the control of the entity (including, but not limited to, weather or traffic conditions affecting all vehicular traffic that were not anticipated at the time a trip was scheduled) shall not be a basis for determining that such a pattern or practice exists.

(g) *Additional service.* Public entities may provide complementary paratransit service to ADA paratransit eligible individuals exceeding that provided for in this section. However, only the cost of service provided for in this section may be considered in a public entity's request for an undue financial burden waiver under §§ 37.151–37.155 of this part.

§ 37.133 Subscription service.

(a) This part does not prohibit the use of subscription service by public entities as part of a complementary paratransit system, subject to the limitations in this section.

(b) Subscription service may not absorb more than fifty percent of the number of trips available at a given time of day, unless there is non-subscription capacity.

(c) Notwithstanding any other provision of this part, the entity may establish waiting lists or other capacity constraints and trip purpose restrictions or priorities for participation in the subscription service only.

§ 37.135 Submission of paratransit plan.

(a) *General.* Each public entity operating fixed route transportation service, which is required by § 37.121 to provide complementary paratransit service, shall develop a paratransit plan.

(b) *Initial submission.* Except as provided in § 37.141 of this part, each entity shall submit its initial plan for compliance with the complementary paratransit service provision by January 26, 1992, to the appropriate location identified in paragraph (f) of this section.

(c) *Annual updates.* Each entity shall submit an annual update to the plan on January 26 of each succeeding year.

(d) *Phase-in of implementation.* Each plan shall provide full compliance by no later than January 26, 1997, unless the entity has received a waiver based on undue financial burden. If the date for full compliance specified in the plan is after January 26, 1993, the plan shall include milestones, providing for measured, proportional progress toward full compliance.

(e) *Plan implementation.* Each entity shall begin implementation of its plan on January 26, 1992.

(f) *Submission locations.* An entity shall submit its plan to one of the following offices, as appropriate:

(1) The individual state administering agency, if it is —

(i) A section 18 recipient;

(ii) A small urbanized area recipient of section 9 funds administered by the State;

(iii) A participant in a coordinated plan, in which all of the participating entities are eligible to submit their plans to the State; or

(2) The FTA Regional Office (as listed in appendix B to this part) for all other entities required to submit a paratransit plan. This includes an FTA recipient under section 9 of the FT Act; entities submitting a joint plan (unless they meet the requirements of paragraph (f)(1)(iii) of this section), and a public entity not an FT Act recipient.

§ 37.137 Paratransit plan development.

(a) *Survey of existing services.* Each submitting entity shall survey the area to be covered by the plan to identify any person or entity (public or private) which provides a paratransit or other special transportation service for ADA paratransit eligible individuals in the service area to which the plan applies.

(b) *Public participation.* Each submitting entity shall ensure public participation in the development of its paratransit plan, including at least the following:

(1) *Outreach.* Each submitting entity shall solicit participation in the development of its plan by the widest range of persons anticipated to use its paratransit service. Each entity shall develop contacts, mailing lists and other appropriate means for notification of opportunities to participate in the development of the paratransit plan;

(2) *Consultation with individuals with disabilities.* Each entity shall contact individuals with disabilities and groups representing them in the community. Consultation shall begin at an early stage in the plan development and should involve persons with disabilities in all phases of plan development. All documents and other information concerning the planning procedure and the provision of service shall be available, upon request, to members of the public, except where disclosure would be an unwarranted invasion of personal privacy;

(3) *Opportunity for public comment.* The submitting entity shall make its plan available for review before the plan is finalized. In making the plan available for public review, the entity shall ensure that the plan is available upon request in accessible formats;

(4) *Public hearing.* The entity shall sponsor at a minimum one public hearing and shall provide adequate notice of the hearing, including advertisement in appropriate media, such as newspapers of general and special interest circulation and radio announcements; and

(5) *Special requirements.* If the entity intends to phase-in its paratransit service over a multi-year period, or request a waiver based on undue financial burden, the public hearing shall afford the opportunity for interested citizens to express their views concerning the phase-in, the request, and which service criteria may be delayed in implementation.

(c) *Ongoing requirement.* The entity shall create an ongoing mechanism for the participation of individuals with disabilities in the continued development and assessment of services to persons with disabilities. This includes, but is not limited to, the development of the initial plan, any request for an undue financial burden waiver, and each annual submission.

§ 37.139 Plan contents.

Each plan shall contain the following information:

(a) Identification of the entity or entities submitting the plan, specifying for each —

(1) Name and address; and

(2) Contact person for the plan, with telephone number and facsimile telephone number (FAX), if applicable.

(b) A description of the fixed route system as of January 26, 1992 (or subsequent year for annual updates), including —

(1) A description of the service area, route structure, days and hours of service, fare structure, and population served. This includes maps and tables, if appropriate;

(2) The total number of vehicles (bus, van, or rail) operated in fixed route service (including contracted service), and percentage of accessible vehicles and percentage of routes accessible to and usable by persons with disabilities, including persons who use wheelchairs;

(3) Any other information about the fixed route service that is relevant to establishing the basis for comparability of fixed route and paratransit service.

(c) A description of existing paratransit services, including:

(1) An inventory of service provided by the public entity submitting the plan;

(2) An inventory of service provided by other agencies or organizations, which may in whole or in part be used to meet the requirement for complementary paratransit service; and

(3) A description of the available paratransit services in paragraphs (c)(2) and (c)(3) of this section as they relate to the service criteria described in § 37.131 of this part of service area, response time, fares, restrictions on trip purpose, hours and days of service, and capacity constraints; and to the requirements of ADA paratransit eligibility.

(d) A description of the plan to provide comparable paratransit, including:

(1) An estimate of demand for comparable paratransit service by ADA eligible individuals and a brief description of the demand estimation methodology used;

(2) An analysis of differences between the paratransit service currently provided and what is required under this part by the entity(ies) submitting the plan and other entities, as described in paragraph (c) of this section;

(3) A brief description of planned modifications to existing paratransit and fixed route service and the new paratransit service planned to comply with the ADA paratransit service criteria;

(4) A description of the planned comparable paratransit service as it relates to each of the service criteria described in § 37.131 of this part — service area, absence of restrictions or priorities based on trip purpose, response time, fares, hours and days of service, and lack of capacity constraints. If the paratransit plan is to be phased in, this paragraph shall be coordinated with the information being provided in paragraphs (d)(5) and (d)(6) of this paragraph;

(5) A timetable for implementing comparable paratransit service, with a specific date indicating when the planned service will be completely operational. In no case may full implementation be completed later than January 26, 1997. The plan shall include milestones for implementing phases of the plan, with progress that can be objectively measured yearly;

(6) A budget for comparable paratransit service, including capital and operating expenditures over five years.

(e) A description of the process used to certify individuals with disabilities as ADA paratransit eligible. At a minimum, this must include —

(1) A description of the application and certification process, including —

(i) The availability of information about the process and application materials inaccessible formats;

(ii) The process for determining eligibility according to the provisions of §§ 37.123–37.125 of this part and notifying individuals of the determination made;

(iii) The entity's system and timetable for processing applications and allowing presumptive eligibility; and

(iv) The documentation given to eligible individuals.

(2) A description of the administrative appeals process for individuals denied eligibility.

(3) A policy for visitors, consistent with § 37.127 of this part.

(f) Description of the public participation process including —

(1) Notice given of opportunity for public comment, the date(s) of completed public hearing(s), availability of the plan in accessible formats, outreach efforts, and consultation with persons with disabilities.

(2) A summary of significant issues raised during the public comment period, along with a response to significant comments and discussion of how the issues were resolved.

(g) Efforts to coordinate service with other entities subject to the complementary paratransit requirements of this part which have overlapping or contiguous service areas or jurisdictions.

(h) The following endorsements or certifications:

(1) A resolution adopted by the board of the entity authorizing the plan, as submitted. If more than one entity is submitting the plan there must be an authorizing resolution from each board. If the entity does not function with a board, a statement shall be submitted by the entity's chief executive;

(2) In urbanized areas, certification by the Metropolitan Planning Organization (MPO) that it has reviewed the plan and that the plan is in conformance with the transportation plan developed under the Federal Transit/ Federal Highway Administration joint planning regulation (49 CFR part 613 and 23 CFR part 450). In a service area which is covered by more than one MPO, each applicable MPO shall certify conformity of the entity's plan. The provisions of this paragraph do not apply to non-FTA recipients;

(3) A certification that the survey of existing paratransit service was conducted as required in § 37.137(a) of this part;

(4) To the extent service provided by other entities is included in the entity's plan for comparable paratransit service, the entity must certify that:

(i) ADA paratransit eligible individuals have access to the service;

(ii) The service is provided in the manner represented; and

(iii) Efforts will be made to coordinate the provision of paratransit service by other providers.

(i) A request for a waiver based on undue financial burden, if applicable. The waiver request should include information sufficient for FTA to consider the factors in § 37.155 of this part. If a request for an undue financial burden waiver is made, the plan must include a description of additional paratransit services that would be provided to achieve full compliance with the requirement for comparable paratransit in the event the waiver is not granted, and the timetable for the implementation of these additional services.

(j) *Annual plan updates.* (1) The annual plan updates submitted January 26, 1993, and annually thereafter, shall include information necessary to update the information requirements of this section. Information submitted annually must include all significant changes and revisions to the timetable for implementation;

(2) If the paratransit service is being phased in over more than one year, the entity must demonstrate that the milestones identified in the current paratransit plans have been achieved. If the milestones have not been achieved, the plan must explain any slippage and what actions are being taken to compensate for the slippage.

(3) The annual plan must describe specifically the means used to comply with the public participation requirements, as described in § 37.137 of this part.

§ 37.141 Requirements for a joint paratransit plan.

(a) Two or more entities with overlapping or contiguous service areas or jurisdictions may develop and submit a joint plan providing for coordinated paratransit service. Joint plans shall identify the participating entities and indicate their commitment to participate in the plan.

(b) To the maximum extent feasible, all elements of the coordinated plan shall be submitted on January 26, 1992. If a coordinated plan is not completed by January 26, 1992, those entities intending to coordinate paratransit service must submit a general statement declaring their intention to provide coordinated service and each element of the plan specified in § 37.139 to the extent practicable. In addition, the plan must include the following certifications from each entity involved in the coordination effort:

(1) A certification that the entity is committed to providing ADA paratransit service as part of a coordinated plan.

(2) A certification from each public entity participating in the plan that it will maintain current levels of paratransit service until the coordinated plan goes into effect.

(c) Entities submitting the above certifications and plan elements in lieu of a completed plan on January 26, 1992, must submit a complete plan by July 26, 1992.

(d) Filing of an individual plan does not preclude an entity from cooperating with other entities in the development or implementation of a joint plan. An entity wishing to join with other entities after its initial submission may do so by meeting the filing requirements of this section.

§ 37.143 Paratransit plan implementation.

(a) Each entity shall begin implementation of its complementary paratransit plan, pending notice from FTA. The implementation of the plan shall be consistent with the terms of the plan, including any specified phase-in period.

(b) If the plan contains a request for a wavier based on undue financial burden, the entity shall begin implementation of its plan, pending a determination on its waiver request.

§ 37.145 State comment on plans.

Each state required to receive plans under § 37.135 of this part shall:

(a) Ensure that all applicable section 18 and section 9 recipients have submitted plans.

(b) Certify to FTA that all plans have been received.

(c) Forward the required certification with comments on each plan to FTA. The plans, with comments, shall be submitted to FTA no later than April 1, 1992, for the first year and April 1 annually thereafter.

(d) The State shall develop comments to on each plan, responding to the following points:

(1) Was the plan filed on time?

(2) Does the plan appear reasonable?

(3) Are there circumstances that bear on the ability of the grantee to carry out the plan as represented? If yes, please elaborate.

(4) Is the plan consistent with statewide planning activities?

(5) Are the necessary anticipated financial and capital resources identified in the plan accurately estimated?

§ 37.147 Considerations during FTA review.

In reviewing each plan, at a minimum FTA will consider the following:

(a) Whether the plan was filed on time;

(b) Comments submitted by the state, if applicable;

(c) Whether the plan contains responsive elements for each component required under § 37.139 of this part;

(d) Whether the plan, when viewed in its entirety, provides for paratransit service comparable to the entity's fixed route service;

(e) Whether the entity complied with the public participation efforts required by this part; and

(f) The extent to which efforts were made to coordinate with other public entities with overlapping or contiguous service areas or jurisdictions.

§ 37.149 Disapproved plans.

(a) If a plan is disapproved in whole or in part, FTA will specify which provisions are disapproved. Each entity shall amend its plan consistent with this information and resubmit the plan to the appropriate FTA Regional Office within 90 days of receipt of the disapproval letter.

(b) Each entity revising its plan shall continue to comply with the public participation requirements applicable to the initial development of the plan (set out in § 37.137 of this part).

§ 37.151 Waiver for undue financial burden.

If compliance with the service criteria of § 37.131 of this part creates an undue financial burden, an entity may request a waiver from all or some of the provisions if the entity has complied with the public participation requirements in § 37.137 of this part and if the following conditions apply:

(a) At the time of submission of the initial plan on January 26, 1992 —

(1) The entity determines that it cannot meet all of the service criteria by January 26, 1997; or

(2) The entity determines that it cannot make measured progress toward compliance in any year before full compliance is required. For purposes of this part, measured progress means implementing milestones as scheduled, such as incorporating an additional paratransit service criterion or improving an aspect of a specific service criterion.

(b) At the time of its annual plan update submission, if the entity believes that circumstances have changed since its last submission, and it is no longer able to comply by January 26, 1997, or make measured progress in any year before 1997, as described in paragraph (a)(2) of this section.

§ 37.153 FTA waiver determination.

(a) The Administrator will determine whether to grant a waiver for undue financial burden on a case-by-case basis, after considering the factors identified in § 37.155 of this part and the information accompanying the request. If necessary, the Administrator will return the application with a request for additional information.

(b) Any waiver granted will be for a limited and specified period of time.

(c) If the Administrator grants the applicant a waiver, the Administrator will do one of the following:

(1) Require the public entity to provide complementary paratransit to the extent it can do so without incurring an undue financial burden. The entity shall make changes in its plan that the Administrator determines are appropriate to maximize the complementary paratransit service that is provided to ADA paratransit eligible individuals. When making changes to its plan, the entity shall use the public participation process specified for plan development and shall consider first a reduction in number of trips provided to each ADA paratransit eligible person per month, while attempting to meet all other service criteria.

(2) Require the public entity to provide basic complementary paratransit services to all ADA paratransit eligible individuals, even if doing so would cause the public entity to incur an undue financial burden. Basic complementary paratransit service in corridors defined as provided in § 37.131(a) along the public entity's key routes during core service hours.

(i) For purposes of this section, key routes are defined as routes along which there is service at least hourly throughout the day.

(ii) For purposes of this section, core service hours encompass at least peak periods, as these periods are defined locally for fixed route service, consistent with industry practice.

(3) If the Administrator determines that the public entity will incur an undue financial burden as the result of providing basic complementary paratransit service, such that it is infeasible for the entity to provide basic complementary paratransit service, the Administrator shall require the public entity to coordinate with other available providers of demand responsive service in the area served by the public entity to maximize the service to ADA paratransit eligible individuals to the maximum extent feasible.

§ 37.155 Factors in decision to grant an undue financial burden waiver.

(a) In making an undue financial burden determination, the FTA Administrator will consider the following factors:

(1) Effects on current fixed route service, including reallocation of accessible fixed route vehicles and potential reduction in service, measured by service miles;

(2) Average number of trips made by the entity's general population, on a per capita basis, compared with the average number of trips to be made by registered ADA paratransit eligible persons, on a per capita basis;

(3) Reductions in other services, including other special services;

(4) Increases in fares;

(5) Resources available to implement complementary paratransit service over the period covered by the plan;

(6) Percentage of budget needed to implement the plan, both as a percentage of operating budget and a percentage of entire budget;

(7) The current level of accessible service, both fixed route and paratransit;

(8) Cooperation/coordination among area transportation providers;

(9) Evidence of increased efficiencies, that have been or could be effectuated, that would benefit the level and quality of available resources for complementary paratransit service; and

(10) Unique circumstances in the submitting entity's area that affect the ability of the entity to provide paratransit, that militate against the need to provide paratransit, or in some other respect create a circumstance considered exceptional by the submitting entity.

(b)(1) Costs attributable to complementary paratransit shall be limited to costs of providing service specifically required by this part to ADA paratransit eligible individuals, by entities responsible under this part for providing such service.

(2) If the entity determines that it is impracticable to distinguish between trips mandated by the ADA and other trips on a trip-by-trip basis, the entity shall attribute to ADA complementary paratransit requirements a percentage of its overall paratransit costs. This percentage shall be determined by a statistically valid methodology that determines the percentage of trips that are required by this part. The entity shall submit information concerning its methodology and the data on which its percentage is based with its request for a waiver. Only costs attributable to ADA-mandated trips may be considered with respect to a request for an undue financial burden waiver.

(3) Funds to which the entity would be legally entitled, but which, as a matter of state or local funding arrangements, are provided to another entity and used by that entity to provide paratransit service which is part of a coordinated system of paratransit meeting the requirements of this part, may be counted in determining the burden associated with the waiver request.

§ 37.157 — 37.159 [Reserved]

Subpart G — Provision of Service

§ 37.161 Maintenance of accessible features: General.

(a) Public and private entities providing transportation services shall maintain in operative condition those features of facilities and vehicles that are required to make the vehicles and facilities readily accessible to and usable by individuals with disabilities. These features include, but are not limited to, lifts and other means of access to vehicles, securement devices, elevators, signage and systems to facilitate communications with persons with impaired vision or hearing.

(b) Accessibility features shall be repaired promptly if they are damaged or out of order. When an accessibility feature is out of order, the entity shall take reasonable steps to accommodate individuals with disabilities who would otherwise use the feature.

(c) This section does not prohibit isolated or temporary interruptions in service or access due to maintenance or repairs.

§ 37.163 Keeping vehicle lifts in operative condition: Public entities.

(a) This section applies only to public entities with respect to lifts in non-rail vehicles.

(b) The entity shall establish a system of regular and frequent maintenance checks of lifts sufficient to determine if they are operative.

(c) The entity shall ensure that vehicle operators report to the entity, by the most immediate means available, any failure of a lift to operate in service.

(d) Except as provided in paragraph (e) of this section, when a lift is discovered to be inoperative, the entity shall take the vehicle out of service before the beginning of the vehicle's next service day and ensure that the lift is repaired before the vehicle returns to service.

(e) If there is no spare vehicle available to take the place of a vehicle with an inoperable lift, such that taking the vehicle out of service will reduce the transportation service the entity is able to provide, the public entity may keep the vehicle in service with an inoperable lift for no more than five days (if the entity serves an area of 50,000 or less population) or three days (if the entity serves an area of over 50,000 population) from the day on which the lift is discovered to be inoperative.

(f) In any case in which a vehicle is operating on a fixed route with an inoperative lift, and the headway to the next accessible vehicle on the route exceeds 30 minutes, the entity shall promptly provide alternative transportation to individuals with disabilities who are unable to use the vehicle because its lift does not work.

§ 37.165 Lift and securement use.

(a) This section applies to public and private entities.

(b) All common wheelchairs and their users shall be transported in the entity's vehicles or other conveyances. The entity is not required to permit wheelchairs to ride in places other than designated securement locations in the vehicle, where such locations exist.

(c) (1) For vehicles complying with part 38 of this title, the entity shall use the securement system to secure wheelchairs as provided in that Part.

(2) For other vehicles transporting individuals who use wheelchairs, the entity shall provide and use a securement system to ensure that the wheelchair remains within the securement area.

(3) The entity may require that an individual permit his or her wheelchair to be secured.

(d) The entity may not deny transportation to a wheelchair or its user on the ground that the device cannot be secured or restrained satisfactorily by the vehicle's securement system.

(e) The entity may recommend to a user of a wheelchair that the individual transfer to a vehicle seat. The entity may not require the individual to transfer.

(f) Where necessary or upon request, the entity's personnel shall assist individuals with disabilities with the use of securement systems, ramps and lifts. If it is necessary for the personnel to leave their seats to provide this assistance, they shall do so.

(g) The entity shall permit individuals with disabilities who do not use wheelchairs, including standees, to use a vehicle's lift or ramp to enter the vehicle. *Provided,* that an entity is not required to permit such individuals to use a lift Model 141 manufactured by EEC, Inc. If the entity chooses not to allow such individuals to use such a lift, it shall clearly notify consumers of this fact by signage on the exterior of the vehicle (adjacent to and of equivalent size with the accessibility symbol).

[56 FR 45621, Sept. 6, 1991, as amended at 58 FR 63103, Nov. 30, 1993]

§ 37.167 Other service requirements.

(a) This section applies to public and private entities.

(b) On fixed route systems, the entity shall announce stops as follows:

(1) The entity shall announce at least at transfer points with other fixed routes, other major intersections and destination points, and intervals along a route sufficient to permit individuals with visual impairments or other disabilities to be oriented to their location.

(2) The entity shall announce any stop on request of an individual with a disability.

(c) Where vehicles or other conveyances for more than one route serve the same stop, the entity shall provide a means by which an individual with a visual impairment or other disability can identify the proper vehicle to enter or be identified to the vehicle operator as a person seeking a ride on a particular route.

(d) The entity shall permit service animals to accompany individuals with disabilities in vehicles and facilities.

(e) The entity shall ensure that vehicle operators and other personnel make use of accessibility-related equipment or features required by part 38 of this title.

(f) The entity shall make available to individuals with disabilities adequate information concerning transportation services. This obligation includes making adequate communications capacity available, through accessible formats and technology, to enable users to obtain information and schedule service.

(g) The entity shall not refuse to permit a passenger who uses a lift to disembark from a vehicle at any designated stop, unless the lift cannot be deployed, the lift will be damaged if it is deployed, or temporary conditions at the stop, not under the control of the entity, preclude the safe use of the stop by all passengers.

(h) The entity shall not prohibit an individual with a disability from traveling with a respirator or portable oxygen supply, consistent with applicable Department of Transportation rules on the transportation of hazardous materials (49 CFR subtitle B, chapter 1, subchapter C).

(i) The entity shall ensure that adequate time is provided to allow individuals with disabilities to complete boarding or disembarking from the vehicle.

(j)(1) When an individual with a disability enters a vehicle, and because of a disability, the individual needs to sit in a seat or occupy a wheelchair securement location, the entity shall ask the following persons to move in order to allow the individual with a disability to occupy the seat or securement location:

(i) Individuals, except other individuals with a disability or elderly persons, sitting in a location designated as priority seating for elderly and handicapped persons (or other seat as necessary);

(ii) Individuals sitting in or a fold-down or other movable seat in a wheelchair securement location.

(2) This requirement applies to light rail, rapid rail, and commuter rail systems only to the extent practicable.

(3) The entity is not required to enforce the request that other passengers move from priority seating areas or wheelchair securement locations.

(4) In all signage designating priority seating areas for elderly persons and persons with disabilities, or designating wheelchair securement areas, the entity shall include language informing persons sitting in these locations that they should comply with requests by transit provider personnel to vacate their seats to make room for an individual with a disability. This requirement applies to all fixed route vehicles when they are acquired by the entity or to new or replacement signage in the entity's existing fixed route vehicles.

[56 FR 45621, Sept. 6, 1991, as amended at 58 FR 63103, Nov. 30, 1993]

§ 37.169 Interim requirements for over-the-road bus service operated by private entities.

(a) Private entities operating over-the-road buses, in addition to compliance with other applicable provisions of this part, shall provide accessible service as provided in this section.

(b) The private entity shall provide assistance, as needed, to individuals with disabilities in boarding and disembarking, including moving to and from the bus seat for the purpose of boarding and disembarking. The private entity shall ensure that personnel are trained to provide this assistance safely and appropriately.

(c) To the extent that they can be accommodated in the areas of the passenger compartment provided for passengers' personal effects, wheelchairs or other mobility aids and assistive devices used by individuals with disabilities, or components of such devices, shall be permitted in the passenger compartment. When the bus is at rest at a stop, the driver or other personnel shall assist individuals with disabilities with the stowage and retrieval of mobility aids, assistive devices, or other items that can be accommodated in the passenger compartment of the bus.

(d) Wheelchairs and other mobility aids or assistive devices that cannot be accommodated in the passenger compartment (including electric wheelchairs) shall be accommodated in the baggage compartment of the bus, unless the size of the baggage compartment prevents such accommodation.

(e) At any given stop, individuals with disabilities shall have the opportunity to have their wheelchairs or other mobility aids or assistive devices stowed in the baggage compartment before other baggage or cargo is loaded, but baggage or cargo already on the bus does not have to be off-loaded in order to make room for such devices.

(f) The entity may require up to 48 hours' advance notice only for providing boarding assistance. If the individual does not provide such notice, the entity shall nonetheless provide the service if it can do so by making a reasonable effort, without delaying the bus service.

§ 37.171 Equivalency requirement for demand responsive service operated by private entities not primarily engaged in the business of transporting people.

A private entity not primarily engaged in the business of transporting people which operates a demand responsive system shall ensure that its system, when viewed in its entirety, provides equivalent service to individuals with disabilities, including individuals who use wheelchairs, as it does to individuals without disabilities. The standards of § 37.105 shall be used to determine if the entity is providing equivalent service.

§ 37.173 Training requirements.

Each public or private entity which operates a fixed route or demand responsive system shall ensure that personnel are trained to proficiency, as appropriate to their duties, so that they operate vehicles and equipment safely and properly assist and treat individuals with disabilities who use the service in a respectful and courteous way, with appropriate attention to the difference among individuals with disabilities.

PART 38 — AMERICANS WITH DISABILITIES ACT (ADA) ACCESSIBILITY SPECIFICATIONS FOR TRANSPORTATION VEHICLES

Subpart A — General

Subpart B — Buses, Vans and Systems

Subpart C — Rapid Rail Vehicles and Systems

Subpart D — Light Rail Vehicles and Systems

38.85 Between-car barriers.
38.87 Public information system.

Subpart E — Commuter Rail Cars and Systems

38.91 General.
38.93 Doorways.
38.95 Mobility aid accessibility.
38.97 Interior circulation, handrails and stanchions.
38.99 Floors, steps and thresholds.
38.101 Lighting.
38.103 Public information system.
38.105 Priority seating signs.
38.107 Restrooms.
38.109 Between-car barriers.

Subpart F — Intercity Rail Cars and Systems

38.111 General.
38.113 Doorways.
38.115 Interior circulation, handrails and stanchions.
38.117 Floors, steps and thresholds.
38.119 Lighting.
38.121 Public information system.
38.123 Restrooms.
38.125 Mobility aid accessibility.
38.127 Sleeping compartments.

Subpart G — Over-the-Road Buses and Systems

38.151 General.
38.153 Doors, steps and thresholds.
38.155 Interior circulation, handrails and stanchions.
38.157 Lighting.
38.159 Mobility aid accessibility. [Reserved]

Subpart H — Other Vehicles and Systems

38.171 General.
38.173 Automated guideway transit vehicles and systems.
38.175 High-speed rail cars, monorails and systems.
38.177 Ferries, excursion boats and other vessels. [Reserved]
38.179 Trams, and similar vehicles, and systems.

FIGURES IN PART 38

APPENDIX TO PART 38 — GUIDANCE MATERIAL

AUTHORITY: Americans with Disabilities Act of 1990 (42 U.S.C. 12101–12213); 49 U.S.C. 322.

SOURCE: 56 FR 45756, Sept. 6, 1991, unless otherwise noted.

Subpart A — General

§ 38.1 Purpose.

This part provides minimum guidelines and requirements for accessibility standards in part 37 of this title for transportation vehicles required to be accessible by the Americans With Disabilities Act (ADA) of 1990 (42 U.S.C. 1201 *et seq.*).

§ 38.2 Equivalent facilitation.

Departures from particular technical and scoping requirements of these guidelines by use of other designs and technologies are permitted where the alternative designs and technologies used will provide substantially equivalent or greater access to and usability of the vehicle. Departures are to be considered on a case-by-case basis under procedures set forth in § 37.7 of this title.

§ 38.3 Definitions.

See § 37.3 of this title.

§ 38.4 Miscellaneous instructions.

(a) *Dimensional conventions.* Dimensions that are not noted as minimum or maximum are absolute.

(b) *Dimensional tolerances.* All dimensions are subject to conventional engineering tolerances for material properties and field conditions, including normal anticipated wear not exceeding accepted industry-wide standards and practices.

(c) *Notes.* The text of these guidelines does not contain notes or footnotes. Additional information, explanations, and advisory materials are located in the Appendix.

(d) *General terminology.* (1) *Comply with* means meet one or more specification of these guidelines.

(2) *If* or *if * * * then* denotes a specification that applies only when the conditions described are present.

(3) *May* denotes an option or alternative.

(4) *Shall* denotes a mandatory specification or requirement.

(5) *Should* denotes an advisory specification or recommendation.

Subpart B — Buses, Vans and Systems

§ 38.21 General.

(a) New, used or remanufactured buses and vans (except over-the-road buses covered by subpart G of this part), to be considered accessible by regulations in part 37 of this title shall comply with the applicable provisions of this subpart.

(b) If portions of the vehicle are modified in a way that affects or could affect accessibility, each such portion shall comply, to the extent practicable, with the applicable provisions of this subpart. This provision does not require that inaccessible buses be retrofitted with lifts, ramps or other boarding devices.

§ 38.23 Mobility aid accessibility.

(a) *General.* All vehicles covered by this subpart shall provide a level-change mechanism or boarding device (e.g., lift or ramp) complying with paragraph (b) or (c) of this section and sufficient clearances to permit a wheelchair or other mobility aid user to reach a securement location. At least two securement locations and devices, complying with paragraph (d) of this section, shall be provided on vehicles in excess of 22 feet in length; at least one securement location and device, complying with paragraph (d) of this section, shall be provided on vehicles 22 feet in length or less.

(b) *Vehicle lift* — (1) *Design load.* The design load of the lift shall be at least 600 pounds. Working parts, such as cables, pulleys, and shafts, which can be expected to wear, and upon which the lift depends for support of the load, shall have a safety factor of at least six, based on the ultimate strength of the material. Nonworking parts, such as platform, frame, and attachment hardware which would not be expected to wear, shall have a safety factor of at least three, based on the ultimate strength of the material.

(2) *Controls* — (i) *Requirements.* The controls shall be interlocked with the vehicle brakes, transmission, or door, or shall provide other appropriate mechanisms or systems, to ensure that the vehicle cannot be moved when the lift is not stowed and so the lift cannot be deployed unless the interlocks or systems are engaged. The lift shall deploy to all levels (i.e., ground, curb, and intermediate positions) normally encountered in the operating environment. Where provided, each control for deploying, lowering, raising, and

stowing the lift and lowering the roll-off barrier shall be of a momentary contact type requiring continuous manual pressure by the operator and shall not allow improper lift sequencing when the lift platform is occupied. The controls shall allow reversal of the lift operation sequence, such as raising or lowering a platform that is part way down, without allowing an occupied platform to fold or retract into the stowed position.

(ii) *Exception.* Where the lift is designed to deploy with its long dimension parallel to the vehicle axis and which pivots into or out of the vehicle while occupied (i.e., "rotary lift"), the requirements of this paragraph prohibiting the lift from being stowed while occupied shall not apply if the stowed position is within the passenger compartment and the lift is intended to be stowed while occupied.

(3) *Emergency operation.* The lift shall incorporate an emergency method of deploying, lowering to ground level with a lift occupant, and raising and stowing the empty lift if the power to the lift fails. No emergency method, manual or otherwise, shall be capable of being operated in a manner that could be hazardous to the lift occupant or to the operator when operated according to manufacturer's instructions, and shall not permit the platform to be stowed or folded when occupied, unless the lift is a rotary lift and is intended to be stowed while occupied.

(4) *Power or equipment failure.* Platforms stowed in a vertical position, and deployed platforms when occupied, shall have provisions to prevent their deploying, falling, or folding any faster than 12 inches/second or their dropping of an occupant in the event of a single failure of any load carrying component.

(5) *Platform barriers.* The lift platform shall be equipped with barriers to prevent any of the wheels of a wheelchair or mobility aid from rolling off the platform during its operation. A movable barrier or inherent design feature shall prevent a wheelchair or mobility aid from rolling off the edge closest to the vehicle until the platform is in its fully raised position. Each side of the lift platform which extends beyond the vehicle in its raised position shall have a barrier a minimum $1\frac{1}{2}$ inches high. Such barriers shall not interfere with maneuvering into or out of the aisle. The loading-edge barrier (outer barrier) which functions as a loading ramp when the lift is at ground level, shall be sufficient when raised or closed, or a supplementary system shall be provided, to prevent a power wheelchair or mobility aid from riding over or defeating it. The outer barrier of the lift shall automatically raise or close, or a supplementary system shall automatically engage, and remain raised, closed, or engaged at all times that the platform is more than 3 inches above the roadway or sidewalk and the platform is occupied. Alternatively, a barrier or system may be raised, lowered, opened, closed, engaged, or disengaged by the lift operator, provided an interlock or inherent design feature prevents the lift from rising unless the barrier is raised or closed or the supplementary system is engaged.

(6) *Platform surface.* The platform surface shall be free of any protrusions over $\frac{1}{4}$ inch high and shall be slip resistant. The platform shall have a minimum clear width of $28\frac{1}{2}$ inches at the platform, a minimum clear width of 30 inches measured from 2 inches above the platform surface to 30 inches above the platform, and a minimum clear length of 48 inches measured from 2 inches above the surface of the platform to 30 inches above the surface of the platform. (See Fig. 1)

(7) *Platform gaps.* Any openings between the platform surface and the raised barriers shall not exceed $\frac{5}{8}$ inch in width. When the platform is at vehicle floor height with the inner barrier (if applicable) down or retracted, gaps between the forward lift platform edge and the vehicle floor shall not exceed $\frac{1}{2}$ inch horizontally and $\frac{5}{8}$ inch vertically. Platforms on semi-automatic lifts may have a hand hold not exceeding $1\frac{1}{2}$ inches by $4\frac{1}{2}$ inches located between the edge barriers.

(8) *Platform entrance ramp.* The entrance ramp, or loading-edge barrier used as a ramp, shall not exceed a slope of 1:8, measured on level ground, for a maximum rise of 3 inches, and the transition from roadway or sidewalk to ramp may be vertical without edge treatment up to $\frac{1}{4}$ inch. Thresholds between $\frac{1}{4}$ inch and $\frac{1}{2}$ inch high shall be beveled with a slope no greater than 1:2.

(9) *Platform deflection.* The lift platform (not including the entrance ramp) shall not deflect more than 3 degrees (exclusive of vehicle roll or pitch) in any direction between its unloaded position and its position when loaded with 600 pounds applied through a 26 inch by 26 inch test pallet at the centroid of the platform.

(10) *Platform movement.* No part of the platform shall move at a rate exceeding 6 inches/second during lowering and lifting an occupant, and shall not exceed 12 inches/second during deploying or stowing. This requirement does not apply to the deployment or stowage cycles of lifts that are manually deployed or stowed. The maximum platform horizontal and vertical acceleration when occupied shall be 0.3g.

(11) *Boarding direction.* The lift shall permit both inboard and outboard facing of wheelchair and mobility aid users.

(12) *Use by standees.* Lifts shall accommodate persons using walkers, crutches, canes or braces or who otherwise have difficulty using steps. The platform may be marked to indicate a preferred standing position.

(13) *Handrails.* Platforms on lifts shall be equipped with handrails on two sides, which move in tandem with the lift, and which shall be graspable and provide support to standees throughout the entire lift operation. Handrails shall have a usable component at least 8 inches long with the lowest portion a minimum 30 inches above the platform and the highest portion a maximum 38 inches above the platform. The handrails shall be capable of withstanding a force of 100 pounds concentrated at any point on the handrail

without permanent deformation of the rail or its supporting structure. The handrail shall have a cross-sectional diameter between $1\frac{1}{4}$ inches and $1\frac{1}{2}$ inches or shall provide an equivalent grasping surface, and have eased edges with corner radii of not less than $\frac{1}{8}$ inch. Handrails shall be placed to provide a minimum $1\frac{1}{2}$ inches knuckle clearance from the nearest adjacent surface. Handrails shall not interfere with wheelchair or mobility aid maneuverability when entering or leaving the vehicle.

(c) *Vehicle ramp* — (1) *Design load.* Ramps 30 inches or longer shall support a load of 600 pounds, placed at the centroid of the ramp distributed over an area of 26 inches by 26 inches, with a safety factor of at least 3 based on the ultimate strength of the material. Ramps shorter than 30 inches shall support a load of 300 pounds.

(2) *Ramp surface.* The ramp surface shall be continuous and slip resistant; shall not have protrusions from the surface greater than $\frac{1}{4}$ inch high; shall have a clear width of 30 inches; and shall accommodate both four-wheel and three-wheel mobility aids.

(3) *Ramp threshold.* The transition from roadway or sidewalk and the transition from vehicle floor to the ramp may be vertical without edge treatment up to $\frac{1}{4}$ inch. Changes in level between $\frac{1}{4}$ inch and $\frac{1}{2}$ inch shall be beveled with a slope no greater than 1:2.

(4) *Ramp barriers.* Each side of the ramp shall have barriers at least 2 inches high to prevent mobility aid wheels from slipping off.

(5) *Slope.* Ramps shall have the least slope practicable and shall not exceed 1:4 when deployed to ground level. If the height of the vehicle floor from which the ramp is deployed is 3 inches or less above a 6-inch curb, a maximum slope of 1:4 is permitted; if the height of the vehicle floor from which the ramp is deployed is 6 inches or less, but greater than 3 inches, above a 6-inch curb, a maximum slope of 1:6 is permitted; if the height of the vehicle floor from which the ramp is deployed is 9 inches or less, but greater than 6 inches, above a 6-inch curb, a maximum slope of 1:8 is permitted; if the height of the vehicle floor from which the ramp is deployed is greater than 9 inches above a 6-inch curb, a slope of 1:12 shall be achieved. Folding or telescoping ramps are permitted provided they meet all structural requirements of this section.

(6) *Attachment.* When in use for boarding or alighting, the ramp shall be firmly attached to the vehicle so that it is not subject to displacement when loading or unloading a heavy power mobility aid and that no gap between vehicle and ramp exceeds $\frac{5}{8}$ inch.

(7) *Stowage.* A compartment, securement system, or other appropriate method shall be provided to ensure that stowed ramps, including portable ramps stowed in the passenger area, do not impinge on a passenger's wheelchair or mobility aid or pose any hazard to passengers in the event of a sudden stop or maneuver.

(8) *Handrails.* If provided, handrails shall allow persons with disabilities to grasp them from outside the vehicle while starting to board, and to continue to use them throughout the boarding process, and shall have the top between 30 inches and 38 inches above the ramp surface. The handrails shall be capable of withstanding a force of 100 pounds concentrated at any point on the handrail without permanent deformation of the rail or its supporting structure. The handrail shall have a cross-sectional diameter between $1\frac{1}{4}$ inches and $1\frac{1}{2}$ inches or shall provide an equivalent grasping surface, and have eased edges with corner radii of not less than $\frac{1}{8}$ inch. Handrails shall not interfere with wheelchair or mobility aid maneuverability when entering or leaving the vehicle.

(d) *Securement devices* — (1) *Design load.* Securement systems on vehicles with GVWRs of 30,000 pounds or above, and their attachments to such vehicles, shall restrain a force in the forward longitudinal direction of up to 2,000 pounds per securement leg or clamping mechanism and a minimum of 4,000 pounds for each mobility aid. Securement systems on vehicles with GVWRs of up to 30,000 pounds, and their attachments to such vehicles, shall restrain a force in the forward longitudinal direction of up to 2,500 pounds per securement leg or clamping mechanism and a minimum of 5,000 pounds for each mobility aid.

(2) *Location and size.* The securement system shall be placed as near to the accessible entrance as practicable and shall have a clear floor area of 30 inches by 48 inches. Such space shall adjoin, and may overlap, an access path. Not more than 6 inches of the required clear floor space may be accommodated for footrests under another seat provided there is a minimum of 9 inches from the floor to the lowest part of the seat overhanging the space. Securement areas may have fold-down seats to accommodate other passengers when a wheelchair or mobility aid is not occupying the area, provided the seats, when folded up, do not obstruct the clear floor space required. (See Fig. 2)

(3) *Mobility aids accommodated.* The securement system shall secure common wheelchairs and mobility aids and shall either be automatic or easily attached by a person familiar with the system and mobility aid and having average dexterity.

(4) *Orientation.* In vehicles in excess of 22 feet in length, at least one securement device or system required by paragraph (a) of this section shall secure the wheelchair or mobility aid facing toward the front of the vehicle. Additional securement devices or systems shall secure the wheelchair or mobility aid facing forward, or rearward with a padded barrier, extending from a height of 38 inches from the vehicle floor to a height of 56 inches from the vehicle floor with a width of 18 inches, laterally centered immediately in back of the seated individual. In vehicles 22 feet in length or less, the required securement device may secure the wheelchair or mobility aid

either facing toward the front of the vehicle or facing rearward, with a padded barrier as described. Additional securement locations shall be either forward or rearward facing with a padded barrier. Such barriers need not be solid provided equivalent protection is afforded.

(5) *Movement.* When the wheelchair or mobility aid is secured in accordance with manufacturer's instructions, the securement system shall limit the movement of an occupied wheelchair or mobility aid to no more than 2 inches in any direction under normal vehicle operating conditions.

(6) *Stowage.* When not being used for securement, or when the securement area can be used by standees, the securement system shall not interfere with passenger movement, shall not present any hazardous condition, shall be reasonably protected from vandalism, and shall be readily accessed when needed for use.

(7) *Seat belt and shoulder harness.* For each wheelchair or mobility aid securement device provided, a passenger seat belt and shoulder harness, complying with all applicable provisions of part 571 of this title, shall also be provided for use by wheelchair or mobility aid users. Such seat belts and shoulder harnesses shall not be used in lieu of a device which secures the wheelchair or mobility aid itself.

§ 38.25 Doors, steps and thresholds.

(a) *Slip resistance.* All aisles, steps, floor areas where people walk and floors in securement locations shall have slip-resistant surfaces.

(b) *Contrast.* All step edges, thresholds and the boarding edge of ramps or lift platforms shall have a band of color(s) running the full width of the step or edge which contrasts from the step tread and riser, or lift or ramp surface, either light-on-dark or dark-on-light.

(c) *Door height.* For vehicles in excess of 22 feet in length, the overhead clearance between the top of the door opening and the raised lift platform, or highest point of a ramp, shall be a minimum of 68 inches. For vehicles of 22 feet in length or less, the overhead clearance between the top of the door opening and the raised lift platform, or highest point of a ramp, shall be a minimum of 56 inches.

§ 38.27 Priority seating signs.

(a) Each vehicle shall contain sign(s) which indicate that seats in the front of the vehicle are priority seats for persons with disabilities, and that other passengers should make such seats available to those who wish to use them. At least one set of forward-facing seats shall be so designated.

(b) Each securement location shall have a sign designating it as such.

(c) Characters on signs required by paragraphs (a) and (b) of this section shall have a width-to-height ratio between 3:5 and 1:1 and a stroke width-to-height ratio between 1:5 and 1:10, with a minimum character height (using an upper case "X") of $\frac{5}{8}$ inch, with "wide" spacing (generally, the space between letters shall be 1/16 the height of upper case letters), and shall contrast with the background either light-on-dark or dark-on-light.

§ 38.29 Interior circulation, handrails and stanchions.

(a) Interior handrails and stanchions shall permit sufficient turning and maneuvering space for wheelchairs and other mobility aids to reach a securement location from the lift or ramp.

(b) Handrails and stanchions shall be provided in the entrance to the vehicle in a configuration which allows persons with disabilities to grasp such assists from outside the vehicle while starting to board, and to continue using such assists throughout the boarding and fare collection process. Handrails shall have a cross-sectional diameter between $1\frac{1}{4}$ inches and $1\frac{1}{2}$ inches or shall provide an equivalent grasping surface, and have eased edges with corner radii of not less than $\frac{1}{8}$ inch. Handrails shall be placed to provide a minimum $1\frac{1}{2}$ inches knuckle clearance from the nearest adjacent surface. Where on-board fare collection devices are used on vehicles in excess of 22 feet in length, a horizontal passenger assist shall be located across the front of the vehicle and shall prevent passengers from sustaining injuries on the fare collection device or windshield in the event of a sudden deceleration. Without restricting the vestibule space, the assist shall provide support for a boarding passenger from the front door through the boarding procedure. Passengers shall be able to lean against the assist for security while paying fares.

(c) For vehicles in excess of 22 feet in length, overhead handrail(s) shall be provided which shall be continuous except for a gap at the rear doorway.

(d) Handrails and stanchions shall be sufficient to permit safe boarding, on-board circulation, seating and standing assistance, and alighting by persons with disabilities.

(e) For vehicles in excess of 22 feet in length with front-door lifts or ramps, vertical stanchions immediately behind the driver shall either terminate at the lower edge of the aisle-facing seats, if applicable, or be "dog-legged" so that the floor attachment does not impede or interfere with wheelchair footrests. If the driver seat platform must be passed by a wheelchair or mobility aid user entering the vehicle, the platform, to the maximum extent practicable, shall not extend into the aisle or vestibule beyond the wheel housing.

(f) For vehicles in excess of 22 feet in length, the minimum interior height along the path from the lift to the securement location shall be 68 inches. For vehicles of 22 feet in length or less, the minimum interior height from lift to securement location shall be 56 inches.

§ 38.31 Lighting.

(a) Any stepwell or doorway immediately adjacent to the driver shall have, when the door is open, at least 2 foot-candles of illumination measured on the step tread or lift platform.

(b) Other stepwells and doorways, including doorways in which lifts or ramps are installed, shall have, at all times, at least 2 foot-candles of illumination measured on the step tread, or lift or ramp, when deployed at the vehicle floor level.

(c) The vehicle doorways, including doorways in which lifts or ramps are installed, shall have outside light(s) which, when the door is open, provide at least 1 foot-candle of illumination on the street surface for a distance of 3 feet perpendicular to all points on the bottom step tread outer edge. Such light(s) shall be located below window level and shielded to protect the eyes of entering and existing passengers.

§ 38.33 Fare box.

Where provided, the farebox shall be located as far forward as practicable and shall not obstruct traffic in the vestibule, especially wheelchairs or mobility aids.

§ 38.35 Public information system.

(a) Vehicles in excess of 22 feet in length, used in multiple-stop, fixed-route service, shall be equipped with a public address system permitting the driver, or recorded or digitized human speech messages, to announce stops and provide other passenger information within the vehicle.

(b) [Reserved]

§ 38.37 Stop request.

(a) Where passengers may board or alight at multiple stops at their option, vehicles in excess of 22 feet in length shall provide controls adjacent to the securement location for requesting stops and which alerts the driver that a mobility aid user wishes to disembark. Such a system shall provide auditory and visual indications that the request has been made.

(b) Controls required by paragraph (a) of this section shall be mounted no higher than 48 inches and no lower than 15 inches above the floor, shall be operable with one hand and shall not require tight grasping, pinching, or twisting of the wrist. The force required to activate controls shall be no greater than 5 lbf (22.2 N).

§ 38.39 Destination and route signs.

(a) Where destination or route information is displayed on the exterior of a vehicle, each vehicle shall have illuminated signs on the front and boarding side of the vehicle.

(b) Characters on signs required by paragraph (a) of this section shall have a width-to-height ratio between 3:5 and 1:1 and a stroke width-to-height ratio between 1:5 and 1:10, with a minimum character height (using an upper case "X") of 1 inch for signs on the boarding side and a minimum character height of 2 inches for front "headsigns", with "wide" spacing (generally, the space between letters shall be $\frac{1}{16}$ the height of upper case letters), and shall contrast with the background, either dark-on-light or light-on-dark.

Subpart C — Rapid Rail Vehicles and Systems

§ 38.51 General.

(a) New, used and remanufactured rapid rail vehicles, to be considered accessible by regulations in part 37 of this title, shall comply with this subpart.

(b) If portions of the vehicle are modified in a way that affects or could affect accessibility, each such portion shall comply, to the extent practicable, with the applicable provisions of this subpart. This provision does not require that inaccessible vehicles be retrofitted with lifts, ramps or other boarding devices.

(c) Existing vehicles which are retrofitted to comply with the "one-car-per-train rule" of § 37.93 of this title shall comply with §§ 38.55, 38.57(b), 38.59 of this part and shall have, in new and key stations, at least one door complying with §§ 38.53 (a)(1), (b) and (d) of this part. Removal of seats is not required. Vehicles previously designed and manufactured in accordance with the accessibility requirements of part 609 of this title or the Secretary of Transportation regulations implementing section 504 of the Rehabilitation Act of 1973 that were in effect before October 7, 1991, and which can be entered and used from stations in which they are to be operated, may be used to satisfy the requirements of § 37.93 of this title.

§ 38.53 Doorways.

(a) *Clear width.* (1) Passenger doorways on vehicle sides shall have clear openings at least 32 inches wide when open.

(2) If doorways connecting adjoining cars in a multi-car train are provided, and if such doorway is connected by an aisle with a minimum clear width of 30 inches to one or more spaces where wheelchair or mobility aid

users can be accommodated, then such doorway shall have a minimum clear opening of 30 inches to permit wheelchair and mobility aid users to be evacuated to an adjoining vehicle in an emergency.

(b) *Signage.* The International Symbol of Accessibility shall be displayed on the exterior of accessible vehicles operating on an accessible rapid rail system unless all vehicles are accessible and are not marked by the access symbol. (See Fig. 6.)

(c) *Signals.* Auditory and visual warning signals shall be provided to alert passengers of closing doors.

(d) *Coordination with boarding platform* — (1) *Requirements.* Where new vehicles will operate in new stations, the design of vehicles shall be coordinated with the boarding platform design such that the horizontal gap between each vehicle door at rest and the platform shall be no greater than 3 inches and the height of the vehicle floor shall be within plus or minus $\frac{5}{8}$ inch of the platform height under all normal passenger load conditions. Vertical alignment may be accomplished by vehicle air suspension or other suitable means of meeting the requirement.

(2) *Exception.* New vehicles operating in existing stations may have a floor height within plus or minus $1\frac{1}{2}$ inches of the platform height. At key stations, the horizontal gap between at least one door of each such vehicle and the platform shall be no greater than 3 inches.

(3) *Exception.* Retrofitted vehicles shall be coordinated with the platform in new and key stations such that the horizontal gap shall be no greater than 4 inches and the height of the vehicle floor, under 50% passenger load, shall be within plus or minus 2 inches of the platform height.

§ 38.55 Priority seating signs.

(a) Each vehicle shall contain sign(s) which indicate that certain seats are priority seats for persons with disabilities, and that other passengers should make such seats available to those who wish to use them.

(b) Characters on signs required by paragraph (a) of this section shall have a width-to-height ratio between 3:5 and 1:1 and a stroke width-to-height ratio between 1:5 and 1:10, with a minimum character height (using an upper case "X") of $\frac{5}{8}$ inch, with "wide" spacing (generally, the space between letters shall be $\frac{1}{16}$ the height of upper case letters), and shall contrast with the background, either light-on-dark or dark-on-light.

§ 38.57 Interior circulation, handrails and stanchions.

(a) Handrails and stanchions shall be provided to assist safe boarding, on-board circulation, seating and standing assistance, and alighting by persons with disabilities.

(b) Handrails, stanchions, and seats shall allow a route at least 32 inches wide so that at least two wheelchair or mobility aid users can enter the vehicle and position the wheelchairs or mobility aids in areas, each having a minimum clear space of 48 inches by 30 inches, which do not unduly restrict movement of other passengers. Space to accommodate wheelchairs and mobility aids may be provided within the normal area used by standees and designation of specific spaces is not required. Particular attention shall be given to ensuring maximum maneuver-ability immediately inside doors. Ample vertical stanchions from ceiling to seat-back rails shall be provided. Vertical stanchions from ceiling to floor shall not interfere with wheelchair or mobility aid user circulation and shall be kept to a minimum in the vicinity of doors.

(c) The diameter or width of the gripping surface of handrails and stanchions shall be $1\frac{1}{4}$ inches to $1\frac{1}{2}$ inches or provide an equivalent gripping surface and shall provide a minimum $1\frac{1}{2}$ inches knuckle clearance from the nearest adjacent surface.

§ 38.59 Floor surfaces.

Floor surfaces on aisles, places for standees, and areas where wheelchair and mobility aid users are to be accommodated shall be slip-resistant.

§ 38.61 Public information system.

(a)(1) *Requirements.* Each vehicle shall be equipped with a public address system permitting transportation system personnel, or recorded or digitized human speech messages, to announce stations and provide other passenger information. Alternative systems or devices which provide equivalent access are also permitted. Each vehicle operating in stations having more than one line or route shall have an external public address system to permit transportation system personnel, or recorded or digitized human speech messages, to announce train, route, or line identification information.

(2) *Exception.* Where station announcement systems provide information on arriving trains, an external train speaker is not required.

(b) [Reserved]

§ 38.63 Between-car barriers.

(a) *Requirement.* Suitable devices or systems shall be provided to prevent, deter or warn individuals from inadvertently stepping off the platform between cars. Acceptable solutions include, but are not limited to, pantograph gates, chains, motion detectors or similar devices.

(b) *Exception.* Between-car barriers are not required where platform screens are provided which close off the platform edge and open only when trains are correctly aligned with the doors.

Subpart D — Light Rail Vehicles and Systems

§ 38.71 General.

(a) New, used and remanufactured light rail vehicles, to be considered accessible by regulations in part 37 of this title shall comply with this subpart.

(b)(1) Vehicles intended to be operated solely in light rail systems confined entirely to a dedicated right-of-way, and for which all stations or stops are designed and constructed for revenue service after the effective date of standards for design and construction in § 37.21 and § 37.23 of this title shall provide level boarding and shall comply with § 38.73(d)(1) and § 38.85 of this part.

(2) Vehicles designed for, and operated on, pedestrian malls, city streets, or other areas where level boarding is not practicable shall provide wayside or car-borne lifts, mini-high platforms, or other means of access in compliance with § 38.83 (b) or (c) of this part.

(c) If portions of the vehicle are modified in a way that affects or could affect accessibility, each such portion shall comply, to the extent practicable, with the applicable provisions of this subpart. This provision does not require that inaccessible vehicles be retrofitted with lifts, ramps or other boarding devices.

(d) Existing vehicles retrofitted to comply with the "one-car-per-train rule" at § 37.93 of this title shall comply with § 38.75, § 38.77(c), § 38.79(a) and § 38.83(a) of this part and shall have, in new and key stations, at least one door which complies with §§ 38.73 (a)(1), (b) and (d) of this part. Vehicles previously designed and manufactured in accordance with the accessibility requirements of part 609 of this title or the Secretary of Transportation regulations implementing section 504 of the Rehabilitation Act of 1973 that were in effect before October 7, 1991, and which can be entered and used from stations in which they are to be operated, may be used to satisfy the requirements of § 37.93 of this title.

§ 38.73 Doorways.

(a) *Clear width* — (1) All passenger doorways on vehicle sides shall have minimum clear openings of 32 inches when open.

(2) If doorways connecting adjoining cars in a multi-car train are provided, and if such doorway is connected by an aisle with a minimum clear width of 30 inches to one or more spaces where wheelchair or mobility aid users can be accommodated, then such doorway shall have a minimum clear opening of 30 inches to permit wheelchair and mobility aid users to be evacuated to an adjoining vehicle in an emergency.

(b) *Signage.* The International Symbol of Accessibility shall be displayed on the exterior of each vehicle operating on an accessible light rail system unless all vehicles are accessible and are not marked by the access symbol (see fig. 6).

(c) *Signals.* Auditory and visual warning signals shall be provided to alert passengers of closing doors.

(d) *Coordination with boarding platform* — (1) *Requirements.* The design of level-entry vehicles shall be coordinated with the boarding platform or mini-high platform design so that the horizontal gap between a vehicle at rest and the platform shall be no greater than 3 inches and the height of the vehicle floor shall be within plus or minus $\frac{5}{8}$ inch of the platform height. Vertical alignment may be accomplished by vehicle air suspension, automatic ramps or lifts, or any combination.

(2) *Exception.* New vehicles operating in existing stations may have a floor height within plus or minus $1\frac{1}{2}$ inches of the platform height. At key stations, the horizontal gap between at least one door of each such vehicle and the platform shall be no greater than 3 inches.

(3) *Exception.* Retrofitted vehicles shall be coordinated with the platform in new and key stations such that the horizontal gap shall be no greater than 4 inches and the height of the vehicle floor, under 50% passenger load, shall be within plus or minus 2 inches of the platform height.

(4) *Exception.* Where it is not operationally or structurally practicable to meet the horizontal or vertical requirements of paragraphs (d) (1), (2) or (3) of this section, platform or vehicle devices complying with § 38.83(b) or platform or vehicle mounted ramps or bridge plates complying with § 38.83(c) shall be provided.

§ 38.75 Priority seating signs.

(a) Each vehicle shall contain sign(s) which indicate that certain seats are priority seats for persons with disabilities, and that other passengers should make such seats available to those who wish to use them.

(b) Where designated wheelchair or mobility aid seating locations are provided, signs shall indicate the location and advise other passengers of the need to permit wheelchair and mobility aid users to occupy them.

(c) Characters on signs required by paragraphs (a) or (b) of this section shall have a width-to-height ratio between 3:5 and 1:1 and a stroke width-to-height ratio between 1:5 and 1:10, with a minimum character height (using an upper case "X") of $\frac{5}{8}$ inch, with "wide" spacing (generally, the space between letters shall be $\frac{1}{16}$ the height of upper case letters), and shall contrast with the background, either light-on-dark or dark-on-light.

§ 38.77 Interior circulation, handrails and stanchions.

(a) Handrails and stanchions shall be sufficient to permit safe boarding, on-board circulation, seating and standing assistance, and alighting by persons with disabilities.

(b) At entrances equipped with steps, handrails and stanchions shall be provided in the entrance to the vehicle in a configuration which allows passengers to grasp such assists from outside the vehicle while starting to board, and to continue using such handrails or stanchions throughout the boarding process. Handrails shall have a cross-sectional diameter between $1\frac{1}{4}$ inches and $1\frac{1}{2}$ inches or shall provide an equivalent grasping surface, and have eased edges with corner radii of not less than $\frac{1}{8}$ inch. Handrails shall be placed to provide a minimum $1\frac{1}{2}$ inches knuckle clearance from the nearest adjacent surface. Where on-board fare collection devices are used, a horizontal passenger assist shall be located between boarding passengers and the fare collection device and shall prevent passengers from sustaining injuries on the fare collection device or windshield in the event of a sudden deceleration. Without restricting the vestibule space, the assist shall provide support for a boarding passenger from the door through the boarding procedure. Passengers shall be able to lean against the assist for security while paying fares.

(c) At all doors on level-entry vehicles, and at each entrance accessible by lift, ramp, bridge plate or other suitable means, handrails, stanchions, passenger seats, vehicle driver seat platforms, and fare boxes, if applicable, shall be located so as to allow a route at least 32 inches wide so that at least two wheelchair or mobility aid users can enter the vehicle and position the wheelchairs or mobility aids in areas, each having a minimum clear space of 48 inches by 30 inches, which do not unduly restrict movement of other passengers. Space to accommodate wheelchairs and mobility aids may be provided within the normal area used by standees and designation of specific spaces is not required. Particular attention shall be given to ensuring maximum maneuverability immediately inside doors. Ample vertical stanchions from ceiling to seat-back rails shall be provided. Vertical stanchions from ceiling to floor shall not interfere with wheelchair or mobility aid circulation and shall be kept to a minimum in the vicinity of accessible doors.

§ 38.79 Floors, steps and thresholds.

(a) Floor surfaces on aisles, step treads, places for standees, and areas where wheelchair and mobility aid users are to be accommodated shall be slip-resistant.

(b) All thresholds and step edges shall have a band of color(s) running the full width of the step or threshold which contrasts from the step tread and riser or adjacent floor, either light-on-dark or dark-on-light.

§ 38.81 Lighting.

(a) Any stepwell or doorway with a lift, ramp or bridge plate immediately adjacent to the driver shall have, when the door is open, at least 2 foot-candles of illumination measured on the step tread or lift platform.

(b) Other stepwells, and doorways with lifts, ramps or bridge plates, shall have, at all times, at least 2 foot-candles of illumination measured on the step tread or lift or ramp, when deployed at the vehicle floor level.

(c) The doorways of vehicles not operating at lighted station platforms shall have outside lights which provide at least 1 foot-candle of illumination on the station platform or street surface for a distance of 3 feet perpendicular to all points on the bottom step tread. Such lights shall be located below window level and shielded to protect the eyes of entering and exiting passengers.

§ 38.83 Mobility aid accessibility.

(a)(1) *General.* All new light rail vehicles, other than level entry vehicles, covered by this subpart shall provide a level-change mechanism or boarding device (e.g., lift, ramp or bridge plate) complying with either paragraph (b) or (c) of this section and sufficient clearances to permit at least two wheelchair or mobility aid users to reach areas, each with a minimum clear floor space of 48 inches by 30 inches, which do not unduly restrict passenger flow. Space to accommodate wheelchairs and mobility aids may be provided within the normal area used by standees and designation of specific spaces is not required.

(2) *Exception.* If lifts, ramps or bridge plates meeting the requirements of this section are provided on station platforms or other stops required to be accessible, or mini-high platforms complying with § 38.73(d) of this part are provided, the vehicle is not required to be equipped with a car-borne device. Where each new vehicle is compatible with a single platform-mounted access system or device, additional systems or devices are not required for each vehicle provided that the single device could be used to provide access to each new vehicle if passengers using wheelchairs or mobility aids could not be accommodated on a single vehicle.

(b) *Vehicle lift* — (1) *Design load.* The design load of the lift shall be at least 600 pounds. Working parts, such as cables, pulleys, and shafts, which can be expected to wear, and upon which the lift depends for support of the load, shall have a safety factor of at least six, based on the ultimate strength of the material. Nonworking parts, such as platform, frame, and attachment hardware which would not be expected to wear, shall have a safety factor of at least three, based on the ultimate strength of the material.

(2) *Controls* — (i) *Requirements.* The controls shall be interlocked with the vehicle brakes, propulsion system, or door, or shall provide other ap-

propriate mechanisms or systems, to ensure that the vehicle cannot be moved when the lift is not stowed and so the lift cannot be deployed unless the interlocks or systems are engaged. The lift shall deploy to all levels (i.e., ground, curb, and intermediate positions) normally encountered in the operating environment. Where provided, each control for deploying, lowering, raising, and stowing the lift and lowering the roll-off barrier shall be of a momentary contact type requiring continuous manual pressure by the operator and shall not allow improper lift sequencing when the lift platform is occupied. The controls shall allow reversal of the lift operation sequence, such as raising or lowering a platform that is part way down, without allowing an occupied platform to fold or retract into the stowed position.

(ii) *Exception.* Where physical or safety constraints prevent the deployment at some stops of a lift having its long dimension perpendicular to the vehicle axis, the transportation entity may specify a lift which is designed to deploy with its long dimension parallel to the vehicle axis and which pivots into or out of the vehicle while occupied (i.e., "rotary lift"). The requirements of paragraph (b)(2)(i) of this section prohibiting the lift from being stowed while occupied shall not apply to a lift design of this type if the stowed position is within the passenger compartment and the lift is intended to be stowed while occupied.

(iii) *Exception.* The brake or propulsion system interlocks requirement does not apply to a station platform mounted lift provided that a mechanical, electrical or other system operates to ensure that vehicles do not move when the lift is in use.

(3) *Emergency operation.* The lift shall incorporate an emergency method of deploying, lowering to ground level with a lift occupant, and raising and stowing the empty lift if the power to the lift fails. No emergency method, manual or otherwise, shall be capable of being operated in a manner that could be hazardous to the lift occupant or to the operator when operated according to manufacturer's instructions, and shall not permit the platform to be stowed or folded when occupied, unless the lift is a rotary lift intended to be stowed while occupied.

(4) *Power or equipment failure.* Lift platforms stowed in a vertical position, and deployed platforms when occupied, shall have provisions to prevent their deploying, falling, or folding any faster than 12 inches/second or their dropping of an occupant in the event of a single failure of any load carrying component.

(5) *Platform barriers.* The lift platform shall be equipped with barriers to prevent any of the wheels of a wheelchair or mobility aid from rolling off the lift during its operation. A movable barrier or inherent design feature shall prevent a wheelchair or mobility aid from rolling off the edge closest to the vehicle until the lift is in its fully raised position. Each side of the lift platform which extends beyond the vehicle in its raised position shall have a barrier a minimum $1\frac{1}{2}$ inches high. Such barriers shall not interfere

with maneuvering into or out of the aisle. The loading-edge barrier (outer barrier) which functions as a loading ramp when the lift is at ground level, shall be sufficient when raised or closed, or a supplementary system shall be provided, to prevent a power wheelchair or mobility aid from riding over or defeating it. The outer barrier on the outboard of the lift shall automatically rise or close, or a supplementary system shall automatically engage, and remain raised, closed, or engaged at all times that the lift is more than 3 inches above the station platform or roadway and the lift is occupied. Alternatively, a barrier or system may be raised, lowered, opened, closed, engaged or disengaged by the lift operator provided an interlock or inherent design feature prevents the lift from rising unless the barrier is raised or closed or the supplementary system is engaged.

(6) *Platform surface.* The lift platform surface shall be free of any protrusions over $\frac{1}{4}$ inch high and shall be slip resistant. The lift platform shall have a minimum clear width of $28\frac{1}{2}$ inches at the platform, a minimum clear width of 30 inches measured from 2 inches above the lift platform surface to 30 inches above the surface, and a minimum clear length of 48 inches measured from 2 inches above the surface of the platform to 30 inches above the surface. (See Fig. 1)

(7) *Platform gaps.* Any openings between the lift platform surface and the raised barriers shall not exceed $\frac{5}{8}$ inch wide. When the lift is at vehicle floor height with the inner barrier (if applicable) down or retracted, gaps between the forward lift platform edge and vehicle floor shall not exceed $\frac{1}{2}$ inch horizontally and $\frac{5}{8}$ inch vertically. Platforms on semi-automatic lifts may have a hand hold not exceeding $1\frac{1}{2}$ inches by $4\frac{1}{2}$ inches located between the edge barriers.

(8) *Platform entrance ramp.* The entrance ramp, or loading-edge barrier used as a ramp, shall not exceed a slope of 1:8 measured on level ground, for a maximum rise of 3 inches, and the transition from the station platform or roadway to ramp may be vertical without edge treatment up to $\frac{1}{4}$ inch. Thresholds between $\frac{1}{4}$ inch and $\frac{1}{2}$ inch high shall be beveled with a slope no greater than 1:2.

(9) *Platform deflection.* The lift platform (not including the entrance ramp) shall not deflect more than 3 degrees (exclusive of vehicle roll) in any direction between its unloaded position and its position when loaded with 600 pounds applied through a 26 inch by 26 inch test pallet at the centroid of the lift platform.

(10) *Platform movement.* No part of the platform shall move at a rate exceeding 6 inches/second during lowering and lifting an occupant, and shall not exceed 12 inches/second during deploying or stowing. This requirement does not apply to the deployment or stowage cycles of lifts that are manually deployed or stowed. The maximum platform horizontal and vertical acceleration when occupied shall be 0.3g.

(11) *Boarding direction.* The lift shall permit both inboard and outboard facing of wheelchairs and mobility aids.

(12) *Use by standees.* Lifts shall accommodate persons using walkers, crutches, canes or braces or who otherwise have difficulty using steps. The lift may be marked to indicate a preferred standing position.

(13) *Handrails.* Platforms on lifts shall be equipped with handrails, on two sides, which move in tandem with the lift which shall be graspable and provide support to standees throughout the entire lift operation. Handrails shall have a usable component at least 8 inches long with the lowest portion a minimum 30 inches above the platform and the highest portion a maximum 38 inches above the platform. The handrails shall be capable of withstanding a force of 100 pounds concentrated at any point on the handrail without permanent deformation of the rail or its supporting structure. Handrails shall have a cross-sectional diameter between $1\frac{1}{4}$ inches and $1\frac{1}{2}$ inches or shall provide an equivalent grasping surface, and have eased edges with corner radii of not less than $\frac{1}{8}$ inch. Handrails shall be placed to provide a minimum $1\frac{1}{2}$ inches knuckle clearance from the nearest adjacent surface. Handrails shall not interfere with wheelchair or mobility aid maneuverability when entering or leaving the vehicle.

(c) *Vehicle ramp or bridge plate.* — (1) *Design load.* Ramps or bridge plates 30 inches or longer shall support a load of 600 pounds, placed at the centroid of the ramp or bridge plate distributed over an area of 26 inches, with a safety factor of at least 3 based on the ultimate strength of the material. Ramps or bridge plates shorter than 30 inches shall support a load of 300 pounds.

(2) *Ramp surface.* The ramp or bridge plate surface shall be continuous and slip resistant, shall not have protrusions from the surface greater then $\frac{1}{4}$ inch, shall have a clear width of 30 inches, and shall accommodate both four-wheel and three-wheel mobility aids.

(3) *Ramp threshold.* The transition from roadway or station platform and the transition from vehicle floor to the ramp to bridge plate may be vertical without edge treatment up to $\frac{1}{4}$ inch. Changes in level between $\frac{1}{4}$ inch and $\frac{1}{2}$ inch shall be beveled with a slope no greater than 1:2.

(4) *Ramp barriers.* Each side of the ramp or bridge plate shall have barriers at least 2 inches high to prevent mobility aid wheels from slipping off.

(5) *Slope.* Ramps or bridge plates shall have the least slope practicable. If the height of the vehicle floor, under 50% passenger load, from which the ramp is deployed is 3 inches or less above the station platform a maximum slope of 1:4 is permitted; if the height of the vehicle floor, under 50% passenger load, from which the ramp is deployed is 6 inches or less, but more than 3 inches, above the station platform a maximum slope of 1:6 is permitted; if the height of the vehicle floor, under 50% passenger load, from

which the ramp is deployed is 9 inches or less, but more than 6 inches, above the station platform a maximum slope of 1:8 is permitted; if the height of the vehicle floor, under 50% passenger load, from which the ramp is deployed is greater than 9 inches above the station platform a slope of 1:12 shall be achieved. Folding or telescoping ramps are permitted provided they meet all structural requirements of this section.

(6) *Attachment* — (i) *Requirement.* When in use for boarding or alighting, the ramp or bridge plate shall be attached to the vehicle, or otherwise prevented from moving such that it is not subject to displacement when loading or unloading a heavy power mobility aid and that any gaps between vehicle and ramp or bridge plate, and station platform and ramp or bridge plate, shall not exceed $\frac{5}{8}$ inch.

(ii) *Exception.* Ramps or bridge plates which are attached to, and deployed from, station platforms are permitted in lieu of vehicle devices provided they meet the displacement requirements of paragraph (c)(6)(i) of this section.

(7) *Stowage.* A compartment, securement system, or other appropriate method shall be provided to ensure that stowed ramps or bridge plates, including portable ramps or bridges plates stowed in the passenger area, do not impinge on a passenger's wheelchair or mobility aid or pose any hazard to passengers in the event of a sudden stop.

(8) *Handrails.* If provided, handrails shall allow persons with disabilities to grasp them from outside the vehicle while starting to board, and to continue to use them throughout the boarding process, and shall have the top between 30 inches and 38 inches above the ramp surface. The handrails shall be capable of withstanding a force of 100 pounds concentrated at any point on the handrail without permanent deformation of the rail or its supporting structure. The handrail shall have a cross-sectional diameter between $1\frac{1}{4}$ inches and $1\frac{1}{2}$ inches or shall provide an equivalent grasping surface, and have "eased" edges with corner radii of not less than $\frac{1}{8}$ inch. Handrails shall not interfere with wheelchair or mobility aid maneuverability when entering or leaving the vehicle.

§ 38.85 Between-car barriers.

Where vehicles operate in a high-platform, level-boarding mode, devices or systems shall be provided to prevent, deter or warn individuals from inadvertently stepping off the platform between cars. Appropriate devices include, but are not limited to, pantograph gates, chains, motion detectors or other suitable devices.

§ 38.87 Public information system.

(a) Each vehicle shall be equipped with an interior public address system permitting transportation system personnel, or recorded or digitized human speech messages, to announce stations and provide other passenger information. Alternative systems or devices which provide equivalent access are also permitted.

(b) [Reserved]

Subpart E — Commuter Rail Cars and Systems

§ 38.91 General.

(a) New, used and remanufactured commuter rail cars, to be considered accessible by regulations in part 37 of this title, shall comply with this subpart.

(b) If portions of the car are modified in such a way that it affects or could affect accessibility, each such portion shall comply, to the extent practicable, with the applicable provisions of this subpart. This provision does not require that inaccessible cars be retrofitted with lifts, ramps or other boarding devices.

(c)(1) Commuter rail cars shall comply with §§ 38.93(d) and 38.109 of this part for level boarding wherever structurally and operationally practicable.

(2) Where level boarding is not structurally or operationally practicable, commuter rail cars shall comply § 38.95 of this part.

(d) Existing vehicles retrofitted to comply with the "one-car-per-train rule" at § 37.93 of this title shall comply with §§ 38.93(e), 38.95(a) and 38.107 of this part and shall have, in new and key stations at least one door on each side from which passengers board which complies with § 38.93(d) of this part. Vehicles previously designed and manufactured in accordance with the program accessibility requirements of section 504 of the Rehabilitation Act of 1973, or implementing regulations of the Secretary of Transportation that were in effect before October 7, 1991; and which can be entered and used from stations in which they are to be operated, may be used to satisfy the requirements of § 37.93 of this title.

§ 38.93 Doorways.

(a) *Clear width.* (1) At least one door on each side of the car from which passengers board opening onto station platforms and at least one adjacent doorway into the passenger coach compartment, if provided, shall have a minimum clear opening of 32 inches.

(2) If doorways connecting adjoining cars in a multi-car train are provided, and if such doorway is connected by an aisle with a minimum clear width of 30 inches to one or more spaces where wheelchair or mobility aid users can be accommodated, then such doorway shall have, to the maximum extent practicable in accordance with the regulations issued under the Fed-

eral Railroad Safety Act of 1970 (49 CFR parts 229 and 231), a clear opening of 30 inches.

(b) *Passageways.* A route at least 32 inches wide shall be provided from doors required to be accessible by paragraph (a)(1) of this section to seating locations complying with § 38.95(d) of this part. In cars where such doorways require passage through a vestibule, such vestibule shall have a minimum width of 42 inches. (See Fig. 3.)

(c) *Signals.* If doors to the platform close automatically or from a remote location, auditory and visual warning signals shall be provided to alert passengers or closing doors.

(d) *Coordination with boarding platform* — (1) *Requirements.* Cars operating in stations with high platforms, or mini-high platforms, shall be coordinated with the boarding platform design such that the horizontal gap between a car at rest and the platform shall be no greater than 3 inches and the height of the car floor shall be within plus or minus $\frac{5}{8}$ inch of the platform height. Vertical alignment may be accomplished by car air suspension, platform lifts or other devices, or any combination.

(2) *Exception.* New vehicles operating in existing stations may have a floor height within plus or minus $1\frac{1}{2}$ inches of the platform height. At key stations, the horizontal gap between at least one accessible door of each such vehicle and the platform shall be no greater than 3 inches.

(3) *Exception.* Where platform setbacks do not allow the horizontal gap or vertical alignment specified in paragraph (d)(1) or (d)(2) of this section, car, platform or portable lifts complying with § 38.95(b) of this part, or car or platform ramps or bridge plates, complying with § 38.95(c) of this part, shall be provided.

(4) *Exception.* Retrofitted vehicles shall be coordinated with the platform in new and key stations such that the horizontal gap shall be no greater than 4 inches and the height of the vehicle floor, under 50% passenger load, shall be within plus or minus 2 inches of the platform height.

(e) *Signage.* The International Symbol of Accessibility shall be displaced on the exterior of all doors complying with this section unless all cars are accessible and are not marked by the access symbol (see Fig. 6). Appropriate signage shall also indicate which accessible doors are adjacent to an accessible restroom, if applicable.

§ 38.95 Mobility aid accessibility.

(a)(1) *General.* All new commuter rail cars, other than level entry cars, covered by this subpart shall provide a level-change mechanism or boarding device (e.g., lift, ramp or bridge plate) complying with either paragraph (b) or (c) of this section; sufficient clearances to permit a wheelchair or mobility aid user to reach a seating location; and at least two wheelchair or mobility aid seating locations complying with paragraph (d) of this section.

(2) *Exception.* If portable or platform lifts, ramps or bridge plates meeting the applicable requirements of this section are provided on station platforms or other stops required to be accessible, or mini-high platforms complying with § 38.93(d) are provided, the car is not required to be equipped with a car-borne device. Where each new car is compatible with a single platform-mounted access system or device, additional systems or devices are not required for each car provided that the single device could be used to provide access to each new car if passengers using wheelchairs or mobility aids could not be accommodated on a single car.

(b) *Car Lift* — (1) *Design load.* The design load of the lift shall be at least 600 pounds. Working parts, such as cables, pulleys, and shafts, which can be expected to wear, and upon which the lift depends for support of the load, shall have a safety factor of at least six, based on the ultimate strength of the material. Nonworking parts, such as platform, frame, and attachment hardware which would not be expected to wear, shall have a safety factor of at least three, based on the ultimate strength of the material.

(2) *Controls* — (i) *Requirements.* The controls shall be interlocked with the car brakes, propulsion system, or door, or shall provide other appropriate mechanisms or systems, to ensure that the car cannot be moved when the lift is not stowed and so the lift cannot be deployed unless the interlocks or systems are engaged. The lift shall deploy to all platform levels normally encountered in the operating environment. Where provided, each control for deploying, lowering, raising, and stowing the lift and lowering the roll-off barrier shall be of a monetary contact type requiring continuous manual pressure by the operator and shall not allow improper lift sequencing when the lift platform is occupied. The controls shall allow reversal of the lift operation sequence, such as raising or lowering a platform that is part way down, without allowing an occupied platform to fold or retract into the stowed position.

(ii) *Exception.* Where physical or safety constraints prevent the deployment at some stops of a lift having its long dimension perpendicular to the car axis, the transportation entity may specify a lift which is designed to deploy with its long dimension parallel to the car axis and which pivots into or out of the car while occupied (i.e., "rotary lift"). The requirements of paragraph (b)(2)(i) of this section prohibiting the lift from being stowed while occupied shall not apply to a lift design of this type if the stowed position is within the passenger compartment and the lift is intended to be stowed while occupied.

(iii) *Exception.* The brake or propulsion system interlock requirement does not apply to a platform mounted or portable lift provided that a mechanical, electrical or other system operates to ensure that cars do not move when the lift is in use.

(3) *Emergency operation.* The lift shall incorporate an emergency method of deploying, lowering to ground or platform level with a lift oc-

cupant, and raising and stowing the empty lift if the power to the lift fails. No emergency method, manual or otherwise, shall be capable of being operated in a manner that could be hazardous to the lift occupant or to the operator when operated according to manufacturer's instructions, and shall not permit the platform to be stowed or folded when occupied, unless the lift is a rotary lift intended to be stowed while occupied.

(4) *Power or equipment failure.* Platforms stowed in a vertical position, and deployed platforms when occupied, shall have provisions to prevent their deploying, falling, or folding any faster than 12 inches/second or their dropping of an occupant in the event of a single failure of any load carrying component.

(5) *Platform barriers.* The lift platform shall be equipped with barriers to prevent any of the wheels of a wheelchair or mobility aid from rolling off the lift during its operation. A movable barrier or inherent design feature shall prevent a wheelchair or mobility aid from rolling off the edge closest to the car until the lift is in its fully raised position. Each side of the lift platform which, in its raised position, extends beyond the car shall have a barrier a minimum $1\frac{1}{2}$ inches high. Such barriers shall not interfere with maneuvering into or out of the car. The loading-edge barrier (outer barrier) which functions as a loading ramp when the lift is at ground or station platform level, shall be sufficient when raised or closed, or a supplementary system shall be provided, to prevent a power wheelchair or mobility aid from riding over or defeating it. The outer barrier of the lift shall automatically rise or close, or a supplementary system shall automatically engage, and remain raised, closed, or engaged at all times that the lift platform is more than 3 inches above the station platform and the lift is occupied. Alternatively, a barrier or system may be raised, lowered, opened, closed, engaged or disengaged by the lift operator provided an interlock or inherent design feature prevents the lift from rising unless the barrier is raised or closed or the supplementary system is engaged.

(6) *Platform surface.* The lift platform surface shall be free of any protrusions over $\frac{1}{4}$ inch high and shall be slip resistant. The lift platform shall have a minimum clear width of $28\frac{1}{2}$ inches at the platform, a minimum clear width of 30 inches measured from 2 inches above the lift platform surface to 30 inches above the surface, and a minimum clear length of 48 inches measured from 2 inches above the surface of the platform to 30 inches above the surface. (See Fig. 1)

(7) *Platform gaps.* Any openings between the lift platform surface and the raised barriers shall not exceed $\frac{5}{8}$ inch wide. When the lift is at car floor height with the inner barrier down (if applicable) or retracted, gaps between the forward lift platform edge and car floor shall not exceed $\frac{1}{2}$ inch horizontally and $\frac{5}{8}$ inch vertically.

(8) *Platform entrance ramp.* The entrance ramp, or loading-edge barrier

used as a ramp, shall not exceed a slope of 1:8, when measured on level ground, for a maximum rise of 3 inches, and the transition from station platform to ramp may be vertical without edge treatment up to $\frac{1}{4}$ inch. Thresholds between $\frac{1}{4}$ inch and $\frac{1}{2}$ inch high shall be beveled with a slope no greater than 1:2.

(9) *Platform deflection.* The lift platform (not including the entrance ramp) shall not deflect more than 3 degrees (exclusive of vehicle roll) in any direction between its unloaded position and its position when loaded with 600 pounds applied through a 26 inch by 26 inch test pallet at the centroid of the lift platform.

(10) *Platform movement.* No part of the platform shall move at a rate exceeding 6 inches/second during lowering and lifting an occupant, and shall not exceed 12 inches/second during deploying or stowing. This requirement does not apply to the deployment or stowage cycles of lifts that are manually deployed or stowed. The maximum platform horizontal and vertical acceleration when occupied shall be 0.3g.

(11) *Boarding direction.* The lift shall permit both inboard and outboard facing of wheelchairs and mobility aids.

(12) *Use by standees.* Lifts shall accommodate persons using walkers, crutches, canes or braces or who otherwise have difficulty using steps. The lift may be marked to indicate a preferred standing position.

(13) *Handrails.* Platforms on lifts shall be equipped with handrails, on two sides, which move in tandem with the lift which shall be graspable and provide support to standees throughout the entire lift operation. Handrails shall have a usable component at least 8 inches long with the lowest portion a minimum 30 inches above the platform and the highest portion a maximum 38 inches above the platform. The handrails shall be capable of withstanding a force of 100 pounds concentrated at any point on the handrail without permanent deformation of the rail or its supporting structure. The handrail shall have a cross-sectional diameter between $1\frac{1}{4}$ inches and $1\frac{1}{2}$ inches or shall provide an equivalent grasping surface, and have eased edges with corner radii of not less than $\frac{1}{8}$ inch. Handrails shall be placed to provide a minimum $1\frac{1}{2}$ inches knuckle clearance from the nearest adjacent surface. Handrails shall not interfere with wheelchair or mobility aid maneuverability when entering or leaving the car.

(c) *Car ramp or bridge plate* — (1) *Design load.* Ramps or bridge plates 30 inches or longer shall support a load of 600 pounds, placed at the centroid of the ramp or bridge plate distributed over an area of 26 inches by 26 inches, with a safety factor of at least 3 based on the ultimate strength of the material. Ramps or bridge plates shorter than 30 inches shall support a load of 300 pounds.

(2) *Ramp surface.* The ramp or bridge plate surface shall be continuous and slip resistant, shall not have protrusions from the surface greater than

657

$\frac{1}{4}$ inch high, shall have a clear width of 30 inches and shall accommodate both four-wheel and three-wheel mobility aids.

(3) *Ramp threshold.* The transition from station platform to the ramp or bridge plate and the transition from car floor to the ramp or bridge plate may be vertical without edge treatment up to $\frac{1}{4}$ inch. Changes in level between $\frac{1}{4}$ inch and $\frac{1}{2}$ inch shall be beveled with a slope no greater than 1:2.

(4) *Ramp barriers.* Each side of the ramp or bridge plate shall have barriers at least 2 inches high to prevent mobility aid wheels from slipping off.

(5) *Slope.* Ramps or bridge plates shall have the least slope practicable. If the height of the vehicle floor, under 50% passenger load, from which the ramp is deployed is 3 inches or less above the station platform a maximum slope of 1:4 is permitted; if the height of the vehicle floor, under 50% passenger load, from which the ramp is deployed is 6 inches or less, but more than 3 inches, above the station platform a maximum slope of 1:6 is permitted; if the height of the vehicle floor, under 50% passenger load, from which the ramp is deployed is 9 inches or less, but more than 6 inches, above the station platform a maximum slope of 1:8 is permitted; if the height of the vehicle floor, under 50% passenger load, from which the ramp is deployed is greater than 9 inches above the station platform a slope of 1:12 shall be achieved. Folding or telescoping ramps are permitted provided they meet all structural requirements of this section.

(6) *Attachment* — (i) *Requirement.* When in use for boarding or alighting, the ramp or bridge plate shall be attached to the vehicle, or otherwise prevented from moving such that it is not subject to displacement when loading or unloading a heavy power mobility aid and that any gaps between vehicle and ramp or bridge plate, and station platform and ramp or bridge plate, shall not exceed $\frac{5}{8}$ inch.

(ii) *Exception.* Ramps or bridge plates which are attached to, and deployed from, station platforms are permitted in lieu of car devices provided they meet the displacement requirements of paragraph (c)(6)(i) of this section.

(7) *Stowage.* A compartment, securement system, or other appropriate method shall be provided to ensure that stowed ramps or bridge plates, including portable ramps or bridge plates stowed in the passenger area, do not impinge on a passenger's wheelchair or mobility aid or pose any hazard to passengers in the event of a sudden stop.

(8) *Handrails.* If provided, handrails shall allow persons with disabilities to grasp them from outside the car while starting to board, and to continue to use them throughout the boarding process, and shall have the top between 30 inches and 38 inches above the ramp surface. The handrails shall be capable of withstanding a force of 100 pounds concentrated at any point on the handrail without permanent deformation of the rail or its sup-

porting structure. The handrail shall have a cross-sectional diameter between $1\frac{1}{4}$ inches and $1\frac{1}{2}$ inches or shall provide an equivalent grasping surface, and have eased edges with corner radii of not less than $\frac{1}{8}$ inch. Handrails shall not interfere with wheelchair or mobility aid maneuverability when entering or leaving the car.

(d) *Mobility aid seating location.* Spaces for persons who wish to remain in their wheelchairs or mobility aids shall have a minimum clear floor space 48 inches by 30 inches. Such spaces shall adjoin, and may overlap, an accessible path. Not more than 6 inches of the required clear floor space may be accommodated for footrests under another seat provided there is a minimum of 9 inches from the floor to the lowest part of the seat overhanging the space. Seating spaces may have fold-down or removable seats to accommodate other passengers when a wheelchair or mobility aid user is not occupying the area, provided the seats, when folded up, do not obstruct the clear floor space required. (See Fig. 2.)

§ 38.97 Interior circulation, handrails and stanchions.

(a) Where provided, handrails or stanchions within the passenger compartment shall be placed to permit sufficient turning and maneuvering space for wheelchairs and other mobility aids to reach a seating location, complying with § 38.95(d) of this part, from an accessible entrance. The diameter or width of the gripping surface of interior handrails and stanchions shall be $1\frac{1}{4}$ inches to $1\frac{1}{2}$ inches or shall provide an equivalent gripping surface. Handrails shall be placed to provide a minimum $1\frac{1}{2}$ inches knuckle clearance from the nearest adjacent surface.

(b) Where provided, handrails or stanchions shall be sufficient to permit safe boarding, on-board circulation, seating and standing assistance, and alighting by persons with disabilities.

(c) At entrances equipped with steps, handrails or stanchions shall be provided in the entrance to the car in a configuration which allows passengers to grasp such assists from outside the car while starting to board, and to continue using such assists throughout the boarding process, to the extent permitted by part 231 of this title.

§ 38.99 Floors, steps and thresholds.

(a) Floor surfaces on aisles, step treads, places for standees, and areas where wheelchair and mobility aid users are to be accommodated shall be slip-resistant.

(b) All thresholds and step edges shall have a band of color(s) running the full width of the step or threshold which contrasts from the step tread and riser or adjacent floor, either light-on-dark or dark-on-light.

§ 38.101 Lighting.

(a) Any stepwell or doorway with a lift, ramp or bridge plate shall have, when the door is open, at least 2 foot-candles of illumination measured on the step tread, ramp, bridge plate, or lift platform.

(b) The doorways of cars not operating at lighted station platforms shall have outside lights which, when the door is open, provide at least 1 foot-candle of illumination on the station platform surface for a distance of 3 feet perpendicular to all points on the bottom step tread edge. Such lights shall be shielded to protect the eyes of entering and exiting passengers.

§ 38.103 Public information system.

(a) Each car shall be equipped with an interior public address system permitting transportation system personnel, or recorded or digitized human speech messages, to announce stations and provide other passenger information. Alternative systems or devices which provide equivalent access are also permitted.

(b) [Reserved]

§ 38.105 Priority seating signs.

(a) Each car shall contain sign(s) which indicate that certain seats are priority seats for persons with disabilities and that other passengers should make such seats available to those who wish to use them.

(b) Characters on signs required by paragraph (a) shall have a width-to-height ratio between 3:5 and 1:1 and a stroke width-to-height ratio between 1:5 and 1:10, with a minimum character height (using an upper case "X") of $\frac{5}{8}$ inch, with "wide" spacing (generally, the space between letters shall be $\frac{1}{16}$ the height of upper case letters), and shall contrast with the background either light-on-dark or dark-on-light.

§ 38.107 Restrooms.

(a) If a restroom is provided for the general public, it shall be designed so as to allow a person using a wheelchair or mobility aid to enter and use such restroom as specified in paragraphs (a) (1) through (5) of this section.

(1) The minimum clear floor area shall be 35 inches by 60 inches. Permanently installed fixtures may overlap this area a maximum of 6 inches, if the lowest portion of the fixture is a minimum of 9 inches above the floor, and may overlap a maximum of 19 inches, if the lowest portion of the fixture is a minimum of 29 inches above the floor, provided such fixtures do not interfere with access to the water closet. Fold-down or retractable seats or

shelves may overlap the clear floor space at a lower height provided they can be easily folded up or moved out of the way.

(2) The height of the water closet shall be 17 inches to 19 inches measured to the top of the toilet seat. Seats shall not be sprung to return to a lifted position.

(3) A grab bar at least 24 inches long shall be mounted behind the water closet, and a horizontal grab bar at least 40 inches long shall be mounted on at least one side wall, with one end not more than 12 inches from the back wall, at a height between 33 inches and 36 inches above the floor.

(4) Faucets and flush controls shall be operable with one hand and shall not require tight grasping, pinching, or twisting of the wrist. The force required to activate controls shall be no greater than 5 lbf (22.2 N). Controls for flush valves shall be mounted no more than 44 inches above the floor.

(5) Doorways on the end of the enclosure, opposite the water closet, shall have a minimum clear opening width of 32 inches. Doorways on the side wall shall have a minimum clear opening width of 39 inches. Door latches and hardware shall be operable with one hand and shall not require tight grasping, pinching, or twisting of the wrist.

(b) Restrooms required to be accessible shall be in close proximity to at least one seating location for persons using mobility aids and shall be connected to such a space by an unobstructed path having a minimum width of 32 inches.

§ 38.109 Between-car barriers.

Where vehicles operate in a high-platform, level-boarding mode, and where between-car bellows are not provided, devices or systems shall be provided to prevent, deter or warn individuals from inadvertently stepping off the platform between cars. Appropriate devices include, but are not limited to, pantograph gates, chains, motion detectors or other suitable devices.

Subpart F — Intercity Rail Cars and Systems

§ 38.111 General.

(a) New, used and remanufactured intercity rail cars, to be considered accessible by regulations in part 37 of this title shall comply with this subpart to the extent required for each type of car as specified below.

(1) Single-level rail passenger coaches and food service cars (other than single-level dining cars) shall comply with §§ 38.113 through 38.123 of this part. Compliance with § 38.125 of this part shall be required only to the extent necessary to meet the requirements of paragraph (d) of this section.

(2) Single-level dining and lounge cars shall have at least one connecting doorway complying with § 38.113(a)(2) of this part connected to a car accessible to persons using wheelchairs or mobility aids, and at least one space complying with §§ 38.125(d) (2) and (3) of this part, to provide table service to a person who wishes to remain in his or her wheelchair, and space to fold and store a wheelchair for a person who wishes to transfer to an existing seat.

(3) Bi-level dining cars shall comply with §§ 38.113(a)(2), 38.115(b), 38.117(a), and 38.121 of this part.

(4) Bi-level lounge cars shall have doors on the lower level, on each side of the car from which passengers board, complying with § 38.113, a restroom complying with § 38.123, and at least one space complying with § 38.125(d) (2) and (3) to provide table service to a person who wishes to remain in his or her wheelchair and space to fold and store a wheelchair for a person who wishes to transfer to an existing seat.

(5) Restrooms, complying with § 38.123 shall be provided in single-level rail passenger coaches and food services cars adjacent to the accessible seating locations required by paragraph (d) of this section. Accessible restrooms are required in dining and lounge cars only if restrooms are provided for other passengers.

(6) Sleeper cars shall comply with §§ 38.113 (b) through (d), 38.115 through 38.121, and 38.125, of this part, and have at least one compartment which can be entered and used by a person using a wheelchair or mobility aid and complying with § 38.127 of this part.

(b)(1) If physically and operationally practicable, intercity rail cars shall comply with § 38.113(d) of this part for level boarding.

(2) Where level boarding is not structurally or operationally practicable, intercity rail cars shall comply with § 38.125.

(c) If portions of the car are modified in a way that it affects or could affect accessibility, each such portion shall comply, to the extent practicable, with the applicable provisions of this subpart. This provision does not require that inaccessible cars be retrofitted with lifts, ramps or other boarding devices.

(d) Passenger coaches or food service cars shall have the number of spaces complying with § 38.125(d)(2) of this part and the number of spaces complying with § 38.125(d)(3) of this part, as required by § 37.91 of this title.

(e) Existing cars retrofitted to meet the seating requirements of § 37.91 of this title shall comply with § 38.113(e), § 38.123, § 38.125(d) of this part and shall have at least one door on each side from which passengers board complying with § 38.113(d) of this part. Existing cars designed and manufactured to be accessible in accordance with the Secretary of Transportation regulations implementing section 504 of the Rehabilitation Act of 1973 that were in effect before October 7, 1991, shall comply with § 38.125(a) of this part.

§ 38.113 Doorways.

(a) *Clear width.* (1) At least one doorway, on each side of the car from which passengers board, of each car required to be accessible by § 38.111(a) and where the spaces required by § 38.111(d) of this part are located, and at least one adjacent doorway into coach passenger compartments shall have a minimum clear opening width of 32 inches.

(2) Doorways at ends of cars connecting two adjacent cars, to the maximum extent practicable in accordance with regulations issued under the Federal Railroad Safety Act of 1970 (49 CFR parts 229 and 231), shall have a clear opening width of 32 inches to permit wheelchair and mobility aid users to enter into a single-level dining car, if available.

(b) *Passageway.* Doorways required to be accessible by paragraph (a) of this section shall permit access by persons using mobility aids and shall have an unobstructed passageway at least 32 inches wide leading to an accessible sleeping compartment complying with § 38.127 of this part or seating locations complying with § 38.125(d) of this part. In cars where such doorways require passage through a vestibule, such vestibule shall have a minimum width of 42 inches. (see Fig. 4)

(c) *Signals.* If doors to the platform close automatically or from a remote location, auditory and visual warning signals shall be provided to alert passengers of closing doors.

(d) *Coordination with boarding platforms.* — (1) *Requirements.* Cars which provide level-boarding in stations with high platforms shall be co-ordinated with the boarding platform or mini-high platform design such that the horizontal gap between a car at rest and the platform shall be no greater than 3 inches and the height of the car floor shall be within plus or minus $\frac{5}{8}$ inch of the platform height. Vertical alignment may be accomplished by car air suspension, platform lifts or other devices, or any combination.

(2) *Exception.* New cars operating in existing stations may have a floor height within plus or minus $1\frac{1}{2}$ inches of the platform height.

(3) *Exception.* Where platform setbacks do not allow the horizontal gap or vertical alignment specified in paragraph (d) (1) or (2), platform or portable lifts complying with § 38.125(b) of this part, or car or platform bridge plates, complying with § 38.125(c) of this part, may be provided.

(4) *Exception.* Retrofitted vehicles shall be coordinated with the platform in existing stations such that the horizontal gap shall be no greater than 4 inches and the height of the vehicle floor, under 50% passenger load, shall be within plus or minus 2 inches of the platform height.

(e) *Signage.* The International Symbol of Accessibility shall be displayed on the exterior of all doors complying with this section unless all cars and doors are accessible and are not marked by the access symbol (see fig. 6). Appropriate signage shall also indicate which accessible doors are adjacent to an accessible restroom, if applicable.

[56 FR 45756, Sept. 6, 1991, as amended at 58 FR 63103, Nov. 30, 1993]

§ 38.115 Interior circulation, handrails and stanchions.

(a) Where provided, handrails or stanchions within the passenger compartment shall be placed to permit sufficient turning and maneuvering space for wheelchairs and other mobility aids to reach a seating location, complying with § 38.125(d) of this part, from an accessible entrance. The diameter or width of the gripping surface of interior handrails and stanchions shall be $1\frac{1}{4}$ inches to $1\frac{1}{2}$ inches or shall provide an equivalent gripping surface. Handrails shall be placed to provide a minimum $1\frac{1}{2}$ inches knuckle clearance from the nearest adjacent surface.

(b) Where provided, handrails and stanchions shall be sufficient to permit safe boarding, on-board circulation, seating and standing assistance, and alighting by persons with disabilities.

(c) At entrances equipped with steps, handrails or stanchions shall be provided in the entrance to the car in a configuration which allows passengers to grasp such assists from outside the car while starting to board, and to continue using such assists throughout the boarding process, to the extent permitted by part 231 of this title.

§ 38.117 Floors, steps and thresholds.

(a) Floor surfaces on aisles, step treads and areas where wheelchair and mobility aid users are to be accommodated shall be slip-resistant.

(b) All step edges and thresholds shall have a band of color(s) running the full width of the step or threshold which contrasts from the step tread and riser or adjacent floor, either light-on-dark or dark-on-light.

§ 38.119 Lighting.

(a) Any stepwell, or doorway with a lift, ramp or bridge plate, shall have, when the door is open, at least 2 foot-candles of illumination measured on the step tread, ramp, bridge plate or lift platform.

(b) The doorways of cars not operating at lighted station platforms shall have outside lights which, when the door is open, provide at least 1 foot-candle of illumination on the station platform surface for a distance of 3 feet perpendicular to all points on the bottom step tread edge. Such lights shall be shielded to protect the eyes of entering and exiting passengers.

§ 38.121 Public information system.

(a) Each car shall be equipped with a public address system permitting transportation system personnel, or recorded or digitized human speech messages, to announce stations and provide other passenger information. Alternative systems or devices which provide equivalent access are also permitted.

(b) [Reserved]

§ 38.123 Restrooms.

(a) If a restroom is provided for the general public, and an accessible restroom is required by § 38.111 (a) and (e) of this part, it shall be designed so as to allow a person using a wheelchair or mobility aid to enter and use such restroom as specified in paragraphs (a) (1) through (5) of this section.

(1) The minimum clear floor area shall be 35 inches by 60 inches. Permanently installed fixtures may overlap this area a maximum of 6 inches, if the lowest portion of the fixture is a minimum of 9 inches above the floor, and may overlap a maximum of 19 inches, if the lowest portion of the fixture is a minimum of 29 inches above the floor. Fixtures shall not interfere with access to and use of the water closet. Fold-down or retractable seats or shelves may overlap the clear floor space at a lower height provided they can be easily folded up or moved out of the way.

(2) The height of the water closet shall be 17 inches to 19 inches measured to the top of the toilet seat. Seats shall not be sprung to return to a lifted position.

(3) A grab bar at least 24 inches long shall be mounted behind the water closet, and a horizontal grab bar at least 40 inches long shall be mounted on at least one side wall, with one end not more than 12 inches from the back wall, at a height between 33 inches and 36 inches above the floor.

(4) Faucets and flush controls shall be operable with one hand and shall not require tight grasping, pinching, or twisting of the wrist. The force required to activate controls shall be no greater than 5 lbf (22.2 N). Controls for flush valves shall be mounted no more than 44 inches above the floor.

(5) Doorways on the end of the enclosure, opposite the water closet, shall have a minimum clear opening width of 32 inches. Doorways on the side wall shall have a minimum clear opening width of 39 inches. Door latches and hardware shall be operable with one hand and shall not require tight grasping, pinching, or twisting of the wrist.

(b) Restrooms required to be accessible shall be in close proximity to at least one seating location for persons using mobility aids complying with § 38.125(d) of this part and shall be connected to such a space by an unobstructed path having a minimum width of 32 inches.

§ 38.125 Mobility aid accessibility.

(a)(1) *General.* All intercity rail cars, other than level entry cars, required to be accessible by §§ 38.111 (a) and (e) of this subpart shall provide a level-change mechanism or boarding device (e.g., lift, ramp or bridge plate) complying with either paragraph (b) or (c) of this section and sufficient clearances to permit a wheelchair or other mobility aid user to reach a seating location complying with paragraph (d) of this section.

(2) *Exception.* If portable or platform lifts, ramps or bridge plates meeting the applicable requirements of this section are provided on station platforms or other stops required to be accessible, or mini-high platforms complying with § 38.113(d) are provided, the car is not required to be equipped with a car-borne device.

(b) *Car Lift* — (1) *Design load.* The design load of the lift shall be at least 600 pounds. Working parts, such as cables, pulleys, and shafts, which can be expected to wear, and upon which the lift depends for support of the load, shall have a safety factor of at least six, based on the ultimate strength of the material. Nonworking parts, such as platform, frame, and attachment hardware which would not be expected to wear, shall have a safety factor of at least three, based on the ultimate strength of the material.

(2) *Controls* — (i) *Requirements.* The controls shall be interlocked with the car brakes, propulsion system, or door, or shall provide other appropriate mechanisms or systems, to ensure that the car cannot be moved when the lift is not stowed and so the lift cannot be deployed unless the interlocks or systems are engaged. The lift shall deploy to all platform levels normally encountered in the operating environment. Where provided, each control for deploying, lowering, raising, and stowing the lift and lowering the roll-off barrier shall be of a monetary contact type requiring continuous manual pressure by the operator and shall not allow improper lift sequencing when the lift platform is occupied. The controls shall allow reversal of the lift operation sequence, such as raising or lowering a platform that is part way down, without allowing an occupied platform to fold or retract into the stowed position.

(ii) *Exception.* Where physical or safety constraints prevent the deployment at some stops of a lift having its long dimension perpendicular to the car axis, the transportation entity may specify a lift which is designed to deploy with its long dimension parallel to the car axis and which pivots into or out of the car while occupied (i.e., "rotary lift"). The requirements of paragraph (b)(2)(i) of this section prohibiting the lift from being stowed while occupied shall not apply to a lift design of this type if the stowed position is within the passenger compartment and the lift is intended to be stowed while occupied.

(iii) *Exception.* The brake or propulsion system interlocks requirement does not apply to platform mounted or portable lifts provided that a mechanical, electrical or other system operates to ensure that cars do not move when the lift is in use.

(3) *Emergency operation.* The lift shall incorporate an emergency method of deploying, lowering to ground or station platform level with a

lift occupant, and raising and stowing the empty lift if the power to the lift fails. No emergency method, manual or otherwise, shall be capable of being operated in a manner that could be hazardous to the lift occupant or to the operator when operated according to manufacturer's instructions, and shall not permit the platform to be stowed or folded when occupied, unless the lift is a rotary lift and is intended to be stowed while occupied.

(4) *Power or equipment failure.* Platforms stowed in a vertical position, and deployed platforms when occupied, shall have provisions to prevent their deploying, falling, or folding any faster than 12 inches/second or their dropping of an occupant in the event of a single failure of any load carrying component.

(5) *Platform barriers.* The lift platform shall be equipped with barriers to prevent any of the wheels of a wheelchair or mobility aid from rolling off the lift during its operation. A movable barrier or inherent design feature shall prevent a wheelchair or mobility aid from rolling off the edge closest to the car until the lift is in its fully raised position. Each side of the lift platform which, in its raised position, extends beyond the car shall have a barrier a minimum $1\frac{1}{2}$ inches high. Such barriers shall not interfere with maneuvering into or out of the car. The loading-edge barrier (outer barrier) which functions as a loading ramp when the lift is at ground or station platform level, shall be sufficient when raised or closed, or a supplementary system shall be provided, to prevent a power wheelchair or mobility aid from riding over or defeating it. The outer barrier of the lift shall automatically rise or close, or a supplementary system shall automatically engage, and remain raised, closed, or engaged at all times that the lift platform is more than 3 inches above the station platform and the lift is occupied. Alternatively, a barrier or system may be raised, lowered, opened, closed, engaged or disengaged by the lift operator provided an interlock or inherent design feature prevents the lift from rising unless the barrier is raised or closed or the supplementary system is engaged.

(6) *Platform surface.* The lift platform surface shall be free of any protrusions over $\frac{1}{4}$ inch high and shall be slip resistant. The lift platform shall have a minimum clear width of $28\frac{1}{2}$ inches at the platform, a minimum clear width of 30 inches measured from 2 inches above the lift platform surface to 30 inches above the surface, and a minimum clear length of 48 inches measured from 2 inches above the surface of the platform to 30 inches above the surface. (See Fig. 1.)

(7) *Platform gaps.* Any openings between the lift platform surface and the raised barriers shall not exceed $\frac{5}{8}$ inch wide. When the lift is at car floor height with the inner barrier (if applicable) down or retracted, gaps between the forward lift platform edge and car floor shall not exceed $\frac{1}{2}$ inch horizontally and $\frac{5}{8}$ inch vertically.

(8) *Platform entrance ramp.* The entrance ramp, or loading-edge barrier

used as a ramp, shall not exceed a slope of 1:8, when measured on level ground, for a maximum rise of 3 inches, and the transition from station platform to ramp may be vertical without edge treatment up to $\frac{1}{4}$ inch. Thresholds between $\frac{1}{4}$ inch and $\frac{1}{2}$ inch high shall be beveled with a slope no greater than 1:2.

(9) *Platform deflection.* The lift platform (not including the entrance ramp) shall not deflect more than 3 degrees (exclusive of car roll) in any direction between its unloaded position and its position when loaded with 600 pounds applied through a 26 inch by 26 inch test pallet at the centroid of the lift platform.

(10) *Platform movement.* No part of the platform shall move at a rate exceeding 6 inches/second during lowering and lifting an occupant, and shall not exceed 12 inches/second during deploying or stowing. This requirement does not apply to the deployment or stowage cycles of lifts that are manually deployed or stowed. The maximum platform horizontal and vertical acceleration when occupied shall be 0.3g.

(11) *Boarding direction.* The lift shall permit both inboard and outboard facing of wheelchairs and mobility aids.

(12) *Use by standees.* Lifts shall accommodate persons using walkers, crutches, canes or braces or who otherwise have difficulty using steps. The lift may be marked to indicate a preferred standing position.

(13) *Handrails.* Platforms on lifts shall be equipped with handrails, on two sides, which move in tandem with the lift, and which shall be graspable and provide support to standees throughout the entire lift operation. Handrails shall have a usable component at least 8 inches long with the lowest portion a minimum 30 inches above the platform and the highest portion a maximum 38 inches above the platform. The handrails shall be capable of withstanding a force of 100 pounds concentrated at any point on the handrail without permanent deformation of the rail or its supporting structure. The handrail shall have a cross-sectional diameter between $1\frac{1}{4}$ inches and $1\frac{1}{2}$ inches or shall provide an equivalent grasping surface, and have eased edges with corner radii of not less than $\frac{1}{8}$ inch. Handrails shall be placed to provide a minimum $1\frac{1}{2}$ inches knuckle clearance from the nearest adjacent surface. Handrails shall not interfere with wheelchair or mobility aid maneuverability when entering or leaving the car.

(c) *Car ramp or bridge plate* — (1) *Design load.* Ramps or bridge plates 30 inches or longer shall support a load of 600 pounds, placed at the centroid of the ramp or bridge plate distributed over an area of 26 inches by 26 inches, with a safety factor of at least 3 based on the ultimate strength of the material. Ramps or bridge plates shorter than 30 inches shall support a load of 300 pounds.

(2) *Ramp surface.* The ramp or bridge plate surface shall be continuous and slip resistant, shall not have protrusions from the surface greater than

$\frac{1}{4}$ inch high, shall have a clear width of 30 inches and shall accommodate both four-wheel and three-wheel mobility aids.

(3) *Ramp threshold.* The transition from station platform to the ramp or bridge plate and the transition from car floor to the ramp or bridge plate may be vertical without edge treatment up to $\frac{1}{4}$ inch. Changes in level between $\frac{1}{4}$ inch and $\frac{1}{2}$ inch shall be beveled with a slope no greater than 1:2.

(4) *Ramp barriers.* Each side of the ramp or bridge plate shall have barriers at least 2 inches high to prevent mobility aid wheels from slipping off.

(5) *Slope.* Ramps or bridge plates shall have the least slope practicable. If the height of the vehicle floor, under 50% passenger load, from which the ramp is deployed is 3 inches or less above the station platform a maximum slope of 1:4 is permitted; if the height of the vehicle floor, under 50% passenger load, from which the ramp is deployed is 6 inches or less, but more than 3 inches, above the station platform a maximum slope of 1:6 is permitted; if the height of the vehicle floor, under 50% passenger load, from which the ramp is deployed is 9 inches or less, but more than 6 inches, above the station platform a maximum slope of 1:8 is permitted; if the height of the vehicle floor, under 50% passenger load, from which the ramp is deployed is greater than 9 inches above the station platform a slope of 1:12 shall be achieved. Folding or telescoping ramps are permitted provided they meet all structural requirements of this section.

(6) *Attachment* — (i) *Requirement.* When in use for boarding or alighting, the ramp or bridge plate shall be attached to the vehicle, or otherwise prevented from moving such that it is not subject to displacement when loading or unloading a heavy power mobility aid and that any gaps between vehicle and ramp or bridge plate, and station platform and ramp or bridge plate, shall not exceed $\frac{5}{8}$ inch.

(ii) *Exception.* Ramps or bridge plates which are attached to, and deployed from, station platforms are permitted in lieu of car devices provided they meet the displacement requirements of paragraph (c)(6)(i) of this section.

(7) *Stowage.* A compartment, securement system, or other appropriate method shall be provided to ensure that stowed ramps or bridge plates, including portable ramps or bridge plates stowed in the passenger area, do not impinge on a passenger's wheelchair or mobility aid or pose any hazard to passengers in the event of a sudden stop.

(8) *Handrails.* If provided, handrails shall allow persons with disabilities to grasp them from outside the car while starting to board, and to continue to use them throughout the boarding process, and shall have the top between 30 inches and 38 inches above the ramp surface. The handrails shall be capable of withstanding a force of 100 pounds concentrated at any point on the handrail without permanent deformation of the rail or its sup-

porting structure. The handrail shall have a cross-sectional diameter between $1\frac{1}{4}$ inches and $1\frac{1}{2}$ inches or shall provide an equivalent grasping surface, and have eased edges with corner radii of not less than $\frac{1}{8}$ inch. Handrails shall not interfere with wheelchair or mobility aid maneuverability when entering or leaving the car.

(d) *Seating* — (1) *Requirements.* All intercity rail cars required to be accessible by §§ 38.111 (a) and (e) of this subpart shall provide at least one, but not more than two, mobility aid seating location(s) complying with paragraph (d)(2) of this section; and at least one, but not more than two, seating location(s) complying with paragraph (d)(3) of this section which adjoin or overlap an accessible route with a minimum clear width of 32 inches.

(2) *Wheelchair or mobility aid spaces.* Spaces for persons who wish to remain in their wheelchairs or mobility aids shall have a minimum clear floor space 48 inches by 30 inches. Such spaces shall adjoin, and may overlap, an accessible path. Not more than 6 inches of the required clear floor space may be accommodated for footrests under another seat provided there is a minimum of 9 inches from the floor to the lowest part of the seat overhanging the space. Seating spaces may have fold-down or removable seats to accommodate other passengers when a wheelchair or mobility aid user is not occupying the area, provided the seats, when folded up, do not obstruct the clear floor space provided (See Fig. 2).

(3) *Other spaces.* Spaces for individuals who wish to transfer shall include a regular coach seat or dining car booth or table seat and space to fold and store the passenger's wheelchair.

[56 FR 45756, Sept. 6, 1991, as amended at 58 FR 63103, Nov. 30, 1993]

§ 38.127 Sleeping compartments.

(a) Sleeping compartments required to be accessible shall be designed so as to allow a person using a wheelchair or mobility aid to enter, maneuver within and approach and use each element within such compartment. (See Fig. 5.)

(b) Each accessible compartment shall contain a restroom complying with § 38.123(a) which can be entered directly from such compartment.

(c) Controls and operating mechanisms (e.g., heating and air conditioning controls, lighting controls, call buttons, electrical outlets, etc.) shall be mounted no more than 48 inches, and no less than 15 inches, above the floor and shall have a clear floor area directly in front a minimum of 30 inches by 48 inches. Controls and operating mechanisms shall be operable with one hand and shall not require tight grasping, pinching, or twisting of the wrist.

Subpart G — Over-the-Road Buses and Systems

§ 38.151 General.

(a) New, used and remanufactured over-the-road buses, to be considered accessible by regulations in part 37 of this title, shall comply with this subpart.

(b) Over-the-road buses covered by § 37.7 (c) of this title shall comply with § 38.23 and this subpart.

§ 38.153 Doors, steps and thresholds.

(a) Floor surfaces on aisles, step treads and areas where wheelchair and mobility aid users are to be accommodated shall be slip-resistant.

(b) All step edges shall have a band of color(s) running the full width of the step which contrasts from the step tread and riser, either dark-on-light or light-on-dark.

(c) To the maximum extent practicable, doors shall have a minimum clear width when open of 30 inches, but in no case less than 27 inches.

§ 38.155 Interior circulation, handrails and stanchions.

(a) Handrails and stanchions shall be provided in the entrance to the vehicle in a configuration which allows passengers to grasp such assists from outside the vehicle while starting to board, and to continue using such handrails or stanchions throughout the boarding process. Handrails shall have a cross-sectional diameter between $1\frac{1}{4}$ inches and $1\frac{1}{2}$ inches or shall provide an equivalent grasping surface, and have eased edges with corner radii of not less than $\frac{1}{8}$ inch. Handrails shall be placed to provide a minimum $1\frac{1}{2}$ inches knuckle clearance from the nearest adjacent surface. Where on-board fare collection devices are used, a horizontal passenger assist shall be located between boarding passengers and the fare collection device and shall prevent passengers from sustaining injuries on the fare collection device or windshield in the event of a sudden deceleration. Without restricting the vestibule space, the assist shall provide support for a boarding passenger from the door through the boarding procedure. Passengers shall be able to lean against the assist for security while paying fares.

(b) Where provided within passenger compartments, handrails or stanchions shall be sufficient to permit safe on-board circulation, seating and standing assistance, and alighting by persons with disabilities.

§ 38.157 Lighting.

(a) Any stepwell or doorway immediately adjacent to the driver shall have, when the door is open, at least 2 foot-candles of illumination measured on the step tread.

(b) The vehicle doorway shall have outside light(s) which, when the door is open, provide at least 1 foot-candle of illumination on the street surface for a distance of 3 feet perpendicular to all points on the bottom step tread outer edge. Such light(s) shall be located below window level and shielded to protect the eyes of entering and exiting passengers.

§ 38.159 Mobility aid accessibility. [Reserved]

Subpart H — Other Vehicles and Systems

§ 38.171 General.

(a) New, used and remanufactured vehicles and conveyances for systems not covered by other subparts of this part, to be considered accessible by regulations in part 37 of this title shall comply with this subpart.

(b) If portions of the vehicle or conveyance are modified in a way that affects or could affect accessibility, each such portion shall comply, to the extent practicable, with the applicable provisions of this subpart. This provision does not require that inaccessible vehicles be retrofitted with lifts, ramps or other boarding devices.

(c) Requirements for vehicles and systems not covered by this part shall be determined on a case-by-case basis by the Department of Transportation in consultation with the U.S. Architectural and Transportation Barriers Compliance Board (Access Board).

§ 38.173 Automated guideway transit vehicles and systems.

(a) Automated Guideway Transit (AGT) vehicles and systems, sometimes called "people movers", operated in airports and other areas where AGT vehicles travel at slow speed, shall comply with the provisions of § 38.53 (a) through (c), and §§ 38.55 through 38.61 of this part for rapid rail vehicles and systems.

(b) Where the vehicle covered by paragraph (a) will operate in an accessible station, the design of vehicles shall be coordinated with the boarding platform design such that the horizontal gap between a vehicle door at rest and the platform shall be no greater than 1 inch and the height of the vehicle floor shall be within plus or minus $\frac{1}{2}$ inch of the platform height under all normal passenger load conditions. Vertical alignment may be accomplished by vehicle air suspension or other suitable means of meeting the requirement.

(c) In stations where open platforms are not protected by platform screens, a suitable device or system shall be provided to prevent, deter or warn individuals from stepping off the platform between cars. Acceptable devices include, but arc not limited to, pantograph gates, chains, motion detectors or other appropriate devices.

(d) Light rail and rapid rail AGT vehicles and systems shall comply with subparts D and C of this part, respectively.

§ 38.175 High-speed rail cars, monorails and systems.

(a) All cars for high-speed rail systems, including but not limited to those using "maglev" or high speed steel-wheel-on-steel rail technology, and monorail systems operating primarily on dedicated rail (i.e., not used by freight trains) or guideway, in which stations are constructed in accordance with part 37, subpart C of this title, shall be designed for high-platform, level boarding and shall comply with § 38.111(a) of this part for each type of car which is similar to intercity rail, §§ 38.111(d), 38.113 (a) through (c) and (e), 38.115 (a) and (b), 38.117 (a) and (b), 38.121 through 38.123, 38.125(d), and 38.127 (if applicable) of this part. The design of cars shall be coordinated with the boarding platform design such that the horizontal gap between a car door at rest and the platform shall be no greater than 3 inches and the height of the car floor shall be within plus or minus $\frac{5}{8}$ inch of the platform height under all normal passenger load conditions. Vertical alignment may be accomplished by car air suspension or other suitable means of meeting the requirement. All doorways shall have, when the door is open, at least 2 foot-candles of illumination measured on the door threshold.

(b) All other high-speed rail cars shall comply with the similar provisions of subpart F of this part.

§ 38.177 Ferries, excursion boats and other vessels. [Reserved]

§ 38.179 Trams, and similar vehicles, and systems

(a) New and used trams consisting of a tractor unit, with or without passenger accommodations, and one or more passenger trailer units, including but not limited to vehicles providing shuttle service to remote parking areas, between hotels and other public accommodations, and between and within amusement parks and other recreation areas, shall comply with this section. For purposes of determining applicability of 49 CFR 37.101, 37.103, or 37.105 the capacity of such a vehicle or "train" shall consist of the total combined seating capacity of all units, plus the driver, prior to any modification for accessibility.

(b) Each tractor unit which accommodates passengers and each trailer unit shall comply with § 38.25 and § 38.29 of this part. In addition, each such unit shall comply with § 38.23 (b) or (c) and shall provide at least one space for wheelchair or mobility aid users complying with § 38.23(d) of this part unless the complete operating unit consisting of tractor and one or more trailers can already accommodate at least two wheelchair or mobility aid users.

FIGURES IN PART 38

Fig. 1 Wheelchair or Mobility Aid Envelope
Fig. 2 Toe Clearance Under a Seat
Fig. 3 Commuter Rail Car (without restrooms)
Fig. 4 Intercity Rail Car (with accessible restroom)
Fig. 5 Intercity Rail Car (with accessible sleeping compartment)
Fig. 6 International Symbol of Accessibility

DEPARTMENT OF JUSTICE REGULATIONS FOR TITLE II OF ADA-CODE OF FEDERAL REGULATIONS TITLE 28

PART 35 — NONDISCRIMINATION ON THE BASIS OF DISABILITY IN STATE AND LOCAL GOVERNMENT SERVICES

Subpart A — General

Subpart B — General Requirements

Subpart C — Employment

Subpart D — Program Accessibility

35.149 Discrimination prohibited.
35.150 Existing facilities.
35.151 New construction and alterations.
35.152–35.159 [Reserved]

Subpart E — Communications

35.160 General.
35.161 Telecommunication devices for the deaf (TDD's).
35.162 Telephone emergency services.
35.163 Information and signage.
35.164 Duties.
35.165–35.169 [Reserved]

Subpart F — Compliance Procedures

35.170 Complaints.
35.171 Acceptance of complaints.
35.172 Resolution of complaints.
35.173 Voluntary compliance agreements.
35.174 Referral.
35.175 Attorney's fees.
35.176 Alternative means of dispute resolution.
35.177 Effect of unavailability of technical assistance.
35.178 State immunity.
35.179–35.189 [Reserved]

Subpart G — Designated Agencies

35.190 Designated agencies.
35.191–35.999 [Reserved]

APPENDIX A TO PART 35 — PREAMBLE TO REGULATION ON NONDISCRIMINATION ON THE BASIS OF DISABILITY IN STATE AND LOCAL GOVERNMENT SERVICES (PUBLISHED JULY 26, 1991)

AUTHORITY: 5 U.S.C. 301; 28 U.S.C. 509, 510; Title II, Pub. L. 101-336 (42 U.S.C. 12134).

SOURCE: Order No. 1512-91, 56 FR 35716, July 26, 1991, unless otherwise noted.

Subpart A — General

§ 35.101 Purpose.

The purpose of this part is to effectuate subtitle A of title II of the Americans with Disabilities Act of 1990 (42 U.S.C. 12131), which prohibits discrimination on the basis of disability by public entities.

§ 35.102 Application.

(a) Except as provided in paragraph (b) of this section, this part applies to all services, programs, and activities provided or made available by public entities.

(b) To the extent that public transportation services, programs, and activities of public entities are covered by subtitle B of title II of the ADA (42 U.S.C. 12141), they are not subject to the requirements of this part.

§ 35.103 Relationship to other laws.

(a) *Rule of interpretation.* Except as otherwise provided in this part, this part shall not be construed to apply a lesser standard than the standards applied under title V of the Rehabilitation Act of 1973 (29 U.S.C. 791) or the regulations issued by Federal agencies pursuant to that title.

(b) *Other laws.* This part does not invalidate or limit the remedies, rights, and procedures of any other Federal laws, or State or local laws (including State common law) that provide greater or equal protection for the rights of individuals with disabilities or individuals associated with them.

§ 35.104 Definitions.

For purposes of this part, the term —

Act means the Americans with Disabilities Act (Pub. L. 101–336, 104 Stat. 327, 42 U.S.C. 12101–12213 and 47 U.S.C. 225 and 611).

Assistant Attorney General means the Assistant Attorney General, Civil Rights Division, United States Department of Justice.

Auxiliary aids and services includes —

(1) Qualified interpreters, note takers, transcription services, written materials, telephone handset amplifiers, assistive listening devices, assistive listening systems, telephones compatible with hearing aids, closed caption decoders, open and closed captioning, telecommunications devices for deaf persons (TDD's), videotext displays, or other effective methods of making aurally delivered materials available to individuals with hearing impairments;

(2) Qualified readers, taped texts, audio recordings, Brailled materials, large print materials, or other effective methods of making visually delivered materials available to individuals with visual impairments;

677

(3) Acquisition or modification of equipment or devices; and

(4) Other similar services and actions.

Complete complaint means a written statement that contains the complainant's name and address and describes the public entity's alleged discriminatory action in sufficient detail to inform the agency of the nature and date of the alleged violation of this part. It shall be signed by the complainant or by someone authorized to do so on his or her behalf. Complaints filed on behalf of classes or third parties shall describe or identify (by name, if possible) the alleged victims of discrimination.

Current illegal use of drugs means illegal use of drugs that occurred recently enough to justify a reasonable belief that a person's drug use is current or that continuing use is a real and ongoing problem.

Designated agency means the Federal agency designated under subpart G of this part to oversee compliance activities under this part for particular components of State and local governments.

Disability means, with respect to an individual, a physical or mental impairment that substantially limits one or more of the major life activities of such individual; a record of such an impairment; or being regarded as having such an impairment.

(1)(i) The phrase *physical* or *mental impairment* means —

(A) Any physiological disorder or condition, cosmetic disfigurement, or anatomical loss affecting one or more of the following body systems: Neurological, musculoskeletal, special sense organs, respiratory (including speech organs), cardiovascular, reproductive, digestive, genitourinary, hemic and lymphatic, skin, and endocrine;

(B) Any mental or psychological disorder such as mental retardation, organic brain syndrome, emotional or mental illness, and specific learning disabilities.

(ii) The phrase *physical* or *mental impairment* includes, but is not limited to, such contagious and noncontagious diseases and conditions as orthopedic, visual, speech and hearing impairments, cerebral palsy, epilepsy, muscular dystrophy, multiple sclerosis, cancer, heart disease, diabetes, mental retardation, emotional illness, specific learning disabilities, HIV disease (whether symptomatic or asymptomatic), tuberculosis, drug addiction, and alcoholism.

(iii) The phrase *physical* or *mental impairment* does not include homosexuality or bisexuality.

(2) The phrase *major life activities* means functions such as caring for one's self, performing manual tasks, walking, seeing, hearing, speaking, breathing, learning, and working.

(3) The phrase has a *record of such an impairment* means has a history of, or has been misclassified as having, a mental or physical impairment that substantially limits one or more major life activities.

(4) The phrase *is regarded as having an impairment* means —

(i) Has a physical or mental impairment that does not substantially limit major life activities but that is treated by a public entity as constituting such a limitation;

(ii) Has a physical or mental impairment that substantially limits major life activities only as a result of the attitudes of others toward such impairment; or

(iii) Has none of the impairments defined in paragraph (1) of this definition but is treated by a public entity as having such an impairment.

(5) The term *disability* does not include —

(i) Transvestism, transsexualism, pedophilia, exhibitionism, voyeurism, gender identity disorders not resulting from physical impairments, or other sexual behavior disorders;

(ii) Compulsive gambling, kleptomania, or pyromania;

(iii) Psychoactive substance use disorders resulting from current illegal use of drugs.

Drug means a controlled substance, as defined in schedules I through V of section 202 of the Controlled Substances Act (21 U.S.C. 812).

Facility means all or any portion of buildings, structures, sites, complexes, equipment, rolling stock or other conveyances, roads, walks, passageways, parking lots, or other real or personal property, including the site where the building, property, structure, or equipment is located.

Historic preservation programs means programs conducted by a public entity that have preservation of historic properties as a primary purpose.

Historic Properties means those properties that are listed or eligible for listing in the National Register of Historic Places or properties designated as historic under State or local law.

Illegal use of drugs means the use of one or more drugs, the possession or distribution of which is unlawful under the Controlled Substances Act (21 U.S.C. 812). The term *illegal use of drugs* does not include the use of a drug taken under supervision by a licensed health care professional, or other uses authorized by the Controlled Substances Act or other provisions of Federal law.

Individual with a disability means a person who has a disability. The term *individual with a disability* does not include an individual who is currently engaging in the illegal use of drugs, when the public entity acts on the basis of such use.

Public entity means —

(1) Any State or local government;

(2) Any department, agency, special purpose district, or other instrumentality of a State or States or local government; and

(3) The National Railroad Passenger Corporation, and any commuter authority (as defined in section 103(8) of the Rail Passenger Service Act).

Qualified individual with a disability means an individual with a disability who, with or without reasonable modifications to rules, policies, or practices, the removal of architectural, communication, or transportation barriers, or the provision of auxiliary aids and services, meets the essential eligibility requirements for the receipt of services or the participation in programs or activities provided by a public entity.

Qualified interpreter means an interpreter who is able to interpret effectively, accurately, and impartially both receptively and expressively, using any necessary specialized vocabulary.

Section 504 means section 504 of the Rehabilitation Act of 1973 (Pub. L. 93–112, 87 Stat. 394 (29 U.S.C. 794)), as amended.

State means each of the several States, the District of Columbia, the Commonwealth of Puerto Rico, Guam, American Samoa, the Virgin Islands, the Trust Territory of the Pacific Islands, and the Commonwealth of the Northern Mariana Islands.

§ 35.105 Self-evaluation.

(a) A public entity shall, within one year of the effective date of this part, evaluate its current services, policies, and practices, and the effects thereof, that do not or may not meet the requirements of this part and, to the extent modification of any such services, policies, and practices is required, the public entity shall proceed to make the necessary modifications.

(b) A public entity shall provide an opportunity to interested persons, including individuals with disabilities or organizations representing individuals with disabilities, to participate in the self-evaluation process by submitting comments.

(c) A public entity that employs 50 or more persons shall, for at least three years following completion of the self-evaluation, maintain on file and make available for public inspection:

(1) A list of the interested persons consulted;

(2) A description of areas examined and any problems identified; and

(3) A description of any modifications made.

(d) If a public entity has already complied with the self-evaluation requirement of a regulation implementing section 504 of the Rehabilitation Act of 1973, then the requirements of this section shall apply only to those policies and practices that were not included in the previous self-evaluation.

(Approved by the Office of Management and Budget under control number 1190–0006)
[56 FR 35716, July 26, 1991, as amended by Order No. 1694-93, 58 FR 17521, Apr. 5, 1993]

§ 35.106 Notice.

A public entity shall make available to applicants, participants, beneficiaries, and other interested persons information regarding the provisions of this part and its applicability to the services, programs, or activities of the public entity, and make such information available to them in such manner as the head of the entity finds necessary to apprise such persons of the protections against discrimination assured them by the Act and this part.

§ 35.107 Designation of responsible employee and adoption of grievance procedures.

(a) *Designation of responsible employee.* A public entity that employs 50 or more persons shall designate at least one employee to coordinate its efforts to comply with and carry out its responsibilities under this part, including any investigation of any complaint communicated to it alleging its noncompliance with this part or alleging any actions that would be prohibited by this part. The public entity shall make available to all interested individuals the name, office address, and telephone number of the employee or employees designated pursuant to this paragraph.

(b) *Complaint procedure.* A public entity that employs 50 or more persons shall adopt and publish grievance procedures providing for prompt and equitable resolution of complaints alleging any action that would be prohibited by this part.

§§ 35.108–35.129 [Reserved]

Subpart B — General Requirements

§ 35.130 General prohibitions against discrimination.

(a) No qualified individual with a disability shall, on the basis of disability, be excluded from participation in or be denied the benefits of the services, programs, or activities of a public entity, or be subjected to discrimination by any public entity.

(b)(1) A public entity, in providing any aid, benefit, or service, may not, directly or through contractual, licensing, or other arrangements, on the basis of disability —

(i) Deny a qualified individual with a disability the opportunity to participate in or benefit from the aid, benefit, or service;

(ii) Afford a qualified individual with a disability an opportunity to participate in or benefit from the aid, benefit, or service that is not equal to that afforded others;

(iii) Provide a qualified individual with a disability with an aid, benefit, or service that is not as effective in affording equal opportunity to obtain the same result, to gain the same benefit, or to reach the same level of achievement as that provided to others;

(iv) Provide different or separate aids, benefits, or services to individuals with disabilities or to any class of individuals with disabilities than is provided to others unless such action is necessary to provide qualified individuals with disabilities with aids, benefits, or services that are as effective as those provided to others;

(v) Aid or perpetuate discrimination against a qualified individual with a disability by providing significant assistance to an agency, organization, or person that discriminates on the basis of disability in providing any aid, benefit, or service to beneficiaries of the public entity's program;

(vi) Deny a qualified individual with a disability the opportunity to participate as a member of planning or advisory boards;

(vii) Otherwise limit a qualified individual with a disability in the enjoyment of any right, privilege, advantage, or opportunity enjoyed by others receiving the aid, benefit, or service.

(2) A public entity may not deny a qualified individual with a disability the opportunity to participate in services, programs, or activities that are not separate or different, despite the existence of permissibly separate or different programs or activities.

(3) A public entity may not, directly or through contractual or other arrangements, utilize criteria or methods of administration:

(i) That have the effect of subjecting qualified individuals with disabilities to discrimination on the basis of disability;

(ii) That have the purpose or effect of defeating or substantially impairing accomplishment of the objectives of the public entity's program with respect to individuals with disabilities; or

(iii) That perpetuate the discrimination of another public entity if both public entities are subject to common administrative control or are agencies of the same State.

(4) A public entity may not, in determining the site or location of a facility, make selections —

(i) That have the effect of excluding individuals with disabilities from, denying them the benefits of, or otherwise subjecting them to discrimination; or

(ii) That have the purpose or effect of defeating or substantially impairing the accomplishment of the objectives of the service, program, or activity with respect to individuals with disabilities.

(5) A public entity, in the selection of procurement contractors, may not use criteria that subject qualified individuals with disabilities to discrimination on the basis of disability.

(6) A public entity may not administer a licensing or certification program in a manner that subjects qualified individuals with disabilities to discrimination on the basis of disability, nor may a public entity establish requirements for the programs or activities of licensees or certified entities that subject qualified individuals with disabilities to discrimination on the basis of disability. The programs or activities of entities that are licensed or certified by a public entity are not, themselves, covered by this part.

(7) A public entity shall make reasonable modifications in policies, practices, or procedures when the modifications are necessary to avoid discrimination on the basis of disability, unless the public entity can demonstrate that making the modifications would fundamentally alter the nature of the service, program, or activity.

(8) A public entity shall not impose or apply eligibility criteria that screen out or tend to screen out an individual with a disability or any class of individuals with disabilities from fully and equally enjoying any service, program, or activity, unless such criteria can be shown to be necessary for the provision of the service, program, or activity being offered.

(c) Nothing in this part prohibits a public entity from providing benefits, services, or advantages to individuals with disabilities, or to a particular class of individuals with disabilities beyond those required by this part.

(d) A public entity shall administer services, programs, and activities in the most integrated setting appropriate to the needs of qualified individuals with disabilities.

(e)(1) Nothing in this part shall be construed to require an individual with a disability to accept an accommodation, aid, service, opportunity, or benefit provided under the ADA or this part which such individual chooses not to accept.

(2) Nothing in the Act or this part authorizes the representative or guardian of an individual with a disability to decline food, water, medical treatment, or medical services for that individual.

(f) A public entity may not place a surcharge on a particular individual with a disability or any group of individuals with disabilities to cover the costs of measures, such as the provision of auxiliary aids or program accessibility, that are required to provide that individual or group with the nondiscriminatory treatment required by the Act or this part.

(g) A public entity shall not exclude or otherwise deny equal services, programs, or activities to an individual or entity because of the known disability of an individual with whom the individual or entity is known to have a relationship or association.

§ 35.131 Illegal use of drugs.

(a) *General.* (1) Except as provided in paragraph (b) of this section, this part does not prohibit discrimination against an individual based on that individual's current illegal use of drugs.

(2) A public entity shall not discriminate on the basis of illegal use of drugs against an individual who is not engaging in current illegal use of drugs and who —

(i) Has successfully completed a supervised drug rehabilitation program or has otherwise been rehabilitated successfully;

(ii) Is participating in a supervised rehabilitation program; or

683

(iii) Is erroneously regarded as engaging in such use.

(b) *Health and drug rehabilitation services.* (1) A public entity shall not deny health services, or services provided in connection with drug rehabilitation, to an individual on the basis of that individual's current illegal use of drugs, if the individual is otherwise entitled to such services.

(2) A drug rehabilitation or treatment program may deny participation to individuals who engage in illegal use of drugs while they are in the program.

(c) *Drug testing.* (1) This part does not prohibit a public entity from adopting or administering reasonable policies or procedures, including but not limited to drug testing, designed to ensure that an individual who formerly engaged in the illegal use of drugs is not now engaging in current illegal use of drugs.

(2) Nothing in paragraph (c) of this section shall be construed to encourage, prohibit, restrict, or authorize the conduct of testing for the illegal use of drugs.

§ 35.132 Smoking.

This part does not preclude the prohibition of, or the imposition of restrictions on, smoking in transportation covered by this part.

§ 35.133 Maintenance of accessible features.

(a) A public entity shall maintain in operable working condition those features of facilities and equipment that are required to be readily accessible to and usable by persons with disabilities by the Act or this part.

(b) This section does not prohibit isolated or temporary interruptions in service or access due to maintenance or repairs.
[56 FR 35716, July 26, 1991, as amended by Order No. 1694-93, 58 FR 17521, Apr. 5, 1993]

§ 35.134 Retaliation or coercion.

(a) No private or public entity shall discriminate against any individual because that individual has opposed any act or practice made unlawful by this part, or because that individual made a charge, testified, assisted, or participated in any manner in an investigation, proceeding, or hearing under the Act or this part.

(b) No private or public entity shall coerce, intimidate, threaten, or interfere with any individual in the exercise or enjoyment of, or on account of his or her having exercised or enjoyed, or on account of his or her having aided or encouraged any other individual in the exercise or enjoyment of, any right granted or protected by the Act or this part.

§ 35.135 Personal devices and services.

This part does not require a public entity to provide to individuals with disabilities personal devices, such as wheelchairs; individually prescribed devices, such as prescription eyeglasses or hearing aids; readers for personal use or study; or services of a personal nature including assistance in eating, toileting, or dressing.

§§ 35.136–35.139 [Reserved]

Subpart C — Employment

§ 35.140 Employment discrimination prohibited.

(a) No qualified individual with a disability shall, on the basis of disability, be subjected to discrimination in employment under any service, program, or activity conducted by a public entity.

(b)(1) For purposes of this part, the requirements of title I of the Act, as established by the regulations of the Equal Employment Opportunity Commission in 29 CFR part 1630, apply to employment in any service, program, or activity conducted by a public entity if that public entity is also subject to the jurisdiction of title I.

(2) For the purposes of this part, the requirements of section 504 of the Rehabilitation Act of 1973, as established by the regulations of the Department of Justice in 28 CFR part 41, as those requirements pertain to employment, apply to employment in any service, program, or activity conducted by a public entity if that public entity is not also subject to the jurisdiction of title I.

§§ 35.141–35.148 [Reserved]

Subpart D — Program Accessibility

§ 35.149 Discrimination prohibited.

Except as otherwise provided in § 35.150, no qualified individual with a disability shall, because a public entity's facilities are inaccessible to or unusable by individuals with disabilities, be excluded from participation in, or be denied the benefits of the services, programs, or activities of a public entity, or be subjected to discrimination by any public entity.

§ 35.150 Existing facilities.

(a) *General.* A public entity shall operate each service, program, or activity so that the service, program, or activity, when viewed in its entirety, is readily accessible to and usable by individuals with disabilities. This paragraph does not —

(1) Necessarily require a public entity to make each of its existing facilities accessible to and usable by individuals with disabilities;

(2) Require a public entity to take any action that would threaten or destroy the historic significance of an historic property; or

(3) Require a public entity to take any action that it can demonstrate would result in a fundamental alteration in the nature of a service, program, or activity or in undue financial and administrative burdens. In those circumstances where personnel of the public entity believe that the proposed action would fundamentally alter the service, program, or activity or would result in undue financial and administrative burdens, a public entity has the burden of proving that compliance with § 35.150(a) of this part would result in such alteration or burdens. The decision that compliance would result in such alteration or burdens must be made by the head of a public entity or his or her designee after considering all resources available for use in the funding and operation of the service, program, or activity, and must be accompanied by a written statement of the reasons for reaching that conclusion. If an action would result in such an alteration or such burdens, a public entity shall take any other action that would not result in such an alteration or such burdens but would nevertheless ensure that individuals with disabilities receive the benefits or services provided by the public entity.

(b) *Methods* — (I) *General.* A public entity may comply with the requirements of this section through such means as redesign of equipment, reassignment of services to accessible buildings, assignment of aides to beneficiaries, home visits, delivery of services at alternate accessible sites, alteration of existing facilities and construction of new facilities, use of accessible rolling stock or other conveyances, or any other methods that result in making its services, programs, or activities readily accessible to and usable by individuals with disabilities. A public entity is not required to make structural changes in existing facilities where other methods are effective in achieving compliance with this section. A public entity, in making alterations to existing buildings, shall meet the accessibility requirements of § 35.151. In choosing among available methods for meeting the requirements of this section, a public entity shall give priority to those methods that offer services, programs, and activities to qualified individuals with disabilities in the most integrated setting appropriate.

(2) *Historic preservation programs.* In meeting the requirements of § 35.150(a) in historic preservation programs, a public entity shall give priority to methods that provide physical access to individuals with disabilities. In cases where a physical alteration to an historic property is not required because of paragraph (a)(2) or (a)(3) of this section, alternative methods of achieving program accessibility include —

(i) Using audio-visual materials and devices to depict those portions of an historic property that cannot otherwise be made accessible;

(ii) Assigning persons to guide individuals with handicaps into or through portions of historic properties that cannot otherwise be made accessible; or

(iii) Adopting other innovative methods.

(c) *Time period for compliance.* Where structural changes in facilities are undertaken to comply with the obligations established under this section, such changes shall be made within three years of January 26, 1992, but in any event as expeditiously as possible.

(d) *Transition plan.* (1) In the event that structural changes to facilities will be undertaken to achieve program accessibility, a public entity that employs 50 or more persons shall develop, within six months of January 26, 1992, a transition plan setting forth the steps necessary to complete such changes. A public entity shall provide an opportunity to interested persons, including individuals with disabilities or organizations representing individuals with disabilities, to participate in the development of the transition plan by submitting comments. A copy of the transition plan shall be made available for public inspection.

(2) If a public entity has responsibility or authority over streets, roads, or walkways, its transition plan shall include a schedule for providing curb ramps or other sloped areas where pedestrian walks cross curbs, giving priority to walkways serving entities covered by the Act, including State and local government offices and facilities, transportation, places of public accommodation, and employers, followed by walkways serving other areas.

(3) The plan shall, at a minimum —

(i) Identify physical obstacles in the public entity's facilities that limit the accessibility of its programs or activities to individuals with disabilities;

(ii) Describe in detail the methods that will be used to make the facilities accessible;

(iii) Specify the schedule for taking the steps necessary to achieve compliance with this section and, if the time period of the transition plan is longer than one year, identify steps that will be taken during each year of the transition period; and

(iv) Indicate the official responsible for implementation of the plan.

(4) If a public entity has already complied with the transition plan requirement of a Federal agency regulation implementing section 504 of the Rehabilitation Act of 1973, then the requirements of this paragraph (d) shall apply only to those policies and practices that were not included in the previous transition plan.

(Approved by the Office of Management and Budget under control number 1190-0004)
[56 FR 35716, July 26, 1991, as amended by Order No. 1694-93, 58 FR 17521, Apr. 5, 1993]

§ 35.151 New construction and alterations.

(a) *Design and construction.* Each facility or part of a facility constructed by, on behalf of, or for the use of a public entity shall be designed and constructed in such manner that the facility or part of the facility is readily accessible to and usable by individuals with disabilities, if the construction was commenced after January 26, 1992.

(b) *Alteration.* Each facility or part of a facility altered by, on behalf of, or for the use of a public entity in a manner that affects or could affect the usability of the facility or part of the facility shall, to the maximum extent feasible, be altered in such manner that the altered portion of the facility is readily accessible to and usable by individuals with disabilities, if the alteration was commenced after January 26, 1992.

(c) *Accessibility standards.* Design, construction, or alteration of facilities in conformance with the Uniform Federal Accessibility Standards (UFAS) (appendix A to 41 CFR part 101-19.6) or with the Americans with Disabilities Act Accessibility Guidelines for Buildings and Facilities (ADAAG) (appendix A to 28 CFR part 36) shall be deemed to comply with the requirements of this section with respect to those facilities, except that the elevator exemption contained at section 4.1.3(5) and section 4.1.6(l)(k) of ADAAG shall not apply. Departures from particular requirements of either standard by the use of other methods shall be permitted when it is clearly evident that equivalent access to the facility or part of the facility is thereby provided.

(d) *Alterations: Historic properties.* (1) Alterations to historic properties shall comply, to the maximum extent feasible, with section 4.1.7 of UFAS or section 4.1.7 of ADAAG.

(2) If it is not feasible to provide physical access to an historic property in a manner that will not threaten or destroy the historic significance of the building or facility, alternative methods of access shall be provided pursuant to the requirements of § 35.150.

(e) *Curb ramps.* (1) Newly constructed or altered streets, roads, and highways must contain curb ramps or other sloped areas at any intersection having curbs or other barriers to entry from a street level pedestrian walkway.

(2) Newly constructed or altered street level pedestrian walkways must contain curb ramps or other sloped areas at intersections to streets, roads, or highways.

[56 FR 35716, July 26, 1991, as amended by Order No. 1694-93, 58 FR 17521, Apr. 5, 1993]

§§ 35.152–35.159 [Reserved]

Subpart E — Communications

§ 35.160 General.

(a) A public entity shall take appropriate steps to ensure that communications with applicants, participants, and members of the public with disabilities are as effective as communications with others.

(b)(1) A public entity shall furnish appropriate auxiliary aids and services where necessary to afford an individual with a disability an equal opportunity to participate in, and enjoy the benefits of, a service, program, or activity conducted by a public entity.

(2) In determining what type of auxiliary aid and service is necessary, a public entity shall give primary consideration to the requests of the individual with disabilities.

§ 35.161 Telecommunication devices for the deaf (TDD's).

Where a public entity communicates by telephone with applicants and beneficiaries, TDD's or equally effective telecommunication systems shall be used to communicate with individuals with impaired hearing or speech.

§ 35.162 Telephone emergency services.

Telephone emergency services, including 911 services, shall provide direct access to individuals who use TDD's and computer modems.

§ 35.163 Information and signage.

(a) A public entity shall ensure that interested persons, including persons with impaired vision or hearing, can obtain information as to the existence and location of accessible services, activities, and facilities.

(b) A public entity shall provide signage at all inaccessible entrances to each of its facilities, directing users to an accessible entrance or to a location at which they can obtain information about accessible facilities. The international symbol for accessibility shall be used at each accessible entrance of a facility.

§ 35.164 Duties.

This subpart does not require a public entity to take any action that it can demonstrate would result in a fundamental alteration in the nature of a service, program, or activity or in undue financial and administrative burdens. In those circumstances where personnel of the public entity believe that the proposed action would fundamentally alter the service, program, or activity or would result in undue financial and administrative burdens, a public entity has the burden of proving that compliance with this subpart would result in such alteration or burdens. The decision that compliance would result in such alteration or burdens must be made by the head of the public entity or his or her designee after considering all resources available for use in the funding and operation of the service, program, or activity and must be accompanied by a written statement of the reasons for reaching that conclusion. If an action required to comply with this subpart would result in such an alteration or such burdens, a public entity shall take any other action that would not result in such an alteration or such burdens but would nevertheless ensure that, to the maximum extent possible, individuals with disabilities receive the benefits or services provided by the public entity.

§§ 35.165–35.169 [Reserved]

Subpart F — Compliance Procedures

§ 35.170 Complaints.

(a) *Who may file.* An individual who believes that he or she or a specific class of individuals has been subjected to discrimination on the basis of disability by a public entity may, by himself or herself or by an authorized representative, file a complaint under this part.

(b) *Time for filing.* A complaint must be filed not later than 180 days from the date of the alleged discrimination, unless the time for filing is extended by the designated agency for good cause shown. A complaint is deemed to be filed under this section on the date it is first filed with any Federal agency.

(c) *Where to file.* An individual may file a complaint with any agency that he or she believes to be the appropriate agency designated under subpart G of this part, or with any agency that provides funding to the public entity that is the subject of the complaint, or with the Department of Justice for referral as provided in § 35.171 (a)(2).

§ 35.171 Acceptance of complaints.

(a) *Receipt of complaints.* (1)(i) Any Federal agency that receives a complaint of discrimination on the basis of disability by a public entity shall promptly review the complaint to determine whether it has jurisdiction over the complaint under section 504.

(ii) If the agency does not have section 504 jurisdiction, it shall promptly determine whether it is the designated agency under subpart G of this part responsible for complaints filed against that public entity.

(2)(i) If an agency other than the Department of Justice determines that it does not have section 504 jurisdiction and is not the designated agency, it shall promptly refer the complaint, and notify the complainant that it is referring the complaint to the Department of Justice.

(ii) When the Department of Justice receives a complaint for which it does not have jurisdiction under section 504 and is not the designated agency, it shall refer the complaint to an agency that does have jurisdiction under section 504 or to the appropriate agency designated in subpart G of this part or, in the case of an employment complaint that is also subject to title I of the Act, to the Equal Employment Opportunity Commission.

(3)(i) If the agency that receives a complaint has section 504 jurisdiction, it shall process the complaint according to its procedures for enforcing section 504.

(ii) If the agency that receives a complaint does not have section 504 jurisdiction, but is the designated agency, it shall process the complaint according to the procedures established by this subpart.

(b) *Employment complaints.* (1) If a complaint alleges employment discrimination subject to title I of the Act, and the agency has section 504 jurisdiction, the agency shall follow the procedures issued by the Department of Justice and the Equal Employment Opportunity Commission under section 107(b) of the Act.

(2) If a complaint alleges employment discrimination subject to title I of the Act, and the designated agency does not have section 504 jurisdiction, the agency shall refer the complaint to the Equal Employment Opportunity Commission for processing under title I of the Act.

(3) Complaints alleging employment discrimination subject to this part, but not to title I of the Act shall be processed in accordance with the procedures established by this subpart.

(c) *Complete complaints.* (1) A designated agency shall accept all complete complaints under this section and shall promptly notify the complainant and the public entity of the receipt and acceptance of the complaint.

(2) If the designated agency receives a complaint that is not complete, it shall notify the complainant and specify the additional information that is needed to make the complaint a complete complaint. If the complainant fails to complete the complaint, the designated agency shall close the complaint without prejudice.

§ 35.172 Resolution of complaints.

(a) The designated agency shall investigate each complete complaint, attempt informal resolution, and, if resolution is not achieved, issue to the complainant and the public entity a Letter of Findings that shall include —

(1) Findings of fact and conclusions of law;

(2) A description of a remedy for each violation found; and

(3) Notice of the rights available under paragraph (b) of this section.

(b) If the designated agency finds noncompliance, the procedures in §§ 35.173 and 35.174 shall be followed. At any time, the complainant may file a private suit pursuant to section 203 of the Act, whether or not the designated agency finds a violation.

§ 35.173 Voluntary compliance agreements.

(a) When the designated agency issues a noncompliance Letter of Findings, the designated agency shall —

(1) Notify the Assistant Attorney General by forwarding a copy of the Letter of Findings to the Assistant Attorney General; and

(2) Initiate negotiations with the public entity to secure compliance by voluntary means.

(b) Where the designated agency is able to secure voluntary compliance, the voluntary compliance agreement shall —

(1) Be in writing and signed by the parties;

(2) Address each cited violation;

(3) Specify the corrective or remedial action to be taken, within a stated period of time, to come into compliance;

(4) Provide assurance that discrimination will not recur; and

(5) Provide for enforcement by the Attorney General.

§ 35.174 Referral.

If the public entity declines to enter into voluntary compliance negotiations or if negotiations are unsuccessful, the designated agency shall refer the matter to the Attorney General with a recommendation for appropriate action.

§ 35.175 Attorney's fees.

In any action or administrative proceeding commenced pursuant to the Act or this part, the court or agency, in its discretion, may allow the prevailing party, other than the United States, a reasonable attorney's fee, including litigation expenses, and costs, and the United States shall be liable for the foregoing the same as a private individual.

§ 35.176 Alternative means of dispute resolution.

Where appropriate and to the extent authorized by law, the use of alternative means of dispute resolution, including settlement negotiations, conciliation, facilitation, mediation, fact-finding, minitrials, and arbitration, is encouraged to resolve disputes arising under the Act and this part.

§ 35.177 Effect of unavailability of technical assistance.

A public entity shall not be excused from compliance with the requirements of this part because of any failure to receive technical assistance, including any failure in the development or dissemination of any technical assistance manual authorized by the Act.

§ 35.178 State immunity.

A State shall not be immune under the eleventh amendment to the Constitution of the United States from an action in Federal or State court of competent jurisdiction for a violation of this Act. In any action against a State for a violation of the requirements of this Act, remedies (including remedies both at law and in equity) are available for such a violation to the same extent as such remedies are available for such a violation in an action against any public or private entity other than a State.

§§ 35.179–35.189 [Reserved]

Subpart G — Designated Agencies

§ 35.190 Designated agencies.

(a) The Assistant Attorney General shall coordinate the compliance activities of Federal agencies with respect to State and local government components, and shall provide policy guidance and interpretations to designated agencies to ensure the consistent and effective implementation of the requirements of this part.

(b) The Federal agencies listed in paragraph (b) (1) through (8) of this section shall have responsibility for the implementation of subpart F of this part for components of State and local governments that exercise responsibilities, regulate, or administer services, programs, or activities in the following functional areas.

(1) *Department of Agriculture:* All programs, services, and regulatory activities relating to farming and the raising of livestock, including extension services.

(2) *Department of Education:* All programs, services, and regulatory activities relating to the operation of elementary and secondary education systems and institutions, institutions of higher education and vocational education (other than schools of medicine, dentistry, nursing, and other health-related schools), and libraries.

(3) *Department of Health and Human Services:* All programs, services, and regulatory activities relating to the provision of health care and social services, including schools of medicine, dentistry, nursing, and other health-related schools, the operation of health care and social service providers and institutions, including "grass-roots" and community services organizations and programs, and preschool and daycare programs.

(4) *Department of Housing and Urban Development:* All programs, services, and regulatory activities relating to state and local public housing, and housing assistance and referral.

(5) *Department of Interior:* All programs, services, and regulatory activities relating to lands and natural resources, including parks and recreation, water and waste management, environmental protection, energy, historic and cultural preservation, and museums.

(6) *Department of Justice:* All programs, services, and regulatory activities relating to law enforcement, public safety, and the administration of justice, including courts and correctional institutions; commerce and industry, including general economic development, banking and finance, consumer protection, insurance, and small business; planning, development, and regulation (unless assigned to other designated agencies); state and local government support services (*e.g.,* audit, personnel, comptroller, administrative services); all other government functions not assigned to other designated agencies.

(7) *Department of Labor:* All programs, services, and regulatory activities relating to labor and the work force.

(8) *Department of Transportation:* All programs, services, and regulatory activities relating to transportation, including highways, public transportation, traffic management (non-law enforcement), automobile licensing and inspection, and driver licensing.

(c) Responsibility for the implementation of subpart F of this part for components of State or local governments that exercise responsibilities, regulate, or administer services, programs, or activities relating to functions not assigned to specific designated agencies by paragraph (b) of this section may be assigned to other specific agencies by the Department of Justice.

(d) If two or more agencies have apparent responsibility over a complaint, the Assistant Attorney General shall determine which one of the agencies shall be the designated agency for purposes of that complaint.

§§ 35.191–35.999 [Reserved]

APPENDIX A TO PART 35 — PREAMBLE TO REGULATION ON NONDISCRIMINATION ON THE BASIS OF DISABILITY IN STATE AND LOCAL GOVERNMENT SERVICES (PUBLISHED JULY 26, 1991)

NOTE: For the convenience of the reader, this appendix contains the text of the preamble to the final regulation on nondiscrimination on the basis of disability in State and local government services beginning at the heading "Section-by-Section Analysis" and ending before "List of Subjects in 28 CFR Part 35" (56 FR 35696, July 26, 1991).

SECTION-BY-SECTION ANALYSIS

SECTION 35.101 Purpose

Section 35.101 states the purpose of the rule, which is to effectuate subtitle A of title II of the Americans with Disabilities Act of 1990 (the Act), which prohibits discrimination on the basis of disability by public entities. This part does not, however, apply to matters within the scope of the authority of the Secretary of Transportation under subtitle B of title II of the Act.

Section 35.102 Application

This provision specifies that, except as provided in paragraph (b), the regulation applies to all services, programs, and activities provided or made available by public entities, as that term is defined in § 35.104. Section 504 of the Rehabilitation Act of 1973 (29 U.S.C. 794), which prohibits discrimination on the basis of handicap in federally assisted programs and activities, already covers those programs and activities of public entities that receive Federal financial assistance. Title II of the ADA extends this prohibition of discrimination to include all services, programs, and activities provided or made available by State and local governments or any of their instrumentalities or agencies, regardless of the receipt of Federal financial assistance. Except as provided in § 35.134, this part does not apply to private entities.

The scope of title II's coverage of public entities is comparable to the coverage of Federal Executive agencies under the 1978 amendment to section 504, which extended section 504's application to all programs and activities "conducted by" Federal Executive agencies, in that title II applies to anything a public entity does. Title II coverage, however, is not limited to "Executive" agencies, but includes activities of the legislative and judicial branches of State and local governments. All governmental activities of public entities are covered, even if they are carried out by contractors. For example, a State is obligated by title II to ensure that the services, programs, and activities of a State park inn operated under contract by a private entity are in compliance with title II's requirements. The private entity operating the inn would also be subject to the obligations of public accommodations under title III of the Act and the Department's title III regulations at 28 CFR part 36.

Aside from employment, which is also covered by title I of the Act, there are two major categories of programs or activities covered by this regulation: those involving general public contact as part of ongoing operations of the entity and those directly administered by the entities for program beneficiaries and participants. Activities in the first category include communication with the public (telephone contacts, office walk-ins, or interviews) and the public's use of the entity's facilities. Activities in the second category include programs that provide State or local government services or benefits.

Paragraph (b) of § 35.102 explains that to the extent that the public transportation services, programs, and activities of public entities are covered by subtitle B of title II of the Act, they are subject to the regulation of the Department of Transportation (DOT) at 49 CFR part 37, and are not covered by this part. The Department of Transportation's ADA regulation establishes specific requirements for construction of transportation facilities and acquisition of vehicles. Matters not covered by subtitle B, such as the provision of auxiliary aids, are covered by this rule. For example, activities that are covered by the Department of Transportation's regulation implementing subtitle B are not required to be included in the self-evaluation required by § 35.105. In addition, activities not specifically addressed by DOT's ADA regulation may be covered by DOT's regulation implementing section 504 for its federally assisted programs and activities at 49 CFR part 27. Like other programs of public entities that are also recipients of Federal financial assistance, those programs would be covered by both the section 504 regulation and this part. Although airports operated by public entities are not subject to DOT's ADA regulation, they are subject to subpart A of title II and to this rule.

Some commenters asked for clarification about the responsibilities of public school systems under section 504 and the ADA with respect to programs, services, and activities that are not covered by the Individuals with Disabilities Education Act (IDEA), including, for example, programs open to parents or to the public, graduation ceremonies, parent-teacher organization meetings, plays and other events open to the public, and adult education classes. Public school systems must comply with the ADA in all of their services, programs, or activities, including those that are open to parents or to the public. For instance, public school systems must provide program accessibility to parents and guardians with disabilities to these programs, activities, or services, and appropriate auxiliary aids and services whenever necessary to ensure effective communication, as long as the provision of the auxiliary aids results neither in an undue burden or in a fundamental alteration of the program.

Section 35.103 Relationship to Other Laws

Section 35.103 is derived from sections 501(a) and (b) of the ADA. Paragraph (a) of this section provides that, except as otherwise specifically provided by this part, title II of the ADA is not intended to apply lesser standards than are required under title V of the Rehabilitation Act of 1973, as amended (29 U.S.C. 790–94), or the regulations implementing that title. The standards of title V of the Rehabilitation Act apply for purposes of the ADA to the extent that the ADA has not explicitly adopted a different standard than title V. Because title II of the ADA essentially extends the anti-discrimination prohibition embodied in section 504 to all actions of State and local governments, the standards adopted in this part are generally the same as those required under section 504 for federally assisted programs. Title II, however, also incorporates those provisions of titles I and III of the ADA that are not inconsistent with the regulations implementing section 504. Judiciary Committee report, H.R. Rep. No. 485, 101st Cong., 2d Sess., pt. 3, at 51 (1990) (hereinafter "Judiciary report"); Education and Labor Committee report, H.R. Rep. No. 485, 101st Cong., 2d Sess., pt. 2, at 84 (1990) (hereinafter "Education and Labor report"). Therefore, this part also includes appropriate provisions derived from the regulations implementing those titles. The inclusion of specific language in this part, however, should not be interpreted as an indication that a requirement is not included under a regulation implementing section 504.

Paragraph (b) makes clear that Congress did not intend to displace any of the rights or remedies provided by other Federal laws (including section 504) or other State laws (including State common law) that provide greater or equal protection to individuals with disabilities. As discussed above, the standards adopted by title II of the ADA for State and local government services are generally the same as those required under section 504 for federally assisted programs and activities. Subpart F of the regulation establishes compliance procedures for processing complaints covered by both this part and section 504.

With respect to State law, a plaintiff may choose to pursue claims under a State law that does not confer greater substantive rights, or even confers fewer substantive rights, if the alleged violation is protected under the alternative law and the remedies are greater. For example, a person with a physical disability could seek damages under a State law that allows compensatory and punitive damages for discrimination on the basis of physical disability, but not on the basis of mental disability. In that situation, the State law would provide narrower coverage, by excluding mental disabilities, but broader remedies, and an individual covered by both laws could choose to bring an action under both laws. Moreover, State tort claims confer greater remedies and are not preempted by the ADA. A plaintiff may join a State tort claim to a case brought under the ADA. In such a case, the plaintiff must, of course, prove all the elements of the State tort claim in order to prevail under that cause of action.

Section 35.104 Definitions

"Act." The word "Act" is used in this part to refer to the Americans with Disabilities Act of 1990, Public Law 101–336, which is also referred to as the "ADA."

"Assistant Attorney General." The term "Assistant Attorney General" refers to the Assistant Attorney General of the Civil Rights Division of the Department of Justice.

"Auxiliary aids and services." Auxiliary aids and services include a wide range of services and devices for ensuring effective communication. The proposed definition in § 35.104 provided a list of examples of auxiliary aids and services that were taken from the definition of auxiliary aids and services in section 3(1) of the ADA and were supplemented by examples from regulations implementing section 504 in federally conducted programs (see 28 CFR 39.103).

A substantial number of commenters suggested that additional examples be added to this list. The Department has added several items to this list but wishes to clarify that the list is not an all-inclusive or exhaustive catalogue of possible or available auxiliary aids or services. It is not possible to provide an exhaustive list, and an attempt to do so would omit the new devices that will become available with emerging technology.

Subparagraph (1) lists several examples, which would be considered auxiliary aids and services to make aurally delivered materials available to individuals with hearing impairments. The Department has changed the phrase used in the proposed rules, "orally delivered materials," to the statutory phrase, "aurally delivered materials," to track section 3 of the ADA and to include non-verbal sounds and alarms, and computer generated speech.

The Department has added videotext displays, transcription services, and closed and open captioning to the list of examples.

Videotext displays have become an important means of accessing auditory communications through a public address system. Transcription services are used to relay aurally delivered material almost simultaneously in written form to persons who are deaf or hearing-impaired. This technology is often used at conferences, conventions, and hearings. While the proposed rule expressly included television decoder equipment as an auxiliary aid or service, it did not mention captioning itself. The final rule rectifies this omission by mentioning both closed and open captioning.

Several persons and organizations requested that the Department replace the term "telecommunications devices for deaf persons" or "TDD's" with the term "text telephone." The Department has declined to do so. The Department is aware that the Architectural and Transportation Barriers Compliance Board (ATBCB) has used the phrase "text telephone" in lieu of the statutory term "TDD" in its final accessibility guidelines. Title IV of the

ADA, however, uses the term "Telecommunications Device for the Deaf" and the Department believes it would be inappropriate to abandon this statutory term at this time.

Several commenters urged the Department to include in the definition of "auxiliary aids and services" devices that are now available or that may become available with emerging technology.

The Department declines to do so in the rule. The Department, however, emphasizes that, although the definition would include "state of the art" devices, public entities are not required to use the newest or most advanced technologies as long as the auxiliary aid or service that is selected affords effective communication.

Subparagraph (2) lists examples of aids and services for making visually delivered materials accessible to persons with visual impairments. Many commenters proposed additional examples, such as signage or mapping, audio description services, secondary auditory programs, telebraillers, and reading machines. While the Department declines to add these items to the list, they are auxiliary aids and services and may be appropriate depending on the circumstances.

Subparagraph (3) refers to acquisition or modification of equipment or devices. Several commenters suggested the addition of current technological innovations in microelectronics and computerized control systems (*e.g.,* voice recognition systems, automatic dialing telephones, and infrared elevator and light control systems) to the list of auxiliary aids. The Department interprets auxiliary aids and services as those aids and services designed to provide effective communications, *i.e.,* making aurally and visually delivered information available to persons with hearing, speech, and vision impairments. Methods of making services, programs, or activities accessible to, or usable by, individuals with mobility or manual dexterity impairments are addressed by other sections of this part, including the provision for modifications in policies, practices, or procedures (§ 35.130 (b)(7)).

Paragraph (b)(4) deals with other similar services and actions.

Several commenters asked for clarification that "similar services and actions" include retrieving items from shelves, assistance in reaching a marginally accessible seat, pushing a barrier aside in order to provide an accessible route, or assistance in removing a sweater or coat. While retrieving an item from a shelf might be an "auxiliary aid or service" for a blind person who could not locate the item without assistance, it might be a method of providing program access for a person using a wheelchair who could not reach the shelf, or a reasonable modification to a self-service policy for an individual who lacked the ability to grasp the item. As explained above, auxiliary aids and services are those aids and services required to provide effective communications. Other forms of assistance are more appropriately addressed by other provisions of the final rule.

"Complete complaint." "Complete complaint" is defined to include all the information necessary to enable the Federal agency designated under subpart G as responsible for investigation of a complaint to initiate its investigation.

"Current illegal use of drugs." The phrase "current illegal use of drugs" is used in § 35.131. Its meaning is discussed in the preamble for that section.

"Designated agency." The term "designated agency" is used to refer to the Federal agency designated under subpart G of this rule as responsible for carrying out the administrative enforcement responsibilities established by subpart F of the rule.

"Disability." The definition of the term "disability" is the same as the definition in the title III regulation codified at 28 CFR part 36. It is comparable to the definition of the term "individual with handicaps" in section 7(8) of the Rehabilitation Act and section 802(h) of the Fair Housing Act. The Education and Labor Committee report makes clear that the analysis of the term "individual with handicaps" by the Department of Health, Education, and Welfare (HEW) in its regulations implementing section 504 (42 FR 22685 (May 4, 1977)) and the analysis by the Department of Housing and Urban Development in its regulation implementing the Fair Housing Amendments Act of 1988 (54 FR 3232 (Jan. 23, 1989)) should also apply fully to the term "disability" (Education and Labor report at 50).

The use of the term "disability" instead of "handicap" and the term "individual with a disability" instead of "individual with handicaps" represents an effort by Congress to make use of up-to-date, currently accepted terminology. As with racial and ethnic epithets, the choice of terms to apply to a person with a disability is overlaid with stereotypes, patronizing attitudes, and other emotional connotations. Many individuals with disabilities, and organizations representing such individuals, object to the use of such terms as "handicapped person" or "the handicapped." In other recent legislation, Congress also recognized this shift in terminology, e.g., by changing the name of the National Council on the Handicapped to the National Council on Disability (Pub. L. 100-630).

In enacting the Americans with Disabilities Act, Congress concluded that it was important for the current legislation to use terminology most in line with the sensibilities of most Americans with disabilities. No change in definition or substance is intended nor should one be attributed to this change in phraseology.

The term "disability" means, with respect to an individual —

(A) A physical or mental impairment that substantially limits one or more of the major life activities of such individual;

(B) A record of such an impairment; or

(C) Being regarded as having such an impairment.

If an individual meets any one of these three tests, he or she is considered to be an individual with a disability for purposes of coverage under the Americans with Disabilities Act.

Congress adopted this same basic definition of "disability," first used in the Rehabilitation Act of 1973 and in the Fair Housing Amendments Act of 1988, for a number of reasons. First, it has worked well since it was adopted in 1974. Second, it would not be possible to guarantee comprehensiveness by providing a list of specific disabilities, especially because new disorders may be recognized in the future, as they have since the definition was first established in 1974.

Test A — A physical or mental impairment that substantially limits one or more of the major life activities of such individual

Physical or mental impairment. Under the first test, an individual must have a physical or mental impairment. As explained in paragraph (1)(i) of the definition, "impairment" means any physiological disorder or condition, cosmetic disfigurement, or anatomical loss affecting one or more of the following body systems: neurological; musculoskeletal; special sense organs (which would include speech organs that are not respiratory such as vocal cords, soft palate, tongue, etc.); respiratory, including speech organs; cardiovascular; reproductive; digestive; genitourinary; hemic and lymphatic; skin; and endocrine. It also means any mental or psychological disorder, such as mental retardation, organic brain syndrome, emotional or mental illness, and specific learning disabilities.

This list closely tracks the one used in the regulations for section 504 of the Rehabilitation Act of 1973 (*see, e.g.,* 45 CFR 84.3(j)(2)(i)).

Many commenters asked that "traumatic brain injury" be added to the list in paragraph (1)(i). Traumatic brain injury is already included because it is a physiological condition affecting one of the listed body systems, *i.e.,* "neurological." Therefore, it was unnecessary to add the term to the regulation, which only provides representative examples of physiological disorders.

It is not possible to include a list of all the specific conditions, contagious and noncontagious diseases, or infections that would constitute physical or mental impairments because of the difficulty of ensuring the comprehensiveness of such a list, particularly in light of the fact that other conditions or disorders may be identified in the future. However, the list of examples in paragraph (1)(ii) of the definition includes: orthopedic, visual, speech and hearing impairments, cerebral palsy, epilepsy, muscular dystrophy, multiple sclerosis, cancer, heart disease, diabetes, mental retardation, emotional illness, specific learning disabilities, HIV disease (symptomatic or asymptomatic), tuberculosis, drug addiction, and alcoholism. The phrase "symptomatic or asymptomatic" was inserted in the final rule after "HIV disease" in response to commenters who suggested the clarification was necessary.

The examples of "physical or mental impairments" in paragraph (1)(ii) are the same as those contained in many section 504 regulations, except for the addition of the phrase "contagious and noncontagious" to describe the types of diseases and conditions included, and the addition of "HIV disease (symptomatic or asymptomatic)" and "tuberculosis" to the list of examples. These additions are based on the committee reports, caselaw, and official legal opinions interpreting section 504. In *School Board of Nassau County v. Arline,* 480 U.S. 273 (1987), a case involving an individual with tuberculosis, the Supreme Court held that people with contagious diseases are entitled to the protections afforded by section 504. Following the Arline decision, this Department's Office of Legal Counsel issued a legal opinion that concluded that symptomatic HIV disease is an impairment that substantially limits a major life activity; therefore it has been included in the definition of disability under this part. The opinion also concluded that asymptomatic HIV disease is an impairment that substantially limits a major life activity, either because of its actual effect on the individual with HIV disease or because the reactions of other people to individuals with HIV disease cause such individuals to be treated as though they are disabled. See Memorandum from Douglas W. Kmiec, Acting Assistant Attorney General, Office of Legal Counsel, Department of Justice, to Arthur B. Culvahouse, Jr., Counsel to the President (Sept. 27, 1988), reprinted in Hearings on S. 933, the Americans with Disabilities Act, Before the Subcomm. on the Handicapped of the Senate Comm. on Labor and Human Resources, 101st. Cong., 1st Sess. 346 (1989).

Paragraph (1)(iii) states that the phrase "physical or mental impairment" does not include homosexuality or bisexuality. These conditions were never considered impairments under other Federal disability laws. Section 511(a) of the statute makes clear that they are likewise not to be considered impairments under the Americans with Disabilities Act.

Physical or mental impairment does not include simple physical characteristics, such as blue eyes or black hair. Nor does it include environmental, cultural, economic, or other disadvantages, such as having a prison record, or being poor. Nor is age a disability. Similarly, the definition does not include common personality traits such as poor judgment or a quick temper where these are not symptoms of a mental or psychological disorder. However, a person who has these characteristics and also has a physical or mental impairment may be considered as having a disability for purposes of the Americans with Disabilities Act based on the impairment.

Substantial Limitation of a Major Life Activity. Under Test A, the impairment must be one that "substantially limits a major life activity." Major life activities include such things as caring for one's self, performing manual tasks, walking, seeing, hearing, speaking, breathing, learning, and working.

For example, a person who is paraplegic is substantially limited in the major life activity of walking, a person who is blind is substantially limited in the major life activity of seeing, and a person who is mentally retarded is substantially limited in the major life activity of learning. A person with traumatic brain injury is substantially limited in the major life activities of caring for one's self, learning, and working because of memory deficit, confusion, contextual difficulties, and inability to reason appropriately.

A person is considered an individual with a disability for purposes of Test A, the first prong of the definition, when the individual's important life activities are restricted as to the conditions, manner, or duration under which they can be performed in comparison to most people. A person with a minor, trivial impairment, such as a simple infected finger, is not impaired in a major life activity. A person who can walk for 10 miles continuously is not substantially limited in walking merely because, on the eleventh mile, he or she begins to experience pain, because most people would not be able to walk eleven miles without experiencing some discomfort.

The Department received many comments on the proposed rule's inclusion of the word "temporary" in the definition of "disability." The preamble indicated that impairments are not necessarily excluded from the definition of "disability" simply because they are temporary, but that the duration, or expected duration, of an impairment is one factor that may properly be considered in determining whether the impairment substantially limits a major life activity. The preamble recognized, however, that temporary impairments, such as a broken leg, are not commonly regarded as disabilities, and only in rare circumstances would the degree of the limitation and its expected duration be substantial. Nevertheless, many commenters objected to inclusion of the word "temporary" both because it is not in the statute and because it is not contained in the definition of "disability" set forth in the title I regulations of the Equal Employment Opportunity Commission (EEOC). The word "temporary" has been deleted from the final rule to conform with the statutory language.

The question of whether a temporary impairment is a disability must be resolved on a case-by-case basis, taking into consideration both the duration (or expected duration) of the impairment and the extent to which it actually limits a major life activity of the affected individual.

The question of whether a person has a disability should be assessed without regard to the availability of mitigating measures, such as reasonable modification or auxiliary aids and services. For example, a person with hearing loss is substantially limited in the major life activity of hearing, even though the loss may be improved through the use of a hearing aid.

Likewise, persons with impairments, such as epilepsy or diabetes, that substantially limit a major life activity, are covered under the first prong of the definition of disability, even if the effects of the impairment are controlled by medication.

Many commenters asked that environmental illness (also known as multiple chemical sensitivity) as well as allergy to cigarette smoke be recognized as disabilities. The Department, however, declines to state categorically that these types of allergies or sensitivities are disabilities, because the determination as to whether an impairment is a disability depends on whether, given the particular circumstances at issue, the impairment substantially limits one or more major life activities (or has a history of, or is regarded as having such an effect).

Sometimes respiratory or neurological functioning is so severely affected that an individual will satisfy the requirements to be considered disabled under the regulation. Such an individual would be entitled to all of the protections afforded by the Act and this part. In other cases, individuals may be sensitive to environmental elements or to smoke but their sensitivity will not rise to the level needed to constitute a disability. For example, their major life activity of breathing may be somewhat, but not substantially, impaired. In such circumstances, the individuals are not disabled and are not entitled to the protections of the statute despite their sensitivity to environmental agents.

In sum, the determination as to whether allergies to cigarette smoke, or allergies or sensitivities characterized by the commenters as environmental illness are disabilities covered by the regulation must be made using the same case-by-case analysis that is applied to all other physical or mental impairments. Moreover, the addition of specific regulatory provisions relating to environmental illness in the final rule would be inappropriate at this time pending future consideration of the issue by the Architectural and Transportation Barriers Compliance Board, the Environmental Protection Agency, and the Occupational Safety and Health Administration of the Department of Labor.

Test B — A record of such an impairment

This test is intended to cover those who have a record of an impairment. As explained in paragraph (3) of the rule's definition of disability, this includes a person who has a history of an impairment that substantially limited a major life activity, such as someone who has recovered from an impairment. It also includes persons who have been misclassified as having an impairment.

This provision is included in the definition in part to protect individuals who have recovered from a physical or mental impairment that previously substantially limited them in a major life activity. Discrimination on the basis of such a past impairment is prohibited. Frequently occurring examples of the first group (those who have a history of an impairment) are persons with histories of mental or emotional illness, heart disease, or cancer; examples of the second group (those who have been misclassified as having an impairment) are persons who have been misclassified as having mental retardation or mental illness.

Test C — Being regarded as having such an impairment

This test, as contained in paragraph (4) of the definition, is intended to cover persons who are treated by a public entity as having a physical or mental impairment that substantially limits a major life activity. It applies when a person is treated as if he or she has an impairment that substantially limits a major life activity, regardless of whether that person has an impairment.

The Americans with Disabilities Act uses the same "regarded as" test set forth in the regulations implementing section 504 of the Rehabilitation Act. *See, e.g.,* 28 CFR 42.540(k)(2)(iv), which provides:

> (iv) "Is regarded as having an impairment" means (A) Has a physical or mental impairment that does not substantially limit major life activities but that is treated by a recipient as constituting such a limitation; (B) Has a physical or mental impairment that substantially limits major life activities only as a result of the attitudes of others toward such impairment; or (C) Has none of the impairments defined in paragraph (k)(2)(i) of this section but is treated by a recipient as having such an impairment.

The perception of the covered entity is a key element of this test. A person who perceives himself or herself to have an impairment, but does not have an impairment, and is not treated as if he or she has an impairment, is not protected under this test.

A person would be covered under this test if a public entity refused to serve the person because it perceived that the person had an impairment that limited his or her enjoyment of the goods or services being offered.

For example, persons with severe burns often encounter discrimination in community activities, resulting in substantial limitation of major life activities. These persons would be covered under this test based on the attitudes of others towards the impairment, even if they did not view themselves as "impaired."

The rationale for this third test, as used in the Rehabilitation Act of 1973, was articulated by the Supreme Court in *Arline,* 480 U.S. 273 (1987). The Court noted that although an individual may have an impairment that does not in fact substantially limit a major life activity, the reaction of others may prove just as disabling. "Such an impairment might not diminish a person's physical or mental capabilities, but could nevertheless substantially limit that person's ability to work as a result of the negative reactions of others to the impairment." *Id.* at 283.

The Court concluded that, by including this test in the Rehabilitation Act's definition, "Congress acknowledged that society's accumulated myths and fears about disability and diseases are as handicapping as are the physical limitations that flow from actual impairment." *Id.* at 284.

Thus, a person who is denied services or benefits by a public entity because of myths, fears, and stereotypes associated with disabilities would be covered under this third test whether or not the person's physical or mental condition would be considered a disability under the first or second test in the definition.

If a person is refused admittance on the basis of an actual or perceived physical or mental condition, and the public entity can articulate no legitimate reason for the refusal (such as failure to meet eligibility criteria), a perceived concern about admitting persons with disabilities could be inferred and the individual would qualify for coverage under the "regarded as" test. A person who is covered because of being regarded as having an impairment is not required to show that the public entity's perception is inaccurate (*e.g.,* that he will be accepted by others) in order to receive benefits from the public entity.

Paragraph (5) of the definition lists certain conditions that are not included within the definition of "disability." The excluded conditions are: transvestism, transsexualism, pedophilia, exhibitionism, voyeurism, gender identity disorders not resulting from physical impairments, other sexual behavior disorders, compulsive gambling, kleptomania, pyromania, and psychoactive substance use disorders resulting from current illegal use of drugs. Unlike homosexuality and bisexuality, which are not considered impairments under either section 504 or the Americans with Disabilities Act (see the definition of "disability," paragraph (1)(iv)), the conditions listed in paragraph (5), except for transvestism, are not necessarily excluded as impairments under section 504. (Transvestism was excluded from the definition of disability for section 504 by the Fair Housing Amendments Act of 1988, Pub. L. 100–430, section 6(b)).

"Drug." The definition of the term "drug" is taken from section 510(d)(2) of the ADA.

"Facility." "Facility" means all or any portion of buildings, structures, sites, complexes, equipment, rolling stock or other conveyances, roads, walks, passageways, parking lots, or other real or personal property, including the site where the building, property, structure, or equipment is located. It includes both indoor and outdoor areas where human-constructed improvements, structures, equipment, or property have been added to the natural environment.

Commenters raised questions about the applicability of this part to activities operated in mobile facilities, such as bookmobiles or mobile health screening units. Such activities would be covered by the requirement for program accessibility in § 35.150, and would be included in the definition of "facility" as "other real or personal property," although standards for new construction and alterations of such facilities are not yet included in the accessibility standards adopted by § 35.151. Sections 35.150 and 35.151 specifically address the obligations of public entities to ensure accessibility by providing curb ramps at pedestrian walkways.

"Historic preservation programs" and "Historic properties" are defined in order to aid in the interpretation of §§ 35.150(a)(2) and (b)(2), which relate to accessibility of historic preservation programs, and § 35.151(d), which relates to the alteration of historic properties.

"Illegal use of drugs." The definition of "illegal use of drugs" is taken from section 510(d)(1) of the Act and clarifies that the term includes the illegal use of one or more drugs.

"Individual with a disability" means a person who has a disability but does not include an individual who is currently illegally using drugs, when the public entity acts on the basis of such use. The phrase "current illegal use of drugs" is explained in § 35.131.

"Public entity." The term "public entity" is defined in accordance with section 201(1) of the ADA as any State or local government; any department, agency, special purpose district, or other instrumentality of a State or States or local government; or the National Railroad Passenger Corporation, and any commuter authority (as defined in section 103(8) of the Rail Passenger Service Act).

"Qualified individual with a disability." The definition of "qualified individual with a disability" is taken from section 201(2) of the Act, which is derived from the definition of "qualified handicapped person" in the Department of Health and Human Services' regulation implementing section 504 (45 CFR § 84.3(k)). It combines the definition at 45 CFR 84.3(k)(1) for employment ("a handicapped person who, with reasonable accommodation, can perform the essential functions of the job in question") with the definition for other services at 45 CFR 84.3(k)(4) ("a handicapped person who meets the essential eligibility requirements for the receipt of such services").

Some commenters requested clarification of the term "essential eligibility requirements." Because of the variety of situations in which an individual's qualifications will be at issue, it is not possible to include more specific criteria in the definition.

The "essential eligibility requirements" for participation in some activities covered under this part may be minimal. For example, most public entities provide information about their operations as a public service to anyone who requests it. In such situations, the only "eligibility requirement" for receipt of such information would be the request for it. Where such information is provided by telephone, even the ability to use a voice telephone is not an "essential eligibility requirement," because § 35.161 requires a public entity to provide equally effective telecommunication systems for individuals with impaired hearing or speech.

For other activities, identification of the "essential eligibility requirements" may be more complex. Where questions of safety are involved, the principles established in § 36.208 of the Department's regulation implementing title III of the ADA, to be codified at 28 CFR, part 36, will be applicable. That section implements section 302(b)(3) of the Act, which provides that a public accommodation is not required to permit an individual to participate in or benefit from the goods, services, facilities, privileges, advantages and accommodations of the public accommodation, if that individual poses a direct threat to the health or safety of others.

A "direct threat" is a significant risk to the health or safety of others that cannot be eliminated by a modification of policies, practices, or procedures, or by the provision of auxiliary aids or services. In *School Board of Nassau County v. Arline,* 480 U.S. 273 (1987), the Supreme Court recognized that there is a need to balance the interests of people with disabilities against legitimate concerns for public safety. Although persons with disabilities are generally entitled to the protection of this part, a person who poses a significant risk to others will not be "qualified," if reasonable modifications to the public entity's policies, practices, or procedures will not eliminate that risk.

The determination that a person poses a direct threat to the health or safety of others may not be based on generalizations or stereotypes about the effects of a particular disability. It must be based on an individualized assessment, based on reasonable judgment that relies on current medical evidence or on the best available objective evidence, to determine: the nature, duration, and severity of the risk; the probability that the potential injury will actually occur; and whether reasonable modifications of policies, practices, or procedures will mitigate the risk. This is the test established by the Supreme Court in *Arline.* Such an inquiry is essential if the law is to achieve its goal of protecting disabled individuals from discrimination based on prejudice, stereotypes, or unfounded fear, while giving appropriate weight to legitimate concerns, such as the need to avoid exposing others to significant health and safety risks. Making this assessment will not usually require the services of a physician. Sources for medical knowledge include guidance from public health authorities, such as the U.S. Public Health Service, the Centers for Disease Control, and the National Institutes of Health, including the National Institute of Mental Health.

"Qualified interpreter." The Department received substantial comment regarding the lack of a definition of "qualified interpreter." The proposed rule defined auxiliary aids and services to include the statutory term, "qualified interpreters" (§ 35.104), but did not define it. Section 35.160 requires the use of auxiliary aids including qualified interpreters and commenters stated that a lack of guidance on what the term means would create confusion among those trying to secure interpreting services and often result in less than effective communication.

Many commenters were concerned that, without clear guidance on the issue of "qualified" interpreter, the rule would be interpreted to mean "available, rather than qualified" interpreters. Some claimed that few public entities would understand the difference between a qualified interpreter and a person who simply knows a few signs or how to fingerspell.

In order to clarify what is meant by "qualified interpreter" the Department has added a definition of the term to the final rule.

A qualified interpreter means an interpreter who is able to interpret effectively, accurately, and impartially both receptively and expressively, using any necessary specialized vocabulary. This definition focuses on the actual ability of the interpreter in a particular interpreting context to facilitate effective communication between the public entity and the individual with disabilities.

Public comment also revealed that public entities have at times asked persons who are deaf to provide family members or friends to interpret. In certain circumstances, notwithstanding that the family member of friend is able to interpret or is a certified interpreter, the family member or friend may not be qualified to render the necessary interpretation because of factors such as emotional or personal involvement or considerations of confidentiality that may adversely affect the ability to interpret "effectively, accurately, and impartially."

The definition of "qualified interpreter" in this rule does not invalidate or limit standards for interpreting services of any State or local law that are equal to or more stringent than those imposed by this definition. For instance, the definition would not supersede any requirement of State law for use of a certified interpreter in court proceedings.

"Section 504." The Department added a definition of "section 504" because the term is used extensively in subpart F of this part.

"State." The definition of "State" is identical to the statutory definition in section 3(3) of the ADA.

Section 35.105 Self-evaluation

Section 35.105 establishes a requirement, based on the section 504 regulations for federally assisted and federally conducted programs, that a public entity evaluate its current policies and practices to identify and correct any that are not consistent with the requirements of this part. As noted in the discussion of § 35.102, activities covered by the Department of Transportation's regulation implementing subtitle B of title II are not required to be included in the self-evaluation required by this section.

Experience has demonstrated the self-evaluation process to be a valuable means of establishing a working relationship with individuals with disabilities, which has promoted both effective and efficient implementation of section 504. The Department expects that it will likewise be useful to public entities newly covered by the ADA.

All public entities are required to do a self-evaluation. However, only those that employ 50 or more persons are required to maintain the self-evaluation on file and make it available for public inspection for three years. The number 50 was derived from the Department of Justice's section 504 regulations for federally assisted programs, 28 CFR 42.505(c). The Department received comments critical of this limitation, some suggesting the requirement apply to all public entities and others suggesting that the number be changed from 50 to 15. The final rule has not been changed. Although many regulations implementing section 504 for federally assisted programs do use 15 employees as the cut-off for this record-keeping requirement, the Department believes that it would be inappropriate to extend it to those smaller public entities covered by this regulation that do not receive Federal financial assistance. This approach has the benefit of minimizing paperwork burdens on small entities.

Paragraph (d) provides that the self-evaluation required by this section shall apply only to programs not subject to section 504 or those policies and practices, such as those involving communications access, that have not already been included in a self-evaluation required under an existing regulation implementing section 504. Because most self-evaluations were done from five to twelve years ago, however, the Department expects that a great many public entities will be reexamining all of their policies and programs. Programs and functions may have changed, and actions that were supposed to have been taken to comply with section 504 may not have been fully implemented or may no longer be effective. In addition, there have been statutory amendments to section 504 which have changed the coverage of section 504, particularly the Civil Rights Restoration Act of 1987, Public Law No. 100-259, 102 Stat. 28 (1988), which broadened the definition of a covered "program or activity."

Several commenters suggested that the Department clarify public entities' liability during the one-year period for compliance with the self-evaluation requirement. The self-evaluation requirement does not stay the effective date of the statute nor of this part. Public entities are, therefore, not shielded from discrimination claims during that time.

Other commenters suggested that the rule require that every self-evaluation include an examination of training efforts to assure that individuals with disabilities are not subjected to discrimination because of insensitivity, particularly in the law enforcement area. Although the Department has not added such a specific requirement to the rule, it would be appropriate for public entities to evaluate training efforts because, in many cases, lack of training leads to discriminatory practices, even when the policies in place are nondiscriminatory.

Section 35.106 Notice

Section 35.106 requires a public entity to disseminate sufficient information to applicants, participants, beneficiaries, and other interested persons to inform them of the rights and protections afforded by the ADA and this regulation. Methods of providing this information include, for example, the publication of information in handbooks, manuals, and pamphlets that are distributed to the public to describe a public entity's programs and activities; the display of informative posters in service centers and other public places; or the broadcast of information by television or radio. In providing the notice, a public entity must comply with the requirements for effective communication in § 35.160. The preamble to that section gives guidance on how to effectively communicate with individuals with disabilities.

Section 35.107 Designation of Responsible Employee and Adoption of Grievance Procedures

Consistent with § 35.105, self-evaluation, the final rule requires that public entities with 50 or more employees designate a responsible employee and adopt grievance procedures. Most of the commenters who suggested that the requirement that self-evaluation be maintained on file for three years not be limited to those employing 50 or more persons made a similar suggestion concerning § 35.107. Commenters recommended either that all public entities be subject to § 35.107, or that "50 or more persons" be changed to "15 or more persons." As explained in the discussion of § 35.105, the Department has not adopted this suggestion.

The requirement for designation of an employee responsible for coordination of efforts to carry out responsibilities under this part is derived from the HEW regulation implementing section 504 in federally assisted programs. The requirement for designation of a particular employee and dissemination of information about how to locate that employee helps to ensure that individuals dealing with large agencies are able to easily find a responsible person who is familiar with the requirements of the Act and this part and can communicate those requirements to other individuals in the agency who may be unaware of their responsibilities. This paragraph in no way limits a public entity's obligation to ensure that all of its employees comply with the requirements of this part, but it ensures that any failure by individual employees can be promptly corrected by the designated employee.

Section 35.107(b) requires public entities with 50 or more employees to establish grievance procedures for resolving complaints of violations of this part. Similar requirements are found in the section 504 regulations for federally assisted programs (*see, e.g.,* 45 CFR 84.7(b)). The rule, like the regulations for federally assisted programs, provides for investigation and resolution of complaints by a Federal enforcement agency. It is the view of the Department that public entities subject to this part should be required to establish a mechanism for resolution of complaints at the local level without requiring the complainant to resort to the Federal complaint procedures established under subpart F. Complainants would not, however, be required to exhaust the public entity's grievance procedures before filing a complaint under subpart F. Delay in filing the complaint at the Federal level caused by pursuit of the remedies available under the grievance procedure would generally be considered good cause for extending the time allowed for filing under § 35.170(b).

Subpart B — General Requirements

Section 35.130 General Prohibitions Against Discrimination

The general prohibitions against discrimination in the rule are generally based on the prohibitions in existing regulations implementing section 504 and, therefore, are already familiar to State and local entities covered by section 504. In addition, § 35.130 includes a number of provisions derived from title III of the Act that are implicit to a certain degree in the requirements of regulations implementing section 504.

Several commenters suggested that this part should include the section of the proposed title III regulation that implemented section 309 of the Act, which requires that courses and examinations related to applications, licensing, certification, or credentialing be provided in an accessible place and manner or that alternative accessible arrangements be made. The Department has not adopted this suggestion. The requirements of this part, including the general prohibitions of discrimination in this section, the program access requirements of subpart D, and the communications requirements of subpart E, apply to courses and examinations provided by public entities. The Department considers these requirements to be sufficient to ensure that courses and examinations administered by public entities meet the requirements of section 309. For example, a public entity offering an examination must ensure that modifications of policies, practices, or procedures or the provision of auxiliary aids and services furnish the individual with a disability an equal opportunity to demonstrate his or her knowledge or ability.

Also, any examination specially designed for individuals with disabilities must be offered as often and in as timely a manner as are other examinations. Further, under this part, courses and examinations must be offered in the most integrated setting appropriate. The analysis of § 35.130(d) is relevant to this determination.

A number of commenters asked that the regulation be amended to require training of law enforcement personnel to recognize the difference between criminal activity and the effects of seizures or other disabilities such as mental retardation, cerebral palsy, traumatic brain injury, mental illness, or deafness. Several disabled commenters gave personal statements about the abuse they had received at the hands of law enforcement personnel. Two organizations that commented cited the Judiciary report at 50 as authority to require law enforcement training.

The Department has not added such a training requirement to the regulation. Discriminatory arrests and brutal treatment are already unlawful police activities. The general regulatory obligation to modify policies, practices, or procedures requires law enforcement to make changes in policies that result in discriminatory arrests or abuse of individuals with disabilities.

Under this section law enforcement personnel would be required to make appropriate efforts to determine whether perceived strange or disruptive behavior or unconsciousness is the result of a disability. The Department notes that a number of States have attempted to address the problem of arresting disabled persons for noncriminal conduct resulting from their disability through adoption of the Uniform Duties to Disabled Persons Act, and encourages other jurisdictions to consider that approach.

Paragraph (a) restates the nondiscrimination mandate of section 202 of the ADA. The remaining paragraphs in § 35.130 establish the general principles for analyzing whether any particular action of the public entity violates this mandate.

Paragraph (b) prohibits overt denials of equal treatment of individuals with disabilities. A public entity may not refuse to provide an individual with a disability with an equal opportunity to participate in or benefit from its program simply because the person has a disability.

Paragraph (b)(1)(i) provides that it is discriminatory to deny a person with a disability the right to participate in or benefit from the aid, benefit, or service provided by a public entity. Paragraph (b)(1)(ii) provides that the aids, benefits, and services provided to persons with disabilities must be equal to those provided to others, and paragraph (b)(1)(iii) requires that the aids, benefits, or services provided to individuals with disabilities must be as effective in affording equal opportunity to obtain the same result, to gain the same benefit, or to reach the same level of achievement as those provided to others. These paragraphs are taken from the regulations implementing section 504 and simply restate principles long established under section 504.

Paragraph (b)(1)(iv) permits the public entity to develop separate or different aids, benefits, or services when necessary to provide individuals with disabilities with an equal opportunity to participate in or benefit from the public entity's programs or activities, but only when necessary to ensure that the aids, benefits, or services are as effective as those provided to others. Paragraph (b)(1)(iv) must be read in conjunction with paragraphs (b)(2), (d), and (e). Even when separate or different aids, benefits, or services would be more effective, paragraph (b)(2) provides that a qualified individual with a disability still has the right to choose to participate in the program that is not designed to accommodate individuals with disabilities. Paragraph (d) requires that a public entity administer services, programs, and activities in the most integrated setting appropriate to the needs of qualified individuals with disabilities.

Paragraph (b)(2) specifies that, notwithstanding the existence of separate or different programs or activities provided in accordance with this section, an individual with a disability shall not be denied the opportunity to participate in such programs or activities that are not separate or different. Paragraph (e), which is derived from section 501 (d) of the Americans with Disabilities Act, states that nothing in this part shall be construed to require an individual with a disability to accept an accommodation, aid, service, opportunity, or benefit that he or she chooses not to accept.

Taken together, these provisions are intended to prohibit exclusion and segregation of individuals with disabilities and the denial of equal opportunities enjoyed by others, based on, among other things, presumptions, patronizing attitudes, fears, and stereotypes about individuals with disabilities. Consistent with these standards, public entities are required to ensure that their actions are based on facts applicable to individuals and not on presumptions as to what a class of individuals with disabilities can or cannot do.

Integration is fundamental to the purpose of the Americans with Disabilities Act. Provision of segregated accommodations and services relegates persons with disabilities to second-class status. For example, it would be a violation of this provision to require persons with disabilities to eat in the back room of a government cafeteria or to refuse to allow a person with a disability the full use of recreation or exercise facilities because of stereotypes about the person's ability to participate.

Many commenters objected to proposed paragraphs (b)(1)(iv) and (d) as allowing continued segregation of individuals with disabilities. The Department recognizes that promoting integration of individuals with disabilities into the mainstream of society is an important objective of the ADA and agrees that, in most instances, separate programs for individuals with disabilities will not be permitted. Nevertheless, section 504 does permit separate programs in limited circumstances, and Congress clearly intended the regulations issued under title II to adopt the standards of section 504. Furthermore, Congress included authority for separate programs in the specific requirements of title III of the Act. Section 302(b)(1)(A)(iii) of the Act provides for separate benefits in language similar to that in § 35.130(b)(1)(iv), and section 302(b)(1)(B) includes the same requirement for "the most integrated setting appropriate" as in § 35.130(d).

Even when separate programs are permitted, individuals with disabilities cannot be denied the opportunity to participate in programs that are not separate or different. This is an important and overarching principle of the Americans with Disabilities Act. Separate, special, or different programs that are designed to provide a benefit to persons with disabilities cannot be used to restrict the participation of persons with disabilities in general, integrated activities.

For example, a person who is blind may wish to decline participating in a special museum tour that allows persons to touch sculptures in an exhibit and instead tour the exhibit at his or her own pace with the museum's recorded tour. It is not the intent of this section to require the person who is blind to avail himself or herself of the special tour. Modified participation for persons with disabilities must be a choice, not a requirement.

In addition, it would not be a violation of this section for a public entity to offer recreational programs specially designed for children with mobility impairments. However, it would be a violation of this section if the entity then excluded these children from other recreational services for which they are qualified to participate when these services are made available to nondisabled children, or if the entity required children with disabilities to attend only designated programs.

Many commenters asked that the Department clarify a public entity's obligations within the integrated program when it offers a separate program but an individual with a disability chooses not to participate in the separate program. It is impossible to make a blanket statement as to what level of auxiliary aids or modifications would be required in the integrated program. Rather, each situation must be assessed individually. The starting point is to question whether the separate program is in fact necessary or appropriate for the individual. Assuming the separate program would be appropriate for a particular individual, the extent to which that individual must be provided with modifications in the integrated program will depend not only on what the individual needs but also on the limitations and defenses of this part. For example, it may constitute an undue burden for a public accommodation, which provides a full-time interpreter in its special guided tour for individuals with hearing impairments, to hire an additional interpreter for those individuals who choose to attend the integrated program. The Department cannot identify categorically the level of assistance or aid required in the integrated program.

Paragraph (b)(1)(v) provides that a public entity may not aid or perpetuate discrimination against a qualified individual with a disability by providing significant assistance to an agency, organization, or person that discriminates on the basis of disability in providing any aid, benefit, or service to beneficiaries of the public entity's program. This paragraph is taken from the regulations implementing section 504 for federally assisted programs.

Paragraph (b)(1)(vi) prohibits the public entity from denying a qualified individual with a disability the opportunity to participate as a member of a planning or advisory board.

Paragraph (b)(1)(vii) prohibits the public entity from limiting a qualified individual with a disability in the enjoyment of any right, privilege, advantage, or opportunity enjoyed by others receiving any aid, benefit, or service.

Paragraph (b)(3) prohibits the public entity from utilizing criteria or methods of administration that deny individuals with disabilities access to the public entity's services, programs, and activities or that perpetuate the discrimination of another public entity, if both public entities are subject to common administrative control or are agencies of the same State. The phrase "criteria or methods of administration" refers to official written policies of the public entity and to the actual practices of the public entity. This paragraph prohibits both blatantly exclusionary policies or practices and nonessential policies and practices that are neutral on their face, but deny individuals with disabilities an effective opportunity to participate. This standard is consistent with the interpretation of section 504 by the U.S. Supreme Court in *Alexander v. Choate,* 469 U.S. 287 (1985). The Court in *Choate* explained that members of Congress made numerous statements during passage of section 504 regarding eliminating architectural barriers, providing access to transportation, and eliminating discriminatory effects of job qualification procedures. The Court then noted: "These statements would ring hollow if the resulting legislation could not rectify the harms resulting from action that discriminated by effect as well as by design." *Id.* at 297 (footnote omitted).

Paragraph (b)(4) specifically applies the prohibition enunciated in § 35.130(b)(3) to the process of selecting sites for construction of new facilities or selecting existing facilities to be used by the public entity. Paragraph (b)(4) does not apply to construction of additional buildings at an existing site.

Paragraph (b)(5) prohibits the public entity, in the selection of procurement contractors, from using criteria that subject qualified individuals with disabilities to discrimination on the basis of disability.

Paragraph (b)(6) prohibits the public entity from discriminating against qualified individuals with disabilities on the basis of disability in the granting of licenses or certification. A person is a "qualified individual with a disability" with respect to licensing or certification if he or she can meet the essential eligibility requirements for receiving the license or certification (see § 35.104).

A number of commenters were troubled by the phrase "essential eligibility requirements" as applied to State licensing requirements, especially those for health care professions. Because of the variety of types of programs to which the definition of "qualified individual with a disability" applies, it is not possible to use more specific language in the definition. The phrase "essential eligibility requirements," however, is taken from the definitions in the regulations implementing section 504, so caselaw under section 504 will be applicable to its interpretation. In *Southeastern Community College v. Davis,* 442 U.S. 397, for example, the Supreme Court held that section 504 does not require an institution to "lower or effect substantial modifications of standards to accommodate a handicapped person," 442 U.S. at 413, and that the school had established that the plaintiff was not "qualified" because she was not able to "serve the nursing profession in all customary ways," *id.* Whether a particular requirement is "essential" will, of course, depend on the facts of the particular case.

In addition, the public entity may not establish requirements for the programs or activities of licensees or certified entities that subject qualified individuals with disabilities to discrimination on the basis of disability. For example, the public entity must comply with this requirement when establishing safety standards for the operations of licensees. In that case the public entity must ensure that standards that it promulgates do not discriminate against the employment of qualified individuals with disabilities in an impermissible manner.

Paragraph (b)(6) does not extend the requirements of the Act or this part directly to the programs or activities of licensees or certified entities themselves. The programs or activities of licensees or certified entities are not themselves programs or activities of the public entity merely by virtue of the license or certificate.

Paragraph (b)(7) is a specific application of the requirement under the general prohibitions of discrimination that public entities make reasonable modifications in policies, practices, or procedures where necessary to avoid discrimination on the basis of disability. Section 302(b)(2)(A)(ii) of the ADA sets out this requirement specifically for public accommodations covered by title III of the Act, and the House Judiciary Committee Report directs the Attorney General to include those specific requirements in the title II regulation to the extent that they do not conflict with the regulations implementing section 504. Judiciary report at 52.

Paragraph (b)(8), a new paragraph not contained in the proposed rule, prohibits the imposition or application of eligibility criteria that screen out or tend to screen out an individual with a disability or any class of individuals with disabilities from fully and equally enjoying any service, program, or activity, unless such criteria can be shown to be necessary for the provision of the service, program, or activity being offered. This prohibition is also a specific application of the general prohibitions of discrimination and is based on section 302(b)(2)(A)(i) of the ADA. It prohibits overt denials of equal treatment of individuals with disabilities, or establishment of exclusive or segregative criteria that would bar individuals with disabilities from participation in services, benefits, or activities.

Paragraph (b)(8) also prohibits policies that unnecessarily impose requirements or burdens on individuals with disabilities that are not placed on others. For example, public entities may not require that a qualified individual with a disability be accompanied by an attendant. A public entity is not, however, required to provide attendant care, or assistance in toileting, eating, or dressing to individuals with disabilities, except in special circumstances, such as where the individual is an inmate of a custodial or correctional institution.

In addition, paragraph (b)(8) prohibits the imposition of criteria that "tend to" screen out an individual with a disability. This concept, which is derived from current regulations under section 504 (*see, e.g.,* 45 CFR 84.13), makes it discriminatory to impose policies or criteria that, while not creating a direct bar to individuals with disabilities, indirectly prevent or limit their ability to participate. For example, requiring presentation of a driver's license as the sole means of identification for purposes of paying by check would violate this section in situations where, for example, individuals with severe vision impairments or developmental disabilities or epilepsy are ineligible to receive a driver's license and the use of an alternative means of identification, such as another photo I.D. or credit card, is feasible.

A public entity may, however, impose neutral rules and criteria that screen out, or tend to screen out, individuals with disabilities if the criteria are necessary for the safe operation of the program in question. Examples of safety qualifications that would be justifiable in appropriate circumstances would include eligibility requirements for drivers' licenses, or a requirement that all participants in a recreational rafting expedition be able to meet a necessary level of swimming proficiency. Safety requirements must be based on actual risks and not on speculation, stereotypes, or generalizations about individuals with disabilities.

Paragraph (c) provides that nothing in this part prohibits a public entity from providing benefits, services, or advantages to individuals with disabilities, or to a particular class of individuals with disabilities, beyond those required by this part. It is derived from a provision in the section 504 regulations that permits programs conducted pursuant to Federal statute or Executive order that are designed to benefit only individuals with disabilities or a given class of individuals with disabilities to be limited to those individuals with disabilities. Section 504 ensures that federally assisted programs are made available to all individuals, without regard to disabilities, unless the Federal program under which the assistance is provided is specifically limited to individuals with disabilities or a particular class of individuals with disabilities. Because coverage under this part is not limited to federally assisted programs, paragraph (c) has been revised to clarify that State and local governments may provide special benefits, beyond those required by the nondiscrimination requirements of this part, that are limited to individuals with disabilities or a particular class of individuals with disabilities, without thereby incurring additional obligations to persons without disabilities or to other classes of individuals with disabilities.

Paragraphs (d) and (e), previously referred to in the discussion of paragraph (b)(1)(iv), provide that the public entity must administer services, programs, and activities in the most integrated setting appropriate to the needs of qualified individuals with disabilities, *i.e.,* in a setting that enables individuals with disabilities to interact with nondisabled persons to the fullest extent possible, and that persons with disabilities must be provided the option of declining to accept a particular accommodation.

Some commenters expressed concern that § 35.130(e), which states that nothing in the rule requires an individual with a disability to accept special accommodations and services provided under the ADA, could be interpreted to allow guardians of infants or older people with disabilities to refuse medical treatment for their wards. Section 35.130(e) has been revised to make it clear that paragraph (e) is inapplicable to the concern of the commenters. A new paragraph (e)(2) has been added stating that nothing in the regulation authorizes the representative or guardian of an individual with a disability to decline food, water, medical treatment, or medical services for that individual. New paragraph (e) clarifies that neither the ADA nor the regulation alters current Federal law ensuring the rights of incompetent individuals with disabilities to receive food, water, and medical treatment. *See, e.g.,* Child Abuse Amendments of 1984 (42 U.S.C. 5106a(b)(10), 5106g(10)); Rehabilitation Act of 1973, as amended (29 U.S.C. 794); the Developmentally Disabled Assistance and Bill of Rights Act (42 U.S.C. 6042).

Sections 35.130(e)(1) and (2) are based on section 501(d) of the ADA. Section 501(d) was designed to clarify that nothing in the ADA requires individuals with disabilities to accept special accommodations and services for individuals with disabilities that may segregate them:

> The Committee added this section [501(d)] to clarify that nothing in the ADA is intended to permit discriminatory treatment on the basis of disability, even when such treatment is rendered under the guise of providing an accommodation, service, aid or benefit to the individual with disability. For example, a blind individual may choose not to avail himself or herself of the right to go to the front of a line, even if a particular public accommodation has chosen to offer such a modification of a policy for blind individuals. Or, a blind individual may choose to decline to participate in a special museum tour that allows persons to touch sculptures in an exhibit and instead tour the exhibits at his or her own pace with the museum's recorded tour.

Judiciary report at 71–72. The Act is not to be construed to mean that an individual with disabilities must accept special accommodations and services for individuals with disabilities when that individual can participate in the regular services already offered. Because medical treatment, including treatment for particular conditions, is not a special accommodation or service for individuals with disabilities under section 501(d), neither the Act nor this part provides affirmative authority to suspend such treatment. Section 501(d) is intended to clarify that the Act is not designed to foster discrimination through mandatory acceptance of special services when other alternatives are provided; this concern does not reach to the provision of medical treatment for the disabling condition itself.

Paragraph (f) provides that a public entity may not place a surcharge on a particular individual with a disability, or any group of individuals with disabilities, to cover any costs of measures required to provide that individual or group with the nondiscriminatory treatment required by the Act or this part. Such measures may include the provision of auxiliary aids or of modifications required to provide program accessibility.

Several commenters asked for clarification that the costs of interpreter services may not be assessed as an element of "court costs." The Department has already recognized that imposition of the cost of courtroom interpreter services is impermissible under section 504. The preamble to the Department's section 504 regulation for its federally assisted programs states that where a court system has an obligation to provide qualified interpreters, "it has the corresponding responsibility to pay for the services of the interpreters." (45 FR 37630 (June 3, 1980)).

Accordingly, recouping the costs of interpreter services by assessing them as part of court costs would also be prohibited.

Paragraph (g), which prohibits discrimination on the basis of an individual's or entity's known relationship or association with an individual with a disability, is based on sections 102(b)(4) and 302(b)(1)(E) of the ADA. This paragraph was not contained in the proposed rule. The individuals covered under this paragraph are any individuals who are discriminated against because of their known association with an individual with a disability. For example, it would be a violation of this paragraph for a local government to refuse to allow a theater company to use a school auditorium on the grounds that the company had recently performed for an audience of individuals with HIV disease.

This protection is not limited to those who have a familial relationship with the individual who has a disability. Congress considered, and rejected, amendments that would have limited the scope of this provision to specific associations and relationships. Therefore, if a public entity refuses admission to a person with cerebral palsy and his or her companions, the companions have an independent right of action under the ADA and this section.

During the legislative process, the term "entity" was added to section 302(b)(1)(E) to clarify that the scope of the provision is intended to encompass not only persons who have a known association with a person with a disability, but also entities that provide services to or are otherwise associated with such individuals. This provision was intended to ensure that entities such as health care providers, employees of social service agencies, and others who provide professional services to persons with disabilities are not subjected to discrimination because of their professional association with persons with disabilities.

Section 35.131 Illegal Use of Drugs

Section 35.131 effectuates section 510 of the ADA, which clarifies the Act's application to people who use drugs illegally. Paragraph (a) provides that this part does not prohibit discrimination based on an individual's current illegal use of drugs.

The Act and the regulation distinguish between illegal use of drugs and the legal use of substances, whether or not those substances are "controlled substances," as defined in the Controlled Substances Act (21 U.S.C. 812). Some controlled substances are prescription drugs that have legitimate medical uses. Section 35.131 does not affect use of controlled substances pursuant to a valid prescription under supervision by a licensed health care professional, or other use that is authorized by the Controlled Substances Act or any other provision of Federal law. It does apply to illegal use of those substances, as well as to illegal use of controlled substances that are not prescription drugs. The key question is whether the individual's use of the substance is illegal, not whether the substance has recognized legal uses. Alcohol is not a controlled substance, so use of alcohol is not addressed by § 35.131 (although alcoholics are individuals with disabilities, subject to the protections of the statute).

A distinction is also made between the use of a substance and the status of being addicted to that substance. Addiction is a disability, and addicts are individuals with disabilities protected by the Act. The protection, however, does not extend to actions based on the illegal use of the substance. In other words, an addict cannot use the fact of his or her addiction as a defense to an action based on illegal use of drugs. This distinction is not artificial. Congress intended to deny protection to people who engage in the illegal use of drugs, whether or not they are addicted, but to provide protection to addicts so long as they are not currently using drugs.

A third distinction is the difficult one between current use and former use. The definition of "current illegal use of drugs" in § 35.104, which is based on the report of the Conference Committee, H.R. Conf. Rep. No. 596, 101st Cong., 2d Sess. 64 (1990) (hereinafter "Conference report"), is "illegal use of drugs that occurred recently enough to justify a reasonable belief that a person's drug use is current or that continuing use is a real and ongoing problem."

Paragraph (a)(2)(i) specifies that an individual who has successfully completed a supervised drug rehabilitation program or has otherwise been rehabilitated successfully and who is not engaging in current illegal use of drugs is protected. Paragraph (a)(2)(ii) clarifies that an individual who is currently participating in a supervised rehabilitation program and is not engaging in current illegal use of drugs is protected. Paragraph (a)(2)(iii) provides that a person who is erroneously regarded as engaging in current illegal use of drugs, but who is not engaging in such use, is protected.

Paragraph (b) provides a limited exception to the exclusion of current illegal users of drugs from the protections of the Act. It prohibits denial of health services, or services provided in connection with drug rehabilitation to an individual on the basis of current illegal use of drugs, if the individual is otherwise entitled to such services. A health care facility, such as a hospital or clinic, may not refuse treatment to an individual in need of the services it provides on the grounds that the individual is illegally using drugs, but it is not required by this section to provide services that it does not ordinarily provide. For example, a health care facility that specializes in a particular type of treatment, such as care of burn victims, is not required to provide drug rehabilitation services, but it cannot refuse to treat a individual's burns on the grounds that the individual is illegally using drugs.

Some commenters pointed out that abstention from the use of drugs is an essential condition of participation in some drug rehabilitation programs, and may be a necessary requirement in inpatient or residential settings. The Department believes that this comment is well-founded. Congress clearly intended to prohibit exclusion from drug treatment programs of the very individuals who need such programs because of their use of drugs, but, once an individual has been admitted to a program, abstention may be a necessary and appropriate condition to continued participation. The final rule therefore provides that a drug rehabilitation or treatment program may prohibit illegal use of drugs by individuals while they are participating in the program.

Paragraph (c) expresses Congress' intention that the Act be neutral with respect to testing for illegal use of drugs. This paragraph implements the provision in section 510(b) of the Act that allows entities "to adopt or administer reasonable policies or procedures, including but not limited to drug testing," that ensure that an individual who is participating in a supervised rehabilitation program, or who has completed such a program or otherwise been rehabilitated successfully is no longer engaging in the illegal use of drugs. The section is not to be "construed to encourage, prohibit, restrict, or authorize the conducting of testing for the illegal use of drugs."

Paragraph 35.131(c) clarifies that it is not a violation of this part to adopt or administer reasonable policies or procedures to ensure that an individual who formerly engaged in the illegal use of drugs is not currently engaging in illegal use of drugs. Any such policies or procedures must, of course, be reasonable, and must be designed to identify accurately the illegal use of drugs.

This paragraph does not authorize inquiries, tests, or other procedures that would disclose use of substances that are not controlled substances or are taken under supervision by a licensed health care professional, or other uses authorized by the Controlled Substances Act or other provisions of Federal law, because such uses are not included in the definition of "illegal use of drugs." A commenter argued that the rule should permit testing for lawful use of prescription drugs, but most commenters preferred that tests must be limited to unlawful use in order to avoid revealing the lawful use of prescription medicine used to treat disabilities.

Section 35.132 Smoking

Section 35.132 restates the clarification in section 501(b) of the Act that the Act does not preclude the prohibition of, or imposition of restrictions on, smoking in transportation covered by title II. Some commenters argued that this section is too limited in scope, and that the regulation should prohibit smoking in all facilities used by public entities. The reference to smoking in section 501, however, merely clarifies that the Act does not require public entities to accommodate smokers by permitting them to smoke in transportation facilities.

Section 35.133 Maintenance of Accessible Features

Section 35.133 provides that a public entity shall maintain in operable working condition those features of facilities and equipment that are required to be readily accessible to and usable by persons with disabilities by the Act or this part. The Act requires that, to the maximum extent feasible, facilities must be accessible to, and usable by, individuals with disabilities. This section recognizes that it is not sufficient to provide features such as accessible routes, elevators, or ramps, if those features are not maintained in a manner that enables individuals with disabilities to use them. Inoperable elevators, locked accessible doors, or "accessible" routes that are obstructed by furniture, filing cabinets, or potted plants are neither "accessible to" nor "usable by" individuals with disabilities.

Some commenters objected that this section appeared to establish an absolute requirement and suggested that language from the preamble be included in the text of the regulation. It is, of course, impossible to guarantee that mechanical devices will never fail to operate. Paragraph (b) of the final regulation provides that this section does not prohibit isolated or temporary interruptions in service or access due to maintenance or repairs. This paragraph is intended to clarify that temporary obstructions or isolated instances of mechanical failure would not be considered violations of the Act or this part. However, allowing obstructions or "out of service" equipment to persist beyond a reasonable period of time would violate this part, as would repeated mechanical failures due to improper or inadequate maintenance. Failure of the public entity to ensure that accessible routes are properly maintained and free of obstructions, or failure to arrange prompt repair of inoperable elevators or other equipment intended to provide access would also violate this part.

Other commenters requested that this section be expanded to include specific requirements for inspection and maintenance of equipment, for training staff in the proper operation of equipment, and for maintenance of specific items. The Department believes that this section properly establishes the general requirement for maintaining access and that further details are not necessary.

Section 35.134 Retaliation or Coercion

Section 35.134 implements section 503 of the ADA, which prohibits retaliation against any individual who exercises his or her rights under the Act. This section is unchanged from the proposed rule. Paragraph (a) of § 35.134 provides that no private or public entity shall discriminate against any individual because that individual has exercised his or her right to oppose any act or practice made unlawful by this part, or because that individual made a charge, testified, assisted, or participated in any manner in an investigation, proceeding, or hearing under the Act or this part.

Paragraph (b) provides that no private or public entity shall coerce, intimidate, threaten, or interfere with any individual in the exercise of his or her rights under this part or because that individual aided or encouraged any other individual in the exercise or enjoyment of any right granted or protected by the Act or this part.

This section protects not only individuals who allege a violation of the Act or this part, but also any individuals who support or assist them. This section applies to all investigations or proceedings initiated under the Act or this part without regard to the ultimate resolution of the underlying allegations. Because this section prohibits any act of retaliation or coercion in response to an individual's effort to exercise rights established by the Act and this part (or to support the efforts of another individual), the section applies not only to public entities subject to this part, but also to persons acting in an individual capacity or to private entities.

For example, it would be a violation of the Act and this part for a private individual to harass or intimidate an individual with a disability in an effort to prevent that individual from attending a concert in a State-owned park. It would, likewise, be a violation of the Act and this part for a private entity to take adverse action against an employee who appeared as a witness on behalf of an individual who sought to enforce the Act.

Section 35.135 Personal Devices and Services

The final rule includes a new § 35.135, entitles "Personal devices and services," which states that the provision of personal devices and services is not required by title II. This new section, which serves as a limitation on all of the requirements of the regulation, replaces § 35.160(b)(2) of the proposed rule, which addressed the issue of personal devices and services explicitly only in the context of communications. The personal devices and services limitation was intended to have general application in the proposed rule in all contexts where it was relevant. The final rule, therefore, clarifies this point by including a general provision that will explicitly apply not only to auxiliary aids and services but across-the-board to include other relevant areas such as, for example, modifications in policies, practices, and procedures (§ 35.130(b)(7)). The language of § 35.135 parallels an analogous provision in the Department's title III regulations (28 CFR 36.306) but preserves the explicit reference to "readers for personal use or study" in § 35.160(b)(2) of the proposed rule. This section does not preclude the short-term loan of personal receivers that are part of an assistive listening system.

Subpart C — Employment

Section 35.140 Employment Discrimination Prohibited

Title II of the ADA applies to all activities of public entities, including their employment practices. The proposed rule cross-referenced the definitions, requirements, and procedures of title I of the ADA, as established by the Equal Employment Opportunity Commission in 29 CFR part 1630. This proposal would have resulted in use, under § 35.140, of the title I definition of "employer," so that a public entity with 25 or more employees would have become subject to the requirements of § 35.140 on July 26, 1992, one with 15 to 24 employees on July 26, 1994, and one with fewer than 15 employees would have been excluded completely.

The Department received comments objecting to this approach. The commenters asserted that Congress intended to establish nondiscrimination requirements for employment by all public entities, including those that employ fewer than 15 employees; and that Congress intended the employment requirements of title II to become effective at the same time that the other requirements of this regulation become effective, January 26, 1992. The Department has reexamined the statutory language and legislative history of the ADA on this issue and has concluded that Congress intended to cover the employment practices of all public entities and that the applicable effective date is that of title II.

The statutory language of section 204(b) of the ADA requires the Department to issue a regulation that is consistent with the ADA and the Department's coordination regulation under section 504, 28 CFR part 41. The coordination regulation specifically requires nondiscrimination in employment, 28 CFR 41.52–41.55, and does not limit coverage based on size of employer. Moreover, under all section 504 implementing regulations issued in accordance with the Department's coordination regulation, employment coverage under section 504 extends to all employers with federally assisted programs or activities, regardless of size, and the effective date for those employment requirements has always been the same as the effective date for nonemployment requirements established in the same regulations. The

Department therefore concludes that § 35.140 must apply to all public entities upon the effective date of this regulation.

In the proposed regulation the Department cross-referenced the regulations implementing title I of the ADA, issued by the Equal Employment Opportunity Commission at 29 CFR part 1630, as a compliance standard for § 35.140 because, as proposed, the scope of coverage and effective date of coverage under title II would have been coextensive with title I. In the final regulation this language is modified slightly. Subparagraph (1) of new paragraph (b) makes it clear that the standards established by the Equal Employment Opportunity Commission in 29 CFR part 1630 will be the applicable compliance standards if the public entity is subject to title I. If the public entity is not covered by title I, or until it is covered by title I, subparagraph (b)(2) cross-references section 504 standards for what constitutes employment discrimination, as established by the Department of Justice in 28 CFR part 41. Standards for title I of the ADA and section 504 of the Rehabilitation Act are for the most part identical because title I of the ADA was based on requirements set forth in regulations implementing section 504.

The Department, together with the other Federal agencies responsible for the enforcement of Federal laws prohibiting employment discrimination on the basis of disability, recognizes the potential for jurisdictional overlap that exists with respect to coverage of public entities and the need to avoid problems related to overlapping coverage. The other Federal agencies include the Equal Employment Opportunity Commission, which is the agency primarily responsible for enforcement of title I of the ADA, the Department of Labor, which is the agency responsible for enforcement of section 503 of the Rehabilitation Act of 1973, and 26 Federal agencies with programs of Federal financial assistance, which are responsible for enforcing section 504 in those programs. Section 107 of the ADA requires that coordination mechanisms be developed in connection with the administrative enforcement of complaints alleging discrimination under title I and complaints alleging discrimination in employment in violation of the Rehabilitation Act. Although the ADA does not specifically require inclusion of employment complaints under title II in the coordinating mechanisms required by title I, Federal investigations of title II employment complaints will be coordinated on a government-wide basis also. The Department is currently working with the EEOC and other affected Federal agencies to develop effective coordinating mechanisms, and final regulations on this issue will be issued on or before January 26, 1992.

Subpart D — Program Accessibility

Section 35.149 Discrimination Prohibited

Section 35.149 states the general nondiscrimination principle underlying the program accessibility requirements of §§ 35.150 and 35.151.

Section 35.150 Existing Facilities

Consistent with section 204(b) of the Act, this regulation adopts the program accessibility concept found in the section 504 regulations for federally conducted programs or activities (e.g., 28 CFR part 39). The concept of "program accessibility" was first used in the section 504 regulation adopted by the Department of Health, Education, and Welfare for its federally assisted programs and activities in 1977. It allowed recipients to make their federally assisted programs and activities available to individuals with disabilities without extensive retrofitting of their existing buildings and facilities, by offering those programs through alternative methods. Program accessibility has proven to be a useful approach and was adopted in the regulations issued for programs and activities conducted by Federal Executive agencies. The Act provides that the concept of program access will continue to apply with respect to facilities now in existence, because the cost of retrofitting existing facilities is often prohibitive.

Section 35.150 requires that each service, program, or activity conducted by a public entity, when viewed in its entirety, be readily accessible to and usable by individuals with disabilities. The regulation makes clear, however, that a public entity is not required to make each of its existing facilities accessible (§ 35.150(a)(1)). Unlike title III of the Act, which requires public accommodations to remove architectural barriers where such removal is "readily achievable," or to provide goods and services through alternative methods, where those methods are "readily achievable," title II requires a public entity to make its programs accessible in all cases, except where to do so would result in a fundamental alteration in the nature of the program or in undue financial and administrative burdens. Congress intended the "undue burden" standard in title II to be significantly higher than the "readily achievable" standard in title III. Thus, although title II may not require removal of barriers in some cases where removal would be required under title III, the program access requirement of title II should enable individuals with disabilities to participate in and benefit from the services, programs, or activities of public entities in all but the most unusual cases.

Paragraph (a)(2), which establishes a special limitation on the obligation to ensure program accessibility in historic preservation programs, is discussed below in connection with paragraph (b).

Paragraph (a)(3), which is taken from the section 504 regulations for federally conducted programs, generally codifies case law that defines the scope of the public entity's obligation to ensure program accessibility. This paragraph provides that, in meeting the program accessibility requirement, a public entity is not required to take any action that would result in a fundamental alteration in the nature of its service, program, or activity or in undue financial and administrative burdens. A similar limitation is provided in § 35.164.

This paragraph does not establish an absolute defense; it does not relieve a public entity of all obligations to individuals with disabilities. Although a public entity is not required to take actions that would result in a fundamental alteration in the nature of a service, program, or activity or in undue financial and administrative burdens, it nevertheless must take any other steps necessary to ensure that individuals with disabilities receive the benefits or services provided by the public entity.

It is the Department's view that compliance with § 35.150(a), like compliance with the corresponding provisions of the section 504 regulations for federally conducted programs, would in most cases not result in undue financial and administrative burdens on a public entity. In determining whether financial and administrative burdens are undue, all public entity resources available for use in the funding and operation of the service, program, or activity should be considered. The burden of proving that compliance with paragraph (a) of § 35.150 would fundamentally alter the nature of a service, program, or activity or would result in undue financial and administrative burdens rests with the public entity.

The decision that compliance would result in such alteration or burdens must be made by the head of the public entity or his or her designee and must be accompanied by a written statement of the reasons for reaching that conclusion. The Department recognizes the difficulty of identifying the official responsible for this determination, given the variety of organizational forms that may be taken by public entities and their components. The intention of this paragraph is that the determination must be made by a high level official, no lower than a Department head, having budgetary authority and responsibility for making spending decisions.

Any person who believes that he or she or any specific class of persons has been injured by the public entity head's decision or failure to make a decision may file a complaint under the compliance procedures established in subpart F.

Paragraph (b)(1) sets forth a number of means by which program accessibility may be achieved, including redesign of equipment, reassignment of services to accessible buildings, and provision of aides.

The Department wishes to clarify that, consistent with longstanding interpretation of section 504, carrying an individual with a disability is considered an ineffective and therefore an unacceptable method for achieving program accessibility. Department of Health, Education, and Welfare, Office of Civil Rights, Policy Interpretation No. 4, 43 FR 36035 (August 14, 1978). Carrying will be permitted only in manifestly exceptional cases, and only if all personnel who are permitted to participate in carrying an individual with a disability are formally instructed on the safest and least humiliating means of carrying. "Manifestly exceptional" cases in which carrying would be permitted might include, for example, programs conducted in unique facilities, such as an oceanographic vessel, for which structural changes and devices necessary to adapt the facility for use by individuals with mobility impairments are unavailable or prohibitively expensive. Carrying is not permitted as an alternative to structural modifications such as installation of a ramp or a chairlift.

In choosing among methods, the public entity shall give priority consideration to those that will be consistent with provision of services in the most integrated setting appropriate to the needs of individuals with disabilities. Structural changes in existing facilities are required only when there is no other feasible way to make the public entity's program accessible. (It should be noted that "structural changes" include all physical changes to a facility; the term does not refer only to changes to structural features, such as removal of or alteration to a load-bearing structural member.) The requirements of § 35.151 for alterations apply to structural changes undertaken to comply with this section. The public entity may comply with the program accessibility requirement by delivering services at alternate accessible sites or making home visits as appropriate.

Historic Preservation Programs

In order to avoid possible conflict between the congressional mandates to preserve historic properties, on the one hand, and to eliminate discrimination against individuals with disabilities on the other, paragraph (a)(2) provides that a public entity is not required to take any action that would threaten or destroy the historic significance of an historic property. The special limitation on program accessibility set forth in paragraph (a)(2) is applicable only to historic preservation programs, as defined in § 35.104, that is, programs that have preservation of historic properties as a primary purpose. Narrow application of the special limitation is justified because of the inherent flexibility of the program accessibility requirement. Where historic preservation is not a primary purpose of the program, the public entity is not required to use a particular facility. It can relocate all or part of its program to an accessible facility, make home visits, or use other standard methods of achieving program accessibility without making structural alterations that might threaten or destroy significant historic features of the historic property. Thus, government programs located in historic properties, such as an historic State capitol, are not excused from the requirement for program access.

Paragraph (a)(2), therefore, will apply only to those programs that uniquely concern the preservation and experience of the historic property itself. Because the primary benefit of an historic preservation program is the experience of the historic property, paragraph (b)(2) requires the public entity to give priority to methods of providing program accessibility that permit individuals with disabilities to have physical access to the historic property. This priority on physical access may also be viewed as a specific application of the general requirement that the public entity administer programs in the most integrated setting appropriate to the needs of qualified individuals with disabilities (§ 35.130(d)). Only when providing physical access would threaten or destroy the historic significance of an historic property, or would result in a fundamental alteration in the nature of the program or in undue financial and administrative burdens, may the public entity adopt alternative methods for providing program accessibility that do not ensure physical access. Examples of some alternative methods are provided in paragraph (b)(2).

Time Periods

Paragraphs (c) and (d) establish time periods for complying with the program accessibility requirement. Like the regulations for federally assisted programs (e.g., 28 CFR 41.57(b)), paragraph (c) requires the public entity to make any necessary structural changes in facilities as soon as practicable, but in no event later than three years after the effective date of this regulation.

The proposed rule provided that, aside from structural changes, all other necessary steps to achieve compliance with this part must be taken within sixty days. The sixty day period was taken from regulations implementing section 504, which generally were effective no more than thirty days after publication. Because this regulation will not be effective until January 26, 1992, the Department has concluded that no additional transition period for non-structural changes is necessary, so the sixty day period has been omitted in the final rule. Of course, this section does not reduce or eliminate any obligations that are already applicable to a public entity under section 504.

Where structural modifications are required, paragraph (d) requires that a transition plan be developed by an entity that employs 50 or more persons, within six months of the effective date of this regulation. The legislative history of title II of the ADA makes it clear that, under title II, "local and state governments are required to provide curb cuts on public streets." Education and Labor report at 84. As the rationale for the provision of curb cuts, the House report explains, "The employment, transportation, and public accommodation sections of * * * (the ADA) would be meaningless if people who use wheelchairs were not afforded the opportunity to travel on and between the streets." *Id.* Section 35.151(e), which establishes accessibility requirements for new construction and alterations, requires that all newly constructed or altered streets, roads, or highways must contain curb ramps or other sloped areas at any intersection having curbs or other barriers to entry from a street level pedestrian walkway, and all newly constructed or altered street level pedestrian walkways must have curb ramps or other sloped areas at intersections to streets, roads, or highways. A new paragraph (d)(2) has been added to the final rule to clarify the application of the general requirement for program accessibility to the provision of curb cuts at existing crosswalks. This paragraph requires that the transition plan include a schedule for providing curb ramps or other sloped areas at existing pedestrian walkways, giving priority to walkways serving entities covered by the Act, including State and local government offices and facilities, transportation, public accommodations, and employers, followed by walkways serving other areas. Pedestrian "walkways" include locations where access is required for use of public transportation, such as bus stops that are not located at intersections or crosswalks.

Similarly, a public entity should provide an adequate number of accessible parking spaces in existing parking lots or garages over which it has jurisdiction.

Paragraph (d)(3) provides that, if a public entity has already completed a transition plan required by a regulation implementing section 504, the transition plan required by this part will apply only to those policies and practices that were not covered by the previous transition plan. Some commenters suggested that the transition plan should include all aspects of the public entity's operations, including those that may have been covered by a previous transition plan under section 504. The Department believes that such a duplicative requirement would be inappropriate. Many public entities may find, however, that it will be simpler to include all of their operations in the transition plan than to attempt to identify and exclude specifically those that were addressed in a previous plan. Of course, entities covered under section 504 are not shielded from their obligations under that statute merely because they are included under the transition plan developed under this section.

Section 35.151 New Construction and Alterations

Section 35.151 provides that those buildings that are constructed or altered by, on behalf of, or for the use of a public entity shall be designed, constructed, or altered to be readily accessible to and usable by individuals with disabilities if the construction was commenced after the effective date of this part.

Facilities under design on that date will be governed by this section if the date that bids were invited falls after the effective date. This interpretation is consistent with Federal practice under section 504.

Section 35.151(c) establishes two standards for accessible new construction and alteration. Under paragraph (c), design, construction, or alteration of facilities in conformance with the Uniform Federal Accessibility Standards (UFAS) or with the Americans with Disabilities Act Accessibility Guidelines for Buildings and Facilities (hereinafter ADAAG) shall be deemed to comply with the requirements of this section with respect to those facilities except that, if ADAAG is chosen, the elevator exemption contained at §§ 36.401(d) and 36.404 does not apply. ADAAG is the standard for private buildings and was issued as guidelines by the Architectural and Transportation Barriers Compliance Board (ATBCB) under title III of the ADA. It has been adopted by the Department of Justice and is published as appendix A to the Department's title III rule in today's Federal Register. Departures from particular requirements of these standards by the use of other methods shall be permitted when it is clearly evident that equivalent access to the facility or part of the facility is thereby provided. Use of two standards is a departure from the proposed rule.

The proposed rule adopted UFAS as the only interim accessibility standard because that standard was referenced by the regulations implementing section 504 of the Rehabilitation Act promulgated by most Federal funding agencies. It is, therefore, familiar to many State and local government entities subject to this rule. The Department, however, received many comments objecting to the adoption of UFAS. Commenters pointed out that, except for the elevator exemption, UFAS is not as stringent as ADAAG. Others suggested that the standard should be the same to lessen confusion.

Section 204(b) of the Act states that title II regulations must be consistent not only with section 504 regulations but also with "this Act." Based on this provision, the Department has determined that a public entity should be entitled to choose to comply either with ADAAG or UFAS.

Public entities who choose to follow ADAAG, however, are not entitled to the elevator exemption contained in title III of the Act and implemented in the title III regulation at § 36.401(d) for new construction and § 36.404 for alterations. Section 303(b) of title III states that, with some exceptions, elevators are not required in facilities that are less than three stories or have less than 3000 square feet per story. The section 504 standard, UFAS, contains no such exemption. Section 501 of the ADA makes clear that nothing in the Act may be construed to apply a lesser standard to public entities than the standards applied under section 504. Because permitting the elevator exemption would clearly result in application of a lesser standard than that applied under section 504, paragraph (c) states that the elevator exemption does not apply when public entities choose to follow ADAAG. Thus, a two-story courthouse, whether built according to UFAS or ADAAG, must be constructed with an elevator. It should be noted that Congress did not include an elevator exemption for public transit facilities covered by subtitle B of title II, which covers public transportation provided by public entities, providing further evidence that Congress intended that public buildings have elevators.

Section 504 of the ADA requires the ATBCB to issue supplemental Minimum Guidelines and Requirements for Accessible Design of buildings and facilities subject to the Act, including title II. Section 204(c) of the ADA provides that the Attorney General shall promulgate regulations implementing title II that are consistent with the ATBCB's ADA guidelines. The ATBCB has announced its intention to issue title II guidelines in the future. The Department anticipates that, after the ATBCB's title II guidelines have been published, this rule will be amended to adopt new accessibility standards consistent with the ATBCB's rulemaking. Until that time, however, public entities will have a choice of following UFAS or ADAAG, without the elevator exemption.

Existing buildings leased by the public entity after the effective date of this part are not required by the regulation to meet accessibility standards simply by virtue of being leased. They are subject, however, to the program accessibility standard for existing facilities in § 35.150. To the extent the buildings are newly constructed or altered, they must also meet the new construction and alteration requirements of § 35.151.

The Department received many comments urging that the Department require that public entities lease only accessible buildings. Federal practice under section 504 has always treated newly leased buildings as subject to the existing facility program accessibility standard. Section 204(b) of the Act states that, in the area of "program accessibility, existing facilities," the title II regulations must be consistent with section 504 regulations. Thus, the Department has adopted the section 504 principles for these types of leased buildings. Unlike the construction of new buildings where architectural barriers can be avoided at little or no cost, the application of new construction standards to an existing building being leased raises the same prospect of retrofitting buildings as the use of an existing Federal facility, and the same program accessibility standard should apply to both owned and leased existing buildings. Similarly, requiring that public entities only lease accessible space would significantly restrict the options of State and local governments in seeking leased space, which would be particularly burdensome in rural or sparsely populated areas.

On the other hand, the more accessible the leased space is, the fewer structural modifications will be required in the future for particular employees whose disabilities may necessitate barrier removal as a reasonable accommodation. Pursuant to the requirements for leased buildings contained in the Minimum Guidelines and Requirements for Accessible Design published under the Architectural Barriers Act by the ATBCB, 36 CFR 1190.34, the Federal Government may not lease a building unless it contains (1) one accessible route from an accessible entrance to those areas in which the principal activities for which the building is leased are conducted, (2) accessible toilet facilities, and (3) accessible parking facilities, if a parking area is included within the lease (36 CFR 1190.34). Although these requirements are not applicable to buildings leased by public entities covered by this regulation, such entities are encouraged to look for the most accessible space available to lease and to attempt to find space complying at least with these minimum Federal requirements.

Section 35.151(d) gives effect to the intent of Congress, expressed in section 504(c) of the Act, that this part recognize the national interest in preserving significant historic structures. Commenters criticized the Department's use of descriptive terms in the proposed rule that are different from those used in the ADA to describe eligible historic properties. In addition, some commenters criticized the Department's decision to use the concept of "substantially impairing" the historic features of a property, which is a concept employed in regulations implementing section 504 of the Rehabilitation Act of 1973. Those commenters recommended that the Department adopt the criteria of "adverse effect" published by the Advisory Council on Historic Preservation under the National Historic Preservation Act, 36 CFR 800.9, as the standard for determining whether an historic property may be altered.

The Department agrees with these comments to the extent that they suggest that the language of the rule should conform to the language employed by Congress in the ADA. A definition of "historic property," drawn from section 504 of the ADA, has been added to § 35.104 to clarify that the term applies to those properties listed or eligible for listing in the National Register of Historic Places, or properties designated as historic under State or local law.

The Department intends that the exception created by this section be applied only in those very rare situations in which it is not possible to provide access to an historic property using the special access provisions established by UFAS and ADAAG. Therefore, paragraph (d)(1) of § 35.151 has been revised to clearly state that alterations to historic properties shall comply, to the maximum extent feasible, with section 4.1.7 of UFAS or section 4.1.7 of ADAAG. Paragraph (d)(2) has been revised to provide that, if it has been determined under the procedures established in UFAS and ADAAG that it is not feasible to provide physical access to an historic property in a manner that will not threaten or destroy the historic significance of the property, alternative methods of access shall be provided pursuant to the requirements of § 35.150.

In response to comments, the Department has added to the final rule a new paragraph (e) setting out the requirements of § 36.151 as applied to curb ramps. Paragraph (e) is taken from the statement contained in the preamble to the proposed rule that all newly constructed or altered streets, roads, and highways must contain curb ramps at any intersection having curbs or other barriers to entry from a street level pedestrian walkway, and that all newly constructed or altered street level pedestrian walkways must have curb ramps at intersections to streets, roads, or highways.

Subpart E — Communications

Section 35.160 General

Section 35.160 requires the public entity to take such steps as may be necessary to ensure that communications with applicants, participants, and members of the public with disabilities are as effective as communications with others.

Paragraph (b)(1) requires the public entity to furnish appropriate auxiliary aids and services when necessary to afford an individual with a disability an equal opportunity to participate in, and enjoy the benefits of, the public entity's service, program, or activity. The public entity must provide an opportunity for individuals with disabilities to request the auxiliary aids and services of their choice. This expressed choice shall be given primary consideration by the public entity (§ 35.160(b)(2)). The public entity shall honor the choice unless it can demonstrate that another effective means of communication exists or that use of the means chosen would not be required under § 35.164.

Deference to the request of the individual with a disability is desirable because of the range of disabilities, the variety of auxiliary aids and services, and different circumstances requiring effective communication. For instance, some courtrooms are now equipped for "computer-assisted transcripts," which allow virtually instantaneous transcripts of courtroom argument and testimony to appear on displays. Such a system might be an effective auxiliary aid or service for a person who is deaf or has a hearing loss who uses speech to communicate, but may be useless for someone who uses sign language.

Although in some circumstances a notepad and written materials may be sufficient to permit effective communication, in other circumstances they may not be sufficient. For example, a qualified interpreter may be necessary when the information being communicated is complex, or is exchanged for a lengthy period of time. Generally, factors to be considered in determining whether an interpreter is required include the context in which the communication is taking place, the number of people involved, and the importance of the communication.

Several commenters asked that the rule clarify that the provision of readers is sometimes necessary to ensure access to a public entity's services, programs or activities. Reading devices or readers should be provided when necessary for equal participation and opportunity to benefit from any governmental service, program, or activity, such as reviewing public documents, examining demonstrative evidence, and filling out voter registration forms or forms needed to receive public benefits. The importance of providing qualified readers for examinations administered by public entities is discussed under § 36.130. Reading devices and readers are appropriate auxiliary aids and services where necessary to permit an individual with a disability to participate in or benefit from a service, program, or activity.

Section 35.160(b)(2) of the proposed rule, which provided that a public entity need not furnish individually prescribed devices, readers for personal use or study, or other devices of a personal nature, has been deleted in favor of a new section in the final rule on personal devices and services (see § 35.135).

In response to comments, the term "auxiliary aids and services" is used in place of "auxiliary aids" in the final rule. This phrase better reflects the range of aids and services that may be required under this section.

A number of comments raised questions about the extent of a public entity's obligation to provide access to television programming for persons with hearing impairments. Television and videotape programming produced by public entities are covered by this section. Access to audio portions of such programming may be provided by closed captioning.

Section 35.161 Telecommunication Devices for the Deaf (TDD's)

Section 35.161 requires that, where a public entity communicates with applicants and beneficiaries by telephone, TDD's or equally effective telecommunication systems be used to communicate with individuals with impaired speech or hearing.

Problems arise when a public entity which does not have a TDD needs to communicate with an individual who uses a TDD or vice versa. Title IV of the ADA addresses this problem by requiring establishment of telephone relay services to permit communications between individuals who communicate by TDD and individuals who communicate by the telephone alone. The relay services required by title IV would involve a relay operator using both a standard telephone and a TDD to type the voice messages to the TDD user and read the TDD messages to the standard telephone user.

Section 204(b) of the ADA requires that the regulation implementing title II with respect to communications be consistent with the Department's regulation implementing section 504 for its federally conducted programs and activities at 28 CFR part 39. Section 35.161, which is taken from § 39.160(a)(2) of that regulation, requires the use of TDD's or equally effective telecommunication systems for communication with people who use TDD's. Of course, where relay services, such as those required by title IV of the ADA are available, a public entity may use those services to meet the requirements of this section.

Many commenters were concerned that public entities should not rely heavily on the establishment of relay services. The commenters explained that while relay services would be of vast benefit to both public entities and individuals who use TDD's, the services are not sufficient to provide access to all telephone services. First, relay systems do not provide effective access to the increasingly popular automated systems that require the caller to respond by pushing a button on a touch tone phone. Second, relay systems cannot operate fast enough to convey messages on answering machines, or to permit a TDD user to leave a recorded message. Third, communication through relay systems may not be appropriate in cases of crisis lines pertaining to rape, domestic violence, child abuse, and drugs. The Department believes that it is more appropriate for the Federal Communications Commission to address these issues in its rulemaking under title IV.

Some commenters requested that those entities with frequent contacts with clients who use TDD's have on-site TDD's to provide for direct communication between the entity and the individual. The Department encourages those entities that have extensive telephone contact with the public such as city halls, public libraries, and public aid offices, to have TDD's to insure more immediate access. Where the provision of telephone service is a major function of the entity, TDD's should be available.

Section 35.162 Telephone Emergency Services

Many public entities provide telephone emergency services by which individuals can seek immediate assistance from police, fire, ambulance, and other emergency services. These telephone emergency services — including "911" services — are clearly an important public service whose reliability can be a matter of life or death. The legislative history of title II specifically reflects congressional intent that public entities must ensure that telephone emergency services, including 911 services, be accessible to persons with impaired hearing and speech through telecommunication technology (Conference report at 67; Education and Labor report at 84–85).

Proposed § 35.162 mandated that public entities provide emergency telephone services to persons with disabilities that are "functionally equivalent" to voice services provided to others. Many commenters urged the Department to revise the section to make clear that direct access to telephone emergency services is required by title II of the ADA as indicated by the legislative history (Conference report at 67–68; Education and Labor report at 85). In response, the final rule mandates "direct access," instead of "access that is functionally equivalent" to that provided to all other telephone users. Telephone emergency access through a third party or through a relay service would not satisfy the requirement for direct access.

Several commenters asked about a separate seven-digit emergency call number for the 911 services. The requirement for direct access disallows the use of a separate seven-digit number where 911 service is available. Separate seven-digit emergency call numbers would be unfamiliar to many individuals and also more burdensome to use. A standard emergency 911 number is easier to remember and would save valuable time spent in searching in telephone books for a local seven-digit emergency number.

Many commenters requested the establishment of minimum standards of service (*e.g.,* the quantity and location of TDD's and computer modems needed in a given emergency center). Instead of establishing these scoping requirements, the Department has established a performance standard through the mandate for direct access.

Section 35.162 requires public entities to take appropriate steps, including equipping their emergency systems with modern technology, as may be necessary to promptly receive and respond to a call from users of TDD's and computer modems. Entities are allowed the flexibility to determine what is the appropriate technology for their particular needs. In order to avoid mandating use of particular technologies that may become outdated, the Department has eliminated the references to the Baudot and ASCII formats in the proposed rule.

Some commenters requested that the section require the installation of a voice amplification device on the handset of the dispatcher's telephone to amplify the dispatcher's voice. In an emergency, a person who has a hearing loss may be using a telephone that does not have an amplification device. Installation of speech amplification devices on the handsets of the dispatchers' telephones would respond to that situation. The Department encourages their use.

Several commenters emphasized the need for proper maintenance of TDD's used in telephone emergency services. Section 35.133, which mandates maintenance of accessible features, requires public entities to maintain in operable working condition TDD's and other devices that provide direct access to the emergency system.

Section 35.163 Information and Signage

Section 35.163(a) requires the public entity to provide information to individuals with disabilities concerning accessible services, activities, and facilities. Paragraph (b) requires the public entity to provide signage at all inaccessible entrances to each of its facilities that directs users to an accessible entrance or to a location with information about accessible facilities.

Several commenters requested that, where TDD-equipped pay phones or portable TDD's exist, clear signage should be posted indicating the location of the TDD. The Department believes that this is required by paragraph (a). In addition, the Department recommends that, in large buildings that house TDD's, directional signage indicating the location of available TDD's should be placed adjacent to banks of telephones that do not contain a TDD.

Section 35.164 Duties

Section 35.164, like paragraph (a)(3) of § 35.150, is taken from the section 504 regulations for federally conducted programs. Like paragraph (a)(3), it limits the obligation of the public entity to ensure effective communication in accordance with *Davis* and the circuit court opinions interpreting it. It also includes specific requirements for determining the existence of undue financial and administrative burdens. The preamble discussion of § 35.150(a) regarding that determination is applicable to this section and further explains the public entity's obligation to comply with §§ 135.160–35.164. Because of the essential nature of the services provided by telephone emergency systems, the Department assumes that § 35.164 will rarely be applied to § 35.162.

Subpart F — Compliance Procedures

Subpart F sets out the procedures for administrative enforcement of this part. Section 203 of the Act provides that the remedies, procedures, and rights set forth in section 505 of the Rehabilitation Act of 1973 (29 U.S.C. 794a) for enforcement of section 504 of the Rehabilitation Act, which prohibits discrimination on the basis of handicap in programs and activities that receive Federal financial assistance, shall be the remedies, procedures, and rights for enforcement of title II.

Section 505, in turn, incorporates by reference the remedies, procedures, and rights set forth in title VI of the Civil Rights Act of 1964 (42 U.S.C. 2000d to 2000d-4a). Title VI, which prohibits discrimination on the basis of race, color, or national origin in federally assisted programs, is enforced by the Federal agencies that provide the Federal financial assistance to the covered programs and activities in question. If voluntary compliance cannot be achieved, Federal agencies enforce title VI either by the termination of Federal funds to a program that is found to discriminate, following an administrative hearing, or by a referral to this Department for judicial enforcement.

Title II of the ADA extended the requirements of section 504 to all services, programs, and activities of State and local governments, not only those that receive Federal financial assistance. The House Committee on Education and Labor explained the enforcement provisions as follows:

It is the Committee's intent that administrative enforcement of section 202 of the legislation should closely parallel the Federal government's experience with section 504 of the Rehabilitation Act of 1973. The Attorney General should use section 504 enforcement procedures and the Department's coordination role under Executive Order 12250 as models for regulation in this area.

The Committee envisions that the Department of Justice will identify appropriate Federal agencies to oversee compliance activities for State and local governments. As with section 504, these Federal agencies, including the Department of Justice, will receive, investigate, and where possible, resolve complaints of discrimination. If a Federal agency is unable to resolve a complaint by voluntary means, * * * the major enforcement sanction for the Federal government will be referral of cases by these Federal agencies to the Department of Justice.

The Department of Justice may then proceed to file suits in Federal district court. As with section 504, there is also a private right of action for persons with disabilities, which includes the full panoply of remedies. Again, consistent with section 504, it is not the Committee's intent that persons with disabilities need to exhaust Federal administrative remedies before exercising their private right of action.

Education & Labor report at 98. See also S. Rep. No. 116, 101st Cong., 1st Sess., at 57–58 (1989).

Subpart F effectuates the congressional intent by deferring to section 504 procedures where those procedures are applicable, that is, where a Federal agency has jurisdiction under section 504 by virtue of its provision of Federal financial assistance to the program or activity in which the discrimination is alleged to have occurred. Deferral to the 504 procedures also makes the sanction of fund termination available where necessary to achieve compliance. Because the Civil Rights Restoration Act (Pub. L. 100–259) extended the application of section 504 to all of the operations of the public entity receiving the Federal financial assistance, many activities of State and local governments are already covered by section 504. The procedures in subpart F apply to complaints concerning services, programs, and activities of public entities that are covered by the ADA.

Subpart G designates the Federal agencies responsible for enforcing the ADA with respect to specific components of State and local government. It does not, however, displace existing jurisdiction under section 504 of the various funding agencies. Individuals may still file discrimination complaints against recipients of Federal financial assistance with the agencies that provide that assistance, and the funding agencies will continue to process those complaints under their existing procedures for enforcing section 504. The substantive standards adopted in this part for title II of the ADA are generally the same as those required under section 504 for federally assisted programs, and public entities covered by the ADA are also covered by the requirements of section 504 to the extent that they receive Federal financial assistance. To the extent that title II provides greater protection to the rights of individuals with disabilities, however, the funding agencies will also apply the substantive requirements established under title II and this part in processing complaints covered by both this part and section 504, except that fund termination procedures may be used only for violations of section 504.

Subpart F establishes the procedures to be followed by the agencies designated in subpart G for processing complaints against State and local government entities when the designated agency does not have jurisdiction under section 504.

Section 35.170 Complaints

Section 35.170 provides that any individual who believes that he or she or a specific class of individuals has been subjected to discrimination on the basis of disability by a public entity may, by himself or herself or by an authorized representative, file a complaint under this part within 180 days of the date of the alleged discrimination, unless the time for filing is extended by the agency for good cause. Although § 35.107 requires public entities that employ 50 or more persons to establish grievance procedures for resolution of complaints, exhaustion of those procedures is not a prerequisite to filing a complaint under this section. If a complainant chooses to follow the public entity's grievance procedures, however, any resulting delay may be considered good cause for extending the time allowed for filing a complaint under this part.

Filing the complaint with any Federal agency will satisfy the requirement for timely filing. As explained below, a complaint filed with an agency that has jurisdiction under section 504 will be processed under the agency's procedures for enforcing section 504.

Some commenters objected to the complexity of allowing complaints to be filed with different agencies. The multiplicity of enforcement jurisdiction is the result of following the statutorily mandated enforcement scheme. The Department has, however, attempted to simplify procedures for complainants by making the Federal agency that receives the complaint responsible for referring it to an appropriate agency.

The Department has also added a new paragraph (c) to this section providing that a complaint may be filed with any agency designated under subpart G of this part, or with any agency that provides funding to the public entity that is the subject of the complaint, or with the Department of Justice. Under § 35.171(a)(2), the Department of Justice will refer complaints for which it does not have jurisdiction under section 504 to an agency that does have jurisdiction under section 504, or to the agency designated under subpart G as responsible for complaints filed against the public entity that is the subject of the complaint or in the case of an employment complaint that is also subject to title I of the Act, to the Equal Employment Opportunity

Commission. Complaints filed with the Department of Justice may be sent to the Coordination and Review Section, P.O. Box 66118, Civil Rights Division, U.S. Department of Justice, Washington, DC 20035-6118.

Section 35.171 Acceptance of Complaints

Section 35.171 establishes procedures for determining jurisdiction and responsibility for processing complaints against public entities. The final rule provides complainants an opportunity to file with the Federal funding agency of their choice. If that agency does not have jurisdiction under section 504, however, and is not the agency designated under subpart G as responsible for that public entity, the agency must refer the complaint to the Department of Justice, which will be responsible for referring it either to an agency that does have jurisdiction under section 504 or to the appropriate designated agency, or in the case of an employment complaint that is also subject to title I of the Act, to the Equal Employment Opportunity Commission.

Whenever an agency receives a complaint over which it has jurisdiction under section 504, it will process the complaint under its section 504 procedures. When the agency designated under subpart G receives a complaint for which it does not have jurisdiction under section 504, it will treat the complaint as an ADA complaint under the procedures established in this subpart.

Section 35.171 also describes agency responsibilities for the processing of employment complaints. As described in connection with § 35.140, additional procedures regarding the coordination of employment complaints will be established in a coordination regulation issued by DOJ and EEOC. Agencies with jurisdiction under section 504 for complaints alleging employment discrimination also covered by title I will follow the procedures established by the coordination regulation for those complaints.

Complaints covered by title I but not section 504 will be referred to the EEOC, and complaints covered by this part but not title I will be processed under the procedures in this part.

Section 35.172 Resolution of Complaints

Section 35.172 requires the designated agency to either resolve the complaint or issue to the complainant and the public entity a Letter of Findings containing findings of fact and conclusions of law and a description of a remedy for each violation found.

The Act requires the Department of Justice to establish administrative procedures for resolution of complaints, but does not require complainants to exhaust these administrative remedies. The Committee Reports make clear that Congress intended to provide a private right of action with the full panoply of remedies for individual victims of discrimination. Because the Act does not require exhaustion of administrative remedies, the complainant may elect to proceed with a private suit at any time.

Section 35.173 Voluntary Compliance Agreements

Section 35.173 requires the agency to attempt to resolve all complaints in which it finds noncompliance through voluntary compliance agreements enforceable by the Attorney General.

Section 35.174 Referral

Section 35.174 provides for referral of the matter to the Department of Justice if the agency is unable to obtain voluntary compliance.

Section 35.175 Attorney's Fees

Section 35.175 states that courts are authorized to award attorneys fees, including litigation expenses and costs, as provided in section 505 of the Act. Litigation expenses include items such as expert witness fees, travel expenses, etc. The Judiciary Committee Report specifies that such items are included under the rubric of "attorneys fees" and not "costs" so that such expenses will be assessed against a plaintiff only under the standard set forth in *Christiansburg Garment Co. v. Equal Employment Opportunity Commission,* 434 U.S. 412 (1978). (Judiciary report at 73.)

Section 35.176 Alternative Means of Dispute Resolution

Section 35.176 restates section 513 of the Act, which encourages use of alternative means of dispute resolution.

Section 35.177 Effect of Unavailability of Technical Assistance

Section 35.177 explains that, as provided in section 506(e) of the Act, a public entity is not excused from compliance with the requirements of this part because of any failure to receive technical assistance.

Section 35.178 State Immunity

Section 35.178 restates the provision of section 502 of the Act that a State is not immune under the eleventh amendment to the Constitution of the United States from an action in Federal or State court for violations of the Act, and that the same remedies are available for any such violations as are available in an action against an entity other than a State.

Subpart G — Designated Agencies

Section 35.190 Designated Agencies

Subpart G designates the Federal agencies responsible for investigating complaints under this part. At least 26 agencies currently administer programs of Federal financial assistance that are subject to the nondiscrimination requirements of section 504 as well as other civil rights statutes. A majority of these agencies administer modest programs of Federal financial assistance and/or devote minimal resources exclusively to "external" civil rights enforcement activities. Under Executive Order 12250, the Department of Justice has encouraged the use of delegation agreements under which certain civil rights compliance responsibilities for a class of recipients funded by more than one agency are delegated by an agency or agencies to a "lead" agency. For example, many agencies that fund institutions of higher education have signed agreements that designate the Department of Education as the "lead" agency for this class of recipients.

The use of delegation agreements reduces overlap and duplication of effort, and thereby strengthens overall civil rights enforcement. However, the use of these agreements to date generally has been limited to education and health care recipients. These classes of recipients are funded by numerous agencies and the logical connection to a lead agency is clear (*e.g.,* the Department of Education for colleges and universities, and the Department of Health and Human Services for hospitals).

The ADA's expanded coverage of State and local government operations further complicates the process of establishing Federal agency jurisdiction for the purpose of investigating complaints of discrimination on the basis of disability. Because all operations of public entities now are covered irrespective of the presence or absence of Federal financial assistance, many additional State and local government functions and organizations now are subject to Federal jurisdiction. In some cases, there is no historical or single clear-cut subject matter relationship with a Federal agency as was the case in the education example described above. Further, the 33,000 governmental jurisdictions subject to the ADA differ greatly in their organization, making a detailed and workable division of Federal agency jurisdiction by individual State, county, or municipal entity unrealistic.

This regulation applies the delegation concept to the investigation of complaints of discrimination on the basis of disability by public entities under the ADA. It designates eight agencies, rather than all agencies currently administering programs of Federal financial assistance, as responsible for investigating complaints under this part. These "designated agencies" generally have the largest civil rights compliance staffs, the most experience in complaint investigations and disability issues, and broad yet clear subject area responsibilities. This division of responsibilities is made functionally rather than by public entity type or name designation. For example, all entities (regardless of their title) that exercise responsibilities, regulate, or administer services or programs relating to lands and natural resources fall within the jurisdiction of the Department of Interior.

Complaints under this part will be investigated by the designated agency most closely related to the functions exercised by the governmental component against which the complaint is lodged. For example, a complaint against a State medical board, where such a board is a recognizable entity, will be investigated by the Department of Health and Human Services (the designated agency for regulatory activities relating to the provision of health care), even if the board is part of a general umbrella department of planning and regulation (for which the Department of Justice is the designated agency). If two or more agencies have apparent responsibility over a complaint, § 35.190(c) provides that the Assistant Attorney General shall determine which one of the agencies shall be the designated agency for purposes of that complaint.

Thirteen commenters, including four proposed designated agencies, addressed the Department of Justice's identification in the proposed regulation of nine "designated agencies" to investigate complaints under this part. Most comments addressed the proposed specific delegations to the various individual agencies. The Department of Justice agrees with several commenters who pointed out that responsibility for "historic and cultural preservation" functions appropriately belongs with the Department of Interior rather than the Department of Education. The Department of Justice also agrees with the Department of Education that "museums" more appropriately should be delegated to the Department of Interior, and that "preschool and daycare programs" more appropriately should be assigned to the Department of Health and Human Services, rather than to the Department of Education. The final rule reflects these decisions.

The Department of Commerce opposed its listing as the designated agency for "commerce and industry, including general economic development, banking and finance, consumer protection, insurance, and small business." The Department of Commerce cited its lack of a substantial existing section 504 enforcement program and experience with many of the specific functions to be delegated. The Department of Justice accedes to the Department of Commerce's position, and has assigned itself as the designated agency for these functions.

In response to a comment from the Department of Health and Human Services, the regulation's category of "medical and nursing schools" has been clarified to read "schools of medicine, dentistry, nursing, and other health-related fields". Also in response to a comment from the Department of Health and Human Services, "correctional institutions" have been specifically added to the public safety and administration of justice functions assigned to the Department of Justice.

The regulation also assigns the Department of Justice as the designated agency responsible for all State and local government functions not assigned to other designated agencies. The Department of Justice, under an agreement with the Department of the Treasury, continues to receive and coordinate the investigation of complaints filed under the Revenue Sharing Act. This entitlement program, which was terminated in 1986, provided civil rights compliance jurisdiction for a wide variety of complaints regarding the use of Federal funds to support various general activities of local governments. In the absence of any similar program of Federal financial assistance administered by another Federal agency, placement of designated agency responsibilities for miscellaneous and otherwise undesignated functions with the Department of Justice is an appropriate continuation of current practice.

The Department of Education objected to the proposed rule's inclusion of the functional area of "arts and humanities" within its responsibilities, and the Department of Housing and Urban Development objected to its proposed designation as responsible for activities relating to rent control, the real estate industry, and housing code enforcement. The Department has deleted these areas from the lists assigned to the Departments of Education and Housing and Urban Development, respectively, and has added a new paragraph (c) to § 35.190, which provides that the Department of Justice may assign responsibility for components of State or local governments that exercise responsibilities, regulate, or administer services, programs, or activities relating to functions not assigned to specific designated agencies by paragraph (b) of this section to other appropriate agencies. The Department believes that this approach will provide more flexibility in determining the appropriate agency for investigation of complaints involving those components of State and local governments not specifically addressed by the listings in paragraph (b). As provided in §§ 35.170 and 35.171, complaints filed with the Department of Justice will be referred to the appropriate agency.

Several commenters proposed a stronger role for the Department of Justice, especially with respect to the receipt and assignment of complaints, and the overall monitoring of the effectiveness of the enforcement activities of Federal agencies. As discussed above, §§ 35.170 and 35.171 have been revised to provide for referral of complaints by the Department of Justice to appropriate enforcement agencies. Also, language has been added to § 35.190(a) of the final regulation stating that the Assistant Attorney General shall provide policy guidance and interpretations to designated agencies to ensure the consistent and effective implementation of this part.

DEPARTMENT OF JUSTICE REGULATIONS FOR TITLE III OF ADA

28 CFR Ch. I (7-1-95 Edition)

PART 36 — NONDISCRIMINATION ON THE BASIS OF DISABILITY BY PUBLIC ACCOMMODATIONS AND IN COMMERCIAL FACILITIES

Subpart A — General

Subpart B — General Requirements

36.606 Procedure following preliminary denial of certification.
36.607 Effect of certification.
36.608 Guidance concerning model codes.

APPENDIX A TO PART 36 — STANDARDS FOR ACCESSIBLE DESIGN

APPENDIX B TO PART 36 — PREAMBLE TO REGULATION ON NONDISCRIMINATION ON THE BASIS OF DISABILITY BY PUBLIC ACCOMMODATIONS AND IN COMMERCIAL FACILITIES (PUBLISHED JULY 26, 1991)

AUTHORITY: 5 U.S.C. 301; 28 U.S.C. 509, 510; 42 U.S.C. 12186(b).

SOURCE: Order No. 1513–91, 56 FR 35592, July 26, 1991, unless otherwise noted.

Subpart A — General

§ 36.101 Purpose.

The purpose of this part is to implement title III of the Americans with Disabilities Act of 1990 (42 U.S.C. 12181), which prohibits discrimination on the basis of disability by public accommodations and requires places of public accommodation and commercial facilities to be designed, constructed, and altered in compliance with the accessibility standards established by this part.

§ 36.102 Application.

(a) *General.* This part applies to any —
(1) Public accommodation;
(2) Commercial facility; or
(3) Private entity that offers examinations or courses related to applications, licensing, certification, or credentialing for secondary or post-secondary education, professional, or trade purposes.
(b) *Public accommodations.* (1) The requirements of this part applicable to public accommodations are set forth in subparts B, C, and D of this part.
(2) The requirements of subparts B and C of this part obligate a public accommodation only with respect to the operations of a place of public accommodation.
(3) The requirements of subpart D of this part obligate a public accommodation only with respect to —
(i) A facility used as, or designed or constructed for use as, a place of public accommodation; or

(ii) A facility used as, or designed and constructed for use as, a commercial facility.

(c) *Commercial facilities.* The requirements of this part applicable to commercial facilities are set forth in subpart D of this part.

(d) *Examinations and courses.* The requirements of this part applicable to private entities that offer examinations or courses as specified in paragraph (a) of this section are set forth in § 36.309.

(e) *Exemptions and exclusions.* This part does not apply to any private club (except to the extent that the facilities of the private club are made available to customers or patrons of a place of public accommodation), or to any religious entity or public entity.

§ 36.103 Relationship to other laws.

(a) *Rule of interpretation.* Except as otherwise provided in this part, this part shall not be construed to apply a lesser standard than the standards applied under title V of the Rehabilitation Act of 1973 (29 U.S.C. 791) or the regulations issued by Federal agencies pursuant to that title.

(b) *Section 504.* This part does not affect the obligations of a recipient of Federal financial assistance to comply with the requirements of section 504 of the Rehabilitation Act of 1973 (29 U.S.C. 794) and regulations issued by Federal agencies implementing section 504.

(c) *Other laws.* This part does not invalidate or limit the remedies, rights, and procedures of any other Federal laws, or State or local laws (including State common law) that provide greater or equal protection for the rights of individuals with disabilities or individuals associated with them.

§ 36.104 Definitions.

For purposes of this part, the term —

Act means the Americans with Disabilities Act of 1990 (Pub. L. 101–336, 104 Stat. 327, 42 U.S.C. 12101–12213 and 47 U.S.C. 225 and 611).

Commerce means travel, trade, traffic, commerce, transportation, or communication —

(1) Among the several States;

(2) Between any foreign country or any territory or possession and any State; or

(3) Between points in the same State but through another State or foreign country.

Commercial facilities means facilities —

(1) Whose operations will affect commerce;

(2) That are intended for nonresidential use by a private entity; and

(3) That are not —

(i) Facilities that are covered or expressly exempted from coverage under the Fair Housing Act of 1968, as amended (42 U.S.C. 3601–3631);

(ii) Aircraft; or

(iii) Railroad locomotives, railroad freight cars, railroad cabooses, commuter or intercity passenger rail cars (including coaches, dining cars, sleeping cars, lounge cars, and food service cars), any other railroad cars described in section 242 of the Act or covered under title II of the Act, or railroad rights-of-way. For purposes of this definition, "rail" and "railroad" have the meaning given the term "railroad" in section 202(e) of the Federal Railroad Safety Act of 1970 (45 U.S.C. 431(e)).

Current illegal use of drugs means illegal use of drugs that occurred recently enough to justify a reasonable belief that a person's drug use is current or that continuing use is a real and ongoing problem.

Disability means, with respect to an individual, a physical or mental impairment that substantially limits one or more of the major life activities of such individual; a record of such an impairment; or being regarded as having such an impairment.

(1) The phrase *physical or mental impairment* means —

(i) Any physiological disorder or condition, cosmetic disfigurement, or anatomical loss affecting one or more of the following body systems: neurological; musculoskeletal; special sense organs; respiratory, including speech organs; cardiovascular; reproductive; digestive; genitourinary; hemic and lymphatic; skin; and endocrine;

(ii) Any mental or psychological disorder such as mental retardation, organic brain syndrome, emotional or mental illness, and specific learning disabilities;

(iii) The phrase physical or mental impairment includes, but is not limited to, such contagious and noncontagious diseases and conditions as orthopedic, visual, speech, and hearing impairments, cerebral palsy, epilepsy, muscular dystrophy, multiple sclerosis, cancer, heart disease, diabetes, mental retardation, emotional illness, specific learning disabilities, HIV disease (whether symptomatic or asymptomatic), tuberculosis, drug addiction, and alcoholism;

(iv) The phrase *physical or mental impairment* does not include homosexuality or bisexuality.

(2) The phrase *major life activities* means functions such as caring for one's self, performing manual tasks, walking, seeing, hearing, speaking, breathing, learning, and working.

(3) The phrase *has a record of such an impairment* means has a history of, or has been misclassified as having, a mental or physical impairment that substantially limits one or more major life activities.

(4) The phrase *is regarded as having an impairment* means —

(i) Has a physical or mental impairment that does not substantially limit major life activities but that is treated by a private entity as constituting such a limitation;

(ii) Has a physical or mental impairment that substantially limits major life activities only as a result of the attitudes of others toward such impairment; or

(iii) Has none of the impairments defined in paragraph (1) of this definition but is treated by a private entity as having such an impairment.

(5) The term *disability* does not include —

(i) Transvestism, transsexualism, pedophilia, exhibitionism, voyeurism, gender identity disorders not resulting from physical impairments, or other sexual behavior disorders;

(ii) Compulsive gambling, kleptomania, or pyromania; or

(iii) Psychoactive substance use disorders resulting from current illegal use of drugs.

Drug means a controlled substance, as defined in schedules I through V of section 202 of the Controlled Substances Act (21 U.S.C. 812).

Facility means all or any portion of buildings, structures, sites, complexes, equipment, rolling stock or other conveyances, roads, walks, passageways, parking lots, or other real or personal property, including the site where the building, property, structure, or equipment is located.

Illegal use of drugs means the use of one or more drugs, the possession or distribution of which is unlawful under the Controlled Substances Act (21 U.S.C. 812). The term "illegal use of drugs" does not include the use of a drug taken under supervision by a licensed health care professional, or other uses authorized by the Controlled Substances Act or other provisions of Federal law.

Individual with a disability means a person who has a disability. The term "individual with a disability" does not include an individual who is currently engaging in the illegal use of drugs, when the private entity acts on the basis of such use.

Place of public accommodation means a facility, operated by a private entity, whose operations affect commerce and fall within at least one of the following categories —

(1) An inn, hotel, motel, or other place of lodging, except for an establishment located within a building that contains not more than five rooms for rent or hire and that is actually occupied by the proprietor of the establishment as the residence of the proprietor;

(2) A restaurant, bar, or other establishment serving food or drink;

(3) A motion picture house, theater, concert hall, stadium, or other place of exhibition or entertainment;

(4) An auditorium, convention center, lecture hall, or other place of public gathering;

(5) A bakery, grocery store, clothing store, hardware store, shopping center, or other sales or rental establishment;

(6) A laundromat, dry-cleaner, bank, barber shop, beauty shop, travel service, shoe repair service, funeral parlor, gas station, office of an account-

ant or lawyer, pharmacy, insurance office, professional office of a health care provider, hospital, or other service establishment;

(7) A terminal, depot, or other station used for specified public transportation;

(8) A museum, library, gallery, or other place of public display or collection;

(9) A park, zoo, amusement park, or other place of recreation;

(10) A nursery, elementary, secondary, undergraduate, or postgraduate private school, or other place of education;

(11) A day care center, senior citizen center, homeless shelter, food bank, adoption agency, or other social service center establishment; and

(12) A gymnasium, health spa, bowling alley, golf course, or other place of exercise or recreation.

Private club means a private club or establishment exempted from coverage under title II of the Civil Rights Act of 1964 (42 U.S.C. 2000a(e)).

Private entity means a person or entity other than a public entity.

Public accommodation means a private entity that owns, leases (or leases to), or operates a place of public accommodation.

Public entity means —

(1) Any State or local government;

(2) Any department, agency, special purpose district, or other instrumentality of a State or States or local government; and

(3) The National Railroad Passenger Corporation, and any commuter authority (as defined in section 103(8) of the Rail Passenger Service Act). (45 U.S.C. 541)

Qualified interpreter means an interpreter who is able to interpret effectively, accurately and impartially both receptively and expressively, using any necessary specialized vocabulary.

Readily achievable means easily accomplishable and able to be carried out without much difficulty or expense. In determining whether an action is readily achievable factors to be considered include —

(1) The nature and cost of the action needed under this part;

(2) The overall financial resources of the site or sites involved in the action; the number of persons employed at the site; the effect on expenses and resources; legitimate safety requirements that are necessary for safe operation, including crime prevention measures; or the impact otherwise of the action upon the operation of the site;

(3) The geographic separateness, and the administrative or fiscal relationship of the site or sites in question to any parent corporation or entity;

(4) If applicable, the overall financial resources of any parent corporation or entity; the overall size of the parent corporation or entity with respect to the number of its employees; the number, type, and location of its facilities; and

(5) If applicable, the type of operation or operations of any parent corporation or entity, including the composition, structure, and functions of the workforce of the parent corporation or entity.

Religious entity means a religious organization, including a place of worship.

Service animal means any guide dog, signal dog, or other animal individually trained to do work or perform tasks for the benefit of an individual with a disability, including, but not limited to, guiding individuals with impaired vision, alerting individuals with impaired hearing to intruders or sounds, providing minimal protection or rescue work, pulling a wheelchair, or fetching dropped items.

Specified public transportation means transportation by bus, rail, or any other conveyance (other than by aircraft) that provides the general public with general or special service (including charter service) on a regular and continuing basis.

State means each of the several States, the District of Columbia, the Commonwealth of Puerto Rico, Guam, American Samoa, the Virgin Islands, the Trust Territory of the Pacific Islands, and the Commonwealth of the Northern Mariana Islands.

Undue burden means significant difficulty or expense. In determining whether an action would result in an undue burden, factors to be considered include —

(1) The nature and cost of the action needed under this part;

(2) The overall financial resources of the site or sites involved in the action; the number of persons employed at the site; the effect on expenses and resources; legitimate safety requirements that are necessary for safe operation, including crime prevention measures; or the impact otherwise of the action upon the operation of the site;

(3) The geographic separateness, and the administrative or fiscal relationship of the site or sites in question to any parent corporation or entity;

(4) If applicable, the overall financial resources of any parent corporation or entity; the overall size of the parent corporation or entity with respect to the number of its employees; the number, type, and location of its facilities; and

(5) If applicable, the type of operation or operations of any parent corporation or entity, including the composition, structure, and functions of the workforce of the parent corporation or entity.

§§ 36.105 — 36.199 [Reserved]

Subpart B — General Requirements

§ 36.201 General.

(a) *Prohibition of discrimination.* No individual shall be discriminated against on the basis of disability in the full and equal enjoyment of the goods, services, facilities, privileges, advantages, or accommodations of any place of public accommodation by any private entity who owns, leases (or leases to), or operates a place of public accommodation.

(b) *Landlord and tenant responsibilities.* Both the landlord who owns the building that houses a place of public accommodation and the tenant who owns or operates the place of public accommodation are public accommodations subject to the requirements of this part. As between the parties, allocation of responsibility for complying with the obligations of this part may be determined by lease or other contract.

§ 36.202 Activities.

(a) *Denial of participation.* A public accommodation shall not subject an individual or class of individuals on the basis of a disability or disabilities of such individual or class, directly, or through contractual, licensing, or other arrangements, to a denial of the opportunity of the individual or class to participate in or benefit from the goods, services, facilities, privileges, advantages, or accommodations of a place of public accommodation.

(b) *Participation in unequal benefit.* A public accommodation shall not afford an individual or class of individuals, on the basis of a disability or disabilities of such individual or class, directly, or through contractual, licensing, or other arrangements, with the opportunity to participate in or benefit from a good, service, facility, privilege, advantage, or accommodation that is not equal to that afforded to other individuals.

(c) *Separate benefit.* A public accommodation shall not provide an individual or class of individuals, on the basis of a disability or disabilities of such individual or class, directly, or through contractual, licensing, or other arrangements with a good, service, facility, privilege, advantage, or accommodation that is different or separate from that provided to other individuals, unless such action is necessary to provide the individual or class of individuals with a good, service, facility, privilege, advantage, or accommodation, or other opportunity that is as effective as that provided to others.

(d) *Individual or class of individuals.* For purposes of paragraphs (a) through (c) of this section, the term "individual or class of individuals" refers to the clients or customers of the public accommodation that enters into the contractual, licensing, or other arrangement.

§ 36.203 Integrated settings.

(a) *General.* A public accommodation shall afford goods, services, facilities, privileges, advantages, and accommodations to an individual with a disability in the most integrated setting appropriate to the needs of the individual.

(b) *Opportunity to participate.* Notwithstanding the existence of separate or different programs or activities provided in accordance with this subpart, a public accommodation shall not deny an individual with a disability an opportunity to participate in such programs or activities that are not separate or different.

(c) *Accommodations and services.* (1) Nothing in this part shall be construed to require an individual with a disability to accept an accommodation, aid, service, opportunity, or benefit available under this part that such individual chooses not to accept.

(2) Nothing in the Act or this part authorizes the representative or guardian of an individual with a disability to decline food, water, medical treatment, or medical services for that individual.

§ 36.204 Administrative methods.

A public accommodation shall not, directly or through contractual or other arrangements, utilize standards or criteria or methods of administration that have the effect of discriminating on the basis of disability, or that perpetuate the discrimination of others who are subject to common administrative control.

§ 36.205 Association.

A public accommodation shall not exclude or otherwise deny equal goods, services, facilities, privileges, advantages, accommodations, or other opportunities to an individual or entity because of the known disability of an individual with whom the individual or entity is known to have a relationship or association.

§ 36.206 Retaliation or coercion.

(a) No private or public entity shall discriminate against any individual because that individual has opposed any act or practice made unlawful by this part, or because that individual made a charge, testified, assisted, or participated in any manner in an investigation, proceeding, or hearing under the Act or this part.

(b) No private or public entity shall coerce, intimidate, threaten, or interfere with any individual in the exercise or enjoyment of, or on account of his or her having exercised or enjoyed, or on account of his or her having aided or encouraged any other individual in the exercise or enjoyment of, any right granted or protected by the Act or this part.

(c) Illustrations of conduct prohibited by this section include, but are not limited to:

(1) Coercing an individual to deny or limit the benefits, services, or advantages to which he or she is entitled under the Act or this part;

(2) Threatening, intimidating, or interfering with an individual with a disability who is seeking to obtain or use the goods, services, facilities, privileges, advantages, or accommodations of a public accommodation;

(3) Intimidating or threatening any person because that person is assisting or encouraging an individual or group entitled to claim the rights granted or protected by the Act or this part to exercise those rights; or

(4) Retaliating against any person because that person has participated in any investigation or action to enforce the Act or this part.

§ 36.207 Places of public accommodation located in private residences.

(a) When a place of public accommodation is located in a private residence, the portion of the residence used exclusively as a residence is not covered by this part, but that portion used exclusively in the operation of the place of public accommodation or that portion used both for the place of public accommodation and for residential purposes is covered by this part.

(b) The portion of the residence covered under paragraph (a) of this section extends to those elements used to enter the place of public accommodation, including the homeowner's front sidewalk, if any, the door or entryway, and hallways; and those portions of the residence, interior or exterior, available to or used by customers or clients, including restrooms.

§ 36.208 Direct threat.

(a) This part does not require a public accommodation to permit an individual to participate in or benefit from the goods, services, facilities, privileges, advantages and accommodations of that public accommodation when that individual poses a direct threat to the health or safety of others.

(b) *Direct threat* means a significant risk to the health or safety of others that cannot be eliminated by a modification of policies, practices, or procedures, or by the provision of auxiliary aids or services.

(c) In determining whether an individual poses a direct threat to the health or safety of others, a public accommodation must make an individualized assessment, based on reasonable judgment that relies on current medical knowledge or on the best available objective evidence, to ascertain: the nature, duration, and severity of the risk; the probability that the potential injury will actually occur; and whether reasonable modifications of policies, practices, or procedures will mitigate the risk.

§ 36.209 Illegal use of drugs.

(a) *General.* (1) Except as provided in paragraph (b) of this section, this part does not prohibit discrimination against an individual based on that individual's current illegal use of drugs.

(2) A public accommodation shall not discriminate on the basis of illegal use of drugs against an individual who is not engaging in current illegal use of drugs and who —

(i) Has successfully completed a supervised drug rehabilitation program or has otherwise been rehabilitated successfully;

(ii) Is participating in a supervised rehabilitation program; or

(iii) Is erroneously regarded as engaging in such use.

(b) *Health and drug rehabilitation services.* (1) A public accommodation shall not deny health services, or services provided in connection with drug rehabilitation, to an individual on the basis of that individual's current illegal use of drugs, if the individual is otherwise entitled to such services.

(2) A drug rehabilitation or treatment program may deny participation to individuals who engage in illegal use of drugs while they are in the program.

(c) *Drug testing.* (1) This part does not prohibit a public accommodation from adopting or administering reasonable policies or procedures, including but not limited to drug testing, designed to ensure that an individual who formerly engaged in the illegal use of drugs is not now engaging in current illegal use of drugs.

(2) Nothing in this paragraph (c) shall be construed to encourage, prohibit, restrict, or authorize the conducting of testing for the illegal use of drugs.

§ 36.210 Smoking.

This part does not preclude the prohibition of, or the imposition of restrictions on, smoking in places of public accommodation.

§ 36.211 Maintenance of accessible features.

(a) A public accommodation shall maintain in operable working condition those features of facilities and equipment that are required to be readily accessible to and usable by persons with disabilities by the Act or this part.

(b) This section does not prohibit isolated or temporary interruptions in service or access due to maintenance or repairs.

§ 36.212 Insurance.

(a) This part shall not be construed to prohibit or restrict —

(1) An insurer, hospital or medical service company, health maintenance organization, or any agent, or entity that administers benefit plans, or similar organizations from underwriting risks, classifying risks, or administering such risks that are based on or not inconsistent with State law; or

(2) A person or organization covered by this part from establishing, sponsoring, observing or administering the terms of a bona fide benefit plan that are based on underwriting risks, classifying risks, or administering such risks that are based on or not inconsistent with State law; or

(3) A person or organization covered by this part from establishing, sponsoring, observing or administering the terms of a bona fide benefit plan that is not subject to State laws that regulate insurance.

(b) Paragraphs (a) (1), (2), and (3) of this section shall not be used as a subterfuge to evade the purposes of the Act or this part.

(c) A public accommodation shall not refuse to serve an individual with a disability because its insurance company conditions coverage or rates on the absence of individuals with disabilities.

§ 36.213 Relationship of subpart B to subparts C and D of this part.

Subpart B of this part sets forth the general principles of nondiscrimination applicable to all entities subject to this part. Subparts C and D of this part provide guidance on the application of the statute to specific situations. The specific provisions, including the limitations on those provisions, control over the general provisions in circumstances where both specific and general provisions apply.

§§ 36.214–36.299 [Reserved]

Subpart C — Specific Requirements

§ 36.301 Eligibility criteria.

(a) *General.* A public accommodation shall not impose or apply eligibility criteria that screen out or tend to screen out an individual with a disability or any class of individuals with disabilities from fully and equally enjoying any goods, services, facilities, privileges, advantages, or accommodations, unless such criteria can be shown to be necessary for the provision of the goods, services, facilities, privileges, advantages, or accommodations being offered.

(b) *Safety.* A public accommodation may impose legitimate safety requirements that are necessary for safe operation. Safety requirements must be based on actual risks and not on mere speculation, stereotypes, or generalizations about individuals with disabilities.

(c) *Charges.* A public accommodation may not impose a surcharge on a particular individual with a disability or any group of individuals with disabilities to cover the costs of measures, such as the provision of auxiliary aids, barrier removal, alternatives to barrier removal, and reasonable modifications in policies, practices, or procedures, that are required to provide that individual or group with the nondiscriminatory treatment required by the Act or this part.

§ 36.302 Modifications in policies, practices, or procedures.

(a) *General.* A public accommodation shall make reasonable modifications in policies, practices, or procedures, when the modifications are necessary to afford goods, services, facilities, privileges, advantages, or accommodations to individuals with disabilities, unless the public accommodation can demonstrate that making the modifications would fundamentally alter the nature of the goods, services, facilities, privileges, advantages, or accommodations.

(b) *Specialties* — (1) *General.* A public accommodation may refer an individual with a disability to another public accommodation, if that individual is seeking, or requires, treatment or services outside of the referring public accommodation's area of specialization, and if, in the normal course of its operations, the referring public accommodation would make a similar referral for an individual without a disability who seeks or requires the same treatment or services.

(2) *Illustration — medical specialties.* A health care provider may refer an individual with a disability to another provider, if that individual is seeking, or requires, treatment or services outside of the referring provider's area of specialization, and if the referring provider would make a similar referral for an individual without a disability who seeks or requires the same treatment or services. A physician who specializes in treating only a particular condition cannot refuse to treat an individual with a disability for that condition, but is not required to treat the individual for a different condition.

(c) *Service animals* — (1) *General.* Generally, a public accommodation shall modify policies, practices, or procedures to permit the use of a service animal by an individual with a disability.

(2) *Care or supervision of service animals.* Nothing in this part requires a public accommodation to supervise or care for a service animal.

(d) *Check-out aisles.* A store with check-out aisles shall ensure that an adequate number of accessible check-out aisles are kept open during store hours, or shall otherwise modify its policies and practices, in order to ensure that an equivalent level of convenient service is provided to individuals with disabilities as is provided to others. If only one check-out aisle is accessible, and it is generally used for express service, one way of providing equivalent service is to allow persons with mobility impairments to make all their purchases at that aisle.

§ 36.303 Auxiliary aids and services.

(a) *General.* A public accommodation shall take those steps that may be necessary to ensure that no individual with a disability is excluded, denied services, segregated or otherwise treated differently than other individuals because of the absence of auxiliary aids and services, unless the public accommodation can demonstrate that taking those steps would fundamentally alter the nature of the goods, services, facilities, privileges, advantages, or accommodations being offered or would result in an undue burden, i.e., significant difficulty or expense.

(b) *Examples.* The term "auxiliary aids and services" includes —

(1) Qualified interpreters, notetakers, computer-aided transcription services, written materials, telephone handset amplifiers, assistive listening devices, assistive listening systems, telephones compatible with hearing aids, closed caption decoders, open and closed captioning, telecommunications devices for deaf persons (TDD's), videotext displays, or other effective methods of making aurally delivered materials available to individuals with hearing impairments;

(2) Qualified readers, taped texts, audio recordings, Brailled materials, large print materials, or other effective methods of making visually delivered materials available to individuals with visual impairments;

(3) Acquisition or modification of equipment or devices; and

(4) Other similar services and actions.

(c) *Effective communication.* A public accommodation shall furnish appropriate auxiliary aids and services where necessary to ensure effective communication with individuals with disabilities.

(d) *Telecommunication devices for the deaf (TDD's).* (1) A public accommodation that offers a customer, client, patient, or participant the opportunity to make outgoing telephone calls on more than an incidental convenience basis shall make available, upon request, a TDD for the use of an individual who has impaired hearing or a communication disorder.

(2) This part does not require a public accommodation to use a TDD for receiving or making telephone calls incident to its operations.

(e) *Closed caption decoders.* Places of lodging that provide televisions in five or more guest rooms and hospitals that provide televisions for patient use shall provide, upon request, a means for decoding captions for use by an individual with impaired hearing.

(f) *Alternatives.* If provision of a particular auxiliary aid or service by a public accommodation would result in a fundamental alteration in the nature of the goods, services, facilities, privileges, advantages, or accommodations being offered or in an undue burden, i.e., significant difficulty or expense, the public accommodation shall provide an alternative auxiliary aid or service, if one exists, that would not result in an alteration or such burden but would nevertheless ensure that, to the maximum extent possible, individuals with disabilities receive the goods, services, facilities, privileges, advantages, or accommodations offered by the public accommodation.

§ 36.304 Removal of barriers.

(a) *General.* A public accommodation shall remove architectural barriers in existing facilities, including communication barriers that are structural in nature, where such removal is readily achievable, i.e., easily accomplishable and able to be carried out without much difficulty or expense.

(b) *Examples.* Examples of steps to remove barriers include, but are not limited to, the following actions —

(1) Installing ramps;

(2) Making curb cuts in sidewalks and entrances;

(3) Repositioning shelves;

(4) Rearranging tables, chairs, vending machines, display racks, and other furniture;

(5) Repositioning telephones;

(6) Adding raised markings on elevator control buttons;

(7) Installing flashing alarm lights;

(8) Widening doors;

(9) Installing offset hinges to widen doorways;

(10) Eliminating a turnstile or providing an alternative accessible path;

(11) Installing accessible door hardware;

(12) Installing grab bars in toilet stalls;

(13) Rearranging toilet partitions to increase maneuvering space;

(14) Insulating lavatory pipes under sinks to prevent burns;

(15) Installing a raised toilet seat;

(16) Installing a full-length bathroom mirror;

(17) Repositioning the paper towel dispenser in a bathroom;

(18) Creating designated accessible parking spaces;

(19) Installing an accessible paper cup dispenser at an existing inaccessible water fountain;

(20) Removing high pile, low density carpeting; or

(21) Installing vehicle hand controls.

(c) *Priorities.* A public accommodation is urged to take measures to comply with the barrier removal requirements of this section in accordance with the following order of priorities.

(1) First, a public accommodation should take measures to provide access to a place of public accommodation from public sidewalks, parking, or public transportation. These measures include, for example, installing an entrance ramp, widening entrances, and providing accessible parking spaces.

(2) Second, a public accommodation should take measures to provide access to those areas of a place of public accommodation where goods and services are made available to the public. These measures include, for example, adjusting the layout of display racks, rearranging tables, providing Brailled and raised character signage, widening doors, providing visual alarms, and installing ramps.

(3) Third, a public accommodation should take measures to provide access to restroom facilities. These measures include, for example, removal of obstructing furniture or vending machines, widening of doors, installation of ramps, providing accessible signage, widening of toilet stalls, and installation of grab bars.

(4) Fourth, a public accommodation should take any other measures necessary to provide access to the goods, services, facilities, privileges, advantages, or accommodations of a place of public accommodation.

(d) *Relationship to alterations requirements of subpart D of this part.* (1) Except as provided in paragraph (d)(2) of this section, measures taken to comply with the barrier removal requirements of this section shall comply with the applicable requirements for alterations in § 36.402 and §§ 36.404–36.406 of this part for the element being altered. The path of travel requirements of § 36.403 shall not apply to measures taken solely to comply with the barrier removal requirements of this section.

(2) If, as a result of compliance with the alterations requirements specified in paragraph (d)(1) of this section, the measures required to remove a barrier would not be readily achievable, a public accommodation may take other readily achievable measures to remove the barrier that do not fully comply with the specified requirements. Such measures include, for example, providing a ramp with a steeper slope or widening a doorway to a narrower width than that mandated by the alterations requirements. No measure shall be taken, however, that poses a significant risk to the health or safety of individuals with disabilities or others.

(e) *Portable ramps.* Portable ramps should be used to comply with this section only when installation of a permanent ramp is not readily achievable. In order to avoid any significant risk to the health or safety of individuals with disabilities or others in using portable ramps, due consideration shall be given to safety features such as nonslip surfaces, railings, anchoring, and strength of materials.

(f) *Selling or serving space.* The rearrangement of temporary or movable structures, such as furniture, equipment, and display racks is not readily achievable to the extent that it results in a significant loss of selling or serving space.

(g) *Limitation on barrier removal obligations.* (1) The requirements for barrier removal under § 36.304 shall not be interpreted to exceed the standards for alterations in subpart D of this part.

(2) To the extent that relevant standards for alterations are not provided in subpart D of this part, then the requirements of § 36.304 shall not be interpreted to exceed the standards for new construction in subpart D of this part.

(3) This section does not apply to rolling stock and other conveyances to the extent that § 36.310 applies to rolling stock and other conveyances.

§ 36.305 Alternatives to barrier removal.

(a) *General.* Where a public accommodation can demonstrate that barrier removal is not readily achievable, the public accommodation shall not fail to make its goods, services, facilities, privileges, advantages, or accommodations available through alternative methods, if those methods are readily achievable.

(b) *Examples.* Examples of alternatives to barrier removal include, but are not limited to, the following actions —

(1) Providing curb service or home delivery;

(2) Retrieving merchandise from inaccessible shelves or racks;

(3) Relocating activities to accessible locations;

(c) *Multiscreen cinemas.* If it is not readily achievable to remove barriers to provide access by persons with mobility impairments to all of the theaters of a multiscreen cinema, the cinema shall establish a film rotation schedule that provides reasonable access for individuals who use wheelchairs to all films. Reasonable notice shall be provided to the public as to the location and time of accessible showings.

§ 36.306 Personal devices and services.

This part does not require a public accommodation to provide its customers, clients, or participants with personal devices, such as wheelchairs; individually prescribed devices, such as prescription eyeglasses or hearing aids; or services of a personal nature including assistance in eating, toileting, or dressing.

§ 36.307 Accessible or special goods.

(a) This part does not require a public accommodation to alter its inventory to include accessible or special goods that are designed for, or facilitate use by, individuals with disabilities.

(b) A public accommodation shall order accessible or special goods at the request of an individual with disabilities, if, in the normal course of its operation, it makes special orders on request for unstocked goods, and if the accessible or special goods can be obtained from a supplier with whom the public accommodation customarily does business.

(c) Examples of accessible or special goods include items such as Brailled versions of books, books on audio cassettes, closed-captioned video tapes, special sizes or lines of clothing, and special foods to meet particular dietary needs.

§ 36.308 Seating in assembly areas.

(a) *Existing facilities.* (1) To the extent that it is readily achievable, a public accommodation in assembly areas shall —

(i) Provide a reasonable number of wheelchair seating spaces and seats with removable aisle-side arm rests; and

(ii) Locate the wheelchair seating spaces so that they —

(A) Are dispersed throughout the seating area;

(B) Provide lines of sight and choice of admission prices comparable to those for members of the general public;

(C) Adjoin an accessible route that also serves as a means of egress in case of emergency; and

(D) Permit individuals who use wheelchairs to sit with family members or other companions.

(2) If removal of seats is not readily achievable, a public accommodation shall provide, to the extent that it is readily achievable to do so, a portable chair or other means to permit a family member or other companion to sit with an individual who uses a wheelchair.

(3) The requirements of paragraph (a) of this section shall not be interpreted to exceed the standards for alterations in subpart D of this part.

(b) *New construction and alterations.* The provision and location of wheelchair seating spaces in newly constructed or altered assembly areas shall be governed by the standards for new construction and alterations in subpart D of this part.

§ 36.309 Examinations and courses.

(a) *General.* Any private entity that offers examinations or courses related to applications, licensing, certification, or credentialing for secondary or postsecondary education, professional, or trade purposes shall offer such examinations or courses in a place and manner accessible to persons with disabilities or offer alternative accessible arrangements for such individuals.

(b) *Examinations.* (1) Any private entity offering an examination covered by this section must assure that —

(i) The examination is selected and administered so as to best ensure that, when the examination is administered to an individual with a disability that impairs sensory, manual, or speaking skills, the examination results accurately reflect the individual's aptitude or achievement level or whatever other factor the examination purports to measure, rather than reflecting the individual's impaired sensory, manual, or speaking skills (except where those skills are the factors that the examination purports to measure);

(ii) An examination that is designed for individuals with impaired sensory, manual, or speaking skills is offered at equally convenient locations, as often, and in as timely a manner as are other examinations; and

(iii) The examination is administered in facilities that are accessible to individuals with disabilities or alternative accessible arrangements are made.

(2) Required modifications to an examination may include changes in the length of time permitted for completion of the examination and adaptation of the manner in which the examination is given.

(3) A private entity offering an examination covered by this section shall provide appropriate auxiliary aids for persons with impaired sensory, manual, or speaking skills, unless that private entity can demonstrate that offering a particular auxiliary aid would fundamentally alter the measurement of the skills or knowledge the examination is intended to test or would result in an undue burden. Auxiliary aids and services required by this section may include taped examinations, interpreters or other effective methods of making orally delivered materials available to individuals with hearing impairments, Brailled or large print examinations and answer sheets or qualified readers for individuals with visual impairments or learning disabilities, transcribers for individuals with manual impairments, and other similar services and actions.

(4) Alternative accessible arrangements may include, for example, provision of an examination at an individual's home with a proctor if accessible facilities or equipment are unavailable. Alternative arrangements must provide comparable conditions to those provided for nondisabled individuals.

(c) *Courses.* (1) Any private entity that offers a course covered by this section must make such modifications to that course as are necessary to ensure that the place and manner in which the course is given are accessible to individuals with disabilities.

(2) Required modifications may include changes in the length of time permitted for the completion of the course, substitution of specific requirements, or adaptation of the manner in which the course is conducted or course materials are distributed.

(3) A private entity that offers a course covered by this section shall provide appropriate auxiliary aids and services for persons with impaired sensory, manual, or speaking skills, unless the private entity can demonstrate that offering a particular auxiliary aid or service would fundamentally alter the course or would result in an undue burden. Auxiliary aids and services

required by this section may include taped texts, interpreters or other effective methods of making orally delivered materials available to individuals with hearing impairments, Brailled or large print texts or qualified readers for individuals with visual impairments and learning disabilities, classroom equipment adapted for use by individuals with manual impairments, and other similar services and actions.

(4) Courses must be administered in facilities that are accessible to individuals with disabilities or alternative accessible arrangements must be made.

(5) Alternative accessible arrangements may include, for example, provision of the course through videotape, cassettes, or prepared notes. Alternative arrangements must provide comparable conditions to those provided for nondisabled individuals.

§ 36.310 Transportation provided by public accommodations.

(a) *General.* (1) A public accommodation that provides transportation services, but that is not primarily engaged in the business of transporting people, is subject to the general and specific provisions in subparts B, C, and D of this part for its transportation operations, except as provided in this section.

(2) *Examples.* Transportation services subject to this section include, but are not limited to, shuttle services operated between transportation terminals and places of public accommodation, customer shuttle bus services operated by private companies and shopping centers, student transportation systems, and transportation provided within recreational facilities such as stadiums, zoos, amusement parks, and ski resorts.

(b) *Barrier removal.* A public accommodation subject to this section shall remove transportation barriers in existing vehicles and rail passenger cars used for transporting individuals (not including barriers that can only be removed through the retrofitting of vehicles or rail passenger cars by the installation of a hydraulic or other lift) where such removal is readily achievable.

(c) *Requirements for vehicles and systems.* A public accommodation subject to this section shall comply with the requirements pertaining to vehicles and transportation systems in the regulations issued by the Secretary of Transportation pursuant to section 306 of the Act.

§§ 36.311–36.399 [Reserved]

Subpart D — New Construction and Alterations

§ 36.401 New construction.

(a) *General.* (1) Except as provided in paragraphs (b) and (c) of this section, discrimination for purposes of this part includes a failure to design and construct facilities for first occupancy after January 26, 1993, that are readily accessible to and usable by individuals with disabilities.

(2) For purposes of this section, a facility is designed and constructed for first occupancy after January 26, 1993, only —

(i) If the last application for a building permit or permit extension for the facility is certified to be complete, by a State, County, or local government after January 26, 1992 (or, in those jurisdictions where the government does not certify completion of applications, if the last application for a building permit or permit extension for the facility is received by the State, County, or local government after January 26, 1992); and

(ii) If the first certificate of occupancy for the facility is issued after January 26, 1993.

(b) *Commercial facilities located in private residences.* (1) When a commercial facility is located in a private residence, the portion of the residence used exclusively as a residence is not covered by this subpart, but that portion used exclusively in the operation of the commercial facility or that portion used both for the commercial facility and for residential purposes is covered by the new construction and alterations requirements of this subpart.

(2) The portion of the residence covered under paragraph (b)(1) of this section extends to those elements used to enter the commercial facility, including the homeowner's front sidewalk, if any, the door or entryway, and hallways; and those portions of the residence, interior or exterior, available to or used by employees or visitors of the commercial facility, including restrooms.

(c) *Exception for structural impracticability.* (1) Full compliance with the requirements of this section is not required where an entity can demonstrate that it is structurally impracticable to meet the requirements. Full compliance will be considered structurally impracticable only in those rare circumstances when the unique characteristics of terrain prevent the incorporation of accessibility features.

(2) If full compliance with this section would be structurally impracticable, compliance with this section is required to the extent that it is not structurally impracticable. In that case, any portion of the facility that can be made accessible shall be made accessible to the extent that it is not structurally impracticable.

(3) If providing accessibility in conformance with this section to individuals with certain disabilities (e.g., those who use wheelchairs) would be structurally impracticable, accessibility shall nonetheless be ensured to persons with other types of disabilities (e.g., those who use crutches or who have sight, hearing, or mental impairments) in accordance with this section.

(d) *Elevator exemption.* (1) For purposes of this paragraph (d) —

(i) *Professional office of a health care provider* means a location where a person or entity regulated by a State to provide professional services related to the physical or mental health of an individual makes such services available to the public. The facility housing the "professional office of a health care provider" only includes floor levels housing at least one health care provider, or any floor level designed or intended for use by at least one health care provider.

(ii) *Shopping center or shopping mall means* —

(A) A building housing five or more sales or rental establishments; or

(B) A series of buildings on a common site, either under common ownership or common control or developed either as one project or as a series of related projects, housing five or more sales or rental establishments. For purposes of this section, places of public accommodation of the types listed in paragraph (5) of the definition of "place of public accommodation" in section § 36.104 are considered sales or rental establishments. The facility housing a "shopping center or shopping mall" only includes floor levels housing at least one sales or rental establishment, or any floor level designed or intended for use by at least one sales or rental establishment.

(2) This section does not require the installation of an elevator in a facility that is less than three stories or has less than 3000 square feet per story, except with respect to any facility that houses one or more of the following:

(i) A shopping center or shopping mall, or a professional office of a health care provider.

(ii) A terminal, depot, or other station used for specified public transportation, or an airport passenger terminal. In such a facility, any area housing passenger services, including boarding and debarking, loading and unloading, baggage claim, dining facilities, and other common areas open to the public, must be on an accessible route from an accessible entrance.

(3) The elevator exemption set forth in this paragraph (d) does not obviate or limit, in any way the obligation to comply with the other accessibility requirements established in paragraph (a) of this section. For example, in a facility that houses a shopping center or shopping mall, or a professional office of a health care provider, the floors that are above or below an accessible ground floor and that do not house sales or rental establishments or a professional office of a health care provider, must meet the requirements of this section but for the elevator.

§ 36.402 Alterations.

(a) *General.* (1) Any alteration to a place of public accommodation or a commercial facility, after January 26, 1992, shall be made so as to ensure that, to the maximum extent feasible, the altered portions of the facility are readily accessible to and usable by individuals with disabilities, including individuals who use wheelchairs.

(2) An alteration is deemed to be undertaken after January 26, 1992, if the physical alteration of the property begins after that date.

(b) *Alteration.* For the purposes of this part, an alteration is a change to a place of public accommodation or a commercial facility that affects or could affect the usability of the building or facility or any part thereof.

(1) Alterations include, but are not limited to, remodeling, renovation, rehabilitation, reconstruction, historic restoration, changes or rearrangement in structural parts or elements, and changes or rearrangement in the plan configuration of walls and full-height partitions. Normal maintenance, re-roofing, painting or wallpapering, asbestos removal, or changes to mechanical and electrical systems are not alterations unless they affect the usability of the building or facility.

(2) If existing elements, spaces, or common areas are altered, then each such altered element, space, or area shall comply with the applicable provisions of appendix A to this part.

(c) *To the maximum extent feasible.* The phrase "to the maximum extent feasible," as used in this section, applies to the occasional case where the nature of an existing facility makes it virtually impossible to comply fully with applicable accessibility standards through a planned alteration. In these circumstances, the alteration shall provide the maximum physical accessibility feasible. Any altered features of the facility that can be made accessible shall be made accessible. If providing accessibility in conformance with this section to individuals with certain disabilities (e.g., those who use wheelchairs) would not be feasible, the facility shall be made accessible to persons with other types of disabilities (e.g., those who use crutches, those who have impaired vision or hearing, or those who have other impairments).

§ 36.403 Alterations: Path of travel.

(a) *General.* An alteration that affects or could affect the usability of or access to an area of a facility that contains a primary function shall be made so as to ensure that, to the maximum extent feasible, the path of travel to the altered area and the restrooms, telephones, and drinking fountains serving the altered area, are readily accessible to and usable by individuals with disabilities, including individuals who use wheelchairs, unless the cost and scope of such alterations is disproportionate to the cost of the overall alteration.

(b) *Primary function.* A "primary function" is a major activity for which the facility is intended. Areas that contain a primary function include, but are not limited to, the customer services lobby of a bank, the dining area of a cafeteria, the meeting rooms in a conference center, as well as offices and other work areas in which the activities of the public accommodation or other private entity using the facility are carried out. Mechanical rooms, boiler rooms, supply storage rooms, employee lounges or locker rooms, janitorial closets, entrances, corridors, and restrooms are not areas containing a primary function.

(c) *Alterations to an area containing a primary function.* (1) Alterations that affect the usability of or access to an area containing a primary function include, but are not limited to —

(i) Remodeling merchandise display areas or employee work areas in a department store;

(ii) Replacing an inaccessible floor surface in the customer service or employee work areas of a bank;

(iii) Redesigning the assembly line area of a factory; or

(iv) Installing a computer center in an accounting firm.

(2) For the purposes of this section, alterations to windows, hardware, controls, electrical outlets, and signage shall not be deemed to be alterations that affect the usability of or access to an area containing a primary function.

(d) *Landlord/tenant:* If a tenant is making alterations as defined in § 36.402 that would trigger the requirements of this section, those alterations by the tenant in areas that only the tenant occupies do not trigger a path of travel obligation upon the landlord with respect to areas of the facility under the landlord's authority, if those areas are not otherwise being altered.

(e) *Path of travel.* (1) A "path of travel" includes a continuous, unobstructed way of pedestrian passage by means of which the altered area may be approached, entered, and exited, and which connects the altered area with an exterior approach (including sidewalks, streets, and parking areas), an entrance to the facility, and other parts of the facility.

(2) An accessible path of travel may consist of walks and sidewalks, curb ramps and other interior or exterior pedestrian ramps; clear floor paths through lobbies, corridors, rooms, and other improved areas; parking access aisles; elevators and lifts; or a combination of these elements.

(3) For the purposes of this part, the term "path of travel" also includes the restrooms, telephones, and drinking fountains serving the altered area.

(f) *Disproportionality.* (1) Alterations made to provide an accessible path of travel to the altered area will be deemed disproportionate to the overall alteration when the cost exceeds 20% of the cost of the alteration to the primary function area.

(2) Costs that may be counted as expenditures required to provide an accessible path of travel may include:

771

(i) Costs associated with providing an accessible entrance and an accessible route to the altered area, for example, the cost of widening doorways or installing ramps;

(ii) Costs associated with making restrooms accessible, such as installing grab bars, enlarging toilet stalls, insulating pipes, or installing accessible faucet controls;

(iii) Costs associated with providing accessible telephones, such as relocating the telephone to an accessible height, installing amplification devices, or installing a telecommunications device for deaf persons (TDD);

(iv) Costs associated with relocating an inaccessible drinking fountain.

(g) *Duty to provide accessible features in the event of disproportionality.* (1) When the cost of alterations necessary to make the path of travel to the altered area fully accessible is disproportionate to the cost of the overall alteration, the path of travel shall be made accessible to the extent that it can be made accessible without incurring disproportionate costs.

(2) In choosing which accessible elements to provide, priority should be given to those elements that will provide the greatest access, in the following order:

(i) An accessible entrance;

(ii) An accessible route to the altered area;

(iii) At least one accessible restroom for each sex or a single unisex restroom;

(iv) Accessible telephones;

(v) Accessible drinking fountains; and

(vi) When possible, additional accessible elements such as parking, storage, and alarms.

(h) *Series of smaller alterations.* (1) The obligation to provide an accessible path of travel may not be evaded by performing a series of small alterations to the area served by a single path of travel if those alterations could have been performed as a single undertaking.

(2) (i) If an area containing a primary function has been altered without providing an accessible path of travel to that area, and subsequent alterations of that area, or a different area on the same path of travel, are undertaken within three years of the original alteration, the total cost of alterations to the primary function areas on that path of travel during the preceding three year period shall be considered in determining whether the cost of making that path of travel accessible is disproportionate.

(ii) Only alterations undertaken after January 26, 1992, shall be considered in determining if the cost of providing an accessible path of travel is disproportionate to the overall cost of the alterations.

§ 36.404 Alterations: Elevator exemption.

(a) This section does not require the installation of an elevator in an altered facility that is less than three stories or has less than 3,000 square feet per story, except with respect to any facility that houses a shopping center, a shopping mall, the professional office of a health care provider, a terminal, depot, or other station used for specified public transportation, or an airport passenger terminal.

(1) For the purposes of this section, "professional office of a health care provider" means a location where a person or entity regulated by a State to provide professional services related to the physical or mental health of an individual makes such services available to the public. The facility that houses a "professional office of a health care provider" only includes floor levels housing by at least one health care provider, or any floor level designed or intended for use by at least one health care provider.

(2) For the purposes of this section, shopping center or shopping mall means —

(i) A building housing five or more sales or rental establishments; or

(ii) A series of buildings on a common site, connected by a common pedestrian access route above or below the ground floor, that is either under common ownership or common control or developed either as one project or as a series of related projects, housing five or more sales or rental establishments. For purposes of this section, places of public accommodation of the types listed in paragraph (5) of the definition of "place of public accommodation" in § 36.104 are considered sales or rental establishments. The facility housing a "shopping center or shopping mall" only includes floor levels housing at least one sales or rental establishment, or any floor level designed or intended for use by at least one sales or rental establishment.

(b) The exemption provided in paragraph (a) of this section does not obviate or limit in any way the obligation to comply with the other accessibility requirements established in this subpart. For example, alterations to floors above or below the accessible ground floor must be accessible regardless of whether the altered facility has an elevator.

§ 36.405 Alterations: Historic preservation.

(a) Alterations to buildings or facilities that are eligible for listing in the National Register of Historic Places under the National Historic Preservation Act (16 U.S.C. 470 *et seq.*), or are designated as historic under State or local law, shall comply to the maximum extent feasible with section 4.1.7 of appendix A to this part.

(b) If it is determined under the procedures set out in section 4.1.7 of appendix A that it is not feasible to provide physical access to an historic property that is a place of public accommodation in a manner that will not threaten or destroy the historic significance of the building or facility, alternative methods of access shall be provided pursuant to the requirements of subpart C of this part.

§ 36.406 Standards for new construction and alterations.

(a) New construction and alterations subject to this part shall comply with the standards for accessible design published as appendix A to this part (ADAAG).

(b) The chart in the appendix to this section provides guidance to the user in reading appendix A to this part (ADAAG) together with subparts A through D of this part, when determining requirements for a particular facility.

Appendix to § 36.406

This chart has no effect for purposes of compliance or enforcement. It does not necessarily provide complete or mandatory information.

	Subparts	ADAAG
Application, General.	36.102(b)(3): public accommodations. 36.102(c): commercial facilities. 36.102(e): public entities. 36.103 (other laws) 36.401 ("for first occupancy"). 36.402(a) (alterations).	1, 2, 3, 4.1.1.
Definitions	36.104: commercial facilities, facility, place of public accommodation, private club, public accommodation, public entity, religious entity.	3.5 Definitions, including: addition, alteration, building, element, facility, space, story.
	36.401(d)(1)(ii), 36.404(a)(2): shopping center or shopping mall. 36.401(d)(1)(i), 36.404(a)(1): professional office of a health care provider. 36.402: alteration; usability. 36.402(c): to the maximum extent feasible.	4.1.6(j), technical infeasibility.

	Subparts	*ADAAG*
New Construction:	36.401(a) General	4.1.2.
General.	36.401(b) Commercial facilities in private residences.	4.1.3.
	36.207 Places of public accommodation in private residences.	
Work Areas		4.1.1(3).
Structural Impracticability.	36.401(c)	4.1.1(5)(a).
Elevator Exemption.	36.401(d) 36.404	4.1.3(5).
Other Exceptions.		4.1.1(5), 4.1.3(5) and throughout.
Alterations:		
General.	36.401(b): commercial facilities in private residences.	
	36.402	4.1.6(1).
Alterations Affecting an Area Containing A Primary Function; Path of Travel; Disproportionality.	36.403	4.1.6(2).
Alterations: Special Technical Provisions.		4.1.6(3).
Additions	36.401–36.405	4.1.5.
Historic Preservation.	36.405	4.1.7.
Technical Provisions.		4.2 through 4.35.
Restaurants and Cafeterias		5.
Medical Care Facilities.		6.
Business and Mercantile.		7.
Libraries		8.
Transient Lodging (Hotels, Homeless Shelters, Etc.).		9.
Transportation Facilities.		10.

[Order No. 1513–91, 56 FR 35592, July 26, 1991, as amended by Order No. 1836–94, 59 FR 2675, Jan. 18, 1994]

§ 36.407 Temporary suspension of certain detectable warning requirements.

The requirements contained in sections 4.7.7, 4.29.5, and 4.29.6 of appendix A to this part are suspended temporarily until July 26, 1996.

[Order No. 1852–94, 59 FR 17446, Apr. 12, 1994]

§§36.408 — 36.499 [Reserved]

Subpart E — Enforcement

§ 36.501 Private suits.

(a) *General.* Any person who is being subjected to discrimination on the basis of disability in violation of the Act or this part or who has reasonable grounds for believing that such person is about to be subjected to discrimination in violation of section 303 of the Act or subpart D of this part may institute a civil action for preventive relief, including an application for a permanent or temporary injunction, restraining order, or other order. Upon timely application, the court may, in its discretion, permit the Attorney General to intervene in the civil action if the Attorney General or his or her designee certifies that the case is of general public importance. Upon application by the complainant and in such circumstances as the court may deem just, the court may appoint an attorney for such complainant and may authorize the commencement of the civil action without the payment of fees, costs, or security. Nothing in this section shall require a person with a disability to engage in a futile gesture if the person has actual notice that a person or organization covered by title III of the Act or this part does not intend to comply with its provisions.

(b) *Injunctive relief.* In the case of violations of § 36.304, §§ 36.308, 36.310(b), 36.401, 36.402, 36.403, and 36.405 of this part, injunctive relief shall include an order to alter facilities to make such facilities readily accessible to and usable by individuals with disabilities to the extent required by the Act or this part. Where appropriate, injunctive relief shall also include requiring the provision of an auxiliary aid or service, modification of a policy, or provision of alternative methods, to the extent required by the Act or this part.

§ 36.502 Investigations and compliance reviews.

(a) The Attorney General shall investigate alleged violations of the Act or this part.

(b) Any individual who believes that he or she or a specific class of persons has been subjected to discrimination prohibited by the Act or this part may request the Department to institute an investigation.

(c) Where the Attorney General has reason to believe that there may be a violation of this part, he or she may initiate a compliance review.

§ 36.503 Suit by the Attorney General.

Following a compliance review or investigation under § 36.502, or at any other time in his or her discretion, the Attorney General may commence a civil action in any appropriate United States district court if the Attorney General has reasonable cause to believe that —

(a) Any person or group of persons is engaged in a pattern or practice of discrimination in violation of the Act or this part; or

(b) Any person or group of persons has been discriminated against in violation of the Act or this part and the discrimination raises an issue of general public importance.

§ 36.504 Relief.

(a) *Authority of court.* In a civil action under § 36.503, the court —

(1) May grant any equitable relief that such court considers to be appropriate, including, to the extent required by the Act or this part —

(i) Granting temporary, preliminary, or permanent relief;

(ii) Providing an auxiliary aid or service, modification of policy, practice, or procedure, or alternative method; and

(iii) Making facilities readily accessible to and usable by individuals with disabilities;

(2) May award other relief as the court considers to be appropriate, including monetary damages to persons aggrieved when requested by the Attorney General; and

(3) May, to vindicate the public interest, assess a civil penalty against the entity in an amount

(i) Not exceeding $50,000 for a first violation; and

(ii) Not exceeding $100,000 for any subsequent violation.

(b) *Single violation.* For purposes of paragraph (a) (3) of this section, in determining whether a first or subsequent violation has occurred, a determination in a single action, by judgment or settlement, that the covered entity has engaged in more than one discriminatory act shall be counted as a single violation.

(c) *Punitive damages.* For purposes of paragraph (a)(2) of this section, the terms "monetary damages" and "such other relief" do not include punitive damages.

(d) *Judicial consideration.* In a civil action under § 36.503, the court, when considering what amount of civil penalty, if any, is appropriate, shall give consideration to any good faith effort or attempt to comply with this part by the entity. In evaluating good faith, the court shall consider, among other factors it deems relevant, whether the entity could have reasonably anticipated the need for an appropriate type of auxiliary aid needed to accommodate the unique needs of a particular individual with a disability.

§ 36.505 Attorneys fees.

In any action or administrative proceeding commenced pursuant to the Act or this part, the court or agency, in its discretion, may allow the prevailing party, other than the United States, a reasonable attorney's fee, including litigation expenses, and costs, and the United States shall be liable for the foregoing the same as a private individual.

§ 36.506 Alternative means of dispute resolution.

Where appropriate and to the extent authorized by law, the use of alternative means of dispute resolution, including settlement negotiations, conciliation, facilitation, mediation, fact-finding, minitrials, and arbitration, is encouraged to resolve disputes arising under the Act and this part.

§ 36.507 Effect of unavailability of technical assistance.

A public accommodation or other private entity shall not be excused from compliance with the requirements of this part because of any failure to receive technical assistance, including any failure in the development or dissemination of any technical assistance manual authorized by the Act.

§ 36.508 Effective date.

(a) *General.* Except as otherwise provided in this section and in this part, this part shall become effective on January 26, 1992.

(b) *Civil actions.* Except for any civil action brought for a violation of section 303 of the Act, no civil action shall be brought for any act or omission described in section 302 of the Act that occurs —

(1) Before July 26, 1992, against businesses with 25 or fewer employees and gross receipts of $1,000,000 or less.

(2) Before January 26, 1993, against businesses with 10 or fewer employees and gross receipts of $500,000 or less.

(c) *Transportation services provided by public accommodations.* Newly purchased or leased vehicles required to be accessible by § 36.310 must be readily accessible to and usable by individuals with disabilities, including individuals who use wheelchairs, if the solicitation for the vehicle is made after August 25, 1990.

§§36.509 — 36.599 [Reserved]

Subpart F — Certification of State Laws or Local Building Codes

§ 36.601 Definitions.

Assistant Attorney General means the Assistant Attorney General for Civil Rights or his or her designee.

Certification of equivalency means a final certification that a code meets or exceeds the minimum requirements of title III of the Act for accessibility and usability of facilities covered by that title.

Code means a State law or local building code or similar ordinance, or part thereof, that establishes accessibility requirements.

Model code means a nationally recognized document developed by a private entity for use by State or local jurisdictions in developing codes as defined in this section. A model code is intended for incorporation by reference or adoption in whole or in part, with or without amendment, by State or local jurisdictions.

Preliminary determination of equivalency means a preliminary determination that a code appears to meet or exceed the minimum requirements of title III of the Act for accessibility and usability of facilities covered by that title.

Submitting official means the State or local official who —

(1) Has principal responsibility for administration of a code, or is authorized to submit a code on behalf of a jurisdiction; and

(2) Files a request for certification under this subpart.

§ 36.602 General rule.

On the application of a State or local government, the Assistant Attorney General may certify that a code meets or exceeds the minimum requirements of the Act for the accessibility and usability of places of public accommodation and commercial facilities under this part by issuing a certification of equivalency. At any enforcement proceeding under title III of the Act, such certification shall be rebuttable evidence that such State law or local ordinance does meet or exceed the minimum requirements of title III.

§ 36.603 Filing request for certification.

(a) A submitting official may file a request for certification of a code under this subpart.

(b) Before filing a request for certification of a code, the submitting official shall ensure that —

(1) Adequate public notice of intention to file a request for certification, notice of a hearing, and notice of the location at which the request and materials can be inspected is published within the relevant jurisdiction;

(2) Copies of the proposed request and supporting materials are made available for public examination and copying at the office of the State or local agency charged with administration and enforcement of the code; and

(3) The local or State jurisdiction holds a public hearing on the record, in the State or locality, at which the public is invited to comment on the proposed request for certification.

(c) The submitting official shall include the following materials and information in support of the request:

(1) The text of the jurisdiction's code; any standard, regulation, code, or other relevant document incorporated by reference or otherwise referenced in the code; the law creating and empowering the agency; any relevant manuals, guides, or any other interpretive information issued that pertain to the code; and any formal opinions of the State Attorney General or the chief legal officer of the jurisdiction that pertain to the code;

(2) Any model code or statute on which the pertinent code is based, and an explanation of any differences between the model and the pertinent code;

(3) A transcript of the public hearing required by paragraph (b)(3) of this section; and

(4) Any additional information that the submitting official may wish to be considered.

(d) The submitting official shall file the original and one copy of the request and of supporting materials with the Assistant Attorney General. The submitting official shall clearly label the request as a "request for certification" of a code. A copy of the request and supporting materials will be available for public examination and copying at the offices of the Assistant Attorney General in Washington, DC. The submitting official shall ensure that copies of the request and supporting materials are available for public examination and copying at the office of the State or local agency charged with administration and enforcement of the code. The submitting official shall ensure that adequate public notice of the request for certification and of the location at which the request and materials can be inspected is published within the relevant jurisdiction.

(e) Upon receipt of a request for certification, the Assistant Attorney General may request further information that he or she considers relevant to the determinations required to be made under this subpart.

(Approved by the Office of Management and Budget under control number 1190-0005) [56 FR 35592, July 26, 1991, as amended by Order No. 1679-93, 58 FR 17522, Apr. 5, 1993]

§ 36.604 Preliminary determination.

After consultation with the Architectural and Transportation Barriers Compliance Board, the Assistant Attorney General shall make a preliminary determination of equivalency or a preliminary determination to deny certification.

§ 36.605 Procedure following preliminary determination of equivalency.

(a) If the Assistant Attorney General makes a preliminary determination of equivalency under § 36.604, he or she shall inform the submitting official, in writing, of that preliminary determination. The Assistant Attorney General shall also —

(1) Publish a notice in the FEDERAL REGISTER that advises the public of the preliminary determination of equivalency with respect to the particular code, and invite interested persons and organizations, including individuals with disabilities, during a period of at least 60 days following publication of the notice, to file written comments relevant to whether a final certification of equivalency should be issued;

(2) After considering the information received in response to the notice described in paragraph (a) of this section, and after publishing a separate notice in the FEDERAL REGISTER, hold an informal hearing in Washington, D.C. at which interested persons, including individuals with disabilities, are provided an opportunity to express their views with respect to the preliminary determination of equivalency; and

(b) The Assistant Attorney General, after consultation with the Architectural and Transportation Barriers Compliance Board, and consideration of the materials and information submitted pursuant to this section and § 36.603, shall issue either a certification of equivalency or a final determination to deny the request for certification. He or she shall publish notice of the certification of equivalency or denial of certification in the FEDERAL REGISTER.

§ 36.606 Procedure following preliminary denial of certification.

(a) If the Assistant Attorney General makes a Preliminary determination to deny certification of a code under § 36.604, he or she shall notify the submitting official of the determination. The notification may include specification of the manner in which the code could be amended in order to qualify for certification.

(b) The Assistant Attorney General shall allow the submitting official not less than 15 days to submit data, views, and arguments in opposition to the preliminary determination to deny certification. If the submitting official does not submit materials, the Assistant Attorney General shall not be required to take any further action. If the submitting official submits materials, the Assistant Attorney General shall evaluate those materials and any other relevant information. After evaluation of any newly submitted materials, the Assistant Attorney General shall make either a final denial of certification or a preliminary determination of equivalency.

§ 36.607 Effect of certification.

(a)(1) A certification shall be considered a certification of equivalency only with respect to those features or elements that are both covered by the certified code and addressed by the standards against which equivalency is measured.

(2) For example, if certain equipment is not covered by the code, the determination of equivalency cannot be used as evidence with respect to the question of whether equipment in a building built according to the code satisfies the Act's requirements with respect to such equipment. By the same token, certification would not be relevant to construction of a facility for children, if the regulations against which equivalency is measured do not address children's facilities.

(b) A certification of equivalency is effective only with respect to the particular edition of the code for which certification is granted. Any amendments or other changes to the code after the date of the certified edition are not considered part of the certification.

(c) A submitting official may reapply for certification of amendments or other changes to a code that has already received certification.

§ 36.608 Guidance concerning model codes.

Upon application by an authorized representative of a private entity responsible for developing a model code, the Assistant Attorney General may review the relevant model code and issue guidance concerning whether and in what respects the model code is consistent with the minimum requirements of the Act for the accessibility and usability of places of public accommodation and commercial facilities under this part.

TABLE OF CASES

B

C

F

G

H

L

McPherson v. Michigan High Sch. Athletic Ass'n, 5.09[M], 6.04[B]

McWilliams v. Logicon, Inc., 9.11[C]

Mears v. Gulfstream Aerospace Corp., 4.06[B][22]

Medical Soc'y v. Jacobs, 5.09[M], 5.12, 9.03, 9.04[A], 9.04[F]

Medoza v. Borden, Inc., 3.03[W]

Meester v. Runyon, 9.24[C]

Mellon v. Federal Express Corp., 3.03[T]

Melton v. Community for Creative Nonviolence, 6.07

Memmer v. Marin County Courts, 5.07[B]

Mengine v. Runyon, 4.05[B][4]

Menkowitz v. Pottstown Mem'l Med. Ctr., 6.03[A]

Meritor Sav. Bank v. Vinson, 9.04[J]

Merry v. A. Sulka & Co., 4.05[B][6]

Michels v. United States, 1.07[A]

Midgett v. Tri-County Metro. Transp. Dist., 9.04[D]

Miller v. Centennial State Bank, 4.10[B][3], 4.11[B][2]

Miller v. City of Springfield, 3.02[C][2]

Miller v. Illinois Dep't of Corrections, 3.03[MM], 4.11[B][2]

Miller v. Maxwell's Int'l Inc., 9.04[G]

Miller v. National Cas. Co., 4.04[A]

Miller v. National Railroad Passenger Corp., 15.02[B][2][a]

Miller v. Public Storage Mgmt., 9.11[C]

Miller v. Solaglas California, Inc., 15.02[B][2][a]

Milton v. Bob Maddox Chrysler Plymouth, 3.03[II]

Milton v. Schrivner, Inc., 3.06, 4.06[B][18], 4.16[G]

Mine Workers v. Gibbs, 9.12

Miners v. Cargill Communications, Inc., 3.03[P]

Misek-Falkoff v. IBM, 9.23[G][1]

Mitchell v. AT&T Corp., 4.06[B][11]

Mitchell v. Qashingtonville Central Sch. Dist., 3.10

Modderno v. King, 4.14

Mohamed v. Marriott Int'l, Inc., 3.06[F], 4.06[B][2]

Mohasco Corp. v. Silver, 9.08[A][1], 9.08[A][2]

Mole v. Buckhorn Rubber Prods., Inc., 3.06[D]

Mondzelewski v. Pathmark Stores, Inc., 3.07, 4.03[K]

Monk v. Doctors' Hosp., 9.17[B]

Montalvo v. Radcliffe, 6.04[E]

Moore v. Harris Corp., 1.07[A]

Moore v. J.B. Hunt Transport, Inc., 3.03[D]

Moore v. Payless Shoe Serv., Inc., 4.05[D]

Moore v. Payless Shoe Source, Inc., 9.24[C]

Moore v. Walker, 8.01

Moreno v. Consolidated Rail Corp., 8.04[B]

Morgan v. City of Albuquerque, 5.07[D]

Morgan v. Hilti, Inc., 4.03[K], 4.11[B][4][c]

Morgan v. Joint Admin. Bd., 3.02[D]

Morgan v. State, 1.07[C]

Morgan v. United States Postal Serv., 8.07

Morisky v. Broward County, 9.18

Moritz v. Frontier Airlines, Inc., 3.03[AA], 4.06[A]

S

U

United Airlines v. McMann,
6.10[A]
United States v. City of Charlotte,
5.13, 9.04[D]
United States v. Colorado,
17.01[B][8]
United States v. Days Inns of
Am., Inc., 6.02[A]
United States v. Fisher,
17.01[B][8]
United States v. Hutson, 16.01[A]
United States v. Illinois, 4.02[E],
4.14, 9.04[K]
United States v. International
Bldg. Co., 17.01[B][6]
United States v. International
Business Machs., Corp.,
9.17[A]
United States v. Marshall,
17.01[B][10]
United States v. Mensik,
17.01[B][10]
United States v. Meyer,
17.01[B][10]
United States v. Miller Bros.
Constr. Co., 9.04[L]
United States v. Morvant, 9.04[G],
9.04[L], 9.17[A]
United States v. NEC Corp.,
9.04[L]
United States v. Northside Realty
Assocs., 9.21
United States v. Oregon,
17.01[B][8]
United States v. Pottorf, 9.21
United States v. Prugh,
17.01[B][10]
United States v. Rylander,
17.01[B][10]
United States v. Sanders, 9.17[B]
United States v. Schiffer,
17.01[B][10]
United States v. Sliker, 16.01[A]
United States v. Southern Mgmt.
Corp., 6.03[A]

United States v. UMWA,
17.01[B][10]
United States v. Vague,
17.01[B][10]
United States v. Venture Stores,
Inc., 214 F.3d 1115, 9.23[G][1]
United States v. Venture Stores,
Inc., 1994 WL 86068,
9.23[G][1]
United States Dep't of Transp. v.
Paralyzed Veterans, 8.04[B],
7.01
University of Tenn. v. Elliott,
9.08[A][6]
Upshur v. Love, 9.08[A][1]
Urban v. Jefferson County Sch.
Dist. R-1, 5.09[M]

V

Vaca v. Sipes, 4.16[D]
Valdez v. Albuquerque Public
Schs., 3.06[A]
Valenzuela v. Kraft, Inc.,
9.08[A][2]
Van Sickle v. Automatic Data
Processing, Inc., 3.03[O]
Van Stan v. Fancy Colours & Co.,
3.05[E]
VandeZande v. State of Wis. Dep't
of Admin., 44 F.3d 538,
4.06[B][17], 4.10[B][3]
VandeZande v. State of Wis. Dep't
of Admin., 851 F. Supp. 353,
4.06[B][17]
Vanguards of Cleveland v. City of
Cleveland, 17.01[B][8]
Varner v. National Super Markets,
Inc., 4.16[E], 9.11[B]
Velasco v. Illinois Dep't of Human
Servs., 5.22
Velazquez-Rivera v. Danzig, 9.18

X

Y

Z

TABLE OF STATUTES

[References are to sections.]

AMERICANS WITH DISABILITIES ACT

Act §	U.S. Code Citation	Text §
101(4)	42 U.S.C. § 12111(4)	4.02[B]
101(5)	42 U.S.C. § 12111(5)	2.03
101(5)(A)	42 U.S.C. § 12111(5)(A)	4.02[C]
101(5)(B)	42 U.S.C. § 12111(5)(B)	4.02[C], 8.01
101(6)	42 U.S.C. § 12111(6)	1.03, 4.13
101(7)	42 U.S.C. § 12111(7)	1.03
101(8)	42 U.S.C. § 12111(8)	3.06, 4.05[D]
101(9)	42 U.S.C. § 12111(9)	4.05[A], 4.05[B][5], 4.10[B][1], 18.08[B][9]
101(10)	42 U.S.C. § 12111(10)	4.10[B][1], 4.10[C], 18.08[B][9]
101(10)(B)(ii)	42 U.S.C. § 12111(10)(B)(ii)	4.10[B][1]
101(10)(B)(iii)	42 U.S.C. § 12111(10)(B)(iii)	4.10[B][1]
	42 U.S.C. § 12111(3)	4.10[C]
	42 U.S.C. § 12111(8)	3.06[D], 4.05[D], 16.01[B][7]
	42 U.S.C. § 12111(9)(B)	4.06[B][23], 4.06[B][27]
102	42 U.S.C. § 12112	3.02, 18.08[B][9]
102(a)	42 U.S.C. § 12112(a)	4.03[F], 4.03[I], 4.03[H][2], 4.11[B][1], 5.26, 9.04[G], 9.08[B], 18.08[B][9]
102(a)–(b)	42 U.S.C. §§ 12112(a)–(b)	18.04[B][6]
102(b)(1)	42 U.S.C. § 12112(b)(1)	4.03[A], 4.03[J], 8.11, 17.01[B][10]
102(b)(2)	42 U.S.C. § 12112(b)(2)	4.03[D], 4.16[B]

Act §	U.S. Code Citation	Text §
102(b)(3)	42 U.S.C. § 12112(b)(3)	4.03[C], 4.05[D], 4.11[B][3]
	42 U.S.C. § 12112(b)(3)(A)	4.06[B][11]
102(b)(4)	42 U.S.C. § 12112(b)(4)	3.11, 4.03[E]
102(b)(5)	42 U.S.C. § 12112(b)(5)	4.03[E], 4.05[A], 4.05[C], 4.10[B][1], 4.11[B][4][b], 8.11
102(b)(5)(A)	42 U.S.C. § 12112(b)(5)(A)	4.03[A], 4.03[E], 4.05[B][5], 4.10[B][1], 12.03[A]
102(b)(5)(B)	42 U.S.C. § 12112(b)(5)(B)	4.03[A]
102(b)(6)	42 U.S.C. § 12112(b)(6)	4.03[G][1], 4.05[D]
102(b)(7)	42 U.S.C. § 12112(b)(7)	4.03[G][1], 8.11
102(c)	42 U.S.C. § 12112(c)	4.14, 18.07[B]
102(c)(1)	42 U.S.C. § 12112(c)(1)	4.03[H][1]
102(c)(1)(A)	42 U.S.C. § 12112 (c)(1)(A)	18.04[B][6]
102(c)(1)(B)	42 U.S.C. § 12112(c)(1)(B)	18.04[B][6]
102(c)(2)(A)	42 U.S.C. § 12112(c)(2)(A)	4.03[H][1], 18.10
102(c)(2)(B)	42 U.S.C. § 12112(c)(2)(B)	4.03[H][1], 18.10
102(c)(3)(A)	42 U.S.C. § 12112(c)(3)(A)	4.03[H][1]
102(c)(3)(B)	42 U.S.C. § 12112(c)(3)(B)	4.03[H][1], 18.10
102(c)(3)(B)(i)	42 U.S.C. § 12112(c)(3)(B)(i)	4.03[H][1]
102(c)(3)(B)(ii)	42 U.S.C. § 12112(c)(3)(B)(ii)	4.03[H][1]
102(c)(3)(B)(iii)	42 U.S.C. § 12112(c)(3)(B)(iii)	4.03[H][1]
102(c)(3)	42 U.S.C. § 12112(c)(3)	4.03[H][1]

825

Act §	U.S. Code Citation	Text §
102(c)(3)(C)	42 U.S.C. § 12112(c)(3)(C)	4.03[H][1]
102(c)(4)(A)	42 U.S.C. § 12112(c)(4)(A)	4.03[H][1]
102(c)(4)(B)	42 U.S.C. § 12112(c)(4)(B)	4.03[H][1], 4.03[H][2]
	42 U.S.C. § 12112(d)	4.03[H][3]
	42 U.S.C. § 12112(d)(2)	4.03[H][2]
	42 U.S.C. §§ 12112(d)(2)–(4)	5.07[E]
	42 U.S.C. §§ 12112(d)(3)–(4)	4.03[H][2]
	42 U.S.C. § 12112(d)(3)(B)	4.03[H][2]
	42 U.S.C. § 12112(d)(3)(C)	4.03[H][2]
	42 U.S.C. § 12112(d)(4)	4.03[H][2]
	42 U.S.C. § 12112(d)(4)(A)	4.03[H][2]
103	42 U.S.C. § 12113	3.04, 4.10[A]
103(a)	42 U.S.C. § 12113(a)	4.10[A], 14.02[B][3]
103(b)	42 U.S.C. § 12113(b)	2.05, 3.04, 4.10[A], 4.10[C], 14.02[B][3]
	42 U.S.C. § 12113(c)(2)	4.15
103(d)	42 U.S.C. § 12113(d)	3.04, 4.10[C]
104	42 U.S.C. § 12114	1.01, 4.13, 5.17
104(a)	42 U.S.C. § 12114(a)	3.12, 4.13
104(b)	42 U.S.C. § 12114(b)	3.12
	42 U.S.C. § 12114(b)(2)	4.13
	42 U.S.C. § 12114(b)(3)	3.12, 4.13
104(c)	42 U.S.C. § 12114(c)	3.12, 4.13

Act §	U.S. Code Citation	Text §
203	42 U.S.C. § 12133	9.02, 9.14, 9.16, 9.22, 9.23[F], 17.01[B][10]
204	42 U.S.C. § 12134	5.05, 9.06, 9.23[G][1]
	42 U.S.C. § 12141(1)	7.02
221(2)	42 U.S.C. § 12141(2)	7.01, 7.02
221(3)	42 U.S.C. § 12141(3)	7.02
222(a)	42 U.S.C. § 12142(a)	7.02, 7.08
222(b)	42 U.S.C. § 12142(b)	7.02, 7.08
222(b)(7)	42 U.S.C. § 12142(b)(7)	7.02
222(c)	42 U.S.C. § 12142(c)	7.02
222(c)(1)	42 U.S.C. § 12142(c)(1)	7.08
222(c)(2)(A)	42 U.S.C. § 12142(c)(2)(A)	7.08
223	42 U.S.C. § 12143	7.02
223(b)	42 U.S.C. § 12143(b)	7.02
223(c)(1)	42 U.S.C. § 12143(c)(1)	7.02
223(d)	42 U.S.C. § 12143(d)	7.02
223(e)	42 U.S.C. § 12143(e)	7.02
224	42 U.S.C. § 12144	7.02
226	42 U.S.C. § 12146	7.02
227(a)	42 U.S.C. § 12147(a)	7.02
227(b)(2)(A)	42 U.S.C. § 12147(b)(2)(A)	7.02
227(b)(2)(B)	42 U.S.C. § 12147(b)(2)(B)	7.02
	42 U.S.C. § 12148	7.02
228(a)(2)	42 U.S.C. § 12148(a)(2)	7.02

Act §	*U.S. Code Citation*	*Text §*
228(a)(3)	42 U.S.C. § 12148(a)(3)	7.02
	42 U.S.C. § 12148(b)	7.02
229	42 U.S.C. § 12149	7.05
	42 U.S.C. § 12162	7.02
242(b)	42 U.S.C. § 12162(b)	7.02
242(e)	42 U.S.C. § 12162(e)	7.02
242(2)(a)	42 U.S.C. § 12162(a)	7.02
244	42 U.S.C. § 12164	7.05
301–310	42 U.S.C. §§ 12181–12189	1.01, 2.05, 3.01, 4.14, 6.01, 7.01, 8.01, 9.01, 11.01, 12.03[A], 18.24
301(a)	42 U.S.C. § 12181(a), 1.05	6.11
301(b)	42 U.S.C. § 12181(b), 1.05	6.11
301(c)	42 U.S.C. § 12181(c), 1.05	6.11
301(2)	42 U.S.C. § 12181(2)	6.01, 9.06
301(3)	42 U.S.C. § 12181(3)	7.02, 7.04
301(4)	42 U.S.C. § 12181(4)	7.02, 7.04
301(5)	42 U.S.C. § 12181(5)	7.04
301(6)	42 U.S.C. § 12181(6)	8.01
	42 U.S.C. § 12181(7)	5.04, 9.06
301(7)(F)	42 U.S.C. § 12181(7)(F)	9.04[K]
301(7)(G)	42 U.S.C. § 12181(7)(G)	7.02
301(7)	42 U.S.C. § 12181(7)(1)	6.02[A]
301(7)	42 U.S.C. § 12181(7)	6.02[A], 8.01

Act §	U.S. Code Citation	Text §
301(9)	42 U.S.C. § 12181(9)	6.03[D][4]
301(9)(A)	42 U.S.C. § 12181(9)(A)	6.03[D][4]
301(9)(B)	42 U.S.C. § 12181(9)(B)	6.03[D][4]
301(9)(C)	42 U.S.C. § 12181(9)(C)	6.03[D][4]
301(9)(D)	42 U.S.C. § 12181(9)(D)	6.03[D][4]
301(10)	42 U.S.C. § 12181(10)	7.01, 7.02
301(11)	42 U.S.C. § 12181(11)	7.02
302	42 U.S.C. § 12182	5.02, 5.09[D], 6.02[A], 6.03[A], 6.04[D], 6.04[E], 7.02
302(a)	42 U.S.C. § 12182(a)	3.02, 6.02[A], 6.03[A], 6.04[D], 6.12
302(b)(1)	42 U.S.C § 12182(b)(1)	6.12
302(b)(1)(A)(i)	42 U.S.C. § 12182(b)(1)(A)(i)	6.03[A]
302(b)(1)(A)(ii)	42 U.S.C. § 12182(b)(1)(A)(ii)	6.03[A]
302(b)(1)(A)(iii)	42 U.S.C. § 12182(b)(1)(A)(iii)	6.03[A]
302(b)(1)(B)	42 U.S.C. § 12182(b)(1)(B)	6.03[A]
302(b)(1)(C)	42 U.S.C. § 12182(b)(1)(C)	6.03[A]
302(b)(1)(D)	42 U.S.C. § 12182(b)(1)(D)	6.03[A]
302(b)(1)(E)	42 U.S.C. § 12182(b)(1)(E)	6.03[A]
302(b)(2)	42 U.S.C. § 12182(b)(2)	6.12
302(b)(2)(A)(i)	42 U.S.C. § 12182(b)(2)(A)(i)	6.03[A], 12.03[A]

Act §	U.S. Code Citation	Text §
302(b)(2)(A)(ii)	42 U.S.C. § 12182(b)(2)(A)(ii)	6.01, 6.03[A], 6.03[B], 6.04[B], 12.03[A]
302(b)(2)(A)(iii)	42 U.S.C. § 12182(b)(2)(A)(iii)	6.01, 6.03[C][1], 6.03[C][3], 6.04[A], 6.04[C], 12.03[A]
302(b)(2)(A)(iv)	42 U.S.C. § 12182(b)(2)(A)(iv)	6.01, 6.03[D][1], 6.03[D][4], 9.22, 12.03[A]
302(b)(2)(A)(v)	42 U.S.C. § 12182(b)(2)(A)(v)	6.01, 6.03[D][4], 12.03[A]
302(b)(2)(B)	42 U.S.C. § 12182(b)(2)(B)	7.02, 7.04
302(b)(2)(C)	42 U.S.C. § 12182(b)(2)(C)	7.02, 7.04
302(b)(2)(C)(ii)	42 U.S.C. § 12182(b)(2)(C)(ii)	7.04
302(b)(2)(D)	42 U.S.C. § 12182(b)(2)(D)	7.02, 7.04
302(b)(3)	42 U.S.C. § 12182(b)(3)	6.04[E]
303	42 U.S.C. § 12183	6.02[A], 6.03[E], 6.12, 9.02, 9.22
303(a)	42 U.S.C. § 12183(a)	9.22
303(a)(1)	42 U.S.C. § 12183(a)(1)	6.01, 6.03[E], 6.10[B], 7.02
303(a)(2)	42 U.S.C. § 12183(a)(2)	6.03[E]
303(b)	42 U.S.C. § 12183(b)	6.03[E]
	42 U.S.C. § 12183(b)(3)	6.04[E]
304	42 U.S.C. § 12184	6.03[J], 6.13, 7.02, 7.03
304(a)	42 U.S.C. § 12184(a)	6.03[I]
304(b)(1)	42 U.S.C. § 12184(b)(1)	6.03[I]
304(b)(2)(C)	42 U.S.C. § 12184(b)(2)(C)	6.03[I]
304(b)(3)	42 U.S.C. § 12184(b)(3)	6.03[I], 7.02

Act §	U.S. Code Citation	Text §
304(c)	42 U.S.C. § 12184(c)	6.03[I]
306	42 U.S.C. § 12186	7.05
306(a)	42 U.S.C. § 12186(a)	6.12
306(a)(1)	42 U.S.C. § 12186(a)(1)	6.12
306(a)(2)(B)(iii)	42 U.S.C. § 12186(a)(2)(B)(iii)	6.12
306(a)(2)(C)	42 U.S.C. § 12186(a)(2)(C)	6.12
306(b)	42 U.S.C. § 12186(b)	6.12
306(c)	42 U.S.C. § 12186(c)	6.12
306(d)(1)	42 U.S.C. § 12186(d)(1)	6.12
307	42 U.S.C. § 12187	6.02[B]
308	42 U.S.C. § 12188	17.01[B][10]
	42 U.S.C. § 12188(a)	9.14
308(a)(1)	42 U.S.C. § 12188(a)(1)	6.08, 9.02, 9.04[E], 9.16, 9.22, 9.23[G][1]
308(a)(2)	42 U.S.C. § 12188(a)(2)	6.08, 9.02, 9.22
	42 U.S.C. § 12188(b)	7.06
308(b)(1)(A)(i)	42 U.S.C. § 12188(b)(1)(A)(i)	6.08, 9.02
308(b)(1)(A)(ii)	42 U.S.C. § 12188(b)(1)(A)(ii)	6.03[E], 6.08, 9.02
308(b)(1)(B)	42 U.S.C. § 12188(b)(1)(B)	6.08, 9.02, 9.04[E], 9.23[F]
308(b)(2)	42 U.S.C. § 12188(b)(2)	9.22
308(b)(2)(C)	42 U.S.C. § 12188(b)(2)(C)	6.08, 9.02
308(b)(4)	42 U.S.C. § 12188(b)(4)	6.08, 9.02
309	42 U.S.C. § 12189	6.03[G]

Act §	U.S. Code Citation	Text §
310(6)	42 U.S.C. § 12181(6)	8.01
	47 U.S.C. §§ 151–613	7.01
	47 U.S.C. § 153	7.16
	47 U.S.C. § 153(10)	7.16
	47 U.S.C. § 223	7.16
	47 U.S.C. § 223(e)(6)	7.16
	47 U.S.C. § 223(h)(1)(B)	7.16
401	47 U.S.C. § 225	1.01, 2.01, 2.08, 3.01, 4.01, 5.01, 6.01, 7.01, 7.09, 7.11, 7.15, 7.16, 8.01, 9.01, 9.03, 10.01, 10.02[A], 11.01, 12.01, 13.01, 14.01, 15.01[A], 16.01[A], 17.01[A], 18.01
401(a)(1)	47 U.S.C. § 225(a)(1)	7.10, 7.16
401(b)	47 U.S.C. § 225(b)	7.16
401(b)(2)	47 U.S.C. § 225(b)(2)	7.15
401(c)	47 U.S.C. § 225(c)	7.16
401(d)	47 U.S.C. § 225(d)	7.09, 7.16
	47 U.S.C. § 225(d)(2)	7.09
	47 U.S.C. § 228	7.16
	47 U.S.C. § 230(b)	7.16
	47 U.S.C. § 230(e)	7.16
	47 U.S.C. § 230(e)(2)	7.16
	47 U.S.C. §§ 610 et seq.	7.15
	47 U.S.C. § 610(a)	7.15
	47 U.S.C. § 610(c)	7.15

Act §	U.S. Code Citation	Text §
402	47 U.S.C. § 711	1.01, 2.01, 2.08, 3.01, 5.01, 4.01, 6.01, 7.01, 7.11, 7.16, 8.01, 9.01, 9.03, 10.01, 10.02[A], 11.01, 12.01, 13.01, 14.01, 15.01[A], 16.01[A], 17.01[A], 18.01
501	42 U.S.C. § 12201	8.02[A]
501–514	42 U.S.C. §§ 12201–12213	1.01, 5.20, 6.07, 7.17
501(a)	42 U.S.C. § 12201(a)	6.14
501(b)	42 U.S.C. § 12201(b)	1.01, 6.08, 9.02, 9.15
501(c)	42 U.S.C. § 12201(c)	4.14
501(c)(3)	42 U.S.C. § 12201(c)(3)	4.14
502	42 U.S.C. § 12202 (1994)	1.01
503	42 U.S.C. § 12203	6.03[A]
504(a)	42 U.S.C. § 12204(a)	6.12
504(b)	42 U.S.C. § 12204(b)	6.12
506(a)(1)	42 U.S.C. § 12206(a)(1)	6.13
506(c)(1)	42 U.S.C. § 12206(c)(1)	6.13
506(c)(2)(C)	42 U.S.C. § 12206(c)(2)(C)	6.13
506(c)(3)	42 U.S.C. § 12206(c)(3)	6.13
506(d)	42 U.S.C. § 12206(d)	6.13
506(e)	42 U.S.C. § 12206(e)	6.13
	42 U.S.C. § 12201(b)	1.07[A], 5.25, 6.14
	42 U.S.C. § 12201(c)	4.14

Act §	U.S. Code Citation	Text §
	42 U.S.C. § 12201(c)(3)	4.14
	42 U.S.C. § 12203	1.01, 4.03[K], 5.20, 6.07
	42 U.S.C. § 12203(a)–(c)	4.03[E]
	42 U.S.C. § 12203(b)	4.03[K]
	42 U.S.C. § 12204	6.10[A]
	42 U.S.C. § 12205	1.08, 9.23[G][1]
509	42 U.S.C. § 12209	4.02[C]
	42 U.S.C. § 12210	2.05, 4.13, 5.17
	42 U.S.C. § 12210(d)(1)	4.13
	42 U.S.C. § 12213	18.27
510(b)	42 U.S.C. § 12210(b)	5.17
510(c)	42 U.S.C. § 12210(c)	4.13
	42 U.S.C. § 12211	3.02
511(a)	42 U.S.C. § 12211(a)	3.13
511(b)	42 U.S.C. § 12211(b)	3.13
	42 U.S.C. § 12212	8.10, 9.11[C]

OTHER UNITED STATES CODE PROVISIONS

2 U.S.C.

§ 1301(3)	2.02, 4.02[D], 5.02, 9.14
§ 1301(9)	2.02, 4.02[D], 5.02, 9.14
§ 1302	4.02[D], 5.02
§ 1302(a)(3)(10)	4.02[D], 5.02
§ 1311	4.02[D], 5.02
§ 1311(a)(3)	4.02[D], 5.02
§ 1311(b)(3)	4.02[D], 5.02, 9.14
§ 1331(a)	9.14
§ 1331(c)	9.14
§ 1331(d)	9.14
§ 1331(d)(1)	9.14
§ 1331(d)(4)	9.14
§ 1361(e)	9.14

§ 1361(f)(3)   9.14

§ 1361(f)(3)	9.14
§ 1381	9.14
§ 1381(b)	9.14
§ 1384	9.14
§§ 1402–1403	9.14
§ 1402(a)	9.14
§ 1403(a)	9.14
§ 1404	9.14
§ 1404(2)	9.14
§§ 1405–1406	9.14
§ 1407	9.14
§ 1408	9.14
§ 1408(c)	9.14
§ 1409	9.14
§ 1410	9.14
§ 1413	9.14
§ 1415	9.14
§ 1431	9.14
§ 1434	9.14
ch. 24	2.02, 4.02[C], 5.01, 8.01, 9.14

5 U.S.C.

§§ 551–559	4.14
§§ 551–706	9.03, 9.14
§ 552	13.02[A]
§§ 701–706	4.14

9 U.S.C.

§ 1	9.11[A], 9.11[C]
§ 9	9.11[A]
§ 10	9.11[A]
§§ 11–12	9.11[A]
§ 201	9.11[A]

11 U.S.C.

§ 348	9.30
§ 706	9.30

18 U.S.C.

§ 1462	7.16
§§ 1961–1968	9.06

49 U.S.C.

§ 41705	7.01, 7.02
app. § 1305(a)	11.02[B][15]
app. § 1374(c)	11.02[B][15]

Constitution

art. I, § 8	5.21, 8.02[B], 8.13
art. III, § 2	9.04[M]
amend. I	6.02[B], 8.02[B], 9.04[M]
amend. VII	9.21, 9.24[A]
amend. X	8.13
amend. XI	1.01, 5.01, 5.04, 5.09[K], 5.22, 8.02[B], 8.13, 9.22, 9.23[F], 9.29
amend. XIV	5.12, 5.21, 5.22, 8.13

CODE OF FEDERAL REGULATIONS

17 C.F.R.

pt. 149	8.04[A]

28 C.F.R.

§ 0.5	6.08, 9.02
§ 0.51	9.04[E]
pt. 35	2.08, 5.05, 9.08[B]
§ 35.102(b)	5.05
§ 35.102	5.04
§ 35.103	5.25
§ 35.105	5.19[B]
§ 35.106	5.19[B]
§ 35.107	5.19[B]
§ 35.107(a)	5.19[B]
§ 35.107(b)	5.19[B]
§ 35.130	5.14
§ 35.130(b)(1)(i)	5.04
§ 35.130(b)(1)(ii)	5.04
§ 35.130(b)(1)(iii)	5.04
§ 35.130(b)(1)(iv)	5.04
§ 35.130(b)(1)(v)	5.04
§ 35.130(b)(1)(vi)	5.04
§ 35.130(b)(1)(vii)	5.04
§ 35.130(b)(2)	5.04
§ 35.130(b)(3)	5.04
§ 35.130(b)(3)(i)	5.04

901(a)	16.01[A]
901(b)	16.01[A]
901(b)(2)	16.01[A]
901(b)(3)	16.01[A]
901(b)(4)	16.01[A]
901(b)(5)	16.01[A]
901(b)(6)	16.01[A]
902	16.01[A]
1001(2)	9.17[B]

STATE STATUTES AND RULES

California

Cal. Gov't Code § 12900	9.17[A]
Cal. Gov't Code § 12926	9.17[A]

Illinois

Ill. Rev. Stat. ch. 68, ¶ 1–103(l)	4.11[B][4][b]
Ill. Rev. Stat. ch. 68, ¶ 1–103(l)(1)	4.11[B][4][b]

Kentucky

Ky. Rev. Stat. § 344.010	4.11[B][5]

Maryland

Md. R. Civ. P. 2–303(c)	9.15
Md. R. Civ. P. 2–305	9.15

Massachusetts

Mass. Gen. L. ch. 123, § 18A	5.09[M]

Missouri

Mo. Rev. Stat. § 213.010(8)	3.02[C][1]

New Jersey

N.J. Stat. Ann. § 10:5–5(q)	4.11[B][4][b]

New York

N.Y. Civ. Prac. L. & R. art. 50–B	5.07[B]

Pennsylvania

42 Pa. Cons. Stat. Ann. § 8302	9.04[L]
Pa. R. Civ. P. 1020	9.15

Washington

Wash. Admin. Code § 162–22–050(3)   4.06[B][8]

Wash. Rev. Code § 49.60.181(1)   4.06[B][8]

West Virginia

W. Va. Code § 5–11–1   8.14

W. Va. Code § 55–2–12   9.16

INDEX